Handbook of Research on Cloud and Fog Computing Infrastructures for Data Science

Pethuru Raj
Reliance Jio Infocomm. Ltd., India

Anupama Raman
Societe Generale Global Solution Center, India

A volume in the Advances in Computer and
Electrical Engineering (ACEE) Book Series

Published in the United States of America by
IGI Global
Engineering Science Reference (an imprint of IGI Global)
701 E. Chocolate Avenue
Hershey PA, USA 17033
Tel: 717-533-8845
Fax: 717-533-8661
E-mail: cust@igi-global.com
Web site: http://www.igi-global.com

Library of Congress Cataloging-in-Publication Data

Names: Raj, Pethuru, editor. | Raman, Anupama C., editor.
Title: Handbook of research on cloud and fog computing infrastructures for
  data science / Pethuru Raj and Anupama Raman, editors.
Description: Hershey, PA : Engineering Science Reference, [2018] | Includes
  bibliographical references.
Identifiers: LCCN 2017059194| ISBN 9781522559726 (hardcover) | ISBN
  9781522559733 (ebook)
Subjects: LCSH: Cloud computing--Handbooks, manuals, etc.
Classification: LCC QA76.585 .H3626 2018 | DDC 004.67/82--dc23 LC record available at https://lccn.loc.gov/2017059194

This book is published in the IGI Global book series Advances in Computer and Electrical Engineering (ACEE) (ISSN: 2327-039X; eISSN: 2327-0403)

British Cataloguing in Publication Data
A Cataloguing in Publication record for this book is available from the British Library.

All work contributed to this book is new, previously-unpublished material. The views expressed in this book are those of the authors, but not necessarily of the publisher.

For electronic access to this publication, please contact: eresources@igi-global.com.

Advances in Computer and Electrical Engineering (ACEE) Book Series

Srikanta Patnaik
SOA University, India

ISSN:2327-039X
EISSN:2327-0403

MISSION

The fields of computer engineering and electrical engineering encompass a broad range of interdisciplinary topics allowing for expansive research developments across multiple fields. Research in these areas continues to develop and become increasingly important as computer and electrical systems have become an integral part of everyday life.

The **Advances in Computer and Electrical Engineering (ACEE) Book Series** aims to publish research on diverse topics pertaining to computer engineering and electrical engineering. **ACEE** encourages scholarly discourse on the latest applications, tools, and methodologies being implemented in the field for the design and development of computer and electrical systems.

COVERAGE

- Qualitative Methods
- VLSI Fabrication
- Circuit Analysis
- Programming
- Digital Electronics
- Microprocessor Design
- Computer Architecture
- Chip Design
- Computer science
- Computer Hardware

IGI Global is currently accepting manuscripts for publication within this series. To submit a proposal for a volume in this series, please contact our Acquisition Editors at Acquisitions@igi-global.com or visit: http://www.igi-global.com/publish/.

Titles in this Series

For a list of additional titles in this series, please visit: www.igi-global.com/book-series

EHT Transmission Performance Evaluation Emerging Research and Opportunities
K. Srinivas (Transmission Corporation of Andhra Pradesh Limited, India) and R.V.S. Satyanarayana (Sri Venkateswara University College of Engineering, India)
Engineering Science Reference • copyright 2018 • 160pp • H/C (ISBN: 9781522549413) • US $145.00 (our price)

Fuzzy Logic Dynamics and Machine Prediction for Failure Analysis
Tawanda Mushiri (University of Johannesburg, South Africa) and Charles Mbowhwa (University of Johannesburg, South Africa)
Engineering Science Reference • copyright 2018 • 301pp • H/C (ISBN: 9781522532446) • US $225.00 (our price)

Creativity in Load-Balance Schemes for Multi/Many-Core Heterogeneous Graph Computing Emerging Research and Opportunities
Alberto Garcia-Robledo (Center for Research and Advanced Studies of the National Polytechnic Institute (Cinvestav-Tamaulipas), Mexico) Arturo Diaz-Perez (Center for Research and Advanced Studies of the National Polytechnic Institute (Cinvestav-Tamaulipas), Mexico) and Guillermo Morales-Luna (Center for Research and Advanced Studies of the National Polytechnic Institute (Cinvestav-IPN), Mexico)
Engineering Science Reference • copyright 2018 • 217pp • H/C (ISBN: 9781522537991) • US $155.00 (our price)

Free and Open Source Software in Modern Data Science and Business Intelligence Emerging Research and Opportunities
K.G. Srinivasa (CBP Government Engineering College, India) Ganesh Chandra Deka (M. S. Ramaiah Institute of Technology, India) and Krishnaraj P.M. (M. S. Ramaiah Institute of Technology, India)
Engineering Science Reference • copyright 2018 • 189pp • H/C (ISBN: 9781522537076) • US $190.00 (our price)

Design Parameters of Electrical Network Grounding Systems
Osama El-Sayed Gouda (Cairo University, Egypt)
Engineering Science Reference • copyright 2018 • 316pp • H/C (ISBN: 9781522538530) • US $235.00 (our price)

Design and Use of Virtualization Technology in Cloud Computing
Prashanta Kumar Das (Government Industrial Training Institute Dhansiri, India) and Ganesh Chandra Deka (Government of India, India)
Engineering Science Reference • copyright 2018 • 315pp • H/C (ISBN: 9781522527855) • US $235.00 (our price)

701 East Chocolate Avenue, Hershey, PA 17033, USA
Tel: 717-533-8845 x100 • Fax: 717-533-8661
E-Mail: cust@igi-global.com • www.igi-global.com

List of Contributors

A., Saleema / *Indian Institute of Information Technology and Management Kerala, India* 360

Akkaya, Murat / *Girne American University, Turkey* 289

Alageswaran, R. / *K. L. N. College of Engineering, India* 33

Amali, S. Miruna Joe / *K. L. N. College of Engineering, India* 33

Ameen, Nabeena / *B. S. Abdur Rahman Crescent Institute of Science and Technology, India* 265

Arunkumar, N. / *Sastra University, India* 231

Aswathy, R. H. / *Vel Tech Rangarajan Dr. Sagunthala R&D Institute of Science and Technology,*
India 124

Balakrishnan, P. / *VIT University, India* 68

Baranidharan, B. / *Madanapalle Institute of Technology and Science, India* 149

Duggirala, Siddhartha / *Bharat Petroleum Corporation Limited, India* 53

G., Keerthana / *VIT University, India* 108

J., Pushpa / *Jain University, India* 1

Jamal, D. Najumnissa / *B. S. Abdur Rahman Crescent Institute of Science and Technology, India* 265

Jayanthiladevi, A. / *Jain University, India* 108,231,344,390

Koteeswaran, S. / *Vel Tech Rangarajan Dr. Sagunthala R&D Institute of Science and*
Technology, India 124

Kousalya, G. / *Coimbatore Institute of Technology, India* 175

Kumar, Abhishek / *M. S. Ramaiah Institute of Technology, India* 312

Lathar, Pankaj / *CBP Government Engineering College, India* 312

M., Dhanya N. / *Amrita Vishwa Vidyapeetham, India* 175

Malarvizhi, N. / *Vel Tech Rangarajan Dr. Sagunthala R&D Institute of Science and Technology,*
India 124

Manivel, K. / *United Health Corporation, India* 390

Megdadi, Khaled / *Girne American University, Turkey* 289

Mohanasundaram, R. / *VIT University, India* 108

Murugan, S. / *Mewer University, India* 390

N., Kalaiyarasi / *Sri Ramakrishna Engineering College, India* 85

P., Ambika / *Kristu Jayanti College, India* 195,209

P., Balarksihnan / *Vellore Institute of Technology, India* 175

R., Dharshana / *Sri Ramakrishna Engineering College, India* 85

R., Madhumathi / *Sri Ramakrishna Engineering College, India* 85

Raj, Pethuru / *Reliance Jio Infocomm. Ltd., India* 1,68,175

Rajkumar, S. / *Bhairava Centre for Technology and Research, India* 265

Sakthivel / *KSR College of Technology, India* 344

Sari, Arif / *Girne American University, Turkey* 289

Siddiqui, Nabeel / *M. S. Ramaiah Institute of Technology, India* 312

Srinivasa, K. G. / *CBP Government Engineering College, India* 312

Sulthana, Reshma / *Coimbatore Institute of Technology, India* 85

Surendararavindhan / *Vignan's University, India* 344

Suresh, P. / *Vel Tech Rangarajan Dr. Sagunthala R&D Institute of Science and Technology, India* 124

Thampi, Sabu M. / *Indian Institute of Information Technology and Management Kerala, India* 360

Thilagamani, S. / *Kumarasamy Engineering College, India* 231

Venkatesh, Veeramuthu / *SASTRA University, India* 68

Table of Contents

Preface..xvii

Chapter 1
Expounding the Edge/Fog Computing Infrastructures for Data Science...............................1
    Pethuru Raj, Reliance Jio Infocomm. Ltd., India
    Pushpa J., Jain University, India

Chapter 2
Evolution of Fog Computing and Its Role in IoT Applications 33
    R. Alageswaran, K. L. N. College of Engineering, India
    S. Miruna Joe Amali, K. L. N. College of Engineering, India

Chapter 3
Fog Computing and Virtualization 53
    Siddhartha Duggirala, Bharat Petroleum Corporation Limited, India

Chapter 4
Fog Computing: Introduction, Architecture, Analytics, and Platforms 68
    P. Balakrishnan, VIT University, India
    Veeramuthu Venkatesh, SASTRA University, India
    Pethuru Raj, Reliance Jio Infocomm. Ltd., India

Chapter 5
A Comprehensive Survey of IoT Edge/Fog Computing Protocols 85
    Madhumathi R., Sri Ramakrishna Engineering College, India
    Dharshana R., Sri Ramakrishna Engineering College, India
    Reshma Sulthana, Coimbatore Institute of Technology, India
    Kalaiyarasi N., Sri Ramakrishna Engineering College, India

Chapter 6
Software-Defined Cloud Infrastructure...108
    R. Mohanasundaram, VIT University, India
    A. Jayanthiladevi, Jain University, India
    Keerthana G., VIT University, India

Chapter 7
Internet of Things (IoT): A Study on Key Elements, Protocols, Application, Research Challenges, and Fog Computing 124
    P. Suresh, Vel Tech Rangarajan Dr. Sagunthala R&D Institute of Science and Technology, India
    S. Koteeswaran, Vel Tech Rangarajan Dr. Sagunthala R&D Institute of Science and Technology, India
    N. Malarvizhi, Vel Tech Rangarajan Dr. Sagunthala R&D Institute of Science and Technology, India
    R. H. Aswathy, Vel Tech Rangarajan Dr. Sagunthala R&D Institute of Science and Technology, India

Chapter 8
Internet of Things (IoT) Technologies, Architecture, Protocols, Security, and Applications: A Survey 149
    B. Baranidharan, Madanapalle Institute of Technology and Science, India

Chapter 9
Fuzzy-Logic-Based Decision Engine for Offloading IoT Application Using Fog Computing 175
    Dhanya N. M., Amrita Vishwa Vidyapeetham, India
    G. Kousalya, Coimbatore Institute of Technology, India
    Balarksihnan P., Vellore Institute of Technology, India
    Pethuru Raj, Reliance Jio Infocomm. Ltd., India

Chapter 10
Data Mining Algorithms and Techniques 195
    Ambika P., Kristu Jayanti College, India

Chapter 11
Machine Learning 209
    Ambika P., Kristu Jayanti College, India

Chapter 12
Data Mining Algorithms, Fog Computing 231
    S. Thilagamani, Kumarasamy Engineering College, India
    A. Jayanthiladevi, Jain University, India
    N. Arunkumar, Sastra University, India

Chapter 13
Remote Elderly Health Monitoring System Using Cloud-Based WBANs 265
    D. Najumnissa Jamal, B. S. Abdur Rahman Crescent Institute of Science and Technology, India
    S. Rajkumar, Bhairava Centre for Technology and Research, India
    Nabeena Ameen, B. S. Abdur Rahman Crescent Institute of Science and Technology, India

Chapter 14
Internet of Things and Smart City Initiatives in Middle Eastern Countries 289
    Khaled Megdadi, Girne American University, Turkey
    Murat Akkaya, Girne American University, Turkey
    Arif Sari, Girne American University, Turkey

Chapter 15
Comparison Study of Different NoSQL and Cloud Paradigm for Better Data Storage
Technology 312
    Pankaj Lathar, CBP Government Engineering College, India
    K. G. Srinivasa, CBP Government Engineering College, India
    Abhishek Kumar, M. S. Ramaiah Institute of Technology, India
    Nabeel Siddiqui, M. S. Ramaiah Institute of Technology, India

Chapter 16
Fast Data vs. Big Data With IoT Streaming Analytics and the Future Applications 344
    A. Jayanthiladevi, Jain University, India
    Surendararavindhan, Vignan's University, India
    Sakthivel, KSR College of Technology, India

Chapter 17
Voice Biometrics: The Promising Future of Authentication in the Internet of Things 360
    Saleema A., Indian Institute of Information Technology and Management Kerala, India
    Sabu M. Thampi, Indian Institute of Information Technology and Management Kerala, India

Chapter 18
Text, Images, and Video Analytics for Fog Computing 390
    A. Jayanthiladevi, Jain University, India
    S. Murugan, Mewer University, India
    K. Manivel, United Health Corporation, India

Compilation of References 411

Index 438

Detailed Table of Contents

Preface.. xvii

Chapter 1

Expounding the Edge/Fog Computing Infrastructures for Data Science................................ 1

Pethuru Raj, Reliance Jio Infocomm. Ltd., India
Pushpa J., Jain University, India

Data is the new fuel for any system to deliver smart and sophisticated services. Data is being touted as the strategic asset for any organization to plan ahead and provide next-generation capabilities with all the clarity and confidence. Whether data is internally sourced or aggregated from different and distributed source, it is essential for all kinds of data to be continuously and consciously collected, transmitted, cleansed, and hosted on storage systems. There are several types of analytical methods and machines to do deeper and decisive analytics on those curated and consolidated data to extract actionable insights in real-time. Precise and concise analytics guarantee perfect decision-making and action. We need competent and highly integrated analytics platform for speeding up, simplifying and streamlining data analytics, which is becoming a hard nut to crack due to the multi-structured and massive quantities of data. On the infrastructure front, we need highly optimized compute, storage and network infrastructure for achieving data analytics with ease. Another noteworthy point is that there are batch, real-time, and interactive processing of data. Most of the personal and professional applications need real-time insights in order to produce real-time applications. That is, real-time capture, processing, and decision-making are being insisted and hence the edge or fog computing concept has become very popular. This chapter is exclusively designed in order to tell all on how to accomplish real-time analytics on fog devices data.

Chapter 2

Evolution of Fog Computing and Its Role in IoT Applications 33

R. Alageswaran, K. L. N. College of Engineering, India
S. Miruna Joe Amali, K. L. N. College of Engineering, India

Fog computing is an evolving technology that brings the benefits achieved by cloud computing to the periphery of the network devices for faster data analytics. This has triggered the usage of fog computing for enabling a new breed of applications and services that require localized and faster decision making. Fog computing has attributes such as location awareness, edge deployment and a large number of geographically distributed nodes, heterogeneity through which fog computing offers better performance in terms of mobility, low latency, and real-time interaction. They can also gracefully handle enormous data flow and provide analytics in reasonable time. Due to these additional attributes, fog computing is considered as the appropriate platform for many applications and especially suited for internet of things

(IoT). Fog computing also provides an intelligent platform to manage the distributed and real-time nature of emerging IoT applications and infrastructures. With the increase in the number of connected objects, the development of fog computing is tremendous and has promising technological future growth.

Chapter 3

Fog Computing and Virtualization 53
Siddhartha Duggirala, Bharat Petroleum Corporation Limited, India

The essence of cloud computing is moving out the processing from the local systems to remote systems. Cloud is an umbrella of physical/virtual services/resources easily accessible over the internet. With more companies adopting cloud either fully through public cloud or hybrid model, the challenges in maintaining a cloud capable infrastructure is also increasing. About 42% of CTOs say that security is their main concern for moving into cloud. Another problem, which is mainly problem with infrastructure, is the connectivity issue. The datacenter could be considered as the backbone of cloud computing architecture. Handling this new generation of requirements of volume, variety, and velocity in IoT data requires us to evaluate the tools and technologies. As the processing power and storage capabilities of the end devices like mobile phones, routers, sensor hubs improve, we can increase leverage these resources to improve your quality and reliability of services. Applications of fog computing is as diverse as IoT and cloud computing itself. What IoT and fog computing have in common is to monitor and analyse real-time data from network connected things and acting on them. Machine-to-machine coordination or human-machine interaction can be a part of this action. This chapter explores fog computing and virtualization.

Chapter 4

Fog Computing: Introduction, Architecture, Analytics, and Platforms 68
P. Balakrishnan, VIT University, India
Veeramuthu Venkatesh, SASTRA University, India
Pethuru Raj, Reliance Jio Infocomm. Ltd., India

The evolutions of world wide web (WWW) promise the revolution in personal, professional, and social aspects of human beings. These evolutions begin with static web pages to more sophisticated brain-computer interfaces. Among them, Web 4.0 plays a significant role that aimed to integrate mobile devices and things into the web to realize smarter environments. Further, it leads to the progression of machine-to-machine communication, wireless sensor networks, cyber physical systems, and internet of things (IoT). The drastic development of IoT applications led to unprecedented growth of data which can be processed using more powerful far-end cloud resources or less powerful local edge devices. Fog computing compromises the demerits of both approaches and conducts the data analysis at the network-end itself. This chapter provides the benefits of fog computing architectures together with the simulator as well as different software platforms for realizing the fog computing.

Chapter 5

A Comprehensive Survey of IoT Edge/Fog Computing Protocols 85
Madhumathi R., Sri Ramakrishna Engineering College, India
Dharshana R., Sri Ramakrishna Engineering College, India
Reshma Sulthana, Coimbatore Institute of Technology, India
Kalaiyarasi N., Sri Ramakrishna Engineering College, India

The IoT device ecosystem is being blessed with a dazzling array of slim and sleek, trendy and handy, purpose-specific and generic, disappearing, disposable yet indispensable, resource-constrained and intensive, and embedded yet networked devices. Therefore, our personal, as well as professional, environments are increasingly being stuffed with such kinds of functionally powerful devices that are instrumented, interconnected, and intelligent. This trend and transition set a stimulating foundation for a variety of connected and smarter environments. By empowering our everyday devices to be computing, communicative, sensitive, and responsive, the newly introduced concept of edge or fog computing is to bring forth a number of innovations, disruptions, and transformations for the IT domain. This chapter conveys how the various protocols contribute immensely to the intended success of fog computing and analytics in the days ahead.

Chapter 6
Software-Defined Cloud Infrastructure.. 108
    R. Mohanasundaram, VIT University, India
    A. Jayanthiladevi, Jain University, India
    Keerthana G., VIT University, India

Cloud computing suggests that the applications conveyed as services over the internet and frameworks programming in the server that give various services and offers in "pay as you go" trend which means pay only for what you use. The information and services are managed as software as a service (SaaS). Some sellers utilize terms, for example, IaaS (infrastructure as a service) and PaaS (platform as a service). The purpose of cloud computing is quickly expanding in everyday life. Today the use of cloud computing is widespread to the point that it is being utilized even in the medicinal services industry. As the development of cloud computing in healthcare is happening at a fast rate, we can expect a noteworthy piece of the healthcare administrations to move onto the Cloud and along these lines more focus is laid on giving cost-effective and efficient services to the general population all around the world. Cloud these days are turning into the new building pieces of significant organizations spread the world over. They offer assistance in servicing to offer different frameworks. Cloud computing has enhanced its technique and technologies in a better way to provide better services. Existing e-healthcare has many difficulties from advancement to usage. In this chapter, the authors discuss how cloud computing is utilized and the services provided by the Cloud and their models and its infrastructure.

Chapter 7
Internet of Things (IoT): A Study on Key Elements, Protocols, Application, Research Challenges, and Fog Computing.. 124
    P. Suresh, Vel Tech Rangarajan Dr. Sagunthala R&D Institute of Science and Technology, India
    S. Koteeswaran, Vel Tech Rangarajan Dr. Sagunthala R&D Institute of Science and Technology, India
    N. Malarvizhi, Vel Tech Rangarajan Dr. Sagunthala R&D Institute of Science and Technology, India
    R. H. Aswathy, Vel Tech Rangarajan Dr. Sagunthala R&D Institute of Science and Technology, India

The physical world entities are communicated via advanced communication technologies without human intervention. Such an evolving advanced version of automation technology is internet of things (IOT), where each smart device is provided with unique identification. The integration part of such technology comprises key elements, protocols, applications, and research challenges. This chapter discusses such terms and addresses the research challenges. The concept of fog computing is analyzed by cognitive approach. Fog computing localizes the processing information and optimizes the communication and storage among enormous smart devices. In addition, it favourably mitigates the need of bandwidth size and delay in communication.

Chapter 8

Internet of Things (IoT) Technologies, Architecture, Protocols, Security, and Applications: A Survey 149

B. Baranidharan, Madanapalle Institute of Technology and Science, India

Internet of things (IoT) is a rapidly developing technology that connects various kinds of smart miniature things such as smart medical alert watches, smart vehicles, smart phones, smart running shoes, etc. Smart devices are connected through internet and can communicate to other smart devices in any part of the world in an automated manner. IoT environment often uses constrained devices with low energy, low processing capability, and low memory space. In order to prevent communication failure, a special kind of architecture is needed for IoT. This chapter presents a review of the basic architecture model, communication protocol of IoT, security aspects of IoT, and various IoT applications such as smart agriculture, water management, smart healthcare, smart home, smart industry, and smart vehicles.

Chapter 9

Fuzzy-Logic-Based Decision Engine for Offloading IoT Application Using Fog Computing........... 175

Dhanya N. M., Amrita Vishwa Vidyapeetham, India
G. Kousalya, Coimbatore Institute of Technology, India
Balarksihnan P., Vellore Institute of Technology, India
Pethuru Raj, Reliance Jio Infocomm. Ltd., India

Mobile is getting increasingly popular and almost all applications are shifting into smartphones. Even though lots of advantages are there for smartphones, they are constrained by limitations in battery charge and the processing capacity. For running resource-intensive IoT applications like processing sensor data and dealing with big data coming from the IoT application, the capacity of existing smartphones is not enough, as the battery will be drained quickly, and it will be slow. Offloading is one of the major techniques through which mobile and cloud can be connected together and has emerged to reduce the complexity and increase the computation power of mobiles. Other than depending on the distant cloud for offloading, the extended version of cloud called fog computing can be utilized. Through offloading, the computationally intensive tasks can be shifted to the edge fog devices, and the results can be collected back at the mobile side reducing the burden. This chapter has developed mobile cloud offloading architecture for decision making using fuzzy logic where a decision is made as to whether we can shift the application to cloud or not depending on the current parameters of both cloud and the mobile side. Cloud computing introduces a number of variables depending on which offloading decision must be taken. In this chapter, the authors propose a fuzzy-logic-based algorithm which takes into consideration all the parameters at the mobile and cloud that will affect the offloading decision.

Chapter 10

Data Mining Algorithms and Techniques.. 195

Ambika P., Kristu Jayanti College, India

Integration of data mining tasks in day-to-day life has become popular and common. Everyday people are confronted with opportunities and challenges with targeted advertising, and data mining techniques will help the businesses to become more efficient by reducing processing cost. This goal of this chapter is to provide a comprehensive review about data mining, data mining techniques, popular algorithms, and their impact on fog computing. This chapter also gives further research directions on data mining on fog computing.

Chapter 11

Machine Learning 209
Ambika P., Kristu Jayanti College, India

Machine learning is a subfield of artificial intelligence that encompass the automatic computing to make predictions. The key difference between a traditional program and machine-learning model is that it allows the model to learn from the data and helps to make its own decisions. It is one of the fastest growing areas of computing. The goal of this chapter is to explore the foundations of machine learning theory and mathematical derivations, which transform the theory into practical algorithms. This chapter also focuses a comprehensive review on machine learning and its types and why machine learning is important in real-world applications, and popular machine learning algorithms and their impact on fog computing. This chapter also gives further research directions on machine learning algorithms.

Chapter 12

Data Mining Algorithms, Fog Computing 231
S. Thilagamani, Kumarasamy Engineering College, India
A. Jayanthiladevi, Jain University, India
N. Arunkumar, Sastra University, India

Different methods are used to mine the large amount of data presents in databases, data warehouses, and data repositories. The methods used for mining include clustering, classification, prediction, regression, and association rule. This chapter explores data mining algorithms and fog computing.

Chapter 13

Remote Elderly Health Monitoring System Using Cloud-Based WBANs 265
D. Najumnissa Jamal, B. S. Abdur Rahman Crescent Institute of Science and Technology, India
S. Rajkumar, Bhairava Centre for Technology and Research, India
Nabeena Ameen, B. S. Abdur Rahman Crescent Institute of Science and Technology, India

Monitoring the physical condition of patients is a major errand for specialists. The development of wireless remote elderly patient monitoring system has been intensive in the past. RPM (remote patient monitoring) is reliant on the person's inspiration to deal with their wellbeing. The flow of patient data requires a group of medicinal services suppliers to deal with the information. RPM sending is reliant on a wireless telecommunication infrastructure, which may not be accessible/practical in provincial territories. Patients' data are shared as service on cloud in hospitals. Therefore, in the current research, a new approach of cloud-based wireless remote patient monitoring system during emergency is proposed as a model to monitor the critical health data. The vital parameters are measured and transmitted. In this chapter, the authors present an extensive review of the significant technologies associated with wireless patient monitoring using wireless sensor networks and cloud.

Chapter 14

Internet of Things and Smart City Initiatives in Middle Eastern Countries 289

Khaled Megdadi, Girne American University, Turkey

Murat Akkaya, Girne American University, Turkey

Arif Sari, Girne American University, Turkey

This chapter presents a systematic review of prior research work that is closely aligned to the subject of interest related with internet of things (IoT) and smart city initiatives in Middle Eastern countries. Since internet of things technology (IoT) is the new revolution in the existing services provision environment due to increased contact with high-speed internet access, and the need to provide services more quickly and with minimal effort, costs and keeping pace with the development witnessed by the rest of the advanced countries of the world at a time connection is no longer limited by political borders of the states. This encompasses articles, unpublished papers and theses, conference papers, and memos. The chapter is an evaluation of previous research on the current research topic and serves as a space for research gap identification and hypotheses development in the field of IoT with smart city development initiatives.

Chapter 15

Comparison Study of Different NoSQL and Cloud Paradigm for Better Data Storage
Technology 312

Pankaj Lathar, CBP Government Engineering College, India

K. G. Srinivasa, CBP Government Engineering College, India

Abhishek Kumar, M. S. Ramaiah Institute of Technology, India

Nabeel Siddiqui, M. S. Ramaiah Institute of Technology, India

Advancements in web-based technology and the proliferation of sensors and mobile devices interacting with the internet have resulted in immense data management requirements. These data management activities include storage, processing, demand of high-performance read-write operations of big data. Large-scale and high-concurrency applications like SNS and search engines have appeared to be facing challenges in using the relational database to store and query dynamic user data. NoSQL and cloud computing has emerged as a paradigm that could meet these requirements. The available diversity of existing NoSQL and cloud computing solutions make it difficult to comprehend the domain and choose an appropriate solution for a specific business task. Therefore, this chapter reviews NoSQL and cloud-system-based solutions with the goal of providing a perspective in the field of data storage technology/ algorithms, leveraging guidance to researchers and practitioners to select the best-fit data store, and identifying challenges and opportunities of the paradigm.

Chapter 16

Fast Data vs. Big Data With IoT Streaming Analytics and the Future Applications 344

A. Jayanthiladevi, Jain University, India

Surendararavindhan, Vignan's University, India

Sakthivel, KSR College of Technology, India

Big data depicts information volume – petabytes to exabytes in organized, semi-organized, and unstructured information that can possibly be broken down for data. Fast data are facts streaming into applications and computing environments from hundreds of thousands to millions of endpoints. Fast data is totally different from big data. There is no question that we will continue generating large volumes of data, especially with the wide variety of handheld units and internet-connected devices expected to grow exponentially. Data streaming analytics is vital for disruptive applications. Streaming analytics permits the processing of terabytes of data in memory. This chapter explores fast data and big data with IoT streaming analytics.

Chapter 17

Voice Biometrics: The Promising Future of Authentication in the Internet of Things 360
Saleema A., Indian Institute of Information Technology and Management Kerala, India
Sabu M. Thampi, Indian Institute of Information Technology and Management Kerala, India

Biometric technology is spearheading the existing authentication methods in the IoT. Considering the balance between security and convenience, voice biometrics seems to be the most logical biometric technologies to be used. The authors present an extensive survey to identify, analyze, and compare various methods and algorithms for the different phases in the process of speaker identification/recognition, which is the part and parcel in voice biometrics. The chapter is intended to provide essential background information to those interested in learning or planning to design voice authentication systems. The chapter highlights the need for a biometric authentication system, the reason why we prefer voice, its present state of affairs, and its scope with fog computing to be used in IoT.

Chapter 18

Text, Images, and Video Analytics for Fog Computing 390
A. Jayanthiladevi, Jain University, India
S. Murugan, Mewer University, India
K. Manivel, United Health Corporation, India

Today, images and image sequences (videos) make up about 80% of all corporate and public unstructured big data. As growth of unstructured data increases, analytical systems must assimilate and interpret images and videos as well as they interpret structured data such as text and numbers. An image is a set of signals sensed by the human eye and processed by the visual cortex in the brain creating a vivid experience of a scene that is instantly associated with concepts and objects previously perceived and recorded in one's memory. To a computer, images are either a raster image or a vector image. Simply put, raster images are a sequence of pixels with discreet numerical values for color; vector images are a set of color-annotated polygons. To perform analytics on images or videos, the geometric encoding must be transformed into constructs depicting physical features, objects and movement represented by the image or video. This chapter explores text, images, and video analytics in fog computing.

Compilation of References 411

Index 438

Preface

Our everyday devices are increasingly instrumented, interconnected, and intelligent. This trend has set in for the massive uptake of the Internet of Devices (IoD) concept. This elegant and extreme connectivity amongst different and distributed devices has laid a stimulating and sparkling foundation for accentuating and articulating a dazzling array of hitherto unknown business, technical and use cases. Precisely speaking, devices are not only talking to other devices in the vicinity but also with remote devices over one or more networks. Further on, devices at the ground level are being integrated with remotely held software applications and data sources. That is, there is a seamless linkage being established between physical and cyber systems in order to envision path-breaking industrial and consumer applications. The integration phenomenon, which has been dominating in the enterprise IT space, is now penetrating onto devices (mechanical, electrical and electronics). We, therefore, hear, read and even experience spectacular services due to the growing device-to-device (D2D) and device-to-cloud (D2C) integration aspects. This deeper integration readily and rewardingly opens up an array of sophisticated and smarter applications for the total mankind.

On the other hand, recent devices are being stuffed with a number of newer capabilities and additional capacities. Devices are becoming sensitive, communicative, computational, responsive and adaptive in their actions and reactions. For example, our smartphones are being intrinsically enabled to run artificial intelligence (AI) applications. Devices themselves form device clusters and clouds through a kind of ad hoc networking in order to accomplish better and bigger assignments. The processing, memory, storage and I/O power of our personal and professional devices are growing steadily. The device ecosystem also is the growth path. There are medical instruments, defence equipment, manufacturing machines, household utensils and ware, consumer electronics, robots, drones, smartphones, wearables, handhelds, portables, fixed devices, etc. That is, there are purpose-specific and agnostic devices catering to various requirements of people and professionals emerging and evolving fast. These two key trends are the fabulous foundation for the emergence of the incredible domains of fog/edge computing and analytics.

These devices typically bring forth an additional layer of abstraction in between the scores of digitized entities/smart objects/sentient materials (Digitized elements mean all kinds of cheap, casual and common objects in our everyday environments becoming digitized through the systematic application of an arsenal of edge technologies such as sensors, stickers, beacons, LED lights, smart dust, speckles, barcodes, chips, microcontrollers, and other kinds of implantables) at the ground level and the family of virtualized and containerised services at the cyber level. These empowered fog/edge devices are innately capable of performing local and logical processing, transaction and operations by aggregating massive and multi-structured data being emitted by hundreds of thousands of digitized entities. Any device that is physically collecting data is an edge or fog device. Fog computing is referring to computation performed right at the source of the data. There are fog computing platforms, frameworks, programming models, gateways and middleware, etc. for accelerating the fog computing phenomenon.

WHY FOG COMPUTING AND ANALYTICS?

Without the fog computing and analytics in place, all kinds of poly-structured data emanating from ground-level digitized elements have to be carried to the faraway cloud environments for storage and processing. This fog-to-cloud interaction kills the concept of real-time analytics and applications. For producing people-centric, situation-aware, and real-time applications, we need real-time data capture, storage, processing, analytics for knowledge discovery and dissemination, decision-making and actuation. Fog computing devices and infrastructures guarantee all these specific needs. The sensor and actuator data security is being maintained by the fog computing. A lot of redundant, repetitive and routine data get eliminated at the source so that the network bandwidth can be optimally used. The data latency is almost nil.

THE CONVERGENCE OF FOG AND CLOUD COMPUTING

This unique combination comes handy in building next-generation applications. That is, real-time processing gets accomplished by fog devices and their clusters/clouds. The historical and comprehensive processing is being performed at cloud centers (private, public, and hybrid). First, the fog analytics happens locally and the pre-processed digital data gets transmitted to powerful cloud servers in order to do big data analytics, which can create big insights.

This book is specially made up for conveying the role and responsibility of fog devices and cloud servers for performing data science activities such as big, real-time, streaming, IoT data analytics. Further on, how cognitive analytics comprising machine and deep learning for generating prognostic, predictive, prescriptive and personalized insights through fog and cloud environments. This edited book beautifully illustrates all aspects of fog computing with a focus on various protocols and associated technologies. The various use cases of fog computing are also elucidated in a nice manner in this book. The associated technologies like IoT, big data analytics, data science, machine learning, security, real-time analytics, sensor mesh, and cloud computing are also covered in this book.

Chapter 1 focuses on the basic aspects of fog computing. Fog computing has a lot of interesting applications in the field of data science. These applications are discussed at length in this chapter. The various interesting use cases of fog/edge computing are also discussed in this chapter.

Chapter 2 focuses on fog computing and its applications in the Internet of Things (IoT) domain. The architecture of fog computing and the main differences from cloud computing architecture are discussed in detail in this chapter. The various interesting use cases of fog computing are also discussed here

Chapter 3 focuses on the need for the evolution of fog computing. The main advantage of fog computing is that it extends cloud computing to the devices which produce, act on or consume data which in turns offers a host of advantages when compared to the traditional cloud computing paradigm. This chapter highlights all the basic aspects of fog computing and clearly illustrates all the differences between fog computing and cloud computing.

Chapter 4 focuses on the evolution of fog computing. Fog computing evolved to address the limitations which are associated with IoT technology. This chapter also provides a detailed explanation of fog computing architecture using iFogSim which is a simulator for creating and testing the various application scenarios.

Chapter 5 focuses on the various IoT/fog protocols. This chapter focuses on how these protocols contribute immensely to the intended success of fog computing and analytics in the days ahead.

Chapter 6 focuses on the basics of software-defined cloud infrastructure. The various aspects associated with the implementation of cloud infrastructure are also covered in detail in this chapter. This chapter also explains the various use cases of cloud computing in the healthcare sector.

Chapter 7 focuses on the evolution of IoT and its impact on other technologies like fog and edge computing. This chapter provides a bird's eye view of IoT empowering, protocols phases, key factors, applications, diverse challenges and fog computing in everyday life.

Chapter 8 focuses primarily on IoT. The basic architecture model, communication protocol of IoT, security aspects of IoT and various IoT applications are covered in detail in this chapter. The key IoT applications which are covered in this chapter are smart agriculture, water management, smart healthcare, smart home, smart industry, and smart vehicle.

Chapter 9 focuses on mobile cloud offloading architecture for decision making using fuzzy logic and its applications in the field of fog computing. This chapter focuses on various parameters which help us make a decision on whether we can shift an application to cloud side or mobile side based on the current parameters which exist on both sides.

Chapter 10 focuses on the impact of data mining techniques on fog computing. This goal of this chapter is to provide a comprehensive review of Data Mining, data mining techniques, popular algorithms and its impact on fog computing. This chapter also highlights futuristic research directions on data mining on Fog Computing.

Chapter 11 focuses mainly on the applications of machine learning in fog computing. This chapter highlights the foundations of machine learning theory and mathematical derivations, which transform the theory into practical algorithms. This chapter also focuses on a comprehensive review of Machine Learning and its types, why machine learning is important in real-world applications.

Chapter 12 focuses on the different types of methods which are used in data mining which in turn are used in fog computing. This chapter covers the following data mining techniques: Clustering, Classification, prediction, regression and association.

Chapter 13 focuses on wireless remote elderly patient monitoring system which has gained a lot of prominence of late. There are several technologies which make remote patient monitoring a reality. This chapter provides an extensive review of these technologies with more emphasis on wireless sensor networks and cloud.

Chapter 14 focuses on the use cases of IoT for development of smart cities in Middle East countries. Smart cities are very common in Europe and US. However, that is not the case in some other parts of the world. The chapter is an evaluation of previous research on smart cities and serves as a space for research gap identification and hypotheses development in the field of IoT with Smart City development initiatives in Middle East countries.

Chapter 15 focuses on the importance of NoSQL databases. NoSQL databases are closely linked to cloud and fog computing because of the features offered by them to support these technologies. The features which make NoSQL databases very important for fog technology is also discussed at length in this chapter.

Chapter 16 focuses on the key features of fast data and big data. Their suitability to work with IoT applications and use cases is also examined in detail in this chapter. The various security challenges while using each type of data with IoT applications is also explained at length in this chapter.

Chapter 17 focuses on voice biometrics which is an emerging technology area. In this chapter, extensive survey to identify, analyze and compare various methods and algorithms for the different phases in the process of speaker identification/recognition which is the part and parcel in voice biometrics is done. The chapter is intended to provide essential background information to those interested in learning or planning to design voice authentication systems. The chapter highlights the need for a biometric authentication system, the reason why we prefer voice, its present state of affairs and its scope with fog computing to be used in IoT.

Chapter 18 focuses on various types of analytics which are performed on data. Some of the different types of analytics are text analytics, image analytics and video analytics. This chapter focuses on the techniques which are used for performing each of these analytics. The interesting applications of each of these analytical techniques are also explained in this chapter.

Chapter 1
Expounding the Edge/Fog Computing Infrastructures for Data Science

Pethuru Raj
Reliance Jio Infocomm. Ltd., India

Pushpa J.
Jain University, India

ABSTRACT

Data is the new fuel for any system to deliver smart and sophisticated services. Data is being touted as the strategic asset for any organization to plan ahead and provide next-generation capabilities with all the clarity and confidence. Whether data is internally sourced or aggregated from different and distributed source, it is essential for all kinds of data to be continuously and consciously collected, transmitted, cleansed, and hosted on storage systems. There are several types of analytical methods and machines to do deeper and decisive analytics on those curated and consolidated data to extract actionable insights in real-time. Precise and concise analytics guarantee perfect decision-making and action. We need competent and highly integrated analytics platform for speeding up, simplifying and streamlining data analytics, which is becoming a hard nut to crack due to the multi-structured and massive quantities of data. On the infrastructure front, we need highly optimized compute, storage and network infrastructure for achieving data analytics with ease. Another noteworthy point is that there are batch, real-time, and interactive processing of data. Most of the personal and professional applications need real-time insights in order to produce real-time applications. That is, real-time capture, processing, and decision-making are being insisted and hence the edge or fog computing concept has become very popular. This chapter is exclusively designed in order to tell all on how to accomplish real-time analytics on fog devices data.

DOI: 10.4018/978-1-5225-5972-6.ch001

INTRODUCTION

The faster maturity and stability of edge technologies (Raj and Deka, 2014) has blossomed into a big factor in realizing scores of digitized elements / smart objects/sentient materials out of common, cheap and casual items in our midst. These empowered entities are data-generating and capturing, buffering, transmitting, etc. That is, tangible things are peppered with and prepared for the future. These are mostly resource-constrained and this phenomenon is called the Internet of Things (IoT). Further on, a wider variety of gadgets and gizmos in our working, walking and wandering locations are futuristically instrumented to be spontaneously interconnected and exceptionally intelligent in their behaviours. Thus, we hear, read and even feel connected and cognitive devices and machines in our everyday life. Once upon of a time, all our personal computers were connected via networks (LAN and WAN) and nowadays our personal and professional devices (fixed, portables, mobiles, wearables, implantables, handhelds, phablets, etc.) are increasingly interconnected (BAN, PAN, CAN, LAN. MAN and WAN) to exhibit a kind of intelligent behavior. This extreme connectivity and service-enablement of our everyday devices go to the level of getting seamlessly integrated with off-premise, online, and on-demand cloud-based applications, services, data sources, and content. This cloud-enablement is capable of making ordinary devices into extraordinary ones. However, most of the well-known and widely used embedded devices individually do not have sufficient computation power, battery, storage and I/O bandwidth to host and manage IoT applications and services. Hence performing data analytics on individual devices is a bit difficult.

As we all know, smart sensors and actuators are being randomly deployed in any significant environments such as homes, hospitals, hotels, etc. in order to minutely monitor, precisely measure, and insightfully manage the various parameters of the environments. Further on, powerful sensors are embedded and etched on different physical, mechanical, electrical and electronics systems in our everyday environments in order to empower them to join in the mainstream computing. Thus, not only environments but also all tangible things in those environments are also smartly sensor-enabled with a tactic as well as the strategic goal of making them distinctly sensitive and responsive in their operations, offerings, and outputs. Sensors are sweetly turning out to be the inseparable eyes and ears of any important thing in near future. This systematic sensor-enablement of ordinary things not only make them extraordinary but also lay out a stimulating and sparkling foundation for generating a lot of usable and time-critical data. Typically sensors and sensors-attached assets capture or generate and transmit all kinds of data to the faraway cloud environments (public, private and hybrid) through a host of standards-compliant sensor gateway devices. Precisely speaking, clouds represent the dynamic combination of several powerful server machines, storage appliances, and network solutions and are capable of processing tremendous amounts of multi-structured data to spit out actionable insights.

However, there is another side to this remote integration and data processing. For certain requirements, the local or proximate processing of data is mandated. That is, instead of capturing sensor and device data and transmitting them to the faraway cloud environments is not going to be beneficial for time-critical applications. Thereby the concept of edge or fog computing has emerged and is evolving fast these days with the concerted efforts of academic as well as corporate people. The reasonably powerful devices such as smartphones, sensor and IoT gateways, consumer electronics, set-top boxes, smart TVs, Web-enabled refrigerators, Wi-Fi routers, etc. are classified as fog or edge devices to form edge or fog clouds to do the much-needed local processing quickly and easily to arrive and articulate any hidden knowledge. Thus, fog or edge computing is termed and tuned as the serious subject of study and research for producing people-centric and real-time applications and services.

BRIEFING FOG / EDGE COMPUTING

Traditional networks, which feed data from devices or transactions to a central storage hub (data warehouses and data marts) can't keep up with the data volume and velocity created by IoT devices. Nor can the data warehouse model meet the low latency response times that users demand. The Hadoop platform in the cloud was supposed to be an answer. But sending the data to the cloud for analysis also poses a risk of data bottlenecks as well as security concerns. New business models, however, need data analytics in a minute or less. The problem of data congestion will only get worse as IoT applications and devices continue to proliferate.

There are certain interesting use cases such as rich connectivity and interactions among vehicles (V2V) and infrastructures (V2I). This emerging domain of IoT requires services like entertainment, education, and information, public safety, real-time traffic analysis and information, support for high mobility, context awareness and so forth. Such things see the light only if the infotainment systems within vehicles have to identify and interact with one another dynamically and also with wireless communication (Wang et al, 2011) infrastructures made available on the road, with remote traffic servers and FM stations, etc. The infotainment system is emerging as the highly synchronized gateway for vehicles on the road. Local devices need to interact themselves to collect data from vehicles and roads/expressways/tunnels/bridges to process them instantaneously to spit out useful intelligence. This is the salivating and sparkling foundation for fog/edge computing.

The value of the data decreases as the time goes. That is, the timeliness and the trustworthiness of data are very important for extracting actionable insights. The moment the data gets generated and captured, it has to be subjected to processing. That is, it is all about real-time capture. Also, it is all about gaining real-time insights through rule / policy-based data filtering, enrichment, pattern searching, aggregation, knowledge discovery, etc. to take a real-time decision and to build real-time applications. The picture below clearly articulates how the delay in capturing and analyzing data costs a lot in terms of business, technical and user values.

The latest trend of computing paradigm is to push the storage, networking, and computation to edge/fog devices for availing certain critical services. As devices are interconnected and integrated with the Internet, their computational capabilities and competencies are uniquely being leveraged in order to lessen the increasing load on cloud infrastructures. Edge devices are adequately instrumented at the design stage itself to interconnect with nearby devices automatically so that multiple devices dynamically can be found, bound, and composed for creating powerful and special-purpose edge clouds. Thus, the concept of fog or edge computing is blooming and booming these days.

The essence and gist of fog computing (Pan et al, 2017; Salman et al, 2015; Raj, 2015) are to keep data and computation close to end-users at the edge of the network and this arrangement has the added tendency of producing a new class of applications and services to end-users with low latency, high bandwidth, and context-awareness. Fog is invariably closer to humans rather than clouds and hence the name 'fog computing' is overwhelmingly accepted across. As indicated and illustrated above, fog devices are typically resource-intensive edge devices. Fog computing is usually touted as the supplement and complement to the popular cloud computing. Students, scholars, and scientists are keen towards unearthing a number of convincing and sellable business and technical cases for fog computing. Being closer to people, the revitalized fog or edge computing is to be extremely fruitful and fabulous in conceptualizing and concretizing a litany of people-centric software applications. Finally, in the era of big, fast, streaming and IoT data, fog/edge computing can facilitate edge analytics. Edge devices can filter out redundant, repetitive and routine data to reduce the precious network bandwidth and the data loads on clouds. Figure 1 vividly illustrates the fast-emerging three-tier architecture for futuristic computing.

The digitized objects (sensors, beacons, etc.) at the lowest level are generating and capturing poly-structured data in big quantities. The fog devices (gateways, controllers, etc.) at the second level are reasonably blessed with computational, communication and storage power in order to mix, mingle and merge with other fog devices in the environment to ingest and accomplish the local or proximate data processing to emit viable and value-adding insights in time. The third and final level is the faraway cloud centres. This introduction of fog devices in between clouds and digitized elements is the new twist brought in towards the ensuing era of knowledge-filled services. Fog devices act as intelligent intermediaries between cloud-based cyber/virtual applications and sensor/actuator (Lee et al, 2016; Tredway et al, 2016; Poole et al, 2015) data at the ground level. Here is another representation of fog computing as articulated in Figure 2.

ILLUSTRATING THE EPOCH-MAKING IOT JOURNEY

The mesmerizing number of smart sensors and actuators being deployed in specific environments ultimately produces massive volumes of data and currently, the collected data is faithfully transmitted over

Figure 1. The End-to-end Fog – Cloud Integration Architecture

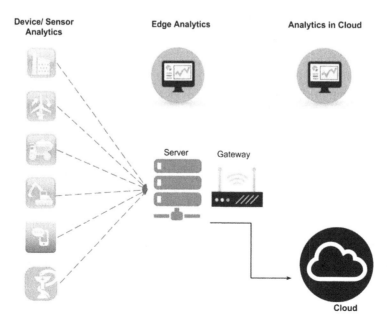

Figure 2. The Fog as the Intermediary between the Physical and the Cyber Worlds

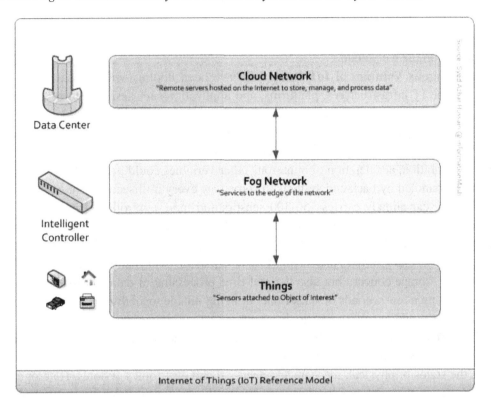

the Internet or any private network to faraway cloud infrastructures in order to be concertedly and calculatedly crunched to extract exceptional insights. As we all know, clouds are the best bet for doing the batch or historical processing through the renowned Hadoop framework. That is, cloud-based analytics is the overwhelming practice. However, the emerging trend is to come with micro-scale clouds in between the ground-level sensors and the cyber-level cloud applications towards fog analytics. This specialized cloud, which is being formed out of networked and resource-intensive devices in that environment, takes out the constricting stress on the traditional clouds. The proximate processing gets accomplished through these micro-clouds whereas the device data security and privacy is maintained. This kind of cloud-in-the-middle approach is capable of unearthing fresh IoT use cases. As any micro-cloud is very near the data-emitting sensors and sensors-attached assets, the faster processing and response are being achieved in an affordable fashion.

- **It Is All About the Extreme and Deeper Connectivity:** As the inventive paradigm of networked embedded devices expands into multiple business domains and industry verticals such as manufacturing facilities and floors, healthcare centers, retail stores, luxury hotels, spacious homes, energy grids and transportation systems, there is a greater scope for deriving sophisticated applications not only for businesses but also for commoners. The world is tending towards the connected world. Recent devices come with the connectivity feature and there are a vast number of hitherto unconnected legacy devices. Further on, there are resource-constrained devices such as heart rate monitors to temperature & humidity sensors, in plenty and enabling them to be integrated with other devices and web applications is definitely a big challenge. Thus, connectivity solutions and platforms are being brought in to enable every tangible device to be connected. The connectivity is not only with adjacent devices in the vicinity but also with the remotely held applications and data sources on the web/cloud.

- **The Humongous Volumes of IoT Data:** We have been fiddling with transaction systems extensively. The IT infrastructures, platforms, and applications are designed to be appropriate for streamlining and speeding up transactions. However, with the faster penetration of devices and digitized entities, there is a relook. That is, operational systems are becoming more prevalent and prominent. In the impending IoT era, a sensor or smart device that is monitoring temperature, humidity, vibration, acceleration or numerous other variables could potentially generate data that needs to be handled by back-end systems in some way every millisecond. For example, a typical Formula One car already carries 150-300 sensors and more controllers, sensors, and actuators are being continuously incorporated to bring in more automation. Today, these hundred sensors already capture data in milliseconds. The racecars generate 100-200 KBs of data per second, amounting to several terabytes in a racing season. There are twin challenges for back-end systems. Not only the storage concern but also the real-time processing of data is also equally important. That is, missing a few seconds of sensor data or being unable to analyze it efficiently and rapidly, can lead to risks and in some cases, to disasters.

- **Major IoT Data Types:** There are three major data types that will be common to most IoT projects:

- **Measurement Data:** Sensors monitor and measure the various parameters of the environment as well as the states of physical, mechanical, electrical and electronics systems. Heterogeneous and multiple sensors read and transmit data very frequently and hence with a larger number of sensors and frequent readings, the total data size is bound to grow exponentially. This is the crux of the IoT era. A particular company in the oil and gas space is already dealing with more than 100TB of such data per day.

- **Event Data:** Any status change, any break-in of the threshold value, any noteworthy incident or untoward accident, and any decision-enabling data are simply categorized event data. With devices assisting people in their daily assignments and engagements, the number of events is likely to shoot up. We have powerful simple and complex event processing engines in order to discover and disseminate knowledge out of event data.

- **Interaction and Transaction Data:** With the extreme and deeper connectivity amongst devices, the quality and quantity of purpose-specific interactions between devices are going to be greater. Several devices with unique functionality can connect and collaborate for achieving composite functions. The transaction operations are also enabled in devices. Not only inter-device communication but also human-device communication is fairly happening.

- **Diagnostics Data:** The delectable advancements in the IoT domain has led to millions of networked embedded devices and smart objects, information, transactional, analytical and operational systems. There are online, off-premise, and on-demand applications, data sources, and services in plenty. The application portfolio is consistently on the rise for worldwide enterprises. There are software infrastructure solutions, middleware, databases, data virtualization and knowledge visualization platforms, and scores of automation tool. The health of each of these systems is very important for the intended success of any business transaction. Diagnostics is the type of data that gives an insight into the overall health of a machine, system or process. Diagnostic data might not only show the overall health of a system but also show whether the monitoring of that system is also working effectively.

Precisely speaking, the IoT data is going to be big and we have techniques and platforms for big data processing. However, the intriguing challenge is to do real-time processing of IoT big data. Researchers are on the job to unearth path-breaking algorithms to extract timely insights out of big data. Fog computing is one such concept prescribed as a viable and venerable answer for the impending data-driven challenges.

The IoT is turning out to be a primary enabler of the digital transformation of any kind of enterprising businesses. Companies are eagerly looking towards pioneering digital technologies to create and sustain their business competitiveness. The IoT and other digital technologies are helping companies to facilitate process enhancement, create newer business models, optimize the IT infrastructures, bring forth competent architectures, empower workforce efficiency and innovation, etc. The IoT closes down the gap between the physical and cyber worlds. helps connect physical and digital environments. Data collected from connected devices are subjected to a variety of investigations to extract dependable insights.

THE USE CASES OF FOG / EDGE COMPUTING

The rapid growth of personal, social and professional devices in our daily environments has seeded this inimitable computing style. The communication becomes wireless, sensors and devices are heterogeneous and large in number, geo-distribution becomes the new normal, the interconnectivity and interactions among various participants emit a lot of data, etc. The amount of data getting generated and gathered at the edge of the network is really massive in volumes.

Usually, this data is transported back to the cloud for storage and processing, which incidentally requires high bandwidth connectivity. In order to save network bandwidth, there is a valid proposition of using a moderately sized platform in between to do a kind of pre-processing in order to filter out the flabs. Differently enabled cameras, for example, generate images and videos that would aggregate easily in the range of terabytes. Instead of clogging expensive and scarce network bandwidths, a kind of fog/ edge processing can be initiated to ease networks. That is, reasonably powerful devices in the environment under monitoring can be individually or collectively leveraged to process cameras-emitted files in real-time. That is, the data gleaned can be subsequently segmented and shared to different devices in the vicinity in order to do the distributed processing quickly. As we all know, with more devices joining in the mainstream computing and the amount of data getting stocked is growing exponentially, the distributed computing concept has soared in the recent past and is being touted as the mandated way forward for the data-centric world.

There are a number of convincing use cases for fog/edge computing. Fog devices locally collect, cleanse, store, process, and even analyze data in order to facilitate real-time analytics towards informed decisions. There are research papers describing how connected vehicles, smart grids, wireless sensor and actuator networks, etc. are more right and relevant for people with the fast-moving fog computing paradigm. Smart building, manufacturing floors, smart traffic and retail, and smart cities are some of the often-cited domains wherein the raging fog idea chips in with real benefits. Augmented reality (AR), content delivery and mobile data analytics are also very well documented as the direct beneficiaries of fog computing. One use case for fog computing is a smart traffic light system, which can change its signals based on surveillance of incoming traffic to prevent accidents or reduce congestion. Data could also be sent to the cloud for longer-term analytics. Other use cases include rail safety; power restoration from a smart grid network; and cybersecurity. There are connected cars (for vehicle-to-vehicle and vehicle-to-cloud communication); and in smart city applications, such as intelligent lighting and smart parking meters.

- **Smart Homes:** There is a home security application profoundly discussed in a research paper. As we all know, there is a myriad of home security products (smart lock, video/audio recorder, security sensors and monitors (alarm, presence, occupancy, motion sensors etc.). These are stand-alone solutions and due to disparate data transport protocols and data formats, these products do not interoperate with one another. However, the emergence and emancipation of fog computing have simplified the process of dynamically integrating these diverse security products in order to enhance the timeliness and trustworthiness of any security information. The uniqueness of fog computing platform is that it can be flexibly deployed on a virtual machine or in a Docker container. Existing and new sensors and actuators register and get connected with the fog platform, which ensures a seamless and spontaneous interoperation between different and distributed devices and machines towards the goal. This ad-hoc collaboration capability senses any kind of security threats and immediately stimulates the necessary countermeasures through connected actuators. Energy management, device clustering and coordination, ambient assisted living (AAL), activity recognition / context-awareness for formulating and firming up people-centric services, etc. are getting streamlined with the fog computing nuances.

- **Smart Grids:** Smart electric grid is an electricity distribution network with smart meters deployed at various locations to measure the real-time power consumption level. A centrally hosted SCADA server frequently gathers and analyzes status data to send out appropriate information to power grids to adapt accordingly. If there is any palpable increment in power usage or any kind of emergency, it will be instantaneously conveyed to the power grid to act upon. Now with the fog idea, the centralized SCADA server can be supplemented by one or more decentralized microgrids. This salient setup improves scalability, cost-efficiency, security and rapid response of the power system. This also helps to integrate distributed and different power generators (solar panels, wind farms, etc.) with the main power grid. Energy load balancing applications may run on edge devices such as smart meters and microgrids. Based on energy demand, availability, and the lowest price, these devices automatically switch to alternative energies like solar and wind.

- **Smart Vehicles:** The fog concept can be extended to vehicular networks also. The fog nodes can be deployed along the roadside. The fog nodes can send to and receive information from vehicles. Vehicles through their in-vehicle infotainment systems can interact with the roadside fog systems as well as with other vehicles on the road. Thus, this kind of ad hoc networks leads to a variety of applications such as traffic light scheduling, congestion mitigation, precaution sharing, parking facility management, traffic information sharing, etc. A video camera that senses an ambulance flashing lights can automatically change streetlights to open lanes for the vehicle to pass through traffic. Smart streetlights interact locally with sensors and detect the presence of pedestrian and bikers, and measure the distance and speed of approaching vehicles.

- **Smarter Security:** Security and surveillance cameras are being fitted in different important junctions such as airports, nuclear installations, government offices, retail stores, etc. Further on, nowadays smartphones are embedded with powerful cameras to click selfies as well as produce photos of others. Still, as well as running images can be captured and communicated to nearby fog nodes as well as to faraway cloud nodes in order to readily process the photos and compare them with the face images of radicals, extremists, fundamentalists, terrorists, arsonists, trouble-makers, etc. in the already stored databases. Further on, through image processing and analytics, it is possible to extract useful information in the form unusual gestures, movements, etc. All these empower security and police officials to proceed in their investigations with clarity and confidence. The Figure 3 pictorially conveys how the fog cloud facilitates real-time sensor data processing and historical sensor data processing at nearby or faraway clouds (public, private and hybrid).

- **Smart Buildings:** Like homes, office and corporate buildings are stuffed with a number of sensors for minute monitoring, precise measurement, and management. There is a school of thought that multiple sensor values, when blended, throw more accurate value. There are advanced sensor data fusion algorithms and hence, smart sensors and actuators work in tandem towards automating and accelerating several manual tasks. For providing a seamless and smart experience to employees and visitors, the building automation domain is on the fast trajectory with a series of innovations and improvisations in the IT space. That is, computing becomes pervasive, communication is ambient, sensing is ubiquitous, actuation is intelligently accomplished, etc. The computer vision and perception topics gather momentum, knowledge engineering and enhancement are becoming common and cheap and decision-enablement becomes perfect. The edge devices participating in and contributing to the edge cloud facilitate multiple things intelligently so that the strategic goal of building automation through networking and integration is getting accomplished.

Figure 3. The Fog ensures zero latency towards Real-time Applications

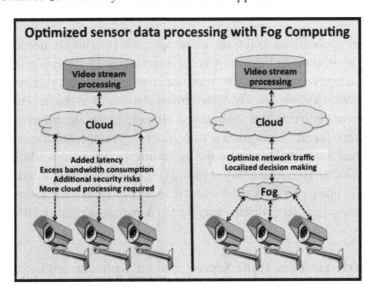

Figure 4.

Today, a medium-sized office building could have hundreds of sensors on its equipment. A great example is chillers, a product needed to cool a building. The product manufacturer (http://www.johnson-controls.com/) monitors chillers remotely using predictive diagnostics to identify and solve issues before they become problems. The company uses internal operational data and historical records to better plan machine maintenance, leading to better operational efficiency and decreasing energy usage, in addition to increase reliability and equipment lifespan. Even better, the company has external data resources like weather patterns and grid demand costs to drive greater operational savings.

There are several other industry verticals and business domains yearning to get immensely benefited out of all the decisive and delectable advancements in the field of fog computing.

WHY EDGE COMPUTING FOR REAL-TIME DATA SCIENCE?

For producing real-time applications, real-time information and insights are needed. Real-time analytics is the way forward for generating timely inputs for empowering IT systems and business workloads accordingly to exhibit adaptive behaviour. Data science covers everything that supports the transition of data to information and to knowledge. There are proven algorithms in the field of data science. There are cloud-based cognitive platforms and applications utilizing those algorithms in a progressive and positive way. Now the time for embedding data science algorithms and applications into edge appliances and clouds to supply real-time intelligence for the increasingly connected world has come. A kind of edge analytics inside vehicles goes a long way in identifying and automating a myriad of vehicle needs. Vehicles' drivers and occupants get a lot of benefits. A variety of spatial and temporal applications are being worked out. In this section, let us discuss why the fog paradigm is right and relevant to the intended success of data science.

- **Weeding out Irrelevant Data at the Source:** The IoT represents trillions of digitized objects, billions of connected devices and millions of software applications. The direct offshoot is that the amount of data getting generated, captured and transmitted is really voluminous. However, most of the data are repetitive, redundant and routine. The edge computing facilitates filtering out the inconsequential data at the edge of the network so that useful and usable data can be communicated to cloud environments in order to have speedy and sagacious analytics. There is very minimal wastage of network bandwidth with this pre-processing at the edges.

- **Real-Time IoT Data Analytics:** For certain scenarios such as historical, comprehensive and posterior processing, the traditional clouds are insisted. Faraway clouds are typically for batch processing or at the most near real-time processing. But the faster maturity and stability of edge computing readily enables real-time processing of device data. That is, there are scenarios craving for real-time data capture and analysis in order to emit out real-time insights. We have discussed the fog/edge analytics in below sections.

- **Instantaneous Response:** There are many use cases wherein faster responses are not needed. Turning on the lights, closing the garage door, or checking the vending machine status, etc. come under this category. However, there are use cases expecting a faster response. For example, vehicles on the road or any moving object has to respond immediately to surrounding situations. Thus, it is indispensable to have fog compute infrastructure in place in order to accomplish actions with very low latency.

- **Resource-Constrained Sensors Behind Fog Devices:** Many sensors do not have enough compute, memory and storage power in order to have their own IPv6 address. Hence, they can hide behind an edge device, which has the power to have its own IPv6 address. It is, therefore, pertinent to configure ground-level and resource-constrained sensors and actuators behind the edge device. The arrival of edge computing has henceforth solidified the sensors to be slimmer, purpose-specific and cheaper.

- **IoT Data Security:** Any external attack on sensors can be stopped at the edge device, which acts as a shelter, strength, stronghold, and saviour for feeble sensors. The idea is to prolong the livelihood of sensors. Also, the sensor data are transmitted to edge devices to be stocked and subjected to specific investigations over any local network only. That is, the sensor data is kept away from the public and porous Internet. Sharing sensor data to public cloud environments is beset with challenges. There can be further advancements on the security front in the days to unfurl.

- **The Formation of Edge Clouds:** All kinds of powerful edge devices can be clubbed together dynamically to form device clusters. Having such edge clouds is an important precursor for doing edge data analytics to emit out real-time intelligent to act upon with all the confidence and clarity. Thus, fog devices with the capability of realizing ad hoc clouds are the real trendsetters for doing local or proximate processing of device and sensor data.

- **Building Composite Applications:** Devices and equipment being deployed in a specific environment (say, a restaurant) communicate to their vendors directly in order to push a variety of data. Specifically, the lighting data would go to the lighting vendor, the kitchen equipment data to the kitchen equipment vendor, and so forth However there is very little for the environment occupants and owners. Now with the surging popularity of fog computing, all kinds of sensor and equipment data get aggregated at the restaurant fog device. Edge device messages are getting accentuated, enriched, secured, and directed to their proper destination through a fog middleware. The messages also can be combined with other relevant messages from other internal as well as external sources to supply viable and venerable insights to decision-making, recommender and expert systems. That is, street traffic data, weather report, demographic information, etc. can be cleansed and enriched to be a stimulant for a range of path-breaking applications including corporate, in-restaurant operational optimization, supply chain, and perhaps a variety of applications for third-party constituents, such as government regulators, suppliers, etc.

- **Policy-Based Fog Devices:** With fog devices being positioned as the most crucial component for the proclaimed success of the IoT idea, it becomes paramount for fog devices to be enabled policy-aware. The brewing idea is to establish and enforce security, governance, role-based access, activation, and configuration policies. Different policies can be inserted in fog devices to have a firm grip and control on all the sensors and actuators attached.

Precisely speaking, the unprecedented and phenomenal acceptance and adoption of the edge computing is a breakthrough for sustaining the strategic journey of the IoT concept. There is this new paradigm of fog or edge computing vigorously and rigorously capturing the imagination of IoT professionals these days. That is, the real-time and relatively small-scale processing is shifted to edge devices instead of aggregating and transmitting device data to faraway cloud servers to squeeze out insights. Localized and personalized decisions are essential in certain scenarios and hence the fast-evolving concept of fog computing is being gleefully received. The edge devices are dynamically discovered and linked through body, personal and local area networks to form ad-hoc edge clouds to accelerate and accentuate edge analytics. With the rapid explosion of connected things, devices, and services, it is understandable that the decentralized networking is the best way forward as it has the inherent potential to reduce infrastructure and maintenance costs. Decentralization guarantees increased robustness by removing single points of failure. By shifting from centralized to decentralized processing, devices at the edges gain greater autonomy to become the core and central point of transactions towards enhanced productivity and value for owners and users.

With the unprecedented success of the pioneering digitization and edge computing technologies and tools, every tangible thing in our daily environments is becoming a digitized / smart/sentient object. It is foreseen that everyone in this world will have one or more smartphones / personal digital assistants/ wearables soon. Every unique asset and artefact (physical, mechanical, electrical, and electronics) participating in our daily deals and deeds is systematically and sagaciously enabled through edge/fog technologies and cloud applications to be computational, communicative, sensitive, perceptive, responsive and cognitive. Ultimately our everyday environments are to be bedecked with a variety of smart sensors and actuators to fulfil the prime goals of precision-centric context-awareness and activity recognition. Further on, cloud-based cyber applications will have a salivating and scintillating role in empowering physical items on the ground. In short, the ensuing era is all about producing and providing knowledge-filled services that are people-centric, situation-aware, and event-driven.

In today's digitally connected society, there will be deeper and decisive affinity among enabled objects, connected devices, and humans in the days ahead. The result is that large volumes of multi-structured data are getting generated at different speeds, sizes, scopes, and schemas through the interactions and collaborations of heterogeneous digital elements, smartphones, technical experiments, social media, healthcare instruments, machines, satellite telemetry, and imagery. These data lead to formulating and firm up various new analytical competencies such as social media analytics, sentiment analytics, predictive, prognostic, prescriptive, personalized analytics etc. for people empowerment. The prickling challenge is how efficiently and effectively subjects the captured and cleansed data to various specific investigations to readily extract real-time intelligence to make right inferences. In this section, we will dig deep and describe at length about the uniqueness of edge analytics.

- **The Greatness of Edge Data:** It is a known fact that the unprecedented rise in data sources has led to the emergence of the strategically sound big data discipline and its allied technologies. The big data landscape is therefore relentlessly and rightly growing. Besides the enormity of the data being produced by knowledge workers and social animals, the growing size of machine-generated data is to get prime importance in the impending big data era. Machine data especially of edge devices is progressively playing a very pivotal role in shaping up the crucial aspect of data-driven insights and insights-driven decisions. The story thus far is that firstly there are a voluminous production and extensive deployment of smart sensors and actuators in a variety of environments (home, industrial, social, entertainment, education, etc.) for different purposes. The much-discussed connectivity, which is constantly becoming deeper and extreme, connects them via different modes: wireless, wireline and the mix of them. That is, there are millions of devices at the edges of networks and it is projected that the number of devices will turn out to be in the range of billions in the years to unfurl.

All these are being intensively deciphered and deliberated these days because of the unparalleled advancements in the embedded and connectivity domains. Both resource-rich and constrained devices are systematically hooked together in an ad hoc fashion to interchange their data and share their unique capabilities. Further on, edge devices are grandly integrated with cyber applications and services hosted at distant cloud environments. These direct, as well as indirect integrations and interactions, have laid a strong and stimulating foundation for a sharp hike in edge data generation. Data is being collected by an enormous variety of equipment, such as smart utility meters, surveillance and security cameras, actuators, robots, RFID readers, biometrics, factory-line sensors, mobile phones, fitness machines, defence equipment and weapons, launchers and satellites, avionics and automobiles, information appliances, household utensils and wares, electronic gadgets and gizmos, lab-experimentation devices, and medical instruments.

The ubiquitous connectivity and the mass production of modern sensors and actuators have opened up a whole new powerhouse for valuable information. It is clear that edge data can bring forth significant value and a rich set of sophisticated services to all stakeholders including end-users. The careful and cognitive capture, processing, and analysis of edge data in time can go a long way in empowering organizations to respond to both positive as well as negative events pre-emptively and solve many problems that were previously out of reach.

The point here is that this untapped resource of edge data has the inherent potential to deliver dependable insights that can transform the operations and strategic initiatives of public and private sector organizations. Incidentally, the edge data is becoming larger, speedier and trickier but the hidden value is definitely greater. And hence, distinct research endeavours on making sense out of edge data are drawing phenomenal attention. On the other hand, there are standards-compliant big data analytics platforms (open source as well as commercial-grade), data ingestion and crunching toolsets, data virtualization and visualization tools, knowledge engineering techniques, high-performance multicore processors, gigabits Ethernet solutions, and inexpensive storage options including object storage to extract and extrapolate knowledge.

In summary, as the size of edge data is growing significantly, there is a bigger challenge to information management professionals to evolve a pragmatic strategy for effectively leveraging all sorts of edge data for the well-being of their organizations. With the faster maturity and stability of data analytics platforms, knowledge systems and services are bound to grow and glow.

THE EDGE ANALYTICS: THE PROMINENT USE CASES

Edge data is carefully captured and crunched using fog devices for generating intelligent immediately. Here are a few interesting use cases for edge analytics.

- **IoT Sensor Data Monitoring and Analysis:** It is clear that the massive deployment of heterogeneous sensors leads to the tremendous amount of sensor data. Moving sensor data analytics to the edge with a platform that can analyze batch, fast and streaming data simultaneously enables organizations to speed and simplify analytics to get the insights they need, right where they need them.
- **Remote Monitoring and Analysis of Oil and Gas Operations:** Edge analytics is a boon for companies in oil and gas exploration, refinement, storage, and distribution. Any kind of delay in sensing and responding to such kinds of rough and risky environments paves for disaster. Cloud-based analytics is time-consuming and it is not possible to expect real-time responses from far-away cloud environments. Having near-instant analysis at the site as the data is being created can help these organizations see the signs of a disaster and take measures to prevent a catastrophe before it starts.
- **Predictive Asset Management:** This capability sharply improves the overall availability and operational performance of physical assets while reducing their total cost of ownership (TCO). Edge analytics enable organizations to move from scheduled maintenance models to predictive ones. That is, it is all about predictive and preventive maintenance giving product managers to gain the expert control over their equipment and maintenance resources. These capabilities help avoid catastrophic failures by identifying critical issues that occur inside the normally scheduled maintenance window, lower costs by eliminating unnecessary maintenance tasks and make more effective use of scarce and expensive resources (both human and capital).
- **Smarter Cities:** Intel defines that the smart city concept mandates the use of smart-grid infrastructures to improve environmental sustainability, manage energy consumption, better coordinate public resources, and protect the quality of life for urban and metropolitan citizens and plan for sustainable growth. The edge data here plays a very incredible role. For example, utility companies and governments are using data from the smart grid to understand the complex relationships between generation, transmission, distribution, and consumption with the goal of delivering reliable energy and reducing operating costs. Consumers are also empowered with insights from the smart grid to better manage their personal energy requirements. For example, a "not home" state might turn off lights, shut down unused equipment and adjust the home temperature. Utility meter readings and grid data are brought into centralized analytical systems to bring forth timely insights.

Thus, edge devices collaboratively contribute immensely to arriving at better decisions than only at a centralized control centre. Communication between devices helps determine when, where, and how much energy should be produced and consumers can use home management tools to monitor and adjust energy consumption accordingly.

- **Smart Retailers:** It is a well-known thing that supermarkets and hypermarkets across the globe duly collect a lot of data every day. If they are properly collected, cleansed, and categorized, worldwide retailers can substantially enhance their grip on their customers and their buying patterns. This incredible knowledge on customers prepares retail stores to think big and to bring forth scores of premium services in time to retain and delight their loyal customers as well as to attract new customers. The enduring challenges thrown by the hugeness in the data being captured and processed is being tackled through highly versatile Hadoop framework / Spark that can totally change the retail economics by radically lowering the cost of data storage and processing, bringing in new flexibilities to gain new insights, automated replenishment and more accurately market to individuals rather than a demographic.

Retailers are using a variety of intelligent systems that gather data and provide immediate feedback to help them to engage shoppers fruitfully. The well-known data-generation systems include digital signage, PoS systems, vending machines, transaction, in-store cameras, dispensing kiosks, etc. The ability to gain reliable insights from the data shared by these systems makes it possible to provide customer-centric "connected stores". Context-awareness is the main theme of these connected machines to precisely and perfectly understand the customer situation. The context information then greatly differentiates in showering customers with a host of unique services. In short, the insights-driven shopping experience is enabling customers immensely in getting items for the best price. Based on the edge data, retailers can integrate their supply chain activities intelligently. Further on, retailers can provide their customers with opportunities to engage with their preferred brands in more meaningful ways to cement customer loyalty.

- **Smart Automobiles:** The number of digital electronics and other automation elements in a vehicle is steadily on the climb for providing different kinds of services to drivers and the occupants. The convenience, care, choice, and comfort induced by these connected devices are definitely awesome. Sensors are being attached to every critical component in a car to pre-emptively get to know the component's status and this reading provides some leeway for drivers to ponder about the next course of action. Another interesting and involving module is the in-vehicle infotainment system, which is emerging as the core and central gateway for securing and strengthening the connectivity outside for a range of use cases. All kinds of communication, computing, and entertainment systems inside vehicles will have a seamless connection with the outside world through the well-defined in-vehicle system so that the occupants can enjoy their trip in a fruitful manner. GPS devices and smart meters of cars throw a lot of data to be captured and analyzed.

Sensors provide information to automated parking systems to substantially lessen the driver's workload. There are sensors-enabled driver assistance systems for automobiles. Location data could be combined with road work and other traffic information to help commuters avoid congestion or take a faster route. Digital signage, cameras and other infrastructures on the roadsides in synchronization with the in-vehicle infotainment module (V2I) aid drivers to give a pleasant travel experience to all. Vehicles today talk to other vehicles (V2V) on the road and interact with remote cloud services and applications (V2C). Vehicles share their data to the remotely held databases in order to facilitate the different aspects of vehicle analytics. Maps are the other salivating tool for reaching out the destination in a cool and controlled manner. Detecting real-time traffic flow from each direction and automatically changing traffic signals are to improve flow.

Autonomous vehicles are tending towards the reality with the realization of the advanced and accurate machine and deep learning algorithms. Further on, there are breakthrough technologies enabling transmission of real-time vehicle telematics, GPS tracking, and geofencing data. These noteworthy improvisations lead to improved safety, mobility, and efficiency and pave the way for new business models such as pay-as-you-go auto insurance. Proactive maintenance decreases costs and reduces vehicle downtime.

Edge data further enable automated, intelligent, and real-time decisions to optimize travel across the transportation infrastructure as cars become capable of connecting to the roadway, safety systems, and one another.

- **Smart Manufacturing:** Every tangible machine and tool in manufacturing floors and production facilities is being stuffed with a manifold of smart sensors, communication modules, etc. That is, today's devices are instrumented to interoperate and be intelligent in their operations and obligations. Machines are not only networked with others in the neighbourhood but also with remote cloud environments. Today all the production-related data are being shared with the centralized systems in the form of excel sheets at the end of the day through emails. But new-generation machines are capable of integrating with cloud-enabled software applications and cloud storages instantly and insightfully. That is, machines transfer all the ground-level information to the cyber-level transaction and analytical systems then and there. This technology-inspired real-time connectivity facilitates a number of fresh possibilities and opportunities for corporates in visualizing hitherto unforeseen competencies. In addition, chief executives and other decision-makers, who are on the move in a far away land, can be provided with decision-enabling productivity details through a real-time notification capability in order to ensure any course correction if necessary, commit something solid to their customers with all the confidence and clarity, ponder about new offerings, bring operational efficiencies, explore newer avenues for fresh revenues, etc.

That is, smart factories connect the boardroom, the factory floor and the supply chain for higher levels of manufacturing control and efficiency. Sensors and actuators in devices such as cameras, robotic machines, and motion-control equipment generate and use data to provide real-time diagnosis and predictive maintenance, increased process visibility and improved factory uptime and flexibility. Thus, edge data lays a sparkling foundation for smart manufacturing.

- **Facilities and Asset Management:** The big data generated by increasingly instrumented, interconnected and intelligent facilities and assets are useful only if transactional systems could extract applicable information and act upon it as needed. The appropriate and real-time usage of this big data is to help improve decisions or generate corrective actions that can create measurable benefits for an organization. Big data analytics can help generate revenue by providing a contextual understanding of information that the business can then employ to its fullest advantage. For example, geographic information systems (GIS) can help location-sensitive organizations such as retailers, telecommunications, and energy companies determine the most advantageous geographies for their business operations. A world's largest wind energy producer has achieved success using a big data modelling solution to harvest insights from an expanded set of location-dependent factors including historical and actual weather to help optimize wind turbine placement and performance. Exact pinpointing the optimal locations for wind turbines enables energy producers to maximize power generation and reduce energy costs as well as to provide its customers with greater business case certainty, quicker results, and increased predictability and reliability in wind power generation.

Effective facilities and asset management solution have to leverage big data analytics to enable organizations to proactively maintain facilities equipment, identify emerging problems to prevent breakdowns, lower maintenance, and operations costs and extend asset life through condition-based maintenance and automated issue-notification. To help mitigate risks to facilities and assets, predictive analytics can detect even minor anomalies and failure patterns to determine the assets that are at the greatest risk of failure. Predictive maintenance analytics can access multiple data sources in real time to predict equipment failure which helps organizations avoid costly downtime and reduce maintenance costs. Sensors could capture the operating conditions of critical equipment such as vibrations from ship engines and communicate the captured data in real time to company's command centre for proceeding with failure analysis and predictive maintenance. Similarly, the careful analysis of environmental and weather-pattern data in real time is another way of mitigating any kind of visible or invisible risks. Organizations can receive alerts of potential weather impacts in time to shut down facilities operations or pre-locate emergency response teams to minimize business disruption in case of any advancing storms.

Big data is admirably advantageous when applied to the management of facilities and assets (everything from office buildings to oil-drilling platforms to fleets of the ship). This is due to the increased instrumentation of facilities and assets, where the digital and physical worlds have synchronized to generate massive volumes of data. Therefore considering the mammoth volume of data, tool-supported analysis of big data can lead to bountiful benefits such as increased revenue, lowered operating expenses, enhanced service availability and reduced risk. In a nutshell, edge data is a ground-breaking phenomenon for all kinds of industrial sectors to zoom ahead with all the required conviction.

IoT Data Edge Analytics for Next-Gen Data Science

Embedded cognitive IoT will become a key focus area for software engineers, experts, and evangelists. One of the key ingredients will be an open source platform for building, tuning, and deploying cognitive applications into edge devices. The ideal development platform for open, embedded, and cognitive IoT applications have to have the following features.

The platform has to facilitate embedding of cognitive analytics capabilities so that IoT devices and services can adapt continuously and react locally to their environments and, as needed, to metrics and commands from neighbouring devices. This has to enable developers to access, configure, and tweak any cognitive computing algorithm that is suited to the IoT analytics requirements. Further on, it has to execute cognitive algorithms on any size IoT device. It also has to present flexible and familiar programming models for IoT development, including Python, Java, and C. The platform has the wherewithal to analyze data as it streams at the device level and thereby eliminates the need to store it persistently. The platform also ought to support the execution of all or most cognitive IoT processing locally, reducing or eliminating the need to round-trip many capabilities back to cloud-based computing clusters. The platform has to accelerate memory-speed local drill down into growing streams of locally acquired and cached sensor data. It also has the connectors, adapters, and drivers to access data from any streaming data platform, as well as from any RDBMS, hub, repository, file system, or another store in any cloud, on-premise, or off-premise.

AD HOC EDGE CLOUDS FOR EDGE ANALYTICS

The ultimate aim of edge clouds is to deliver low-latency, bandwidth-efficient, and resilient applications. Edge clouds are being formed out of connected and resource-intensive fog devices in order to do certain functionalities locally. Edge clouds stand in between faraway clouds in the cyber world and scores of sensors/actuators in the physical world. Edge clouds store every machine and sensor data, subject them to specific investigations and spit out actionable insights that can be given directly to fog devices and to resource-constrained actuators at the ground level. This level of extreme and deeper connectivity and process integration leads to the consistent eruption of path-breaking and people-centric applications. Similarly, the insights emitted out by edge clouds can be readily integrated with cloud-based applications in order to build sophisticated applications.

The edge cloud facilitates a kind of new-generation architecture for seamlessly integrating local edge networks and cloud networks. This is to keep latency-sensitive computation and user interaction components close to end-users at the edge nodes while hosting additional heavy-duty processing and database components in cloud center nodes. Another perceptible benefit is the bandwidth gets conserved by doing the initial activities at the edge so that only highly compressed and compact data get transmitted to cloud environments over the Internet communication infrastructure. The edge cloud is able to access various physical assets, mechanical and electrical devices, consumer electronics, etc. and receives their data. Edge clouds contribute to the application and system resilience. If edge cloud or one of its components fails for any reason, then the traditional cloud environment takes care of the processing. On the reverse side, when something happens to the cloud center due to network failure, natural calamities, or power outage, etc., then the edge cloud takes care of the processing. Thus, edge cloud comes as a complementary cloud environment for faster sensing and responding.

Edge computing is pushing computing applications, data, and services away from centralized cloud data centers to the edges of the underlying network. The objective is to perform data analytics near the source of data to quickly raise right alerts and indulge inappropriate actions immediately. Finally, edge clouds enable end-users getting empowered with knowledge-filled services. In short, edge clouds are for local data processing. Traditional clouds are being realized through a set of homogeneous server machines, storage appliances, and network solutions. Edge clouds are, on the other hand, is formed through clubbing together of decentralized and heterogeneous devices. Edge clouds are generally ad hoc.

The public cloud idea typically represents the online, off-premise and on-demand computing whereas the fog computing is for proximity computing. Of course, there are private and hybrid clouds that use dynamically changing clusters of commodity server machines for data processing and logic execution. The fog computing paradigm extends the computing to the network of edge devices. The fog vision was conceived and aptly concretized in order to comprehensively attend some specific use cases for the smarter computing era. There are specific applications such as gaming, video conferencing, etc. mandating very low and predictable latency. Then there are geo-distributed applications (smarter traffic, grid, etc., pipeline monitoring, environmental monitoring and management through the sensor and actuator networks, etc.). Further on, mobility applications such as connected cars and transports are pitching for the fog paradigm. The next logical step is to have hybrid environments by seamlessly and spontaneously integrating edge and traditional cloud environments for availing advanced and aggregated analytics.

In summary, clouds have been the prominent and dominant infrastructures to develop, debug, deploy, and deliver pioneering business and IT applications. However, cloud computing cannot solve all problems due to its own drawbacks. Applications, such as real-time gaming, augmented reality, and data streaming, are too latency-sensitive to be deployed in the cloud. The networks are clogged due to the growth in data transmission. Sharing sensor and device data over any network is beset with security and privacy challenges and concerns. Real-time analytics is being positioned as the most important requirements for generating real-time insights and making timely decision-making. Since cloud centers are geographically distributed, those applications and services will suffer unacceptable round-trip latency, when data are transmitted from/to end devices to/from the cloud data center through multiple gateways. Cloud-based data analytics sometimes misses the real-time mandate and hence there are efforts in order to craft ad hoc clouds out of devices in the local environment. Multiple and heterogeneous devices in the vicinity are readily identified and connected with one another to form edge or fog clouds to tackle the rising volume of device and sensor data to make sense out of it. The Figure 5 clearly depicts how edge clouds come handy in fulfilling the real-time data capture, processing, decision-making, and actuation requirements.

EDGE APPLICATION AND ANALYTICS PLATFORMS

Fog devices individually cannot do much. They need to be integrated and empowered through a pioneering platform. In other words, we need highly efficient and elegant platform for accomplishing and acquiring the originally envisaged benefits of fog computing and analytics. The traditional enterprise, cloud, and web-based platforms are not suitable for fog computing, as fog devices are not resource-

Figure 5. The Edge Clouds is the Next-Gen Real-time Clouds

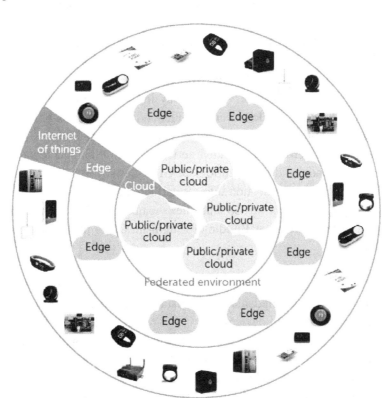

intensive. We need highly modular and extremely adaptive platforms to activate and accentuate the fog computing ideals and ideas. Any fog computing platforms need to be fully synchronized for performing IoT data ingestion, processing, analytics, decision-making, and actuation. The platform has to have the device management and gateway capabilities. This is due to the fact that devices are typically dynamic and nomadic and can come, join and even go out of the network. In this section, we are to discuss the breakthrough techniques in building competitive fog platforms that in turn lead to highly competitive IoT gateways (Raj and Raman, 2016).

The typical fog or edge devices include reasonably powerful controllers, communication gateways, Wi-Fi routers, smartphones, consumer electronics, robots, etc. On the other side, these fog devices interact with a variety of resource-constrained sensors, actuators, digitized objects, sensors-attached physical assets, etc. with the intention of getting, cleansing, curating, translating, and transforming the IoT data. Further on, fog devices crunch the data to discover actionable insights to perform many things intelligently. Fog devices, based on the inputs and insights obtained through the stringent analytics process, activate IoT devices to do many things. Fog devices contribute as a well-intended broker and bus to enable fruitful interactions between IoT entities at the ground with cloud-based applications.

As technology continuously advances, the product vendors are steadily incorporating advanced operational as well as management capabilities into IoT elements, especially in fog devices. These capabilities vary ranging from the simple ability to turn a device on and off to more complex actions such as updating software, managing Wi-Fi connections, configuring security policies, or changing data parameters. Now the next major requirement is to have an intelligent and policy-aware platform to emphatically empower and manage fog/edge devices and the ground-level IoT devices. Raspberry Pi controllers and Arduino boards are the well-known and widely used intermediaries and gateways at this point in time for gathering data from sensors and passing them to centralized control systems. The issue here is that these microcontroller-based solutions do not exhibit any kind of sophisticated management capabilities.

- **The OSGi Standard for Building Device Management Frameworks:** Many times, we have experienced the power of the open service gateway initiative (OSGi) solutions towards having modular applications. OSGi provides a vendor-independent, standards-based approach to modularizing Java software applications, and its proven services model allows software components to communicate locally and across a distributed network. The OSGi specification defines modular based software management and its execution. OSGi makes software management and its execution simpler by making large application into a small bunch of pieces (called as modules). These modules are working independent way so that when we need them, we can start and stop modules. As for OSGi, a module is termed as Bundle or Plugin-in. OSGi provides execution environment enabling modul6.

Java-based applications or components come as an OSGi deployment bundle and can be remotely installed, started, discovered, stopped, updated, and uninstalled. OSGi inherently offers advanced remote management capabilities of embedded devices. An OSGi-based device application framework brings forth a layer between the OS and the business application on the OSGi platform. This growing collection of cohesive software components lets customers modify, reconfigure, and maintain their application over time as per the changes mandated. That is, application evolves with the changes happening around. Furthermore, the adaptability and flexibility of the OSGi application architecture provide competitive advantages. The ability to easily modify functionality is a must-have for device application frameworks

Figure 6. The OSGi Stack Model

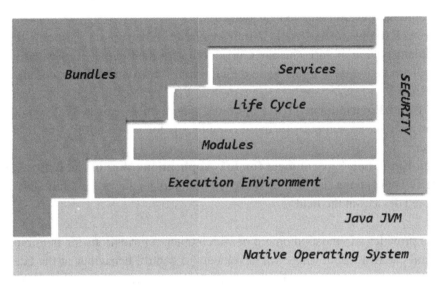

today. A device application framework built on open standards enables communication with multiple management systems, and any platform based on the Java/OSGi deployment model can manage various parts of the device from an application standpoint. The OSGi model can be ingeniously extended to develop an IoT device management framework to build powerful IoT gateways and scores of next-generation IoT applications that are generally dynamic.

- **The Eclipse Kura - An IoT Device Management & Analytics Platform:** The Eclipse Kura framework is being developed on the proven and potential OSGi idea to build next-generation IoT gateways/fog devices with device management capabilities. This Kura framework has been fitted with innovative device management features. For example, the Kura solution is exceptional here. Consider a vending machine company with machines distributed worldwide. Parameters change frequently to reflect inventory, price, and preference, and operators can benefit from remote management in order to fix the broken machine, update software, add new product lines or services, and more. That is, the Kura-empowered fog device monitors and manages different and distributed vending machines at the ground. There can be one or multiple fog devices interacting with one another. That is, fog devices are locally distributed and clubbed together on a need basis to tackle compute and data-intensive needs. In other words, fog or edge devices form an ad hoc compute and data cluster, which is touted as the fog or edge cloud. The Kura framework facilitates the formation and deployment of edge clouds.

Eclipse Kura is an open-source project that provides a platform for building IoT gateways through the use of a smart application container that enables remote management and provides a wide range of developer APIs. The goals of the Eclipse Kura project can be summarized as:

- **Provide an OSGi-Based Container for IoT Applications Running in Service Gateways:** Kura complements the Java and OSGi platforms with APIs and services covering the most common requirements of IoT applications. These extensions include I/O access, data services, watchdog, network configuration, and remote management.

- **Kura Adopts Existing Javax.* APIs When Available:** When possible, Kura will select an open-source implementation of APIs that are compatible with the Eclipse license and package it in an OSGi bundle to be included in the Kura default build (for example, javax.comm, javax.usb, and javax.bluetooth).

- **Design a Build Environment:** The Kura build environment isolates native code components and makes it simple to add ports of these components for new platforms in the Kura build and distribution.

- **Provide an Emulation Environment for IoT Applications Within the Eclipse IDE:** From the Eclipse IDE, applications can then be deployed on a target gateway and remotely provisioned to Kura-enabled devices in the field.

Eclipse Kura provides a foundation on top of which other contributions for field bus protocols and sensor integration can reside, allowing Java developers to control behaviour at the edge. The built-in functionalities include turning the serial port on or off, Wi-Fi management, remote data processing, and more. These remote management services also allow IoT applications installed in Kura to be continuously configured, upgraded, and deployed.

- **Everyware Software Framework (ESF):** ESF is a commercial and enterprise-ready edition of Eclipse Kura, the open source Java/OSGi middleware for IoT gateways. Distributed and supported by Eurotech, ESF adds advanced security, diagnostics, provisioning, remote access and full integration with Everyware Cloud, Eurotech's IoT Integration Platform. ESF is a smart application container that enables remote management of IoT gateways and provides a wide range of APIs allowing you to write and deploy your own IoT application. ESF runs on top of the Java Virtual Machine (JVM) and leverages OSGi, a dynamic component system for Java, to simplify the process of writing reusable software building blocks. ESF APIs offer easy access to the underlying hardware including serial ports, GPS, watchdog, USB, GPIOs, I2C, etc. They also offer OSGi bundles to simplify the management of network configurations, the communication with IoT servers, and the remote management of the gateway.

ESF components are designed as configurable OSGi Declarative Services exposing the service API and raising events. While several ESF components are pure Java, others are invoked through Java Native Interface (JNI) and depend on the Linux operating system. The Eurotech Everyware Software Framework (ESF) provides extensions in the areas of security, field protocol support, and native integration with the Everyware Cloud IoT service and application enablement platform. Through ESF, Eurotech provides a set of the common device, network, and service abstraction tools for Java developers building IoT applications, including I/O access, data services, network configuration, and remote management.

- **Apache Edgent Edge Analytics Platform:** Edgent is a new edge analytics platform and can be used at the edge of any networks. That is, every kind of edge devices, machines, engines, vehicles, robots, drones, rigs, equipment, wares, utensils, consumer electronics, wearables, portables, implantables, sensors-attached physical assets, etc. can be empowered to be intelligent in their operations, offerings, and outputs. Edgent could be hosted on the device itself or a gateway device collecting data from local and resource-constrained devices. It is possible to write an edge application on Edgent and connect it to an IoT application and analytics platform at cloud environments (public and private). Edgent can also be used for enterprise data collection and analysis. Applications are developed using a functional flow API to define operations on data streams that are executed as a graph of "oplets" in a lightweight embeddable runtime. The Edgent SDK provides capabilities like windowing, aggregation, and connectors with an extensible model for the community to expand its capabilities.

Edgent supports connectors for MQTT, HTTP, JDBC, File, Apache Kafka and IBM Watson IoT Platform. Edgent is extensible. It is possible to add any connector. Edgent supports open source technologies and tools such as Apache Spark, Apache Storm, Flink and samza, IBM Streams (on-premises or IBM Streaming Analytics on Bluemix), or any custom application. Edgent is designed for the edge, rather than a more centralized system. It has a small footprint, suitable for running on devices. Edgent provides simple analytics, allowing a device to analyze data locally and to only send to the centralized system if there is a need, reducing communication costs.

- **The IBM Watson IoT Platform Edge Analytics:** This capability enables running Watson IoT Platform Analytics on a gateway device. It leverages a streaming engine which is optimized for edge processing. In the Watson IoT Platform, edge analytics is defined and managed in the cloud but distributed out into the IoT network to collect, analyze and respond to conditions at the source with very low latency and without the need to send data to the cloud. Device data can also be forwarded to Watson IoT Platform for a) additional analytic processing, b) dashboard visualization, c) as input to other analytics and d) storage in a cloud-based historian repository.
- **Watson IoT Edge Analytics on a Dell Edge Gateway 3000:** The IBM Watson IoT Platform Edge Analytics Agent (EAA) enables analytics to be run at the edge of devices and gateways. The Edge Analytics Agent (EAA) is available as an SDK for devices that support Java. The SDK supports a number of different types of connectors between the gateway, IoT devices, and the Edge Analytics Agent, including MQTT, Kafka and file connectors. It is possible to configure the EAA on the Dell gateway to communicate and manage our Raspberry Pi using an MQTT connector. Here is a simplified view of the architecture with the Raspberry Pi and Dell gateway.
- **Microsoft Azure Stream Analytics (ASA):** on edge devices is a freshly incorporated feature of Azure IoT edge analytics. This enables customers to deploy analytical intelligence closer to the IoT devices and unlock the full value of the device-generated data. Azure Stream Analytics on edge

Figure 7.

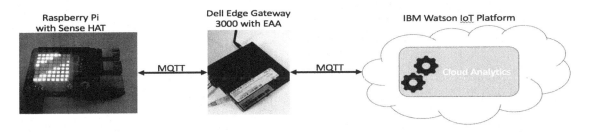

devices extends all the benefits of the Azure's unique streaming technology from the cloud down to devices. With ASA on edge devices, Microsoft Azure is offering the power of the Complex Event Processing (CEP) solution on edge devices to easily develop and run real-time analytics on multiple streams of data. One of the key benefits of this feature is the seamless integration with the cloud: Users can develop, test, and deploy their analytics from the cloud, using the same SQL-like language for both cloud and edge analytics jobs. Like in the cloud, this SQL language notably enables temporal-based joins, windowed aggregates, temporal filters, and other common operations such as aggregates, projections, and filters. Users can also seamlessly integrate custom code in JavaScript for advanced scenarios. The reference architecture of IoT edge analytics is given below.

Azure IoT edge analytics lets you build different IoT solutions. It facilitates to connect new or existing devices, regardless of protocol, process the data in an on-premises gateway using many programming and script languages before sending it to the cloud.

In the image below, an existing device has been connected to the cloud using edge intelligence. The on-premises gateway not only performs protocol adaptation which allows the device to send data to the cloud, it also filters the data so that only the most important information is uploaded.

Figure 8.

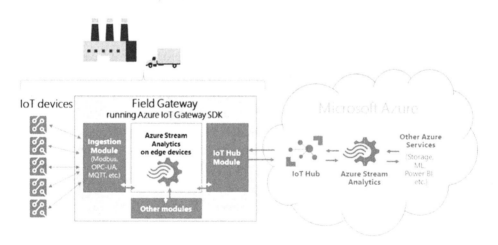

Figure 9.

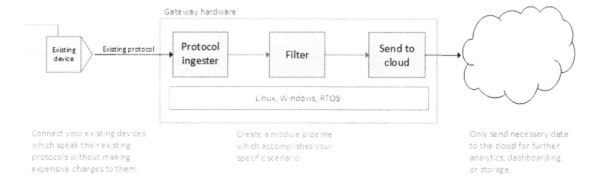

Using existing modules from the Azure IoT Edge ecosystem significantly reduces the development and maintenance costs. Running the gateway on-premises opens up all kinds of scenarios like communicating between devices in real time, operating IoT solution with an intermittent cloud connection, or enforcing additional security requirements.

- **Predixion Software:** According to ABI Research, 90% of machine data never makes it to the cloud. Predixion Software helps to capture and use this data and analyze and act on it at the edge. Predixion Software is the only advanced analytics technology that enables real-time analytics on the device, on the gateway, and in the cloud. Predixion Software has solved big problems in healthcare, fleet, telecommunications, energy, and manufacturing. With Predixion Software, various analytic models can be embedded on the device, can gather real-time data from devices and push it to the gateway, and can aggregate all this information in the cloud. This flexibility, combined with an advanced predictive model, leads to predict when a failure will occur and prescribes what action to be taken when.

With predictive maintenance, real-time predictive insights are delivered to the point of action – whether that's into the hands of a front-lines operator, the dashboard of a project manager, or back onto the device for emergency protocols. All the empowered assets will send alert signals when they are likely to fail. The prediction capability at the edge removes the delays and expenses that result from unplanned downtime Businesses today collect and crunch historical data to gain workable intelligence. That is not sufficient anymore. All kinds of IoT device data need to be combined with historical data in order to activate comprehensive analysis to extract both tactical as well as strategic insights in time to initiate appropriate actions at different levels with all the clarity and confidence. Predixion Software's unique PredixionIQ technology allows analytic models to be deployed on the device, on the gateway, and in the cloud, so actionable insights are delivered at the point of decision. With Predixion, hospitalists know which interventions to apply to high-risk patients, technicians know where to focus their resources, productivity goes up, and costs plummet.

- **ClearBlade IoT Platform:** ClearBlade enables companies to build IoT solutions that make streaming data actionable by combining business rules and machine learning with powerful visualizations and integrations to existing business systems. Built from an enterprise-first perspective, the ClearBlade Platform runs securely in any cloud, on-premise, and at the edge.
- **The ClearBlade IoT EDGE:** This is extremely performant, small and scalable enabling companies to synchronize, configure, manage state and deploy IoT systems with one common software stack. The reference architecture of this platform is pictorially represented below.

ClearBlade IoT Edge powers activities at the edge of any IoT solutions including real-time business rules, filtering, online/offline modes and messaging. This platform carries several distinct advantages and the corporate website (https://clearblade.com/clearblade-iot-edge.html) has more interesting and inspiring details.

The Solair Smart Gateway

The Solair smart gateway is an industrial grade smart device that provides communications, computation power and a lightweight, flexible application framework for the IoT platform integration. It is designed to streamline safe and secure bidirectional communication

- Collect, store and process sensor data at the edge of the network.
- Streamline safe bidirectional communication between the field and the cloud.
- Ensure that only meaningful data is sent to the cloud.
- Enable local intelligence and performance optimization. The Solair gateway technology is based on Kura.

The Solair Platform – IoT Devices: The Integration Options

- **Direct Collection:** A common industrial scenario is when data is transmitted directly from the machine to the Solair platform by using its own internal connectivity, for example, Wi-Fi, Ethernet or 3G/4G.
- **Mobile Bridge:** The data exchange between objects and the Solair cloud is typically managed through mobile phones, via Wi-Fi or Bluetooth.
- **Smart Gateway:** The gateway collects data from machines or equipment through a series of possible protocols - most frequently field protocols such as Modbus - and submits them to the platform while optimizing a number of processes at the edge. Different sensors-attached physical assets and devices get connected to the Solair platform through a bevy of protocols. The Solair smart gateway supports communications through multiple interfaces and multiple protocols, enabling various types of devices and sensors to interact and exchange encrypted data and commands seamlessly.

With edge analytics, it is all about moving the data capture, processing, and analytics processes from the traditional cloud to edge analytics gateway that might dramatically reduce the amount of device data traffic to the cloud by doing the analytics processing close to the device. Edge devices and digitized objects send their data to an edge analytics gateway, which aggregates, segregates, slices, processes and produce actionable insights quickly. There are rules/policies and other knowledge bases being attached to enable the gateway to take right decisions.

- **Cisco Streaming Analytics (CSA):** CSA is an embeddable, horizontal and hierarchically scalable distributed in-memory streaming database designed and built for analytics at the edge. CSA runs in routers, switches, small compute and commercial servers. The streaming engine enables multi-stream, concurrent processing of "raw streams" and the generation of multiple "derived streams" from simple aggregates to advanced machine learning algorithms. CSA applies predicates, aggregates and joins with metadata tables and contextual data to identify anomalies and detect trends.
- **Cisco ParStream:** Cisco ParStream is a distributed massively parallel processing columnar database designed and built for the IoT. The small footprint of ParStream enables implementation at network edges and inside the network, as well as in data centers. Its innovative compression and

bit-mapped indexing technologies enable Cisco ParStream to meet IoT historian and buffering requirements such as providing sub-second response times on billions of data records and thousands of columns, while continuously importing new data.

- **Altiux Innovations:** GWStax, a part of Altiux's IoTStax product portfolio, is a comprehensive framework of modular components that enables seamless connectivity, interoperability, security, remote management, edge analytics, and application enablement in IoT gateways. It enables OEMs to quickly develop and deploy gateway products for IoT that essentially connect end nodes to the cloud. This is built on industry standards and technologies such as 6LoWPAN (Lorwan, 2017) IPv6, Thread, CoAP, LWM2M, etc. and scalable to support application layer protocols such as OIC, AllJoyn etc. GWStax is suitable for applications such as smart home gateways, building automation, smart parking and lighting, industrial automation etc.

NodeStax is a comprehensive framework of modular components that enables seamless connectivity, security, remote management, and application enablement in constrained IoT devices. End node devices in IoT deployments are typically constrained in terms of processing power, memory availability, power availability, communication bandwidth supported, cost considerations etc. Addressing the needs of such devices, NodeStax enables OEMs to quickly develop and deploy constrained end node products for IoT. This is built on industry standards and technologies such as 6LoWPAN, IPv6, Thread, CoAP, LWM2M, etc. and is scalable to support proprietary protocols, NodeStax is suitable for constrained devices in smart homes, building automation, smart appliances, industrial automation, smart cities use cases.

- **Dell Edge Gateway:** It is all about collecting, analyzing, relaying and acting on IoT data at the edge of the network with this IoT gateway, which is purpose-built for building and industrial automation applications. The Dell Edge Gateway is designed to aggregate, secure and relay data from diverse sensors and equipment. The Intel processor provides the capacity to perform local analytics so only meaningful information is sent to the next tier, which could be another gateway, the data center or the cloud. This minimizes consumption of expensive network bandwidth and reduces overall solution latency. The Dell Edge Gateway is designed to attach to a wall or DIN rail in commercial and industrial environments. This is engineered with an industrial-grade form factor and fanless, solid-state design. The Dell gateway can reliably run 24x7 with long life at extended temperatures, in addition to withstanding the higher levels of humidity and dust typical of industrial environments.

On summary, remote management saves time and money by enabling updates, configuration, and troubleshooting without physically reaching out the device. In the medical field, the remote management capability impacts a network of thousands of devices. That is, end-user devices can be updated remotely at once, so patients can access the most up-to-date care available. In the industrial market, managing devices remotely save money by eliminating the need for technicians to service devices in the field. Advanced Java-based device application frameworks that abstract the complexity of hardware and networking subsystems simplify the development, reuse, and remote management of cross-platform IoT applications. The emergence of an Internet of Things (IoT) service gateway model, running modern software stacks and operating on the edge of an IoT deployment as an aggregator and controller, has opened up the possibility of enabling enterprise-level technologies to IoT gateways.

NoSQL Database for IoT Data Edge Analytics

Time series data is any data that has a timestamp, like IoT device data, stocks, commodity prices, tide measurements, solar are tracking, and health information. Collecting, storing, accessing, and analyzing the massive amount of sensor and actuator data with traditional databases is often not possible. Applications need to scale out, up, and down predictably and linearly as the data grows. The challenge of time series data is that reads and writes to the database must be fast, reliable, and scalable. Riak TS is a key/value store that easily scales using commodity hardware. It supports rapid ingestion of time series data from connected devices through extremely fast reads and writes. Riak TS enables application processing of this data to generate actionable information. It is designed to scale horizontally with commodity hardware, making it easy for administrators to add capacity without creating complex sharding

Traditionally, data is analyzed at the core of your network, but with the growth of IoT sensors and devices, data must be analyzed closer to its source and aggregated for core analysis. From cruise ships to health monitoring to system utilization, edge analytics create a better user experience and faster response times. Riak TS requires fewer hardware resources for the same computational power, making it an ideal choice for edge analytics, plus Riak TS makes it easy to do analysis using SQL range queries.

CONCLUSION

Fog or edge computing is gaining a lot of traction these days due to the wider articulation of various business, technical and user cases. Especially for performing and providing real-time data analytics, the role of fog or edge clouds is on the rise. There are edge appliances from different product vendors accelerating the rollout of edge analytics. There are integrated platforms for producing ad hoc fog clouds quickly to accomplish edge data capture, storage, and analytics. The deployment of digitized entities in any environment is made easier. Devices are expertly instrumented and interconnected to be intelligent. Software applications and services are finding their new rewarding residence in cloud infrastructures. Data science is a hugely popular subject of intense study and research in order to make sense out of IoT data. There are a machine and deep learning algorithms to automate the process of doing data analytics. The goal of real-time and automated analytics can be casually accomplished through fog analytics platforms and infrastructures. In this chapter, we have vividly depicted the concept of fog computing, which is the need of the hour for real-time data analytics.

REFERENCES

Lee, W., Nam, K., Roh, H. G., & Kim, S. H. (2016). A gateway based fog computing architecture for wireless sensors and actuator networks. In *Advanced Communication Technology (ICACT). 18th Int. Conf. on Advanced Communication Technology (ICACT)*. Pyeongchang, South Korea: IEEE. doi: 10.1109/ICACT.2016.7423331

LoRaWAN. (2017). *The Things Network*. Retrieved November 11, 2017, from https://www.thethingsnetwork.org/wiki/LoRaWAN/Home

Pan, Y., Beyah, R. A., Goscinski, A., & Ren, J. (2017). Edge Computing for the Internet-of-Things. *IEEE Network*. Retrieved November 3, 2017, from https://www.comsoc.org/netmag/cfp/edge-computing-internet-things

Poole, I. (2015). *RFID Standards. Radio-Electronics*. Retrieved November 11, 2017, from http://www.radio-electronics.com/info/wireless/radio-frequency-identification-rfid/iso-epcglobal-iec-standards.php

Raj. (2015). *High-Performance Big Data Analytics: the Solution Approaches and Systems*. Springer-Verlag, UK. Retrieved from http://www.springer.com/in/book/9783319207438

Raj & Deka. (2014). *Cloud Infrastructures for Big Data Analytics*. IGI Global. Retrieved from http://www.igi-global.com/book/cloud-infrastructures-big-data-analytics/95028

Raj & Raman. (2016). *The Internet of Things (IoT): the Technologies and Tools*. CRC Press. Retrieved from https://www.crcpress.com/The-Internet-of-Things-Enabling-Technologies-Platforms-and-Use-Cases/Raj-Raman/p/book/9781498761284

Salman, O., Elhajj, I., & Kayssi, A. (2015). Edge computing enabling the Internet of Things. In *IEEE 2nd World Forum on the Internet of Things (WF-IoT)*. Milan, Italy. IEEE. 10.1109/WF-IoT.2015.7389122

Schmidt, S. (2016). *6LoWPAN: An Open IoT Networking Protocol*. Open IoT Summit. Retrieved November 14, 2017, from http://events.linuxfoundation.org/sites/events/files/slides/6lowpan-openiot-2016.pdf

Treadway, J. (2016). Using an IoT gateway to connect the "Things" to the cloud. IoT Agenda. *TechTarget Network*. Retrieved November 21, 2017, from http://internetofthingsagenda.techtarget.com/feature/Using-an-IoT-gateway-to-connect-the-Things-to-the-cloud

Wang, W., He, G., & Wan, J. (2011). Research on Zigbee Wireless Communication Technology. In *Int. Conf. on Electrical and Control Engineering (ICECE)*. Yichang, China: IEEE. doi: 10.1109/ICECENG.2011.6057961

APPENDIX

The Prominent Fog-Like Approaches

There are multiple trends emanating and evolving in the information and communication technologies (ICT) spaces. The number of smartphones across the globe is already more than 3 billion empowering people to do both communication and computation seamlessly on a single device. Similarly every specific environment such as homes, luxury cars, and heavy vehicles, manufacturing floors, shopping malls, eating joints and junctions, entertainment and edutainment centers, nuclear installations, research labs, business parks, etc. are being stuffed and sandwiched by a number of purpose-specific as well as generic sensors and actuators. Thus, the prediction that there will be trillions of digitized objects, billions of connected devices and millions of software services in near future is all set to become true sooner than later. There are different approaches and articulations in order to pointedly focus on this fog/edge computing concept. There are myriad of nomenclatures and buzzwords. Figure 10 clearly tells the various options for localized and nearby data processing in real-time.

- **Local / Proximate Clouds:** We have public, private and hybrid clouds in order to cater different requirements. There are specific clouds such as mobile, storage, knowledge, science, data, device, and sensor clouds. Specific communities even have their own clouds. Now with the accumulation of sensors and sensor-attached physical assets, there is a demand for localized and nearby cloud environments for performing proximate processing. Local clouds, a kind of dedicated IT environments, can interoperate with other traditional clouds (private, public, hybrid, and community) for doing comprehensive and historical data processing.

Figure 10.

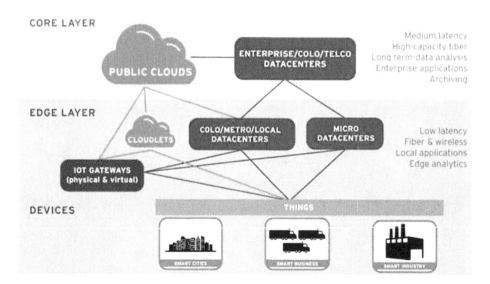

There is literature eulogizing and expressing local clouds as micro or nano clouds considering their slim and sleek nature. As it turns out, there will be thousands of local clouds in the near future. That is, every noteworthy environment has its own local cloud. The various computation and communication devices apart from consumer electronics in the neighbourhood come together to collaboratively form local clouds.

- **Cloudlet Facilities:** There are highly reliable and resilient cloud appliances and hyper-converged clouds in the form of bars and boxes these days. Instead of using commodity servers, powerful, integrated and turnkey appliances are also being used in specific contexts. Cloudlet is "a cloud in a box", which follows the same cloud paradigm but relies on high-end server machines. Cloudlets are very easy and quick to setup and activate and are being recommended to provide delay-sensitive and bandwidth-limited applications. A cloudlet is a new architectural element that arises from the convergence of mobile computing and cloud computing. It represents the middle of a three-tier hierarchy: mobile device, cloudlet, and cloud.

The following use cases for crowdsourced videos insist the need for cloudlet facilities.

The aspect of crowdsourcing has seen a phenomenal growth these days with the widespread deployment of security and surveillance cameras in important junctions. There are sellable and workable use cases being unearthed for sustaining its surging popularity. Here are a few.

- **Marketing and Advertising:** Crowd-sourced videos can provide a lot of real-time and decision-enabling insights based on observational data. For example, which billboards attract the most user attention? How successful is a new store window display in attracting interest? Which clothing colours and patterns attract the most interest? etc.
- **Capturing Theme Parks' Visit:** Visitors to places like Disneyworld can capture and share their delectable experiences, including rides, throughout the entire day. With video, audio, and accelerometer capture, the recreation of rides can be quite realistic and mesmerizing.
- **Locating People, Pets, and Things:** A missing child was last seen walking home from school. A search of crowd-sourced videos from the area shows that the child was near a particular spot an hour ago. The parent remembers that the child has a friend close to that location. She calls the friend's home and locates the child. When a dog owner reports that his dog is missing, a search of crowd-sourced videos captured in the last few hours may help locate the dog before it strays too far.
- **Fraud Detection:** A driver reports that his car was hit while it was parked at a restaurant. However, his insurance claims adjuster finds a crowdsourced video in which the car is intact when leaving the restaurant.
- **Why is Cloudlet-Like Arrangement Mandated?:** Video footages from a mobile device only travel up to its currently associated cloudlet. Computer vision analytics are run on the cloudlet platform in near real time. Only the results (recognized objects, recognized faces, and so on), along with metadata (such as the owner, capture location, and timestamp) are then sent to the remote cloud. The tags and mctadata can guide deeper and more customized searches of the content of a video segment during its (finite) retention period on a cloudlet. Automated modification of video streams to preserve its privacy is done at cloudlet level.

Mobile Edge Computing (MEC)

We have mobile base stations in many locations in order to fail-safe relay mobile communication. These facilities are being recommended for doing the edge data processing and analytics. The utilization rates of those base stations go up significantly with this extra flavour. Base stations act as an intelligent intermediary between smartphones and the faraway cloud environments.

Mobile Cloud Computing (MCC)

As we all know, smartphones do not have sufficient processing, memory and storage capabilities as a typical and traditional cloud does (Off course, as per newspaper reports, there are smartphones empowered with 6 GB memory). Therefore, there are research works initiated in order to bring in an appropriate partition of software applications into a set of easily manageable modules. The specific and smaller modules are kept within smartphones whereas the common and reusable service modules are being taken to cloud environments. The data sources are being kept in cloud environments and smartphones can access the data on a need basis. Now with cloudlets and MEC models are maturing fast, there will be a consolidation and MCC will slowly disappear from the scene altogether.

Thus having understood the need for pioneering intermediaries between devices, machines, equipment, instruments, sensors, robots, actuators, etc. at the ground level and a bevy of software applications and data sources at the cyber level, researchers have proposed several propositions as described above. With the overwhelming acceptance of fog computing, all these diverging concepts are bound to converge to fulfill all the originally envisaged benefits of fog or edge computing.

It is all shifting from the "connected device" to the "intelligent device" through the computing on the edge. Making a connected device adaptive, autonomic and articulate is the important goal. This strategically sound transformation comes handy in realizing people-centric and situation-aware services.

Chapter 2
Evolution of Fog Computing and Its Role in IoT Applications

R. Alageswaran
K. L. N. College of Engineering, India

S. Miruna Joe Amali
K. L. N. College of Engineering, India

ABSTRACT

Fog computing is an evolving technology that brings the benefits achieved by cloud computing to the periphery of the network devices for faster data analytics. This has triggered the usage of fog computing for enabling a new breed of applications and services that require localized and faster decision making. Fog computing has attributes such as location awareness, edge deployment and a large number of geographically distributed nodes, heterogeneity through which fog computing offers better performance in terms of mobility, low latency, and real-time interaction. They can also gracefully handle enormous data flow and provide analytics in reasonable time. Due to these additional attributes, fog computing is considered as the appropriate platform for many applications and especially suited for internet of things (IoT). Fog computing also provides an intelligent platform to manage the distributed and real-time nature of emerging IoT applications and infrastructures. With the increase in the number of connected objects, the development of fog computing is tremendous and has promising technological future growth.

INTRODUCTION

Cloud computing is used as a delivery platform which is a promising way for storing user data and provides a secure access to personal and business information. The users are provided with on-demand services through the Internet. Fog computing has emerged as a promising technology that can bring the cloud applications closer to the physical IoT devices at the network edge. Fog computing extends the Cloud computing paradigm to the edge of the network, thus enabling a new breed of applications and services. Fog computing (also referred to as an edge computing) extends from the core of network to the edge of the network. It provides computation, storage, and services between end devices and traditional

DOI: 10.4018/978-1-5225-5972-6.ch002

cloud servers. Servers and other intermediate nodes are considered as core part of the network. Desktop machine, mobile, smart device, machine or any equipment connected in a network as end point device or machine are considered as edge devices.

Nowadays, more number of devices are connected to the Internet. Internet of Things (IoT) is the network of physical objects or "Things" embedded with Software, sensors and connectivity to enable it to achieve value and service by exchanging data with the manufacturer, operator and/or other connected devices through advanced communication protocols without human operation. The advantage of integrating IoT applications with cloud is the flexibility that the services offered by the cloud provider can be accessed by the user through a web interface.

Cloud systems are part of the Internet, which is a large heterogeneous network with numerous technologies, topologies and types with no central control. Due to heterogeneous and loosely controlled nature of the Internet, there are many issues such as quality of service. The other issue with cloud computing is that security and privacy. In the cloud systems, user requests, data transmission and system responses need to traverse a large number of intermediate networks in Internet depending on the distance between the users and systems. If the number of intermediate nodes to be traversed is more, the risk is higher as the data has to travel a long distance to and from the user's computer to the cloud system, even if the data is encrypted. Similarly the availability of the cloud systems can also be attacked using various methods.

In addition to location awareness and low latency features, IoT requires mobility support and wide range of Geo-distribution. Hence, a new platform is required to meet all these requirements. Fog provides data, processing, storage, and application services to end-users. The unique characteristics of Fog are proximity to end-users, dense geographical distribution, and support for mobility. Services are hosted at the edge of the network or end devices such as set-top-boxes or access points. Fog reduces service latency, and improves QoS, resulting in superior user-experience (Patil, 2015). Fog Computing supports emerging Internet of Everything (IoE) applications that demand real-time and predictable latency.

FOG Computing

Fog computing, also known as Fog networking or Fogging, is a decentralized computing infrastructure in which data, process, storage and applications are distributed in the most logical, efficient place between the data source and the cloud. Fog computing basically extends cloud computing and services to the edge of the network, bringing the advantages and power of the cloud closer to where data is created and acted upon.

The goal of Fogging is to improve efficiency and reduce the amount of data transported to the cloud for processing, analysis and storage. For many IoT applications, where cloud computing is not viable, Fog computing can be effectively used. In IoT applications, the huge amount of data is generated by smart sensors and IoT devices. It is costly and time-consuming to send the data to the cloud for processing, analysis and storage. Fog computing reduces the bandwidth needed and back-and-forth communication between sensors and the cloud and improves overall performance of the IoT application.

How FOG Computing Works?

The edge devices and sensors connected in the application generate and collect the data but those devices and sensors don't have the compute and storage resources to perform advanced analytics and machine-learning tasks. Even though cloud servers have the power to do those tasks, it is too far away from the edge devices to process the data and respond in a timely manner. In addition, having all endpoints connecting to and sending raw data to the cloud through internet can have privacy, security and legal implications.

In a fog environment, the processing takes place in a data hub on a smart device, or in a smart router or gateway, thus reducing the amount of data to be sent to the cloud. Fogging allows for short-term analytics at the edge, where as the cloud performs resource-intensive, longer-term analytics.

Characteristics of FOG Computing

The different characteristics of FOG computing are:

- **Edge Location, Location Awareness, and Low Latency:** Fog computing support endpoints with finest services at the edge of the network.
- **Geographical Distribution:** The services and application objective of the Fog is widely distributed. For example, Fog will play an important role in delivering high quality streaming to connected vehicles through proxies and access points positioned nearby.
- **Support for Mobility:** Fog devices provide mobility techniques like decouple host identity for location identity.
- **Real Time Interactions:** Fog computing requires real time interactions for speedy service.
- **Heterogeneity:** Fog nodes can be deployed in a wide variety of environments.
- **Interoperability:** Fog components must be able to interoperate in order to give wide range of services like streaming.

Fog Computing vs. Edge Computing

The terms Fog computing and edge computing are used interchangeably, as both involve bringing intelligence and processing closer to where the data is created. The key difference is where the intelligence and compute power is placed.

In a Fog environment, intelligence is at the local area network. Data is transmitted from endpoints to a gateway where it is then transmitted to sources for processing and return transmission. In edge computing, intelligence and power of the edge gateway or appliance are in devices such as programmable automation controllers (Shi, Cao, Zhang, Li & Xu, 2016). The difference between Edge and Fog environment is given in Table 1 and Table 2 presents the difference between Edge and Fog computing.

Table 1. Difference between Edge and Fog Environment

Features	Edge	Fog
App Hosting	Limited	Yes
Data Service at Edge	Yes	Yes
Device & App Management	Yes	Yes
Security	Partial Point Solution VPN, FW	E2E, Data Protection, Session & Hardware level
Elastics Compute/Resource Pooling Modular Hardware	No	Yes
Ream -time Control High Availability	No	Yes

Table 2. Difference between Edge and Fog Computing

Edge Computing	Fog Computing
Device aware and few services aware, unaware of the entire domain	Device independent, intelligent, and aware of the entire fog domain
Limited control in the edge domain	Controls all devices in the domain
Cloud unaware	Extends cloud to Fog level
Limited network scope	Complete network scope
No IoT vertical awareness	Supports and enabler for multiple IoT verticals
No IoT vertical integration	Integrates multiple verticals
Uses Edge Controllers that are focused on edge device command and control	Uses fog Nodes that are very versatile and capable of performing a variety of functions like RT Control, application hosting and management
Security scope is limited to devices	End-to-End security
Analytics scoped to a single device	Fog Analytics enables collection, processing and analysis of data from multiple devices in the edge for analysis, machine learning, anomaly detection and system optimization.

Cloud Computing vs. Fog Computing

Table 3 depicts the major differences between cloud and FOG environment. From Table 3 it reveals that Cloud Computing characteristics have very severe limitations with respect to quality of service demanded by real time applications requiring almost immediate action by the server (Osanaiye et al., 2017).

Table 4 presents the difference between cloud computing and FOG Computing.

Table 3. Difference between Cloud and Fog Environment

Features	Cloud	Fog
Latency	High	Low
Location of Service	Within the Internet	At the edge of the Local Network
Distance between client and server	Multiple hops	One hop
Security	Undefined	Can be defined
Attack on dada enroute	High Probability	Very low probability
Location awareness	No	Yes
Geo-distribution	Centralized	Distributed
No. of server nodes	Few	Very Large
Support for mobility	Limited	Supported
Real time interactions	Supported	Supported
Type of Last mile connectivity	Leased Line	Wireless

Table 4. Cloud computing and Fog Computing

Cloud Computing	Fog Computing
Data and applications are processed in a cloud which is time consuming task for large data	As FOG operates on network edge, it consumes less time.
Problem of bandwidth, as a result of sending every bit of data over cloud channels	Less demand for bandwidth, as every bit of data is aggregated at certain access points instead of sending to cloud.
Slow response time and scalability problems as a result of depending servers that are located at remote places.	By setting small servers called edge servers in visibility of users, FOG computing platform avoid response time and scalability issues.

Advantages of FOG Computing

- The significant reduction in data movement across the network resulting in reduced congestion, cost and latency, elimination of bottlenecks resulting from centralized computing systems.
- Improves security of encrypted data as it stays closer to the end user reducing exposure to hostile elements.
- Improves scalability arising from virtualized systems.
- Eliminates the core computing environment, thereby reducing a major block and a point of failure.
- Consumes less amount of band width.

Limitations of FOG Computing

- Complex and more compute intensive applications need services from cloud server.
- Fog devices do not provide data storage service to store data generated over long time and it require storage on cloud server.
- Due to heterogeneity nature of Fog, there may be issues of compatibility.
- If edge devices do not get enough connectivity and bandwidth, there will be issue of latency in service.

Applications of FOG Computing

The FOG computing platform has a wide range of applications including smart grid and Wireless Sensor and Actuator Networks (WSAN) etc. (Peter, 2015). The major Applications are:

Health Care

Smart health gadgets and devices can receive best services from fog devices at network edge. No need to send service request to cloud server.

Connected Car

Fog device enables cars to talk with each other to avoid accidents. It also helps in getting information about low crowded path.

Smart Traffic Lights

Fog enables automatic opening of signals based on dynamic situation of traffic signals. Also, it can detect ambulance and open lanes for it.

Smart Building Control

All sensors in the building can communicate and exchange with each other and with Fog device. Fog device performs analysis on combined data. Connected devices may react in response to data analysis and distributed decision making.

Smart Grids

Smart electric devices can switch to other energy sources like solar and winds based on demand for energy, its attainability and low cost.

Architecture of FOG Computing

Fog Computing is a highly virtualized platform that provides compute, storage, and networking services between end devices and traditional Cloud Computing. Data Centers, typically, but not exclusively located at the edge of network. Figure 1 presents the idealized information and computing architecture supporting IoT applications, and depicts the role of Fog Computing.

Figure 1. Architecture of FOG Computing

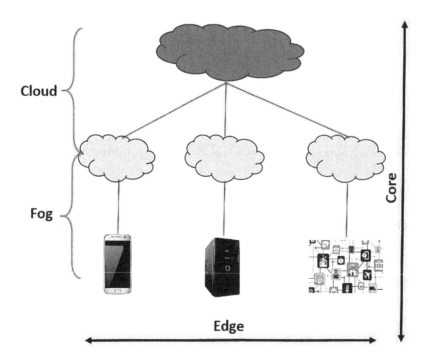

Fog computing are used in the following situations:

- Data is collected at the extreme edge: vehicles, ships, factory floors, roadways, Railways, etc.
- Thousands or millions of things across a large geographic area are generating data.
- Analyze and act on the data in less than a second.

The most time sensitive data is analyzed by the Fog node closest to the things generating the data. For example, in a smart grid application, the time sensitive requirement is to verify whether protection and control loops are operating properly. Hence the Fog nodes closest to the grid sensors can check for signs of problems and then prevent them by sending control commands to actuators.

Data that can tolerate seconds or minutes response is passed to an aggregation node for analysis and action. In the smart grid example, each substation has its own aggregation node that reports the operational status of each downstream feeder and lateral.

Data that is less time sensitive is sent to the cloud for historical analysis, big data analytics, and long term storage. For example, hundreds and thousands of fog nodes can send periodic summary of grid data to the cloud for historical analysis and storage.

Role of Fog nodes:

- Receive feeds from IoT devices using any protocol, in real time.
- Run IoT enabled applications for real time control and analytics, with less response time.
- Provide transient storage, often 1–2 hours.
- Send periodic data summary to the cloud.

Role of the cloud platform in Fog Environment:

- Receives and aggregates data summary from many fog nodes.
- Performs analysis on the IoT data and data from other sources to gain business insight.
- Sends new application rules to the fog nodes based on these insight.

Fog Computing and Internet of Things

IoT environments consist of heterogeneously connected devices as a network. The main purpose of building the IoT network is to collect and process data from the connected devices. The collected data is then mined to detect hidden patterns and retrieve undiscovered information which can be used for predictive analysis or optimization and to make smarter decision in a timely manner. IoT applications have proliferated to every aspect of life and have many interesting application from health care to smart cities. The fabrication of sensors to monitor various physical phenomena is the main driving force of IoT applications. Various IoT applications like jet aircraft running data, smart cities etc generate a huge volume of data. The quantum of data generated is in the order of TB for even a few hours of sensing that the centralized cloud servers cannot deal with such velocity of data in real-time.

Some of the IoT application like health care generate confidential data that users have privacy concerns and are not comfortable to transfer and store their track data into the cloud even if they require statistical report on their activities. This has motivated the need of alternative paradigm that is capable of bringing the computation to more capable devices that are geographically closer to the sensors than to the higher end clouds. Such devices, which are in the edge of the network and therefore referred to as edge devices, can build local views of data flows and can aggregate data to be sent to the cloud for further off-line analysis. This attributed to the formation of Fog computing especially suited for IoT applications.

Fog computing is a distributed computing model that does most of the computation including data storage and processing at the network edge devices. Fog computing is a technique that is locally hosted and easily accessible to the user. In fog computing model all IOT data processing is done locally near the smart devices instead of sending to cloud. In fog computing data collected by sensors are not sent to cloud server instead it is sent to devices at the network edge like set top box, routers, access point for processing (Alrawais, Alhothaily, Hu & Cheng, 2017). This reduces the traffic due to low bandwidth. Fog computing improves the Quality of service and also reduces latency.

Small computing works are locally processed and responses are sent back to the end users without the use of cloud. Thus, fog computing is emerging as a better option than cloud computing for smaller computing works. Fog computing plays an important role by reducing the traffic of data to the cloud. Since fog system is placed near to the data sources computation and communication are not delayed. Fog Computing is used for real time interactions but cannot totally replace cloud computing as it is preferred for high end batch processing.

The main reason for the success of Fog computing is the real time processing as centrally processing large volumes of sensor data slows decision making and increases bandwidth demand. It can encompass, proliferate and impact several enhanced features such as rapid analysis, interoperability among devices, increased response time, centralized or machine-to-machine management, low bandwidth consumption, efficient power consumption, device abstraction and many others.

With the increasing number of smart devices, most of the requests pertain to the surroundings of the device. Hence, such requests can be served without the help of the global information present at the cloud. For example, a smart connected vehicle needs to capture events only about a hundred meters from it and does not require vast data analysis. In Fog computing the communication distance is closer to the physical distance.

The main defining characteristics of the Fog computing as a best match for IoT applications are

- Low latency as they are available at the edge of the network.
- Location awareness as they are closer to the device generating the data.
- Wide-spread geographical distribution.
- Mobility.
- Streaming large data can be performed easily with much less bandwidth.
- Real time decision making.
- Scalability as Fog computing resources can be increased on-demand.
- They can be both dense and sparsely distributed based on geographical location.
- They support Machine-to-Machine communication and wireless connectivity.
- Support with low specification devices like switches and IP cameras.

Fog – IoT Architecture

IoT applications are beginning to embrace a multi-layer architecture for control and data analysis due to rate of increase in the number of connected devices and their heterogeneous nature. Data generated from devices, including sensors and industrial equipment, is being processed by the compute nodes between the actual location of the sensors and the Internet. This is at the boundary of the sensor deployment network. If required some of the data is relayed over from the edge to a remote data center for further analysis and action. The communication between the devices and the edge nodes may be achieved using WiFi, if the devices are WiFi-enabled, or based on specialized protocols like LoRa, or even serial ModBus in an industrial environment. However, the communication between the edge nodes and the Cloud-resident application happens over a Wide-Area TCP-IP network (Bonomi, Milito, Natarajan & Zhu, 2014).

As IoT is evolving, the 'edge' devices with computing power are being manifested in various forms:

1. **An Intelligent Gateway:** A Gateway node is primarily responsible for intercepting data from devices and transmitting it to a cloud-enabled application over TCP-IP. Many Gateway vendors, like Dell manufacture gateway nodes that can filter, aggregate, and apply rules to the device-generated data before transmitting it over to the cloud.
2. **Edge Computing Nodes:** In an industrial environment, Programmable Automation Controllers (PACs) are employed to run a pre-defined set of control functions on a set of plant equipments. When these plant equipments are IoT-enabled, the PAC nodes may be additionally programmed to run data processing functions on data transmitted by such equipment. This capability is referred to as Edge Computing.
3. **Fog Nodes:** 'Fog' refers to a set of computing nodes that perform a large subset of data analytics and control functions that would normally be performed by an application on the cloud, that receives large volumes of data from IoT devices. However, these nodes are located closer to the IoT devices, typically in the same Local Area Network. And unlike gateways and edge nodes, the fog layer consists of both storage and compute capacity.

Figure 2. FOG for IoT Applications

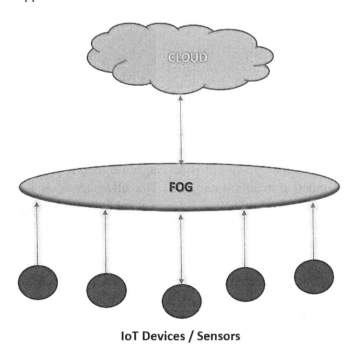

Typically, for an IoT enabled application, the fog layer complements the cloud-hosted applications. The fog layer is generally used to act upon data streams and send out control signals on a frequent basis, while relaying part of the data to the cloud where large volumes of historical data can be stored, analyzed and modeled for running predictive analytics. Thus the fog layer cannot completely replace the computing or storage benefits of cloud servers.

The main applications areas of Fog computing in IoT are detailed below,

- **Low Latency:** There are many applications which require time critical real-time data processing. Few IoT applications which are time critical include control of fly-by-wire aircraft, anti-lock brakes on vehicle, robot motion control etc. These applications depend on the data collected by the sensors and the feedback of the control system. To extract decisions from the cloud may make the process slow or unavailable due to communication failures. Thus in such cases fog computing helps by perform the processing required for control system very close to the sensors and making real-time response possible.
- **Geographically Dispersed Applications:** There are many widely dispersed applications like smart cities which has challenges like traffic congestion, public safety, high energy use, sanitation and other services. These challenges are addressed by a single IoT network and can be maintained by Fog computing. Smart decision making can be done much better by Fog computing then cloud computing.
- **Create Terabytes of Data:** Large volumes of data cannot be practically streamed to the cloud and back for analytics.
- **Fast Mobile Applications:** The exponentially increasing use of smart mobile devices, the computing infrastructure must be able to accommodate variable demands, while relying on elasticity to balance the processing load when necessary.

There are many IoT application scenarios using Fog computing. Two of the most prominent application is detailed below.

Use Case 1: Smart Grid

Smart grid is the next generation electrical energy distribution network that consists of transmission lines, substations, transformers etc. Compared to the traditional model, smart grid uses two-way flow of electricity and information. This creates an automated and distributed advanced energy delivery network. Smart grid enables both the service providers and customers to monitor and control their pricing, production and consumption in almost real time. The advantage of establishing a smart grid for the service providers is to achieve effective load balancing and reliable energy transmission and for the customers to reduce their electricity bill. The features of smart grid that has facilitated the introduction of Fog computing are as follows,

- Smart grid uses smart meters that can collect and deliver not only electricity consumption information but also private data about customers such as device level usage information etc. These sensitive data are usually stored in cloud based data centers. These data must be secured and preserved from misuse.

- ○ Analysis of electricity consumption at the device level can give information about the number of people currently in a house. Charging locations and consumption of the electrical vehicles gives clue about people frequently visited and their availability, usage frequency analysis of electrical devices may be used for behavior analysis illegally.
- Data from smart meters transmitted to the cloud, must ensure reliability, security, flexibility and scalability.
- Smart grid does not hold only consumers but also producers thus as the number of customers connected to smart grid increases complexity also increases.
- With the addition of producers like solar and wind has introduced additional complexities as they are intermittent and require rapid, yet coordinated control actions over a geographically large area.
- The data generated by the sensor (about ~1GB/day) is too large to be transmitted to the cloud for processing. It drastically increases the data traffic.
- The timing requirements of some control loops necessitate rapid and robust decision making. Transmitting large volume of data for analytics to the cloud for decision making is very time consuming.
- Scalable real-time services must be provided to the customers to monitor electricity usage information in almost real time. Congestion or server failures when processing huge amount of data affects cloud services thereby result in latency.

In order to overcome these pitfalls, fog computing can be effectively used. Fog computing address the above issues by maintain the data and computation tasks at the network edge. Compared to cloud based systems, locally keeping private data enables customers to reach that data in a fast and secure manner. As far as providing service both fog and cloud offer similar services. However, there are various communication and computational needs to build a smart grid with a very low latency and improved privacy. The main benefits of using fog computing for smart grid is given below,

- **Proximity:** Fog data are closer to the end users and it gives the customers direct access to the data source. Fog splits big data to sub data that it is easier to manage. It can simplify extracting key information when dealing with big data.
- **Privacy:** Data privacy is about securing the consumer and producer information from third parties. Fog computing separates the public and private data making it easy to provide data privacy.
- **Latency:** As proximity is achieved, it also reduces the reaction time and congestion. As global information will not be required for most of the analytics, the latency is much less with localized data.
- **Geo-Distribution:** Power generators, energy transformers and distribution networks which form the main components of smart grid are geographically distributed. Geographically distributed fog services can provide services with reduced latency compared to a centralized cloud.
- **Location Awareness:** As fog servers are geographically distributed they are location aware. This location information can be used to provide location based services and analytics.

Smart Grid Architecture

The basic architecture of a smart grid consists of three layers. The first layer is composed of smart meters and the second layer is the fog servers. The third layer is cloud layer. The basic fog architecture for smart grid is given in Figure 3.

- **Smart Sensors:** The first layer is responsible for the communication among smart grid devices such as smart meters, smart appliances, electrical vehicles, mobile devices etc. The device level communicate is enabled for business purposes, location based services and billing purposes. For example, an electrical vehicle can be charged at a nearby power outlet that does not belong to the owner of the vehicle. In this case, the smart meter of the power outlet should communicate with the vehicle owner's smart meter in his residential location.
- **Fog Servers:** The second layer connects smart meters to cloud. Each fog server interacts with smart meters in its coverage area and collects the data coming from end users. Data processing is also done by the fog servers and they separate them as private or public. In order to ensure privacy of the customers, fog servers usually store the private data temporarily. The public data is aggregated and sent for storage at the cloud layer. Customers can access their private data such as device level electricity consumption amounts or hourly energy consumption analysis over fog servers. Devices can communicate each other directly as they are connected to same fog server.
- **Cloud Server:** At the highest layer is the cloud server and it is responsible for further aggregating and storing public data that is sent by fog servers. This data can be accessed mainly by the service providers for billing purposes. Customers can also access their current and historical bills over a web interface or a mobile application.

Figure 3. Smart Grid architecture

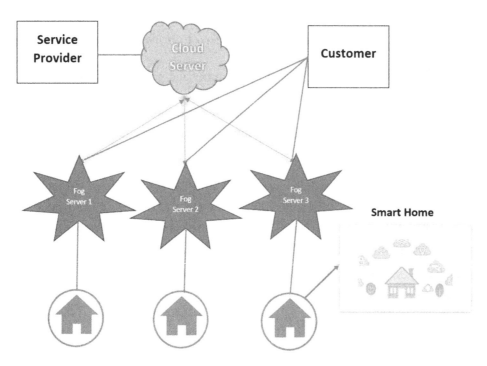

This type of fog computing based smart grid model provides data privacy, latency and location awareness. Consider for example, a smart home with many end devices including washing machine, dishwasher, television, mobile devices or smart devices like sensors. Each smart house has a smart meter and is connected to a fog server. Fog servers are owned and operated by the energy service providers. Each smart meter shares a secret key with the fog server to keep customer data private. Thus smart grid can offer its customers very detailed information about their electricity usage even at the device level, consumption analysis based on their daily/weekly/monthly electric consumption (Okay & Ozdemir, 2016). Detailed analysis of electricity consumption information may reveal important private data about customers, hence it must be treated as private data.

Energy load balancing applications can be run on network edge devices, such as micro-grids and hence based on energy demand, availability and the lowest price, these devices can be automatically switched to alternative energies like solar and wind. Fog collectors at the network edge process the data generated by the grid sensors and can be used to issue control commands. They also filter the data to be consumed locally, and send the rest to the cloud layer for visualization, real-time reports and transactional analytics.

Use Case 2: Vehicular Adhoc Networks

A Mobile Adhoc Network (MANET) is formed using mobile nodes. A Vehicular Ad Hoc Network is a specific type of MANET in which the mobile nodes are moving vehicles. This network has strong connectivity and interaction such as cars to cars, cars to access points like Wi-Fi, 3G, LTE, roadside units [RSUs], smart traffic lights etc. With the upcoming development of sensors and connectivity, all new cars on the road will have the capability to connect to cars nearby and internet. The main requirement for the success of VANET will be real time interaction between the nodes. Depending on the cloud data for all forms of decision making and analytics will be very time consuming. Thus VANETs require a low latency, geographically distributed system for real time analytics. Fog computing has a number of attributes that make it the ideal platform to deliver many services like

- Infotainment
- Safety
- Traffic support, and analytics
- Geo-distribution
- Mobility
- Location awareness
- Low latency
- Heterogeneity
- Real-time interactions.

Cars, access point and traffic lights will be able to interact with each other for better safety and effective driving experience.

In VANETs every vehicle is equipped with an on-board unit and a group of sensors. This radio interfaces or on-board unit enables short range wireless ad hoc networks to be formed. VANETs offer both vehicle to vehicle and vehicle to roadside communication. Every vehicle in the network plays the role of a sender, receiver and a router to broadcast data to the vehicular network and the roadside units which then uses the data to ensure safe and congestion free traffic. VANETs are an important part of smart cities for improved safety and better transportation.

VANETs have been depending primarily on cloud computing services for communication, computing and storage facilities. The main driving factors which has initiated the transfer from cloud computing to Fog computing are,

- Delay in transfer of data and information from the vehicles to the remote cloud server and back to the vehicles after storage and processing.
- As there is a steep rise in the number of connected vehicles and mobility the demand on the cloud servers increases exponentially.
- Communication, computation and analytics using cloud computing is not efficient with the emergence of latest and advanced vehicular applications.
- Real time analytics for efficient decision making by the vehicles cannot be supported by cloud computing.
- Various vehicular applications designed for latest high speed vehicles will require powerful communication and computational support.

Fog computing can be effectively used to alleviate the problems faced by cloud computing. Fog computing introduces an intermediate fog layer between the cloud and the mobile vehicular devices. Devices with computing and communication capabilities called fog nodes are deployed in this fog layer near to the user devices. Extending fog computing to vehicular networks helps to provide powerful communication and computational support to the latest applications in vehicular networks.

The architecture for a fog based vehicular network is given in Figure 4. Fog computing deploys a network of fog nodes between the vehicular network and the clouds servers. The sensors and other devices in the vehicles gather data and this data is stored and processed in the locally available fog servers rather than the centralized cloud servers. Thus the fog servers are able to provide immediate analytics and better communication which are more context aware. Most of the data from the vehicles are processed at the fog servers and immediate response is provided to the vehicles (Baccarelli, Naranjo, Scarpiniti, Shojafar, & Abawajy, 2017). Fog computing provides applications with are widely distributed. The fog servers are connected to the cloud server for wider applications and historical data storge for later analysis. Fog computing is highly beneficial for low latency applications such as video streaming and gaming.

Advantages of Vehicular Fog Computing

- **Low Latency:** Real time data processing takes place much closer to the vehicle and thus provides faster results which can be send as messages to other vehicles and road side units. This also increases the quality of service.
- **Pooling of Resources:** Idle processing power and sensing ability within the devices can be pooled for better services in a fog network.
- **Reduced Bandwidth Utilization:** Fog computing avoids the back-and-forth traffic between cloud servers and devices in vehicles. This saves the bandwidth in the network.
- **Reduced Energy Consumption:** Reduced traffic within the network helps to conserve energy in the devices. Energy conservation in devices with limited battery support is a very important advantage of fog computing.

Figure 4. Architecture for VANETS

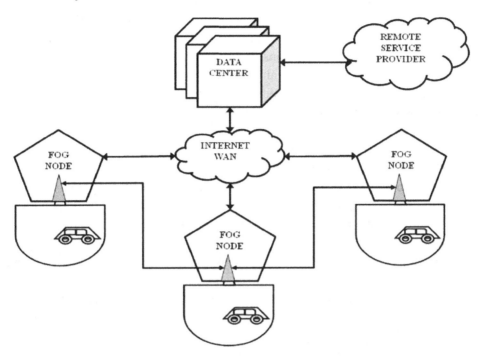

- **Better Services for Customers:** Users can easily customize new applications that are available much nearer to them based on their specific requirements.

Data Protection and Security in Fog Computing

Fog computing platform is a virtualised environment and it is affected by similar threats as that of cloud computing. It is a distributed system and suffers from cyber threats as well. Intrusion attacks, smart device tampering, spoofing, man-in-the-middle attack etc are also prevalent in fog computing. The main components to realize Fog computing are Fog providers which provides the necessary infrastructure to the users, the services providers which utilizes the infrastructure to provides applications to the users and finally the consumers who demand the infrastructure and services. Each component has specific requirements and separate security management system. This decentralized nature can result is loss of security control at any location resulting is total collapse of the system. The security of the data stored in the fog nodes is the major concern. The main driving factors of the fog system namely, decentralized nature, geographical distribution, distributed protocols, limited resources etc become the major security concern for their actual implementation (Khan, Parkinson & Qin, 2017). The major threats as identified by reviews is listed below,

- Smaller computing resources and hence it would be difficult to execute complex security solutions that are able to detect and prevent various attacks.
- Relatively more accessible based on network configuration and physical location, which increases the probability of an attack.

- Advance Persistent Threats is a type of cyber attacks with the desire to steal data and intellectual property.
- Access Control Issues results in unauthorised user being able to acquire data and permissions to install software and change configurations.
- Account Hijacking is where an attack aims to hijack the user accounts for malicious purpose. Phishing is a potential technique for account hijacking.
- Denial of Service (DoS) where legitimate users are prevented from using a service.
- Data Attacks happen when sensitive, protected or confidential data is misused by attacker or when data is lost accidentally or intentionally.
- Insecure APIs can also result in security issues.
- Software Vulnerabilities are exploitable pitfalls from software and configuration faults that can be used by an attacker to compromise a system.
- Malicious Users has authorised access to the network and system for the purpose of compromising the system.
- Shared Technology can also result in loss of security due to sharing infrastructures, platforms or applications.
- Web Security issues like code injection attacks, where SQL code provided by the user is automatically executed resulting in the potential for unauthorised data access and modification.

Fog computing can enable users to take full control and management of the network by providing Network Level Virtualization (NLV) and real-time data services. The use of shared technology is critical because it takes a minor vulnerability or misconfiguration to damage all Fog services, user operations and allows attackers to gain access to exploit Fog resources.

Web security issues could result in the compromise of entire Fog system's database or the forwarding of modified information to a central server. Insecure APIs results in attacks like session and cookie hijacking, illegal data access, malicious redirections and drive-by attacks. Web attacks can also be used for targeting other applications in the same Fog platform by embedding malicious scripts and potentially damage sensitive information.

Although sophisticated database software and high storage capacity hardware are used for aggregation and processing, data can easily be replicated, shared, modified and deleted by any malicious intermediate or fake external node. In addition, it is difficult for a Fog platform to centrally define, set and maintain access control attributes of user ownership in a large amount of moving data. Fog nodes are continuously processing, analysing and accumulating data to produce information and it becomes difficult to retain data integrity and prevent data loss. The tolerance at which a failure occurs is also very low as the exact point of error is hard to identify in a system.

Security Solutions for Fog Computing

Fog computing is an upcoming technology and hence there are no well defined standard security certifications and measures for Fog computing. The possible security solutions which can be applied to fog computing implementation includes,

- User data isolation.
- Attribute or identity based encryption.

- Role-Based and user based Access Control model.
- Data masking, classification and isolation.
- Light weight encryption methods for communication and device level data encryption.
- Implementation of public key infrastructure.
- Intrusion Detection System.
- Network monitoring and wireless security.
- Prompt backup methods to the cloud for better recovery.
- Periodic auditing and policy enforcement.

Future Directions and Scope of Fog Computing

Fog computing is in its initial stages and still it is being adapted by many service providers due to its varied applications. In spite of its advantages compared to cloud computing there are many open issues that needs to be addressed to extract full benefits of the Fog computing system (Chiang & Zhang, 2016). This has given rise to various research issues in order to realize the full potential of Fog computing.

- **Security and Privacy:** Enforcing security protocols over a distributed fog system is very challenging compared to a centralized cloud model. Privacy of user information and sensitive data becomes a crucial issue. As there are no well defined methods to enforce privacy various attacks on user data is possible. Methods to properly enforce security and privacy measures are necessary for the secure working of fog system.
- **Reliability:** Reliability issues in the form of failure of individual sensors, network, service platform, and the application are possible. In the IoT application, the sensor readings can be affected by noise or they can be easily tampered. This leads to information accuracy problem can be solved by redundancy.
- **Authentication:** Authentication is required at various levels of fog nodes. As fog is basically a distributed architecture, authentication issues must be strictly addressed.
- **Policy Management:** Fog computing is still in the evolution phase and hence propose policy-driven security management approach is mandatory. Such an approach is critical for supporting secure sharing, and data reuse in heterogeneous Fog environments.
- **Resource Management:** They are resource constrained in nature as opposed to the vast cloud environment. Thus judicious management of resources is essential for an efficient operation of a fog computing environment.
- **Energy Minimization:** Earlier analysis has revealed that fog computing can significantly cut down the communication latency by incurring slightly greater energy consumption. This problem has led to the introduction of optimization methods to trade off between latency and energy consumption. A method to optimize the allocation of workloads between the fog and cloud should also be considered.
- **Locating Failed Nodes:** Physically locating a failed fog node and repairing then is difficult and costly in the Fog model due to its decentralized nature. Hence methods to isolate region of failure and recovery is an active research problem.
- **Network Connectivity:** An unreachable fog node cannot provide service to the customer even if it is computationally functional. Simple tasks such as regular testing and auditing of hardware

are immensely more complicated and costly in fog computing, due to the necessary coordination among different organizations, geographical distribution of hardware, and unreliable network connectivity. Therefore identifying network errors is vital.

- **Malicious user Identification and Abuse of Fog Services:** Providing the Service level agreement for end user and service provider is mandatory for avoiding related security problems. Access control, Separation of work in the management level should be analyzed to resolve such issues.
- **Communication:** The fog system has three levels of communication namely, between fog and user devices, between fog and cloud and between fog nodes. The Fog server completely depends on wireless communication to connect with the mobile users and peers. The communication channel must be secured and available without disruption.
- **Programmability:** The computation capability in fog nodes is most likely heterogeneous in nature. There are sever programming difficult as the configuration and runtime of these nodes differ from each other. Application development and deployment could be a serious concern for programmers.
- **Optimization Metrics:** Workload allocation between the distributed servers is a big issue. There are multiple allocation strategies based on various criteria to complete a allocated workload. To choose an optimal allocation strategy, several optimization metrics namely, latency, bandwidth, energy and cost must be considered.

SUMMARY

Cloud computing has established itself as an efficient alternative to owning and maintaining computer resources and applications for many small and medium sized organizations due to the pay and use model and other characteristics like, on-demand, self-service, resource pooling and rapid elasticity. But as the demand on the cloud resources increases and as the number of connected devices has increase dramatically in recent times other technologies like fog computing has emerged to the rescue of the cloud services. In fog computing cloud resources are extended to the edge of the network, which include portable devices, smart objects, wireless sensors and other Internet of Things (IoT) devices to decrease latency and network congestion.

Cloud and fog computing have many common features. In addition fog computing has further attributes as discussed which enables fog computing to offers better performance in real-time. They are also robust enough to process sufficiently large data flow and provide analytics in reasonable time. Fog computing also provides an intelligent platform to manage the distributed and real-time nature of emerging IoT infrastructures. With the increase in the number of connected objects, the data generated by IoT and mobile applications is too large to be streamed to the cloud for acquiring useful analytics in reasonable time.

Fog computing resolves the problems related to congestion and latency. Implementing user and application specific services at the edge of the network of sensors through fog computing, will lead to new business models and opportunities for network operators. They provide lower operational costs and better user experience. It also saves both the bandwidth cost and energy consumptions. The emergence of fog computing is mainly due to the localized nature of the user request during most of the scenarios. The mobile user requests are mostly predictable and hence it does not require cloud intelligence. The Fog computing model includes resources in three-dimensions namely, storage, compute and communications, hence three-dimensional service-oriented resource allocations are possible through Fog computing. Fog computing follows a three layer architecture, Sensor nodes-Fog-Cloud and thus has rich potential applications in both mobile networking and IoT. The major IoT application which has already embraced the fog technology are Smart-home, smart-city, smart-grid, vehicular network etc. These applications use a layer of sensors to obtain useful information from the field of the user to improve the quality of life and improve life experiences.

Fog computing is still in the evolutionary phase and much research and policy establishment has to be done for extracting its full potential. There are open research issues in the areas of network management, traffic engineering, big data, novel service delivery, architecture establishment and resource management. Various researches are in progress to establish a trouble free standard implementation of fog computing. Even after standard implementation of fog computing, the cloud system cannot be completely over ruled. The fog servers has to be connected to the cloud servers for long term storage, historical analysis of data and for complex analytics.

Fog computing represents a scalable, sustainable and efficient solution to enable the convergence of cloud-based Internet and the mobile computing. Thus fog computing will play a big role in Internet of things applications and with eventual resolving of the various issues, fog computing will bring about revolutionary changes in the daily life of its customers.

REFERENCES

Alrawais, A., Alhothaily, A., Hu, C., & Cheng, X. (2017). Fog Computing for the Internet of Things: Security and Privacy Issue. *IEEE Internet Computing*, *21*(2), 34–42. doi:10.1109/MIC.2017.37

Baccarelli, E., Vinueza Naranjo, P. G., Scarpiniti, M., Shojafar, M., & Abawajy, J. H. (2017). Fog of Everything: Energy-Efficient Networked Computing Architectures, Research Challenges, and a Case Study. *IEEE Access: Practical Innovations, Open Solutions*, *5*, 9882–9910. doi:10.1109/ACCESS.2017.2702013

Bonomi, F., Milito, R., Natarajan, P., & Zhu, J. (2014). Fog Computing: A Platform for Internet of Things and Analytics. Big Data and Internet of Things: A Roadmap for Smart Environments. *Studies in Computational Intelligence*, *546*, 169–186.

Chiang, M., & Zhang, T. (2016). Fog and IoT: An Overview of Research Opportunities. *IEEE Internet of Things Journal*, *3*(6), 854–864. doi:10.1109/JIOT.2016.2584538

Khan, Parkinson, & Qin. (2017). Fog computing security: a review of current applications and security solutions. *Journal of Cloud Computing Advances, Systems and Applications, 6*(1), 6-19.

Okay, F. Y., & Ozdemir, S. (2016). A Fog Computing Based Smart Grid Model. *International Symposium on Networks, Computers and Communications (ISNCC)*. 10.1109/ISNCC.2016.7746062

Osanaiye, Chen, Yan, Lu, Choo & Dlodlo (2017). From Cloud to Fog Computing: A Review and a Conceptual Live VM Migration Framework. *Recent Advances in Computational Intelligence paradigms for Security and Privacy for Fog and Mobile Edge Computing, 5*, 8284 – 8300.

Patil, P. V. (2015). Fog Computing. *National Conference on Advancements in Alternate Energy Resources for Rural Applications*, 1-6.

Peter, N. (2015). FOG Computing and Its Real Time Applications. *International Journal of Emerging Technology and Advanced Engineering*, 5(6), 266–269.

Chapter 3
Fog Computing and Virtualization

Siddhartha Duggirala
Bharat Petroleum Corporation Limited, India

ABSTRACT

The essence of cloud computing is moving out the processing from the local systems to remote systems. Cloud is an umbrella of physical/virtual services/resources easily accessible over the internet. With more companies adopting cloud either fully through public cloud or hybrid model, the challenges in maintaining a cloud capable infrastructure is also increasing. About 42% of CTOs say that security is their main concern for moving into cloud. Another problem, which is mainly problem with infrastructure, is the connectivity issue. The datacenter could be considered as the backbone of cloud computing architecture. Handling this new generation of requirements of volume, variety, and velocity in IoT data requires us to evaluate the tools and technologies. As the processing power and storage capabilities of the end devices like mobile phones, routers, sensor hubs improve, we can increase leverage these resources to improve your quality and reliability of services. Applications of fog computing is as diverse as IoT and cloud computing itself. What IoT and fog computing have in common is to monitor and analyse real-time data from network connected things and acting on them. Machine-to-machine coordination or human-machine interaction can be a part of this action. This chapter explores fog computing and virtualization.

INTRODUCTION

Cloud computing has completely transformed how businesses function and handle their IT infrastructures. By consolidating all the available resources and providing software defined resources based on the demand has been an efficiency driver. The main reasons the cloud computing really took off are the resource utilisation, efficiency, on demand resource delivery and financial benefits associated with them.

Up until the recent years the processing power, storage available at the end points like user PCS, embedded devices room mobile phones is limited. So it made logical sense to move the burden of processing and storage to the cloud. An effective example of this is Chrome book from Google or any one of the plethora of cloud services we use every day. The only big disadvantage of these services or

DOI: 10.4018/978-1-5225-5972-6.ch003

products is that they are completely network dependent. Heavy usage of network bandwidth and latency expectations places a higher demand on the network infrastructure. This sometimes reduces the quality of experiences for the end users and in extreme cases can even be fatal.

Right now in 2017, there are about 2 devices connected to internet per every human on Earth and the number of devices estimated to be connected to internet is estimated to be 50 billion by 2020. These include the mobile phones, smart routers, home automation hubs, smart industrial machines, sensors smart vehicles (Hou, X., Li, Y., Chen, M., Wu, D., Jin, D., & Chen, S., 2016) and the whole gamut of smart devices. To give an idea of how much needs to be pushed through the Internet due to these devices, Boeing flight generate about 1 TB of data or even more for one hour of operation, the weather sensors generate about 500gb of data per day. Our mobile phone sensors are capable of generating more than 500mb of logs per data and that multiplied by number of smart phones is staggering amount of data. This along with the increasing rich media usage in the Internet will be a huge challenge for the next generation networks.

As the processing power and storage capabilities of the end devices like mobile phones, routers, and sensor hubs improve us can increase leverage these resources to improve your quality and reliability of services. Processing or even caching the data near wherever it is generated or utilized frequently not only of loads of the burden on the networks but also improves the decision making capabilities for commercial or industrial installments, quality of experience for personal usage.

Handling this new generation of requirements of volume, variety and velocity in IOT data requires us to evaluate the tools and technologies. For effective implementation of these use cases places the following requirements on the infrastructure:

1. **Minimize Latency:** Milliseconds, even micro-seconds matter when you are trying to prevent a failure at a nuclear power station, or preventing of some calamity or to make a buyable impression on a customer. Analysing data and gaining actionable insights are near as the device itself makes all the difference between a cascading system failure and averting disaster.
2. **Optimising Network Utilisation:** Data generated by the sensors is huge. And not all the data generated is useful. It is not even practical to transport this vast amount of data to centralised processing stations/Data centre nor is it necessary.
3. **Security and Privacy:** Data needs to be protected both in transit and at rest. This requires efficient encryption, monitoring and automated response in case of any breach (Stojmenovic, I., & Wen, S. (2014, September)).
4. **Reliability:** As more and more intelligent systems are deployed, their effect on the safety of citizens and critical infrastructure cannot be undermined.
5. **Durability:** As the devices they can be deployed across wide area of environment conditions. The devices themselves need to be durable and made rugged to work efficiently in harsh environments likes railways, deep oceans, utility field substations and vehicles 9 Hou, X., Li, Y., Chen, M., Wu, D., Jin, D., & Chen, S. (2016)).
6. **Geographic Distribution and Mobility:** The Fog devices should be dispersed geographically as to provide the storage and processing resources to the sensors/actuators producing and acting based on the decisions made. The sensors themselves can be highly mobile. The fog environment should be able to provide consistent resources even in these highly dynamic scenarios. This is especially the case with Wireless sensor area networks, Personal body area networks, Vehicular area network (MANET/VANET).

7. **Interoperability:** The fog devices are intended to be connected to all sorts of devices. Many of these devices have proprietary communication protocols and are not based on IP. In these cases the fog nodes should be able to communicate and even translate them to IP protocols incase the data needs to be pushed to cloud.

Fog Computing

In simple terms, Fog computing (Yi, S., Li, C., & Li, Q. (2015, June)) or Edge computing extends the cloud to be closer to the things that produce, act on and consume data. The devices at the edge are called fog nodes can be deployed anywhere with network connectivity, alongside the railway track, traffic controllers, parking meters, or anywhere else. Any device with sufficient network, storage and computing resources can be a Fog node. For example network switches, embedded servers, CCTV cameras, and industrial controllers can be utilized as fog nodes.

Analysing data close to where it is collected/generated minuses network latency and offloads gigabytes of less valuable data from the core network, keeping the critical, sensitive data inside the network.

Cisco coined the term Fog computing and defined it as an extension of cloud computing paradigm from the core of network to the edge of network, a highly virtualized platform providing computation, storage (Wu, F., & Sun, G. (2013)) and networking services between end devices and tradition cloud servers. In other work authors defined "Fog computing as a scenario where a huge number of heterogeneous ubiquitous and decentralised devices communicate and potentially cooperate among them and with the network to perform storage and processing tasks without any third party intervention. These tasks can be basic network functions or sophisticated, novel services and applications that run in virtualized environments. Users leasing a part of their devices to host these services get incentives for doing so," Although the exact definition of Fog computing is still being constructed it is essential to separate this from related technologies.

Similar concepts such as Mobile cloud computing and Mobile Edge computing overlap with Fog computing. In Mobile Edge computing (Hu, Y. C., Patel, M., Sabella, D., Sprecher, N., & Young, V. (2015)), cloud server running at the edge of the mobile network performs specifics tasks that cannot be accomplished with traditional network infrastructure. While Mobile Cloud computing refers to infrastructure in which data storage and processing occurs outside the mobile devices. MCC pushes the data and computation to the cloud making it feasible for the non-Smartphone users to use mobile applications and services. Fog computing is a more generalised platform with virtual resources and application aware processing.

Applications of Fog computing is as diverse as IoT and Cloud computing itself. What IoT and Fog computing have in common is to monitor and analyse real-time data from network connected things and acting on them. Machine-to-machine coordination or human-machine interaction can be a part of this action. Unlimited possibilities.

As we have seen in earlier sections, the following scenarios make a good case for Fog computing:

1. Data is generated from thousands or millions of things/sensors distributed geographically.
2. Data is collected at the extreme edges of the infrastructure: factory floors, warehouses, roadways, etc.
3. The time taken to analyse, take a decision and act on the data is in range of milliseconds.

Figure 1. Fog platform high level architecture

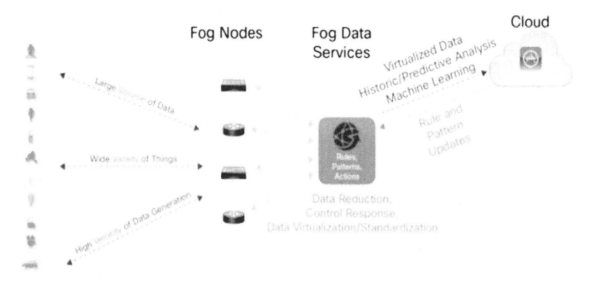

Difference Between Fog Computing and Cloud Computing

The core difference comes in the way resources are organised. In cloud computing the resources are centralized whereas in Fog computing the resources are scattered and available possibly nearer the client. Cloud service providers are generally single tiered organisations where as the fog ecosystem as such is multi-tiered. Fog computing supports dynamic, mobility better than cloud computing as the resources allocated are near-by the usage itself. Due to the service locality and geographic distribution of resources the latency in transmission of data is highly reduced. This mode of processing has an added benefit of adhering to local security and privacy norms. The differences are highlighted in Table 1.

If you look at the financial side of implementing fog computing, a study at Wikibon found that cloud-only infrastructure is costlier to maintain as compared to Cloud with Fog/Edge computing infrastructure. One of the main reasons for this is the average life cycle of a cloud server is a measly 2 years. In proper Fog computing infrastructure the servers' life time is up to 8 years. This would make a huge difference for companies small and large in both short term and long term technology infrastructures.

As we have already seen the major demerit with cloud computing is latency (Bonomi, F., Milito, R., Zhu, J., & Addepalli, S. (2012, August)). Latency in feeding the data into the system to analysing it and producing tangible insights. These insights in many cases help in making split-second decisions. Some data is valuable at the moment it is recorded. For example a pressure gauge going critical in a manufacturing plant, or a security breach at a critical site or Complex event processing. Fog computing helps in analysing at the sources and give results with-in milliseconds range. And the insights are fed to visualisation tools to communicate and coordinate with other systems, the data is then sent to cloud for archiving, aggregation and further batch analysis can be done at the cloud level. As shown in Figure 2. As we move on to transactional analytics and Historical analysis cloud become the ideal choice to do run the analyses.

Table 1. Cloud computing vs. fog computing

Requirement	Cloud Computing	Fog Computing
Latency	High	Low
Delay Jitter	High	Very low
Location of server nodes	Within the internet	At the edge of the local network
Distance between the client and the server.	Multiple hops	One hop
Security	Undefined	Can be defined
Attack on data enroute	High probability	Very low probability
Location awareness	No	Yes
Geographical distribution.	Centralized	Distributed
Number of server nodes	Few	Very large
Support for mobility	Limited	Supported
Real time interactions	Supported	Supported
Type of last mile connectivity.	Leased line	Wireless

Another advantage in analysing the data near the source is all the data generated need to be fed into cloud system. The data generated will have a lot of noise or unnecessary data which doesn't provide us with any significant insight. So pushing the data just wastes precious network bandwidth and cloud storage.

Data thinning removes this unnecessary data and strips away all the noise just leaving us with only the data that really matters. For example a driverless car might generate Petabytes of image data a year of bumpers or speed breakers or any line it crosses and that generated data in entirety is so useful. A Boeing jet generates 2.5TB data per 1 hour of flight operation. An oil drill sensors generate more than 10 GB of data per second.

As the minimalist principle states "More is not always better". The processing of the data at the fog nodes not only reduces the time to insight but them in-turn help in making emergency responses more efficient.

Application Scenarios

In the above sections we have studied the characteristics of Fog computing. The above characteristics make Fog computing ideal for IoT installations, Vehicular intelligence, augmented reality, smart homes, and content distribution. Fog computing is ideal to deal with the scalability challenges in 5G and RCANs. SDN and Fog computing is being studied in the context of VANETs. In this section, we will study some of these major applications.

Figure 2. Processing latency from fog computing to cloud computing

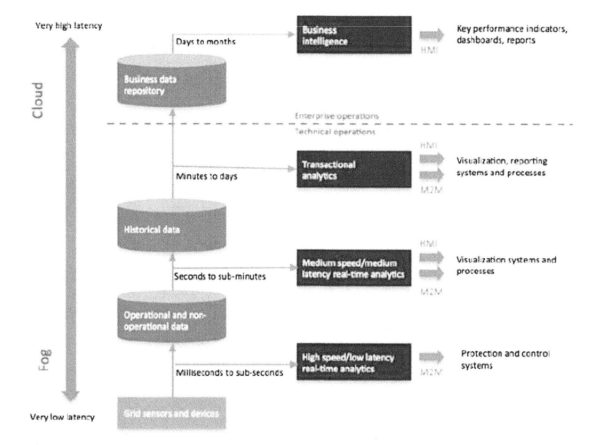

Heart Attacks Fall Monitoring

According to global statistics, every year 17.3 million death are caused by heart diseases. This is expected to rise to more than 23.6 million by 2030. (Arnet et all 2016). This poses a huge challenge to the hospitals and health infrastructure of every country. The chances of the heart attack increases with the age, and previous ailments. This overburdens the already congested and over utilised infrastructures. Instead admitting high risk patients, hospitals and health providers can monitor continuously the high risk patients and with smart preemptive strategy, hospitals can provide much needed care just in time, that too without overburdening themselves.

One of important ways the Fog computing might help in Health care is to take conservative snap decisions and escalate the risky situations for deep analysis which can further help in reducing the risk of false negatives. One such effective implementation is for alerting doctor of cardiac arrests (Stantchev, V., Barnawi, A., Ghulam, S., Schubert, J., & Tamm, G. (2015))

Traditionally, patients are required to strapped sensors sophisticated sensors around chest. They need to wear continuously severely restricting their mobility. More handling their sensors can be difficult for these patients. The advent of Smartphone and smart devices made it easier to monitor patient movements in real-time. Traditional sensors are not just big, bulky; they are aesthetically ugly and horribly expensive. Smartphone being lighter and cheaper have clear advantage in user tracking and movement monitoring. The Smartphone accelerometer data is continuously captured and relayed to cloud for processing. If any patient falls dangerously are detected and the medical services are immediately provided. The drawback is that the patients need to keep the phone at all times. Moreover the phone orientation should be in certain angle for the sneers to be detecting correct and valid patterns over time.

The smart watches overcome these two limitations of Smartphone based solutions. They are extremely mobile. They are lighter and don't require the devices to be in any orientations. The patients can easily wear a smart watch at all times. The accelerator data is continuously related to cloud through a router or a Smartphone. The data is processed there for pattern recognition. With the help of a sophisticated algorithm recognises the fall and alert medical services. The limitation is that since this approach requires the data to be pushed to cloud and then processing to be done there. This carries an inherent latency, which is not affordable in this case. Another approach is to use a Smartphone or a smart router as the processing engine and run a simple frequency-based pattern recognition algorithm, as the processing power is low compared to the cloud based scenario. This reduces the latency to a great bit. This results in a scenario where there are lot false-positives. This scenario although not completely bad one, will result in inefficient utilisation of already scarce resources.

Using Smartphone or a smart router as a fog node and interlacing it with cloud based processing for further analysis we can achieve the required solution which has a permissible error rate in a very low latency. The wearable (mostly smart watch) will monitor the user and relay the data to the fog device which utilises a simple classification algorithm. The hospital is immediately informed without much latency and the fog device will further relay the data to cloud for further processing. This reduces the effect of false-positives to an extent. Thus saving lives without much using a wearable which has heart rate monitoring by default and movement monitoring the physicians can prompt the users to healthier lifestyle.

These analyses also come under the broad class of Mobile Big Data analytics use cases. Fog computing provides elastic resources to large scale systems without the latency concerns of cloud computing (Buyya, R., Yeo, C. S., Venugopal, S., Broberg, J., & Brandic, I. (2009)). As explained in the health care monitoring case, federation of cloud and fog will take care of data acquisition, aggregation and pre-processing, reducing bandwidth overload and data processing. F. Bonomi, et al. (Bonomi, F., Milito, R., Zhu, J., & Addepalli, S. (2012, August))

Content Delivery and Caching

Traditional caching or content delivery techniques are heavily server dependent. Even they provide a sense of geo-graphic locality for multi-datacenter implementations. Delivering content to end-users is a not efficient. What a particular client or set of client want and network level statistics are only available at a local level. This knowledge can be leveraged to optimise the web performance. Since fog nodes lie in the vicinity of the user it can gather statistics and usage knowledge to optimise the user experience. And this reduces the requirement of bandwidth as the data most required will most probably in the vicinity of the user itself. J. Zhu, et al. consider web optimisation from this new perspective in the context of fog computing (Zhu, J., Chan, D. S., Prabhu, M. S., Natarajan, P., Hu, H., & Bonomi, F. (2013, March)).

Software Defined Networking

In broadest terms, the network is connection between various servers and storage clusters inside as well as outside a datacenter. This is the fundamental contributor to QoS and delivery performance of applications. Businesses creating their cloud environments should have a keener look at their whole infrastructure mainly the network which glues every component together. Many of the large enterprises' work are distributed geographically, while the applications that are pre-dominantly media based, time-sensitive. This puts pressure on QoS (Quality of Service) for applications delivered over the network. (Nunes, B. A. A., Mendonca, M., Nguyen, X. N., Obraczka, K., & Turletti, T. (2014)).

Networking has traditionally been completely about hardware. With almost all the major functions are hardcoded in the hardware making it difficult and expensive to upgrade firmware. With the sophistication of software, these functionalities are slowly moved into the software layer, this is called network function virtualization (Martins, J., Ahmed, M., Raiciu, C., Olteanu, V., Honda, M., Bifulco, R., & Huici, F. (2014, April)). Software defined networking is a complete reproduction of physical network at software level, while being more flexible and can be customised according to the application's requirements. The applications can run exactly the same as if they are run on physical network.

A protocol is a set of rules governing communications. Networking protocols lay down the format of message, how they will be identified and what actions need to be taken. (Barroso, L. A., Clidaras, J., & Hölzle, U., 2013)

NETWORK FUNCTION VIRTUALIZATION

If Overlay networks gives the capability of creating network tunnels per flow. The next logical step is offload the functions of hardware based networking services like Firewalls, Load Balancers and provide them as a service on the tunnel. This is Network Function Virtualisation. Network function Virtualization proposes to virtualise entire classes of network node functions in to building blocks using virtualization. The popular functions for this are firewalls and IDS/IPS systems from companies like PLUMgrid or Embrane (Wu, F., & Sun, G., 2013).

Network Function Virtualization runs on x86 platforms, instead of having its own hardware appliance. The NFV architecture has the following three important components:

1. **Virtualized Network Function:** Software implementation of network functions.
2. **Network function Virtualization Infrastructure:** The combination of software+ hardware on which VNFs are deployed.
3. Network Function virtualization management and Orchestration architecture.

Table 2. Network packet

8 Bytes	6 bytes	6 Bytes	2 Bytes	0-1500 Bytes	0-46 Bytes	4 Bytes
Preamble	Destination Address	Source Address	Frame Length	Data	Pad	Checksum

Figure 3. Virtual network

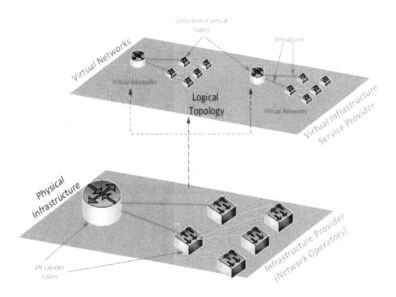

Instead of buying huge, expensive IDS for handling the whole network, one can simply buy specific functions to be deployed.

Software Defined Networking

SDN simply is about making datacenter networking infrastructure pooled and automated resource which can be configured and maintained through software and can seamlessly extend across public/private cloud boundaries. How will this help? Centralized control of networking infrastructure, optimum utilisation of existing physical network, workload optimisation to name a few clear benefits we derive using SDN.

The key of computing trends driving the need of network programmability and a new network paradigm include: changing traffic patterns of applications, big-data computations, consumerisation of IT (Jain, R., & Paul, S., 2013).

SDN starts with abstracting applications form underlying physical networks. Then it provides consistent platform to specify and enforce policy across all clouds. And finally it provides with a standards based mechanism for automatic deployment of networks while being extensible (Barroso, L. A., Clidaras, J., & Hölzle, U., 2013).

By separating the control plane from the data plane, SDN makes it possible to build programmable network. It relies on network switches which can be programmed through an SDN controller. Unlike the Overlay networks and NFVs which work on top of physical networks, SDN changes the physical network itself. SDN is implemented on network switches unlike other network virtualization (Jain, R., & Paul, S. (2013)) techniques. BigSwitch and Pica8 are two notable names selling SDN products. This reduces the necessity to buy black proprietary box switches which are expensive. Instead one can easily buy a cheap white box switches and install SDN controller.

Few characteristics of SDN architecture are: Network control is directly programmable, agile as it is easy for the network manager to enforce changes in policies efficiently and quickly, software based SDN controllers centrally manage the network, the networking resources can be configured programmatically.

Figure 4. Software defined networking architecture

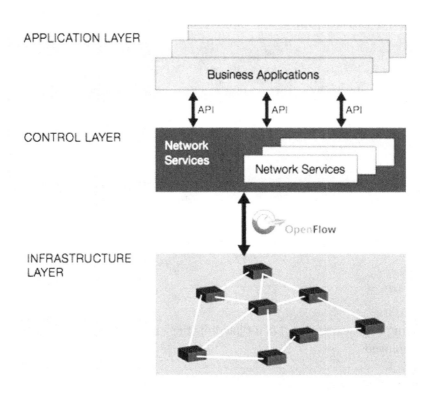

Figure 5. Control and forwarding element separation within a router

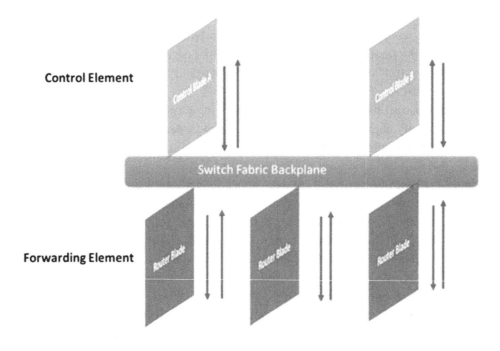

Vehicular Fog Computing

The world is moving towards a rapid urbanisation. The urban roads are heavily congested. Governments are struggling to provide better alternatives to the movement of people and goods. It takes an average 1.5-2 hours of travelling time many major cities in many parts of the world. This is a huge drain productive man hours. As the vehicular density increases so does the associated affects of pollution, parking unavailability and difficult traffic management. As the traffic increase the risk associated with the vehicular collisions and accidents increase exponentially. Either human causes or road conditions or wildlife or lighting conditions or road surface or are some of the major reasons for this. Earlier VANETs used vehicle to vehicle communication to form an ad hoc network. This network will be able to relay the information and transition alters. This somewhat reduces the vehicle to vehicle collisions. With fog computing this can be extended to an extent that the control and processing of the functions is separated. Each device will have an onboard device which tracks driving conditions, vehicle condition, speed, occupancy and temperature. These onboard are connected to road side units through Wi-max or 4G. These onboard units support MQTT or CoAP protocols to connect to various vehicular sensors. Vehicle to vehicle communication is done through peer to peer mechanism through each road sides units are places at regular intervals usually at the range of 300-500 meters. These road side units provides at the computation and semi-permanent storage required by the vehicles on the move. As vehicles moves from one location to another these computations or VMs are offloaded from one road side unit to another. This facilitates the mobility of processing. These road side units are intern connected to each other through Wi-Max//4G/LTE. These roadside units are in-turn connected to each other and to the central cloud trough 4G or Broadband. These road side units not only measure vehicular traffic details. They can also support user functions like entertainment through CDN or route mapping or location driven marketing and services or even health analytics where the road side units function as the fog nodes.

Smart traffic light system can be implemented through the existing architecture to decongest the roads, reroute the traffic. The traffic lights capture the details of the vehicles and pedestrians at every crossing. The road side units can provide details about the speed and number of vehicles at any point of time. The traffic controllers at each signal will utilise these details to minimise the vehicle congestion and pedestrian wait times. The central traffic controller which decides alternate routes based on the aggregate data at all points in the system.

The road side units can also have emergency service notification system. In case of any untimely accident or vehicle breakdown these services will be run at road side units and relevant authorities can be alerted if necessary, thereby reducing the number of casualties on roads.

Smart Grids

Smart grids are electricity distribution networks with smart meters deployed at various locations to measure real time usage statistics. A smart meter is a simple electricity meter which has location identifier and by virtue home broadband network data is pushed to central server called SCADA. Users will also see the real time usage through their mobile app and even create alerts if particular usage levels cross defined limits. The data sent to SCADA is collated and if required SCADA sends command to respond to change in demand or emergency to stabilise the power grid. Fog computing can distribute the functions of a SCADA throughout fog device network forming micro-grids. This improves the scalability, security and cost efficiencies. In addition to that alternative power generators can also be included into the main power grid. This creates a multi-level hierarchy where the fog devices will control the micro-grid and communicate with eh neighboring fog devices. The top layer will be SCADA which communicates with all the fog devices to provide long-term econometric and repository analytics.

Smart Home

More and more devices and smart sensors are being connected to internet at home, managing different walks of everyone's lives. Technology dominates us from the moment we wake up to the moment we sleep. Through internet connected thermostats to CCTVs to smart TVs, smart refrigerators and washing machines, we take help from the technological advances to help us make our lives easier. With different devices from different vendors, interoperability becomes a major hurdle. Real time video analytics for security and information alerts require huge amounts of computation and storage. By using elastic resources, the security and heavy processing can be easily being catered to. One information alert based application is pet monitoring or child monitoring.

High-end home security systems use multi-modal inputs from varied sources like smart locks, ambient temperature, motion sensors, and occupancy sensors along with audio and video recording devices. Fog devices can enable integration, interoperability and provide low latency computational resources. With each sensor having its own processing VMs on the fog devices, cooperation between the devices is as simple as standard network pipe or distributed queues. For example, a motion sensor detects suspicious motion in a room; it directs the security camera to check the exact location. The video feed is analysed on the fog devices and check if there is a security break-in, if so alerts the authorities and house owner.

Augmented Reality

Augmented reality applications are latency intolerant as any delay deteriorates the user experience. In paper (Zao et al 2014) authors built an augmented brain computation interactive game based on Fog computing and linked data. When a player plays the game, row streams of data collected by EFG sensors are generated and classified to detect brain state of the player. This classification is among the most computationally intensive signal processing tasks. Yet to achieve tolerable performance this classification should be carried out in real time. By using fog servers, systems performs continuous real-time brain state classification while the model training is done at the cloud servers based on the EFG reading at the sensors.

Ha et all proposes a wearable cognitive assistance system based on Google glass devices. This is intended to assist people with reduced mental ability. Due to constrained resources at the Google glass, the computer intensive workload of this application needed to be offloaded to an external server. The user experience tradeoff we discussed earlier is equally applicable in this scenario as well. As the cloud offloading is considerably latency ridden, fog devices are employed. These devices in turn communicated with the cloud for the delay tolerant jobs like error reporting and logging.

RESEARCH CHALLENGES IN FOG COMPUTING

The fog computing is slowly clutching its way into mainstream. There are still several issues that need to be tackled. The Fog layer should be interoperable and fault resilient. To achieve this goal in a non-compromising way we need to work on security protocols which don't flood the Fog or create any bottleneck. As the emphasis on standardisation evolves, surely certain challenges will be tackled. We will identify issues and research challenges in implementing and realising full potential of fog computing.

1. **Networking and Interconnectivity:** The Fog nodes are located at the edge of the networks. Fog nodes form interlink between the sensor layer and internet infrastructure. Because of that the Fog network is predominantly heterogeneous. It needs to support various communication protocols which are not necessarily IP based. The sensor and IoT devices (Aazam, M., & Huh, E. N. (2014, August)) for example support ZigBee, MQTT and various other protocols. The fog nodes needs to understand and possibly translate the communications to IP based protocols to push data to cloud. There are other interesting questions like how to deal with node churn, updating, predicting and maintaining the connectivity graph of network in different granularity; how to cooperate different controllers such as constantly connected controller (at the edge infrastructures) or intermittently connected controller (at the end devices) and where to place controllers in fog network.
2. **Quality of Service:** Four important metrics for QoS in Fog networks are connectivity, reliability, bandwidth and latency. Bandwidth refers to the amount of network bandwidth and storage bandwidth at the individual nodes. The reliability and latency requirements are especially critical for use cases control systems.
3. **Interfacing and Programming Model:** A unified interfacing and programming model is required to ease the porting of applications to fog computing platform. It would be difficult for each application developer to orchestrate heterogeneous, dynamic resources to build compatible applications on diverse platforms. And the applications should be aware of the platform level optimisations.
4. **Security and Privacy:** The main advantage of Fog computing is the data locality. This reduces the effect of privacy leakage. However machine to machine authentication and authorisation, user client access control and enforcement of policies is a challenge. This can rectified using privacy preserving techniques and end-to-end encryption of data. However this needs more to be done (Stojmenovic, I., & Wen, S., 2014, September).
5. **Provisioning and Resource Management:** The challenges lie in the mobility of end node since metrics such as bandwidth, storage, computation and latency will be changed dynamically. Resource discovery and sharing Resource discovery and sharing are critical for application performance in fog. The dynamic provisioning of resources and application aware hardware provisioning also is one interesting challenge.
6. **Accounting, Billing and Monitoring:** Sustainable business model with sufficient incentives and benefits for the fog services providers and users to make Fog computing viable. How are the incentives decided and how the pricing policies are set is going to one challenge for widespread adoption of Fog computing. And how the pricing policies are enforced. Research directions looks at the similar pricing models of cloud computing (Buyya, R., Yeo, C. S., Venugopal, S., Broberg, J., & Brandic, I. (2009)). However they pose additional challenges on Fog computing platforms.

CONCLUSION

Fog computing will help businesses be more agile and efficient in their operations, help in de-cluttering and reduces information overload at the higher decision making levels. Fog computing is an extension to the cloud bringing the virtual resources called fog nodes nearby the data generation and consumption. Its application areas are as vast as IoT deployment, 5G network deployment, SDN, Personal Area network, Plant management. Cisco IoX platform is pioneer in this domain providing production level platform for the companies to introduce fog in their environments. The major research challenges include the deployment of fog nodes, International device communication protocols.

REFERENCES

Aazam, M., & Huh, E. N. (2014, August). Fog computing and smart gateway based communication for cloud of things. In *Future Internet of Things and Cloud (FiCloud), 2014 International Conference on* (pp. 464-470). IEEE. doi:10.1145/2757384.2757397

Barroso, L. A., Clidaras, J., & Hölzle, U. (2013). The datacenter as a computer: An introduction to the design of warehouse-scale machines. *Synthesis Lectures on Computer Architecture, 8*(3), 1-154.

Bonomi, F., Milito, R., Zhu, J., & Addepalli, S. (2012, August). Fog computing and its role in the internet of things. In *Proceedings of the first edition of the MCC workshop on Mobile cloud computing* (pp. 13-16). ACM. 10.1145/2342509.2342513

Buyya, R., Yeo, C. S., Venugopal, S., Broberg, J., & Brandic, I. (2009). Cloud computing and emerging IT platforms: Vision, hype, and reality for delivering computing as the 5th utility. *Future Generation Computer Systems, 25*(6), 599–616. doi:10.1016/j.future.2008.12.001

Ha, K., Chen, Z., Hu, W., Richter, W., Pillai, P., & Satyanarayanan, M. (2014, June). Towards wearable cognitive assistance. In *Proceedings of the 12th annual international conference on Mobile systems, applications, and services* (pp. 68-81). ACM.

Hou, X., Li, Y., Chen, M., Wu, D., Jin, D., & Chen, S. (2016). Vehicular fog computing: A viewpoint of vehicles as the infrastructures. *IEEE Transactions on Vehicular Technology, 65*(6), 3860–3873. doi:10.1109/TVT.2016.2532863

Hu, Y. C., Patel, M., Sabella, D., Sprecher, N., & Young, V. (2015). *Mobile edge computing—A key technology towards 5G.* ETSI White Paper, 11.

Jain, R., & Paul, S. (2013). Network virtualization and software defined networking for cloud computing: A survey. *IEEE Communications Magazine, 51*(11), 24–31. doi:10.1109/MCOM.2013.6658648

Martins, J., Ahmed, M., Raiciu, C., Olteanu, V., Honda, M., Bifulco, R., & Huici, F. (2014, April). ClickOS and the art of network function virtualization. In *Proceedings of the 11th USENIX Conference on Networked Systems Design and Implementation* (pp. 459-473). USENIX Association.

Mozaffarian, D., Benjamin, E. J., Go, A. S., Arnett, D. K., Blaha, M. J., Cushman, M., ... Howard, V. J. (2016). Heart disease and stroke statistics—2016 update. *Circulation, 133*(4), e38–e360. doi:10.1161/CIR.0000000000000350 PMID:26673558

Nunes, B. A. A., Mendonca, M., Nguyen, X. N., Obraczka, K., & Turletti, T. (2014). A survey of software-defined networking: Past, present, and future of programmable networks. *IEEE Communications Surveys and Tutorials, 16*(3), 1617–1634. doi:10.1109/SURV.2014.012214.00180

Stantchev, V., Barnawi, A., Ghulam, S., Schubert, J., & Tamm, G. (2015). Smart items, fog and cloud computing as enablers of servitization in healthcare. *Sensors & Transducers*, *185*(2), 121.

Stojmenovic, I., & Wen, S. (2014, September). The fog computing paradigm: Scenarios and security issues. In *Computer Science and Information Systems (FedCSIS), 2014 Federated Conference on* (pp. 1-8). IEEE.

Wu, F., & Sun, G. (2013). *Software-defined storage. Report*. Minneapolis, MN: University of Minnesota.

Yi, S., Li, C., & Li, Q. (2015, June). A survey of fog computing: concepts, applications and issues. In *Proceedings of the 2015 Workshop on Mobile Big Data* (pp. 37-42). ACM.

Zao, J. K., Gan, T. T., You, C. K., Chung, C. E., Wang, Y. T., Méndez, S. J. R., ... Chu, S. L. (2014). Pervasive brain monitoring and data sharing based on multi-tier distributed computing and linked data technology. *Frontiers in Human Neuroscience*, 8. PMID:24917804

Zhu, J., Chan, D. S., Prabhu, M. S., Natarajan, P., Hu, H., & Bonomi, F. (2013, March). Improving web sites performance using edge servers in fog computing architecture. In *Service Oriented System Engineering (SOSE), 2013 IEEE 7th International Symposium on* (pp. 320-323). IEEE.

ADDITIONAL READING

Feng, D. G., Zhang, M., Zhang, Y., & Xu, Z. (2011). Study on cloud computing security. *Journal of Software*, *22*(1), 71–83. doi:10.3724/SP.J.1001.2011.03958

Joshi, Y., & Kumar, P. (Eds.). (2012). *Energy efficient thermal management of data centers*. Springer Science & Business Media. doi:10.1007/978-1-4419-7124-1

Sotomayor, B., Montero, R. S., Llorente, I. M., & Foster, I. (2009). Virtual infrastructure management in private and hybrid clouds. *IEEE Internet Computing*, *13*(5), 14–22. doi:10.1109/MIC.2009.119

Zhang, Q., Cheng, L., & Boutaba, R. (2010). Cloud computing: State-of-the-art and research challenges. *Journal of Internet Services and Applications*, *1*(1), 7–18. http://wikibon.org/wiki/v/. doi:10.100713174-010-0007-6

Chapter 4
Fog Computing:
Introduction, Architecture, Analytics, and Platforms

P. Balakrishnan
VIT University, India

Veeramuthu Venkatesh
SASTRA University, India

Pethuru Raj
Reliance Jio Infocomm. Ltd., India

ABSTRACT

The evolutions of world wide web (WWW) promise the revolution in personal, professional, and social aspects of human beings. These evolutions begin with static web pages to more sophisticated brain-computer interfaces. Among them, Web 4.0 plays a significant role that aimed to integrate mobile devices and things into the web to realize smarter environments. Further, it leads to the progression of machine-to-machine communication, wireless sensor networks, cyber physical systems, and internet of things (IoT). The drastic development of IoT applications led to unprecedented growth of data which can be processed using more powerful far-end cloud resources or less powerful local edge devices. Fog computing compromises the demerits of both approaches and conducts the data analysis at the network-end itself. This chapter provides the benefits of fog computing architectures together with the simulator as well as different software platforms for realizing the fog computing.

INTRODUCTION

The ever-increasing Internet usage absolutely induces profound impact in several aspects over the society as well as the industry in last two decades. This evolution and revolution of Internet redefine the way people or industries interact, work and play with each other which open up new avenues for revenues. Consequently, every evolution in World Wide Web (WWW) changed the mode of business transactions and nature of the companies themselves. This technological progress on the Internet is not only just because

DOI: 10.4018/978-1-5225-5972-6.ch004

of reduction in manufacturing cost of semiconductor components, but also the outstanding applicability of Internet Protocol (IP) and broader adoption of Internet. The rumblings and mumblings of web begin with the interconnection of faraway computers using ARPANET followed by the introduction of TCP/IP and WWW. As a consequence, the read-only web is evolved which allows the users only to read the information from the static web pages (refer to Figure 1). This evolution of the web is called the web of content (Web 1.0) which is primarily meant for reading the content and lacks in active communication or participation from the user side. However, Web 2.0 (web of communication or read-write web) allows any user to contribute their content to the web and communicates with any other web users. Some of the notable Web 2.0 developments are blogs, Twitter, Facebook, and Youtube. Conversely, Web 2.0 failed to associate the context with the data, and hence the actual requirements of the humans are not appropriately communicated to the software applications. For instance, during any search operation on the Internet, if the context of a keyword entered by the human is not understood by the search application (software) then the search operation may end up with limited results since the application does not have the intelligence to distinguish the relevant and irrelevant data for that context. This communication gap leads to the birth of Web 3.0 (web of context or read-write-execute web) where the context of the data is provided using semantic mark-up whereas, the inter-application communication support is provided using web services. In the meantime, the technological advancements in electronics extremely reduce the cost of mobile devices and the subsequent adoption of wireless Internet using mobile networks associate numerous people and businesses to the Internet. This situation sets the goal for the new web version, Web 4.0 (web of things or mobile web) with an objective to interconnect all the mobile devices in the real and virtual world. For instance, the smart agent in Web 4.0 may automatically recognize you using its camera and say to you: "Good Morning, Bob! You are going to NY today. Don't forget to take the raincoat; it is raining there. Also, I came to know the tickets for your favorite 'Wicked' musical show is available. If you say 'yes,' I will book the tickets for the show," and if you replied with 'yes,' it might say, "I have booked the ticket with the row 'M' and seat no. 108 which is your favorite most of the times."

Remember! Web 4.0, not a new technology rather it integrates the mobile devices into the web. Even though the Web 4.0 is not yet matured and still continuously developing, vision for Web 5.0 is proposed. Web 5.0 (web of thoughts or symbiotic web or emotive web) perceives the feelings and emotions of users during the communication between the humans and computers. For example, using the brain wave sensors implanted in the headphone, the users can relate their emotions with the content thereby enabling personalization which is an affable feature of Web 5.0. This chapter mainly deals with Wireless Sensor Networks (WSN), Machine to Machine (M2M) communications, Cyber-Physical Systems (CPS), Internet of Things (IoT) and fog computing which are the ingredients of Web 4.0.

MACHINE TO MACHINE, CYBER-PHYSICAL SYSTEMS, AND INTERNET OF THINGS

The persistent advancements in information and communication technology (ICT) vouch for the transformation in social, personal and professional aspects of human life. In 2025, all the physical objects in our dwelling, relaxing and working places are anticipated to be entrenched with several embedded electronic devices. These devices sense their surrounding physical environments and communicate with humans via different modalities thereby enhancing their lifestyle. The computing elements of these devices communicate with the sensors that collect the data from the surrounding physical environment, analyses

Figure 1. Evolution of World Wide Web

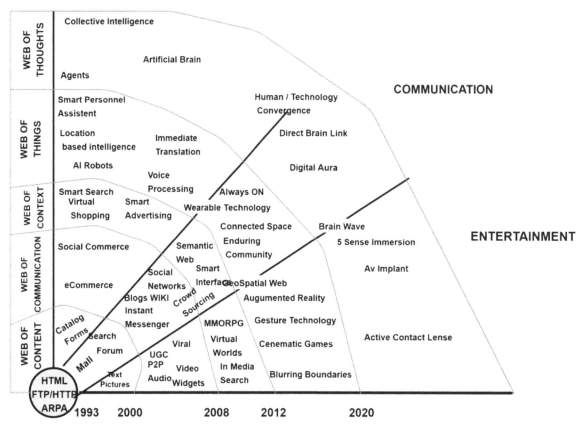

the data to gain a deeper understanding of the context and counteract through their control components. These innovative systems are referred as cyber-physical systems (CPS) which have the competency to cooperate as well as expand the physical world capabilities using their computation, communication and control components. Eventually, the CPS is the evolution of M2M communications. Generally, M2M systems refer the communication (wired or wireless) among the computers, sensors and actuators with or without human involvement. Further, the M2M systems usually contain sensors, actuators, WiFi or cellular network and a software component which receives and analyses the data to conclude. Mostly, the M2M systems are task- or device- specific and lack device-neutral connected platform. By integrating decision-support and instantaneous control mechanisms, the M2M systems are elevated to CPS to augment human-human, human-object and object-object communications in both physical and virtual world. Additionally, WSN contains several distributed independent sensors that are implanted in a physical environment which cooperatively transmits their values via different networks to the destination. However, IoT is a comprehensive infrastructure to facilitate innovative applications or services by enabling the interconnection and interaction among several physical as well as virtual things through existing or evolving communication techniques. In concise, the WSN, M2M, CPS, and IoT have sensors, processors, connectivity and application/services however they differ of design among these components.

ARCHITECTURE OF IOT

The explosion of interconnected things will be expected to reach 24 billion by the year 2020. This unprecedented growth of things transforms the societal, personal and professional lifestyle of people. A drastic evolution of Internet (Web 4.0) acclimatizes the things and their interconnection, leads to gathering environment information (sensing), transfer it to processing elements using existing Internet standards (communication/networking), apply the analytics over the collected data at the embedded device-level or remote cloud-level for extracting the context (processing/analysing) and react to through control devices (applications). At a higher level, the IoT platform consists of hardware layer which contains sensors, actuators, Radio Frequency Identification (RFID) and networking hardware, middleware layer for storage and computational resources to conduct data analysis, application layer for data visualization and interpretation.

Hardware Layer

Radio Frequency Identification (RFID)

Recent advancement in embedded communication hardware design proposes RFID technology which facilitates tags for wireless data communication. They can be used to automatically identify and track any objects they attached to. There are two different kinds of RFID tags: Passive and Active. Passive RFID tags do not have a battery and hence they utilize the power of reader's interrogating radio waves for communication. Nowadays, passive RFID tags are used in access control, retail, supply chain, transportation, bank cards and toll tickets. In contrast, the active RFID tags have local battery power with the capacity to instantiate communication. Predominantly, active tags are used in cargo monitoring and tracking. These RFID tags can be embedded anywhere in the target object since it does not require line of sight with the reader.

Wireless Sensor Network (WSN)

WSNs are geographically distributed independent sensors to measure physical quantities like air quality, temperature, atmospheric pressure, etc. and co-operatively transmit the gathered data to a central location via different network topologies. Usually, the WSN infrastructure consists of the following components:

- **Sensor Node:** A typical WSN node contains hardware interface for sensors, radio transceiver, processing units and a power source.
- **Sensor Node Communication Stack:** Each node in WSN need to communicate with each other to transmit the collected sensor data to the base station via gateway (sink) node. This node interconnects the outside world and WSN subnet using the Internet. Since the WSN nodes are implanted in an ad-hoc manner, routing is a critical concern in managing scalability and longevity of overall network. Besides, WSN frequently suffers from node energy drain out as well as reduced overall network lifetime.
- **Middleware:** Each sensor node can talk with nearby as well as distant sensor nodes, applications, and platforms using any network. However, an application may be interested in a set of

specific sensor data which enables the need-based networking of sensors with the far-end applications. Moreover, every sensor node may be from different manufacturers and requires seamless and spontaneous integration of all sorts of sensors, actuators, and appliances. Middleware is a software solution which supports application/service orchestration, arbitration, and composition, integration of heterogeneous sensor nodes together with sensor data fusion and sits in between application layer which utilize the sensor data and the hardware layer that produce the data. For instance, Open Sensor Web Architecture (OSWA) is an Open Geospatial Consortium (OGC) based autonomous middleware for building sensor applications.

- **Sensor Data Accretion:** The most critical segment of WSN is secure as well as reliable data aggregation. Also, the WSN should be equipped with an appropriate fault-tolerance mechanism to cope up with node drop outs. As the system is integrated with actuators, it is essential to accommodate a suitable intrusion detection mechanism to ensure the security of the system.

Addressing

The capacity to exclusively identify 'Things' is essential for the accomplishment of IoT. This will enable us to uniquely identify the huge amount of nodes and to control remote nodes using the internet. The proposed mechanism for creating the unique address should ensure the uniqueness, reliability, persistence, and scalability. However, the existing IPv4 can identify a group of sensor nodes geographically and lacks to identify each of them individually. Similarly, the IPv6 provides a limited support for nodes identification with its internet mobility features. Since the WSN stack is completely different from the internet, it is not possible to accommodate IPv6 stack to address them individually. Additionally, the heterogeneous sensor nodes, a variety of data types and aggregation of data from several sources aggravate this issue further. These issues are sorted out by Uniform Resource Name (URN) which duplicates the resources that can be accessed using Uniform Resource Locator (URL). At the subnet level, the sensor gateway node having a URN provides the layer for addressing the sensor nodes individually. The URN of each sensor node is a unique ID which is maintained in a lookup table of sensor gateway node. Besides, each sensor in a sensor node has a URN which is to be addressed by sensor gateway node. In concise, at the network level, users communicate with sensors that are addressed using URN, accessed via URL and controlled by Uniform Resource Controller (URC).

Middleware Layer

Data Storage and Analytics

The most important outcome of IoT is the generation of an unprecedented volume of data. The data produced by the IoT environment can be of measurement, event, transaction or diagnostics data. Usually, the measurement data is frequently obtained from several heterogeneous sensors that measure the environment parameters. At present, Oil and Natural gas sector handling the huge volume of measurement data (~100 TB) per day. Any data which leads to decision-making such as, status change, the breaking of the threshold value and notable incident or unwanted accident are categorized as event data. As already mentioned, the sensor networking enables the grouping of sensors which are coordinated to accomplish a specific (atomic) function. Further, any composite function can be realized on top of this by interacting, interconnecting, integrating and collaborating with these set of sensors. The data related to these transactions are transaction data. Finally, the diagnostics data provides the perception of healthiness as well as the proper working of machine or process. This huge amount of data needs to be cleaned, processed and archived in energy as well as cost efficient manner. The deeper insights obtained from the data analytics (processing) are intelligently used to realize controlled smarter environments. Hence, it is essential to devise new centralized or distributed artificial intelligence algorithms that can be used for data processing. Here, the data processing can be done at three different localities: embedded processing at the local node (edge computing), processing in far-off servers (cloud computing) and process the data in between these two locations (fog computing). The detailed explanation of these three technologies will be expounded in the subsequent sections.

Apart from analysis, it is equally important to understand the context of the environment. Context is nothing but an awareness or knowledge of the surroundings inferred from its environment data. For that, data from disparate sensors need to be combined where the resultant data has less uncertainty than if used individually. The process of combining sensor data is sensor fusion that lays the foundation for context-awareness which in-turn opens-up new avenues for more sophisticated intelligent services. In concise, the IoT middleware layer supports the seamless integration of heterogeneous sensors, multi-sensor data fusion, storage as well as analysis of sensor data and much more.

APPLICATION LAYER

Data Visualization

The success of IoT application lies in an efficient display of meaningful information, insights or knowledge from the data than plotting the raw data either individually or collectively. Alternatively, the visualization component of IoT is flexible enough to handle the needs of non-computer savvy professionals and helps to make up efficient and fast decisions. Additionally, it compasses event detection capability by analyzing raw data.

EMERGING IOT APPLICATIONS

A wide variety of emerging smart sensors, connected things, software applications and cloud connectivity introduce several innovative and sophisticated applications in our living as well as working environments.

Smart Homes

The smart home is a personalized place intended to control the equipment such as, air conditioners, heater, washing machines and lights which will provide enhanced energy management. Similarly, IoT platform enables the realization of personalized healthcare with Body Area Network (BAN) which uses Smartphones to interact with several sensors that are measuring the physiological parameters through different interfaces such as, Bluetooth.

Smart Healthcare

The personalized healthcare solutions can be easily extended to Smart healthcare for elderly people where the health data collected from the body area network are sent to doctor via gateway server which is located in the home. This facilitates the doctor to monitor as well as treat the elderly people who are staying in remote places at the earliest.

Smart Cities

Smart cities are the technology vision for urban development to harmonize the ICT and IoT in a secured manner to effectively admin the city's resources. These resources not limited to water supply network, electricity distribution network, hospitals, power generation plants and transportation systems. Further, the smart city started to use urban informatics to enhance the quality of service of services. With ICT, the authorities can monitor the day to day activities of city, and understand the progression of city which will be used to improvise the quality of life.

Smart Transportation

Transportation is a critical cog in constructing smart cities. Nowadays, vehicles are equipped with smart sensors thereby increasingly connected through the extensive usage of IT. These smart sensors ensure the safe and secure journey with more comfort and sophistication.

GAME-CHANGING FACTORS OF IOT JOURNEY

The IoT technology demonstrates drastic deployment of sensors, controllers and communication infrastructure over a widespread of application domains (IoT Analytics Across Edge and Cloud Platforms, n.d). These applications may vary from utility services like smart power to simple devices such as Nest. Hence, the next hype of IoT will be directed by the data analytics and processing in a centralized or distributed platforms using heterogeneous computing hardware at local edge nodes or far-end cloud servers. In general, the software stacks of IoT architectures are either Cloud-centric or Thing-centric (i.e. device-centric) (refer to Figure 2).

In cloud-centric realization, the data gathered from sensors are up-streamed to cloud servers where the analytics and subsequent decision-making are accomplished and down-streamed to controllers located at the edge nodes. Though this approach lowers the processing cost and provides strong security, it introduces more network latency (100's of ms) since it requires the transfer of a sheer amount of data from multiple input data sources to a centralized cloud server for processing. This huge amount of delay is not accepted in real-time or delay-sensitive applications. Additionally, the internet connectivity may be intermittent that leads to discontinuity of service, if the cloud connectivity lost.

However, in Thing-centric implementation, the analytics logic is embedded inside the things itself, operates over the sensor data and generates local conclusions. This approach seems to be appropriate since most of the data sources to be monitored such as, sensors, devices and gateways are located at the edge. Besides, the controllers for administering the infrastructure are also located at the edge. This approach introduces low network latency as it does not require the data transfer. But, the edge devices are

Figure 2. Different interaction models for IoT architectures

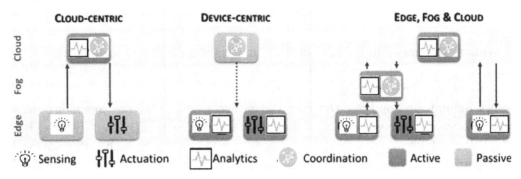

energy-constraint devices and also they have very limited computational as well as storage capabilities which cannot process a continuous stream of data.

In concise, none of the single model (cloud-only or edge-only) is suitable for any IoT applications as each model has their own merits and demerits. The emerging trend in distributed analytics combines both Cloud- and Things- centric approaches (edge+cloud) thereby enabling seamless spanning of devices from edge to cloud servers. Though this combined methodology helps edge devices to coordinate with cloud resources, offload their computation during heavy duty processing or battery draining situations, still it suffers from demerits of both approaches.

Recent advancements in processor technology embed non-trivial computing power at the sensor gateways. For instance, Raspberry Pi which is a single board computer and a well-known IoT gateway has four core processors where each core is equivalent to third of processing power of Xeon cloud instance. These gateways are located between edge nodes and cloud resources down the line in the data-path and overcome the computational power as well as network bandwidth limitations. This new wave in IoT proposes an innovative style of analytics which brings down high-end computing facilities to network-end thereby supports real-time processing and fast-decision making and is known as Fog computing. Alternatively, the Fog computing expanding the cloud-like computational and storage resources as Fog devices and locate them closer to edge nodes which in turn process delay-sensitive application data. These Fog devices can be gateways, servers, cameras, routers and switches. The following statements define Fog computing:

- Processes and analyses the data at the edge which is closer to the location where it is originated, infer knowledge/decisions and actuate the controllers accordingly.
- Useful data alone are up-streamed to cloud for historical data analytics.
- Faster decision-making time (in ms) and mostly avoids the sheer amount of data transfer to the cloud.

SIGNIFICANCES OF FOG COMPUTING FOR THE SUCCESS OF IOT

- **Eradicating Extraneous Data at the Edge:** The fog devices at the network edge eliminate the repetitive and redundant data from the source, ensure that only relevant, useful data alone is transmitted to cloud for conducting analytics.

- **Enabling Real-Time Data Analytics:** The evolution and revolution of edge/fog devices cater the needs of real-time data capture and analytics applications thus eliminating the need of cloud for data processing.
- **Momentary Response:** In the case of delay intolerant applications such as, vehicle collision avoidance system, the fog computing infrastructure is in evitable to provide instantaneous response to retaliate the surrounding situations.
- **Sensors Behind the Fog/Edge Devices:** The advancements in the fog computing enhance the compute, storage and networking capabilities as well as enable them to identify through IPv6 address. This capability allows resource-restraint sensors to identify themselves through fog devices.
- **Data Security:** The fog device provides isolation between the sensor data and the cloud environment. For instance, any intrusion on the sensors can be easily identified and blocked at the edge device itself. Further, the sensor data are completely investigated in a local network which isolates them from Internet and cloud environment.
- **Device-Clouds:** The powerful fog devices grouped to create a device cluster to do the analysis on the sensor data at the network edge.
- **Intricate Applications:** With fog computing, the data from several sensors and devices are routed to the proper destination via fog middleware. Additionally, message-based device/service orchestration is also supported to develop composite applications. For instance, the sensor data collected from various locations of a restaurant can be used in restaurant operational optimization.
- **Security:** The security of IoT data can be further improvised by restricting the access to sensors and fog/edge devices. Besides, several access-control, activation and configuration policies can also be integrated into fog devices to gain fine-grained control over sensors and actuators.

FOG COMPUTING AND ITS COMPANIONS

The technological revolution in ICT empowers the people to do their computation and communication on a single Smartphone. Likewise, several environments ranging from homes, luxury cars to shopping malls are implanted with numerous general-purpose as well as application-specific sensors and actuators. Hence, sooner or later there will be ample amount of things, sensors, and services in realizing fog/edge computing which in-turn proposes several articulation, approaches and methods. In this regard, it is essential to know the nomenclature of fog-like concepts together with their commonalities and difference with fog computing.

Proximate Clouds

There are varieties of general cloud offerings such as private, public and hybrid cloud are available to cater the needs of different analytics applications. Contrastingly, there is a domain or community specific cloud environment with an objective only to meet out their specific requirements. Today, the new generation sensor applications demand proximate cloud environments to accomplish data analysis at the network edge itself. These proximate clouds are a sort of out-and-out infrastructure for performing comprehensive data analysis. Besides, the nearby computation, as well as communication devices, join together to collaboratively realize proximate cloud environment. In future, it is envisioned that there are numerous proximate cloud offerings around us.

Cloudlets

Cloudlet is a turnkey cloud appliance which provides a cloud environment using powerful server machines for a specific context. A cloudlet emerges as an important architectural element in Mobile Cloud Computing (MCC) which sits in between mobile and cloud resources. Interestingly, the cloudlets can be easily configured and activated to realize the delay-intolerant and bandwidth-constraint real-time applications. For instance, locating target objects by analyzing the crowd-sensed videos using a cloudlet is an important use-case of cloudlet facilities. Or else, these videos need to be transmitted to the far-end cloud servers, processed and the results will be returned to the user which is a time consuming one.

Mobile Edge Computing

The MEC deploys cloud computing facilities as well as service provisioning environments in the cellular base stations thereby carry out the processing tasks closer to the cellular customer which in-turn reduces the congestion in the network and improvises the performance.

Mobile Cloud Computing

The primary objective of MCC is to execute complex mobile applications by offloading their computations to a faraway or nearby cloud resources or mobile base stations.

SIMULATING THE FOG COMPUTING ENVIRONMENT: IFOGSIM

The Internet of Things (IoT) represents a massive opportunity for integrating real world objects online. These objects generate a huge amount of data which in-turn poses a major concern on storage and data analysis. Cloud computing on joint co-ordination with IOT tries to solve the problem of managing this tremendous amount of data. However, this technology offers a solution with increased latency and reduced performance since it demands the movement of data towards the processing units present in the far-end cloud environment. Conversely, the next generation applications such as, healthcare-monitoring and emergency response are delay-intolerant whose quality metrics cannot be satisfied by the cloud environments. This situation can be enhanced by extending the cloud services to the network end which leads to the existence of new computing arena named fog or edge computing. The edge computing gives a decentralized architectural design pattern that connects the computing resources and the application services closer to the edge where the data is originally originated. The major concern in the edge is the formulation of resource management techniques that decides the appropriate positioning of computing modules in the edge with minimized latency and increased throughput. The evaluation of such positioning strategy that lies behind the resource management techniques is made through an evaluation platform named iFogSim (H. (2017, June 17)). In concise, many applications (Health care systems and Emergency systems) necessitate both fast processing and minimum delay time between the end user and cloud environment. These two metrics can be achieved by integrating the Edge or Fog Computing environment. The details of Fog Computing for IoT devices will enhance the network as well as computational performance.

The term "fog computing" or "edge computing" insists on conducting the data analysis at the network end instead of establishing channels for cloud storage and utilization. Alternatively, Fog computing can be defined as a distributed computing paradigm that extends the services provided by the cloud to the edge of the network. It enables seamless leveraging of cloud and edge resources along with its infrastructure.

Architecture of iFogSim

Mostly, all of the Fog computing applications have the following three main layers at the higher level (refer to Figure 3): *IoT Device Layer, Fog Layer, and Cloud Computing Layer*. At the bottom level, the *IoT device layer* contains IoT devices, sensors, and actuators. These sensors and IoT devices are connected with the Fog Nodes which are available in the *Fog layer*. The Fog Nodes can be deployed anywhere in the network. Any device that has a computing, storage and network connectivity can be treated as a fog node. The following devices such as industrial controllers, switches, routers, embedded servers, and video surveillance cameras satisfy the abovementioned property hence considered to be fog nodes.

The detailed architecture of fog computing environment is shown in Figure 4 which employs fog nodes in between the sensors at the bottom layer and the cloud environment.

- **Fabric Layer:** Sensor nodes and actuators are employed at the lowest layer. The sensors are scattered around several topographical locations to gather some physical quantities and to propagate the sensed data to higher layers through Fog Gateway for cleaning, processing, and analysis. Likewise, IoT Actuators are placed in the same layer of the architecture which is engaged to control or react to environment changes.
- **Resources Layer:** The resources layer contain fog devices and gateways. Any network device that has the capability to host application modules are called as Fog devices. Further, a fog device which interconnects the sensors with the internet is a Fog gateway. Besides, Fog devices also have the capacity to integrate cloud resources from far-end datacenter in an on-demand fashion,

Figure 3. High-level view of fog computing environment

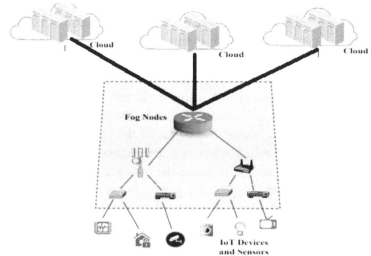

Figure 4. Fog Computing Architecture

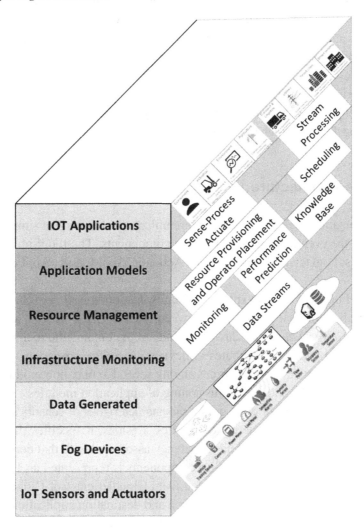

- **Data Layer:** The data layer comprises of IoT data streams which are a stream of immutable data acquired by the sensor nodes.
- **Information Layer:** The configuration and current status of the resources in the resources layer are continuously observed by the monitoring components. Usually, they have the availability as well as utilization information of applications, services, sensors, fog devices, and gateways. This information is up-streamed to resource management layer which helps in decision making. Since the energy consumption is a critical concern in IoT devices, the resource management layer accommodates power monitoring component to monitor the energy consumption of fog devices.
- **Resource Management Layer:** This is the central component of the architecture that efficiently manages the resources with an objective to provide the assured QoS to the applications along with maximum resource utilization. The resource provisioning and scheduling components of this layer utilize the monitoring information to identify the best-breed resources for an application module.

- **Application Layer:** In general, the Fog computing applications use Distributed Data Flow (DDF) model that is represented as Directed Acyclic Graph (DAG) in which the vertices are application modules whereas and edges are data flow between modules. There are two different kinds of application models are supported in iFogSim: Sensor-Process-Actuate and Stream Processing model. The Sensor-Process-Actuate model gathers the sensor data as data streams that are processed by the applications running on Fog devices to make up the decisions, and the respective commands will be sent to actuators. The Stream Processing model comprises of a group of application modules hosted in Fog devices which are constantly mine the data streams transmitted from the sensor nodes.

iFogSim Software Architecture

The software implementation of iFogSim architecture utilizes the basic event simulation functionalities of Cloudsim to notify the events among the iFogSim components. The iFogSim encompasses the following primary classes: FogDevice, Sensor, Tuple, Actuator, AppModule, AppEdge and AppLoop.

- **FogDevice:** The FogDevice class explains the hardware configuration of the device together with the information about the interconnection between other devices, sensors, and actuators. Since it is extended from *PowerDatacenter* class of Cloudsim, it contains the memory, processor capacity, storage size and bandwidth attributes of devices. Also, the properties of this class precisely define the sharing of Fog device's resources among several application modules together with the strategy for commissioning and decommissioning of application modules.
- **Sensor:** The attributes of sensor class depict the characteristics of sensors starting from connectivity, output parameters, and tuple characteristics. Besides, it specifies the identity of the Fog gateway device to which it is linked and the latency associated with that connection.
- **Tuple:** The data flow between the iFogSim components is represented as Tuples that are created by Tuple class of iFogSim which is extended from Cloudlet class of Cloudsim. Additionally, it contains the information about tuple type, source and destination application module, the amount of data encapsulated and the Million Instructions required to process them.
- **Actuator:** The attributes of actuator class defines the network connection properties and the action to be delivered upon the reception of Tuple. Besides, it specifies the identity of the Fog gateway device to which it is linked and the latency associated with that connection.
- **AppModule:** The application module is characterized by its processing elements, the number of output tuples per input tuple and the selectivity model. The AppModule class which is extended from PowerVM class of Cloudsim does this characterization for an application module.
- **AppEdge:** The AppEdge class defines the data-dependency, TupleType, the length of data together with its processing requirements. There are two different types of edges are supported by iFogSim: periodic and event-based. The periodic edges generate the tuples at regular intervals whereas event-based edges allow the transmission of a tuple from a source module to destination module only when the selectivity model of source module allows it.
- **AppLoop:** The iFogSim supports the end-to-end latency measurement by specifying the target origin and destination modules in the form of process control loops.

Apart from these classes, the iFogSim also provides the following services: Power Monitoring Service and Resource Monitoring Service. The Power Monitoring Service defines the appropriate power model that estimates the power consumption of devices by considering the resource utilization. The Resource Management Service firstly places the application modules across the devices by considering end-to-end latency, network utilization, operational cost, and energy consumption. During placement, the application modules can be placed in two different fashions: Cloud-only or Edge-ward. The Cloud-only placement hosts all the application modules in a cloud datacenters whereas the Edge-ward placement deploys the application modules closer to the network edge. Secondly, it schedules the resources of Fog devices among the application modules. By default, the resources of fog device are equally shared among all the application modules. This strategy can be easily modified by overriding the default scheduling policy. Further, the iFogSim facilitates the user to design their application logic by choosing the appropriate device, sensor, and actuator using either java APIs or Graphical User Interface (GUI). These newly designed topologies can be stored and re-loaded by transforming them into a JSON file representation.

EDGE SOFTWARE PLATFORMS

Edge computing emerged as a critical element of Industrial IoT applications that offers additional compute as well as storage device nearer to the data source itself. GE's Predix edge technology becomes a prominent IoT platform which provides both edge and cloud software stack thereby delivering a distributed software platform for industries. The Predix edge technology contains Predix machine, a runtime environment, Predix Edge Manager and Edge management solution.

Predix IoT Platform

Predix Machine (Predix | Cloud-Based Platform for the Industrial Internet. (2017, December 11)). is a device-agnostic flexible and customizable software development kit which helps to associate any edge device/machine with minimum configuration to the Predix cloud environment. Alternatively, it provides a deterministic control system that hosts and integrates any device/machine with GE's control systems. After connecting to the target machine/device, it consumes as well as filters the data from desperate data sources. Also, it manages several storage resources to accumulate the data. Apart from this, it establishes a bi-directional communication between edge and cloud stack via a dedicated data bus. Finally, it has the capability to integrate data from several data sources and provides support to develop as well as execute applications and analytics over the edge devices.

The Predix Machine may be installed in either of one ways: Host operating system deployment and Docker container deployment. The Host operating system deployment may install the OS directly on the hardware (i.e. bare-metal) or on a Virtual Machine. The Predix Machine of this deployment reconfigures its industrial adapters to collect the data from industrial equipment and transport it to Predix cloud services directly. This type of deployment is best suited for edge devices which have inferior performance capabilities. In contrast, the Docker deployments permit the users to execute custom applications developed using C, C++ or Java and communicate with the Predix Machine via publish/subscribe mechanism using a containerized data bus. However, this mode of operation demands additional hardware facilities in the edge devices.

The Predix Edge Manager is a component of Predix Edge Technology that manages multiple Predix Manager enabled devices. Also, it manages the applications, services and connectivity on the edge devices. Besides, it provides scalability by managing their devices, users and applications centrally from the cloud. Also, it offers better reliability and manageability for applications and devices. In concise, the Predix Edge Manager offers following capabilities: Application and software lifecycle management, Device lifecycle management, connectivity and user management.

Application and Software lifecycle management: This component manages the deployment, installation and upgrading of the software/applications over the edge devices. Further, it creates, executes commands over multiple edge devices, debugs and reacts to the message alerts from the devices.

- **Device Lifecycle Management:** This capability is responsible for configuration, secure commissioning and decommissioning of individual devices, create and admin device groups, search the devices of Specific interests.
- **Connectivity Management:** The connectivity capability of Predix Edge Manager configures and manages connection and communication with edge devices. Besides, it monitors the network as well as data usage of edge devices.
- **User Management:** Finally, the user management component assigns and manages the roles and responsibilities to the users.

In concise, the Predix Edge Technology elevates the industrial machines into intelligent connected machines together with the capability to faster data analytics thereby enabling quicker decisions.

Cisco Kinetic IoT Platform

Cisco kinetic (Cisco Kinetic. (2017, December 15)) is an emerging IoT platform which contains connections management, fog computing and data delivery for different types of connected wired and wireless devices. Alternatively, it eases the integration of distributed devices thus senses and transports the data securely to several distributed applications. Also, it enforces the rules of data owners during processing. Firstly, it extracts the data from things and transforms it to application specific data types. Secondly, it provides additional computational resources at the edge nodes thereby attain faster decisions. Finally, it moves the right data to right applications at the right time.

IBM Watson IoT Platform

IBM Watson (The Internet of Things becomes the Internet that thinks with Watson IoT. (n.d.)) IoT platform is a powerful toolkit which has the capability to manage several devices, integrate gateway devices and application access. It has the following features: connect, analyze, information management, risk and security management.

- **Connect:** This feature allows the customers to integrate their own devices, sensors and gateways to the IoT platform. Suppose, if they don't have the devices to connect, it allows the customers to create and connect the devices through Node-RED device simulator.
- **Analyze:** This feature allows the customers to monitor and analyse their device/sensor data in real-time which is guided by rules. Besides, it also triggers automatic alerts through e-mails.

- **Information Management:** The captured data can be archived for future purpose. Further, it also triggers data transformation operations to integrate with other services.
- **Risk and Security Management:** This feature ensures the integrity of the proposed IoT solution using secure connection and access control mechanisms. Also, it assesses the associated risks and mitigate them using policy driven actions.

Above all, it also supports the development of new external analytical applications which can be integrated with the real-time as well as historical data.

Apache Kura

Apache kura (E. (n.d.)) is a project which provides a platform for developing IoT gateways. It also has a smart application container which allows the management of remote gateways. Further, it offers wide range of APIs through which users are allowed to develop and deploy their own customized application. Apache Kura has the following built-in services:

- **I/O Services:** These services enable the access to devices via serial port, blue tooth, USB and GPIO.
- **Data Services:** These services enable the publishing of data to the remote servers using store and forward functionality. Besides, it hides the complexity of network layer and protocol from the application developer.
- **Cloud Services:** With this capability, the IoT application can communicate with any remote server.
- **Configuration Service:** This service offers a snapshot service with which the configuration of all registered devices can be imported or exported from or to the container.
- **Remote Management:** This facility enables the remote management of all the IoT applications deployed in Kura environment. Further, it depends on the configuration service and cloud service.
- **Networking:** This API discovers and configures the network interfaces present in the gateway.
- **Watchdog Service:** Monitors the critical elements of IoT network and forces the system to reset whenever the problem is occurred.
- **Web Administration Interface:** This management console is used to administer the entire IoT gateway.

CONCLUSION

The development of web 4.0 leads to the existence of IoT technology which transforms the several characteristics of human life. The integration of sensors and devices into mainstream computing demands smarter platforms to aggregate them as device groups to do the local processing. Fog computing is truly a game-changer for IoT by which real-time applications with real-time analytics can be easily achieved. This chapter covers up the basic definitions about IoT, edge computing, and fog computing. Additionally, it explains about iFogSim through which anybody can design their fog computing environment.

REFERENCES

E. (n.d.). Retrieved December 22, 2017, from http://www.eclipse.org/kura//

H. (2017, June 17). *Harshitgupta1337/fogsim*. Retrieved December 22, 2017, from https://github.com/harshitgupta1337/fogsim

IoT Analytics Across Edge and Cloud Platforms. (n.d.). Retrieved December 22, 2017, from https://iot.ieee.org/newsletter/may-2017/iot-analytics-across-edge-and-cloud-platforms.html

Kinetic, C. (2017, December 15). Retrieved December 22, 2017, from http://www.cisco.com/c/en/us/solutions/internet-of-things/iot-kinetic.html

Predix | Cloud-Based Platform for the Industrial Internet. (2017, December 11). Retrieved December 22, 2017, from http://www.ge.com/digital/predix

The Internet of Things becomes the Internet that thinks with Watson IoT. (n.d.). Retrieved December 22, 2017, from http://www.ibm.com/internet-of-things

Chapter 5
A Comprehensive Survey of IoT Edge/Fog Computing Protocols

Madhumathi R.
Sri Ramakrishna Engineering College, India

Dharshana R.
Sri Ramakrishna Engineering College, India

Reshma Sulthana
Coimbatore Institute of Technology, India

Kalaiyarasi N.
Sri Ramakrishna Engineering College, India

ABSTRACT

The IoT device ecosystem is being blessed with a dazzling array of slim and sleek, trendy and handy, purpose-specific and generic, disappearing, disposable yet indispensable, resource-constrained and intensive, and embedded yet networked devices. Therefore, our personal, as well as professional, environments are increasingly being stuffed with such kinds of functionally powerful devices that are instrumented, interconnected, and intelligent. This trend and transition set a stimulating foundation for a variety of connected and smarter environments. By empowering our everyday devices to be computing, communicative, sensitive, and responsive, the newly introduced concept of edge or fog computing is to bring forth a number of innovations, disruptions, and transformations for the IT domain. This chapter conveys how the various protocols contribute immensely to the intended success of fog computing and analytics in the days ahead.

INTRODUCTION TO IoT EDGE/FOG COMPUTING

Edge computing refers to the processing of data nearby the IoT devices which reduces the transmission of data to be sent through long routes. Computing of data is done closer to the network which helps in the organization of data for various industries. Here, the IoT devices are used to collect massive bulks of data to send it to the cloud data center for processing. Some of the data are processed locally in order to

DOI: 10.4018/978-1-5225-5972-6.ch005

reduce the traffic in a central repository. This can be done by transmitting all the data from IoT devices to local devices and performing the common compute storage and networking process. The edge of the network processes the data and some of the data is sent to the central repository. An example of edge computing is the 5G cellular networks. It is done by adding micro data centers to the 5G towers.

Fog refers to the interconnection between the cloud and edge devices. Edge refers to space where the processing or computing is done being closer to the edge devices.

Some of the important terms and definitions for edge computing given by (Butler, 2017):

- **Edge Devices:** These are devices that produce data. It can be sensors or any other machine which capture or produce data.
- **Edge:** The edge differs in every case. In telecommunications, the cell tower is the edge.
- **Edge Gateway:** It is the buffer between the fog network and where the processing is done. It acts like a window above the edge of the network.
- **Edge Computing Equipment:** It uses a range of devices and machines, after enabling the Internet accessibility in them. An example for this is Amazon Web Service's Snowball.

Most of the data management is done in the cloud data center. In an edge computing model, the devices transmit the data to the closest edge computing equipment, which acts as a gateway helps in the processing of data rather than sending it back to the cloud or the data centre. Therefore, edge computing helps in the processing of data on the nearest edge rather than taking the data to the cloud, which increased the transmission cost and signal strength. By 2020, most of the enterprises will make use of edge computing. It is better suited for capturing and processing using IoT devices than doing it in the cloud. All the manufacturing industries, factories, organizations can adopt this technology easily into their environment. The deployment is a difficult task but the standards could do it easily. Hence the dependency over the cloud is minimized and the management of data becomes simple.

The definition given by NIST is

Fog computing is a horizontal, physical or virtual resource paradigm that resides between smart end-devices and traditional cloud or data centers. This paradigm supports vertically-isolated, latency-sensitive applications by providing ubiquitous, scalable, layered, federated, and distributed computing, storage, and network connectivity.

Edge computing helps in improving the scalability, energy efficiency and provision of contextual information processing of cloud (Pan, Beyah, Goscinski, & Ren, 2017). It emphasizes the usage of different types of edge devices, such as smart phones, routers, etc.

Advantages

Some of the advantages of edge computing are:

- **Reduction of IoT Solution Costs:** It reduces the amount of data flowing back and forth to the cloud through the network and thus lowering the cost.

- **Security:** Edge computing address security and prevents some of the industries to use the cloud. It can filter the valuable information to process locally and sending the unprocessed data to the cloud for processing.
- **Quick Response Time:** It analyses the data instantly and lowers the possibility of the worst situation to take place, such as terminating the machines before it fails.
- **Dependable Operation:** The edge devices operate without any interference even when the connection is intermittent.
- **Interoperability:** The edge computing protocols helps in understanding the language between different devices and the cloud.
- **Preserving Privacy:** When the data is captured from one device, it is important that the data might be sensitive or insensitive and should be preserved for privacy.
- **Reducing Latency:** When the accuracy is affected, edge computing applications implement machine learning algorithms to interact with the IoT devices.

There are different modules in an edge computing applications, where each one of them runs at different levels. For instance, the data from edge gateway and devices in an analytic module runs in the cloud (Butler, 2017). Each module should clearly describe the components and communications between them.

Mobile Edge Computing (MEC) is also an extension of edge computing and it was developed to connect most of the things to the internet. This was developed because of the increased usage of smart phones today. This makes IoT scalable over a wide region and can be extended using the Software Defined Network (SDN) (Salman, Elhajj, & Kayssi, 2015).

The need for using IoT in edge computing is because the cloud models are not designed as well as IoT in managing a huge volume of data generated. Handling the data using IoT helps in minimizing the latency, address the security concerns, operate reliably, secure the data over a wide geographical area and this proves that it is the best place for processing data.

The Amazon IoT Approach

It captures all the data at once and deals with it. These data are of massive amounts i.e. it collects as much data as possible at one stroke without even caring if they are useful or not. The advantages of using this approach are:

- No data is left remained
- Big data tools for analyzing

The Dell IoT Cloud Edge Approach

Unlike Amazon which grabs all the data, Dell works with only useful and meaningful data. By analyzing the data which is nearer, it can reduce the network traffic and keeps all important information inside the network. The advantages are:

- Only useful information is taken
- Calculations are done before sending the data

- Lower bandwidth costs
- Real-time processing

SENSOR AND ACTUATOR NETWORKING

The sensors and actuators are mostly wired less and so they are called wireless sensors and actuators networks (WSANs). It is a network of sensor nodes which has the ability to change the environment. All the elements interact wirelessly and are autonomous. They are linked to a wireless medium to perform distributed sensing and actuation tasks.

Actuators are heterogeneous and have more energy. It is a device that converts an electrical signal to physical action. It has the mechanism by which the agent acts upon the environment. It is a network entity and has the capability to perform functions such as, transmit, receive, process and relay data. They control a system with various dimensions. The information flow is bidirectional between the sink and the sensors (Lee, Nam, Roh, & Kim, 2016).

Sensor hubs can be used to improve consumer services with the help of location awareness. In order to achieve this, all the devices should enable location awareness including buildings (Haughn, 2015). In these cases, combined sensors are being used. For example, a numerous range of smartphone usage can form a WSAN to control the populations.

Sensors and actuators are the central elements of control systems. They can involve more than a single actuator on a point. WSANs are made of multiple nodes ranging into thousands, with hubs and actors. When used in locations having exact measurement and control, processing of data and CPU allows for actors to change input immediately. However, WSANs and WSNs share common properties, such as connectivity, reliability, energy efficiency, some of the differences between them are:

- Sensor nodes are small inexpensive with communication and computation capabilities and actors are rich in resources which have stronger transmitting powers and long battery life.
- WSANs respond based on the environment. The sensor data must be valid at the time of acting. Therefore, real-time communication is important in WSANs.
- The number of actors is lower than the sensors because all of the actors cannot be deployed and satisfied.
- A distributed local communication between the sensors and actors is the most important.

Sensors are mainly used to gather information about the environment and send the data to actuators through single-hop or multi-hop communications. Sensor nodes are low in cost and use low power and have limited sensing capacity. WSAN can be stationary or mobile based on the target applications. WSANs also have challenges for control applications. The wireless channels have various useful properties such as path loss, adjacent channel interference, multipath fading, etc. (Xia, Tian, Li, & Sun, 2007). They are also unreliable. Due to this, there might be a time delay and packet loss which will degrade the performance. Packet loss is merely a delay which has an impact on performance. To avoid these problems, there are several solutions, for instance, the link quality between the sensors and actuators should be good. The design and evaluation of the deployment are of major concern.

Some of the applications of WSANs are

- Advanced target tracking
- Disaster response
- Precision agriculture
- Ultra-precise chemical production

Some of the constraints on protocols are

- The transport layer is responsible for getting accurate reports of exact type, intensity, and location based on the reliability. The aggregation and dissemination should be reliable.
- The routing layer should route to sink, or coordinate.
- The MAC layer should use the mobility for connectivity between sensors and actuators.

IoT GATEWAY SOLUTIONS

IoT gateways perform functions as device connectivity, protocol translation, processing, security, updating, etc. Some latest gateways operate platforms for application code which processes data. It is the intersection of edge systems such as devices, controllers, sensors and the cloud (Figure 1)

Traditional gateways could not process complex data and were not intelligent. But today's gateways are able to perform with modern operating systems. These are called intelligent gateways. These gateways can push the data closer to the edge, process them, and improve the responsiveness. It helps to filter out routine information and pass alert which are important. Recent developing companies are Wind River and Dell (Treadway, 2016). The Wind River Intelligent Device Platform XT can build its own gateway devices that can modify according to their needs. The Dell Edge Gateway 5000 series targets multiple use cases to build its own gateways. The IoT gateways should support the following functionalities:

- **Reliable Connectivity and Security:** It ensures integrity and network of the system.
- **Protocol and Data Bridge:** Can exchange data between different systems having different protocols and formats

Figure 1. IoT gateway architecture

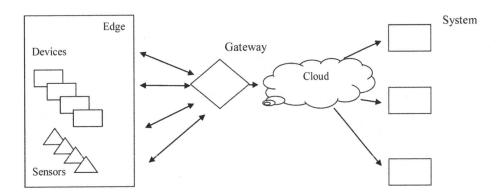

- **Storage and Analysis:** Storage of data and intelligent decision making closer to the device.
- **Management:** It provides control access to devices with policy based permissions.

The Aricent IoT gateway is a middleware which is flexible to deal with the bottom layers of devices and the top layers of cloud platforms like, Microsoft Azure, AWS IoT, and IBM BlueMix. These solutions extend to multiple domains. For example, home automation, smart metering & smart city domains. Some of the features it provides are:

- It is designed to support various use cases across domains like home automation, Smart city, etc, using the REST API based SDK for application development.
- It uses one M2M specification to connect to cloud applications.
- The interfaces that support at the bottom layers are Zigbee, WiFi, BLE, and PLC.
- For device management such as software upgrade, OMA-DM is used.
- It is scalable to support a number of devices.
- It helps in the faster end to end realization.

SENSOR TO CLOUD COMMUNICATION

There are different ways the data can get transmitted from the sensor to the cloud (Burgess, 2015).

- **Sensor to Cloud Over Ethernet:** It is the simplest method which was developed in the 1970s before radio links were invented. The sensor has a processor to configure the data to be sent to the cloud. The Ethernet connection is a wired network service. The disadvantage is that wired connection is not possible in some places.
- **Sensor to Mobile Phone Network to Cloud:** The mobile phones were invented in the 1980s. Cellular networks use radio links for connecting sensors to the cloud. The drawback is that the sensor will need a wired connection, the uplink transmitter needs more power and the user has to pay for the service provider.
- **Sensor to Long Range Radio to Cloud:** Some of the free radio bands available are 902-928MHz and 2400-2483MHz, which are the frequencies used in IEEE 802.15.4 standard. It uses mesh network with many power radios interconnected to relay data from remote sensors. Each collected data has access to the cloud. This allows a wide area to deploy the sensors.
- **Sensor to a WiFi Router to Cloud:** The 2400-2483 MHz band and 5130-5835 MHz were the original frequency bands of the 802.11 Wi-Fi standards. Most of these routers are placed in homes, businesses, and other public places. It is the most widely used method. There are remote sensors available which could directly connect to WiFi.
- **Sensor to a Mobile Phone to Cloud:** The sensor will need a mobile phone to connect. These are served by Bluetooth standards. It can maintain its own group. Bluetooth Low Energy (BLE) is suited for sensors with low data rates

IoT COMMUNICATION PROTOCOLS

Wireless Protocols

RFID

It is a standard which enables manufacturers to differentiate between the qualities of same products from different markets (Poole, 2015). There are two different international standards:

- **ISO (International Standards Organisation):** Most of the standards fall into this category. It includes various areas, such as data content and formatting, conformance testing, etc.
- **EPCglobal (Electronics Product Code Global Incorporated):** It main aim was researching and standardizing. Majority of these activities are associated with RFID using the Auto-ID center.

RFID Standards

RFID is an air-interface protocol, depending on the type of RFID system used there are many "standards" for such protocols. Listed are the most commonly used air-interface protocol standards ratified by the International Organization for Standardization (ISO):

- **ISO 14443:** It is the high frequency (HF) standard created for the secure payment purpose. It is designed to have short read range and includes encryption and it was created for proximity cards.
- **ISO 15693:** Its development purpose is for vicinity cards. It is a longer read range than ISO 14443-based systems and no encryption is done here. It is used in many access-control systems, inventory management, and other applications.
- **ISO 18000-3:** Most of the companies use this standard for item management.
- **ISO 18000-6C:** It uses ultra-high frequency based on EPC Gen 3 air-interface and is widely used for UHF systems.
- **ISO 24730:** It monitors the communication of RFID transponders and is used in real time.

Zigbee

Zigbee wireless communication technology is a kind of newly arisen wireless network technology; the characteristic is short distance communication, low speed, low power dissipation, and low cost. It, application of Zigbee wireless communication technology, makes that inconvenient wire repeat can be avoided in the area of home, factory, hospital, etc. With the rapid development of IT industry and the strong functional expansion of SCM, Zigbee wireless communication technology will play an important role in the wireless sensor network (WSN). The basis of Zigbee is IEEE 802.15.4 standard, but it only defines the lower two layers: the physical (PHY) layer and the medium access control (MAC) sub-layer, then the Zigbee Alliance builds on this foundation by providing the network (NWK) layer and the API is standardized. It could be embedded in all kinds of devices, support Geo-location function, and be used widely in the area of industrial monitoring, safety system, smart home, etc; the protocol is realized by protocol stack (Wang, He, & Wan, 2011).

Application Layer Protocols

LoRa WAN

The LoRa physical layer establishes the communication link. Therefore, LoRaWAN defines a media access control protocol (MAC) and also the network architecture. Optimized for low-power consumption and supporting large networks with millions and millions of devices, data rates range from 0.3 kbps to 50 kbps.

- **Standard:** LoRa WAN
- **Frequency:** Various
- **Range:** 2-5km (urban environment), 15km (suburban environment)
- **Data Rates:** 0.3-50 kbps.

Some of the important terminologies of LoRaWAN are

- **Device or Node:** It is an object with the low power communication device.
- **Network:** It is the route to send and receive signals to the application back and forth.
- **Gateway:** It consists of antennas to send and receive broadcasts from nodes.
- **Application:** It is software running on the server.
- **Uplink Message:** It sends a message from device to application.
- **Downlink Message:** It sends a message from the application to device.

BLE (Bluetooth Low Energy)

It is an object code in a single library file. The latest version is 4.2 and it allows two types of wireless technologies. They are:

- Basic rate
- Bluetooth low energy

It was created to transmit small data packets using less power. It supports the following features:

- LE Secure connection
- LE Data length extension
- LE privacy 1.2

It mainly consists of a controller, host and an application (Townsend, Cufi, Akiba & Robert Davidson, 2016). The application refers to the user application with Bluetooth protocol stack. It is responsible for containing the logic and data handling. The host is present at the top layers of the Bluetooth and the controller is present at the bottom layers. Host Controller Interface (HCI) helps to communicate with the host and BLE module.

The purpose is to interface the controller with the host. The host consists of the following layers:

- Generic Access Profile (GAP)
- Generic Attribute Profile (GATT)
- Logical Link Control and Adaptation Protocol (L2CAP)
- Attribute Protocol (ATT)
- Security Manager (SM)
- Host Controller Interface (HCI), host side

The controller includes the following layers:

- Host Controller Interface (HCI), controller side
- Link Layer (LL)
- Physical Layer (PHY)

6LowPAN

It is an open IoT networking protocol. It is designed and developed in public. It is accessible to anybody without any membership. IoT makes all things aware of the internet. Hence, there is the usage of the IPv6 to make use of internet protocols. The sensors used in 6LowPAN have restricted wireless connectivity. But using IPv6 we can drive the protocols over the internet. It uses direct IP addressing of nodes. It is designed to send these packets over IEEE 802.14.4 along with some standards using the addressing nodes (Schmidt, 2016). It has a mesh network and is robust scalable. It defines encapsulation and header compression mechanisms.

CoAP

CoAP stands for Constrained Application Protocol and is an application layer protocol. It mainly focuses on document transfer. CoAP packets are much smaller than HTTP TCP flows. Bit fields and mappings from strings to integers are used extensively to save space. Generations of the packets are simple. Consumption of extra RAM space for the parsing of the packets is not required. CoAP runs over UDP, not TCP. Clients and servers communicate through connectionless datagrams. CoAP follows a client/server model. Clients make requests to servers, servers send back responses. Clients may GET, PUT, POST and DELETE resources.

The CoAP interaction model is similar to HTTP client/server model but the CoAP implementation acts as both client and server in the typical machine to machine interactions. CoAP is comprised of two layers. They are the message layer which is responsible for UDP communication and reliability and another layer is responsible for request or response interactions. CoAP also uses asynchronous message exchange between endpoints. CoAP defines four types of messages as Confirmable, Non-confirmable, Acknowledgement and Reset. The embedded Method Codes and Response Codes in some of these messages mark them as requests or responses (Joshi, & Kaur, 2015).

The four security modes defined for CoAP which are:

- **NoSec:** This alternative assumes that security is not provided in this mode or in the CoAP transmitted message.
- **PreshardKey:** This mode is enabled by sensing devices preprogrammed with symmetric cryptographic keys. This mode is suitable for applications that support devices that are unable to employ the public key cryptography. Also, applications can use one key per device or one key for a group of devices.
- **RawPublicKey:** The mandatory mode for devices that require authentication based on the public key. The devices are programmed with a pre-provisioned list of keys so that devices can initiate a DTLS session without a certificate.
- **Certificates:** Supports authentication based on public key and application that participate in certification chain. The assumption of this mode is that security infrastructure is available. Devices that include asymmetric key and have unknown X.509 certificates can be validated using the certificate mode and provisioning trusted root keys (Granjal, Monteiro, & Silva, 2015).

Applications

- Basic CoAP based System setup
- Real-Time Condition-based Monitoring in Smart Grid
- Building Automation
- Defence, Aircraft equipment, etc.

AMQP

The application layer protocol generally implied for messaging is the Advanced Message Queuing Protocol (AQMP). It creates full functional interoperability between conforming clients and messaging middleware servers. It is an openly published wire specification for asynchronous messaging. The AMQP protocol is a binary protocol with modern features: it is multi-channel, negotiated, asynchronous, secure, portable, neutral, and efficient. AMQP is usefully split into two layers:

- The functional layer defines a set of commands (grouped into logical classes of functionality) that do useful work on behalf of the application.
- The transport layer that carries these methods from application to server, and back, and which handles channel multiplexing, framing, content encoding, heart-beating, data representation, and error handling.

Applications

The programming language the developer uses determines the actual API through which applications interact with AMQP implementations. For example, you can map AMQP's capabilities such that Java applications cause them through JMS APIs. For C++, Python, and Ruby applications, however, there are no popular open messaging API standards like JMS for Java, so those languages support their own AMQP APIs, which typically reflect the AMQP application-level protocol classes and methods (Vinoski, 2006).

Communication Protocols

DDS

A distributed application can use "Data-Centric Publish-Subscribe" (DCPS) as a communication mechanism since Data Distribution Service (DDS) specification standardizes the software application programming interface (API). DDS is implemented as an "infrastructure" solution and hence it can be added to the communication interface for any software application (Gerardo, Farabaugh, & Warren, 2005). DDS is supported by Linux as well as Windows; the source code provided is complete and well supported/documented by the open DDS website. Created as a networking middleware to circumvent the disadvantages of centralized publish-subscribe architecture, DDS is a TCP-based protocol that features decentralized nodes of clients across a system and allows these nodes to identify themselves as subscribers or publishers through a localization server (Figure 2). The use of this system negates the need for users to identify where other potential nodes are or which topics they are interested in, as the DDS nodes self-discover across a network and send/receive telemetry anonymously based only on topics. After linking publishers and subscribers, the connections between these clients bypass the server and are peer-to-peer (Chen, & Kunz, 2016).

Advantages

- Based on a simple "publish-subscribe" communication paradigm.
- Flexible and adaptable architecture that supports "auto-discovery" of new or stale endpoint applications.
- **Low Overhead:** Can be used with high-performance systems.
- Deterministic data delivery.
- Dynamically scalable.
- Efficient use of transport bandwidth.
- A large number of configuration parameters that give developers complete control of each message in the system.

Figure 2. DDS Communication Architecture

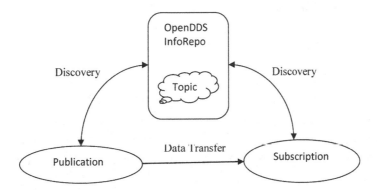

LTE Cat-M

The LTE Cat-M standard is a cellular standard. It has a number of benefits compared to the non-cellular technologies. One obvious benefit is the existing infrastructure for LTE, where operators around the world have been rolling out this technology since 2009. According to GSA, there are now 480 LTE networks launched in 157 countries. It supports up to up to 150Mbits/s in the downlink. LTE supports both frequency division duplex (FDD) and time division duplex (TDD) modes using a common subframe structure of 1ms. Having such a short subframe length allows for latency to be minimized, thus ensuring a good user experience. LTE-M operates on a 1.4 MHz carrier or 6 PRB. The IoT device will always listen to the center 6 PRB for control information like any normal device. When the device is scheduled for IoT traffic, it will be allocated a number of PRBs (up to 6) at any consecutive location within the spectrum of operation. This means that the device will be allocated a 1.4 MHz carrier within a, for example, 20 MHz carrier. Ignoring the legacy control information, the dedicated control and data are multiplexed in the frequency domain. This enables LTE IoT devices to be scheduled within any legacy LTE system and share the carrier capacity, antenna, radio, and hardware at the site.

NB-IoT

NB-IoT, however, is a new narrowband IoT system built from existing LTE functionalities. It can be deployed in three different operation modes.

- Stand-alone as a dedicated carrier
- In-band within the occupied bandwidth of a wideband LTE carrier
- Within the guard-band of an existing LTE carrier

In stand-alone deployment, NB-IoT can occupy one GSM channel (200 kHz) while for in-band and guard-band deployment, it will use one physical resource block (PRB) of LTE (180 kHz). The design targets of NB-IoT include low-cost devices, high coverage (a 20-dB improvement over GPRS), long device battery life (more than 10 years), and massive capacity (greater than 52K devices per channel per cell). Latency is relaxed although a delay budget of 10 seconds is the target for exception reports. Since NB-IoT is expected to adopt a design based on existing LTE functionalities, it is possible to reuse the same hardware and also to share spectrum without coexistence issues. In addition, NB-IoT can simply plug into the LTE core network. This allows all network services such as authentication, security, policy, tracking, and charging to be fully supported (Ratasuk, Vejlgaard, Mangalvedhe, & Ghosh, 2016).

Transmission Protocols

RPL

It is a distance vector and source routing protocol. The distance vector protocol manipulates the vectors of distances to other nodes in the network. It is also an intra-domain routing protocol. It has the ability to change the topology based on the requirement. It has less computational complexity (Richardson, & Robles, 2017).

Distance Vector (DV) is used to calculate the distance and direction of a link. It also finds the path which has minimum cost. It maintains a vector table to determine the shortest path. The total cost of traveling is found using routing metrics.

Source routing also known as path addressing, allows the sender of a packet to completely or partially specify the route of the packet to the network. It determines all possible routes to a host. It organizes the topology using the directed acyclic graph which is divided into one or more graphs. It uses RPL Instance ID which identifies a unique network. Since the root destines a location, the graph is also called Destination Oriented Directed Acyclic Graph (DODAG).

A grounded DODAG connects the host after satisfying the application goal. A floating DODAG doesn't satisfy the goal; rather it provides all the routes to the nodes. An RPL can have multiple instances, which can be local or global. An RPL instance field consists of control and data packets.

USB Protocol

USB, Universal Serial Bus is a polled bus for transferring data, where the nodes initiate all packet exchanges. The packet is transferred in so-called transactions. Normally, they consist of three packets:

- The token packet is the header defining the direction as well as the transmission type, the device address, and the endpoint.
- The packet is transferred in a data packet.
- The final status of the transmission is to acknowledge.

In a transmission, packets are transferred either from the Host to a Device or vice-versa. The mode of transaction is specified in the token packet that is sent from the Host. Then, a data packet indicating that it has no data to transfer is sent by the source. In general, the destination responds with a handshake packet indicating whether the transfer was successful.

MQTT

Message Queue Telemetry Transport protocol (MQTT) is based on Client-Server architecture (Ala, Guizani, & Mohammadi, 2015). This messaging protocol is introduced by an IBM developer Andy Stanford-Clark in 1993 and was internationally standardized in 2013. Embedded devices and networks are connected with the application through MQTT. MQTT provides communication facilities among connected embedded devices and application. Using MQTT, data packets can follow three routing mechanisms (one-to-one, one-to-many, many-to-many).MQTT follow the publish/subscribe pattern for communication where publisher publishes the topic and subscriber subscribes the topic. The architecture of MQTT has three main components, Subscriber, Publisher, and Broker. All three components have their independent work mechanism. Both Subscriber and Publisher are MQTT clients where Subscriber would be registered by an interesting device and subscribes to topics through Broker which acts as a server. The publisher client acts as a data generator that publishes the interesting information to a subscriber through Brokcr (Dhar, & Gupta, 2016). For Internet of Things and M2M, MQTT protocol proves itself an ideal messaging protocol for communication.

Applications

- Healthcare by keeping track of victims besides they go away from the clinic, upgrading the effectiveness of the consequent tests.
- In energy and utilities by making Virtual Power Plant (VPP).
- Social Networking.

XMPP

Instant Messaging (IM) service can be carried out by the standard specified by the Internet Engineering Task Force (IETF) is the eXtensible Messaging and Presence Protocol (XMPP). It is an open XML protocol for near-real-time messaging, presence, and request/response services. It is formalized by the IETF as an approved messaging and communication of structured data between two entities. Every device is identified by a unique address referred to as "bare JID" which consists of a "local part", "domain part", and "resourcepart" and represented as "<localpart@domainpart/resourcepart>". Structured data is transmitted asynchronously over the network to the global address of the given device concurrently (Valluri, 2014). Jabber open-source community was initially proposed XMPP. Later, it was formally approved and archived by the IETF in four Internet specifications (Nie, 2006).

The general procedure of a successful Transport Layer Security (TLS) + Simple Authentication and Security Protocol (SASL) negotiation is as follows:

1. The client establishes the TCP connection to the server and initiates the XML streams.
2. The server sends a STARTTLS extension to the client, including the supported authentication mechanisms.
3. The client responds to the STARTTLS command.
4. The server informs the client that it is ok to proceed.
5. The client and the server complete the TLS setup of the TCP connection.
6. Given that the success of the previous step, the client initiates a new stream to the server.
7. The response of the server can be identified by sending a stream header to client along with any available stream features.
8. The client picks up an appropriate authentication mechanism.
9. The server sends a Base64-encoded challenge to the client.
10. The client responds to the challenge with the credential.
11. The server sends another challenge to the client, as the session token.
12. The client again responds to the challenge.
13. The server informs the client of successful authentication.
14. The client triggers a new stream to the server for the application-purpose communication.

PLC (CLICK)

The communications ability of the CLICK PLC system for transmission of data between the PLC unit and other connected devices covers:

- Electrical connections used for communications
- Networking routing between the PLC and other devices,
- Setting the port communication parameters,
- Selecting the protocols and the available data addressing types to use, and
- Ladder logic program instructions that make it all work together.

Two built-in RS-232 ports are there in CLICK Basic and Standard PLCs. Both ports are 6-pin RJ12 phone type jacks. It has fixed Port 1 communication parameters and is used primarily as the programming port. Modbus RTU protocol slave device can also be used as Port 1. The Port 2 which is used for general purpose and user configurable. Modbus RTU master or slave protocol device can also be used as Port 2, or handle ASCII data in or Out (ASCII stands for American Standard Code for Information Interchange) and defines a character encoding method for text that is used in computers and other communication devices.

3-pin RS-485 port is available in Standard and Analog PLC versions. Like Port 2, Port 3 is also a general purpose port with its communication parameters being user-configurable from the programming software. Modbus RTU master or slave protocol device is used by Port 3, or handle ASCII data in or out. CLICK Ethernet Basic, Standard and Analog PLC units have one built-in Ethernet communications port and one RS-232 serial communication port. RS-485 port has Ethernet Standard and Analog PLC units. The CLICK PLC can be networked to other CLICK PLCs, data input devices, and data output devices.

CLICK PLC to other 3rd party PLCs can be networked and devices can be communicated through the Modbus RTU protocol. There are three different data addressing, CLICK addressing, Modbus 984 addressing, or Modbus HEX addressing. The CLICK addressing makes convenient to exchange of data. The other addressing choices are selected based on the Modbus protocol addressing the networked devices.

Z-Wave

Z-Wave is a low-power RF communications technology that is primarily designed for home automation for products such as lamp controllers and sensors among many others. Optimized for reliable and low-latency communication of small data packets with data rates up to 100kbit/s, it operates in the sub-1GHz band and is impervious to interference from WiFi and other wireless technologies in the 2.4-GHz range such as Bluetooth or ZigBee. It supports full mesh networks without the need for a coordinator Node and is very scalable, enabling control of up to 232 devices. Z-Wave uses a simpler protocol than some others, which can enable faster and simpler development, but the only maker of chips is Sigma Designs compared to multiple sources for other wireless technologies such as ZigBee and others.

- **Standard:** Z-Wave Alliance ZAD12837 / ITU-T G.9959
- **Frequency:** 900MHz (ISM)
- **Range:** 30m
- **Data Rates:** 9.6/40/100kbit/s

Thread

A new IP-based IPv6 protocol used for home-based automation environment is called as Thread. It is not an IoT applications protocol like Bluetooth or ZigBee and based on 6LowPAN. However, it is primarily designed to reside WiFi as it recognizes that while WiFi is good for many consumer devices that limit to a particular area.

Thread, launched in mid-2014 by the Thread Group, a free protocol is based on various standards including IEEE802.15.4 (air-interface protocol), IPv6 and 6LoWPAN, and offers an IP-based solution for the IoT. Designed to work on existing IEEE 802.15.4 wireless silicon from chip vendors such as free scale. Thread provides a mesh network using IEEE802.15.4 radio transceivers and is able of handling up to 250 nodes with high levels of authentication, encryption, and decryption. A very simple software upgrade should allow users to run a thread on existing IEEE802.15.4-enabled devices.

- **Standard:** Thread, based on IEEE802.15.4 and 6LowPAN
- **Frequency:** 2.4GHz (ISM)
- **Range:** N/A
- **Data Rates:** N/A

Cellular

Any sensor devices that need operation over long range can take advantage of GSM/3G/4G cellular communication capabilities. While cellular is capable of sending a large number of data, especially for LTE, the cost and also energy consumption will be high for many applications, but it can be the intelligent way for using sensor-based low-bandwidth-data projects that will send very low amounts of data over the web. A key product in this area is the SparqEE range of products, including the original tiny CELLv1.0 low-cost development board and a series of shield connecting boards for use with the Raspberry Pi and Arduino platforms.

- **Standard:** GSM/GPRS/EDGE (2G), UMTS/HSPA (3G), LTE (4G)
- **Frequencies:** 900/1800/1900/2100MHz
- **Range:** 35km max for GSM; 200km max for HSPA
- **Data Rates (Typical Download):** 35-170kps (GPRS), 120-384kbps (EDGE), 384Kbps-2Mbps (UMTS), 600kbps-10Mbps (HSPA), 3-10Mbps (LTE)

Sigfox

Sigfox ranges between WiFi and cellular. It uses the ISM bands, which is an open source, to communicate data over a very narrow spectrum to and from connected objects. The key factor for Sigfox is that for many M2M applications that run on a small battery and data transfer level is low, then WiFi's range is too short and cellular is too expensive and also power consumption is high. A Sigfox uses Ultra Narrow Band (UNB) which is designed to handle low data-transfer speeds of 10 to 1,000 bits per second. It consumes 50 microwatts compared to 5000 microwatts for M2M communication or can deliver a typical standby time 20 years with a 2.5Ah battery while M2M is only 0.2 years.

It is already applied for tens of thousands of connected objects, the network is currently being rolled out in major cities across Europe, for example including ten cities in the UK. The robust, ultra-low power consumption and the scalable network are offered by the network that can do its transmission over millions of battery-operated devices across the long range, making it suitable for various M2M applications such as smart meters, patient monitors, security devices, street lighting and environmental sensors. The Sigfox system contains a silicon called EZRadioPro wireless transceivers from Silicon Labs, which gives an industry-leading wireless performance, long range and very low power consumption for wireless networking applications operating in the sub-1GHz band.

- **Standard:** Sigfox
- **Frequency:** 900MHz
- **Range:** 30-50km (rural environments), 3-10km (urban environments)
- **Data Rates:** 10-1000bps

Nuel

Nuel is similar to Sigfox and rangessub-1GHz band, very small slices of the TV White Space spectrum to deliver high scalability, a large range of distance, low energy consumption and very least cost wireless networks are leveraged by Nuel. Iceni chip, which makes transmission using the white space radio to work the high-quality UHF spectrum, now available due to the analog to digital TV transition is the one system based. There are huge communications technologies which are called Weightless and is a new large area wireless networking technology designed for the sensor related things that largely challenges against existing GPRS, 3G, CDMA and LTE WAN solutions (Sethi, & Sarangi, 2017).

- **Standard:** Neul
- **Frequency:** 900MHz (ISM), 458MHz (UK), 470-790MHz (White Space)
- **Range:** 10km
- **Data Rates:** Few bps up to 100kbps

Security Protocols

Internet Protocol Security

A network protocol suite that authenticates and encrypts the packets of data sent over a network is the Internet Protocol Security (IPSec). It includes protocols for establishing mutual authentication between agents at the beginning of the session and negotiation of cryptographic keys to use during the session. IPSec is an open standard. Internet Key Exchange (IKE) Protocol, Security Association (SA) is the supporting protocols. There is two header formats namely authentication header (Figure 3) and ESP header (Figure 4).

- The Authentication Header (AH) provides support for data integrity and authentication of IP packets. The data integrity service ensures that data inside IP packets is not altered during transit. The authentication service enables an end user or computer system to authenticate the user or application at other end and decide whether to accept or reject packets accordingly. Authentication is based on the use of a Message Authentication Code (MAC) which means the two parties must share a secret key.
- Encapsulating Security Payload (ESP) adds a header and trailer. ESP is based on symmetric key cryptography techniques. It can be used in isolation or can be combined with AH. It provides source authentication, integrity, and privacy (Singh, & Gahlawat, 2012).

Figure 3. Authentication Header

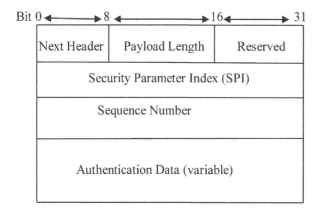

Figure 4. ESP Header

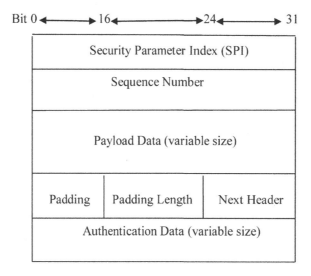

IPsec operates in two different modes.

- The default mode for IPSec is the Transport mode. It is used for end-to-end communications. When transport mode is used, IPSec encrypts only the IP payload. Transport mode provides the protection of an IP payload through an AH or ESP header. Typical IP payloads are TCP segments, a UDP message or an ICMP message. IPSec in the transport mode does not protect the IP header; it only protects the information coming from the transport layer. This mode is normally used when we need the host-to-host protection of data.
- Tunnel mode protects the entire IP packet. The tunnel mode is normally used between two routers, between a host and a router, or between a router and a host. When IPSec tunnel mode is used, IPSec encrypts the IP header and the payload, whereas transport mode only encrypts the IP payload. The protection of an entire IP packet is provided by the Tunnel mode by treating it as an

AH or ESP payload. The IP addresses of the outer IP header are the tunnel endpoints, and the IP addresses of the encapsulated IP header are the ultimate source and destination addresses. When traffic must pass through an intermediate, untrusted network, the protecting of traffic between different networks is aided by the IPSec tunnel mode. Tunnel mode can be used in the following configurations namely Gateway-to-gateway, Server-to-gateway, and Server-to-server.

Kerberos

The computer network authentication protocol that works on the basis of tickets is Kerberos protocol. The concept of tickets allows the nodes to communicate with one another and prove their identity in a secure manner. It executes client-server model and provides mutual authentication. Kerberos builds on symmetric key cryptography and requires a trusted third party and optionally may use public-key cryptography during certain phases of authentication. Kerberos uses UDP port 88 by default.

Drawbacks

The protocol weaknesses can be summarized as follows:

1. Kerberos requires continuous availability of the KDC. When the Kerberos server is down, the system will be vulnerable to the single point of failure problem. This can be mitigated by using multiple Kerberos servers.
2. The system clocks of the hosts that are involved in the protocol should be synchronized. A time availability period has been assigned to the tickets and if the host clock is not synchronized with the Kerberos server clock, the authentication will fail. In practice, Network Time Protocol daemons are usually used to keep the host clocks synchronized.
3. "Password guessing" attacks are not solved by Kerberos. A poor password must be chosen by the user. This is because it is possible for an attacker to successfully mount an offline dictionary attack by repeatedly attempting to decrypt messages obtained which are encrypted under a key derived from the user's password (Eman, Koutlo, Kelash, & Allah, 2009).
4. There are no standards for the administration of the Kerberos protocol. This will differ between server implementations.

Secure Shell Protocol

Secure Shell Protocol (SSH), also known as Secure Socket Shell, is a UNIX based command interface and a cryptographic network protocol used to protect data in transmission between devices providing strong authentication and establishes a secure channel over an insecure network in a client-server architecture, connecting an SSH client application with an SSH server. Secure Shell is a secure method to access the remote computer over a network, in order to execute commands in a remote machine and to move files from one machine to another. It is comprised of a suite of three utilities, Slogin, Ssh and SCP. RSA public key cryptography is used by Secure Shell protocol for connection and authentication. Working of SSH mainly relies on the exchange and verification of information, using public and private keys, to identify hosts and users. Client refers to a workstation or PC that you are already logged in to, e.g., your own personal workstation or a group workstation that provides XDM session management for several X terminals. The term server means a secondary remote workstation that you wish to log in to do some work, for example, a login session server. The client is where you type "rlogin server" or "RCP file server: newfile" and the server is where you get a new login session and shell prompt or are copying files. A user can generate an identity in the client system by running the ssh-keygen program. As a system administrator; you generate a public and private key pair for the system itself. This information contained within the system itself, greatly reduces the possibility of someone spoofing the system's identity by faking IP addresses or mugging up DNS records that associate IP addresses and domain names (Garimella, & Kumar, 2015).

Advantages

- Username and password authentication mechanisms prevent eavesdropping by attackers who would otherwise trap sensitive data.
- Using secure shell the malicious use of IP source routing can be avoided.
- As the data is encrypted, it only appears in the form of some random characters, so data manipulation at routers along the network cannot be done.
- Easy to manage a dedicated server remotely.

Disadvantage

- Port ranges & dynamic ports can't be forwarded.
- SSH server daemon problem. We cannot restrict what ports may or may not be forwarded, per user. When a user is authenticated by password, the client's RSA identity is not verified against Ssh known hosts.
- Performance is not too high on old machines.
- Licensing the original source has become very restrictive.

WiFi Protected Access Protocol (WPA)

WPA is a standard for secure communication protocol. WPA stands for WiFi Protected Access. WPA has been accepted in 2002 as a temporary solution by the WiFi Alliance, as a response to the delayed development of the IEEE 802.11i standard. The standard WPA specifies two operation manners.

1. Personal WPA or WPA-PSK (Key Pre-Shared) that use for small office and home for domestic use authentication which does not use an authentication server and the data cryptography key can go up to 256 bits. This can be any alphanumeric string and is used only to negotiate the initial session with the AP. Because both the client and the AP already possess this key, WPA provides mutual authentication, and the key is never transmitted over the air (Lashkari, & Danesh, 2009).
2. Enterprise WPA or Commercial that the authentication is made by an authentication server 802.1x, generating an excellent control and security in the users' traffic of the wireless network. This WPA uses 802.1X+EAP for authentication but again replaces WEP with the more advanced TKIP encryption. No preshared key is used here, but you will need a RADIUS server. And you get all the other benefits 802.1X+EAP provides, including integration with the Windows login process and support for EAP-TLS and PEAP authentication methods.

Advancements in WPA

- A cryptographic message integrity code, or MIC, called Michael, to defeat forgeries.
- A new IV sequencing discipline, to remove replay attacks from the attacker's arsenal. In order to de-correlate the public IVs from weak keys, a per-packet key mixing function.
- A rekeying mechanism, to provide fresh encryption and integrity keys, undoing the threat of attacks stemming from key reuse.

CONCLUSION

Protocols play a very vital role in shaping up any computing and communication paradigm. For fog/edge computing, there are several protocols being bandied about widely in the literature. This chapter has listed and detailed a number of recent protocols for enabling the paradigm of fog/edge computing. The chapter is to assist the respective architects, consultants, and professionals with the sufficient knowledge on each of the popular protocols and how they fit into the scheme of things. Further on, the study on these protocols opens up fresh possibilities and opportunities for research scholars and scientists to bring forth additional capabilities for the fog world.

REFERENCES

Ala, A. F., Guizani, M., & Mohammadi, M. (2015). Internet of Things: A Survey on Enabling Technologies, Protocols, and Applications. *IEEE Communications Surveys and Tutorials*. doi:10.1109/COMST.2015.2444095

Bluetooth Low Energy Protocol Stack. (2016). Bluetooth Low Energy Software Developer's Guide. *Texas Instruments*. Retrieved November 14, 2017, from http://dev.ti.com/tirex/content/simplelink_cc2640r2_sdk_1_00_00_22/docs/blestack/html/ble-stack/index.html

Burgess, L. (2015). How Does Sensor Data Go From Device To Cloud? *readwrite*. Retrieved November 22, 2017, from https://readwrite.com/2015/10/13/sensor-data-device-to-cloud/

Butler, B. (2017). *Internet of Things. What is edge computing, how it's changing the network?* Retrieved November 1, 2017, from https://www.networkworld.com/article/3224893/internet-of-things/what-is-edge-computing-and-how-it-s-changing-the-network.html

Butler, B. (2017). *Internet of Things. What is edge computing, how it's changing the network?* Retrieved November 3, 2017, from https://www.networkworld.com/article/3224893/internet-of-things/what-is-edge-computing-and-how-it-s-changing-the-network.html

Chen, Y., & Kunz, T. (2016). Performance Evaluation of IoT Protocols under a Constrained Wireless Access Network. In *International Conference on Selected Topics in Mobile and Wireless Networking*. Cairo, Egypt. IEEE. 10.1109/MoWNet.2016.7496622

Dhar, P., Gupta, P., (2016). Intelligent Parking Cloud Services based on IoT using MQTT Protocol. *Int. J. of Engineering Research, 5*(6/12), 457-461.

Eman, E. E., Koutlo, M., Kelash, H., & Allah, O. F. (2009). A Network Authentication Protocol Based on Kerberos. Int. *J. of Computer Science and Network Security.*, 9(8/12), 18–26.

Garimella, D., Kumar, R., (2015). Secure Shell-Its significance in Networking (SSH). *Int. J. of Application or Innovation in Engineering & Management, 4*(3/12), 187-196.

Gerardo, P. C., Farabaugh, B., & Warren, R. (2005). *An Introduction to DDS and Data-Centric Communications*. Real Time Innovations.

Granjal, J., Monteiro, E., & Silva, J. (2015). Security for the Internet of Things: A Survey of Existing Protocols and Open Research Issues. *IEEE Communications Surveys and Tutorials, 17*(3), 1294–1312. doi:10.1109/COMST.2015.2388550

Haughn, M. (2015). Wireless Sensor and Actuator Network. IoT Agenda. *TechTarget Network*. Retrieved November 20, 2017, from http://internetofthingsagenda.techtarget.com/definition/WSAN-wireless-sensor-and-actuator-network

Joshi, M., & Kaur, B. P. (2015). CoAP Protocol for Constrained Networks. Int. *J. of Wireless and Microwave Technologies, 6*, 1–10.

Lashkari, A. H., & Danesh, M. M. S. (2009). A Survey on Wireless Security Protocols (WEP, WPA and WPA/802.11i). 2nd *Int. Conf. on Computer Science and Information Technology (ICCSIT)*, 49-52.

Lee, W., Nam, K., Roh, H. G., & Kim, S. H. (2016). A gateway based fog computing architecture for wireless sensors and actuator networks. In *Advanced Communication Technology (ICACT). 18th Int. Conf. on Advanced Communication Technology (ICACT)*. Pyeongchang, South Korea. IEEE. doi: 10.1109/ICACT.2016.7423331

LoRaWAN. (2017). *The Things Network*. Retrieved November 11, 2017, from https://www.thethingsnetwork.org/wiki/LoRaWAN/Home

Nie, P., (2006). *A Open Standard for Instant Messaging: eXtensible Messaging and Presence Protocol*. TKK T-110.5190 Seminar on Internetworking.

Pan, Y., Beyah, R. A., Goscinski, A., & Ren, J. (2017). Edge Computing for the Internet-of-Things. *IEEE Network*. Retrieved November 3, 2017, from https://www.comsoc.org/netmag/cfp/edge-computing-internet-things

Poole, I. (2015). *RFID Standards. Radio-Electronics*. Retrieved November 11, 2017, from http://www.radio-electronics.com/info/wireless/radio-frequency-identification-rfid/iso-epcglobal-iec-standards.php

Ratasuk, R., Vejlgaard, B., Mangalvedhe, N., & Ghosh, A. (2016). NB-IoT System for M2M Communication. *Workshop on Device to Device Communications for 5G NETWORKS*.

Richardson, M., & Robles, I. (n.d.). *RPL- Routing over Low Power and Lossy Networks*. Retrieved November 21, 2017, from https://www.ietf.org/proceedings/94/slides/slides-94-rtgarea-2.pdf

Salman, O., Elhajj, I., & Kayssi, A. (2015). Edge computing enabling the Internet of Things. In *IEEE 2nd World Forum on the Internet of Things (WF-IoT)*. Milan, Italy. IEEE. 10.1109/WF-IoT.2015.7389122

Schmidt, S. (2016). 6LoWPAN: An Open IoT Networking Protocol. *Open IoT Summit*. Retrieved November 14, 2017, from http://events.linuxfoundation.org/sites/events/files/slides/6lowpan-openiot-2016.pdf

Sethi, P., & Sarangi, S.R. (2017). Internet of Things: Architectures, Protocols, and Applications. *Journal of Electrical and Computer Engineering*, *17*.

Singh, A., & Gahlawat, M. (2012). Internet Protocol Security (IPSec). *International Journal of Computer Networks and Wireless Communications.*, *2*(6), 717–720.

Townsend, K., Cufi, C. A., & Davidson, R. (2016). Bluetooth Low Energy - Part 1: Introduction to BLE. *MikroElektronika*. Retrieved November 14, 2017 from https://learn.mikroe.com/bluetooth-low-energy-part-1-introduction-ble/

Treadway, J. (2016). Using an IoT gateway to connect the "Things" to the cloud. IoT Agenda. *TechTarget Network*. Retrieved November 21, 2017, from http://internetofthingsagenda.techtarget.com/feature/Using-an-IoT-gateway-to-connect-the-Things-to-the-cloud

Valluri, S. P. (2014). Secure Internet of Things Environment using XMPP Protocol. *International Journal of Computers and Applications*, *106*(4). doi:10.5120/18511-9589

Vinoski, S., (2006). Advanced Message Queuing Protocol. *IEEE Internet Computing, 10*(6).

Wang, W., He, G., & Wan, J. (2011). Research on Zigbee Wireless Communication Technology. In *Int. Conf. on Electrical and Control Engineering (ICECE)*. Yichang, China. IEEE. doi: 10.1109/ICECENG.2011.6057961

Xia, F., Tian, Y. C., Li, Y., & Sun, Y. (2007). Wireless Sensor/Actuator Network Design for Mobile Control Applications. *Journal of Sensors*, *7*(10), 2157–2173. doi:10.33907102157 PMID:28903220

Chapter 6
Software–Defined Cloud Infrastructure

R. Mohanasundaram
VIT University, India

A. Jayanthiladevi
Jain University, India

Keerthana G.
VIT University, India

ABSTRACT

Cloud computing suggests that the applications conveyed as services over the internet and frameworks programming in the server that give various services and offers in "pay as you go" trend which means pay only for what you use. The information and services are managed as software as a service (SaaS). Some sellers utilize terms, for example, IaaS (infrastructure as a service) and PaaS (platform as a service). The purpose of cloud computing is quickly expanding in everyday life. Today the use of cloud computing is widespread to the point that it is being utilized even in the medicinal services industry. As the development of cloud computing in healthcare is happening at a fast rate, we can expect a noteworthy piece of the healthcare administrations to move onto the Cloud and along these lines more focus is laid on giving cost-effective and efficient services to the general population all around the world. Cloud these days are turning into the new building pieces of significant organizations spread the world over. They offer assistance in servicing to offer different frameworks. Cloud computing has enhanced its technique and technologies in a better way to provide better services. Existing e-healthcare has many difficulties from advancement to usage. In this chapter, the authors discuss how cloud computing is utilized and the services provided by the Cloud and their models and its infrastructure.

DOI: 10.4018/978-1-5225-5972-6.ch006

INTRODUCTION

Cloud Computing

Cloud computing might be characterized as the utilization of registering assets both Hardware and programming that are conveyed as an administration over a system probably the Internet. Cloud comprises of three fundamental administration models (IaaS, PaaS, and SaaS). Infrastructure a Service (IaaS) gives clients professional workings, space, topology, and other registering foundation assets. Platform as a Service (PaaS) empowers clients to convey applications created utilizing indicated programming or systems and devices onto the Cloud framework. Software as a Service (SaaS) empowers clients to get to applications running on a Cloud foundation from different end-client gadgets (by and large through a web program).For example, if you are travelling in a bus and you are going to reach your destination and pay for it using the services provided by the bus team by paying them for the used services. In the same way, you are going to pay for the services that are provided by the cloud which can be used virtually from any where for storing your data and information in a secured way by paying them for what you used. This is known as "Pay as you go" (where you are going to use for the services what you used).

Cloud also provides services to on demand self servicing, Rapid elasticity, Resource pooling, Broad network access, Measured services(Armbrust et al.,2010). On demand self service refers to the space or the power that are enabled to the clients or the end users in a very easy and accessible way. Many of the end users start by using little resources and then increases to wide range. Rapid elasticity refers to Scalable supervising and also capability to provide services when ever required. Resource pooling explains about the solutions to a problem that serve multiple clients or customers with supervised scaling services (Marcos D. Assunçãoa, Rodrigo N. Calheirosb, Silvia Bianchic, Marco A.S. Nettoc, Rajkumar Buyya,2015). Broad network access briefs about the possessions that are available in private cloud (i.e., used within an organization) for handling devices like mobiles, Macs and systems. Figure 1 explains about the cloud services.

Figure 1. Cloud computing

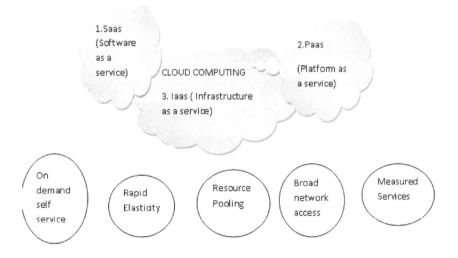

Cloud Services

The cloud services are the one that are provided for the clients virtually. The first intellect of cloud services fulfills the biggest range of possessions (i.e.,resources) that a service provider provides to the clients through the internet which in other words formed up into "cloud". The main feature of cloud services are the self – supervising and flexibility to its clients. The customers or clients can use them as according to their demands. The clients can use whenever it is essential or required or they are allowed to close them (Ch Chakradhara Rao, Mogasala Leelarani, Y Ramesh Kumar, 2013). The payment mode for the usage of cloud are made available to the clients in a monthly billing mode, That is they are given with a license of particular duration and they can access their stored information and data when ever needed. The transactions are also made online through internet. The usage of cloud resources are with usual assistances like Saas (software as a service), Paas (platform as a service), Iaas (infrastructure as a service).

Infrastructure as a Service

Iaas acts an organizations with the communications that are used to own the business. This also consists of communications, computing possessions such as servers or spaces and other resources. In this case, the organization manages the OS and the applications and the frameworks. For example, A hospital may consists many servers to protect and store its confidential data and information related to the patients. The hospital management also maintains a copy of all the information in case of any loss of information. The infrastructure is carried in a daily basis for the maintenance of data. This diagrammatically given in Figure 3.

Figure 2. Cloud services

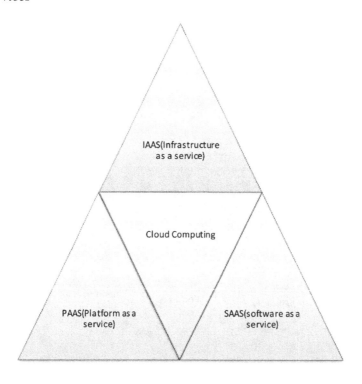

Paas (Platform as a Service)

Platform as a service is a type of cloud services that helps in giving the platform or a support to the clients to create, execute and also maintain the applications with no difficulties of creating or managing the communications that are related with creating and deploying an applications. This also can be delivered in different ways like as a public cloud from where the clients are allowed to mange only limited programming configurations and the service providers only manages the newtworks, servers, spaces for storing the information and other services. This is given in Figure 4.

Figure 3. Iaas (Infrastructure as a service)

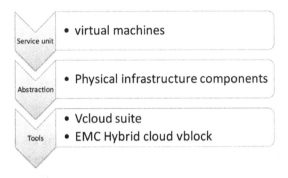

Figure 4. Paas(Platform as a service)

Saas (Software as a Service)

Saas is a software approved model where the software are approved based on the subscriptions basis and are centralized. They are also otherwise termed as "on demand services" and also termed as "software plus services". This is also accessed by clients and customers through a web browser. Saas has become a usual delivery model for many of the enterprise services like office software, messaging software. This is diagrammatically can be represented as shown in Figure 5.

Iaas vs. Paas vs. Saas

Table 1 gives a comparision of Iaas vs. Paas vs. Saas.

CLOUD INFRASTRUCTURE

Cloud Infrastructure Platform

Cloud infrastructure consists of hardware and software elements i.e., Servers, Space for storing the information and virtualization software and they are used for assisting the essential services of a cloud managing model(Bhardwaj,Jain,&jain,2010). Here, virtualization refers to the state of creating a virtual (duplications) of some resources that also comprises of virtual computer hardware platforms, Space for

Figure 5. Saas(software as a service)

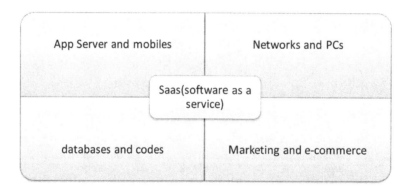

Table 1. Iaas vs Paas vs Saas

S.NO	Iaas	Paas	Saas
1.	Infrastructure as a service.	Platform as a service.	Software as a service.
2.	Automatic updates and maintenance.	Web based Creation tools and collaboration tools.	Cost saving.
3.	Remote access from various devices.	Fully managed development environment.	Security and reliability.
4.	Scalability and spreading costs over time.	Integration with other services and built in scalability for deployed softwares.	Scalability

storing devices, and other communicating devices. The cloud computing platforms includes managing resources, application resources, Storage resources.

Cloud Computing Stack

Cloud computing is more often referred to as a comeback to the wide range of services that are on the high level of each other under cloud. The general explanation of this rises from NIST(National Institute of Standards and Technology) that explains Cloud is a modeling for flexible on demand network access to resources such as networks, Communications, Storage and other application services. The features include On demand self servicing, Resource pooling, Rapid elasticity, Measured services. This is also given as shown in Figure 6.

Cloud Computing Infrastructure Components

1. **Cloud Infrastructure:** Comprises of servers, storage spaces, connection arrangements, cloud Organization software, deployment software, and platform virtualization.
2. **Hypervisor:** This is a particular or low level program which performs as a virtual maintenance machine. It also allows sharing the individual request of cloud assets.
3. **Management Software:** It helps to manage and Organize the infrastructure.
4. **Deployment Software:** It helps to deploy and incorporate the application on the cloud.
5. **Network:** It is the major element of cloud infrastructure. It allows to communicate cloud services through the internet. It is possible providing a utility via internet i.e., the clients can modify the network and the rules.

Figure 6. Cloud stack model

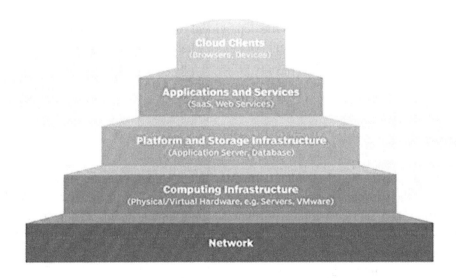

113

Figure 7. Infrstructural Components

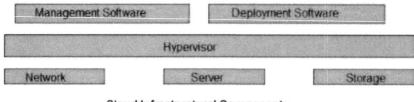

Cloud Infrastructural Components

6. **Server:** The server helps to work out the resources that is to be shared and other offers like space allocation and supervising the resources, security.
7. **Storage:** Cloud manages to have duplications of information. If one fails, the other can be made to use and that is why it is more reliable.

SOFTWARE DEFINED CLOUD

Definition

This is an come up to initiate valuable cloud environments by extending virtualization to variety of possessions that comprises of managing, Storing, communicating of a particular data centre is Software defined cloud computing, or simply software defined clouds(SDC). They also enable simple adaption of physical resources to better accommodate the demand on quality of service (stantchev,Colombo-palacious & Niedermayer,2014). This also decreases the difficulties that are linked for operating the infrastructure which would ease the maintenance of cloud infrastructure that makes the managing of cloud environment simple.

Deployment Models of Cloud

The key components of cloud computing is the deployment model. There are many numbers of various concepts and paths to explain the components of cloud. There are no proper standards to define them (Karnwal,Sivakumar, &Aghila,2011). There are different understanding of deployment model with no betterment than other. The deployment model comprises of Private cloud, Public cloud, Hybrid cloud, Community cloud.

Private Cloud

A private cloud is a specific model of cloud computing that includes a distinct and secure cloud based environment where the particular client can perform its own tasks. As like the other models, this also provides computing as a service within a virtualized environment using an underlying network of resources(Rauscher & Acharya,2013). Under this, the cloud is only accessible by individual institutions or organizations with great privacy and security.

Ex: Servers, Networking, Storage.

Figure 8. Software defined Cloud computing environments

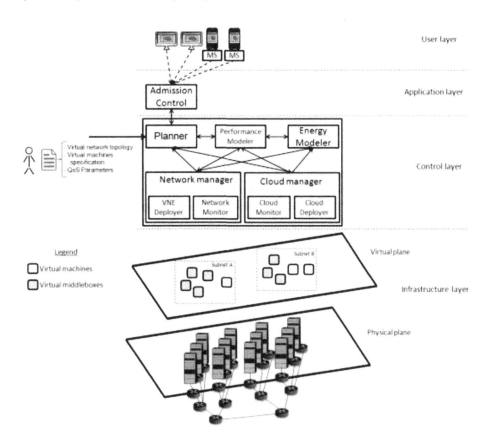

Figure 9. Cloud deployment models

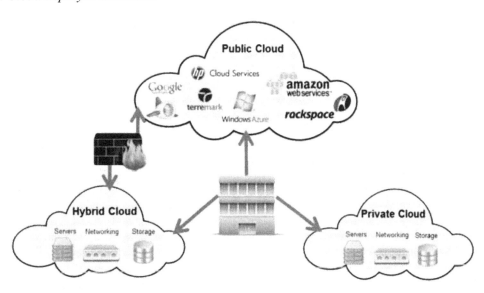

Public Cloud

A Public cloud is based on the standard cloud computing models, where the service providers creates possessions like virtual machines (VMs), applications o storage, available to the public over the internet. Public cloud services is pay as you go i.e., pay only for what you use.

Ex: Cloud services, Amazon web services, Google, Rack space etc.,

Hybrid Cloud

A hybrid cloud is the one that is integrated with the characteristics of both private and public cloud. The public and private partitions of hybrid cloud are put together, they remain unique. This allows a hybrid to cloud to provide the efficiency of multiple deployment models at the same time. They vary greatly in simplicity. Example, Few hybrid clouds give out connection between the on premise and public clouds.

Ex: Servers, Networking, Storage.

Community Cloud

A community cloud in management is mutual or shared resources where the infrastructure is mutual between many organizations from a particular community with common protocols like security, fulfillment, authority) Whether maintained inside or by third party and hosted internally or externally. This is managed by a group of organizations that have shared interests.

Flexibility in Cloud

The flexibility in cloud relies on the five flexible concepts like consumption flexibility, Platform flexibility, pricing flexibility, Business user flexibility, Vendor selection flexibility.

Table 2. Private cloud vs. Public cloud vs. Hybrid cloud vs. Community cloud

S.NO	Private Cloud	Public Cloud	Hybrid Cloud	Community Cloud
1.	Operated solely for single organizations.	Available to the general public and owned by a single.	Any combination of two or more private/ community or public clouds.	Shared by several entities that have a common purpose.
2.	It may be managed by the organization or a third party and may exists on premise or off premise.	This is owned by an organization selling cloud services.	It is private, public or community. This enables data and application portability.	E.g. mission, security, policy, compliance and considerations.
3.	Leverages existing capex.	Shifts to capex to opex.	Bridges one or moreprivate, public or community clouds.	Allows sharing of capex and opex to reduce costs.
4.	Can help reduce opex.	Offers a pay a you go model	Allows manipulation of capex or opex to reduce costs.	Brings together groups or organizations with a common goal/interests.
5.	Intended for a single tenant.	Supports multiple tenants.	Supports Resources portability.	Supports resource portability.
6.	Iaas	Paas, Saas	Iaas, Saas	Paas, saas
7	On or off premise	Off premise at provider.	On or off premise	On or off premise

Where Capex and opex refer to Capital expenditure and operational expenditure respectively.

They are further explained in a way the following:

Consumption Flexibility

You're not purchasing programming licenses in the cloud world. Rather, you are paying for what you expend. On the off chance that you have a need to staff extra operators for a promoting effort, you pay for the utilization of the administration/application, at that point quit paying once the crusade closes.

Platform Flexibility

IT has for some time been constrained into a space where wedding the required programming with the required equipment frequently didn't fit with the range of abilities of the IT association or the capacity to help it. Cloud arrangements expel this equipment programming similarity and bolster issue. Rather, the application benefit is chosen and the cloud supplier stresses over the equipment stage.

Pricing Flexibility

The capacity to pay for application use after some time (and in accordance with your utilization as expressed in thing one) makes budgetary adaptability. No compelling reason to compose the one-time, in advance, extensive check. Rather the expenses are spread out finished the life of utilization of the administration

Business User Flexibility

IT sourced the product and equipment that the organization would purchase. With the cloud, business clients are considerably more engaged with choosing the administrations that address their issues. They at that point leave a great part of the fundamental IT work to the cloud supplier.

Vendor Selection Flexibility

Changing arrangements starting with one seller then onto the next is a major ordeal. Clients must be retrained, and much of the time, business forms should be reclassified. The cloud doesn't take out the agony and cost of exchanging merchants, however it increases your adaptability to do as such. In the premises-based programming world, once you purchase an item, you're entirely very much secured for quite a long time.

THE FUTURE OF INFRASTRUCTURE

Software Defined Everything Infrastructure

This mainly we work for how we perform; software is designing the path to how we live. Software defined networking (SDN), Cloud computing and networking and network functions Virtualization (NFV) are the familiar examples of IT (Wei & Brain Blake, n.d). Cloud based services and software is turning into how we engage with the substantial world and experience day by day. Cloud computing has dimmed the level and limit in the work environment, so we have the capability to work from anywhere in the world and the applications that are running in our mobile devices do everything help us live a very easy and comfortable zoned life.

We refer this renovation as "SDx" for the purpose of Software defined everything, and the change to SDx is upsetting the business models in just about every organization. The quantity of data and information required deploying and communicating all these software defined applications and diplomacy is unbelievable. SDx is quickly growing the capability of traditional communication. This is the next generation of infrastructure required to communicate software defined devices and applications to their networks.

Software Defined Networking and Networking Virtualization Use Case Taxonomy

Given in Figure 10.

Network Access Control

This set suitable right for the clients or devices accessing the communications, that comprises of access control limits, integration of service chains, and suitable quality of service. To manage the security and conformity while giving comfortable benefits, users, devices as they connect from different parts of the network.

Network Virtualization

This generates an distant virtual network on the high of physical network, allowing a large quantity of various tenant networks to execute to run over a physical network spanning numerous spaces in the data centre or localities if needed, including fine-grained rights as well as isolations of security services.

Virtual Customer Edge

Virtualise the clients end model by generating a virtualized stand on client premises or by pulling in the functionalities nearer to the core network on a virtualized numerous tenants stage in a delivery service point of presence, data centre also called the virtual CE.

Figure 10. SDN and NFV use case Taxonomy

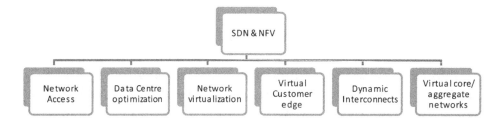

Dynamic Interconnects

Generate active relations between locations, together with data centers, enterprise, and other enterprise locations, as well as energetically applying proper QoS and bandwidth distribution to those links (including bandwidth-on-demand, or BWoD).

Virtual Core/Aggregate Network

Virtualize core systems for service providers including mobile support infrastructure such as vIMS, vEPC, as well as active mobile backhaul, virtual PE, and NFV GiLAN infrastructure.

Data Centre Optimization

Using SDN and NFV, optimize networks to get better application presentation by detecting and taking into account affinities workloads with networking arrangement

CHALLENGES IN CLOUD ENVIRONMENT

The cloud computing environment is yet facing many threats and it is not completely secured environment for many purposes (Agarwal, Das, & Abbadi. n.d).The cloud computing specifies the challenges of encountering the essentials of future trends private, Public and hybrid cloud computing architecture (Assuncao, Calheiros, Bianchi, Netto, & Buyya, 2015). Many of the issues of not completely not solved while the new challenges are merging day by day. Some of the research challenges are:

1. Service level agreements(SLA's)
2. Cloud information maintenance
3. Data encryption etc.,

The brief explanations of the above are given below:

Service Level Agreements

SLA is explained as an official obligation that exists between a service provider and a customer. Some specific aspects of the service like quality, availability, responsibilities and are decided between the service provider and the user. The usual element of SLA is that the services should be decided upon the contract.

Cloud Information Maintenance

Cloud Data Management is a stage that arranges mission basic application information crosswise over private and open mists while conveying information administration capacities, for example, reinforcement, fiasco recuperation, recorded, consistence, look, examination, and duplicate information administration in a solitary, run-anyplace stage. This vision to convey a product texture for information administration is established in our cloud merchant rationalist stage, avoiding seller secure to a specific cloud.

Data Encryption

Data encryption converts the information into different form or code then only persons with rights or access to a confidential key or password can use it. Encrypted data is referred to as cipher text, where the un encrypted data is called plain text. This is one of the usual popular and effective data security methods.

APPLICATIONS OF CLOUD COMPUTING

The cloud applications are in wide range and they provide a on demand services that are much beneficial to the clients (Reddy&Reddy,2013). They also provide services on the basis of "pay as you go " which refers to pay only for the services what we use and there much more other benefits also provided by cloud computing like,

1. Flexibility
2. Disaster recovery
3. Automatic software updates
4. Capital-expenditure Free
5. Increased collaboration
6. Work from anywhere
7. Document control
8. Security
9. Competitiveness
10. Environmental friendly

Benefits of Cloud Apps

Fast Response to Business Needs

Cloud applications can be updated, tested and deployed quickly, providing enterprises with fast time to market and agility. This speed can lead to culture shifts in business operations.

Simplified Operation

Infrastructure management can be outsourced to third-party cloud providers.

Instant Scalability

As demand rises or falls, available capacity can be adjusted.

Table 3. Cloud computing applications

Service type	IaaS	PaaS	SaaS
Service category	VM Rental, Online Storage	Online Operating Environment, Online Database, Online Message Queue	Application and Software Rental
Service Customization	Server Template	Logic Resource Template	Application Template
Service Provisioning	Automation	Automation	Automation
Service accessing and Using	Remote Console, Web 2.0	Online Development and Debugging, Integration of Offline Development Tools and Cloud	Web 2.0
Service monitoring	Physical Resource Monitoring	Logic Resource Monitoring	Application Monitoring
Service level management	Dynamic Orchestration of Physical Resources	Dynamic Orchestration of Logic Resources	Dynamic Orchestration of Application
Service resource optimization	Network Virtualization, Server Virtualization, Storage Virtualization	Large-scale Distributed File System, Database, Middleware etc	Multi-tenancy
Service measurement	Physical Resource Metering	Logic Resource Usage Metering	Business Resource Usage Metering
Service integration and combination	Load Balance	SOA	SOA, Mashup
Service security	Storage Encryption and Isolation, VM Isolation, VLAN, SSL/SSH	Data Isolation, Operating Environment Isolation, SSL	Data Isolation, Operating Environment Isolation, SSL, Web Authentication and Authorization

CONCLUSION

The present situation of cloud computing in the health care will enhance the features and various collaborative information issues in health care organizations as well as cost efficient, Standardized cloud based applications will bring many benefits to patients, insurance companies, imaging centre etc., When sharing information in medical industries yields better results. The security issues and challenges are overcome through many algorithms etc., The adoption of the cloud is progressing good in these days. The future growth of cloud based systems will overcome all the obstacles and hurdles if properly maintained. Software Defined cloud is an upcoming results of advanced technologies in the area of cloud computing, System virtualizations, Software defined networks, Software defined networking etc, There are many challenges to overcome . The data intensity and the enterprise environments of SDCs in the two cases- quality of services, energy efficient, bandwidth allocation, etc.

REFERENCES

Agrawal, D., Das, S., & El Abbadi, A. (2011, March). Big data and cloud computing: current state and future opportunities. In *Proceedings of the 14th International Conference on Extending Database Technology* (pp. 530-533). ACM. 10.1145/1951365.1951432

Ahuja, S. P., Mani, S., & Zambrano, J. (2012). A survey of the state of cloud computing in healthcare. *Network and Communication Technologies*, *1*(2), 12.

Armbrust, M., Fox, A., Griffith, R., Joseph, A. D., Katz, R., Konwinski, A., ... Zaharia, M. (2010). A view of cloud computing. *Communications of the ACM*, *53*(4), 50–58. doi:10.1145/1721654.1721672

Aziz, H. A., & Guled, A. (2016). *Cloud Computing and Healthcare Services. Academic Press.*

Bhardwaj, S., Jain, L., & Jain, S. (2010). Cloud computing: A study of infrastructure as a service (IAAS). *International Journal of Engineering and Information Technology*, *2*(1), 60–63.

Buyya, R., Calheiros, R. N., Son, J., Dastjerdi, A. V., & Yoon, Y. (2014, September). Software-defined cloud computing: Architectural elements and open challenges. In *Advances in Computing, Communications and Informatics (ICACCI, 2014 International Conference on* (pp. 1-12). IEEE.

Chowdhary, S. K., Yadav, A., & Garg, N. (2011, April). Cloud computing: Future prospect for e-health. In *Electronics Computer Technology (ICECT), 2011 3rd International Conference on* (Vol. 3, pp. 297-299). IEEE.

Guo, Y., Kuo, M. H., & Sahama, T. (2012, December). Cloud computing for healthcare research information sharing. In *Cloud Computing Technology and Science (CloudCom), 2012 IEEE 4th International Conference on* (pp. 889-894). IEEE. 10.1109/CloudCom.2012.6427561

GV, R. L., & Annappa, B. (2015, November). An Efficient Framework and Access control scheme for cloud health care. In *Cloud Computing Technology and Science (CloudCom), 2015 IEEE 7th International Conference on* (pp. 552-557). IEEE.

Hitachi Data System. (2016). *How to improve health care with cloud computing.* Author.

Karnwal, T., Sivakumar, T., & Aghila, G. (2011). Cloud Services in Different Cloud Deployment Models. An Overview. *International Journal of Computer Applications*.

Kumar, S., & Goudar, R. H. (2012). Cloud Computing-Research Issues, Challenges, Architecture, Platforms and Applications: A Survey. *International Journal of Future Computer and Communication*, *1*(4), 356–360. doi:10.7763/IJFCC.2012.V1.95

Li, H., Chen, Q., & Zhou, X. (2017, June). An analysis of the health care platform in the cloud environment. In *Software Engineering Research, Management and Applications (SERA), 2017 IEEE 15th International Conference on* (pp. 99-102). IEEE. 10.1109/SERA.2017.7965713

Lupşe, O. S., Vida, M. M., & Tivadar, L. S. (2012). Cloud computing and interoperability in healthcare information systems. In *The First International Conference on Intelligent Systems and Applications* (pp. 81-85). Academic Press.

Mireku, K., FengLi, Z., NiiAyeh, M. D., Khan, A., & Khan, I. (2016, March). Secured cloud database health care mining analysis. In *Computing for Sustainable Global Development (INDIACom), 2016 3rd International Conference on* (pp. 3937-3740). IEEE.

Niedermayer, M. (n.d.). *Cloud Computing Based Systems for Healthcare*. Academic Press.

Rao, C. C., Leelarani, M., & Kumar, Y. R. (2013). Cloud: Computing Services and Deployment Models. *International Journal Of Engineering And Computer Science, 2*(12), 3389–3390.

Rauscher, R., & Acharya, R. (2013, December). Performance of private clouds in health care organizations. In *Cloud Computing Technology and Science (CloudCom), 2013 IEEE 5th International Conference on* (Vol. 1, pp. 693-698). IEEE. 10.1109/CloudCom.2013.113

Reddy, B. E., Kumar, T. S., & Ramu, G. (2012, December). An efficient cloud framework for health care monitoring system. In *Cloud and Services Computing (ISCOS), 2012 International Symposium on* (pp. 113-117). IEEE. 10.1109/ISCOS.2012.11

Reddy, G. N., & Reddy, G. J. (2014). *Study of Cloud Computing in HealthCare Industry.* arXiv preprint arXiv:1402.1841

Sobhy, D., El-Sonbaty, Y., & Elnasr, M. A. (2012, December). MedCloud: healthcare cloud computing system. In *Internet Technology And Secured Transactions, 2012 International Conference for* (pp. 161-166). IEEE.

Stantchev, V., Colomo-Palacios, R., & Niedermayer, M. (2014). Cloud computing based systems for healthcare. *The Scientific World Journal.* PMID:24892070

Ullah, S., & Xuefeng, Z. (2013). *Cloud Computing Research Challenges.* arXiv preprint arXiv:1304.3203

Velte, A. T., Velte, T. J., Elsenpeter, R. C., & Elsenpeter, R. C. (2010). *Cloud computing: a practical approach.* New York: McGraw-Hill.

Wei, Y., & Blake, M. B. (2010). Service-oriented computing and cloud computing: Challenges and opportunities. *IEEE Internet Computing, 14*(6), 72–75. doi:10.1109/MIC.2010.147

Zhang, Q., Cheng, L., & Boutaba, R. (2010). Cloud computing: State-of-the-art and research challenges. *Journal of Internet Services and Applications, 1*(1), 7–18. doi:10.100713174-010-0007-6

Chapter 7
Internet of Things (IoT):
A Study on Key Elements, Protocols, Application, Research Challenges, and Fog Computing

P. Suresh
Vel Tech Rangarajan Dr. Sagunthala R&D Institute of Science and Technology, India

S. Koteeswaran
Vel Tech Rangarajan Dr. Sagunthala R&D Institute of Science and Technology, India

N. Malarvizhi
Vel Tech Rangarajan Dr. Sagunthala R&D Institute of Science and Technology, India

R. H. Aswathy
Vel Tech Rangarajan Dr. Sagunthala R&D Institute of Science and Technology, India

ABSTRACT

The physical world entities are communicated via advanced communication technologies without human intervention. Such an evolving advanced version of automation technology is internet of things (IOT), where each smart device is provided with unique identification. The integration part of such technology comprises key elements, protocols, applications, and research challenges. This chapter discusses such terms and addresses the research challenges. The concept of fog computing is analyzed by cognitive approach. Fog computing localizes the processing information and optimizes the communication and storage among enormous smart devices. In addition, it favourably mitigates the need of bandwidth size and delay in communication.

INTRODUCTION

The term IoT is spawned by Kevin Ashton in 1999, he explained the potential of net of factors. IoT is a machine of interrelated computing gadgets, mechanical and digital machines, where gadgets, animals, humans are furnished with UID (Unique Identifier) and capable of transfer records over a community without require any H2H or H2M interaction. IoT has grown within the confluence of exiting technol-

DOI: 10.4018/978-1-5225-5972-6.ch007

ogy like MEMS ,micro services, wireless technology and internet. Devices embedded with electronics, softwares, sensors and community connectivity that allows object to collect and exchange data. The IoT empower physical objects to engage with every other to percentage international information and appearing collectively to accomplish a selection. Currently we could connect approximately 12 billion gadgets over the internet and it is estimated that around 50 billion gadgets could be connected by 2020,(Ala Al-Fuquha et al.,2015).This new technology will playing a remarkable role in everyday life to increase productivity, improve efficiency in all fields like healthcare, home automation, industrial, retail, logistics and smart applications etc. However, challenges have been recorded as in term of security, storage, interoperability and some other cases.

The outline of the benefaction of this paper relative to the contemporary literature inside the area summarized as follows. In section 2, we present the crucial key elements of IoT which include sensing, communication, cloud consolidation and capture and delivery of data. In section 3, we identify the most appropriate protocols which is suitable for IoT such as MQTT,XMPP, CoAP, AMQP and DTLS with its detailed architecture. In section 4, we present the application of IoT in various fields. In section 5,we identify the most common issues and research challenges.

KEY ELEMENTS OF IoT

Smart applications in IoT are driven by the composition of sensors and actuators, connectivity, people and processes. Major key elements of IoT are sensing, communication, cloud based capture and consolidation and delivery of information, that depicted in Figure 2.

Sensing

In IoT, the first step is sensing. It is a detection of physical presence and the conversion of the data into signal that can be readable by an equipment or observer. It can be done by any wearable device, smart

Figure 1. Overall architectural view of IoT

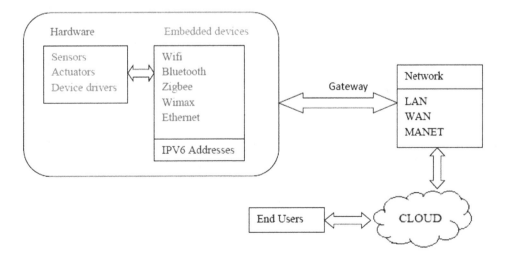

device, wall mounted device or fixed device in an instrument. The sensing can be used in biological experiment, manufacturing, machinery, aerospace, robotics etc. According to needs, sensors gets varies and many types of sensors are available. They are pressure sensor, color sensor, humidity sensor, ultrasonic sensor, temperature sensor, gas sensor, etc.. Organizations like Wemo presents lot of smart objects or devices and mobile application, that enable to monitor and control home equipments and millions of smart devices (Palo Alto et al.,2014). For example, biochips on cattle, heart tracking implants, manufacturing line sensors in factories, vehicles with integrated sensors, or area operation devices that help fire fighters,(Li et al.,2011).

Communication

Data collection and manage message delivery are the main part of IoT and Communication Infrastructure can be enable that dual directional communication. Transmitting the information sensed at a sensor level is send to the cloud based services for further processing for communication. Depending upon the range, the communication device is used, for instance Bluetooth, Zigbee, Z-wave, 6LowPan, Thread, Wifi and so on. There are Radio Frequency Identification tags and that can be active, passive, semi passive/active. Active RFID tags are powered with the aid of battery even as passive ones do no longer want battery. Semi-passive/lively tags use board electricity when wanted.

Cloud Based Capture and Consolidation

The data which is collected by sensors transmitted to cloud service through gateway is aggregated with other cloud based service to provide useful information for end user. This service must receive all data, act upon with relevant data from their surroundings quickly and cost effectively. There is an existence of many new technologies and emerging solutions to enable the break-through of tiny factors, ultra power and performance.

Delivery of Information

The final process is delivery of information to the end user. End user may be client, customer, industrial or commercial user. The goal is to provide information in a simple and transparent method as possible, properly designed interface provides an optimized experience across multiple device platforms-Tablets, Smartphones, desktop across multiple operating systems-Android, ios, Windows.

Figure 2. Key elements of IoT

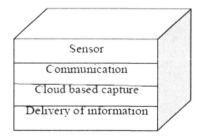

IoT PROTOCOLS

Different protocols have been developed to support IoT use the efforts caused by Internet Engineering Task Force (IETF), World Wide Web Consortium (W3C), Institute of Electrical and Electronics Engineers (IEEE) and so on. IoT protocols can be classified into five broad categories, namely Message Queue Telemetry Transport (MQTT), Constrained Application Protocol (CoAP), Extensible Messaging Presence Protocol (XMPP), Advanced Message Queuing Protocol (AMQP) and Data Distribution Service (DDS) protocol. The Phases of IoT are shown in Figure 3.

Figure 3. Phases of IoT

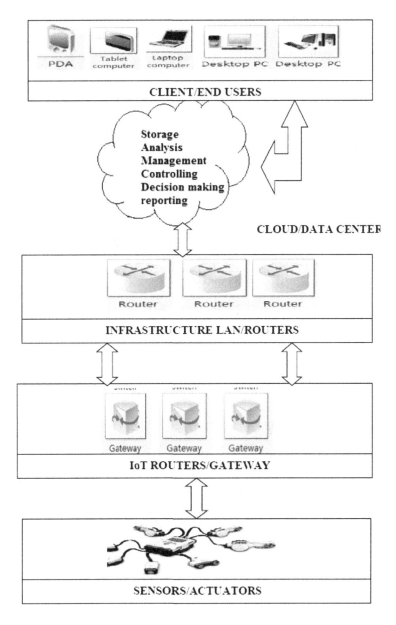

Message Queue Telemetry Transport (MQTT)

The working principle of MQTT is client- server publish/subscribe messaging protocol and it's a light-weight protocol, became introduced via Andy Stanford Clark of IBM and Arlen Nipper of Arcom in 1999 and it become standardized in 2013 at oasis, (Nikhita Reddy et al.,2016). It is simple and easy to implement. It collects data from many devices and transports to other infrastructure. It is a open standard protocol for constrained devices, it works with low bandwidth and high latency devices. It flows on the top of the Transmission Control Protocol. In every message has a discrete chunk of data, not visible to the broker. Device to cloud communication can be achieved by using this protocol.

Figure 4 shows the architecture of MQTT, which defined with three elements publisher, subscriber and intermediate /Broker .The attentive device would register the needed data to the subscriber through the broker. The publisher can be act as a producer of the specific data. The functionality of the broker is to store, forward, prioritize and filtering the data provide with the QoS. The routing mechanism of MQTT is flow through in Figure 5.

The structure of MQTT control packet contains three parts that are fixed header, variable header and payload, (Locke et al., 2010). It works by exchanging a series of MQTT control packet in a specified manner. Each MQTT control packet contains fixed header, (Locke et al., 2010) and it described in Figure 6.

Figure 4. MQTT-Overall architecture

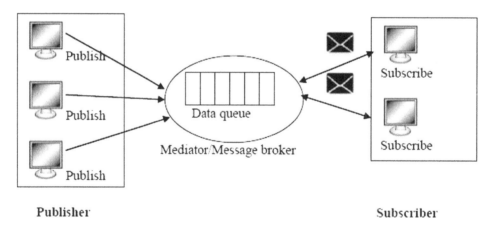

Figure 5. Routing mechanism of MQTT

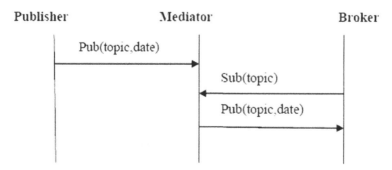

Figure 6. Fixed header of MQTT

Bit	7	6	5	4	3	2	1	0
Byte1	Control Packet				Flag			
Byte 2...	Length							

In MQTT, message contain a fixed length header (2 bytes), variable header is an optional message and message payload. MQTT is optimized for bandwidth constrained and unreliable networks. Optional field are used to mitigate the transmission, (Nikhita Reddy et al., 2016). A variety of messages can be seen in the message field along with PUBLISH, SUBSCRIBE, PUBACK, PUBREC, PUBREL, PUB-COMP, CONNECT and so on (Locke et al., 2010).DUP suggests the message is duplicated, if DUP is ready to zero, it shows client or server has to try to send this MQTT submit packet. If DUP is about to 1, it suggests that is the redelivery of in advance try packet. If preserve flag is ready to 1, the submit packet sent by means of a client to the server, the server stock up the submission message and its QOS, it could be introduced to destiny subscribers, whose subscribers matching its topic call. Figure 7 represents the common feature of MQTT.

CoAP (Constrained Application Protocol)

COAP is an web based protocol developed by IETF, it inherits the features of REST (Representational State Transfer Protocol) architecture generally designed for accessing the internet resources in constraint devices, HTTP defines many methods GET, POST, PUT, CONNECT, HEAD, OPTIONS, TRACE etc. CoAP bind over UDP and exactly suited for IoT applications, CoAP entitle UDP broadcast and multicast for addressing the client server model. Client make request to server and responds. The overall process is exhibits in Figure 8.

Figure 7. Features of MQTT

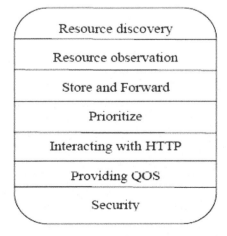

Figure 8. Overall architecture of CoAP

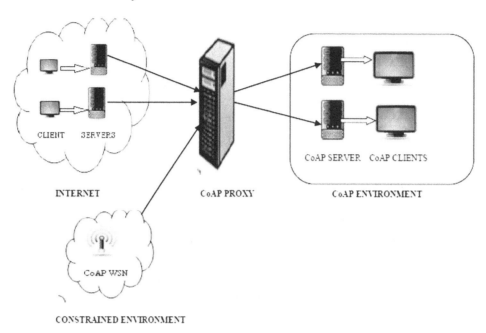

The layer of CoAP is divided into two sub layer Request/Response messages. In this protocol, Message sub layer detect the duplication and ensure the reliable communication over UDP. Device to device communication can be achieved by using this protocol. CoAP works with four types of messages CON, NON, ACK, RESET. The protocol in different layer is shown in Figure 9.

Confirmable message can be acknowledged with ACK or RESET, while non-conformable message does not require any ACK, (Nikhita Reddy et al., 2016) that can be explained in Figure 10 and Figure 11. Request/Response layer model in CoAP use three types of responses named piggy backed, separate response, Non-confirmable request/response.

A number of the crucial capabilities furnished with the aid of CoAP encompass (Borman et al.,2012),(Lerche et al.,2012): Useful resource observation, Lower overhead, simple proxy,DTLS,M2M Communication, Block-wise resource transport, Resource discovery, Interacting with HTT, Security and so on. The features of CoAP are depicted in Figure 12.

Figure 9. Protocols in different layer

PROTOCOLS IN DIFFERENT LAYERS	
APPLICATION LAYER	HTTP,CoAP
NETWORK/COMMUNICATION LAYER	TCP/UDP,IPV4,IPV6,6LowPAN
PHYSICAL/MAC LAYER	IEEE802.11,IEEE802.15,IEEE2.3,Z-Wave

Figure 10. Conformable message

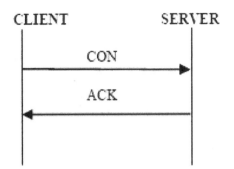

Figure 11. Non-conformable message

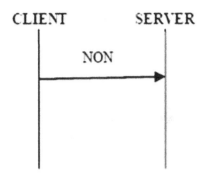

Figure 12. Features of CoAp

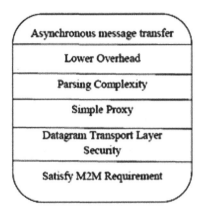

XMPP (Extensible Messaging Presence Protocol)

In view of XML (Extensible Mark-up Language) XMPP is a message oriented middleware. The basic syntax and semantics is developed by Jabber, open source community in 1999.It is a communication protocol, make a real-time data exchange between any two or more network entities,("Extensible Messaging") which is suitable for instant messaging (IM),XMPP allows IM to attain authentication access control, security, privacy, end-to-end encryption and communication with other protocol, (Nikhita Reddy et al.,.2016). Device to cloud and cloud to cloud communication can be achieved by using this protocol.

The Figure 14 illustrates the entire conduct of XMPP protocol, the gateway can be bridge among overseas messaging network ("Advanced Messaging,2008"). XMPP present an era for synchronous, quit-to-cease exchange of dependent data.XML streams which is globally addressable. This global address (unique Id address) is used to route and deliver message over network, (Nikhita Reddy et al.,2016). XML stanza is the basic protocol unit in XMPP which is shown in Figure 14, fragment of XML send over a stream.

A piece of code is separated into three segments, characterized by XML stanza: Presence, Message and IQ (Info/Query: get, set). The XML stanza consists of routing attributes such as from and to addresse ("Extensible Message").To retrieve the data XMPP entity uses PUSH method. Subject, message title, body field and content are included in stanza. Presence stanza and iq stanza notifies client fame, updates

Figure 13. Architecture of XMPP

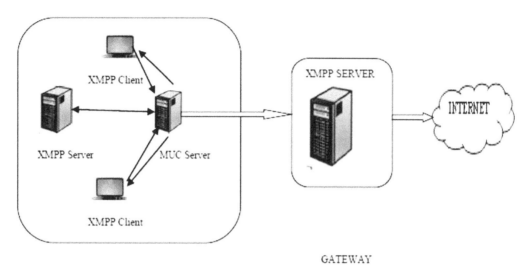

GATEWAY

Figure 14. XMPP message Stanza

if legal and couples message senders and receivers respectively. This protocol is designed to publish-subscribe system, signalling file transfer, gaming and many IoT applications like social networking, Industrial automation and smart grid. The features of XMPP is shown in Figure 15.

AMQP (Advanced Message Queuing Protocol)

It is the arrangement of segments that course and store message with in the intermediary administration by TCP based transmission. The characteristics of AMQP are message-oriented, routing, queuing, routing (Publish-and –subscribe), reliability, security, multi channel, portable, neutral and efficient. Device to cloud, Device to device and cloud to cloud communication can be achieved by using this protocol.

The architecture of AMQP model denotes the set of components (Figure 16) and specific rule for connecting the components.

Figure 15. Features of XMPP

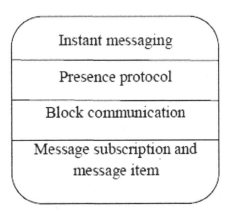

Figure 16. Overall architecture of AMQP

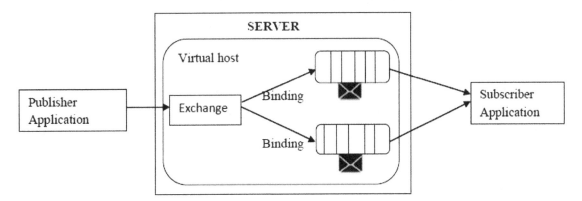

Server receives the message and processes depends upon the arbitrary standards routes to diverse subscribers and stores the message temporarily in memory or disk. Whilst subscribers are not capable of be given message at once, AMQP provides runtime programmable semantics through most important thing("Advanced Messaging",2008).

1.   To create arbitrary trade and message queue kinds.
2.   Message processing system to be created by using wi-fi exchanges and message queues together.

The main components of AMQP is Publisher, Exchange, Message Queue, and Subscriber.

The publisher is issuers, who publish the messages, message queue reserves messages in disk and deliver those in series to one or many applications. Messages can be stores in message queue and it performs distribution operation. Message queue can be standardized by middleware architecture. Store and forward queues-message queue store, collect and forward message in a technique called round robin. Messages are tremendously durable and shared between more than one subscribers. Private reply queue-it store messages and forward the message to handiest one subscriber. Reply queue is a transient queue and own with the aid of most effective one subscriber. Non-public subscription queue-shops messages accrued from numerous "requested" assets and ahead it to single subscriber. Exchange-It accepts messages for manufacturer software and direction messages according to pre-planned order that is known as "binding". Matching and routing engines are exchanges. Check messages using their binding desk and plan the way to ship these messages to message queue. It never store messages as an alternative it change messages. Alternate approach, it suggests magnificence of algorithm and instance of an algorithm, how to publish message and bind queues can be specified by the exchange.

Exchanges are executed using single key known as routing key. The routing secret is a digital cope with, it change messages and it decide a way to direction the messages. Two types of routing are factor-to –factor and put up-subscribe. AMQP is cognitive to email message, here mail box is a message queue. The capabilities of message queue fetches, delete electronic mail, MTA(Message switch Agent),inspects e-mail and comes to a decision on the idea of routing tables and keys, how to send the e-mail to at least one or greater mail boxes. Overall performance assessment of AMQP and REST is mentioned in,(Fernandes et al.,2013). To carry out their have a look at, the authors used the common range of change messages among the consumer and the server in a selected break to degree the overall performance. Beneath a excessive extent of message exchanges, AMQP proven higher effects than RESTful web services, (Nikhita Reddy et al.,2016).

Data Distribution Service

DDS is a middleware protocol in an object management group. It is publish-subscribe protocol by M2M communication. DDS is an excellent protocol used with multicasting and provide low latency data connectivity, reliability and scalable architecture. It relies with Broker-less architecture with P2P communication (Figure 17).

Figure 17. Overall architecture of DDS

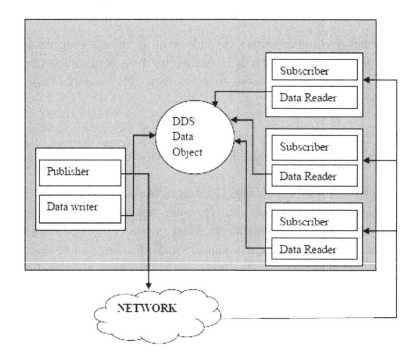

There are two layers defined by DDS architecture, Data-Centric Publish-Subscribe (DCPS) and Data-Local Reconstruction Layer (DLRL). Delivery of information to the subscriber handled by DCPS and the functionalities of DCPS to be served by DLRL, its an optional layer and serves as a middleware. It enables the sharing of allotted records amongst disbursed gadgets (Modadugu et al, 2004).The decrease layer API's programs use to change topic statistics with different DDS enabled utility consistent with QoS regulations. The upper layer API's define how to build a local object cache, so application access topic data if it is local. DCPS layer consists of five entities that are concerned with flow of facts (Ala Al-Faqaha et al,2015). (1) Publisher that propagate information. (2) Information creator is used by the software to interact with the publisher approximately the values and modifications of data particular to given kind. (3)Subscriber that gets published facts and supplies them to software.(4) Records Reader is hired with the aid of the join get entry to the obtained records.(5)Topic is diagnosed with the aid of a records kind and call.

DDS specification only defines polices and interfaces between application and services. DDS is a put up-subscribe messaging: DDS makes use of the publish/subscribe version for dynamic discovery and number one management of statistics flows among relevant DDs entities such as publishers, subscribers, sturdiness offerings and reply offerings. DDS have the salient features of portability, interoperability, data-centricity, high performance and Qos regulations.

DDS provide high-performance data communications suitable for real time and non real-time applications. Today several commercial and open source implementations of the DDS standards are available.

Table 1. DDS Protocols and its features

Protocol → Features ↓	MQTT	CoAP	XMPP	AMQP	DDS
Transport	TCP/IP	UDP/IP	TCP/IP	TCP/IP	UDP/IP TCP/IP (Unicast +Mcast)
Paradigm	Publish / Subscribe	Request/ Reply (ReST)	Point-Point Msg Exchange	Point-Point Msg Exchange	Publish/ Subscribe Request/ Reply
Scope	D2C	D2D	D2C C2C	D2D D2C C2C	D2D D2C C2C
Automatic Discovery	No	Yes	No	No	Yes
Content Awareness	-	-	-	-	Content based routing queries
Data Centricity	Undefined	Encoding	Encoding	Encoding	Encoding Declaration
Interoperability	Foundational	Semantic	Structural	Structural	Semantic
Security	TLS	DTLS	TLS	TLS	TLS, DTLS, DDS Security
Fault Tolerance	Broker is SPoF	Decentralized	Server is SPoF	Implementation Specific	Decentralized

APPLICATIONS IN IoT

The application of IoT is enormous and it is utilized in every domain. These applications drive our life comfort in all aspects. The application of IoT is depicted in the Figure 18 and each application is elucidated below.

Smart Home, Smart Building and Smart Infrastructure

Electronic gadgets have become part of home IP network (TV, Refrigerators, Washing machine, Mobile gadgets and PDA's) because of growing charge of human usability. Many researchers are trying to furnish domestic with technologies that enable occupants to apply single device to control digital gadgets and appliances. To screen the surroundings, dealing with the energy and living consolation we need smart surroundings. To perform this we need clever sensors to monitor air con, lights, security, heating, electricity generation and surroundings key indicators (Ovidiuvermison et al., 2014). IoT applications, for example the usage of sensors gather statistics approximately the operating condition with cloud hosted analytics software program, Operating collectively with internet and power management machine gives an opportunity to access a building a power facts manage device from a mobile tool or smart phone placed anywhere in the global. This smart feature helps the managers, proprietors and inhabitancies of constructing with energy intake remarks and potential to behave on those records. Smart buildings enforce high safety ranges by means of constantly tracking those who input and depart the building, (Nikhita Reddy et al.,2016). Far flung monitoring and tracking-Command, manipulate and routing functions are generally performed manually or it done remotely. For example, these days many homes running with guide procedure to show on and rancid washing machine. In near destiny doors, home windows electrical home equipment and many other types of equipment will have become smart with particular id. These clever devices can communicate through stressed and wi-fi communication, it allows user to display their personal domestic remotely.

Smart Applications, (Nikhita Reddy et al.,2016)

IoT application satisfies the social wishes and the advancements to allow technology that consists of nano electronics and cyber bodily systems, stay challenged by way of a spread of medical, engineering, institutional and economic issues. Clever town is a evolved urban area that creates sustainable monetary development and high quality in existence with the aid of excelling in a couple of key regions: economic system, Mobility, environment, people, residing and government, (Ovidiuvermison et al.,2014). It has been predicted that through clever towns2020, the development of smart metropolis can be widespread more than 60% of world populace live in cities by 2025.

Clever towns via 2020, the development of smart metropolis is widespread with more than 60% of world populace live in city cities by way of 2025. The evolution of clever is manifested by the aid of many smart features including smart power, smart financial system, clever building, clever mobility, smart planning, clever data communiqué and so forth. There might be possible to develop 20 clever towns in India with the aid of IoT by 2020.Clever metropolis is described as a city that monitors and integrate

Figure 18. Smart Applications in Internet of Things(IoT)

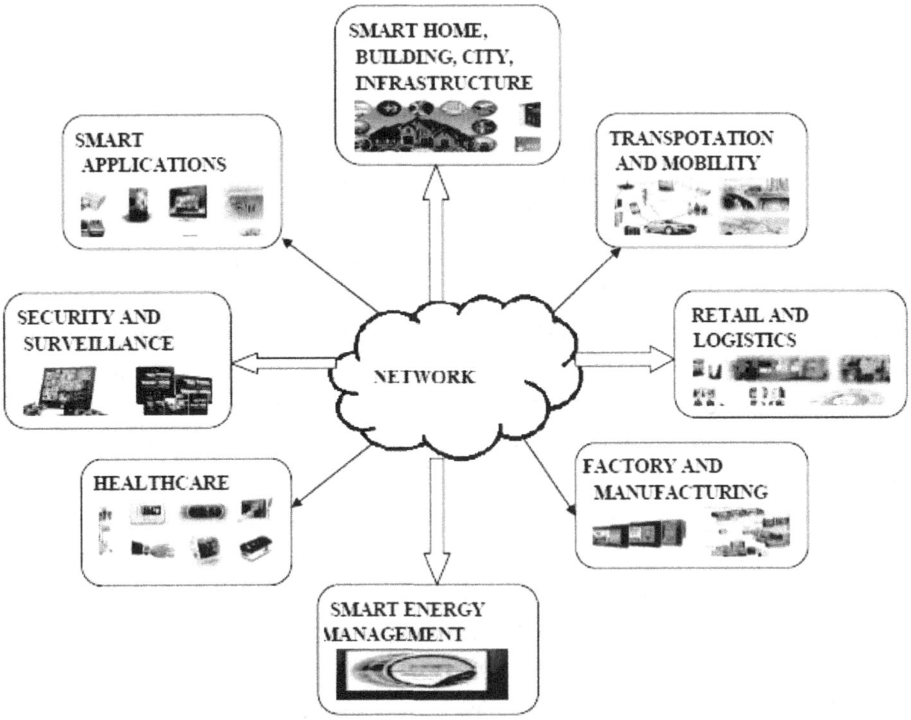

situations of all crucial infrastructure which includes roads, bridges, tunnels, rail, subway, airport, seaport, communiqué, water, power and tracking safety elements, emergency response for both man-made and natural disasters. This to be fulfils both long and quick time period smart metropolis vision. Clever IoT infrastructure will be reveal their own circumstance and carry out self restore as wished.

Smart Energy Management

Power is the tough paradigm in our world these days. Now we are unconditionally depending upon fossil assets or nuclear strength. Be that as it may, with the utilization of numerous renewable assets the future vitality supply needs can be accomplished. For energy storage, power distribution, communication and grid monitoring a revolutionary idea has provided by IoE (Internet of Electricity). That permit to transfer the energy when and where its required. Electricity utilization observing could be done on all reaches from neighbourhood gadgets up to national and worldwide degree, (Ovidiuvermison et al.,2014).Shrewd meters convey the records about the prompt power utilization to the individual, as a result allowing the personality and disposal of quality squandering gadgets and for supplying tips for improving individual vitality utilization. Developing the notice for saving electricity intake is the pillar for future electricity control. Smart meters give all the information about immediate power intake to the person, identification and elimination of electricity losing machine and provide tips for optimizing the energy intake and effective electricity use.

Mobility and Transport

The relationship of cars to the net provides upward to the wealth of recent possibilities and packages which bring new capability to the users for simple and safe shipping, (Ovidiuvermison et al.,2014). In IoE, creating new cellular environment primarily based on confidence, security and convenience to cellular/transportation utility. IoT permitting visitors control and manage-vehicles must experience or speak with each other to arrange themselves with a purpose to keep away from accidents. It can be achieved by coordination and collaboration of smart city management system and traffic control. Aside from this, parking in crowd regions, parking tax can be important detail of IoT enabled structures. Self communication between the infrastructure and vehicle enable new techniques intended for reduce injuries and safety improving. Independent driving and interfacing-there are numerous challenged which addresses the interaction among the vehicle and the surroundings(Sensors, Actuators, communication, Processing, statistics trade and so forth) by thinking about avenue navigation system which joins street shape and street localization estimation to power on streets. Through the utilization of programmed chips that can be utilized to help engines secure with the guide of identifying traffic light, walker, crash and languid drivers. Auto producers, that offer stages for application change, usually don't make their responses to be had on more established styles. A number of auto creators reported that they're running on transforming this dependency. In venture with Gartner's predictions, by 2020 in experienced vehicle markets more prominent than 80% of recently sold vehicles will be set up with related vehicle usefulness. Many companies are imparting computer managed automobile Ex: Google, Volvo and other many groups running on, (Ovidiuvermison et al.,2014). The computerization era is a key features of the smart grid which lets the grid to regulate and manage single or huge number of gadgets from a single location associated with it, (Nikhita Reddy et al.,2016). Automobiles, Sensors in road and visitors controlled infrastructure need to accumulate statistics about road and traffic status. There will be 152 million linked vehicles by 2020, that has estimated by HIS (Laslo et al.,2015).

Factory and Smart Manufacturing

In smart manufacturing facility, the external stake holders interact with IoT enabled production structures. The stake holders are the suppliers of production gear (ex: Machines and robots), manufacturing logistics (deliver chain control, material flow), keeping and re-tooling actors. The design of IoT that difficulties the various levelled and closed manufacturing facility computerization, by method for allowing the above expressed partners to run their offerings in several level generation device (Ovidiuvermison et al.,2014). are proposed. Organisations are the use of many strategies to collect the large quantity of records, enterprise analytics, cloud offerings, company mobility and many different ways to improve the enterprise. Those technology encompass large records, cloud offerings, commercial enterprise analytics software, sensor networks, embedded technology, sensing era, GPS, RFID, M2M, security, mobility, identification, stressed out network, wireless community and so forth.

Healthcare

IoT play an essential position in clinical care in which hospitalized man or woman's physiological repute requires close attention may be monitored frequently by the usage of IoT pushed, non invasive monitoring. The sensors of RFID tags, gather the psychological statistics and bypass to the cloud infrastructure to keep data and improve the first-class of care through the care giver. It addition, real innovation in disease tracking and manage chronic disorders need to be intended to work with negligible influenced individual instruction and collaboration, (Ovidiuvermison et al.,2014). Smart beds are one idea that is being, the market size will grow up to $117 billion by means of 2020. Remote patient monitoring-In this implant sensing node that track biometrics and sends a signal related to abnormal readout for an elderly patient. If patient does not take a medication, the node inform a person from a contact list, if no answer it could called next person and so on. If the last person also doesn't response, it contacts a clinic or provide it emergency assistance.

Logistics and Retail

The logistics operation consists of warehousing operation, freight transportation and final mile shipping. The impact areas are safety, protection and operational performance. In logistics, we can monitor the fame of belongings, parcels and people in real time during the cost chain. The consumers can degree how the assets are acting and impact change in what they may be doing. We will optimize how people, structures and asserts worth together and coordinate and coordinate their sports. Sensing is the monitoring of different asserts within a deliver chain via special technology and mediums. Connectivity is the important thing to be connected every time, everywhere with any devices. Retailers additionally are utilizing sensors, reference points, examining instrument and other IoT advancements to upgrade inside: stock, armada, helpful asset and accessory administration through continuous examination, computerized renewal and notice, group and more noteworthy. The huge facts generated now offers outlets a genuine information of ways their products, customers, representatives and outer components. This is a $1.6T open door for shops with $81B in value effectively acknowledged in 2013, (Ovidiuvermison et al.,2014)..Product and shelf sensors gather records during the entire convey chain. They regularly provide from dock to shelf logs. Predictive analytics programs system those facts and optimize the convey chain,(Lerche et al.,2012).

Security and Surveillance

IP enabled cameras represent a growth area of IoT. It can be used in secure communication of data in defence ad speed limitations in Vehicles (bus, cars etc).Traffic controllers is a centralized operating systems can monitor the speed, status and location of every vehicles with some IP based network that provide Wi-Fi access to passengers. The entire system is heavily secured against virtual and physical intruders. There are 3 main axes for IoT protection (i) Context-conscious and user centric privacy, (ii) Powerful protection for tiny embedded networks and (iii) The systemic and cognitive approach,(Couldry et al.,2014).

CHALLENGES IN IoT

IoT can be employ in different plane views, now we are in the early stage of an IoT, its technology and application is tremendous and impact is good. Even though, we are facing many potential risk and technical challenges day by day. Some challenges are in networking sector, software development, security, communication and cloud storage.

Interoperability

Principles are critical in developing substitute for brand punishing new innovation. On the off chance that gadgets from excellent makers, they did not utilize the equivalent prerequisites. Interoperability will be additional difficult to sketches with it. Innovation covets more portals to make an interpretation from one across the board to some other. An association that works with extraordinary parts of a vertical business sector (e.g. Obtaining of data, coordination, and the use of those records streams to give you imaginative arrangements or to offer offerings) may moreover overwhelm a business sector, rivalry and making issues for little industrialist and advertisers. Contrasting data norms are difficult to bolt clients into one circle of relatives of items: in the event that the buyer can't exchange their information when they supplant one gadget with another from the diverse producer ("Anonymous", 2015). Interoperability should be considered through both programming designers and IoT device produces. As an instance, the majority of the shrewd phones as of late help typical discussion innovation alongside WiFi, NFC, and GSM to guarantee the interoperability in particular circumstances. Additionally, software engineers of the IoT ought to fabricate their projects to take into account incorporating new abilities without incurring issues or dropping capacities in the meantime as keeping joining with unique discussion advancements. Thus, interoperability is a huge rule in planning and building IoT offerings to fulfil clients' necessities (Dunkels et al.,2011).

Security and Privacy

There are number of security related challenges addressed by research community. IoT gives some of protection related issues both in clients and organizations. Cybercriminals seize touchy information by way of interrupting wi-fi communiqué. Culprits assault servers or Cloud-based absolutely environment ere the enormous amounts of accumulated records. Hackers objective neighbourhood group changing the element and control the contraption, e.g. by means of conveying garbage mail, cutting down an as-sembling office or vitality lattice, disturbing the ordinary working of a non-open wellness gadget or it focus on the vehicle resulting in an accident. To minimize the security risk the encryption technique can be implemented strictly, because sensor device have lack of battery power and computation capacity to accomplish the encryption of data. During the design and manufacturing of IoT product the company has to take an account with protection from threats, access control mechanism, and updating software regularly to patch vulnerabilities. To keep accuracy of data, the database must help high pace study and write continuously to collect the information at uniform durations with none loss. Large scale industries working with IoT are been higher susceptible for assault or facts theft. In IoT, many areas we have to safeguard in the terms of security. Some of the malicious attacks that harms the IoT security are DOS attacks, Compromised Node, Malicious code hacking, Cyber situation, Need to be work individually without any human intervention ("Anonymous",2015).

Privacy is the major problem in today's IoT environment. Users are seriously worried about data protection. IoT system should protect the personal data by using some restrictive access mechanism. IoT client gadgets gather private or individual records, from the clients' place, their everyday conduct or state of their wellbeing information might be transmitted to focal server, or imparted to different gadgets or outsiders, without the open door for the client to audit that information. Numerous gadgets, for example, wearable armlets need huge shows or touch screen making it hard to give data to the cus-tomer about conceivable uses and get client assent. Some cryptographic techniques for authentication fine grain process, self configuring access mechanism to Preserving location privacy, Process controlling personal information and Keep information locally. In such manner, a few arrangements have been proposed, for example, gathering inserted gadgets into virtual systems and just present craved gadgets inside each virtual system. Another methodology is to bolster access control in the application layer on a for each seller premise.

Scalability

In 2003 around 3 billion of gadgets is associated with half million IP address square and more than 50 thousand independently administrated systems. Be that as it may, today arrange conventions are intended for stationary gadgets with sensible computational and memory assets, IoT handle the request of amplify more gadgets, large portions of which are irregular associated and low power, (Rajeev Alur.,2015).The versatility of the IoT alludes to the capacity to include new devices, services and capacities for clients without contrarily influencing the nature of existing administrations. Including new operations and supporting new gadgets is not a simple assignment particularly within the sight of assorted equipment stages and interchanges conventions. Utilizing ground up to empower extensible administrations and operations, the IoT applications to be outlined.

Low Power Communication

Numerous gadgets in IoT are small and do not have enough power packages. The significant imperatives are battery size, life time, quality and communication. For the resource compelled devices, IEEE802.15.4 has built up a low power consumption, low cost, low many-sided quality, low to medium reach correspondence guidelines at connection and physical layer. The foreseen development in the quantity of Wi-Fi gadgets will require more radio range. The spectrum could be apportioned depending upon the technology utilized. Mobile gadgets and Wi-Fi gadgets are employed in IoT. The range of choices are more troublesome is that IoT devices tend to have a long lifetime (around 30 years) rather than the bounty shorter normal lifespan of PDAs 5 to 7 years. For instance, administrators in Europe may have issues later on in closing down 2Gwi-fi help for the reason that may render outmoded sharp meters that at present utilize that innovation.

Connectivity and Addressing

Connectivity is the major research challenge in IoT. In such scalable IoT environment, providing connectivity for all devices and servers in a large scale IoT application may be the crucial part. Over two hundred millions of devices connected to our global real time data stream network average of 60 to 70 transactions per second over 4 million of devices. Addressing problem can be solved by IPv6 address. Example: Devices which are connected in automotive, home automation and wearable devices are needed connectivity.

FOG COMPUTING: EDGE WORK WITH CLOUD

The internet technology crossed the peak of expectation stage ie Internet of things (IoT). IoT intensify the quality of life and refers to the network of objects, tools, techniques and electronic devices. The IoT can be visualized as the wireless sensors that interconnect the entire object in our day-to-day life and objects will rely with each other to exchange the data. Moreover, the real innovations of front end technology that supports IoT is cloud computing. In this innovative technology, the information will be efficiently caught and stored. The cache data is transfiguring into significant learning and actionable knowledge. The framework of the cloud will be utilized to a) change information to understanding b) drive beneficial and cost effective actions. Through this procedure the cloud servers act as the brain to enhance the Internet associated collaborations. This countless new type of objects produced unprecedented magnitude of information, difficult for traditional system for processing.

Research community estimate that 50 billion devices connected to the Internet at 2020 and 2025 this ubiquitous computing have economic impact of 11$ trillion per year which would constitute about 11 percentage of world economy.

Some sensitive application like fire alarm in industry, Health care monitoring system, Disaster detection, Emergency response and other latency sensitive applications make delay for exchanging data to cloud and back to application is unsatisfactory. As mentioned above 50 billion connected devices may produce vast volume of data and transfer the same to cloud for analysis require huge amount of bandwidth. The enormous volume of data for storage and processing cause of latency, network bandwidth, operational reliability, security concerns and so on. For managing enormous, velocity and diverse of data require alternate computing paradigm. The main requirements are to

1. Minimize latency
2. Mitigate the requirements of network bandwidth
3. Improve security of data
4. Increase reliability
5. Collect and secure data across diverse environment
6. Efficient data processing.

To meet all these requirements, the traditional cloud computing paradigm not enough, because all data from edge to the data centre leads to latency. Data from thousands of nodes increase the needs of bandwidth capacity, security and privacy of data leads to high cost. The new paradigm mitigate all such limitation, which analyze data near to the IOT devices that generated and act on it is called as Fog computing.

What Is Fog Computing?

Fog computing is a heterogeneous infrastructure with the aggregation of hardware and software solutions. The smart devices or fog nodes are supervised the processes and services at the edge. Also a device or node with storage, computing and network connectivity can act as a fog node. IDC gauges that the amount of data analyzed that are physically close to IoT is 40 percent ("Fog Computing").The effective process in fog computing is to minimize the network latency is to analyze the data close to the node where it is collected. It reduces the analytics time of data that helps to keep sensitive data inside the network and offloads the network traffic from the core network.

The deployment of fog nodes can be anywhere with the network connection and data from the devices can be analyzed at the edge. The mean line between the cloud and hardware enable efficient analytics,

Figure 19. Fog based network architecture

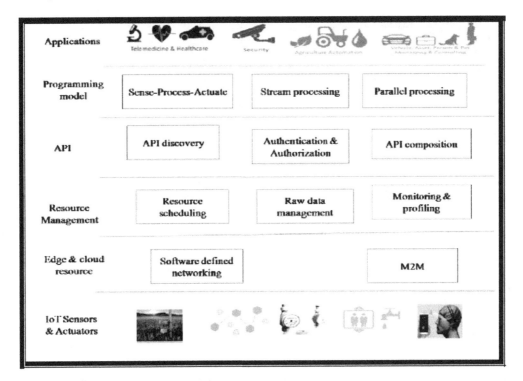

data processing, fetch and storage of data can be attained by minimizing the amount of data which needs to be carry to the cloud.

The fog nodes are diverse in nature and deployed in different environments including access network, core, edge, access points and end points, that uses more collective edge-users to complete a notable volume of storage and communication. The fog architecture promotes a resourceful and seamless management across the different set of platforms.

How Fog Computing Works

At the network edge, developers have to inscribe IoT application for fog nodes at the network edge. The data from the IoT devices are grab by the fog node and it dispatch the divergent data to the optimal location for dissection.

The node at the device edge (fog node) investigate the generated data. Time sensitive data is analyses at the network edge and directs the other data to cloud. The protection and control of time sensitive data has been monitored by fog. The fog nodes in the divergence environment notice the barrier indications and block the barriers by forward the control command to actuators

The aggregation node analysis the data at the network edge so the data remain for milliseconds or seconds to resume the action. In Smart grid application, each subnet have its own aggregation node, the working condition is reported to the downstream node feeder.

The data for historical analysis is send to cloud and big data analytics for long term storage.

Figure 20. Extension of cloud to the fog node (Network edge)

	proximity of Fog nodes	Fog Aggregation nodes	Cloud Infrastructure
Response time	Milliseconds to subseconds	Seconds to minutes	Seconds,minutes,days,weeks
Application examples	Emergency response,Health care	Simple analytics,Visualization	Big data analytics,Historical analysis
IoT data storage	Transient	Short duration:Hours,days or weeks	Months or years
Operating expenses	lower	medium	Comparatively high
Geographic coverage	local	Wider	Global

Features of Fog Computing

Low Latency and Location Awareness

Fog examines most time-sensitive data close to the network edge instead of sending the enormous volume of data to cloud for analysis.

Traffic Proximity

The fog computing carry data close to the user for analytics, cloud catches the numerous volume of data is delivered by the network connected devices and other services. To improve the latency, the services are located close to the user edge. Instead of processing information at cloud or remote data centres fog analyze data at edge of end users.

Geographical Distribution

In centralized cloud environment, fog focus the application and services are widely dispersed environment. For better outcome, data analytics with big data can be done. Location based mobility is helps to traverse over the entire WAN. So edge based computing (fog) can be contented such a way that real time data analytics is turned massive segment.

Mobility and IoT

The mobility of smart device require scheduling technique and resource management, it influence the application performance. The billion of devices connected over the network and data transformation is enormous. The administrators are able to strictly leverage the fog and monitor the access control of users. The control will help to solve security and privacy issues of fog computing. It integrates the heterogeneous data centres with core cloud services

Smart Grid

Smart grid employ smart devices which are responsible for perform a variety of operations which includes smart meters, smart appliances, energy efficient resources, renewable energy resource and manage energy consumptions. During this operation smart grid produce large amount of information that are very difficult to process in cloud. Fog is an edge computing technique and it propose a place for gather, store and process information before direct to cloud servers.

Streaming Applications

Streaming is the real time data generation and continuous process of data in which IoT, the billions of devices connected over the internet and exchange data concurrently to accomplish a specific task. During this concurrent execution data produced by event monitoring, video mining, email, Social media, Ecommerce, Financial transaction, web services etc. At this level the created data series are carry from end device to servers

Security

The sensitive data and applications like health care, emergency response, location based and military applications security is the crucial part. Data requires to be dissembling before sending to the cloud for processing. So time sensitive data can be analyzed at the edge of the network to avoid the latency as well as security. Security is mainly classified into two parts communication and data security. Communication security is termed as data is exchange through secure channel. Data security, data is delivered to anonymous or unintended users. Fog computing helps to eradicate the flaws happen in communication because it process all information at edge instead of transferring to cloud.

Applications of Fog Computing

Apply Fog Computing for various application and few of them are listed.

Healthcare and Activity Tracking

Conventionally, in healthcare the real-time processing and event response are critical. However, Fog computing could be useful in healthcare because the fall-detection learning algorithms are dynamically deployed across edge devices and cloud resources in a proposed work,(Cuo.,2015). Finally the experiments, that concluded with lower response time and energy consumption mitigated than cloud only approaches. Also a fog computing based smart healthcare enables location, privacy awareness, mobility support and low latency,(Stantcher.,2015).

Intelligent Utility Services

Smart cities face challenges from public safety, high energy consumption, sanitation, providing municipal services and traffic congestion, (Zao.,2014). The mentioned, challenges can be addressed by using fog nodes within a IoT networks, fog node capable to compute, store and transfer traffic. An envisioned smart city context require enormous amount of bandwidth space to handle huge volume of traffic generated by diverse smart applications. Most modern smart cities have one or two network providing adequate coverage, that satisfies the needs of existing subscribers and leave little amount of bandwidth for smart municipal services. In order to overcome this challenge and make network optimization, construct fog computing architecture which allows fog nodes to localize the process and storage.

Smart Buildings

Smart building may contains thousand of sensors to measure the operational parameters of building such as key card readers, parking space occupancy, and temperature. Traffic from these sensors is analyzed and takes actions when required, for instance fire alarm may accelerate once smoke is sensed. Edge node or fog node can be making localized processing and optimize the control functions.

CONCLUSION AND FUTURE WORK

The promising thought of the Internet of Things (IoT) is make the modern life, aiming to get better quality life by linking many intelligent and smart devices, technologies, and applications. Everything around us can be get automated by using IoT. This article provides an overview of IoT concept, its permitting technologies, protocols, packages, and the latest studies demanding situations. Also offer an awesome groundwork for researchers and practitioners who are showing interest to know-how within the region of IoT and its technology, protocols to recognize the overall architecture and the functionalities. In addition, a portion of the difficulties and issues that relate to the outline and deployment of IoT implementation and the role of fog computing to optimize the connectivity and storage were discussed.

In future this research can be enhanced with performance evaluation of best suitable protocols for transport layer, application layer in an IoT application and develop a proposed algorithms which is appropriate to provide more security to the IoT systems, all together can be make a IoT structure and implementation can be done using the structure in an effective way, that can be part of the smart city.

REFERENCES

Advanced Message Queuing Protocol. (2008). AMQP-Protocol specification Version 0-9-1, 13.

Ajit, A., Chavana, Mininath, K., & Nighotb. (2015). *Secure and Cost-effective Application Layer Protocol with Authentication Interoperability for IOT*. ICISP 2015, Nagpur, India.

Al-Fuqaha, Guizani, Mohammadi, Aledhari, & Ayyash. (2015). *Internet of Things: A Survey on Enabling Technologies, Protocols, and Applications*. Academic Press.

Alur, R., & Berger, E. (2015). Systems Computing Challenges in the Internet of Things. Academic Press.

Bormann, C., Castellani, A. P., & Shelby, Z. (2012). CoAP: An application protocol for billions of tiny Internet nodes. *IEEE Internet Computing*, *16*(2), 62–67. doi:10.1109/MIC.2012.29

Cao, Y. (2015). FAST: A Fog Computing Assisted Distributed Analytics System to Monitor Fall for Stroke Mitigation. *Proc. 10th IEEE Int'l Conf. Networking, Architecture and Storage (NAS 15)*, 2–11. 10.1109/NAS.2015.7255196

Couldry, N., & Turow, J. (2014). Advertising, big data, and the clearance of the public realm: Marketers' new approaches to thecontent subsidy. *International Journal of Communication*, 8, 1710–1726.

Dunkels, A., Eriksson, J., & Tsiftes, N. (2011). Low-power interoperabilityfor the IPv6-based Internet of Things. *Proc. 10thScandinavian Workshop Wireless ADHOC*, 10-11.

Esposito, C., Russo, S., & Di Crescenzo, D. (2008). Performance assessment of OMG compliant data distribution middleware. *Proc. IEEE IPDPS*, 1–8. 10.1109/IPDPS.2008.4536566

Extensible Messaging Presence Protocol. (n.d.). Retrieved from http//tools.ietf.org.rfc6120

Fernandes, J. L., Lopes, I. C., Rodrigues, J. J. P. C., & Ullah, S. (2013). Performance evaluation of RESTful web services and AMQP protocol. *Proc. 5th ICUFN*, 810–815.

Fog Computing and the Internet of Things. (n.d.). Retrieved from www.cisco.com/go/iot-Whitepaper

Gade, Gade, & Ugander Reddy. (2016). *Internet of Things (LOT) for Smart Cities- The Future Technology Revolution*. Academic Press.

Lengyel, L., & Ekler, P. (2015). SensorHUB: An IoT Driver Framework for Supporting Sensor Networks and Data. Hindawi Publishing Corporation.

Lerche, C., Hartke, K., & Kovatsch, M. (2012). Industry adoption of the Inter-net of Things: A constrained application protocol survey. *Proc. IEEE17th Conf. ETFA*, 1–6.

Li, S., Wang, H., Xu, T., & Zhou, G. (2011). Application study on internet of things in environment protection field. *LectureNotes in Electrical Engineering*, *133*(2), 99–106.

Locke, D. (2010). *MQ telemetry transport (MQTT) v3. 1 protocol specification*. Available Http://Www. Ibm.Com/Developerworks/ Webservices/Library/Ws-Mqtt/Index.Html

Modadugu, N., & Rescorla, E. (2004). The Design and Implementation of Datagram TLS. *Proceedings of the Network and Distributed System Security Symposium*.

Ovidiuvermison & Friess. (2014). Internet of things-From research, innovation to market deployment. River Publishers.

Riahi, Challal, Natalizio, Chtourou, & Bouabdallah. (2013). A systemic approach for IoT security. IEEE.

SmartThings I Home automation, home security, and peace of mind. (2014). Available: http://www. smartthings.com

Stantchev, V. (2015). Smart Items, Fog and Cloud Computing as Enablers of Servitization in Healthcare. *J. Sensors & Transducers*, *185*(2), 121–128.

What the Internet of Things (IoT) needs to become a reality. (2015). Retrieved from www.freescale. com-White paper-2015

Zao, J. (2014). Augmented Brain Computer Interaction Based on Fog Computing and Linked Data. *Proc. 10th IEEE Int'l Conf. Intelligent Environments (IE 14)*, 374–377. 10.1109/IE.2014.54

Chapter 8

Internet of Things (IoT) Technologies, Architecture, Protocols, Security, and Applications:
A Survey

B. Baranidharan
Madanapalle Institute of Technology and Science, India

ABSTRACT

Internet of things (IoT) is a rapidly developing technology that connects various kinds of smart miniature things such as smart medical alert watches, smart vehicles, smart phones, smart running shoes, etc. Smart devices are connected through internet and can communicate to other smart devices in any part of the world in an automated manner. IoT environment often uses constrained devices with low energy, low processing capability, and low memory space. In order to prevent communication failure, a special kind of architecture is needed for IoT. This chapter presents a review of the basic architecture model, communication protocol of IoT, security aspects of IoT, and various IoT applications such as smart agriculture, water management, smart healthcare, smart home, smart industry, and smart vehicles.

INTRODUCTION

Internet of Things (IoT) is the technology which enables these smart devices to connect with each other through internet to exchange data among themselves without any human interference. These devices are characterized of low processing and memory (Atzori, Iera, & Morabito, 2010). IoT promises to change the entire world by connecting very large number of devices which is also termed as things and software which results in effective analytics over the large volume of collected data from these devices. This kind of Big Data analytics enables the users to get the more accurate information and reveal the hidden details of the phenomena which improve the decision making process a lot (Sun, Song, Jara, & Bie, 2016). IoT

DOI: 10.4018/978-1-5225-5972-6.ch008

connects things such as personal digital assistant devices, vehicles, buildings, animals, plants, soil etc. to the internet. Smart devices contains different types of sensor for sensing various physical phenomena and special kind of device called an actuator can also be added in order to control the environment.

With the help of IoT gateway, the sensed data will be transmitted to the cloud system where the data will be processed and stored for the future analytics. Certain high rank application of IoT: smart home, smart farming, smart city, smart healthcare, smart vehicle, smart industry, etc. Beyond these applications, novel IoT application has been proposed in sports, Ikram, Alshehri, & Hussain, (2015) discussed about IoT Football architecture for monitoring footballer in a match or training period. In future, sports become one of the applications in IoT, but there are some obstacles in IoT like standardized protocol demands, security challenges, etc. The main advantage of IoT is assuring the communication between anyone to anything at any time.

Traditional Machine to Machine (M2M) communication like point to point (P2P) tumble into IoT based communication model. Verma et al. (2016) reviewed M2M applications needs like interoperability, ultra-scalable connectivity, and heterogeneity. IoT satisfies the application needs and it builds a Ubiquities connectivity using M2M communication to bring smartness to the applications. To build an IoT application the following technologies play a major role, they are: (i) Radio Frequency Identifier (RFID), (ii) Bluetooth Low Energy (BLE), (iii) IPv6 over Low power Wireless Personal Area Networks (6LoWPAN), (iv) ZigBee, etc. Jara, Ladid, & Gómez-Skarmeta (2013) surveyed IPv6 Challenges, Solutions and Opportunities for IoT and suggested to enable devices with IPv6 technology is to be the first step to connect people, things, and services.

WSN in IoT

Wireless Sensor Network (WSN) is an important part of an IoT application (Kim & Jung, 2017). WSN is the inter-network of miniature sensor nodes in large scale. These sensor nodes collect the real time data about the environment and report it periodically or event base. Periodic data collection requires the data reporting at fixed time intervals whereas event based requires reporting when an event occurs. Since the sensor nodes are having battery power supply lifetime is an important problem in it. Also, the IoT applications suffer because of this lifetime problem in WSN. So the WSN should be designed and modeled considering the nature of IoT application in which it is used.

Key Challenges in IoT

Still now, IoT is in the budding stage of development and needs lot of focus in it. Some of the major challenges (Granjal, Monteiro, & Silva, 2015) in the implementation of IoT are mentioned below.

1. **Connectivity:** An IoT application is built upon heterogeneous devices such as sensor nodes, gateway nodes, RFID devices, electronic readers, actuation devices, etc. When these devices are connected together for an application in wireless fashion there is a need for commonly accepted standard. Unfortunately, for any IoT application there is no such universally accepted standard for connectivity.
2. **Confidentiality:** It is about keeping the data hidden to the users apart from those authorized for that. Since the devices used in IoT are of low processing power, suitable cryptographic algorithms should be designed for it.

3. **Authentication:** It is the process of verifying the users who are the authenticated to use the data.
4. **Access:** Various levels of users will be there for an application. According to the given privileges, users should be allowed to access the data and apply analytics over that.

Country Wise Investment in IoT

- **Europe:** IoT European Research Cluster (IERC) (European Research Commission, 2015) is a consortium for promoting Europe as an information and knowledge society. More than 100 million Euros have been invested in various research projects for building smart cities, smart grids, intelligent transportation, Health care, etc.
- **USA:** According to BI intelligence, US have invested $8.8 billion in 2015 and $7.7 billion in 2014 which clearly depicts $1.1 billion rise in a year (Business Insider, 2016). Between 2011 and 2015, $35 billion is invested by the US government for IoT which is higher than any other fields in the same time. According to the Samsung Corporation (2017), an investment worth of $1.2 billion is planned to be invested for IoT based R&D in US market.
- **China:** China has given prominent importance for the implementation of IoT based smart cities, transportation in their new 12th five year plan (Ministry of Industry and Information Technology of China, 2012; Muralidharan, Roy, & Saxena, 2016).
- **South Korea:** Korea comes next to US in terms of state investment in the development of IoT technology. So far, $27.8 million (Muralidharan, Roy, & Saxena, 2016) has been invested by the government for developing smart cities, smart grids, etc.

The rest of this paper is organized as follows: Section 2 explains about IoT building blocks, Section 3 about layered architecture of the IoT, Communication protocols are discussed in Section 4, Section 5 presents some of the IoT implementations in various domains, Section 6 discusses about security issues in IoT, Section 7 about the role of Big Data Analytics and Section 8 about Fog computing in IoT applications. Finally, Section 9 concludes with a summary.

Figure 1. Represent the general model of IoT framework

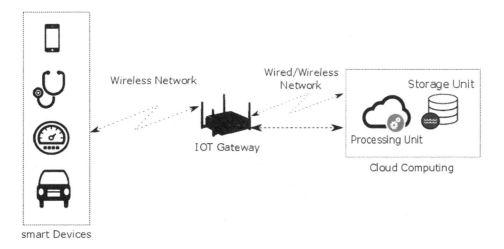

IOT BUILDING BLOCKS

IoT is built of so many subsystems. The basic building blocks (Al - Fuqaha, Guizani, Mohammadi, Aledhari, & Ayyash, 2015) is given below,

1. **Identification:** Each object should be identified uniquely using an Electronic Product Code (EPC) or unique code (uCode). Since, there is no universal standard for addressing like IP for computers, separate kind of addressing can be used for IoT devices.
2. **Sensing:** Sensor nodes are the important component of the IoT applications. Any type of sensors like temperature, pressure, humidity, etc. connected in the Arudino, Raspberry Pi kits will be the part of this component.
3. **Communication:** Since IoT is made of heterogeneous devices, the communication technologies like Wi-Fi, LTE, LTE-A, Bluetooth, Bluetooth Low Energy (BLE), Zigbee, RFID tags and reader are used according to the need.
4. **Computation:** It involves both hardware and software components. Arduino, Raspberry Pi, Intel Galileo are the most familiar microcontroller used in most of the applications. Conitiki Real Time Operating System, TinyOS, LiteOS, RiteOS are the familiar operating system for the IoT hardware devices.
5. **Services:** Services are the application end needs to be provided by the IoT hardware and software. Smart homes, smart grids, smart cities are some of the major services of the IoT applications.
6. **Semantics:** It is the capability of the IoT to infer new knowledge from the collected data. A proper data modeling is required to extract maximum information from it.

Thus, the above mentioned entities are essential for building and implementing an IoT application.

IOT ARCHITECTURE

Institute of Electrical and Electronics Engineers Standards Association (IEEE Standard Associations, 2016) project P2413 has recommended a three layered architecture for the IoT applications. The layers are as follows: (i) Sensing layer, (ii) Networking and Data Communication, (iii) Application layer. Figure 2 illustrate the IoT layer blocks. But in general a four layered architecture which is given below is more suitable for most of the IoT applications.

Perception Layer

The first layer of is perception layer is also called as device layer or sensing layer. The physical device like sensors, actuators and other sensing devices which will collect the environmental data are the components in this layer. The collected data will be sent to the network layer either directly or with the help of IoT gateway. To transfer data between sensing device and IoT gateway which will make use of wireless communication technologies like Zigbee, Bluetooth, BLE, 6LowPAN. RFID tags used for identification of a product also fall under this layer only.

Figure 2. Architecture model of IoT framework

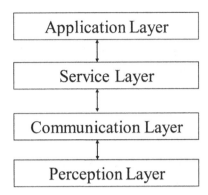

Communication Layer

The data communication happens in this layer, the data collected from the sensing layer are transferred to the application layer via this communication layer. The data collected from the IoT gateway will be sent to the remote location (cloud unit) for storing and processing. All the gateway nodes will be coming under this layer. In general, to send data to the higher layer the telecommunication network technologies are used: PSTN, ISDN, 2G/3G or LTE networks.

Service Layer

Cloud storage and analytics processing are the part of this layer. This layer used for storing, processing, visualizing the sensed data. Sensing layer data are processed and stored in the form of information which satisfies customer request.

Application Layer

It is the user interface part of an IoT application. The outcome of this layer is based on customer initiative service request. The service request is categories into different types: smart home, smart industry, smart city, smart healthcare, smart vehicle, and smart agriculture. Application layer also provides manageability option for sensing layer devices.

COMMUNICATION PROTOCOL IN IOT

Traditional communication protocols are not suitable in the constrained node network (IoT network). Different protocols development organizations are working to create new protocols for IoT and currently proposed Many IoT standard protocols. Some protocol standard groups like Internet Engineering Task Force (IETF), EPC global, Institute of Electrical and Electronics Engineers (IEEE) and the European Telecommunications Standards Institute (ETSI), some common protocols and it is functions are discussed in this section.

Application Protocol

- **Message Queuing Telemetry Transport (MQTT):** Andy Stanford-Clark and Arlen Nipper was designing the first version of the MQTT protocol in 1999.The Organization for the Advancement for Structured Information System (OASIS) released MQTT version 3.1.1 in 29 the October 2014. It is a too simple and lightweight publish/subscribe messaging protocol, designed for constrained devices and low-bandwidth, high-latency or unreliable networks. The protocol is mainly designed for minimizing network bandwidth and device resource requirements. These principles also turn out to make the protocol ideal of the emerging "machine-to-machine" (M2M) or "Internet of Things" world of connected devices, and for mobile applications where bandwidth and battery power are at a premium. The connection modes using MQTT are: (i) one to one, (ii) one to many and (iii) many to many. *Subscriber*, *Publisher* and *Broker* are the three main elements of MQTT. Any devices which are interested in data of a particular type would register itself as a *Subscriber* to the *Broker* element. When a device generates data it reports the data to the *Broker* as the *Publisher*.

Aziz (2016) analyzed three levels of MQTT Quality of Service (QOS): (i) At most once, (ii) At least once, (iii) Exactly once between sender and receiver message. Finally he concluded that the third QOS level was potentially vulnerable.

Various application like personal health care, environmental monitoring, notifications App uses MQTT as their communication model.

- **Constrained Application Protocol (CoAP):** Shelby, Hartke, & Bormann (2014) worked together for CoAP in Request for Comments (RFC) publication (RFC 7252). Internet Engineering Task Force (IETF) Constrained RESTful environments (CoRE) Working Group develop and standardized CoAP protocol. This protocol is designed for the low power device to communicate through the web. CoAP has the request/response communication model between client and server. This protocol is designed for low- power Machine to Machine communication. It uses HTTP's get, put, post and delete method in mobile application environment. CoAP features are Asynchronous message exchanges, simple proxy and caching capabilities, URI and Content-type support, etc. COAP provide reliability in unicast and multicast request.

CoAP has two layers:

1. **Message Layer:** It controls the message flow between two end points of the IoT application. It uses four types of messages and they are,
    a. **Confirmable:** Needs confirmation from other end. The response can be sent as a separate message or piggybacked.
    b. **Non-Confirmable:** It does not need any confirmation or acknowledgement.
    c. **Acknowledgement:** Used for giving acknowledgement to the previous messages.
    d. **Reset**: Used when confirmation messages cannot be processed for any reasons.
2. **Request/Response Layer:** It matches the response to the given request thus ensures reliability over the message exchanges.

- **Extensible Messaging and Presence Protocol (XMPP):** Initially, Jabber open-source community was developing this protocol in 1999, then The Internet Engineering Task Force (IETF) formed an XMPP working group in 2002.The protocol is designed for XML (Extensible Markup Language) based message-oriented middleware. XMPP is allowed to send the small pieces of structured data (XML stanzas) over a network between any two or more things. Saint - Andre (2009) reviewed the XMPP protocol and summarized, Thus, XMPP protocol is services codebase and not a single protocol. It has rich features and various technology ecosystems.

- **Advanced Message Queuing Protocol (AMQP):** The Advancement of Structured Information System (OASIS) organization released AMQP protocol version 1.0on 29 October 2012. AMQP is an open standard application layer protocol initially for business messaging like transaction message. AMQP is a binary protocol and it support heterogeneous messaging applications. Message broker is used between publisher and subscriber. It uses two key component exchange and queues to ensure publisher message is sent to correct subscriber. Luzuriaga, Perez, Boronat, Cano, Calafate, & Manzoni (2015) evaluated AMQP in mobile or dynamic networks like vehicular networks. In this paper he presented an experimental evaluation of protocol in different scenarios. Based on the results, it is proved that AMQP supports to build reliable, scalable, and advanced clustering messaging infrastructures over an ideal wireless local area network (WLAN) and offers better security.

- **Data-Distribution Service for Real-Time Systems (DDS):** DDS is also a broker-less based publish and subscribe architecture. DDS is machine to machine (M2M) middleware standard developed by the Object Management Group (OMG). It uses multicasting to provide Quality of Service (QoS) and high reliability of its applications. Broker-less publish-subscribe architecture is highly suitable for real-time constraints which occurs frequently in M2M communications. Thus DDS ensures scalable, real-time, dependable, high-performance and interoperable data exchanges between publishers and subscriber.

Service Discovery Protocols

- **Multicast DNS (mDNS):** Cheshire & Krochmal (2013) had contributed to develop mDNS. It uses existing DNS protocol DNS message structure, name syntax, and resource record types. Clients send DNS-like queries via IP multicast. Generally, miniature network devices will be having less configuration details and not suitable to interact with DNS servers directly. Multicast DNS (mDNS) performs like DNS in the local link of these miniature device networks without a conventional Unicast DNS server. In addition, Multicast DNS provides free DNS namespace for local use. The benefits of Multicast DNS names are that (i) they require little or no configuration details, (ii) they can work without any major infrastructure, and (iii) they work during infrastructure failures.

- **DNS Service Discovery (DNS-SD):** DNS Service Discovery is a way of using standard DNS programming interfaces, servers, and packet formats to browse the network for services. DNS-SD and mDNS are the complementary technologies that can be used together. DNS-SD is not dependent on Multicast DNS, it also works with unicast. Hybrid unicast and multicast DNS service discovery can help the device for wide-area service discovery. Jara, Martinez-Julia, & Skarmeta (2012) proposed Light-weight multicast DNS and DNS-SD (lmDNS-SD) for IOT devices. lmDNS-SD is used for resource discovery for the devices connected on IPv6. The Sender uses Multicast IP for broadcasting name query in the network. When a device name is matched with the name in the query a reply message is sent back to the sender along with the IP address of the device. All the devices in the network receive the reply message and update the IP address along with the device name in its name cache. lmDNS-SD technique supports the IoT devices for its name query operation in Local Area Network (LAN). Minimum name length is also used in lmDNS-SD techniques. lmDNS-SD addresses many issues like scalability, IoT device mobility, switching between sleep and wakeup mode, etc in a typical IoT network.

Infrastructure Protocols

- **IPv6 Over Low Power Wireless Personal Area Networks (6LowPAN):** Kushalnagar, Montenegro, & Schumacher (2007) documented Request for Comments: 4919 (RFC 4919) for 6LoWPAN. The IETF 6LoWPAN working group has started developing specifications for transmitting IPv6 over IEEE 802.15.4 networks. 6LoWPAN is a low-power wireless network where every node has its own IPv6 address, allowing it to connect directly to the Internet. 6LoWPAN compress packet header to reduce packet size suitable for IoT device communication. IPv6 packet structure is also designed to be easily sent and received over IEEE 802.15.4 network. 6LowPAN has small packet size supports low bandwidth, star and mesh topologies, battery enabled devices, and long idle periods during which communication interfaces are turned off to save energy. Packet fragmentation also enables the packets to get fit in IEEE 802.15.4 network. Based on this approach, physical layer bandwidth utilization will be reduced a lot.
- **Bluetooth Low Energy (BLE):** Bluetooth Special Interest Group designed BLE and specification version is 4.0. BLE is not supported with previous version of the Bluetooth classic for backward compatibility and it had been mainly developed to reduce power consumption and new applications like smart healthcare, smart home, etc. In the lowest level of BLE's stack there is a Physical Layer which transmits and receives bits and above Link Layer services includes medium access, connection establishment, error control, and flow control mechanisms. Then, the Logical Link Control and Adaptation Protocol (L2CAP) provide multiplexing of data channels, fragmentation and reassembly of larger packets. The other upper layers are Generic Attribute protocol (GATT) which provides efficient data collection from sensors, and Generic Access Profile (GAP) that allows the application for configuration and operation in different modes such as advertising or scanning, connection initiation and management. BLE performance was analyzed by Cho, Park, Cho, Seo, Han (2016), and it is found out that the wide range of BLE parameters provide high flexibility for BLE devices to get customized efficiently in various applications scenarios.
- **Z-Wave:** Z-Wave is a wireless communication protocol used primarily for home automation. ZenSys was initially developed this protocol later took over by Sigma Designs. Now, the formal association of Z-Wave alliance focuses on both expansion of Z-Wave and the continued interoperability between the devices which uses Z-Wave. Z-Wave covers about 30 meter point-to-point communication and particularly suitable for applications that need tiny data transmission like light control, household appliance control, smart energy and HVAC, access control, wearable health care control and fire detection. There are two different types of nodes are used in Z-Wave architecture: (i) Controller and (ii) Slave nodes. Controller node governs the slave node and it is maintaining the routing table. Source based routing method is used where the destination path is specified inside the packet by the controller. Gomez & Paradells (2010) used Z-Wave for their Wireless Home Automation Network model since it is proprietary free.

- **ZigBee:** It is a yet another wireless networking technology developed by the ZigBee Alliance for low-data rate and short-range applications. ZigBee is built on 2.4 GHz industrial, scientific and medical (ISM) radio band which is freely available worldwide. ZigBee provides security function across the four main layer layers in protocol stacks: (i) Physical layer (PHY), (ii) Medium access control layer (MAC), (iii) Network layer, and (iv) Application (APL) layer. The two layers PHY and MAC are defined as same as in IEEE 802.15.4 standard and other layers are defined by the ZigBee alliance. Latest version ZigBee is capable of determining device types including home automation, lighting, energy management, smart appliance, security, sensors, and health care monitoring products. Elarabi, Deep, & Rai (2015) mentioned that ZigBee is more suitable for IoT because of its low power and low data rate nature.

- **IEEE 802.15.4:** IEEE proposed the IEEE 802.15.4 (2015) standard for Low Rate Wireless Personal Area Network (LR-WPAN). IEEE 802.15.4 gives the specifications for physical (PHY) and medium access layers (MAC). PHY layers specifies frequency, power, modulation, and other wireless conditions of the link and MAC layer specifies the format of the data in LR-WPAN. IEEE802.15.4 is widely used in IoT, M2M, and WSNs due to its low power consumption, low data rate, low cost and high message throughput. It provides a reliable communication, operability on different platforms and can handle large number of nodes in a LR-WPAN. It also provides the high level of security, encryption and authentication services but the main disadvantage is it's incompatibility to provide QoS guarantees. To avoid collisions, IEEE 802.15.4 MAC layer uses the CSMA/CA protocol.

- **EPC Global:** It is an organization for the development of Electronic Product Code (EPC) and RFID technology. EPC is a unique identification number which is stored on an RFID tag for identifying things. It is a promising technique to support the primary IoT requirements such as objects IDs and service discovery. The RFID system can be divided into two main components: (i) Radio signal transponder (tag) and (ii) Tag reader. In tag, a chip is used to store the unique identity of the object and an antenna for communication with tag readers through radio waves. The tag reader generates a radiofrequency field to identify objects through reflected radio waves of the tag. RFID works by sending the tag's number to the tag reader through radio waves. After that, the reader passes that identification number to a specific computer application to get the tag's details from a database. The underlying architecture uses Internet based RFID technologies along with cheap RFID tags and readers to share product information.

- **XBee:** XBee (n.d.) is the brand name of the wireless communication technology from Digi International. It is designed based on IEEE802.15.4 with the bit rate of 250Kbps. The performance of XBee is better than Bluetooth and Wi-Fi because of it's comparatively less wakeup time and improved security features.

IOT APPLICATIONS

From home to manufacturing industry all environments are getting smarter with help of IoT, this kind of approaches are specified into special names such as connected or smart home, smart healthcare, smart agriculture, smart vehicle or connected vehicle, smart cities, smart wearable device, smart industries, etc. in this section some potential area of IoT application are discussed.

IoT Application in Agriculture

Smart farming system utilizes the agricultural resources like water supply, from lands, seeds, fertilizer, etc. in the most efficient and optimized manner and increases the agricultural productivity. IoT implementations in agriculture increase the quality, quantity, sustainability and cost effectiveness of agricultural production and also support quick delivery to the market. In this section, IoT based smart agriculture models are reviewed.

Rad, Hancu, Takacs, & Olteanu (2015) proposed precision agriculture or satellite, forming prototype in monitoring potato crops vegetation status based on Cyber-Physical System (CPS). CPS model is most of the time based on IOT, WSN, M2M technologies. CPS architecture has four layers and they are (i) Sensing layer, (ii) Network layer, (iii) Decision layer and (iv) Application layer. In physical layer, the vegetation status of potato crop is collected through different types of sensors, human, multispectral terrestrial mobile mechatronics system, multispectral autonomous (a real mobile mechatronics) system. In network level, the sensor nodes are connected through wireless mode and acts as interface between physical and decision layer. In decision layer, the spatial information of the farm field is processed and analyzed. In the application layer, a suitable solution for the crop problems is given to the end users. Based on this approach, the effort of the human workers will be reduced. At the end, continuous monitoring of the crop leads to increased productivity.

Hu & Qian (2011) proposed the Crop Growth Model (CGM) for IOT based agriculture. This model has three layers: (i) sensor layer, (ii) network layer and (iii) application layer. The sensor layer consists of temperature, humidity and carbon dioxide density sensors. For a better crop growth, suitable temperature, humidity and carbon dioxide are required, so these sensors are used in this model. CGM works based on the software approach at the application layer. WSN collect crop condition from the farm field and report to the network layer through the base station. Then, the network layer takes the responsibility of transferring the data to the application layer. From application layer, the data will be further sent to the database. CGM accesses the stored data from the database for further processing. CGM algorithm computes the parameters like time to irrigate, time to fertilize and time to alarm using the analytical model. Irrigation model helps to find the future water consumption of crop based on the farm land condition data and daily weather data. Fertilize model also functions in the same way like irrigation model. Suppose if crop faces inappropriate environment for its growth, an alarm will be given to the farmers. To get better solution from CGM model, more number of input parameter can be used.

Novel technique of smart beehive is proposed by Edward - Murphy, Magno, Whelan, Halloran, & Popovici (2016). Wireless Sensor Networks (WSN) is used to boost up the development of smart beehive. WSN helps to find beehive internal condition and bee colony activities without beekeeper interaction. In the system design, Zigbee enabled wireless sensor nodes are fixed inside the beehive. Each sensor node is connected to the base station to transmit the generated data. Again the base station reports to the cloud environment for predicting the condition of the individual beehive. Two types of sensor nodes are used: Gas Level Node (GLN) and General Condition Node (GCN). GLN monitor air contamination and GCN monitor temperature, humidity and acceleration of the beehive. The entire activities are controlled by two algorithms: (i) Threshold Based Algorithm (TBA) and (ii) Decision Tree Algorithm (DTA). TBA is used for beekeeping and biological analysis. DTA is used for classifying the condition of the beehive based on collected beehive status data. Proposed techniques help for automatic maintenance the bee colony.

Baranwal & Pateriya (2016) proposed a smart security mechanism for implementing IoT in agriculture. Agriculture level securities are prevention from insects, rodent attacks in farm field or grain stores.

The proposed smart security architecture has three layers. In Perception layer, different sensors and web cameras are used for identifying agricultural attack. Heat sensor identifies the motion of the rodent whereas URD sensor calculates the distance of the rodent and activates the web camera for snapshots. Like in other works, Network layer acts as interface between perception layer and application layer. After processing the data in the application layer, the event will be notified to the user through SMS.

Ryu, Yun, Miao, Ahn, Choi, &Kim (2016) developed smart farm prototype with the help of IOT technology. IOT helps to connect farmland into internet for building an automated farm system. Two major infrastructure components are used in the proposed prototype: Cube and Mobius. Cube is the IOT gateway software and Mobius is the IOT service platform. Sensors will collect the farmland information and transmits to the IoT gateway, then from gateway to Mobius. Representational State Transfer (REST) interface is used at the Mobius. Through smart phone, users can control the farm land activities using Mobius service. An automated controlled farming system is envisaged and it consists of controller likes intake fan and exhausts fan, an air conditioner with heating and cooling, an irrigation and nutrient management system.

Ruan & Shi (2016) provides an IOT based framework for monitoring and maintaining fruit freshness in the e- commerce industry. The framework consists of eight modules and they are farmed module, vehicle module, Local Processing Center (LPC) module, End Distribution Center (EDC) module, customer module, communication module, server module, terminal module. All modules are between the two extreme ends: farm land and the end customer. These modules collects data regarding farm land conditions, fruit freshness, fruit location, etc. through the specialized sensors and IOT devices. Prediction and assessment technique used in this work is based on four attributes: fruit, operation, environment and time. Fruit represent values of perish ability and pressure resistance, operation represent what operations are present between farm land and customer like transport to LPC, transport to EDC, environment about transit level and time about how much time taken for each operation. Based on the above attributes, new fruit environment is constructed and gives an optimal solution for controlling the freshness of the fruit

IoT Application in Smart Home

Few branded smart home devices are currently occupying our homes like nest learning thermistor, Philips smart home lighting and air quality egg, etc. But in the future, home refrigerator may send message to home owners and intimate to purchase unavailable food items. Bedroom Television may show the status of automated cooking devices in kitchen whereas television remote can provide an option to control the kitchen device. In a smart home environment, all the electrical devices including light and fan can be remotely controlled. Smart home system saves time, energy and money for homeowners. In this section, IoT applications in smart home models are reviewed.

Khan, Din, Jabbar, Gohar, Ghayvat, & Mukhopadhyay (2016) developed the context- aware low power intelligent smart home which is an IoT based smart home architecture model. CLP-i-smart Home is based on internet centric approach where the cloud environment is responsible for storage, computing, visualization, and analytics. CLP-i-smart home consist of three units, (i) application unit, (ii) data analysis unit, and (iii) visualization unit. Application unit represents the smart home end devices, personal health care system, etc. In personal health care application unit, multiple sensors will be attached over the different parts of our body. Among them a coordinator node is responsible for communicating with the primary mobile device (PMD). For end to end communication, each sensor node at smart home level and PMD level has a Global unique device identifier (GDDI). For device connectivity two communication models are used and they are: (i) BLE and (ii) Zigbee. The BLE is choice for communication within a room and ZigBee is used for the entire house coverage. The sensor and actuator devices can be controlled from outside the home environment also by using 3G/4G networks. Thus CLP-i provided a new framework for device connectivity in a Home automation system.

Collotta & Pau (2015) has proposed a new energy aware scheduling of field device in the home automation applications. In this work, the internal device level optimization is given more importance than in design level. In general, Bluetooth Low Energy (BLE) works in the optimized way compared to the Bluetooth mechanism. In this work, further the energy saving techniques of BLE is enhanced using Fuzzy Logic approach. In the proposed techniques all the field devices (FD) have to report its status like remaining energy and TH/WL (ratio of throughput and work load) to the centralized master node. The master node calculates the sleeping time of each FD using the Fuzzy logic where devices remaining energy and TH/WL are the inputs and the sleeping time is the output. Thus, based on the above factors, each field device will be activated to conserve the energy of the networked device.

Chhabra & Gupta (2016) proposes IoT based smart home design for energy and security management. The proposed model has three elements: (i) End sensors, (ii) single board computer, and (iii) smart phone. Three types of sensors are used and they are temperature sensors, smoke sensor, and Passive Infrared (PIR) motion sensor. An Ethernet based Intel Galileo 2nd Generation Board is used for connecting sensors into internet for monitoring and it use relay module to control home devices. Data generated by the sensors is sent to the server for user view and the energy consumption details of the home device to user smart phone. Smart phone application can switch off or switch on home device through voice command or touch the control buttons. The smoke sensing unit is helping to fire alert to the home owner on internet. Based on this approach, home device lifetime will be increased and maintenance risk will be reduced.

Mano, et al (2016) proposed IoT based smart home for healthcare monitoring system. Smart Architecture for In- Home Health care (SAHHc) consist of two components: sensors and decision maker. Wearable sensors are used for monitor patient health and cameras are used for home ambient monitoring, etc. SAHHc levels are divided into three levels. In level 0, embedded devices are used for patient identification, measuring the face expression of the patients, etc. In level 1, local server is used for decision making over the collected sensed data. In level 2, cloud server is used for processing, storing and applying analytics over it. When a person enters the home, SAHHc detect whether he is the authenticated resident person, then the entered person is a patient or not. Visual-based resident tracking technique is used for monitoring face expression of the patients and their current health status. Decision maker use the technique and send intimation to patient helper (nurse) via mobile notification. Based on this approach, home healthcare system gets smarter than ever.

Bhide & Wagh (2015) proposed an IoT based Intelligent Self-Learning System (ISLS) for home automation. Sensors are used for monitoring home appliances. Light sensor, temperature sensor, etc. are used and the generated information is sent to the home PC. Analysis happens over the collected information in home PC and based on that PC controls the home appliances through driver control. Suppose any device fault is identified, immediately home PC send the information to server for data mining. In remote server, a particular service provider may be chosen and the information is forwarded to them through SMS or E-Mail. ISLS system is designed in such a way to identify faults in home appliances and send notification to service provider. Service provider will directly visit to home for service without resident contribution.

Wang, Lo, Bhimani, & Sugiura (2015) proposed an another such IoT based home appliances monitoring and controlling system. The proposed model has three components: (i) Environment sensor, (ii)

User controller and (iii) User interface. Sensors are used for measuring home temperature, luminance, flow velocity, humidity, etc. Then, the sensor data are sent to the connected single board controller for further processing of it. At last, the necessary control is given to the home appliances. Also, Smart hand held devices (smart phone) are used to control the home appliance manually. User can set task based on environmental changes and a single triggering action can control multiple home appliances. In this system home users are free from the worry of device operation.

Kalaivanan & Manoharan (2016) has proposed an IoT based smart home using Low Power Wireless (LPW) technology. It is made up of five components: (i) Sensor devices and ZigBee module, (ii) Control module, (iii) Local Area Network (LAN), (iv) Internet server and (v) Smart phone application. LPW ZigBee module is used for communication between sensors and control modules. Control module is connected with LAN which sends data to server. Internet server store received data and process it for further actions. ZigBee gets easily connected with different sensors and home appliances control units like air quality sensor, gas sensor, fan control, etc. Based on this approach, home automation monitoring and control module power consumption will be reduced and made much simpler than other models.

IoT Application in Smart Industry

IoT is playing a major role in the Fourth industrial revolution (industry 4.0). Automation and industry data exchange become much smarter than ever in the industrial history. Some of the benefits of using IoT in industries are increased efficiency in the utilization of machines and workers, workers safety, Easiness in handling machines, etc. In this section, the application of IoT in smart industry is reviewed.

Kaur &Sood (2015) proposed cognitive based employee evaluation in smart industry. Manual decision making in employee evaluation have lot of error and less accurate. In the proposed work, employee evaluation is automated with the help of the IOT devices. In the industry prototype, the working environments are monitored with IOT sensing devices and the location of the employee is tracked with the help of GPS. The sensors placed at the work place sends the report about the employee involvement in each task to the Information processing system (IPS). Then in IPS the employee involvement in the task or particular work is evaluated. IPS is made up of data conversion block (DCB), employee evaluation block (EEB) and decision making block (DMB). DCB classify the employee activities into positive, negative, natural from different kind of employee activities. Based on these activities, profit and loss of the industries is calculated. EEB helps to find the relation between particular activity and employee. DMB uses the game theory model for evaluating the employee for the getting rewards or not. At the end, cognitive decision making system provides greater accuracy compared to manual decision making system in employee evaluation.

Almobaideen, Allan, & MahaSaadeh (2016) proposed IOT technology in tourism industry. Convenience and Accessibility based Smart Tourism-destination Approach (CASTA) is the IoT model proposed in this work. Three main components of CASTA are wireless sensors, control unit and Hand Held Device (HHD). In the tourist spots, wireless sensors will be monitoring the important parameters like air quality, visitor's count, etc. The information of the tourist spot is sent to the sensor gateway, and then it is transferred to Control Unit (CU). CU stores received data into Tourism Location Database (TLD). TLD is one of the database among the geographical and transportation database, the network coverage database, which are connected to CU for computation. CU is enabled at cloud and process based on tourist request. GPS enabled HHD (smart phone) is used on tourist side for communication with CASTA. Tourist send message request about particular tourism site to CU. CU send appropriate information likes shortest path to reach the destination, transportation information to tourist.

Shih & Wang (2016) developed a Cold Chain management System (CCM) targeted for food industry. Wireless Sensors (WS) are used for monitoring temperature of frozen food from cooking point up to the end delivery point. CCS framework also helps to find the appropriate time of moving a food product from frozen storage to cool storage. Four types of sensors are used to monitor the situation during the preparation of braised pork (food product), they are: (i) Portable wireless sensors, (ii) wire thermocouple sensors, (iii) needle thermocouple sensors, and (iv) environmental wireless sensors. In different stages of food processing such as cooking, ambient, cool-storage warehouse, tally process, cabinet and vehicle deliveries, and re-cooking processes temperature needs to be monitored. CCM will support various services of corporate food industry such as cold chain home delivery service, CVS indirect delivery, CVS direct delivery and flight kitchen service.

Hao, Zhang, Liu, & Qin (2015) has come with an integrated IOT solution for managing the chemical industrial park. IOT based Industrial Information Management (IIM) easily provides pre-accident warning and post-accident rescue necessary with service support and provides a valuable decision-making support system. IIM framework is divided into three levels: (i) sensing level, (ii) network level and (iii) cloud computing level. In sensing level, different sensing devices like infrared along with RFID devices are used. Data transfer to cloud through wire and wireless communication is handled in network level. In cloud computing level, collected data is processed into information for different user interface application like environmental monitoring, logistic management, emergency rescues, etc. The entire application can be handled by park administration center, government surveillance department for taking necessary action based on industrial park condition. Based on this approach, industry management mechanism will be improved a lot.

Lee, Yoo, & Kim (2016) developed an IOT framework for energy management in smart factory. A smart factory consists of sensors, smart meters and controller. Sensor collects the surrounding environmental data and smart meters about energy consumption. Finally, the entire data is sent to the database via IOT gateway. Factory Energy Management System (FEMS) has four different databases (DB) and they are Energy DB for store sensed raw data, Context DB used for store energy information, profile DB for store factory profile and rule DB for store control information. IOT gateway sends energy consumption data to FEMS framework in periodic interval of time. FEMS framework compares the collected data with the previous energy consumption or factory energy profile information to find any abnormalities in energy consumption. Based on the result CEO or energy manger can alter energy consumption level in factory.

Qiu, Luo, Xu, Zhong, & Huang (2015) proposed Supply Hub in Industrial Park (SHIP). SHIP has three major sub systems: (1) Physical Asset Service System (PASS), (2) Information Infrastructure (II), and (3) Decision Support Systems (DSS). PASS provide different physical assets and services likes warehousing, transportation for enterprises customers based on rental. II sub system has four layers: (1) RFID-enabled smart asset layer for collecting real time information, (2) gateways and Gateway Operating System (GOS) layer for transfering collected information to next level Management Platform Layer (MPL), (3) MPL for managing services, data and network and (4) applications layer for provide interface to user for access SHIP information. DSS is used for pricing the services for enterprises usages, allocate product in storage space, etc. SHIP provides automatic check in and out to warehousing and transportation for member enterprises. Real time route optimization in the vehicle transportation is supported by SHIP. Also, it provides accurate monitoring about stocks, vehicle status and real time information among different participating enterprises.

Liu, Ma, Alhussein, Zhang, & Peng (2016) proposed a cloud based temperature control system for the data center (DC). The proposed system is based on energy efficient multi-level temperature cooling system and cloud based data management. The sensor nodes are attached at ease in various parts of the DC and connected to the central monitoring node using Zigbee technology. By using the different temperature threshold levels, the ventilation system between computer center, maintenance center and natural environment is activated. When the temperature reaches above the maximum threshold level of DC the air-conditioning system will be activated. Using various control levels, the DC is made energy efficient using well-built IoT devices.

IoT Application in Smart Vehicle

In near future, internet enabled vehicles on the road side will create a big revolution. IoT devices fixed in these vehicles will be tracking the vehicle and also guiding the drivers for optimized route, finding nearby hotels, hospitals and some public places where they are new to the environment.

Olariu, Khalil, & Abuelela (2011) have developed a model for Vehicular Ad Hoc Networks (VANETs). The proposed model fixes IoT devices in the vehicles, and then these devices will be communicating the data to the cloud environment continuously. Driver's safety, traffic update, emergency warning, and road assistance are some of the important features addressed in this model.

Kumar, Kaur, Jindal, & Rodrigues (2015) proposed an IOT based healthcare services called Internet of Vehicle (IoV) during the travel. IOV architecture consists of two layers: (i) Acquisition Layer (AL), and (ii) Communication and Computation Layer (CCL). In AL, each vehicle is represented as like in game theory and a learning algorithm (Learning Automata) is used for interaction with travelling environment or with other vehicles. Vehicles and patients are prefixed with sensors for collecting the information regarding body and environment. Sensed data are then sent to Road Side Unit (RSU), which is usually a mobile cloud. Again, RSU is connected with centralized cloud (CC). Short range communication techniques like ZigBee, Bluetooth Low Energy (BLE), etc. can be used for communication between RSU and other vehicles. Connections established between vehicles are of peer to peer type. RSU measures payload value for providing the services. Suppose payload has value, that task will execute with help of CC. Some patient's information will be already stored in RSU cloud to provide faster request service. Handoff technique is used resolve mobility problem in Virtual Machine (VM) level.

He, Yan, & Da Xu (2014) proposed IOT based Vehicular Data Cloud (VDC) for providing intelligent transportation services. There are two services in this model: (i) Intelligent Parking Cloud Services (IPCS), and (ii) Vehicular Data Mining Cloud Services (VDMCS). In IPCS each and every parking lot is monitored for parking lot availability, miss parked cars, etc. Parking lot data is sent to the cloud continuously for processing and storage purpose. In VDMCS, road side infrastructures like traffic control signals, surveillances cameras, etc. are connected to the cloud. Each vehicle also needs to be connected to the cloud environment. The collected data provide solution for driver behavior monitoring, traffic control, movement of different types of vehicles, etc. Further improving the performance, two data mining models are used: Naive Bayes Model and Logistic Regression model. Based on the author approach road safety will increase, easy to maintain and traffic control system and vehicles.

Razzaque & Clarke (2015) proposed an IoT based smart management system for vehicle transportation along with the integration of smart bikes. Proposed framework consist of seven layers: (1) application layer, (2) sensing layer, (3) communication layer, (4) operating system layer, (5) middleware layer, (6) external services layer and (7) safety services layer. Wi-Fi, Dedicated Short Range Communication

(DSRC) are used for communication between the involved entitites. Bike safety and security operation (BSSO) model has two communication infrastructures: (i) Bike to Vehicle (B2V) and (ii) Bike to Infrastructure (B2I). BSSO always connected with biker and travelling vehicle through gateways for providing information. Each bike is monitored to collect data about misbehavior riding, collision detection and collected data are sent to two security support authority unit or IoT gateway. For warning purpose vehicle on board device or mobile phones are used. Misbehavior detection (MD) and Collision Perdition and Detection (CPD) schemas are developed for analyzing the collected data. Based on the above approach biker speed will be monitored so that accident rate can be reduced.

Chatrapathi, Rajkumar, & Venkatesakumar (2015) proposed IoT based smart accident management framework for vehicle users. The proposed model has four major units and they are: i) vehicular unit, ii) central processor, iii) Road side Unit, and iv) Hospital. Each vehicle is enabled with biomedical sensors for monitoring user health conditions and mechanical sensors for detecting vehicle accident. Sensed data are then sent to centralized server via Vehicle Area Network (VANET). Ambulance, Road Side Unit (RSU), VANET are connected with centralized server. Centralized server sends information about an accident to the nearest ambulance unit. Ambulance continuously communicates the patient health condition to the server for arranging immediate needs in the hospital before the patient arrival. Based on this approach, timely first aid services can be provided to the patient.

Kiefer &Behrendt(2016) proposed IOT based Smart e-bike monitoring system. Smart e-bike Monitoring System (SEMS) has integrated IOIO microcontroller board in the vehicle which gets connected with the rider's mobile phone to access GPS services. Sensors are used to collect e-bike user trip situation details. IOIO board analyzes the collected data before sending the control signals to handlebar assistant control device and mobile phone. Then the collected data is stored into server for future analysis. Each e-bike trip is documented and also can be shared to social media easily by user.

IoT Application in Healthcare

The improvement in the micro device technology has led to development of lot of smart medical devices. These devices continuously monitor the health condition of the patient and report to it to the hospital. There are three major advantages in this remote monitoring system,

1. The continuous monitoring helps the doctor to detect the early symptoms of the disease and treat accordingly.
2. Remote monitoring helps the medical field expert to record the patient history properly which is not possible even by frequent visits also.
3. Sudden health deterioration symptoms will appears few minute before which can be detected by these IoT devices and patients can be alerted to go to the nearest hospital.

As a whole, medical IoT devices help the remote patient monitoring an easier and more efficient.

Lemey, et al (2016) studied flexible RFID Tag which is suitable to be human wearable. In future, all wearable devices may be of this kind, because of its flexibility to be fixed in the body or clothes. In IoT healthcare applications, wearable device plays a major role as it allows you to stay better engaged with your environment. IoT devices make the healthcare environment much smarter.

La (2016) has developed a framework for IOT based personal health care system. Five types of disease diagnosis schemes are included in the model and they are: (i) Range-based diagnosis, (ii) Abruption-based diagnosis, (iii) Pattern matching-based diagnosis, (iv) Abnormality frequency-based diagnosis and (v) Abnormality persistency-based diagnosis. All these diagnosis are based on trajectories model. In accordance with the above five schemes, Disease Diagnosis Knowledge Base (DDKB) is designed and implemented in the IOT environment. DDKB is the source which has diagnosis research articles, physician's knowledge about disease, etc. By using DDKB, machine readable schemes are formed and used for diagnosis. A Smart Toilet System (STS) is used for demo purpose. In that, STS client (i.e.) smart IoT devices collect data of Personal Health Care (PHC) device measurement values and sent to the STS server. Then the diagnosis scheme unit in STS server analyzes the STS client data to identify disease. Using Bayes machine learning algorithm, the accuracy of the diagnosis is improved by comparing the diagnosis result with different disease parameters. Benefits of IOT based PHC are early detection of ongoing diseases without frequent clinic visits, frequent monitoring of health condition and continuous assessment.

Spanò, Di Pascoli, & Iannaccone (2016) proposed remote healthcare platform in ECG monitoring System. IOT platform for ECG monitoring system consist of three part and they are: (i) Wireless Sensor Network (WSN), (ii) IOT server and (iii) user interface. Chest belt type ECG sensors are used for monitoring human health and communicate data to IOT gateway through the Zigbee module. IOT gateway compress sensed data to reduce bandwidth utilization without any data loss before sending to IOT server. IOT server is the middleware component between WSN part and user interface (web application) part. IOT server process received raw data and visualizes it to user through web interface. Also, it gets command from user for altering WSN works flow likes changing monitoring time interval. Benefit of the platform is reduced health care expenditure.

Seo, et al (2016) proposed identification of food contamination via Internet of Things (IOT) with the help of packet sized immune sensor system (PSIS). PSI consists of two major parts: (i) Elisa on Chip (EOC) and (ii) CMOS Image Sensor (CIS). PSIS test the contaminated food sample with help of EOC reader to find pathogen. Suppose analysis result is positive PSIS generate light signal, when the light signal is captured by CIS and Wi-Fi module enabled send test results to smart phone. Smart phone is used for controlling PSIS and send analyzed report to the centralized server. In server, hosting service is used for giving warning about contaminated food product to consumer before they purchase it. IOT based PSIS helps to reduce time for advertising about condition of the tested food in global space.

Jarmakiewicz, Parobczak, & Maślanka (2016) proposed IOT based healthcare network using nano sensors. Nano sensors are implanted in the human body for monitoring health condition and it is called as Implanted Body Area Network (IBAN). Nano sensors are capable to communicate with outer device to transmit its sensed data. Magnetic coupling and Radio communication are the two kinds of links used for communication between device and nano sensors. Later, the outer device sends the collected data to server for its users (smartphones) analysis over their body condition.

Catarinucci, et al (2015) proposed IOT based architecture model for Smart Hospital System (SHS). Two major technologies are used in SHS: Ultra High Frequency Radio Frequency Identification (UHF RFID) and Wireless Sensor Network (WSN). The combination of UHF RFID and WSN is called Hybrid Sensor Network (HSN). Architecture is classified into three part and they are (1) HSN, (2) IOT smart gateway and (3) user interface. HSN is used for collecting hospital environment details like temperature, ambient light condition and also patient location. Then the data is sent to the IOT gateway. The IPv6 over Low power Wireless Personal Area Networks (6LoWPAN) technology is used for communication in HSN level. Monitoring application analyzes the received data from IOT gateway and stored into database. Web based user interface or special mobile application are used for controlling HSN and view the monitoring or historical data of patient. Proper authentication mechanism for doctors or hospital staff is implemented for security reasons.

Lee & Ouyang (2014) designed an IOT based healthcare device for treating chronic disease. Self-management is the most important factor for coming over chronic diseases. Separate IOT devices are fixed for identifying risk factor of metabolic syndrome. IOT based blood pressure meter is used to measure hypertension, likewise IOT glucose meter for identifying diabetes and IOT weight scale for measuring obesity. All individual IOT device output will be sent to IOT server for processing. Already in server, patient general information like age, family history, etc. will be stored.

SECURITY ISSUES IN IOT

Since the IoT concept evolved gradually by connecting devices over the conventional internet, there is no need of any big changes in the existing network architecture. But when IoT continuously evolve over the time, the existing cryptographic algorithms are found to be not suitable for these miniature devices. The threats and requirements of each layer are discussed below in brief.

- **Perceptual Layer:** Malicious and compromised nodes are the major threats in this layer. Apart from that authenticity, integrity and confidentiality of the data are also the associated threats. Proper authentication of device level mechanism and lightweight cryptographic algorithms may reduce the security risks in this layer.
- **Communication Layer:** Middle man attack, Virus attacks, Denial of service (DoS) are the possible kinds of security issues associated with communication layer. Network layer security mechanism can only reduce the security threats in this layer.
- **Service Layer:** Malicious information from the compromised nodes will be stored and cause lot of problems in the cloud environment during analysis of the data. High level security algorithms for the cloud environment are required for this layer.
- **Application Layer:** User level data privacy is the big threat of application layer. Well defined user level privileges, authentication mechanisms and educating users regarding proper password management may reduce the risks.

BIG DATA ANALYTICS AND IOT

Big data means large volume and velocity of data. Data is an important resource for an organization for its survivability and maintaining competiveness in the market. A closer look at the collected data will provide lot of facts about our business environment. In a typical IoT application too, large volume of data will be generated by thousands of IoT devices continuously. These data should be stored and analyzed properly at regular interval of time. This analysis will provide the accurate facts about their business or about the environment to their stackholders.

Stages of Big Data Analytics

The Big data analytics framework has the following four stages,

1. **Data Collection:** Collecting large volume of data from the surrounding environment through IoT devices.
2. **Data Transfer:** Transferring the collected data to the central or distributed warehouses needs efficient communication technologies since the volume of data is huge compared with conventional applications. IEEE802.15.4, ZigBee, BLE, etc. are the commonly used communication technologies between IoT device and gateway nodes.
3. **Data Processing:** The nature of data from IoT devices will be of complex datasets and non uniformity will be there. Storing, sorting, searching, analyzing and visualizing from these datasets will not be an easy or normal task. Improved data processing algorithms are required for this purpose. Machine learning algorithms are used in this stage.
4. **Data Leverage:** The useful new insights obtained by analyzing the large volume of datasets is Data leverage. The end users will get benefited through this process and it improves their business.

Analytics Platforms

Some of the widely used Big Data analytics platforms are discussed in brief.

1. **Apache Hadoop:** It is an open source analytics platform from Apache (Nandimath et al, 2013). It has two major components: (i) Hadoop Distributed File System (HDFS) used for storing the large volume of data in the distributed file system, and (ii) MapReduce, for analyzing the stored data in HDFS. Facebook is using the improved version of Hadoop for analyzing their user behaviors.
2. **MapR:** It is based on Hadoop framework (MapR, n.d.). But it replaced HDFS in Hadoop with Network File System (NFS) to improve security features. Search and stream processing used in LucidWorks is added in MapR which enhances its predictive capability.
3. **CloudEra:** Bhardwaj, et al (2014) developed CloudEra, a Hadoop based framework where the performance is improved using Cloudera manager and navigator. But, still the security issues are handled with third party support only.
4. **1010data:** Morabito (2015) developed 1010data which handles and processes semi-structured efficiently than others. Advanced analytic options are the major advantage of it.
5. **Pivotal Big Data Suite:** Zhuang, et al (2016) started used in public clouds for its massive parallel processing capability. Also, predictive analytics is supported well in this platform.

Thus, the effective Big Data analytics capability is an important factor for the success of IoT application.

FOG COMPUTING AND IOT

Mostly, all the IoT devices are designed in the way that their data should be deposited to the centralized cloud environment. Cloud services are easier to access, low cost and third party services can be easily used. Since IoT devices also continuously generate data over the time a large storage space is required which is offered by the cloud environment. Application specific data analytics would be applied in this centralized cloud server. This way of collecting the data from low level IoT devices, analytics process and sending back the control signals from the centralized point will be taking considerable time. But in certain application domains where this time delay is intolerable, immediate response from the cloud environment is required. A mini cloud like structures called Fogs are built at the network edge, where the data from these IoT devices will be stored, analyzed in these Fogs and appropriate control signals will be sent to the end devices as quick as possible. The other name of Fog computing is Edge computing. Fog computing is exactly located between end IoT devices and the centralized cloud environment. Low power communication technologies such as ZigBee, BLE, etc. are used for communication between IoT devices and Fogs or edge nodes. MQTT, CoAP are the protocols used for communication between Fogs and cloud. Thus Fogs nodes have to support different communication technologies and protocol.

Benefits of Fog Computing in IoT

The main needs of Fog computing in an IoT environment are,

1. **Reduced Latency:** The data from the IoT devices will be processed immediately at the network edges than at the remote cloud server so that appropriate actions can be taken immediately.
2. **Reduced Network Traffic:** Since the huge volume of data is processed within the fog edges of the network itself, the network traffic is greatly reduced.
3. **Distribute Management:** The fog computing model enables to develop distributed applications based on the local conditions. Instead of depending too much on the centralized cloud infrastructure for data processing, Fog computing offers distributed processing of the data which is needed for most IoT applications. Also, it reduces the overload at the cloud environment.
4. **Large Scale Control System:** Scalability of the control system improves with fog computing model. Since the workload at the cloud is shared by the distributed Fogs, it seems to be scalable with the network size.
5. **Data Filtering:** All the generated data need not be transmitted to the cloud since it increases the network traffic a lot. Fog nodes are the right points where these unnecessary data can be filtered.
6. **Mobility:** Since the Fog computing is considered to be the cloud units close to the network devices; it is also called as mobile unit of cloud.

Fog Computing in IoT Applications

The following are some of the major application areas where Fog computing will enhance the performance of the IoT applications,

*   **Smart Agriculture:** Large amount of data will be generated from the agricultural fields like data from humidity, temperature, soil light, gaseous sensors. These data can be processed at the network edge itself so that certain localized issues can be handled well. The benefits of Fog in smart agriculture:
    *   Ideal harvesting time localized to the environment can be computed at the edge nodes.
    *   Location tracking, monitoring health condition of the animals is easier.
    *   Ideal model to the rural locations where internet connectivity is still a major problem.

- **Vehicular Transportation:** It is one another area, where network latency is a major issue. Generally, Traffic light controller needs fast response for its switching between the signals. If the computation occurs near to the traffic point, more accurate signals can be passed to the approaching vehicles.

- **Health Care:** Depending on the health conditions of the patients, the medical data can be processed at the edge nodes for fast counter actions can be done in the case of medical emergency.

- **Augmented Reality:** Most of the Augmented Reality applications are time sensitive. Instead of forwarding all the data to the cloud and get assistance, processing at the edge nodes will enhance the performance of certain cognitive applications. Google glass is one such device using this fog computing model.

- **Smart Grid:** Smart grid is one another area where fog computing is essential. Transmission lines, distribution center, etc. needs continuous monitoring and immediate actions are to be done in the case of emergency, fogs are to be built at the distributed locations.

Currently, Cisco Corporation is developing lot of software to support device management, data analytics, etc. for Fog computing model.

CONCLUSION

An overview of IoT technology is reviewed in this article. In Section 1, introduction to IoT, key challenges in it and the role of WSN in IoT is studied. In Section 2, the basic building blocks for building an IoT application are presented. Various layered architecture models followed for IoT applications is discussed in Section 3 and various communication protocols and technologies in Section 4. Implementations of IoT technology in various domains like agriculture, home automation, smart industries, vehicles and health care is briefly reviewed in Section 5. Security issues are studied in Section 6 and Section 8 about the need of Fog computing for an IoT environment. Thus, this paper presented different dimensions of IoT technology.

REFERENCES

Al-Fuqaha, A., Guizani, M., Mohammadi, M., Aledhari, M., & Ayyash, M. (2015). Internet of things: A survey on enabling technologies, protocols, and applications. *IEEE Communications Surveys and Tutorials, 17*(4), 2347–2376. doi:10.1109/COMST.2015.2444095

Almobaideen, W., Allan, M., & Saadeh, M. (2016). Smart archaeological tourism: Contention, convenience and accessibility in the context of cloud-centric IoT. *Mediterranean Archaeology & Archaeometry, 16*(1).

Atzori, L., Iera, A., & Morabito, G. (2010). The internet of things: A survey. *Computer Networks, 54*(15), 2787–2805. doi:10.1016/j.comnet.2010.05.010

Aziz, B. (2016). A formal model and analysis of an IoT protocol. *Ad Hoc Networks, 36*, 49–57. doi:10.1016/j.adhoc.2015.05.013

Baranwal, T., & Pateriya, P. K. (2016, January). Development of IoT based smart security and monitoring devices for agriculture. In *Cloud System and Big Data Engineering (Confluence), 2016 6th International Conference* (pp. 597-602). IEEE. 10.1109/CONFLUENCE.2016.7508189

Bee, X. (n.d.). *Digi XBee Ecosystem - Everything you need to explore and create wireless connectivity - Digi International*. Retrieved from https://www.digi.com/xbee

Bhardwaj, A., Bhattacherjee, S., Chavan, A., Deshpande, A., Elmore, A. J., Madden, S., & Parameswaran, A. G. (2014). *Datahub: Collaborative data science & dataset version management at scale*. arXiv pre-print arXiv:1409.0798

Bhide, V. H., & Wagh, S. (2015, April). i-learning IoT: An intelligent self learning system for home automation using IoT. In *Communications and Signal Processing (ICCSP), 2015 International Conference on* (pp. 1763-1767). IEEE.

Business Insider. (2016). *The US government is pouring money into the Internet of Things*. Retrieved from http://www.businessinsider.com/the-us-government-is-pouring-money-into-the-internet-of-things-2016-5?IR=T

Catarinucci, L., De Donno, D., Mainetti, L., Palano, L., Patrono, L., Stefanizzi, M. L., & Tarricone, L. (2015). An IoT-aware architecture for smart healthcare systems. *IEEE Internet of Things Journal, 2*(6), 515–526. doi:10.1109/JIOT.2015.2417684

Chatrapathi, C., Rajkumar, M. N., & Venkatesakumar, V. (2015, February). VANET based integrated framework for smart accident management system. In *Soft-Computing and Networks Security (ICSNS), 2015 International Conference on* (pp. 1-7). IEEE. 10.1109/ICSNS.2015.7292411

Cheshire, S., & Krochmal, M. (2013). *Rfc 6762: Multicast dns*. Internet Engineering Task Force (IETF) standard.

Chhabra, J., & Gupta, P. (2016). IoT based Smart Home Design using Power and Security Management. 2016 *1st International Conference on Innovation and Challenges in Cyber Security (ICICCS 2016)*.

Cho, K., Park, G., Cho, W., Seo, J., & Han, K. (2016). Performance analysis of device discovery of Bluetooth Low Energy (BLE) networks. *Computer Communications, 81*, 72–85. doi:10.1016/j.comcom.2015.10.008

Collotta, M., & Pau, G. (2015). Bluetooth for Internet of Things: A fuzzy approach to improve power management in smart homes. *Computers & Electrical Engineering, 44*, 137–152. doi:10.1016/j.compeleceng.2015.01.005

Edwards-Murphy, F., Magno, M., Whelan, P. M., O'Halloran, J., & Popovici, E. M. (2016). b+ WSN: Smart beehive with preliminary decision tree analysis for agriculture and honey bee health monitoring. *Computers and Electronics in Agriculture, 124*, 211–219. doi:10.1016/j.compag.2016.04.008

Elarabi, T., Deep, V., & Rai, C. K. (2015, December). Design and simulation of state-of-art ZigBee transmitter for IoT wireless devices. In *Signal Processing and Information Technology (ISSPIT), 2015 IEEE International Symposium on* (pp. 297-300). IEEE. 10.1109/ISSPIT.2015.7394347

European Research Commission. (2015). *European Research Cluster on Internet of Things*. Retrieved from http://www.internet-of-things-research.eu/

Gomez, C., & Paradells, J. (2010). Wireless home automation networks: A survey of architectures and technologies. *IEEE Communications Magazine, 48*(6), 92–101. doi:10.1109/MCOM.2010.5473869

Granjal, J., Monteiro, E., & Silva, J. S. (2015). Security for the internet of things: A survey of existing protocols and open research issues. *IEEE Communications Surveys and Tutorials, 17*(3), 1294–1312. doi:10.1109/COMST.2015.2388550

Hao, Q., Zhang, F., Liu, Z., & Qin, L. (2015). Design of chemical industrial park integrated information management platform based on cloud computing and IOT (the internet of things) technologies. *International Journal of Smart Home, 9*(4), 35–46. doi:10.14257/ijsh.2015.9.4.04

He, W., Yan, G., & Da Xu, L. (2014). Developing vehicular data cloud services in the IoT environment. *IEEE Transactions on Industrial Informatics, 10*(2), 1587–1595. doi:10.1109/TII.2014.2299233

Hu, X., & Qian, S. (2011, November). IOT application system with crop growth models in facility agriculture. In *Computer Sciences and Convergence Information Technology (ICCIT), 2011 6th International Conference on* (pp. 129-133). IEEE.

IEEE 802.15.4 (2015). *IEEE Standard for Low-Rate Wireless Networks*. Retrieved from https://standards.ieee.org/findstds/standard/802.15.4-2015.html

IEEE Standards Association. (2016). *Standard for an Architectural Framework for the Internet of Things (IoT)*. New York: Institute of Electrical and Electronics Engineers.

Ikram, M. A., Alshehri, M. D., & Hussain, F. K. (2015, December). Architecture of an IoT-based system for football supervision (IoT Football). In *Internet of Things (WF-IoT), 2015 IEEE 2nd World Forum on* (pp. 69-74). IEEE.

Jara, A. J., Ladid, L., & Gómez-Skarmeta, A. F. (2013). The Internet of Everything through IPv6: An Analysis of Challenges, Solutions and Opportunities. *JoWua, 4*(3), 97–118.

Jara, A. J., Martinez-Julia, P., & Skarmeta, A. (2012, July). Light-weight multicast DNS and DNS-SD (lmDNS-SD): IPv6-based resource and service discovery for the Web of Things. In *Innovative mobile and internet services in ubiquitous computing (IMIS), 2012 sixth international conference on* (pp. 731-738). IEEE.

Jarmakiewicz, J., Parobczak, K., & Maślanka, K. (2016, May). On the Internet of Nano Things in healthcare network. In *Military Communications and Information Systems (ICMCIS), 2016 International Conference on* (pp. 1-6). IEEE. 10.1109/ICMCIS.2016.7496572

Kalaivanan, S., & Manoharan, S. (2016). Monitoring and Controlling of Smart Homes using IoT and Low Power Wireless Technology. *Indian Journal of Science and Technology, 9*(31). doi:10.17485/ijst/2016/v9i31/92701

Kaur, N., & Sood, S. K. (2015). Cognitive decision making in smart industry. *Computers in Industry, 74*, 151–161. doi:10.1016/j.compind.2015.06.006

Khan, M., Din, S., Jabbar, S., Gohar, M., Ghayvat, H., & Mukhopadhyay, S. C. (2016). Context-aware low power intelligent SmartHome based on the Internet of things. *Computers & Electrical Engineering*, *52*, 208–222. doi:10.1016/j.compeleceng.2016.04.014

Kiefer, C., & Behrendt, F. (2016). Smart e-bike monitoring system: Real-time open source and open hardware GPS assistance and sensor data for electrically-assisted bicycles. *IET Intelligent Transport Systems*, *10*(2), 79–88. doi:10.1049/iet-its.2014.0251

Kim, D. Y., & Jung, M. (2017). Data transmission and network architecture in long range low power sensor networks for IoT. *Wireless Personal Communications*, *93*(1), 119–129. doi:10.100711277-016-3482-7

Kumar, N., Kaur, K., Jindal, A., & Rodrigues, J. J. (2015). Providing healthcare services on-the-fly using multi-player cooperation game theory in Internet of Vehicles (IoV) environment. *Digital Communications and Networks*, *1*(3), 191–203. doi:10.1016/j.dcan.2015.05.001

Kushalnagar, N., Montenegro, G., & Schumacher, C. (2007). *IPv6 over low-power wireless personal area networks (6LoWPANs): overview, assumptions, problem statement, and goals* (No. RFC 4919).

La, H. J. (2016). A conceptual framework for trajectory-based medical analytics with IoT contexts. *Journal of Computer and System Sciences*, *82*(4), 610–626. doi:10.1016/j.jcss.2015.10.007

Lee, B. M., & Ouyang, J. (2014). Intelligent healthcare service by using collaborations between IoT personal health devices. *International Journal of Bio-Science and Bio-Technology*, *6*(1), 155–164. doi:10.14257/ijbsbt.2014.6.1.17

Lee, H., Yoo, S., & Kim, Y. W. (2016, January). An energy management framework for smart factory based on context-awareness. In *Advanced Communication Technology (ICACT), 2016 18th International Conference on* (pp. 685-688). IEEE.

Lemey, S., Agneessens, S., Van Torre, P., Baes, K., Vanfleteren, J., & Rogier, H. (2016). Wearable flexible lightweight modular RFID tag with integrated energy harvester. *IEEE Transactions on Microwave Theory and Techniques*, *64*(7), 2304–2314. doi:10.1109/TMTT.2016.2573274

Liu, Q., Ma, Y., Alhussein, M., Zhang, Y., & Peng, L. (2016). Green data center with IoT sensing and cloud-assisted smart temperature control system. *Computer Networks*, *101*, 104–112. doi:10.1016/j.comnet.2015.11.024

Luzuriaga, J. E., Perez, M., Boronat, P., Cano, J. C., Calafate, C., & Manzoni, P. (2015, January). A comparative evaluation of AMQP and MQTT protocols over unstable and mobile networks. In *Consumer Communications and Networking Conference (CCNC), 2015 12th Annual IEEE* (pp. 931-936). IEEE. 10.1109/CCNC.2015.7158101

Mano, L. Y., Faiçal, B. S., Nakamura, L. H., Gomes, P. H., Libralon, G. L., Meneguete, R. I., ... Ueyama, J. (2016). Exploiting IoT technologies for enhancing Health Smart Homes through patient identification and emotion recognition. *Computer Communications*, *89*, 178–190. doi:10.1016/j.comcom.2016.03.010

MapR. (n.d.). *The only converged data platform*. Retrieved from https://mapr.com/

Ministry of Industry and Information Technology of China. (2012). *The National 12th Five-Year Plan Including IoT Development (2011–2015)*. Retrieved from http://www.gov.cn/zwgk/2012-02/14/content2065999.html

Morabito, V. (2015). Managing Change for Big Data Driven Innovation. In *Big Data and Analytics* (pp. 125–153). Springer International Publishing. doi:10.1007/978-3-319-10665-6_7

Muralidharan, S., Roy, A., & Saxena, N. (2016). An Exhaustive Review on Internet of Things from Korea's Perspective. *Wireless Personal Communications*, *90*(3), 1463–1486. doi:10.100711277-016-3404-8

Nandimath, J., Banerjee, E., Patil, A., Kakade, P., Vaidya, S., & Chaturvedi, D. (2013, August). Big data analysis using Apache Hadoop. In *Information Reuse and Integration (IRI), 2013 IEEE 14th International Conference on* (pp. 700-703). IEEE. 10.1109/IRI.2013.6642536

Olariu, S., Khalil, I., & Abuelela, M. (2011). Taking VANET to the clouds. *International Journal of Pervasive Computing and Communications*, *7*(1), 7–21. doi:10.1108/17427371111123577

Qiu, X., Luo, H., Xu, G., Zhong, R., & Huang, G. Q. (2015). Physical assets and service sharing for IoT-enabled Supply Hub in Industrial Park (SHIP). *International Journal of Production Economics*, *159*, 4–15. doi:10.1016/j.ijpe.2014.09.001

Rad, C. R., Hancu, O., Takacs, I. A., & Olteanu, G. (2015). Smart monitoring of potato crop: A cyber-physical system architecture model in the field of precision agriculture. *Agriculture and Agricultural Science Procedia*, *6*, 73–79. doi:10.1016/j.aaspro.2015.08.041

Razzaque, M. A., & Clarke, S. (2015, December). A security-aware safety management framework for IoT-integrated bikes. In *Internet of Things (WF-IoT), 2015 IEEE 2nd World Forum on* (pp. 92-97). IEEE. 10.1109/WF-IoT.2015.7389033

Ruan, J., & Shi, Y. (2016). Monitoring and assessing fruit freshness in IOT-based e-commerce delivery using scenario analysis and interval number approaches. *Information Sciences*, *373*, 557–570. doi:10.1016/j.ins.2016.07.014

Ryu, M., Yun, J., Miao, T., Ahn, I. Y., Choi, S. C., & Kim, J. (2015, November). Design and implementation of a connected farm for smart farming system. In SENSORS, 2015 IEEE (pp. 1-4). IEEE.

Saint-Andre, P. (2009). XMPP: Lessons learned from ten years of XML messaging. *IEEE Communications Magazine*, *47*(4), 92–96. doi:10.1109/MCOM.2009.4907413

Samsung Corporation. (2017). *Samsung Shows Dedication to IoT with $1.2 Billion Investment and R&D*, Retrieved from https://news.samsung.com/global/samsung-electronics-announces-vision-for-a-human-centered-internet-of-things-planning-1-2-billion-for-u-s-research-and-development-of-iot

Seo, S. M., Kim, S. W., Jeon, J. W., Kim, J. H., Kim, H. S., Cho, J. H., ... Paek, S. H. (2016). Food contamination monitoring via internet of things, exemplified by using pocket-sized immunosensor as terminal unit. *Sensors and Actuators. B, Chemical*, *233*, 148–156. doi:10.1016/j.snb.2016.04.061

Shelby, Z., Hartke, K., & Bormann, C. (2014). *The constrained application protocol (CoAP)*. Academic Press.

Shih, C. W., & Wang, C. H. (2016). Integrating wireless sensor networks with statistical quality control to develop a cold chain system in food industries. *Computer Standards & Interfaces*, *45*, 62–78. doi:10.1016/j.csi.2015.12.004

Spanò, E., Di Pascoli, S., & Iannaccone, G. (2016). Low-power wearable ECG monitoring system for multiple-patient remote monitoring. *IEEE Sensors Journal*, *16*(13), 5452–5462. doi:10.1109/JSEN.2016.2564995

Sun, Y., Song, H., Jara, A. J., & Bie, R. (2016). Internet of things and big data analytics for smart and connected communities. *IEEE Access: Practical Innovations, Open Solutions*, *4*, 766–773. doi:10.1109/ACCESS.2016.2529723

Verma, P. K., Verma, R., Prakash, A., Agrawal, A., Naik, K., Tripathi, R., ... Abogharaf, A. (2016). Machine-to-Machine (M2M) communications: A survey. *Journal of Network and Computer Applications*, *66*, 83–105. doi:10.1016/j.jnca.2016.02.016

Wang, D., Lo, D., Bhimani, J., & Sugiura, K. (2015, July). Anycontrol--iot based home appliances monitoring and controlling. In *Computer Software and Applications Conference (COMPSAC), 2015 IEEE 39th Annual* (Vol. 3, pp. 487-492). IEEE. 10.1109/COMPSAC.2015.259

Zhuang, Y., Wang, Y., Shao, J., Chen, L., Lu, W., Sun, J., ... Wu, J. (2016). D-Ocean: An unstructured data management system for data ocean environment. *Frontiers of Computer Science*, *10*(2), 353–369. doi:10.100711704-015-5045-6

Chapter 9
Fuzzy–Logic–Based Decision Engine for Offloading IoT Application Using Fog Computing

Dhanya N. M.
Amrita Vishwa Vidyapeetham, India

G. Kousalya
Coimbatore Institute of Technology, India

Balarksihnan P.
Vellore Institute of Technology, India

Pethuru Raj
Reliance Jio Infocomm. Ltd., India

ABSTRACT

Mobile is getting increasingly popular and almost all applications are shifting into smartphones. Even though lots of advantages are there for smartphones, they are constrained by limitations in battery charge and the processing capacity. For running resource-intensive IoT applications like processing sensor data and dealing with big data coming from the IoT application, the capacity of existing smartphones is not enough, as the battery will be drained quickly, and it will be slow. Offloading is one of the major techniques through which mobile and cloud can be connected together and has emerged to reduce the complexity and increase the computation power of mobiles. Other than depending on the distant cloud for offloading, the extended version of cloud called fog computing can be utilized. Through offloading, the computationally intensive tasks can be shifted to the edge fog devices, and the results can be collected back at the mobile side reducing the burden. This chapter has developed mobile cloud offloading architecture for decision making using fuzzy logic where a decision is made as to whether we can shift the application to cloud or not depending on the current parameters of both cloud and the mobile side. Cloud computing introduces a number of variables depending on which offloading decision must be taken. In this chapter, the authors propose a fuzzy-logic-based algorithm which takes into consideration all the parameters at the mobile and cloud that will affect the offloading decision.

DOI: 10.4018/978-1-5225-5972-6.ch009

INTRODUCTION

The proliferations of smartphones are increasing dramatically during recent years. Billions of users are using smartphones and various applications. A large number of applications and sensors are coming along with mobile phones such as real time gaming applications, powerful GPS sensors, NFC readers, etc. Hence it is easy to create an IOT application with the sensors which are available in the mobile devices. Majority of these applications are computationally intensive and processing intensive which will drain the battery faster (Buyya et al., 2009). More over currently most of the smart phones are equipped with processors and batteries which are not capable of doing all these works. Hence the critical problem that smart phones are facing is the ability to carry out the above mentioned applications with the existing battery and processing capabilities.

A large number of hardware technologies such as maintaining leakage power, parallel execution, runtime voltage scaling is existing nowadays. Recently cloud computing came into popularity where all the applications are migrating to cloud. The cloud computing with mobile technologies such as ubiquitous computing devices, location based devices, lead to a novel computing technology called Mobile Cloud Computing (MCC). This provides the mobile users with all advantages of cloud including infinite storage space and unlimited computing power. But the main disadvantage of cloud computing is the connection latency. So we need a low latency connection to the server which can save both energy and time. The extension of cloud computing called Fog computing can be utilized for this. Hence for energy and time efficiency and total performance improvement of the application offloading to the Fog servers are the best suitable solution. Therefore, there is strong need for research into smart system based on the concept of offloading to Fog edge servers.

Offloading is the process of transferring the calculations to the cloud in order to achieve energy savings and improved efficiency. The shortcomings of mobile devices can be overcome by the use of offloading. Another question that arises is "Whether offloading is beneficial always?" The answer is "No". Only if enough energy savings and speed up can be achieved by offloading, applications can be offloaded, otherwise it can be executed in the local mobile itself. So a decision has to be taken for offloading. If the situations are favorable for offloading where it will lead to significant performance improvement a decision can be taken to offload the application. Otherwise the decision should be not to offload but to use a local execution. This decision has to be taken logically by looking at the current situation and take an offloading decision. For such decision making Fuzzy logic decision provides an efficient mechanism. The parameters that are going to be considered in this decision can be formulated as fuzzy parameters.

In this chapter, the offloading is considered as a decision problem. This depends on various features on mobile side and the cloud side. Here a fuzzy logic based approach is used to take a decision on whether to execute locally on the mobile itself or remotely in the cloud. After the decision the application is partitioned into local and remote fragments and the remote part is executed in the cloud server. Therefore, the main contributions of this chapter are:

1. Develop Mobile Offloading architecture.
2. **A Decision Algorithm Using Fuzzy Logic:** The offloading decision is taken with the help of a fuzzy logic based system which will take into consideration of both mobile and cloud side parameters. Based on these parameters a decision is taken and is conveyed to the mobile for further processing.

3. **Performance Analysis:** The performance of the system is analyzed based on the error rate in the decision and time taken for the decision. The execution time for local and remote execution is compared for the applications. Even though the execution time in cloud is lesser, it shows much fluctuation compared to the local execution.

This chapter has been divided into five sections: Section 1 introduces the concept and our approach; section 2 provides background; section 3 discusses the proposed software architecture based on Fuzzification and algorithm; section 4 discusses the evaluation of our approach and section 5 concludes the work.

BACKGROUND

Cloud offloading has become a popular technique for mobile application; where cloud based remote servers execute the resource intensive part of the application there by saving the energy consumed by the application and the performance efficiency. Over the past few years significant studies have been done on the resource constraint mobile devices to make it energy efficient. Offloading is one of the techniques which can be applied. Many research works is going on in the field of offloading and offloading decision making.

Clone cloud (Chun et al., 2009) proposes a thread level granularity, where the device dependent classes are maintained in the mobile and rest of the application are offloaded. It uses static and dynamic code analysis to find out which part of the code should be offloaded. It does not need programmer support for conversion of the application. The application partitioning technique is fully dynamic in nature. The migration points are calculated by static analysis and dynamic profiling.

Cuckoo framework (Kempet al., 2012) is targeted for android platform where it supports local and remote execution. It is integrated with the existing development platform. It is having a service re-writer and remote service deriver for supporting the offloading. Partially the applications are offloaded to the nearby infrastructure. The main modules are Cuckoo Remote Service Deriver(CRSD) and Cuckoo Service Rewriter(CSR). A dummy remote implementation is created by CRSD and stub/proxy is created by CSR for each AIDL interface so that the methods can be invoked remotely or locally. The applications which are offloaded can be run in a JVM on the remote infrastructure or the cloud. The main disadvantage of Cuckoo is that it needs programmer support to rewrite the applications.

MAUI architecture (Cuervo et al., 2010) describes the code offloading in Common Language Run (CLR) in .NET platform. MAUI creates offloading decision based on the classes with @remotable annotation. It takes a runtime decision of which method to offload. it creates an offloading decision which maximizes the energy saving and minimizes the programmer burden. In "Offload or not to offload" (Barbera et al., 2013) the feasibility of both local and remote execution is calculated. It uses a real time clone of the device in the cloud for application offloading. One more clone is available for data and app backup. Based on the decision of mobile data traffic and network availability a decision is taken.

(Wolski et al., 2008) is taking offloading decision based on Bandwidth data. This chapter deals with an offloading decision which is based on Bayesian decision. The offloading problem is formulated as a Bayesian decision problem and it compared with a number of other decision strategies. A prediction strategy is used for predicting the bandwidth and based on this information a decision is taken for offloading. the parameters takes into consideration are only bandwidth. Depending on the predicted bandwidth offloading decision is taken (Wolski 2008)(Wolski, Spring & Hayes, 1999). An offloading decision proposed by (Wu, Huang & Bouzefrane, 2013) is dealing with an offloading decision which is taking into consideration of the network unavailability. Network disconnection can be deciding factor in making offloading decision. An adaptive algorithm is designed for this. The author takes time and energy as the parameters for the offloading decision. But no other features like current battery charge, load on the cloud, etc. are not taken into consideration at all.

(Gurun et al., 2008) is dealing with offloading decision to a grid. A scheduler is deciding when to offload the computations. A prediction is done on when the remote execution is better than local execution. This decision is based on the bandwidth and Bayesian decisions strategy. Adaptive code offloading by (Macario & Srirama 2013) introduces a fuzzy decision engine for offloading. The decision is based on evidence based learning. The proposed work is an extension of this work where all extensive parameters which will affect the offloading are considered and a prediction strategy is included for more accurate decision. The bandwidth prediction helps the system to add future bandwidth into the algorithms so that dynamism can be incorporated into our work.

(Oueis, Strinati & Barbarossa, 2014) proposed an Energy-efficient and network-aware offloading algorithm for mobile cloud computing. This chapter deals with a middleware that lies between the mobile and the cloud. This is called cloudlets and is a decision is taken either to offload the task to cloud or cloudlet. The main considerations for the decision are energy efficiency. (Ellouze, Gagnaire & Haddad, 2015) offloading architecture is one of the latest work for offloading. This chapter is dealing with the off loading of application considering the current CPU load and State of Charge (SoC) of the mobile phones. The offloading decision is taken based on the delay for offloading and Quality of Experience (QoE). The critical delay, energy balance and the state of charge of battery is calculated mathematically and a decision is taken for offloading. A chess game, speech recognition and a virus scan application is considered and the results are compared based on the energy gain and rejection ratio.

(Mukherjee, Gupta & De, 2013) multi-parameter Decision Algorithm for Mobile Computation Offloading proposes an algorithm for offloading decision to femtocloud. This considers multiple parameters such as Local capacity of the mobile, battery level, channel capacity and takes a decision while reducing the handset energy utilization while increasing the user experience. All tasks are classified based on the criteria and urgency as Offloadable, non offloadable, urgent, not urgent, etc and a decision is taken for each module for offloading.

(Dhanya, Kousalya & Balakrishnan 2017) suggested an offloading prediction algorithm based on statistical regression. Since regression is a simple machine learning approach and with reasonable accuracy it can be used in the mobile devices for decision making. But for high accuracy the algorithms will be much complex and running such algorithms on the mobile devices will reduces the energy efficiency of the devices further.

(Dhanya & Kousalya 2016) proposed an offloading decision algorithm based on regression and based on this decision the application is partitioned into local and remote partition. The application is converted into a Weighted Object relational Graph and a Kernighan Lin algorithm is used for partitioning.

The existing work provides interesting approaches to various issues on offloading. However, they lack comprehensive approach to offloading decision making, in detail, how this decision has been achieved based on requirements constraints on functionality and performances. This need to be precise when offloading decision has been made. In summary, there are a lot of interesting approaches to various issues in offloading. However they lack comprehensive approach in decision making and taking all parameters which are related to the offloading scenario. Comparing to the existing work, the aim of our approach is to improve the offloading decision making using a fuzzy based approach, where all parameters for offloading can be modeled as a fuzzy set, which is more suitable.

OFFLOADING ARCHITECTURE

Today's mobile users are expecting their phones to do all the sophisticated applications and there is ubiquitous access to 3G or Wi-Fi always. But this is not happening in practical cases. There are lots of limitations for smartphones in terms of storage, computation capacity and so on. In order to achieve performance efficiency there should be some augmentation for your mobile devices with a technology which will overcome all the limitations of the mobile devices. Fog computing is the possible alternative to augment smartphones because of the ubiquitous connectivity. We can offload some part of the application to the attached fog server for better performance. Offloading is a process by which resource intensive part of an application is executed at the cloud side in order to make the smartphones more efficient in terms of performance and battery utilization.

Fog computing supports lots of augmentation strategies such as memory augmentation, energy augmentation and computational augmentation. Storage augmentation and computational augmentation are two very important functions that can be achieved using cloud which will help mobile devices a lot.

Offloading Decision in Fog Offloading

In the Smartphone environment the user mobility is highly dynamic and the resource availability is very limited. For example, in mobile environment the bandwidth fluctuates significantly when the user is moving around. Similarly the remaining battery charge, load and memory utilization depends on how many applications are running in parallel in the Smartphone. The decision making also depends on the parameters of the fog server such as load on the server and number of Virtual machines available, to which application offloading is being done. To do efficient processing an intelligent decision should be taken whether to offload or not. The offloading engine should take right decision and right amount of application to be transferred to the server for execution to maintain low offloading overhead and efficient application execution. For example if we have high bandwidth and battery charge is less without much overhead the major portion of the applications can be offloaded. On the other hand, if the bandwidth is medium, the offloading engine should decide to offload only the necessary portion to the fog server for execution to avoid offloading overhead. Because of this dynamic nature of smartphones, an intelligent decision should be taken for offloading considering the various dynamic parameters.

The offloading architecture is shown in Figure 1. The dynamic parameters such as bandwidth, residual battery charge, etc. are constantly monitored by the profiler. With the input from the profiler a Fuzzy logic decision engine decides whether to offload or not. The offloading decision is taken for the dataset given in offloading traces. The offloading decision is taken at the server side on the basis of the residual battery charge and the bandwidth at the mobile side and the load and number of virtual machines at the server side.

The main advantage of this architecture is that the decision making is happening outside the mobile phone which will save a lot of energy. The execution sequence is shown below.

Figure 1. The Offloading Architecture

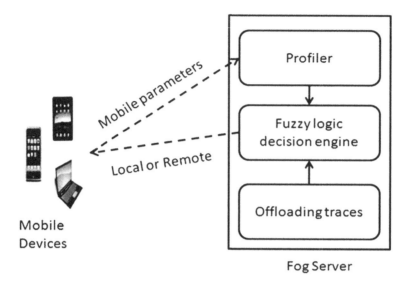

1. When the application is switched on the mobile device it contacts the cloud through the application provider.
2. From the mobile, the residual battery charge, data size, memory, load and the predicted bandwidth is transferred to the cloud for calculation.
3. At the cloud side, the cloud load and number of virtual machines available are added with the data obtained from the mobile.
4. Applying fuzzy logic on the offloading data traces cloud will take a decision on local or remote execution.
5. This decision is conveyed to the mobile for further processing.

The following are the factors which will contribute to the decision making.

Mobile Devices

From the Smartphone perspective, the decision making parameters are the resources such as CPU load, memory, storage, residual battery charge and the current bandwidth. The current bandwidth is measured and is given to the cloud for decision making. The amount of data to be transferred is also taken into consideration for offloading decision. In this chapter, the sizes of all components except non offloadable components are considered when the data to be transferred is calculated.

Fog Servers

The offloading decision depends on the server side parameters such as resources and its characteristics. The main factors are performance, availability, elasticity, security and vulnerability. Utilizing cloud resources reduces overall delay and battery consumption and increases the performance and can use the property of pay-as-you-use of the cloud. The server parameters taken into consideration are the number of users connected to the server and number of virtual machines available.

Fuzzy Logic Offloading Decision Maker

The context aware offloading decision making can be formulated as a decision tree based structure. Using decision tree the rules can be written in the form of an IF-THEN-ELSE structure and the output represents whether to offload or not. The inputs can be simple to more complex rules which will combine multiple parameters together. This approach may lead to a hard threshold on the context variable which may lead to inadvertent results to some of the inputs. On the other hand fuzzy logic approach handles all the input parameters in a more natural way. Since the mobile and cloud parameters are a part of environmental behavior, it is inherently fuzzy, described using degrees of confidence rather than absolutes.

The decision making of whether to execute remotely or locally is a complex process to control in mobile cloud infrastructure. The environment is distributed in nature and is difficult to manage. The natures of factors that affect offloading decision are highly variable and are having real time constraints. In such situations the inference can be made based on the previous experience. The best suitable method for such situations is fuzzy logic based solutions.

The fuzzy logic based systems must be capable of adapting to the continuous changes in the environment. This is a strong reason fuzzy based decision engine is selected. The fuzzy decision system consists of the following parts. 1) Fuzzifier 2) Rules 3) decision engine 4) defuzzifier. The Figure 2 shows the process of fuzzy logic.

The crisp set input parameters are given as input to the fuzzy logic engine. It is then converted into the fuzzy input values. Based on the rules given in the rule base a decision is taken for offloading. This fuzzy decision is converted into crisp decision values and is given as the output. The final decision is Local/Remote execution.

The steps are as follows

1. Definition of input/output fuzzy variables which is the crisp set.
2. The decision making engine along with the input and the rule base make an inference regarding the output.
3. Resulting output is mapped to crisp set using defuzzifier.

Figure 2. The Fuzzy Logic

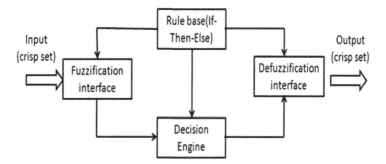

The input parameters under consideration are
Mobile side:

- Residual battery charge
- Bandwidth
- Data size to be transferred
- Load on the mobile side
- Memory

Cloud side:

- Load on the cloud
- Number of VMs available

The offloading engine implements the fuzzy-logic-based mapping. It takes the confidence values of fuzzy sets (e.g., low, medium, and high) as inputs and generates outputs in the form of confidence values of fuzzy sets for output variables (e.g., Remote Execution/Local Execution). Hence, to use the generic fuzzy inference engine, the offloading inference engine provides two functions, Fuzzification to prepare input fuzzy sets for the generic fuzzy inference engine, and defuzzification to convert the output fuzzy sets to actual offloading decisions, such as remote/local execution.

Fuzzification and Membership Functions

Fuzzification is the first step for applying fuzzy interface system. The crisp variables are converted into fuzzy variables. The decision engine considers each of the input parameter as crisp set and is converted to fuzzy set. Each parameter is given a name and is converted into ranges. The following are the specification for the parameters. Each variable is represented as three ranges such as low, medium and high, which represents the linguistic variables.

bandwidth = (bw_low,bw_medium,bw_high) - Bandwidth at mobile side. The ranges for bandwidth are
(0,40), (35,70) and (65-100) mbps.

The bandwidth is varying from 0 to 100. In my experiments 72 and 54 are the most frequent values. The linguistic variable bandwidth is set in such a way that 54 is classified in the medium range and 72 is classified in the high range. All the variables are selected accordingly.

Residual battery charge = (bat_low, bat_medium, bat_high) - Battery charge remaining - (0,35),(25,75),(60,100) %
Data size = (data_low,data_medium,data_high) - Data size to be offloaded(0,360),(250,590),(450,600) KB
Load = (load_low,load_medium,load_high) - CPU load on the mobile (0,40), (35,70) and (65-100) %
Memory = (mem_low,mem_medium,mem_high) - Memory on the mobile(0,40), (35,70) and (65-10)
Virtual machines available = (vm_low, vm_medium, vm_high)- Number of virtual machine available(0,20),(15,35),(30,50)

Number of concurrent users=(user_low, user_medium, user_high) - Number of concurrent users for the same application (0,40),(30,70),(60,100)

Each of these inputs can be represented as trapezoidal membership functions. The following represents membership function definition for the linguistic variable and the graph representation of bandwidth membership is shown in the Figure 3.

Linguistic variable - Bandwidth[0,100]
bw_low [0 20 30 40]
bw_medium [35 45 60 70]
bw_high [65 75 90 100]

Fuzzy Control Rules (Rule Base)

The output linguistic term has two values local processing and remote processing. The fuzzy rules are formulated based on the basic operations like AND, OR, XOR, etc. The following are the parameters and some rules considered for the decision engine.

Some sample Rules considered are given in Table 1.

The above mentioned is a sample set of rules and a rich set of rules are used for analyzing the offloading traces at the cloud. As the fuzzy logic system infers a decision expressed in terms of degree of truth, the system is designed in terms of quantifying the execution in terms of local and remote execution in percentages. The result is a decision in percentage, depending on the input parameters (both mobile and cloud side) whether to execute the application locally or remotely.

Fuzzy Mapping Rules

Fuzzy mapping rules provide a functional mapping between input parameters and the output linguistic variables. The sample mapping rule is shown in Table 2.

Figure 3. The Sample Fuzzy Rule

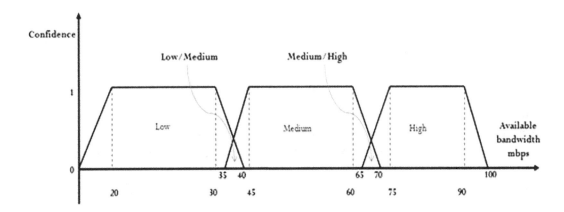

Table 1. Fuzzy IF_THEN_ELSE Rules

	Synchronous eLearning
R1	if bw_high AND data_low then remote _ processing
R2	if bw_high AND load_low then remote_processing
R3	if bw_high AND bat_low then remote_processing
R4	if bw_high AND vm_high then remote_processing
R5	if bw_medium AND vm_high then remote_processing
R6	if bw_low AND data_high then local_processing
R7	if bw_low AND load_high then local_processing
R8	if bw_low AND bat_high then local_processing
R9	if bw_low AND vm_low then local_processing

Table 2. Fuzzy Mapping Rules

BandwidthBattery	**Low**	**Medium**	**High**
Low	Local processing	Remote processing	Remote processing
Medium	Local processing	Remote processing	Remote processing
High	Local processing	Remote processing	Remote Processing

Defuzzification

A fuzzy logic system maps the input variable to a crisp output value. In order to get the crisp output, which can be easily understood by the users, we need defuzzification process. The input to the defuzzifier is fuzzy values, which is obtained from the fuzzy logic. The output is a single value after defuzzification. There are several methods used for defuzzification. This includes centroid method, maximum, mean of maximum, height and modified height. The most popular defuzzifier is the centroid or centre of gravity method. This returns the centre of gravity of the aggregated fuzzy set.

The defuzzification is done using Center of Gravity Method. The following formula is used to calculate the centroid.

$$COG\left(Execution\right) = \frac{\sum_{x}\mu_{execution}\left(x\right) \times x}{\sum_{x}\mu_{execution}\left(x\right)}$$

This function will give the grade of truth for the execution. The defuzzification is applied for the Remote Execution or Local Execution, which is the output parameter.

The response is formulated as a trapezoidal membership function as Local Execution (0, 12, 24, 48) and Remote Execution (36, 60, 72, 100).

Offloading Traces

The offloading traces are collected by creating an android application and distributed randomly among 5 people. At frequent intervals the residual battery charge, bandwidth, current CPU load and memory status is updated into a dataset and this data is used for the analysis. The data size for application calculated based on the maximum application size except the non-offloadable components. A server system as the cloud and the load on the server is calculated and entered. The number of VMs is taken randomly assuming there are only up to 100 parallel users and 50 VMs. At each usage of the App the data is filled in the dataset and this information is passed to the fuzzy decision engine for taking the offloading decision. This decision is also loaded into the data set. The following Figure shows the data set which is collected. Table 3 shows the sample dataset collected.

Sample Applications for Evaluation

An IOT application is created to check the performance of our offloading decision. The application is developed in the IBM Bluemix platform to collect the accelerometer and the GPS information of the mobile device. From the collected information a predictive system is generated to predict the location of the mobile device. The application will do both local processing and remote processing. A decision based on fuzzy logic is made whether to offload the computations or not. If the decision is yes the computations are done at the fog server and if the decision is "no" the prediction is done at the mobile device locally. Table 3 shows architecture of the sample IOT application.

Since mobile is having limited storage capacity, the application is designed in such a way that the local device will store the last 50 entries of the dataset. The fog server contains the entire dataset. If

Table 3. Sample Dataset Collected

Battery	Bandwidth	Latitude	Longitude	CPU Load %	Memory %	Data KB	Cloud Load	VMs
12	18	10 9056749	76 898556	54 310345	18 96373057	4	50 90909	35
12	18	10 9057687	76 8984582	61 702126	18 86010363	4	81 818184	14
100	18	10 9057503	76 898518	18 292683	16 89119171	4	75 268814	41
100	18	10 9057503	76 898518	43 589745	18 75647668	4	59 139782	12
99	18	10 9057819	76 8984201	6 779661	18 65284974	4	45 16129	36
99	18	10 9057819	76 8984201	10	18 86010363	4	42 718445	2
97	18	10 9057819	76 8984201	15 873016	18 86010363	4	10 344828	19
97	18	10 9057819	76 8984201	16 666668	18 65284974	4	35 338345	40
89	18	10 9057819	76 8984201	13 207547	18 65284974	4	49 152542	36
89	18	10 9057262	76 898497	13 793103	18 44559585	4	14 035088	37
89	18	10 9057262	76 898497	24 193548	18 5492228	4	11 864407	48
53	18	10 9057262	76 898497	18 181818	18 65284974	4	18 181818	10
53	18	10 9058474	76 8984411	5 555556	18 03108808	4	70 96774	33
23	18	10 9058484	76 8983998	25	14 61139896	4	18 181818	13
99	18	10 9056432	76 898546	13 114754	14 61139896	4	5 16129	46
99	54	10 9056432	76 898546	10	14 50777202	4	13 559322	48
99	72	10 9057768	76 8983674	21 818182	16 06217617	4	52 63158	49
97	18	10 9057633	76 8984127	13 793103	15 75129534	4	7 692308	19
97	18	10 9057554	76 8984236	12 903225	15 64766839	4	16 981133	5
89	54	10 9438116	76 9261363	31 081081	20 82901554	4	52 307693	37
89	54	10 9438116	76 9261363	25 454544	21 4507772	4	16 666668	21
89	54	10 9438114	76 9261365	29 508198	23 41968912	4	5 555556	23
53	54	10 9395911	76 9300612	25 287357	23 00518135	4	17 460318	33

the prediction is done locally, these 50 entries are used for prediction and if it is done at the fog server all values can be used for learning and prediction. Hence the local prediction is less accurate then the remote prediction. This application can be used to locate Alzheimer's patients in case they are missing or can be associated with school children to locate them if they found missing. The continuous location information along with context information is stored in the dataset and with that information an efficient prediction can be done for the current location. The architecture of the application can be shown below.

Any IOT application can be made efficient with the offloading technology. Smart home Applications for example, can be enhanced using offloading. An application which switches on the Air conditioner when you are near to the home can also be considered. The location can be constantly updated and when you are near to the location of the house the Air conditioner can be switched on. All smart applications with resource constraint devices can take the advantage of offloading like this.

Energy Model

The energy model calculation is used to calculate the prediction accuracy of the fuzzy logic based decision making. The local execution energy and remote execution energies are calculated based on the context information. If the local execution energy is greater than the calculated remote execution energy, the decision of offloading is "yes" or else a decision is taken not to offload the application but to execute it locally. The local and remote execution time based on the bandwidth information can be calculated as

$$\text{Time for local execution, } T_{mobile} = \frac{N}{S_{mobile}} \tag{1}$$

Time for offloading can be calculated as

$$T_{offload} = T_{trans} + T_{cloud} \tag{2}$$

$$T_{trans} = \frac{D}{b} \tag{3}$$

$$\text{Time for cloud execution, } T_{cloud} = \frac{N}{S_{cloud}} \tag{4}$$

If, the $T_{mobile} > T_{cloud} + \frac{D}{b}$ remote execution else, local execution.

If optimization choice is energy saving, the local execution energy and remote execution energy are calculated. If the local energy is higher than remote energy, the choice of offloading is "yes" else local execution is preferred. The local and remote energy based on the current network bandwidth can be calculated as

Local execution energy $E_{mobile} = P_{mobile} * T_{mobile}$ (5)

Energy for offloading can be calculated as

$$E_{offload} = E_{trans} + E_{cloud}$$ (6)

$$E_{trans} = P_{trans} * \frac{D}{b}$$ (7)

Energy for cloud execution, $E_{cloud} = P_{idle} * T_{cloud}$ (8)

If, $E_{mobile} > E_{cloud} + P_{trans} * \frac{D}{b}$ remote execution else, local execution.

If the optimization selection is based on both energy and time we are defining a new metrics called Energy Response time Weighted Sum (ERWS). ERWS is the combination of execution energy and response time. For a trade-off between the energy and response time, ERWS can be used.

$$ERWS_{mobile} = \omega * E_{mobile} + \left(1 - \omega\right) * T_{mobile}$$ (9)

$$ERWS_{offload} = \omega * E_{offload} + \left(1 - \omega\right) * T_{offload}$$ (10)

$ERWS_{mobile} > ERWS_{offload}$ remote execution else local execution.

where ω is the weighing factor, and if the value of $\omega > 0.5$ the importance is given to the energy of execution and $\omega < 0.5$ the consideration to save time and if the value is $\omega = 0.5$, both energy and time is considered equally. In our experiments we calculated the estimated time and energy based on $\omega = 0.5$.

Table 4 specifies all the symbols and their meanings.

Evaluation of Algorithm

The application which is considered is an IOT Application to predict the GPS location based on the pervious entries. The fuzzy logic for decision making is evaluated based on the following conditions. All the experiments are performed on a Gionee V4S Smartphone with a 1GHz Cortex- A8 CPU, 1GB RAM, and a 100-Mbps wireless LAN, MotoG Smartphone with 1GB RAM, Gionee P4 with 1GB RAM and 2 Samsung Galaxies with 1GB RAM. Each application is executed several times with different input datasets and operations. A server system is acting as the cloud server with a specification of 8GB RAM,

Table 4. Tradeoff Parameters

Symbol	Meanings
T_{mobile}	Execution time on mobile device
T_{cloud}	Execution time of the service on the cloud server
$T_{offload}$	Total time for offloading
T_{trans}	Transmission time between mobile and cloudlet/cloud
D	Transmitted data between mobile and cloud
b	Bandwidth between mobile device and cloud
P_{mobile}	Power for computing in mobile
P_{idle}	Idle power
P_{trans}	Power for transmission
$ERWS_{mobile}$	ERWS metrics for mobile
$ERWS_{offload}$	ERWS metrics for offloading
E_{mobile}	Energy for mobile device
$E_{offload}$	Energy for offloading
E_{trans}	Energy for transmission

64Bit Ubuntu with a 1TB hard disc where a replica of The IOT application is running. The parameters are passed to the Cloud for decision making and according to the decision the application is executed either on the server or locally. All the decision logic is executed at the cloud and the results are sent back to the mobile for further processing. Figure 4 shows the sample application architecture.

The application is executed randomly and the results are calculated.

Table 5 shows the result of execution for the application.

The test data is given as an input to the algorithms and the training data is given for verifying the accuracy of the system. The measures used for calculating the prediction accuracy are as follows.

False positive (FP), false negative (FN), true positive (TP), true negative (TN), sensitivity, specificity, accuracy, precision or positive predictive value (PPV), negative predictive value (NPV), F-measure and total mis-classification cost (TC).

False positive (FP) is the number of entries where local execution is beneficial but classified as remote execution. False negative (FN) is the number of entries that belong to a remote execution but

Figure 4. Sample IOT Application

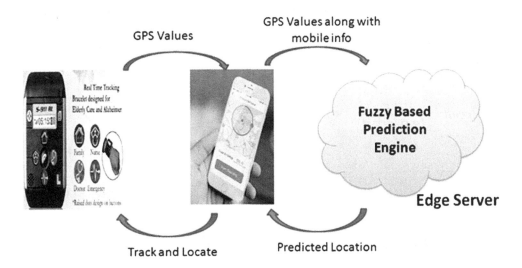

Table 5. Comparative Results with basic Classification Algorithms

Application Parameters	IOT Application				
	Offloading Decision with regression	Offloading Decision with Decision Tree	Decision with Naïve bayes	Offloading Decision with SVM Offloading	Offloading Decision with Fuzzy Logic
FP	18	11	9	7	3
FN	25	32	25	6	5
TP	502	478	460	521	556
TN	191	215	242	202	172
Sensitivity	0.9526	0.937255	0.948454	0.9886	0.991087
specificity	0.9139	0.951327	0.964143	0.9665	0.982857
Accuracy	0.9416	0.941576	0.953804	0.9823	0.98913
Precision	0.9654	0.977505	0.98081	0.9867	0.994633
NPV	0.8843	0.870445	0.906367	0.9712	0.971751
F-Measure	0.9589	0.956957	0.964361	0.9876	0.992857
Misclassification Rate	0.0584	0.058424	0.046196	0.0177	0.01087

were not allocated to it. True positive (TP) is number of entries that are correctly predicted as remote execution. True negative (TN) is the number of entries that did get predicted as remote execution and it is not beneficial to do remote execution (Gupta 2015).

Sensitivity is also called as true positive rate or recall. Sensitivity relates to the test's ability to identify positive results. It measures the proportion of actual positives which are correctly identified. Specificity relates to the ability of the test to identify negative results. It measures the proportion of negatives which are correctly identified. Accuracy is defined as proportion of sum of TP and TN against all positive and negative results. Positive predictive value or precision is defined as proportion of the TP against all the positive results (both TP and FP). Negative predictive value is defined as proportion of the TN against all the negative results (both TN and FN) (Fielding & Bell, 1997). The F-measure can be used as a single measure of performance of the test. The F-measure is the harmonic mean of precision and recall (Japkowicz & Shah, 2009). The total misclassification cost (TC) depends on the number of FP, FN and unclassified (UC) (Pham & Triantaphyllou, 2008). The formulas are given below:

$$Sensitivity\,or\,Recall = \frac{TP}{\left(TP + FN\right)}$$

$$Specificity = \frac{TN}{\left(TN + FP\right)}$$

$$Accuracy = \frac{\left(TP + TN\right)}{\left(TP + FN + TN + FP\right)}$$

$$Positive\,Prediction\,Value\,or\,Precision = \frac{TP}{\left(TP + FP\right)}$$

$$Negative\,Prediction\,Value = \frac{TN}{\left(TN + FN\right)}$$

$$F - Measure = 2 * \frac{\left(Precision * Recall\right)}{\left(Precision + Recall\right)}$$

$$TC = \left(CFP * FP\right) + \left(CFN * FN\right) + \left(CUC * UC\right)$$

$$Misclassification\,Rate = \frac{\left(FP + FN\right)}{\left(TP + FN + TN + FP\right)}$$

The approach proposed in this chapter is compared against the existing decision making algorithms such as regression, SVM, decision tree and Naïve bayes classifier. The following tables represent the accuracy of this algorithm with already existing algorithm which is considering only bandwidth as a decision parameter.

The results show that this algorithm which combines all the possible parameters is giving a better result and the misclassification rate is reduced. The possibility of a local execution mapped to a remote execution and remote execution mapped to local execution is reduced through this approach. The following table shows the evaluation of the fuzzy logic based method and simple linear regression based offloading decision.

Figure 5 and 6 represents the energy and time taken for different classification algorithms. Since the algorithm is executing on the cloud side the energy taken for fuzzy logic based algorithm is better than any other algorithms. Since the data is constantly send to the cloud and the decision algorithm is running at the cloud side the time efficiency at some times is lesser than other machine learning techniques. Since the accuracy is much higher than other algorithms our proposed fuzzy based approach will perform better than other classification algorithms.

Table 5 shows the F-measure comparison of various algorithms. The SVM shows closer performance to our proposed algorithm. But Fuzzy algorithm shows much better results than other classification algorithms.

Table 6 shows the grade of truth for perfect local and remote execution. With the proposed algorithm the accuracy is close to 100%.

CONCLUSION AND FUTURE WORK

This chapter is dealing with a decision algorithm for offloading. The decision considers all the possible parameters which will affect the offloading decision. The offloading decision making is taking place at the cloud side so that complex process and not executed at the mobile side to overload the mobile.

Figure 5. Comparison Chart of Time for Different Classification Techniques

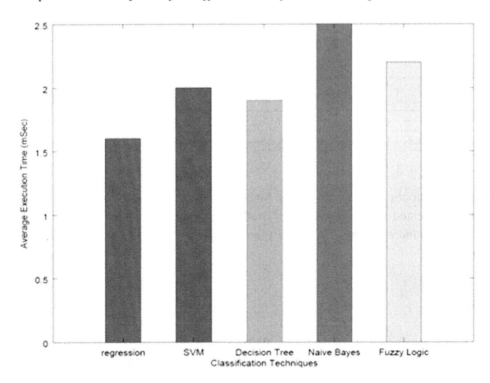

Figure 6. Comparison Chart of Energy for Different Classification Techniques

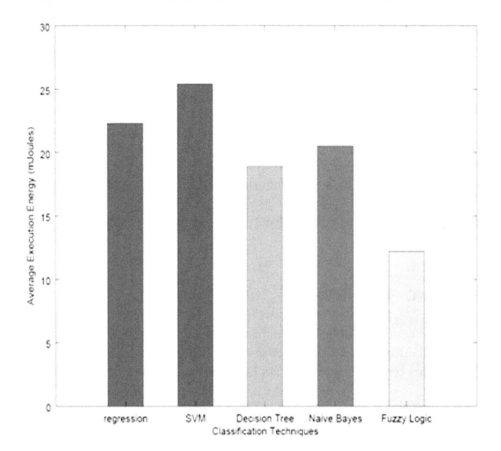

Table 6. Grade of Truth

Parameters	Decision	Grade of truth
Low Bandwidth + High Battery + High datasize+ Low VMs+ High users + High memory+ Low load	Local Execution	99.7
High Bandwidth + Low Battery + Low datasize+ High VMs+ Low users + Low memory+ High load	Remote Execution	99.8

Only the prediction process is happening at the Smartphone where a simple and much energy efficient algorithm is implemented so that it will never overburden the mobile side. But at the same time the bandwidth prediction increases the efficiency of the decision as the future bandwidth is considered for decision making.

REFERENCES

Barbera, M. V., Kosta, S., Mei, A., & Stefa, J. (2013). To offload or not to offload? The bandwidth and energy costs of mobile cloud computing. *2013. Proceedings - IEEE INFOCOM*, 1285–1293.

Buyya, R., Yeo, C. S., Venugopal, S., Broberg, J., & Brandic, I. (2009). Cloud computing and emerging IT platforms: Vision, hype, and reality for delivering computing as the 5th utility. *Future Generation Computer Systems*, *25*(6), 599–616. doi:10.1016/j.future.2008.12.001

Chun, B., Ihm, S., Maniatis, P., Naik, M., & Patti, A. (2011). CloneCloud. *Proceedings of the sixth conference on Computer systems - EuroSys '11*, 301–314. 10.1145/1966445.1966473

Cuervo, E., Balasubramanian, A., Cho, D., Wolman, A., Saroiu, S., Chandra, R., & Bahl, P. (2010). Maui. *Proceedings of the 8th international conference on Mobile systems, applications, and services - MobiSys '10*, 49-62.

Dhanya, N.M., & Kousalya, G. (2016) Context Aware Offloading Decision and Partitioning in Mobile Cloud Computing. *Asian Journal of Information Technology, 15*(13), 2177-2185.

Dhanya, N. M., Kousalya, G., & Balakrishnan, P. (2017). Dynamic mobile cloud offloading prediction based on statistical regression. *Journal of Intelligent & Fuzzy Systems*, *32*(4), 3081–3089. doi:10.3233/JIFS-169251

Ellouze, A., Gagnaire, M., & Haddad, A. (2015). A Mobile Application Offloading Algorithm for Mobile Cloud Computing. *2015 3rd IEEE International Conference on Mobile Cloud Computing, Services, and Engineering*, 34-40.

Fielding, A. H., & Bell, J. F. (1997). A review of methods for the assessment of prediction errors in conservation presence/absence models. *Environmental Conservation*, *24*(1), 38–49. doi:10.1017/S0376892997000088

Gupta, G. K. (2015). *Introduction to data mining with case studies*. Delhi: PHI Learning Private Limited.

Gurun, S., Wolski, R., Krintz, C., & Nurmi, D. (2008). On the Efficacy of Computation Offloading Decision-Making Strategies. *International Journal of High Performance Computing Applications*, *22*(4), 460–479. doi:10.1177/1094342007095289

Japkowicz, N., & Shah, M. (2009). *Evaluating Learning Algorithms: a classification perspective*. Cambridge, UK: Cambridge University Press.

Kemp, R., Palmer, N., Kielmann, T., & Bal, H. (2012). Cuckoo: A Computation Offloading Framework for Smartphones. *Lecture Notes of the Institute for Computer Sciences, Social Informatics and Telecommunications Engineering Mobile Computing, Applications, and Services*, 59-79.

Macario, H. R., & Srirama, S. (2013). Adaptive code offloading for mobile cloud applications. *Proceeding of the fourth ACM workshop on Mobile cloud computing and services - MCS '13*, 9-16. 10.1145/2497306.2482984

Mukherjee, A., Gupta, P., & De, D. (2014). Mobile cloud computing based energy efficient offloading strategies for femtocell network. *2014 Applications and Innovations in Mobile Computing (AIMoC)*, 22-33.

Oueis, J., Strinati, E. C., & Barbarossa, S. (2014). Multi-parameter decision algorithm for mobile computation offloading. *2014 IEEE Wireless Communications and Networking Conference (WCNC)*, 3005-3010. 10.1109/WCNC.2014.6952959

Pham, H. N., & Triantaphyllou, E. (2008). The Impact of Overfitting and Overgeneralization on the Classification Accuracy in Data Mining. *Soft Computing for Knowledge Discovery and Data Mining,* 391-431.

Wolski, R. (2003). Experiences with predicting resource performance on-line in computational grid settings. *Performance Evaluation Review, 30*(4), 41. doi:10.1145/773056.773064

Wolski, R., Gurun, S., Krintz, C., & Nurmi, D. (2008). Using bandwidth data to make computation offloading decisions. *2008 IEEE International Symposium on Parallel and Distributed Processing,* 1–8. 10.1109/IPDPS.2008.4536215

Wolski, R., Spring, N. T., & Hayes, J. (1999). The network weather service: A distributed resource performance forecasting service for metacomputing. *Future Generation Computer Systems, 15*(5-6), 757–768. doi:10.1016/S0167-739X(99)00025-4

Wu, H., Huang, D., & Bouzefrane, S. (2013). Making Offloading Decisions Resistant to Network Unavailability for Mobile Cloud Collaboration. *Proceedings of the 9th IEEE International Conference on Collaborative Computing: Networking, Applications and Worksharing,* 168 - 177. 10.4108/icst.collaboratecom.2013.254106

KEY TERMS AND DEFINITIONS

Energy Efficiency: Dealing with energy efficiency in mobile using offloading.

Fog Computing: Instead of distant cloud, the nearby fog server can be used for offloading for better energy and time efficiency.

Fuzzy Logic: Fuzzy logic can be used for making offloading decision.

IOT Application: Any IOT applications can take advantage of offloading.

Mobile Cloud Offloading: The resource constraint mobile can be attached with cloud for better energy and time efficiency.

Offloading Decision Making: Offloading is not always beneficial. Hence, a decision must be made about whether to offload or not.

Time Efficiency: The application can be completed with lesser time than running on the mobile devices.

Chapter 10
Data Mining Algorithms and Techniques

Ambika P.
Kristu Jayanti College, India

ABSTRACT

Integration of data mining tasks in day-to-day life has become popular and common. Everyday people are confronted with opportunities and challenges with targeted advertising, and data mining techniques will help the businesses to become more efficient by reducing processing cost. This goal of this chapter is to provide a comprehensive review about data mining, data mining techniques, popular algorithms, and their impact on fog computing. This chapter also gives further research directions on data mining on fog computing.

INTRODUCTION

Development of IoT and the prevalence of ubiquitously connected smart devices are main source of computing. Computing paradigms process big data which categorize rapidly generated, wide variety of huge volumes of data. Gartner – technology research and advisory corporate said nearly 26 billion devices will be connected in the Internet of Things by 2020. Intelligent data mining and analysis plays a key role to achieve benefits in the following fields: Business, medicine, science and engineering etc.,

What Is Data Mining?

Data mining is a method of analysing data and finding out new patterns from large data set. Data mining contains lot of definitions from different authors Agrawal et al. (1991), Han & Yu(1996), Zomya et al(1999) and Jong (1995). In other words, it is a convenient way of extracting useful knowledge from the massive data sets like trends, patterns and rules. In recent days, large amount of data is created from multiple sources and mining tasks focus on issues related to feasibility, usefulness, scalability and effectiveness. Data mining is a process of Knowledge Discovery from Data which extracts implicit, previously unknown and useful patterns or rules from historical data (Jiawei, Kamber & Pei, 2012).

DOI: 10.4018/978-1-5225-5972-6.ch010

Why Data Mining

Data mining is needed for any organisational tasks because of many reasons. While analysing and generating relationships between features, analysts and knowledge engineers often do mistakes, data mining techniques possibly applied to these kinds of problems to find solutions.

Computing paradigms like Cloud, grid, fog and roof computing are all aimed at allowing access to large amounts of computing power in a fully virtualized environment by connecting resources in to a single view. In other words, these computing paradigms offer storage, computing and software as a utility to the consumers. Cloud computing signifies a computing infrastructure in which businesses and individuals access applications anywhere in the world on demand (Buyya, 2009). Vaquero et al. (2009) said clouds provide large pool of virtualised resources like hardware, platform and services. These resources can be customized to achieve optimum resource utilization. Those resources utilized as pay-per use model and Service Level Agreements (SLA) ensures negotiable services between service providers and consumers.

Though cloud computing is a popular computing paradigm and widely used in many applications and has its own limitations such as latency, lack of mobility support and location awareness. Result of these limitations a new computing paradigm fog computing have emerged to provide elastic resources at the edge of the network. Fog Computing is a technology that enables data processing in smart devices. Fog computing motivates promising computing paradigm by ubiquitously connected smart devices. It also makes data and computation close to users by processing data at the network level of smart devices. Due to data processing at network level fog computing achieves the following advantages such as low latency, high bandwidth and location awareness

In fog computing, fog nodes facilitate resources at the edge of the network. Like cloud computing elastic resources (computation, storage and networking) are the building blocks of fog computing and most of the cloud computing technologies can be directly applied to fog computing.

Fog computing has several unique properties; some of them are listed below.

1. Very close to end users.
2. Location-awareness which allows the fog node to infer its own location and track end user devices to support mobility.
3. Edge analytics and stream mining helps to reduce data volume at a very early stage and cut down delay which saves bandwidth.

There are several techniques emerged to keep computing resource at the edge of the network to support latency-sensitive applications and services. In recent years, data mining techniques have evolved and become used in cloud and fog computing. Cloud/fog providers use data mining to provide clients better service. Data mining allows organisation to centralize the data storage and management of software with a reliable secure service to the users. Goal of data mining includes prediction and description. Prediction helps us to predict unknown by identifying new inferences and description focuses on finding patterns on existing data and helps for user interpretation.

Data mining helps the process of extracting structured information from unstructured or semi-structured web data sources in fog computing. Mining techniques through fog computing allows everyone to centralize the management of software and data storage, with assurance of efficient, reliable and secure services. It allows us to retrieve meaningful information from virtually integrated data warehouse that reduces the costs of infrastructure and storage.

Data Mining Process

Cross Industry Standard Process for Data Mining (CRISP-DM) (Shearer, 2000) breaks the iterative process of data mining in to six phases represented in Figure 1.

- Problem definition
- Data exploration
- Data preparation
- Modelling
- Evaluation
- Deployment

Problem Definition

Initial step of data mining process starts to formulate a problem definition depends on business. Business Problem must be clearly defined and it is easier to translate the business objective in to data mining task. Business experts, domain experts and data mining experts work closely and derive requirements at this phase.

Data Exploration

This phase includes finding the right source of data and domain experts understand the meaning of metadata. It includes data collection, description and exploration.

Figure 1. CRISP- Data Mining Process (source: http://www.crisp-dm.org/Process/index.htm)

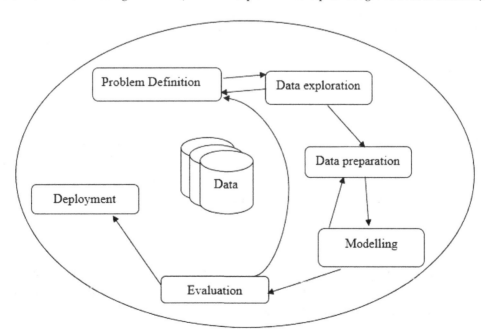

Data Preparation

Data pre-processing is required before modelling, this phase includes tasks like cleaning, data integration and transformation. An ETL (extraction, transformation and loading) tool is used at this level.

Modelling

Model is constructed based on the business requirement. Various modelling techniques are selected and applied with the help of data mining tools. Usually it is an iterative process in which more than one data mining techniques are experimented to achieve optimal values. It can also be coupled with evaluation process.

Evaluation

Evaluation step involve checking model accuracy and effectiveness. If the model does not perform well then we have to rebuild the model by changing its parameters until optimal results are achieved.

Deployment

Interpreting the results of data mining to the decision makers is the final and important step in data mining process. Data mining tools often visualize the results using various methods.

Data Mining Tasks

Data Mining techniques plays vital role in many area of applications such as education, healthcare, fraud detection, market basket analysis etc.,. Data mining tasks are distinct and are needed to find different kind of patterns. Data Summarisation, Data Clustering, Data Classification, Detection of Outliers, Association Rule Mining and trend analysis are basic data mining techniques.

Data Summarization

It is a process of abstraction or generalization of data and relevant data are summarized. The results of the abstraction are small which gives us an overview of the data or aggregated data. This process can have different abstraction level and can be viewed from different angles. Different combination of abstraction levels or dimensions reveals various kinds of patterns. Yoo-Kang Ji et al. (2014) used data summarisation method to extract semantic feature in distributed network. Splunk cloud knowledge manager uses summarization and indexing to increase report efficiency.

Classification

It is a process of classifying objects based on their attributes. Set of objects in the training dataset is represented by vector of attributes. Classification model is built by analysing the relationship between attributes and the objects in the training set. It can also accurately predict the class to which a new case belongs.

Popular Data Mining Algorithms

This chapter puts forward the most important data mining algorithms used in the research field of cloud and fog computing.

C4.5

Decision tree is a classification method used in many data mining applications and also assists decision making process Witten & Frank (2005), Berryand & Linoff (1997) and Quinlan (1990). A decision tree is a directed tree with a root node and has no incoming edges and exactly one incoming edges with all other nodes.

ID3, C4.5 and CART are most popular decision tree algorithms which require training data sample datasets to do classification. Each internal node split the instance in to two or more parts at the training stage with objective of optimizing the performance of the classifier. Every path from the root node to the leaf node forms a decision rule to determine the sample to which class belongs to. The core algorithm to build decision tree is ID3 by J.R.Quinlan uses top-down greedy search through possible branches with no back tracking. ID3 uses entropy and information gain to construct decision trees. Authors Nikam, Katkar and Umathe (2016) have implemented ID3 classification algorithm for intrusion detection on cloud. They promised solution for malware prone host computers mainly computer using windows based operating system. CART (Classification and Regression Trees) deals with both continuous and categorical attributes and also handles missing values.

CART algorithm is the foundation for decision trees, random forest and boosted decision trees. CART algorithm selects input variables and spilt points on those variables until a suitable tree is constructed. On the selected input variable specific spilt is chosen using greedy algorithm to minimize the cost function. Finally, tree is constructed using with a predefined stopping criteria mostly minimum count on the number of training instances assigned to each leaf node. It also uses cost complexity pruning to remove the unreliable from the decision tree to improve the accuracy. Other well-known decision tree algorithm is C4.5 (Quinlan, 1993) (Quinlan, 1996). Some of the improvements of C4.5 compared to ID3 are C4.5 employs information gain, handles continuous attributes, handles incomplete training data with missing values also prunes the tree to avoid overfitting (Ventura & Martinez, 1995 and Li & Hu, 2008). Its successor C5.0 is devised Ross Quinlan in the 1970s. Major differences between C4.5 and C5.0 are respectively,

- C5.0 rulesets have low error rates and both have same predictive accuracy
- C5.0 is faster and optimized
- C5.0 requires less memory

Algorithm

- Given set if S samples, C4.5 constructs initial tree using divide and conquer algorithm
- If all the samples in X belong to same class or X is small, the leaf is labelled with most frequent class in X.

- Else choose a test for an attribute with two or more outcomes. Build the tree with the chosen initial test and each outcome become its branches. Partition X in to corresponding subsets $X_1, X_2, ...$, apply the same procedure recursively to each subset according to the outcome.

K Means

The k-means algorithm is a simple iterative clustering method to partition a given data set in to a user specified number of clusters, k. Items are moved among sets of clusters until the desired set is achieved. High degree of similarity among elements in clusters is obtained while high degree of dissimilarity among elements indifferent clusters is also achieved simultaneously. The clusters mean of $K_i = \{t_{i1}, t_{i2}, ..., t_{im}\}$ is defined as:

$$m_i = \frac{1}{m} \sum_{j=1}^{m} t_{ij} \tag{1}$$

This algorithm operates on m- dimensional vectors where t_i denotes the ith data point. Initially the algorithm chooses k points as centroids which could be assigned randomly and setting them as solution of clustering a small subset or global mean of k times. Then the algorithm iterates till the centroid converges.

Algorithm

- Assign initial values for means $m_1, m_2, ..., m_k$
- Repeat the following
  - Assign each item t_i to the cluster which has the closest
  - Calculate the new mean for each cluster
  - Until convergence criteria is met

Cluster samples closest property is determined by Euclidean distance. K-means finds local optimum but it actually misses the global optimum. K-means does not work on categorical data since mean must be defined on the attribute type. Many cloud applications use this algorithm to process the documents and also used in parallel programming (Zhao, Huifang & He, 2009) to scale well and efficiently process large data sets. Juan et al (2017) have also experimented unsupervised k-means clustering on utilizing cloud computing technologies for efficient process of hyper spectral data.

Support Vector Machines (SVM)

A supervised learning method which analyse data and recognise patterns that can be used for classification and regression analysis. SVM is a statistical learning which minimizes the empirical training error through maximizing the margin between the separating hyper plane and the data. SVM can operate either linear or non-linear way.

Linear SVM

Linear SVM classifies the linearly separable data set by constructing decision hyper plane that passes through the middle of the two classes. When a new testing data is added, it can be classified by testing the sign of the hyper plane function. The distance between the hyper plane and the nearest data point from any of the data set is referred as margin. The aim of the SVM is to find a hyper plane with maximum margin. Best classification performance is found by maximizing the margin between the two classes. If we select a hyper-plane having low margin then there is high chance of miss-classification. The algorithm selects the hyper-plane which classifies the classes accurately prior to maximizing margin. In Figure 2, hyper-plane B has a classification error and A has classified all correctly.

Non-Linear SVM

It is hard to classify the real-life problems in linear way, in which data will be mapped from input space in to high dimensional feature space by a non-linear transformation. Cover's theorem stated that if the transformation is non-linear and the dimensionality is high enough, then the input space may be transformed in to a new feature space where the patterns are linearly separable with high probability. Non - linear transformations did using kernel functions. The kernel function used to define a variety of non-linear relationship between its inputs. The use of implicit kernels allows reducing the dimension of the problem and overcoming dimension curse problem. Many researches in recent years have gone in to experimenting different kernel functions (Scholkopf & Smola, 2002) for classification and for other tests. For example, if we have following non-linear data sample can be transformed in to high dimensional space which can be linearly separable (Figure 3).

Figure 2. Example for misclassification of B hyperplane

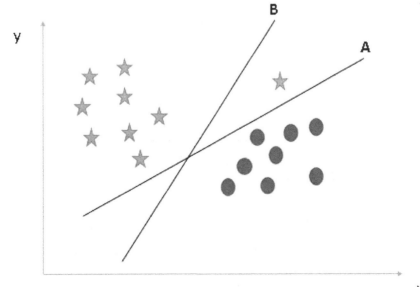

Figure 3. Non-linear class samples transformed in to high dimensional space

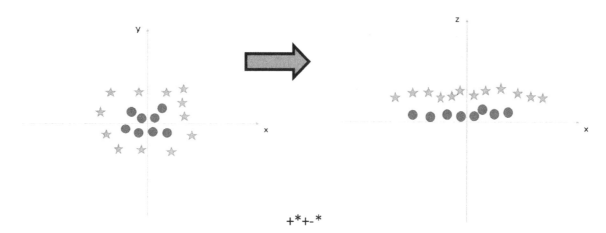

+*+-*

There are different variations in kernel functions $K\left(X_i, X_j\right)$ to construct different hyperplane in feature space. Table 1 shows three typical kernel functions.

SVM can be further extended to perform two different tasks, one to perform regression analysis other extension to rank elements rather classification.

Apriori Algorithm

Apriori Algorithm is a frequent item set mining by identifying the frequent individual items in the data base. Once frequent item sets are determined then association rules are generated with higher confidence. The frequent item sets can be used to determine association rules which highlight the general trends in the data base.

It is proposed by R. Agarwal and R. Srikant in 1994 to determine frequent item sets for Boolean association rules. It is an iterative approach where k-item sets are used to explore (k+1) item sets. First, a set of frequent 1 item sets determined by scanning the data base and collect those items that satisfy minimum support, result set is denoted as R1. R1 is used to find R2 which could be frequent 2 item sets

Table 1.

Kernel Function	Inner product kernel $K\left(X_i, X_j\right), i = 1, 2, \ldots, N$
Polynomial kernel	$K\left(X_i, X_j\right) = \left(X^T X_i + 1\right)^d$
Gaussian Kernel	$K\left(X_i, X_j\right) = \exp\left(-X - X_i^2 / 2\sigma^2\right)$
Multi-layer perceptron	$K\left(X_i, X_j\right) \tanh\left(\beta_0 X^T X_i + \beta_1\right)$ $\beta_0 \, and \, \beta_1 \, are \, decided \, by \, the \, user$

that could be used to find R3 and so on till no frequent k-item sets can be found. Finding all frequent item sets requires repetitive scanning of data base. In order to improve the efficiency of the algorithm, Apriori algorithm uses a special property called Apriori property which reduces the search space. If an item set *i* does not satisfy the minimum support threshold, then it is not frequent item set and cannot be included in the candidate set. It has the following two-step process:

Step 1: Join
To find R_k, a set of candidate k-itemsets can be generated by joining R_{k-1} with itself. All these have denoted as candidate set C_k
Let r_1 and r_2 be item sets in R_{k-1} then r_1 and r_2 are joined if their first (k-2) items are in common $(r_1[1]=r_2[1]).(r_1[2]=r_2[2])\ldots(r_1[k-2]=r_2[k-2].r_1[k-1]<r_2[k-1])$
Step 2: Prune
Ck is a superset of r_k. Determine the count of each candidate in C_k that would result in determining r_k. Pruning is done by applying apriori property.
Any (k-1) item set is not frequent then it can be removed from C_k
Apriori Algorithm
R_1 = (find frequent 1 itemsets(D))
for $(k=2;R_{k-1}\neq\varnothing;k++)$ begin
Ck=apriori_gen(R_{k-1})
For each transactions $t \epsilon D$
C1=subset (C_k,t)
For each candidate $c \epsilon C_t$
c.count ++;
end
R_k = {$c \epsilon C_k$ | c.count >= min_support
end
end
Return $R = \cup_k R_k$

Apriori algorithm is transplanted in Hadoop framework (Zhang, Yu & Zheng, 2014) to improve the parallel mining. The algorithm has an inbuilt map reduce and also reduces the scanning time significantly. The author Jongwook (2012) proposed Apriori-Map/Reduce Algorithm and illustrated its time complexity, which theoretically shows that the algorithm gains much higher performance than the sequential algorithm as the map and reduce nodes get added. The item sets produced by the algorithm can be adopted to compute and produce Association Rule for market analysis.

K-Nearest Neighbor (KNN)

KNN is one of the sophisticated learners used in pattern recognition. It is a classification technique learns by comparing n given test sample with the training sample that are similar to it. The similarity is determined by distance metric. There are many existing distance measures; KNN uses Euclidean distance measure to evaluate the distance between two samples.

Example: Assume X and Y are two different samples with n attributes, then distance between the two sample can then be calculated using the following Euclidean formula,

$$distance\left(X_{ij}, Y_{ij}\right) = \sqrt{\sum_{i,j=1}^{n}\left(X_{ij} - Y_{ij}\right)^{2}}$$

In KNN, all samples are represented in n-dimensional space where each sample is a point in the space. In the testing phase, if an unknown sample is entered, KNN algorithm searches for a space for the unknown sample to which closest training sample.

KNN algorithm

Input: T – set of training samples and test sample S = (x',y')
Start
Compute the distance d(x',y'), the distance between S=(x',y') do
Select D from the set of k closest training samples to S

Output: y' = argmax $\displaystyle\sum_{\left(x_i, y_i\right) \in D_z} I\left(v = y_i\right)$

Naïve Bayes

It is a classification algorithm works based on Bayes Theorem which assumes the presence of a particular feature in a class is unrelated to the presence of any other feature. All the features are depending on each other and independently contribute to the probability. It is a lazy learner and useful for very large datasets

Bayes theorem provides a way of calculating posterior probability P(A|B) from P(A), P(B) and P(A|B). Look at the equation below:

$$P\left(A \mid B\right) = \frac{P\left(B \mid A\right) P\left(A\right)}{P\left(B\right)}$$

$$P\left(A \mid B\right) = P\left(b_1 \mid A\right) \times \left(b_2 \mid A\right) \times \ldots \ldots \times P\left(b_n \mid A\right) \times P\left(A\right)$$

$P\left(A \mid B\right)$ – Posterior Probability of the target sample for the given predictor

$P\left(A\right)$ – Prior probability

$P\left(B \mid A\right)$ – Likelihood which is the probability of predictor

$P\left(B\right)$ – prior probability of the predictor

Krunal et al used naïve Bayes' statistical classifier to predict the probability of a given network event belong to a particular class (normal or intrusion). He has proved higher accuracy and speed than the

ANN classifier (Krunal & Rohit, 2013). Naïve Bayes model size is low and quite constant with respect to the data. The Naïve Bayes models cannot represent complex behaviour so it won't get into over fitting.

Most interesting part of Naïve Bayes is it performs when we have multiple classes like text classification. Some of the advantages of Naïve Bayes Classifier are it is simple if the conditional independence assumption exists and requires less training time to train the model. It also quickly converges than other discriminative models.

Naïve Bayes classifier also handles missing values by ignoring the sample during model building and classification. It is robust for irrelevant attributes. If A_i is an irrelevant attribute, then $P (A_i \mid B)$ become distributed. The class conditional probability for A_i has no impact on the overall computation of the posterior probability. Correlated attributes can degrade the performance of the model because the conditional independence assumption no longer holds for such attributes. It is mostly used in text classification and with problems having multiple classes.

Some of the merits and demerits of Naïve Bayes classifier are as follows:

- Easy and fast prediction in multiclass
- It performs well in categorical inputs compared to numerical variables
- If categorical variable is not observed and assigned as zero, for smoothing we have to go for Laplace estimation
- Another limitation is assumption of independent predictors.

Applications of Naïve Bayes Classifier

Text Classification: Naïve Bayes used as most powerful algorithm to do text classification to identify sentiments of different people in social media and can do spam filtering to identify spam emails

Recommender Systems: Naïve Bayes classifier and machine learning algorithms works with collaborative filtering filters unseen information and can predict whether a user would like the given service or not.

Successful Data Mining Tasks Towards Fog Computing

Edge or fog computing is a process of optimizing cloud systems by providing data processing at the edge of the network to where the data is created. The goal of fogging is to improve efficiency and reduce the amount of data transported to the cloud for processing, analysis and storage.

There are numerous opportunities for data mining algorithms on edge computing which creates a competitive edge for IoT devices. For example: IoT devices and applications on some traffic lights or manufacturing companies. These devices capture real data and can be used to prevent from failing, reroute traffic and optimize production. When the cloud and its services are not available then data analysis is done at the edge of the network. Data mining algorithms play a vital role in Edge Analytics.

When huge amount of priceless data moved to cloud, data loss and slow decisions are not accepted by the user. Edge computing platform provides instant intelligence by enabling data analytics using different data mining algorithms at the edge.

Some of the data mining techniques helps in edge computing (Table 2).

Table 2.

Data Mining Task	Purpose
Clustering	Data exploration applied to find customer segments
Classification	Prediction for predicting a specific outcome as response
Association	Frequent item set mining used for market basket analysis, cross-sell and root cause analysis
Regression	Prediction for predicting continuous numerical outcome
Anomaly detection	Identifying unusual and deviation from the normal behaviour. Example are fraud detection
Feature Extraction	Identifying patterns by identifying linear combination of existing attributes.

FUTURE OF DATA MINING

Data mining in cloud computing is the process of extracting structured information from unstructured or semi-structured web data sources. Cloud computing allowed organisations to centralize the management of software and data storage. It also assured efficient, reliable and secure services to the users. Data mining implementation on cloud allows the user to retrieve meaningful information from virtually integrated data warehouse that reduces the costs of infrastructure and storage. Most of the organisations are emphasizing on distributed nature of the data instead of size. Privacy is often overlooked and an important area of research which also consider how data mining activities affects users whose data are being mined.

Edge mining enables data mining on wireless, battery powered and smart sensing devices at the edge points of the IoT. Though the local data reduces the transformation, energy usage and remote storage requirement but has risk on personal privacy. IoT Edge Analytics is typically applicable for Oil Rigs, Mines and Factories which operate in low bandwidth, low latency environments. Edge Analytics could apply not just to sensor data but also to richer forms of data such as Video analytics.

Impact of data mining tasks on fog computing has two stages, first one is creating analytical model and executing analytics model. Creating involves collecting, storing and preparing the data, choosing the analytics program, training the algorithms and validating the goodness of the model. Executing the built analytical model at the edge is the second stage. Predictive Model Mark-up Language (PMML) is an XML based predictive model provide a way for the analytical applications to explicitly describe the model which is created.

SUMMARY

Data mining is a broad area which integrates techniques from different fields like machine learning, pattern recognition, statistics, artificial intelligence and data warehouse. This chapter gives information about overview of data mining, data mining tasks, popular data mining algorithms, applications of data mining algorithms, data mining on Fog computing. It also provides necessity and utility of data mining algorithms in Fog computing. As the need of user is growing every day, the ability of integrating data mining algorithms and techniques on the Fog computing become more stringent.

REFERENCES

Agrawal, R., Imienski, D., & Swamy, A. (1991). *Database Mining: A Performance Perspective. IEEE Tran. on Knowledge and Data Engg.*

Berryand, M. J., & Linoff, G. S. (1997). *Data mining techniques: For marketing, sales, and customer support.* John Wiley & Sons, Inc.

Buyya, R., Yeo, C. S., Venugopal, S., Broberg, J., & Brandic, I. (2009). Cloud Computing and emerging IT platforms:Vision,hype, and reality for delivering computing as the 5th utility. *Future Generation Computer Systems, 25*(6), 599–616. doi:10.1016/j.future.2008.12.001

Han, J., & Yu, P. S. (1996). Data Mining: An Overview from a Database Perspective. *IEEE Tran. on Knowledge and Data Engg.*

Han, J., Kamber, M., & Pei, J. (1996). *Data Mining Concept and Technique* (3rd ed.). Morgan Kaufmann.

Haut, Paoletti, Plaza, & Plaza. (2017). Cloud implementation of the K-means algorithm for hyperspectral image analysis. *Journal of Supercomputing, 73*, 514–529. DOI: 10.1007/s11227-016-1896-3

Ji, Y.-K., Kim, Y.-I., & Park, S. (2014). Big Data Summarization Using Semantic Feature for IoT on Cloud. *Contemporary Engineering Sciences, 7*(22), 1095–1103. doi:10.12988/ces.2014.49137

Li, H., & Hu, X. M. (2008). Analysis and comparison between ID3 Algorithm and C4.5 Algorithm in Decision Tree. *Water Resources and Power, 26*(2), 129–132.

Nikam, V. R., Katkar, G. S., & Umathe, M. K. (2016). Statistical Pattern Classification and Data Mining Approach through Cloud Computing. *IOSR Journal of Computer Engineering*, 24-29.

Park, Chen, &Yu, S.(1995). An effective hashbased algorithm for mining association rules. *Proceedings of ACM-SiGMOID international Conference on Management of Data.*

Patel, K., & Srivastava, R. (2013). Classification of Cloud Data using Bayesian Classification. *International Journal of Science and Research, 2*(6), 80–85.

Quinlan, J. R. (1990). Decision trees and decision-making. *IEEE Transactions on Systems, Man, and Cybernetics, 20*(2), 339–346. doi:10.1109/21.52545

Quinlan, J. R. (1993). *C4.5 programs for machine learning.* Morgan Kaufmann Publishers.

Quinlan, J. R. (1996). Improved use of continuous attributes in C4.5. *Journal of Artificial Intelligence Research, 4*(1), 77–90.

Scholkopf, B., & Smola, A. J. (2002). *Learning with kernels.* MIT Press.

Shearer, C. (2000). The CRISP-DM model: The new blueprint for data mining. *Journal of Data Warehousing, 5*, 13–22.

Vaquero, L. M., Rodero-Merio, L., Caceres, J., & Lindner, M. (2009). A break in the clouds: Towards a cloud definition. *Computer Communication Review, 39*(1), 50–55. doi:10.1145/1496091.1496100

Ventura, D., & Martinez, T. R. (1995). An empirical comparison of discretization methods. *Proceedings of the tenth international symposium on Computer and information sciences*, 443-450.

Witten, H. I., & Frank, E. (2005). *Data Mining: Practical machine learning tools and techniques*. Morgan Kaufmann.

Woo, J. (2012). Apriori-Map/Reduce Algorithm. *WORLDCOMP'12 - The 2012 World Congress in Computer Science, Computer Engineering, and Applied Computing*.

Zhang, D., Yu, H., & Zheng, L. (2014). Apriori Algorithm Research Based on Map-Reduce in Cloud Computing Environments. *The Open Automation and Control Systems Journal*, 6(1), 368–373. doi:10.2174/1874444301406010368

Zhao, W., Ma, H., & He, Q. (2009). Parallel K-Means Clustering Based on MapReduce. *IEEE International Conference on Cloud Computing*.

Zomya, A. Y., Ghazawi, T. E., & Frieder, O. (1999). Parallel and Distributed Computing for Data Mining. *IEEE Concurrency*, 7(4), 11–13. doi:10.1109/MCC.1999.806974

Chapter 11
Machine Learning

Ambika P.
Kristu Jayanti College, India

ABSTRACT

Machine learning is a subfield of artificial intelligence that encompass the automatic computing to make predictions. The key difference between a traditional program and machine-learning model is that it allows the model to learn from the data and helps to make its own decisions. It is one of the fastest growing areas of computing. The goal of this chapter is to explore the foundations of machine learning theory and mathematical derivations, which transform the theory into practical algorithms. This chapter also focuses a comprehensive review on machine learning and its types and why machine learning is important in real-world applications, and popular machine learning algorithms and their impact on fog computing. This chapter also gives further research directions on machine learning algorithms.

INTRODUCTION

Machine learning (ML) was introduced in the late 1950's as a technique for artificial intelligence (AI) (Ayodele, 2010). Over time, its focus evolved and shifted more to algorithms that are computationally viable and robust. In the last decade, machine learning techniques have been used extensively for a wide range of tasks including classification and regression in a variety of application areas such as bioinformatics, speech recognition, spam detection, computer vision and fraud detection. The algorithms and techniques used come from many diverse fields including statistics, mathematics, neuroscience, and computer science.

Classical Definitions of Machine Learning

- The development of computer models for learning processes that provide solutions to the problem of knowledge acquisition and enhance the performance of developed systems (Duffy,1997).
- The adoption of computational methods for improving machine performance by detecting and describing consistencies and patterns in training data (Langley & Simon, 1995).

DOI: 10.4018/978-1-5225-5972-6.ch011

A learning algorithm takes training data as input that represents experience and output will perform some actions. There are two general types of learning Supervised and Unsupervised Learning. Both learning methods need some interaction between learner and the environment. Difference between both learning is explained in the following example. In the task of detecting spam email and anomaly detection, the model gets input as email messages and the task in to detect and assign labels spam or not spam. The above type of learning is referred as supervised. It can also be used to predict the missing portion in the unseen sample. Unsupervised learning processes the input data with the goal of grouping similar objects. Clustering is the typical example of unsupervised learning.

What Is Machine Learning?

Smart data analysis become more pervasive and a necessary ingredient for technological process due to increasing amount of data. Machine Learning is an emerging field of research that deeply focuses on the theory, performance and properties of learning systems and algorithms. Machine Learning algorithms concerned about the problems of making decisions from limited information. Machine Learning literature describes it as a problem of "predicting from expert advice". It is explained as "A learning algorithm is given the task each day of predicting whether it will rain or not today". To make such decisions, a prediction algorithm is given with the advice of n "experts" as input. Each expert predicts yes or no and then the learning algorithm must use this information in order to make its own prediction. After making such prediction then it is told to that system whether it is rained or not.

Machine Learning teaches computers to do that comes naturally to humans. Machine Learning algorithms use computational methods that learn information through experience from data without relying on a predetermined equation as a model. It finds natural patterns in data that generate insight and help to make better decisions and predictions.

It is an interdisciplinary field from many different fields such as Artificial Intelligence (AI), statistics, optimization theory, mathematics, information theory, optimal control and many other fields Mitchell (1997), Russell & Norvig (1995), Cherkassky & Mulier (2007) and Mitchell (2006). Machine Learning has covered almost every scientific domain application that has also brought major impact in the society (Rudin & Wagstaff, 2014). Some of the applications (Bishop, 2006) include recommendation systems, recognition systems and autonomous control systems. It can also be used every day to make critical decisions in

medical diagnosis, stock trading and energy load forecasting. We would always have dilemma when to use machine learning algorithms and how would it differ from traditional algorithms. Consider a complex task or problem involving large volume of data and has lot of variables, but no existing formula or equation then machine learning is a good option to handle.

A machine learning (ML) algorithm would be trained on a training data to 'learn' how to recognize any face, where a simple algorithm would not be of performing this task, a ML algorithm would not only be able to categorize the photos as trained, it would continuously learn from testing data and add to its "learning" to become more accurate in its predictions. How often Facebook prompts us to tag the person in the picture. Among billions of users, Face Book Machine Learning algorithms are able to correctly match different pictures of the same person and identify her. There are many key industries where Machine Learning is making a huge impact: Financial services, Delivery, Marketing and Sales, Health Care to name a few shown in Figure 1. It is expected that in a couple of decades the mechanical,

Figure 1. Machine Learning tasks

Hand written recognition

Fraud Detection

Automated Trading

repetitive tasks will be over. Machine learning and improvements in Artificial intelligence techniques have made impossible possible.

Machine learning systems made up of three major parts. Model, Parameters and learner are major parts of any machine learning systems shown in Figure 2. Model is the real system that makes predictions or identifications, signals or factors used by the model are the parameters used to make predictions. Learner is a system that adjusts the parameters and looks for difference in predictions.

Model Building

A predictive model that takes input from user and it depends on the parameters passed in the input used to make predictions. For example, a teacher wants to identify optimal amount of time study should learn to get the best grade on a test. Teacher will tell the model to assume that studying five hours will lead to score perfect. Then the model make calculations depends on time spent for learning and test score. Assumptions are 1 hour – 50%, 2 hours – 60%, …. 6hours – 100%. Machine learning system uses

Figure 2. Machine Learning workflow

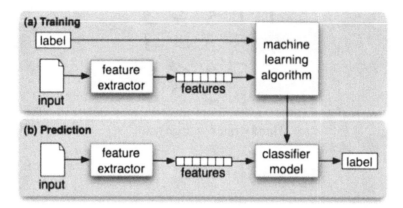

mathematical equation to express the above. It is represented with a trend line y=mx+b. y is test score depends on no of hours spent to learn x.

Initial Input

Number of hours learned and the teacher enters test score of different students.

Learning Model

The data entered in to the machine-learning model is training data that can be used by the learning model to train itself to create a better model. The learning model uses more maths and adjust initial assumptions. The above list of assumptions is altered 1 hour = 55% score, 2 hours = 65% score,6 hours = 100% score. The new prediction is predicted to earn perfect score. The learning model make adjustments on the parameters to redefine the model. The model run repeatedly to adjust the parameters. Those real scores compared against the revised score.

Why Machine Learning?

Machine learning has several practical applications that propel the kind of real business results into positive note such as time and money. We see tremendous interactive applications in customer care industry and virtual assistant solutions that allow people to get things done more quickly and effectively. Further improvement in interaction, which eliminates the request, sent to human by the live agents. Using Adaptive understanding technology, the machine learns to be aware of its limitations that eliminates human interaction when it has low confidence. Virtual Assistant Solutions mixed with Artificial and true human intelligence that provide the highest level of accuracy and understanding

Challenges

This section discusses the challenges faced by the machine learning models.

1. Data Shape

Real world data sets are incomplete, unstructured, offline stored, messy and in variety of formats. Abundant yet scattered data creates lot of challenges and inconsistency. Due to different type and incompleteness, specialized knowledge and tools are required for pre-processing the data.

2. Finding Right Model to Fit the Data

Choosing the right model is the biggest challenge in the machine learning. Highly flexible models tend to over-fit the data by modelling minor variations that could be noise. On the other hand, simple models may assume too much. There is always trade-off between model speed, accuracy and complexity.

3. Unclear Questions and Metric

Communication – prior to any analysis or data engineering is crucial factor to solve Machine Learning problem quickly and painlessly. These questions have to be specific and formulated in a way that the people responsible for identifying the problem and its domain such as management or marketing etc.,

4. Feature Engineering

Feature selection is playing vital role in Machine Learning task. Machine Learning expects significant time and energy spent on looking over the data itself that identify additional information that may be 'hiding' in the features already included. Feature engineering is a combination of subject matter expertise and general intuition that can pull the maximum amount of useful information out of a given set of input data that gives informative data to a Machine Learning model.

5. Cost of Computational Resources

Cost estimation of Computational resources for ML can be tricky. Over-budgeting and under-budgeting cause problems like wasting significant money on powerful computing systems and produce severe bottlenecks in model construction and deployment. However, edge computing has taken intense steps towards making computational pipelines more expandable. Example systems like Amazon's AWS allows for the deployment of larger virtual machines with relatively low cost and high speed. Edge computing ensures elastic-computing framework and is much easier to budget appropriately when setting up a Machine Learning system, especially when working with very large data sets.

6. Merging of Training and Testing Data

Conflation of training and testing data sets is an important task in data science. Machine Learning models draw estimations and generate values that used to guide future decisions in the learning process. Because of this, it is completely critical to separate 'training' data that used to fit an original model from 'testing' data that is used to assess the model's accuracy. Generalised thumb rule is 75-80% of data are used to build the model and 20-25% of the original data set used as test data.

7. Choice of Algorithm

Classification tasks have range of algorithms like Decision trees, Random forests, Support Vector Machines, neural networks and Bayesian estimation models etc., the question of which algorithm is suitable for the given data set and some algorithms might work better than others on some questions. Generally, modelling approach will dominate all other options that determine best answer for any Machine Learning approach.

Machine Learning vs. Artificial Intelligence

Machine Learning and Artificial Intelligence are not interchangeable rather Machine Learning is an approach to the field of Artificial Intelligence. AI found at a conference at Dartmouth in 1956. It is the way of simulating intelligence in computers that encompasses a range of approaches from simple to complex. For example encoding set of rules for a simple tic-tac-toe game. Other way, AI makes computer to learn by itself to complete a task like human does that brought many research interest over last few years. Interesting question is how do machines learn? there may be number of ways to make machines to learn but Deep Learning has got more attention in the recent breakthroughs. Its core function started from Artificial Neural Networks. Learning system encourages the computers to mimic the way the human brain learns. Artificial Neural Networks (ANN) is a mathematical representation of how brain operates.

Neural Network is a series of units modelled as brain neuron. Brain neuron is a cell has two components. Dendrites that can receive impulses and an axon that can send impulses. When dendrites receive enough impulses, the neuron sends an impulse down the axon and then the axon to other neurons dendrites and so on. The connection between an axon and dendrite is a synapse. The same concept represented as perceptron. The perceptron has a number of inputs corresponding to the axons of other neurons.

Inputs x_i for $i = 1, \ldots, n$, weight w_i for each input. $\sum_{i=1}^{n} w_i x_i > 0$. When it is electrified, its output is 1, -1 otherwise. Perceptron can output only these two values. Perceptron learns by changing its weight w_i and it starts with random weights then it makes mistake by predicting 1 when the correct answer is -1, we change all weights as follows

$$w_i = w_i - r x_i$$

Learning rate is represented as r, if we choose r as large value then the perceptron may give erroneous output rather than settle down. Artificial Neural Network (ANN) is a complex network that has three layers. The first is input layer, which are not really neurons of the network, and it just feed attributes to the neurons of the next layer. Second layer is hidden layer, which has several neurons that should adapt to the input. These neurons process the inputs into useful information like detecting feature of a picture. Choosing the right number of neurons for this layer is an art. Figure 3 includes five neurons in the hidden layer with every input node connected to every neuron. The final layer is the output layer that has an output neuron for each output that the ANN should produce.

Figure 3. Artificial Neural Network

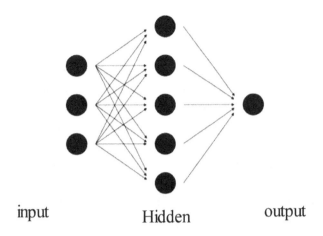

input   Hidden   output

Sigmoid Function

To modify the behaviour of the hidden neurons, researchers found a practical way to do modification on the perceptron called sigmoid unit. These units produce an output between 0 and 1. A sigmoid unit has a weight w_i for each Sigmoid function x_i that process the weighted sum using sigmoid function defined as

$$\sigma\left(y\right) = \frac{1}{1+e^{-y}}$$

It is a smoothed approximation to the threshold function used by perceptron, to make prediction given input x_i, the sigmoid unit computes the output as

$$\sigma(\sum_i w_i x_i)$$

The output will be a number between 0 and 1. To illustrate how they work, how a neural network like the one above can be used to train a computer to with a black-and-white image it's shown has a dog in it.

The column of units on the left is the input layer; you can set these up to represent some input you want to pass the neural network (in our case a black-and-white image). To do that, you make each unit in the input layer correspond to a pixel in the image, with 'on' representing a black pixel and 'off' representing a white pixel. That way, the input layer can 'see' the image—its units can represent the image in its entirety.

A neural network whose input layer is shown an image. The units in the input layer, when they 'see' that image, trigger the connections to the next layer of units. Each of these connections has some weighting, with some stronger than others. Each of the units in that next layer (the ones in the middle column) triggers its own connections if the combined weightings of all the triggered connections coming into that unit cross a certain threshold.

Two things to consider—(i) the image the network is shown and (ii) what exactly all the weightings between its units are set to—create a complex chain reaction of triggered connections that works its way through the network (from left to right) and that directly effects which connections into the final layer are triggered.

This final layer has single unit out on the right—is the output layer. Like the units in the middle layer, it takes the combined weightings of all the triggered connections coming into it and—in our case—if these are above a certain threshold, we treat this as an output of 'yes' from the network (with a 'no' given by a sum below that threshold). In this way, the network gives us an answer to the question, 'Does this image contain a dog?'

A neural network, shown in Figure 4, gives an output 'yes'. The first time this whole process takes place, that answer is likely to be wrong. The weightings of the connections between the layers are essentially random, which means the output is essentially random; the network can't successfully tell you whether or not the image features a dog.

But—and this is the clever part—if you tell the network whether it was right or wrong, it can go and change the weightings of the connections between its units (using a technique called *backpropagation*), in an attempt to get closer to the right answer. In this case, it learns the ability to tell you whether or not an image shown has a cat in it. And this same technique can be used for a whole range of tasks, from translating speech to composing music.

Types of Machine Learning

The basic learning process is similar to any learner whether is a human or machine, the basic learning process is similar. It can be divided into four components shown in Figure 5.

- **Data Storage:** Utilizes observation, memory, and recall to provide a factual basis for further reasoning.
- **Abstraction:** Involves the translation of stored data into broader representations and concepts.
- **Generalization:** Uses abstracted data to create knowledge and inferences that drive action in new contexts.
- **Evaluation:** Provides a feedback mechanism to measure the utility of learned knowledge and inform potential improvements.

Figure 4. Artificial Neural Network example

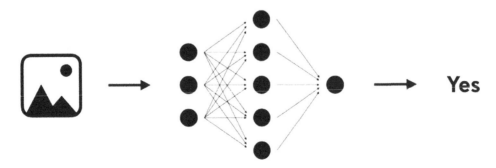

Figure 5. Learning Process

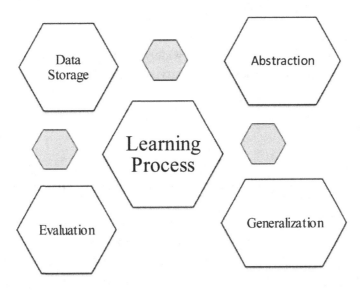

Machine Learning Algorithm Categories

Machine learning algorithm categories are shown in Figure 6.

Supervised Learning (Predictive Model, "Labeled" Data)

This algorithm consists of a target / outcome variable (or dependent variable) which is to be predicted from a given set of predictors (independent variables). Using these set of variables, we generate a function that map inputs to desired outputs. The training process continues until the model achieves a desired level of accuracy on the training data. Examples of Supervised Learning: Regression, Decision Tree, Random Forest, KNN, Logistic Regression etc.

- Classification (Logistic Regression, Decision Tree, KNN, Random Forest, SVM, Naive Bayes, etc)
- Numeric prediction (Linear Regression, KNN, Gradient Boosting & AdaBoost, etc)

Figure 6. Machine Learning Categories

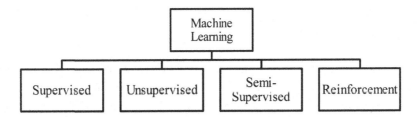

Unsupervised Learning (Descriptive Model, "Unlabeled" Data)

In this algorithm, we do not have any target or outcome variable to predict / estimate. It is used for clustering population in different groups, which is widely used for segmenting customers in different groups for specific intervention. Examples of Unsupervised Learning:

- Apriori algorithm, K-means.
- Clustering (K-Means)
- Pattern discovery

Semi-Supervised Learning (Mixture of "Labeled" and "Unlabeled" Data)

Semi-supervised learning (SSL) is halfway between supervised and unsupervised learning. The algorithm takes unlabeled data with some supervision information – but not necessarily for all examples. The data of Semi Supervised Learning set $X = (xi)$ $i \in [n]$ can be divided into two parts: the points $X_l :=$ $(x_1,...,x_l)$, for which labels $Y_l := (y_1,...,y_l)$ are provided, and the points $X_u := (x_{l+1},...,x_{l+u})$, the labels of which are not known.

Reinforcement Learning

Using this algorithm, the machine is trained to make specific decisions. It works this way: the machine is exposed to an environment where it trains itself continually using trial and error. This machine learns from past experience and tries to capture the best possible knowledge to make accurate business decisions. Example of Reinforcement Learning: Markov Decision Process.

Semi-supervised learning is powerful whenever there are far more unlabeled data than labeled. This is likely to occur if obtaining data points is cheap, but obtaining the labels costs a lot of time, effort, or money. It is applied in speech recognition, it costs almost nothing to record huge amounts of speech, but labeling requires some human to listen to it and type a transcript. Billions of webpages are directly available for automated processing, but to classify them reliably, humans have to read them. Protein sequences are nowadays acquired at industrial speed (by genome sequencing, computational gene finding, and automatic translation), but to resolve a three dimensional (3D) structure or to determine the functions of a single protein may require years of scientific work.

Common Machine Learning Algorithms

List of commonly used machine learning algorithms discussed in this section.

1. Linear Regression

A regression model works based on the complete case data for a given feature is developed. This model treats the feature as the outcome and uses the other features as predictors. It is a tool for modeling the relationship between variables, and used to predict the change of target variable with respect to changes of decision variables. For example, we assume energy as the target variable *y* and utilizations of components as independent decision vector x. The relationship of x and y represented as $y = \mu(x)$, and this method is called regression analysis.

Linear Method: In linear method, the target variable called dependent variable and the decision variables are called independent variables. Multivariate linear regression models the relationship between dependent variable and multiple independent variables. If there are m independent variables, then the regression model is

$$y = \beta_0 + \beta_1 x_1 + \beta_2 x_2 + \ldots + \beta_n x_n + \varepsilon$$

$$E(\varepsilon) = 0$$

$D(\varepsilon) = \sigma^2 < +\infty$ where y is the dependent observation from the independent observations $x_i \left(1 \le i \le n\right)$ by utilization of $\beta_i \left(0 \le i \le n\right)$ co-efficient of regression model, ε is the random error which is assumed from the expected outcome and the variance(0 and σ^2).

Nonlinear Methods: Nonlinear regression is represented by transforming function and adding factors as follows

$$f\left(x\right) = w.\varnothing\left(x\right) + b$$

Transformation can be of any form. This section discusses three functions for the transformation.

Polynomial + Lasso

Instead of linear model, we use polynomial to model the relationship between dependent and independent variable. Here, we set $(x) = \left\{x_i^a : 1 \le a \le 3, 1 \le i \le m\right\}$, and its coefficient is w. Lasso constraint on (x) and final objective is
$$f\left(x\right) = w.\varnothing\left(x\right) + b + \lambda \phi\left(x\right)$$

Polynomial + Exponential + Lasso

Based on polynomial and lasso regression, we add exponential transform for each coefficient and get the following equation:

$$f\left(x\right) = w.\exp\left(\varnothing\left(x\right)\right) + b + \lambda \phi\left(x\right)$$

Support Vector Regression

Other than the above two we can also have support vector machine based regression model. Given a collection of samples $(xi \ yi)$, $_1 \le i \le n$, where $xi \in Rm$ are independent Journal of Electrical and Computer Engineering 5 variables, $yi \in R$ is dependent variable, and n is the number of samples, the regression model is

$$f(x) = w \cdot x + b$$

Regression models are quite common task and employed in various applications, Authors Fei Chen et al.,(2014) proposed two protocols which enables secure and efficient outsourcing of linear regression problems to the cloud. Those protocols can protect the client's data privacy well and has good efficiency. They used linear regression problem to get a new problem which is sent to the cloud; and then transforming the answer returned back from the cloud to get the true solution to the original problem. Dynamic resource scaling for an enterprise by measuring resource and provision strategies achieved in (Islam, Keung & Lee, 2012). Authors developed prediction models to enable proactive resource scaling in the cloud using regression models. They predicted future utilization based on history data and current utilization.

2. Logistic Regression

It is true that we can't use any algorithm in any condition. For example: trying linear regression on a categorical dependent variable?. No business would be interested for getting extremely low values of adjusted R2 and F statistic. Logistic Regressing is the best choice in such situations. Logistic Regression is a classification algorithm. It is used to predict a binary outcome (1 / 0, Yes / No, True / False) given a set of independent variables. Categorical output can be represented using dummy variables. Logistic regression as a special case of linear regression when the outcome variable is categorical, where we are using log of odds as dependent variable. Nelder and Wedderburn proposed this model and also predicts the probability of occurrence of an event by fitting data to a logit function.

The fundamental equation of model is:

$$g\Big(E\big(y\big)\Big) = \alpha + \beta x_1 + \gamma x_2$$

g() is the link function, E(y) is the expectation of target variable and α + βx1 + γx2 is the linear predictor (α,β,γ to be predicted). The role of link function is to 'link' the expectation of y to linear predictor.

For example, we have a sample of 1000 customer records. We need to predict the probability whether a customer will buy (y) a particular product or not. We can use logistic regression to predict a categorical outcome variable. To do so, we rewrite linear regression equation with dependent variable enclosed in a link function:

$$g\big(y\big) = \beta_0 + \beta x\big(it\,can\,be\,any\,indepedent\,variable\big)$$

From the above, we are concerned about the probability of output variable that takes a value 0 when the probability is of success and 1 in case of probability of failure. An estimated logistic regression equation can be formulated from generalised linear model. The coefficients a and b_k (k = 1, 2, ..., p) are determined according to a maximum likelihood approach, and it allow us to estimate the probability of the dependent variable y taking on the value 1 for given values of x_k (k = 1, 2, ..., p). Logistic regression seeks to

- Model the probability of an event occurring based on the values of independent variables (Credit score)

- Estimate the probability that an event occurs for a randomly selected observation versus probability that event does not occur
- Classify the observations by estimating the probability of event (Loan approved or not)

Estimated logistic equation is represented as follows:

$$\hat{p} = \frac{e^{\beta_0 \beta_1 x_1}}{1 + e^{\beta_0 + \beta_1 x_1}}$$

Authors Kuswantoa, Asfihanib, Sarumahab & Ohwada (2015) used logistic regression ensemble to predict customer defection for companies producing cloud based software. They build a new model has been formed without considering both insignificant variables.

The constraints are

3. Decision Tree

Decision tree is a supervised learning algorithm that deal with a pre-defined target variable. A classification algorithm works for both categorical and continuous input and output variables. It is expressed as a recursive partition of the instance space. The decision tree consists of nodes that form a rooted tree called "root" that has no incoming edges. All other nodes have exactly one incoming edge. A node with outgoing edges is called an internal or test node. A decision tree, each internal node splits the instance space into two or more sub-spaces according to a certain discrete function of the input attributes values. Each test considers a single attribute, and instance space partitioned according to the attribute's value. In case of numeric attributes, the above condition refers to a range. Each leaf assigned to one class representing the most appropriate target value. For example a classifier, the analyst can predict the response of a potential customer and understand the behavioural characteristics of them regarding direct mailing. In that case, each node labelled with the attribute it tests, and its branches labeled with its corresponding values. It automatically construct a decision tree from a given dataset and the goal is to find the optimal decision tree by minimizing the generalization error. Heuristics methods applied for solving the problem that classified in to two groups: top-down and bottom-up. ID3 (Quinlan,1986), C4.5 (Quinlan,1993), CART (Breiman, Friedman, Olshen & Stone, 1984) are top-down decision tree algorithms. These algorithms consist of two phases: growing and pruning

Decision Tree Types

Based on target variable it can be of two types:

1. **Binary Variable Decision Tree:** It has a binary target. For example: scenario of student problem, where the target variable was "Student will play cricket or not" i.e. YES or NO.
2. **Continuous Variable Decision Tree:** It has continuous target variable for example predict customer income based on occupation, product and various other variables.

Two Phases

- **Splitting:** It is a process of dividing a node into two or more sub-nodes.
- **Pruning:** Removing sub-nodes of a decision node called pruning.

A Decision tree can be transformed to set of decision rules by mapping from the root to the leaf nodes

Issues With Decision Trees

- **Overfitting:** Not possible and we can use random forest for the same.
- Working on continuous attributes.
- **Super Attributes:** Working with many attributes.
- Working with missing values.

SVM

Support Vector Machine (SVM) is supervised machine learning technique that can be used as classification or regression algorithm. It is based on the concept of decision planes that define decision boundaries. A decision plane is one that separates between a set of objects having different class memberships. A classifier formally defined by a separating hyperplane. Given labelled training data (supervised learning), the algorithm outputs an optimal hyperplane which categorizes new examples. In two-dimensional space this hyperplane is a line dividing a plane in two parts where in each class lay in either side.

When we draw line that separates black circles and blue squares, SVM does *Separation of classes*. It fairly separates the two classes. Any point that is left of line falls into black circle class and on right falls into blue square class. A discriminative classifier formally defined by a separating hyperplane. This algorithm deal with lines and points in the Cartesian plane instead of hyperplanes and vectors in a high dimensional space. A line is bad if it passes too close to the points because it will be noise sensitive and it will not generalize correctly. Goal is to find the line passing as far as possible from all points. SVM operates based on finding the hyperplane that gives the largest minimum distance to the training examples. Optimal separating hyperplane *maximizes* the margin of the training data.

Figure 7. Linearly separable classes

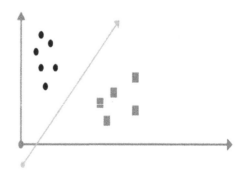

Optimal Hyperplane Computation

Define formally a hyperplane: $f\left(x\right) = \beta_0 + \beta_x^T$, where β and β_0 are weight vector and bias respectively. The optimal hyperplane represented in an infinite number of different ways by scaling of β and β_0, among all the possible representations of the hyperplane, the one chosen is $\left|\beta_0 + \beta_x^T\right| = 1$ where χ symbolizes the training examples closest to the hyperplane. In general, the training examples that are closest to the hyperplane are called support vectors. This representation known as the canonical hyperplane. Support Vector Machines (SVM) is a powerful, state-of-the-art algorithm with strong theoretical foundations based on the Vapnik-Chervonenkis theory. SVM has strong regularization properties. Regularization refers to the generalization of the model to new data.

Advantages of SVM

- SVM models complex real world problems such as image classification, hand-written recognition
- Performs better classification for data set that have many attributes
- Kernel based algorithm that transforms the input data in to high-dimensional space.

4. Naive Bayes

Naïve Bayes is a classification algorithm works based on Bayes Theorem that uses conditional probability. Conditional probability calculates a probability by counting the frequency of values and combinations of values in the historical data. Naïve Bayes is simple to build, useful for very large data sets and outperforms that other classification methods.

Bayes Theorem

Bayes theorem provides a way of calculating posterior probability P(A|B) from P(A), P(B) and P(A|B). Look at the equation below:

$$P\left(A \mid B\right) = \frac{P\left(B \mid A\right)P\left(A\right)}{P\left(B\right)}$$

$$P\left(A \mid B\right) = P\left(b_1 \mid A\right) \times \left(b_2 \mid A\right) \times \ldots \ldots \times P\left(b_n \mid A\right) \times P\left(A\right)$$

$P\left(A \mid B\right)$ – Posterior Probability of the target sample for the given predictor

$P\left(A\right)$ – Prior probability

$P\left(B \mid A\right)$ – Likelihood, which is the probability of predictor

$P\left(B\right)$ – Prior probability of the predictor

Due to independence assumption, it can handle independent continuous and categorical variables. Large feature spaces learning takes an exponentially large amount of training data in the dimension, the number of features. This is known as the curse of dimensionality, which intuitively says that as the number of features grows, the number of "bins" in the space spanned by those features grows exponentially fast. Accurately learning a distribution requires an amount of data proportional to the number of bins so learning classifiers on high dimensional data with small datasets presents a problem.

5. KNN

Nearest Neighbour classification is one of the simplest and oldest methods for performing non-parametric classification. Non-parametric technique means that it does not make any assumptions on the underlying data distribution. Typical theoretical assumptions made (eg Gaussian mixtures, linearly separable etc). It is also named as lazy algorithm. Because it does not use the training data points to do any generalization or no explicit training phase. Lack of generalization means that KNN keeps all the training data. All the training data is needed during the testing phase. Keller et al designed KNN classifier in 1985.

For example, task of classifying a new object among a number of known examples. KNN assumes that the data is in a feature space. The data points are in a metric space. The data can be scalars or multidimensional vectors. The data points are in feature space, they have a notion of distance. Each of the training data consists of a set of vectors and class label associated with each vector. It will be either + or – (for positive or negative classes). But KNN, can work equally well with arbitrary number of classes.

Given a single number, "k" decides how many neighbors that defined based on the distance metric influence the classification. If k=1, then the algorithm is simply called the nearest neighbor algorithm. Define a metric for measuring the distance between the query point and cases from the examples sample. Most popular distance known as Euclidean. Euclidean, Manhattan, Minkowski and Chebyshev are other distance measures.

Geometry Distance Functions

Manhattan distance $d\left(x,z\right)=\sum_{i=1}^{n}\left|x_i-z_i\right|$

Euclidean distance $d\left(x,z\right)=\sqrt{\sum_{i=1}^{n}\left(x_i-z_i\right)^2}$

Minkowski distance $d\left(x,z\right)=\left(\sum_{i=1}^{n}\left|x_i-z_i\right|^p\right)^{1/p}$

Chebyshev distance $d\left(x, z\right) = \lim_{p \to \infty} \left(\sum_{i=1}^{n} \left| x_i - z_i \right|^p \right)^{1/p}$

6. K-Means

K-means clustering is a simple unsupervised machine-learning algorithm that is trained on a test data set and then able to classify a new data set. This clustering algorithm separates data into the best-suited group based on the information the algorithm has. Data is grouped in different clusters, which are usually chosen to be far enough apart from each other spatially, in Euclidean Distance, to be able to produce effective data mining results. Each cluster has a center, called the *centroid,* and a data point is clustered into a certain cluster based on how close the features are to the centroid.-means algorithm iteratively minimizes the distances between every data point and its centroid in order to find the most optimal solution for all the data points.

Steps

1. Random points of the data set are chosen to be centroids.
2. Distances between every data point and the centroids are calculated and stored.
3. Based on distance calculates, each point is assigned to the nearest cluster
4. New cluster centroid positions are updated: similar to finding a mean in the point locations
5. If the centroid locations changed, the process repeats from step 2, until the calculated new center stays the same, which signals that the clusters' members and centroids are now set.

Finding the minimal distances between all the points implies that data points are separated in order to form the most compact clusters possible, with the least variance within them. The K-means algorithm defined above aims at minimizing an objective function, which in this case is the squared error function.

Advantages

K-Means clustering is a fast, robust, and simple algorithm that gives reliable results when data sets are distinct or well separated from each other in a linear fashion. It is best used when the number of cluster centers, is specified due to a well-defined list of types shown in the data. However, it is important to keep in mind that K-Means clustering may not perform well if it contains heavily overlapping data, if the Euclidean distance does not measure the underlying factors well, or if the data is noisy or full of outliers (Naik, 2016).

7. Random Forest

Random forest algorithm is a supervised classification algorithm that creates the forest with a number of trees. Random forest classifier that has *higher the number* of trees in the forest gives *the high accuracy* results. Constructing the decision with information gain or gini index approach.is not enough to model more number of decision trees in the forest.

Reason for Random Forest

- Random forest classifier can use for both classification and the regression task.
- Random forest classifier will handle the missing values.
- When we have more trees in the forest, random forest classifier won't overfit the model.
- Random forest classifier can model the categorical values.

8. Dimensionality Reduction Algorithms

There has been a tremendous increase in the way sensors are being used in the industry. These sensors continuously record data and store it for analysis at a later point. In the way data are captured, there can be a lot of redundancy. The problem of unwanted increase in dimension is closely related to fixation of measuring data at a far granular level then it was done in past. It has started gaining more importance lately due to pre-process in data. For example, a motorbike rider in racing competitions. Position and movement measured by GPS sensor on bike, gyro meters, multiple video feeds and his smart watch. Data analyst analyze the racing strategy of the biker – he/ she would have a lot of variables / dimensions which are similar and of little (or no) incremental value. This is the problem of high unwanted dimensions and needs a treatment of dimension reduction.

Dimension Reduction

Process of converting a set of data having vast dimensions into data with lesser dimensions ensuring that it conveys similar information concisely. These techniques used to obtain better features for a classification or regression task.

For example, measurements of several object in cm (x1) and inches (x2) is given and we want to use both dimensions in machine learning that convey similar information and become redundant information in the system. In that system, we can reduce the dimensions of data set to k dimensions ($k < n$) . These k dimensions can be directly identified (filtered) or can be a combination of dimensions (weighted averages of dimensions) or new dimension(s) that represent existing multiple dimensions well. Popular application of this technique is Image processing. Example popular application is Facebook "Which Celebrity Do You Look Like? Application uses this technique. How does it work? Celebrity image can be identified by using pixel data and each pixel is equivalent to one dimension. In every image has high number of pixels i.e. high number of dimensions. In such situation, dimension reduction techniques that find the significant dimension using various method.

Advantages of Dimension Reduction

- Data compressing and reducing the storage space required
- It fastens the time required for performing same computations.
- Avoids multi-collinearity that improves the model performance. It removes redundant features.
- Reducing the dimensions of data to 2D or 3D may allow us to plot.

Dimension Reduction Techniques

- **Missing Values:** While exploring data, if we encounter missing values, method to to handle missing value is to impute missing values/ drop variables using appropriate methods. There is threshold of missing values for dropping a variable. If the information contained in the variable is not that much, then we can drop the variable if it has more than ~40-50% missing values.
- **Low Variance:** In case of data set has a constant variable that all observations have same value. it cannot improve the power of model, because it has zero variance. In case of high number of dimensions, we should drop variables having low variance compared to others because these variables will not explain the variation in target variables.
- **Decision Trees:** It is one of the best method that can be used as a ultimate solution to tackle multiple challenges like missing values, outliers and identifying significant variables.
- **High Correlation:** Dimensions exhibiting higher correlation can lower down the performance of model. it is not good to have multiple variables of similar information or variation also known as "Multicollinearity". *Pearson* correlation matrix allow us to identify the variables with high correlation and select one of them using VIF (Variance Inflation Factor). Variables having higher value (VIF > 5) can be dropped.

Backward Feature Elimination

This method takes all n dimensions and compute the sum of square of error (SSR) by eliminating each variable (n times). Then, identifying variables whose removal has produced the smallest increase in the SSR and removing it finally, leaving us with *n-1* input features. Repeat this process until no other variables can be dropped.

Factor Analysis

For example, some variables are highly correlated in a data set. These variables can be grouped by their correlations i.e. all variables in a particular group can be highly correlated among themselves but have low correlation with variables of other group(s). Each group represents a single underlying construct or factor. These factors are small in number as compared to large number of dimensions. Factors are difficult to observe that is identified using the following two methods

- EFA (Exploratory Factor Analysis)
- CFA (Confirmatory Factor Analysis)
- **Principal Component Analysis (PCA):** In this technique, variables are transformed into a new set of variables, which are linear combination of original variables. New set of variables are known as principle components. Each principle component is identified with possible variation of original data after which each succeeding component has the highest possible variance. The second principal component must be orthogonal to the first principal component. In other words, it does its best to capture the variance in the data that is not captured by the first principal component. For two-dimensional dataset, there can be only two principal components.

Boosting Algorithms

Boosting algorithms are one of the most widely used algorithm in data science. Boosting algorithms grants power to machine learning models to improve their accuracy of prediction. The term 'Boosting' refers to a family of algorithms that converts weak learner to strong learners. For example, we have to classify email are spam or not. Boosting combines weak learner to form a strong rule. Each time base learning algorithm is applied, it generates a new weak prediction rule. This is an iterative process. After many iterations, the boosting algorithm combines these weak rules into a single strong prediction rule.

Steps

1.	The base learner takes all the distributions and assign equal weight to each observation.
2.	If there is any prediction error caused by first base learning algorithm, then we apply the next base learning algorithm.
3.	Iterate Step 2 till the limit of base learning algorithm is reached or higher accuracy is achieved.
4.	Finally, it combines the outputs from weak learner and creates a strong learner, which eventually improves the prediction accuracy of the model.

Types of Boosting Algorithms

1.	AdaBoost (Adaptive Boosting)
2.	Gradient Boosting

AdaBoost

AdaBoost (Adaptive Boosting) fits a sequence of weak learners on different weighted training data. It predicts original data set and gives equal weight to each observation. If prediction is incorrect using the first learner, then it gives higher weight to observation, which have been predicted incorrectly. Being an iterative process, it continues to add learner(s) until a limit is reached in the number of models or accuracy. Decision stamps with AdaBoost can use any machine learning algorithms as base learner if it accepts weight on training data set. AdaBoost algorithms used for both classification and regression problem.

Gradient Boosting

Gradient boosting trains many model sequentially and new model gradually minimizes the loss function using Gradient Descent method. The learning procedure consecutively fit new models to provide a more accurate estimate of the response variable. It constructs new base learners that can be maximally correlated with negative gradient of the loss function

SUMMARY

ABI Research estimates that by 2020, there will be more than 30 billion connected devices(ABI.2013). These Big Data possess tremendous potential in terms of business value in a variety of fields such as health care, biology, transportation, online advertising, energy management, and financial services (Raghupathi, 2014) and (Al-Jarrah, Yoo, Muhaidat, Karagiannidis & Taha, 2015). However, traditional approaches are struggling when faced with these massive data. This chapter provides a perspective on the domain and research gaps and opportunities in the area of machine learning with Big Data. This chapter gives information about overview of Machine Learning, tasks, popular Machine Learning algorithms, applications of each algorithms. It also provides necessity and utility of Machine Learning algorithms in Fog computing. As the need of data is growing every day, the ability of integrating Machine Learning algorithms and techniques on the Edge computing become more significant.

REFERENCES

ABI. (2013). *Billion Devices Will Wirelessly Connect to the Internet of Everything in 2020*. ABI Research. Available: https://www.abiresearch.com/press/more-than-30-billion-devices-willwirelessly- conne/

Al-Jarrah, O.Y., Yoo, P. D., Muhaidat, S., Karagiannidis, G. K., & Taha. (2015 Efficient machine learning for big data: A review. *Big Data Res., 2*(3), 87-93.

Ayodele, T. O. (2010). Introduction to machine learning. In *New Advances in Machine Learning*. InTech.

Bishop, C. M. (2006). *Pattern recognition and machine learning*. New York: Springer.

Breiman, L., Friedman, J., Olshen, R., & Stone, C. (1984). *Classification and Regression Trees*. Wadsworth Int. Group.

Chen, F., Xiang, T., Lei, X., & Chen, J. (2010). Highly Efficient Linear Regression outsourcing to a cloud. *IEEE Transactions on Cloud Computing, 2*(4), 499-508.

Cherkassky, V., & Mulier, F. M. (2007). *Learning from data: concepts, theory, and methods. John Wiley & Sons*. doi:10.1002/9780470140529

Duffy, A. H. (1997). The "what" and "how" of learning in design. *IEEE Expert, 12*(3), 71–76. doi:10.1109/64.590079

Islam, S., Keung, J., Lee, K., & Liu, A. (2012). Empirical prediction models for adaptive resource provisioning in the cloud. *Future Generation Computer Systems, 28*(1), 155–162. doi:10.1016/j.future.2011.05.027

Kuswantoa, H., Asfihanib, A., Sarumahab, Y., & Ohwada, H. (2015). Logistic Regression Ensemble for Predicting Customer Defection with Very Large Sample Size. *Proceedings of Third Information Systems International Conference, 72*, 86 – 93. 10.1016/j.procs.2015.12.108

Langley, P., & Simon, H. A. (1995). Applications of machine learning and rule induction. *Communications of the ACM, 38*(11), 54–64. doi:10.1145/219717.219768

Mitchell, T. M. (1997). *Machine learning*. New York: McGraw-Hill.

Mitchell, T. M. (2006). *The discipline of machine learning*. Carnegie Mellon University, School of Computer Science, Machine Learning Department.

Naik, A. (2016). *k-Means Clustering Algorithm*. Retrieved June 14,2016, from https://sites.google.com/site/dataclusteringalgorithms/k-means-clustering-algorithm

Quinlan, J. R. (1983). *C4.5: Programs for Machine Learning*. Los Altos, CA: Morgan Kaufmann.

Quinlan, J. R. (1986). Induction of decision trees. *Machine Learning*, *1*(1), 81–106. doi:10.1007/BF00116251

Raghupathi. (2014). Big data analytics in healthcare: Promise and potential. *Health Inf. Sci. Syst.*, *2*(1).

Rudin, C., & Wagstaff, K. L. (2014). Machine learning for science and society. *Machine Learning*, *95*(1), 1–9. doi:10.100710994-013-5425-9

Russell, S., & Norvig, P. (1995). *Artificial intelligence: a modern approach*. Englewood Cliffs, NJ: Prentice-Hall.

Chapter 12
Data Mining Algorithms, Fog Computing

S. Thilagamani
Kumarasamy Engineering College, India

A. Jayanthiladevi
Jain University, India

N. Arunkumar
Sastra University, India

ABSTRACT

Different methods are used to mine the large amount of data presents in databases, data warehouses, and data repositories. The methods used for mining include clustering, classification, prediction, regression, and association rule. This chapter explores data mining algorithms and fog computing.

INTRODUCTION

A cluster is a subset of targets which are "similar". A subset of objects such that the length between any two targets in the cluster is less than the space between any object in the cluster and any object not located inside it. A connected region of multidimensional space containing the relatively high density of target. Clustering is a process of partitioning a set of data (or objects) into a lot of meaningful sub-divisions, called clusters. Help users understand the natural grouping or structure in a data set.

Clustering is unsupervised classification and it has no predefined categories. Unsupervised classification is where the outcomes (groupings of pixels with common characteristics) are based on the software analysis of an image without the user providing sample classes. The information processing system uses techniques to see which pixels are related and groups them into categories. Used either as a stand-alone tool to bring insight into data distribution or as a preprocessing step for other algorithms (Shridhar D et al (2014).

DOI: 10.4018/978-1-5225-5972-6.ch012

Figure 1. Clustering

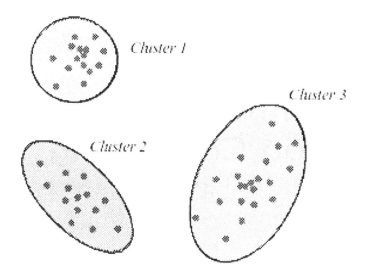

The good clustering method will create high quality clusters in which, the intra-class similarity is high and the inter-class similarity is low. The character of a clustering result also depends on both the similarity measure used by the method and its execution. The character of a clustering method is also evaluated by its ability to disclose some or all of the hidden rules.

Type of Clustering

The clustering can be divided into two subgroups:

1. **Hard Clustering:** In hard clustering, each data point either belongs to a cluster completely or not. For instance, in the above instance, each customer is put into one group out of the 10 groups.
2. **Soft Clustering:** In soft clustering, instead of putting each data point into a separate cluster, a probability or likelihood of that data point to be in those clusters is specified. For instance, from the above scenario, each customer is assigned a probability to be in either of 10 clusters of the retail shop.

Clustering Model

Since the task of clustering is subjective, the substances that can be applied for attaining this goal are plenty. Every methodology follows a different set of regulations for determining the 'similarity' among data points explained by Eli J. Finkel et al., (2012). In fact, there are more than 100 clustering algorithms known. Only a few of the algorithms are used, these are:

- **Connectivity Models:** As the name indicates, these examples are founded on the opinion that the data points closer in the data space exhibit more similar to each other than the data points lying farther out. These models can follow two approaches. In the first attack, they begin by classifying all data points into separate clusters & then aggregating them as the distance decreases. In the second approach, all data points are sorted as a single clump and then partitioned as the length increments. Likewise, the choice of distance function is subjective. These examples are very comfortable to read, but lacks scalability for handling large datasets. Instances of these models are hierarchical clustering algorithm and its variations.

- **Centroid Models:** These are iterative clustering algorithms in which the feeling of similarity is derived by the stuffiness of a data point to the centroid of the clumps. K-Means clustering algorithm is a popular algorithm that falls into this class. In these examples, the ordinal number of clusters required at the end has to be noted in advance, which makes it important to have prior knowledge of the dataset. These models run iteratively to determine the local optima.

- **Distribution Models:** These clustering modes are founded on the notion of how likely is it that all data points in the cluster belong to the same distribution (For example: Normal, Gaussian). These models often suffer from overfitting. A popular example of these models is Expectation-maximization algorithm which uses multivariate normal distributions.

- **Density Models:** These models search the data space for areas of varied density of data points in the data space. It isolates various different density regions and specify the data points within these regions in the same bunch. Popular models of density models are DBSCAN and OPTICS .

Types of Clustering Algorithm

1. **Partition Clustering:** It's simply a division of the set of data objects into non-overlapping clusters such that each object is in exactly one subset.
2. **Hierarchical Clustering:** Also known as 'nesting clustering' as it also clusters to exist within bigger clusters to form a tree.
3. **Exclusive Clustering:** They assign each value to a single cluster.
4. **Overlapping Clustering:** It is used to reflect the fact that an object can simultaneously belong to more than one group.
5. **Fuzzy Clustering:** Every object belongs to every cluster with a membership weight that goes between 0: if it absolutely doesn't belong to cluster and 1: if it absolutely belongs to the cluster.
6. **Complete Clustering:** It performs a hierarchical clustering using a set of dissimilarities on 'n' objects that are being clustered. They tend to find compact clusters of an approximately equal diameter. (Soni Madhulatha et al., 2012).

Applications of Clustering

Clustering has a large number of applications spread across various domains. Some of the most popular applications of clustering are:

1. Recommendation engines
2. Market segmentation
3. Social network analysis
4. Search result grouping
5. Medical imaging
6. Image segmentation
7. Anomaly detection

Other applications are,

1. **Marketing:** Finding groups of customers with similar behavior given a large database of customer data containing their properties and past buying records;
2. **Biology:** Classification of plants and animals given their features;
3. **Libraries:** Book ordering;
4. **Insurance:** Identifying groups of motor insurance policy holders with a high average claim cost; identifying frauds;
5. **City-Planning:** Identifying groups of houses according to their house type, value and geographical location;
6. **Earthquake Studies:** Clustering observed earthquake epicenters to identify dangerous zones;
7. **WWW:** Document classification; clustering weblog data to discover groups of similar access patterns.

Partitioning Based Clustering

Given a database of n objects or data tuples, a partitioning method constructs k partitions of the data, where each partition represents a cluster and k<= n.

- Each group must contain at least one object
- Each object must belong to exactly one group

In k-means algorithm, each cluster is represented by the mean value of the objects in the cluster.

Algorithm:
Input:
k: the number of clusters,

Figure 2. Partitioning Based Clustering

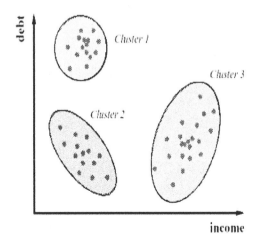
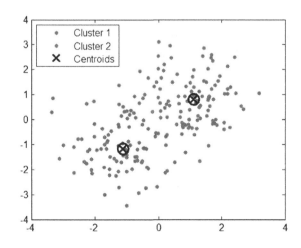

D: a data set containing n objects.

Output: A set of k clusters.

Method:

1. Arbitrarily choose k objects from D as the initial cluster centers;
2. Repeat
3. (Re)Assign each object to the cluster to which the object is the most similar, based on the mean value of the objects in the cluster;
4. Update the cluster means, i.e., calculate the mean value of the objects for each cluster;
5. Until no change;

Example 1

Cluster the following eight points (with (x, y)) into three clusters

A1 (2,10)
A2 (2, 5)
A3 (8, 4)
A4 (5, 8)
A5 (7, 5)
A6 (6, 4)
A7 (1, 2)
A8 (4, 9).

Solution

Here k=3

Initial cluster centers are: A1 (2, 10), A4 (5, 8) and A7 (1, 2).

The distance function between two points a= (x1, y1) and b=(x2, y2) is defined as: $\rho(a, b) = |x2 - x1| + |y2 - y1|$.

Iteration 1

Table 1 shows Iteration 1.

Now the clusters are

Cluster 1: (2, 10)

Cluster 2: (8, 4) (5, 8) (7, 5) (6, 4) (4, 9)

Cluster 3: (2, 5) (1, 2)

Clusters:

c1: {A1},

C2:{ A3, A4, A5, A6, A8},

C3: {A2, A7}

Table 1. Iteration 1

		(2, 10)	(5, 8)	(1, 2)	
	Point	Dist Mean 1	Dist Mean 2	Dist Mean 3	Cluster
A1	(2, 10)	0	5	9	1
A2	(2, 5)	5	6	4	3
A3	(8, 4)	12	7	9	2
A4	(5, 8)	5	0	10	2
A5	(7, 5)	10	5	9	2
A6	(6, 4)	10	5	7	2
A7	(1, 2)	9	10	0	3
A8	(4, 9)	3	2	10	2

= dist b/w (4, 9) and (2, 10) =| (2-4) + (10-9)|=2+1=3

Next, we need to re-compute the new cluster centers (means). We do so, by taking the mean of all points in each cluster.

- For Cluster 1, we only have one point A1 (2, 10), which was the old mean, so the cluster center remains the same.
- For Cluster 2, we have ((8+5+7+6+4)/5, (4+8+5+4+9)/5) = (6, 6)
- For Cluster 3, we have ((2+1)/2, (5+2)/2) = (1.5, 3.5)
- Now cluster centers are: A1 (2, 10), A4 (6, 6) and A7 (1.5, 3.5).

Iteration 2

Table 2 shows Iteration 2.

Now the clusters are
Cluster 1: (2, 10) (4, 9)

Table 2. Iteration 2

		(2,10)	(6,6)	(1.5,3.5)	
	Point	Dist Mean 1	Dist Mean 2	Dist Mean 3	Cluster
A1	(2, 10)	0	8	7	1
A2	(2, 5)	5	5	2	3
A3	(8, 4)	12	4	7	2
A4	(5, 8)	5	3	8	2
A5	(7, 5)	10	2	7	2
A6	(6, 4)	10	2	5	2
A7	(1, 2)	9	9	2	3
A8	(4, 9)	3	5	8	1

Cluster 2: (8, 4) (5, 8) (7, 5) (6, 4)
Cluster 3: (2, 5) (1, 2)
Clusters:
C1: {A1, A8},
C2:{ A3, A4, A5, A6},
C3: {A2, A7}

Next, we need to re-compute the new cluster centers (means). We do so, by taking the mean of all points in each cluster.

- For Cluster 1, we have((2+4)/2,(10+9)/2)=(3,9.5)
- For Cluster 2, we have ((8+5+7+6)/4, (4+8+5+4)/4) = (6.5, 5.25)
- For Cluster 3, we have ((2+1)/2, (5+2)/2) = (1.5, 3.5)
- Now cluster centers are: A1 (3, 9.5), A4 (6.5, 5.25) and A7 (1.5, 3.5).

Iteration 3

Table 3 shows Iteration 3.

Now the clusters are
Cluster 1: (2, 10) (4, 9) (5, 8)
Cluster 2: (8, 4) (7, 5) (6, 4)
Cluster 3: (2, 5) (1, 2)
Clusters:
C1: {A1, A4, And A8},
C2:{ A3, A5, A6},
C3: {A2, A7}

Table 3. Iteration 3

		(3,9.5)	(6.5,5.25)	(1.5,3.5)	
	Point	Dist Mean 1	Dist Mean 2	Dist Mean 3	Cluster
A1	(2, 10)	1.5	9.25	7	1
A2	(2, 5)	5.5	4.75	2	3
A3	(8, 4)	9.5	2.75	7	2
A4	(5, 8)	3.5	4.25	8	1
A5	(7, 5)	8.5	.75	7	2
A6	(6, 4)	8.5	1.75	5.5	2
A7	(1, 2)	9.5	8.75	2	3
A8	(4, 9)	1.5	6.25	5.5	1

Next, we need to re-compute the new cluster centers (means). We do so, by taking the mean of all points in each cluster.

- For Cluster 1, we have((2+4+5)/3,(10+9+8)/3)=(3.66,9)
- For Cluster 2, we have ((8+7+6)/3, (4+5+4)/3) = (7,4.33)
- For Cluster 3, we have ((2+1)/2, (5+2)/2) = (1.5, 3.5)
- Now cluster centers are: A1 (3.66, 9), A4 (7, 4.33) and A7 (1.5, 3.5).

Iteration 4

Table 4 shows Iteration 4.

The means do not change anymore. Finally, we get

Clusters: C1: {A1, A4, and A8}, C2:{ A3, A5, A6} C3: {A2, A7}

K-Medoids

The k-medoids algorithm is a clustering algorithm related to the k-means algorithm and the medoid shift algorithm. Both the k-means and k-medoids algorithms are partition (breaking the dataset up into groups) and both attempt to minimize the distance between points labeled to be in a cluster and a point designated as the center of that cluster. In contrast to the k-means algorithm, k-medoids chooses data points as centers (medoids or exemplars) and works with an arbitrary matrix of distances between data points instead of. This method was proposed in 1987 for the work with norm and other distances explained by Abhishek Patel (2013).

- K- Medoid is a classical partitioning technique of clustering that clusters the data set of n objects into k clusters known a priori.
- It is more robust to noise and outliers as compared to k-means because it minimizes a sum of pair wise dissimilarities instead of a sum of squared Euclidean distances.

Table 4. Iteration 4

		(3.66,9)	(7,4.33)	(1.5,3.5)	
	Point	**Dist Mean 1**	**Dist Mean 2**	**Dist Mean 3**	**Cluster**
A1	(2, 10)	2.66	10.67	7	1
A2	(2, 5)	5.66	5.66	2	3
A3	(8, 4)	9.34	1.33	7	2
A4	(5, 8)	2.34	5.66	8	1
A5	(7, 5)	7.34	.66	7	2
A6	(6, 4)	7.34	1.33	5.5	2
A7	(1, 2)	9.66	8.33	2	3
A8	(4, 9)	0.34	9.66	5.5	1

Table 5. Data set of ten objects

Samples	Attribute1	Attribute 2
X_1	2	6
X_2	3	4
X_3	3	8
X_4	4	7
X_5	6	2
X_6	6	4
X_7	7	3
X_8	7	4
X_9	8	5
X_{10}	7	6

- A medoid can be defined as the object of a cluster whose average dissimilarity to all the objects in the cluster is minimal. i.e. it is a most centrally located point in the cluster.
- The most common realization of k-medoid clustering is the Partitioning around Medoids (PAM) algorithm and is as follows:

1. Initialize: randomly select (without replacement) k of the n data points as the medoids
2. Associate each data point to the closest medoid. ("closest" here is defined using any valid distance metric, most commonly Euclidean distance, Manhattan distance or Minkowski distance)
3. For each medoid m
   a. For each non-medoid data point o
      i. Swap m and o and compute the total cost of the configuration
4. Select the configuration with the lowest cost.
5. Repeat steps 2 to 4 until there is no change in the medoid.

Example 1

Cluster the following data set of ten objects into two clusters i.e. k = 2.

Consider a data set of ten objects as shown in Table 5.

Solution

Initialize k centers. Let us assume x_2 and x_8 are selected as medoids, so the centers are $c_1 = (3, 4)$ and $c_2 = (7,4)$

Calculate distances to each center so as to associate each data object to its nearest medoid. Cost is calculated using Euclidian distance. Costs to the nearest medoid are shown bold in the Table 6.

Then the clusters become:

$Cluster_1 = \{(3, 4), (2, 6)\ (3, 8)\ (4, 7)\} = \{x1, x2, x3, x4\}$

Table 6. Costs to the nearest mediod

Samples	Attribute1	Attribute 2	Cost distance or dist mean (3,4)	Cost distance or dist mean (7,4)	clustering	Total cost
X_1	2	6	3	7	C1	3
X_2	3	4	0	4	C1	0
X_3	3	8	4	8	C1	4
X_4	4	7	4	6	C1	4
X_5	6	2	5	3	C2	3
X_6	6	4	3	1	C2	1
X_7	7	3	5	1	C2	1
X_8	7	4	4	0	C2	0
X_9	8	5	6	2	C2	2
X_{10}	7	6	6	2	C2	2

$Cluster_2 = \{(7,4)(6,2)(6,4)(7,3)(8,5)(7,6)\}=(X5,X6,X7,X8,X9,X10\}$

So the total cost involved is 20.

Iteration 2

Select one of the non medoids O′ Let us assume O′ = (7, 3) =x7

So now the medoids are c_1 (3, 4) and O′ (7, 3) If c1 and O′ are new medoids, calculate the total cost involved by using the formula in the step 1 (Table 7).

So cost of swapping medoid from c_2 to O′ is = 22 so moving to O′ would be a bad idea, so the previous choice was good. So we try other non medoids and found that our first choice was the best. So the configuration does not change and algorithm terminates here (i.e. there is no change in the medoids).

Table 7 . Calculating total cost from step 1

Samples	Attribute1	Attribute 2	Cost distance or dist mean (3,4)	Cost distance or dist mean (7,3)	clustering	Total cost
X_1	2	6	3	8	C1	3
X_2	3	4	0	5	C1	0
X_3	3	8	4	9	C1	4
X_4	4	7	4	7	C1	4
X_5	6	2	5	2	C2	2
X_6	6	4	3	2	C2	2
X_7	7	3	5	0	C2	0
X_8	7	4	4	1	C2	1
X_9	8	5	6	3	C2	3
X_{10}	7	6	6	3	C2	3

Analysis in K-Medoids

- Pam is more robust than k-means in the presence of noise and outliers because a medoid is less influenced by outliers or other extreme values than a mean
- Pam works efficiently for small data sets but does not scale well for large data sets.
  - $O(k(n-k)^2)$ for each iteration where n is # of data, k is # of clusters
- Sampling based method, CLARANS (Clustering Large Applications based on randomized search)
- CLARA (Kaufmann and Rousseeuw in 1990)
  - Built in statistical analysis packages, such as S+
- It draws multiple samples of the data set, applies PAM on each sample, and gives the best clustering as the output
- Strength: deals with larger data sets than PAM
- Weakness:
  - Efficiency depends on the sample size
  - A good clustering based on samples will not necessarily represent a good clustering of the whole data set if the sample is biased

Hierarchical Clustering

Ultimate time, we delivered the undertaking of hierarchical clustering, wherein we purpose to produce nested clusterings that reflect the similarity among clusters. This contrasts sharply with our former discussion of "flat" or structureless clustering strategies like ok-means which do no longer model relationships between clusters. in this lecture, we are able to preserve our discussion of the usual version-loose techniques to hierarchical clustering by way of considering both of the predominant paradigms for hierarchical clustering:

1. Agglomerative / backside-Up Clustering, wherein we recursively merge comparable clusters.
2. Divisive / top-Down Clustering, in which we recursively sub-divide into multiple sub clusters the usual procedures in both settings are greedy fashion and so usually now not choicest in any feel.

Agglomerative clustering is the more commonplace of the two paradigms. The same old greedy set of rules proceeds as follows is begin with all information factors in their personal clusters and Repeat until best one cluster stays. Discover 2 clusters (C1, C2) that are most similar (that have the smallest pairwise cluster dissimilarity d(C1, C2)) Merge C1, C2 into one cluster so as to perform the above set of rules we need to recognise the way to assemble cluster dissimilarity from a degree of statistics factor similarity d(x, xt)? The three maximum not unusual measures, outlined below, are single linkage, complete linkage, and common linkage. Single Linkage is an linkage measure dsl (C1, C2) =minx1 ∈C1, x2 ∈C2d(x1, x2) judges cluster similarity with the aid of the maximum similar factors inside the clusters being compared. an instantaneous implementation of this algorithm would require order of (# clusters)2 paintings to select clusters and update the minimum dissimilarity to the newly merged cluster. The complexity may be decreased considerably with suitable information systems. A disadvantage of this desire is that single Linkage may additionally yield long, prolonged clusters or chains of factors ("chaining") so factors inside the same cluster could be quite varied. Complete Linkage is a complete linkage measured cl(C1,C2)=maxx1∈C1,x2 ∈C2d(x1,x2)judges cluster similarity by the least similar points inside the clusters being as compared. a direct implementation of this algorithm could require order of (# clusters)2 work to pick out clusters and update the maximum dissimilarity to the newly merged cluster. The complexity might be reduced substantially with appropriate records structures. A downside of this choice is that points in a single cluster can be in the direction of factors in another cluster than to any of its own cluster. The average linkage measured (C,C)=1|C1||C2|.x1∈C1,x2 ∈C2d(x1,x2) judges cluster similarity via average similarity of all of the points in the clusters being as compared. This metric may be considered a compromise between unmarried linkage and entire linkage. an immediate implementation of this set of rules would require order of (# clusters)2 work to select clusters and update the common dissimilarity to the newly merged cluster. The complexity may be decreased appreciably with suitable facts structures. A disadvantage of this preference is that common linkage isn't invariant to growing or decreasing modifications of dissimilarity matrix d. This property can be regained through the usage of the median dissimilarity instead of the average. Divisive clustering is the second, much less common paradigm for hierarchical clustering. it may be effective to use divisive clustering over agglomerative while you handiest need a small variety of general clusters. here are commonplace options for implementation.

Density-Based Methods

Partitioning and hierarchical methods are considered to find spherical-shaped clusters. It is complexity finding clusters of arbitrary shape such as the "S" shape and oval clusters in Figure 3. Given such type of data, they would likely incorrectly identify convex regions, where noise or outliers are included in the clusters.

To find clusters of arbitrary shape, alternatively, we can model clusters as dense regions in the data space, divided by sparse regions. This is the main strategy behind density-based clustering methods, it can discover clusters of no spherical shape.

The basic techniques of density-based clustering methods are,

- DBSCAN
- OPTICS
- DENCLUE.

Figure 3. Clusters of arbitrary shape

DBSCAN: Density-Based Clustering Based on Connected Regions With High Density

"How to find dense regions in density-based clustering?" The density of an object **o** can be measured by the number of objects close to o. DBSCAN (Density-Based Spatial Clustering of Applications with Noise) discover core objects, Which objects that have dense neighborhoods. It join core objects and their neighborhoods to form the dense regions as clusters.

"How does DBSCAN quantify the neighborhood of an object?" A user-specified parameter $\epsilon > o$ is used to specify the radius of a neighborhood we consider for every object. The ϵ-neighborhood of an object o is the space within a radius ϵ centered at o.

Due to the fixed neighborhood size parameterized by ϵ, the density of a neighborhood can be measured simply by the number of objects in the neighborhood. To determine whether a neighborhood is dense or not, DBSCAN uses another user-specified parameter, MinPts, which specifies the density threshold of dense regions. An object is a core object if the ϵ-neighborhood of the object contains at least MinPts objects. Core objects are the pillars of dense regions explained by Anjali B. Raut et al. (2017).

Given a set, D, of objects, we can identify all core objects with respect to the given parameters, ϵ and MinPts. The clustering task is therein reduced to using core objects and their neighborhoods to form dense regions, where the dense regions are clusters. For a core object q and an object p, we say that p is directly density-reachable from q (with respect to ϵ and MinPts) if p is within the ϵ-neighborhood of q. Clearly, an object p is directly density-reachable from another object q if and only if q is a core object and p is in the ϵ-neighborhood of q. Using the directly density-reachable relation, a core object can "bring" all objects from its ϵ-neighborhood into a dense region.

"How can we assemble a large dense region using small dense regions centered by core objects?" In DBSCAN, p is density-reachable from q (with respect to ϵ and MinPts in D) if there is a chain of objects $p_1, ..., p_n$, such that $p_1 = q$, $p_n = p$, and p_{i+1} is directly density-reachable from p_i with respect to ϵ and MinPts, for $1 \leq i \leq n$, $p_i \in D$. Note that density-reachability is not an equivalence relation because it is not symmetric. If both o_1 and o_2 are core objects and o_1 is density-reachable from o_2, then o_2 is density-reachable from o_1. However, if o_2 is a core object but o_1 is not, then o_1 may be density-reachable from o_2, but not vice versa.

To connect core objects as well as their neighbors in a dense region, DBSCAN uses the notion of density-connectedness. Two objects $p_1, p_2 \in D$ are density-connected with respect to ϵ and MinPts if there is an object $q \in D$ such that both p_1 and p_2 are density-reachable from q with respect to ϵ and MinPts. Unlike density-reachability, density-connectedness is an equivalence relation. It is easy to show that, for objects $o_1, o_2,$ and o_3, if o_1 and o_2 are density-connected, and o_2 and o_3 are density-connected, then so are o_1 and o_3.

Density-Reachability and Density-Connectivity

Consider the following for a given ϵ represented by the radius of the circles, and, say, let MinPts = 3 (Figure 4).

Of the labeled points, m, p, o, r are core objects because each is in an ϵ-neighborhood containing at least three points. Object q is directly density-reachable from m. Object m is directly density-reachable from p and vice versa.

Figure 4. Density-reachability and density-connectivity in density-based clustering

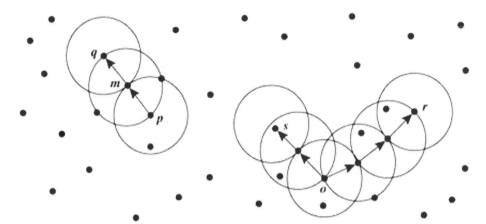

Object q is (indirectly) density-reachable from p because q is directly density-reachable from m and m is directly density-reachable from p. However, p is not density-reachable from q because q is not a core object. Similarly, r and s are density-reachable from o and o is density-reachable from r. Thus, o, r, and s are all density-connected.

We can use the closure of density-connectedness to find connected dense regions as clusters. Each closed set is a density-based cluster. A subset $C \subseteq D$ is a cluster if (1) for any two objects $o_1, o_2 \in C$, o_1 and o_2 are density-connected; and (2) there does not exist an object $o \in C$ and another object $o' \in (D - C)$ such that o and o' are density-connected.

"How does DBSCAN find clusters?" Initially, all objects in a given data set D are marked as "unvisited." DBSCAN randomly selects an unvisited object p, marks p as "visited," and checks whether the ϵ-neighborhood of p contains at least MinPts objects. If not, p is marked as a noise point. Otherwise, a new cluster C is created for p, and all the objects in the ϵ-neighborhood of pare added to a candidate set, N. DBSCAN iteratively adds to C those objects in N that do not belong to any cluster. In this process, for an object p' in N that carries the label "unvisited," DBSCAN marks it as "visited" and checks its ϵ-neighborhood. If the ϵ-neighborhood of p' has at least MinPts objects, those objects in the ϵ-neighborhood of p' are added to N. DBSCAN continues adding objects to C until C can no longer be expanded, that is, N is empty. At this time, cluster C is completed, and thus is output.

To find the next cluster, DBSCAN randomly selects an unvisited object from the remaining ones. The clustering process continues until all objects are visited.

The pseudocode of the DBSCAN algorithm is given in Figure 5.

If a spatial index is used, the computational complexity of DBSCAN is O(n log n), where n is the number of database objects. Otherwise, the complexity is $O(n^2)$. With appropriate settings of the user-defined parameters, ϵ and MinPts, the algorithm is effective in finding arbitrary-shaped clusters.

OPTICS: Ordering Points to Identify the Clustering Structure

In DBSCAN can cluster objects given input parameters such as ϵ (the maximum radius of a neighborhood) and MinPts (the minimum number of points required in the neighborhood of a core object), it encumbers users with the responsibility of selecting parameter values that will lead to the discovery of

Figure 5. DBSCAN algorithm

Algorithm: DBSCAN: a density-based clustering algorithm.

Input:

- *D*: a data set containing *n* objects,
- ϵ: the radius parameter, and
- *MinPts*: the neighborhood density threshold.

Output: A set of density-based clusters.

Method:

```
(1)    mark all objects as unvisited;
(2)    do
(3)         randomly select an unvisited object p;
(4)         mark p as visited;
(5)         if the ε-neighborhood of p has at least MinPts objects
(6)              create a new cluster C, and add p to C;
(7)              let N be the set of objects in the ε-neighborhood of p;
(8)              for each point p' in N
(9)                   if p' is unvisited
(10)                       mark p' as visited;
(11)                       if the ε-neighborhood of p' has at least MinPts points,
                           add those points to N;
(12)                  if p' is not yet a member of any cluster, add p' to C;
(13)             end for
(14)             output C;
(15)        else mark p as noise;
(16)   until no object is unvisited;
```

acceptable clusters. This is a problem associated with many other clustering algorithms. Such parameter settings are usually empirically set and difficult to determine, especially for real-world, high-dimensional data sets. Most algorithms are sensitive to these parameter values: Slightly different settings may lead to very different clusterings of the data. Moreover, real-world, high-dimensional data sets often have very skewed distributions such that their intrinsic clustering structure may not be well characterized by a single set of global density parameters.

Note that density-based clusters are monotonic with respect to the neighborhood threshold. That is, in DBSCAN, for a fixed MinPts value and two neighborhood thresholds, $\epsilon_1 < \epsilon_2$, a cluster C with respect to ϵ_1 and MinPts must be a subset of a cluster C' with respect to ϵ_2 and MinPts. This means that if two objects are in a density-based cluster, they must also be in a cluster with a lower density requirement Ricardo et al., (2015).

To overcome the difficulty in using one set of global parameters in clustering analysis, a cluster analysis method called OPTICS was proposed. OPTICS does not explicitly produce a data set clustering. Instead, it outputs a cluster ordering. This is a linear list of all objects under analysis and represents the density-based clustering structure of the data. Objects in a denser cluster are listed closer to each other in the cluster ordering. This ordering is equivalent to density-based clustering obtained from a wide range of parameter settings. Thus, OPTICS does not require the user to provide a specific density threshold. The cluster ordering can be used to extract basic clustering information (e.g., cluster centers, or arbitrary-shaped clusters), derive the intrinsic clustering structure, as well as provide a visualization of the clustering (Adil Fahad et al., (2014).

To construct the different clustering simultaneously, the objects are processed in a specific order. This order selects an object that is density-reachable with respect to the lowest ϵ value so that clusters with higher density (lower ϵ) will be finished first. Based on this idea, OPTICS needs two important pieces of information per object:

- The core-distance of an object p is the smallest value ϵ' such that the ϵ'-neighborhood of p has at least MinPts objects. That is, ϵ' is the minimum distance threshold that makes p a core object. If p is not a core object with respect to ϵ and MinPts, the core-distance of p is undefined.
- The reachability-distance to object p from q is the minimum radius value that makes p density-reachable from q. According to the definition of density-reachability, q has to be a core object and p must be in the neighborhood of q. Therefore, the reachability-distance from q to p is max{core-distance(q), dist(p, q)}. If q is not a core object with respect to ϵ and MinPts, the reachability-distance to p from q is undefined.

An object p may be directly reachable from multiple core objects. Therefore, p may have multiple reachability-distances with respect to different core objects. The smallest reachability-distance of p is of particular interest because it gives the shortest path for which p is connected to a dense cluster.

Figure 6 illustrates the concepts of core-distance and reachability-distance. Suppose that #x03F5; = 6 mm and MinPts = 5. The core-distance of p is the distance, ϵ', between p and the fourth closest data object from p. The reachability-distance of q_1 from p is the core-distance of p (i.e., $\epsilon' = 3$ mm) because this is greater than the Euclidean distance from p to q_1. The reachability-distance of q_2 with respect to p is the Euclidean distance from p to q_2 because this is greater than the core-distance of p.

Figure 6. OPTICS terminology

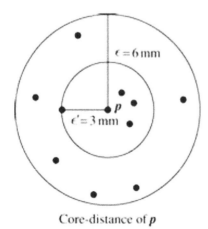

Core-distance of **p**

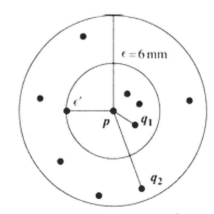

Reachability-distance $(p, q_1) = \epsilon' = 3$ mm
Reachability-distance $(p, q_2) = dist (p, q_2)$

OPTICS computes an ordering of all objects in a given database and, for each object in the database, stores the core-distance and a suitable reachability-distance. OPTICS maintains a list called OrderSeeds to generate the output ordering. Objects in OrderSeeds are sorted by the reachability-distance from their respective closest core objects, that is, by the smallest reachability-distance of each object.

OPTICS begins with an arbitrary object from the input database as the current object, p. It retrieves the ε-neighborhood of p, determines the core-distance, and sets the reachability-distance to undefined. The current object, p, is then written to output. If p is not a core object, OPTICS simply moves on to the next object in the OrderSeeds list (or the input database if OrderSeeds is empty). If p is a core object, then for each object, q, in the ε-neighborhood of p, OPTICS updates its reachability-distance from p and inserts q into OrderSeeds if q has not yet been processed. The iteration continues until the input is fully consumed and OrderSeeds is empty as explored by (Mihael Ankerst et al. 2011).

A data set's cluster ordering can be represented graphically, which helps to visualize and understand the clustering structure in a data set. For example, Figure 7 is the reachability plot for a simple 2-D data set, which presents a general overview of how the data are structured and clustered. The data objects are plotted in the clustering order (horizontal axis) together with their respective reachability-distances (vertical axis). The three Gaussian "bumps" in the plot reflect three clusters in the data set. Methods have also been developed for viewing clustering structures of high-dimensional data at various levels of detail.

The structure of the OPTICS algorithm is very similar to that of DBSCAN. Consequently, the two algorithms have the same time complexity. The complexity is O(n log n) if a spatial index is used, and O(n²) otherwise, where n is the number of objects.

Figure 7. Cluster ordering in OPTICS

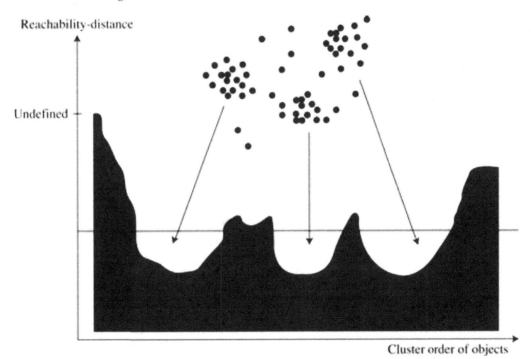

DENCLUE: Clustering Based on Density Distribution Functions

Density estimation is a core issue in density-based clustering methods. DENCLUE (DENsity-based CLUstEring) is a clustering method based on a set of density distribution functions. We first give some background on density estimation, and then describe the DENCLUE algorithm.

In probability and statistics, density estimation is the estimation of an unobservable underlying probability density function based on a set of observed data. In the context of density-based clustering, the unobservable underlying probability density function is the true distribution of the population of all possible objects to be analyzed. The observed data set is regarded as a random sample from that population.

In DBSCAN and OPTICS, density is calculated by counting the number of objects in a neighborhood defined by a radius parameter, ϵ. Such density estimates can be highly sensitive to the radius value used. For example, in Figure 8 the density changes significantly as the radius increases by a small amount.

To overcome this problem, kernel density estimation can be used, which is a nonparametric density estimation approach from statistics. The general idea behind kernel density estimation is simple. We treat an observed object as an indicator of high-probability density in the surrounding region. The probability density at a point depends on the distances from this point to the observed objects.

Formally, let $\mathbf{x}_1, \ldots, \mathbf{x}_n$ be an independent and identically distributed sample of a random variable f. The kernel density approximation of the probability density function is

$$\hat{f}_h = \frac{1}{nh} \sum_{i=1}^{n} K\left(\frac{x - x_i}{h}\right)$$

where K() is a kernel and h is the bandwidth serving as a smoothing parameter. A kernel can be regarded as a function modeling the influence of a sample point within its neighborhood. Technically, a kernel K() is a non-negative real-valued integrable function that should satisfy two requirements: $\int_{-\infty}^{+\infty} K(u)du = 1$ and K(−u) = K(u) for all values of u. A frequently used kernel is a standard Gaussian function with a mean of 0 and a variance of 1:

Figure 8. The subtlety in density estimation in DBSCAN and OPTICS: Increasing the neighborhood radius slightly from 1 to 2 results in a much higher density

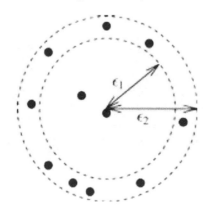

$$K\left(\frac{x - x_i}{h}\right) = \frac{1}{\sqrt{2\pi}}\, e^{-\frac{(x-x_i)^2}{2h^2}}$$

DENCLUE uses a Gaussian kernel to estimate density based on the given set of objects to be clustered. A point $\mathbf{x}^*$ is called a density attractor if it is a local maximum of the estimated density function. To avoid trivial local maximum points, DENCLUE uses a noise threshold, ξ, and only considers those density attractors $\mathbf{x}^*$ such that $\hat{f}(x^*) \geq \xi$. These nontrivial density attractors are the centers of clusters.

Objects under analysis are assigned to clusters through density attractors using a stepwise hill-climbing procedure. For an object, x, the hill-climbing procedure starts from x and is guided by the gradient of the estimated density function. That is, the density attractor for x is computed as

$$x^0 = x$$

$$x^{j+1} = x^j + \delta\frac{\nabla\hat{f}(x_j)}{\left|\nabla\hat{f}(x_j)\right|},$$

where δ is a parameter to control the speed of convergence, and

$$\nabla\hat{f}(x) = \frac{1}{h^{d+2}n\sum_{i=1}^{n} K\left(\dfrac{x - x_i}{h}\right)(x_i - x)}$$

The hill-climbing procedure stops at step k> 0 if $\hat{f}(x^{k+1}) < \hat{f}(x^k)$, and assigns x to the density attractor $\mathbf{x}^* = \mathbf{x}^k$. An object x is an outlier or noise if it converges in the hill-climbing procedure to a local maximum $\mathbf{x}^*$ with $\hat{f}(x^*) \geq \xi$.

A cluster in DENCLUE is a set of density attractors X and a set of input objects C such that each object in C is assigned to a density attractor in X, and there exists a path between every pair of density attractors where the density is above ξ. By using multiple density attractors connected by paths, DENCLUE can find clusters of arbitrary shape.

DENCLUE has several advantages. It can be regarded as a generalization of several well-known clustering methods such as single-linkage approaches and DBSCAN. Moreover, DENCLUE is invariant against noise. The kernel density estimation can effectively reduce the influence of noise by uniformly distributing noise into the input data.

CLASSIFICATION

Classification is a data mining technique that assigns groups to a collection of data in order to help in more accurate forecasting and analysis of the data.

Need for Classification

Nowadays databases are becoming very large which has increased from mega bytes to terabytes of data. (A terabyte is one trillion bytes of data). These are called as big data

Social media like facebook alone occupies 600 terabytes of data every day. These data are to be made sensible.

The big data which is diverse, unstructured and fast changing in nature is to be made sensible. The data like audio, video, social media posts, 3D and geospatial data cannot be easily categorized or organized.

So we need to classify it into groups, which can be easily retrieved. To meet this challenge, a range of automatic methods for extracting useful information has been developed, called classification.

Working of Classification

To make classification work, we need to frame a set of classification rules that will answer a question, make a decision, or predict the behavior.

The main function of the classification algorithm is to discover how that set of attributes produces the conclusion.

Training Data Set

A set of training data is developed that contains a certain set of attributes as well as the likely outcome. (ie the conditions and their results to be given)

Types of Classification

1. Supervised Classification
   a. The set of possible classes is known in advance.
2. Unsupervised Classification
   b. Set of possible classes is not known.
3. **Scenario:** Perhaps a credit card company is trying to determine which prospects should receive a credit card offer.

This might be its set of training data (Table 8).

Based on the Age, gender and annual income of a person credit card is to be offered by the company. Here Age, gender and annual income are called as Predictor columns.

Credit card offer is called as the Predictor attribute. In a training set, the predictor attribute is known. The classification algorithm then tries to determine

Table 8. Training Data

Name	Age	Gender	Annual Income	Credit Card Offer
John Doe	25	M	$39,500	No
Jane Doe	56	F	$125,000	Yes

- How the value of the predictor attribute was reached
- What relationships exist between the predictors and the decision?
- It will develop a set of prediction rules, usually an IF/THEN statement

I.e. IF (Age>18 OR Age <75) AND Annual Income >40,000 THEN Credit Card Offer=yes

Examples

Classification is used in Weather predictions to report whether the day will be rainy, sunny or cloudy. The medical profession might analyze health conditions to predict medical outcomes.

CLASSIFICATION-DECISION TREE

Classification is a technique of identifying predefined categories or class from assigned objects. They are two types of data sets, training set and test set (Table 9).

TRAINING SET

It has collection of records in which each record contains a set of attributes, in which one of the attribute is a class. By using this set of records the model can be built easily.

TEST SET

Records in test set are basically used to determine the correctness of the model and this set of records are used for validating.

This chapter introduces the basic idea of classification and it mainly focuses on various techniques for implementing decision tree induction.

DECISION TREE: CLASSIFICATION

Yan Song (2004) explained decision tree is a classification or regression model that can be used to divide a large collection of records in to smaller set of tree structure. Implementation of tree structure includes

Figure 9. Classification

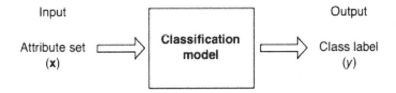

Figure 10. Test Set

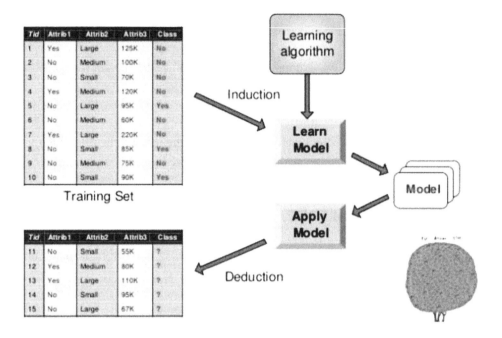

root node, leaf node and its branches. The root node is also called as decision node and it has two or more branches. Leaf node represents a class label, where as internal node represents an tested attributes. Decision tree classification handles both textual and numerical data. Decision tree representation of textual data is shown in Figure 11.

TYPES OF DECISION TREE

Basically Decision tree can be build with two steps:

Figure 11. Decision tree representation of textual data

Predictors				Target
Outlook	Temp	Humidity	Windy	Play Golf
Rainy	Hot	High	False	No
Rainy	Hot	High	True	No
Overcast	Hot	High	False	Yes
Sunny	Mild	High	False	Yes
Sunny	Cool	Normal	False	Yes
Sunny	Cool	Normal	True	No
Overcast	Cool	Normal	True	Yes
Rainy	Mild	High	False	No
Rainy	Cool	Normal	False	Yes
Sunny	Mild	Normal	False	Yes
Rainy	Mild	Normal	True	Yes
Overcast	Mild	High	True	Yes
Overcast	Hot	Normal	False	Yes
Sunny	Mild	High	True	No

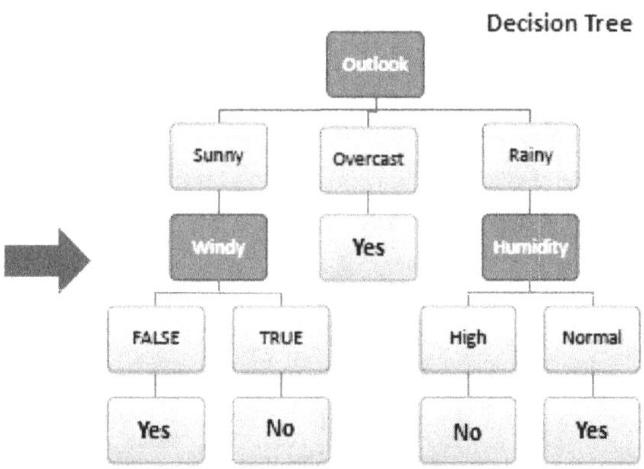

1. **Tree Construction:** A Class of records is split in to multiples based on attributes or conditions.
2. **Tree Pruning:** Classification accuracy is increased based on finding and removing unwanted branches.

HUNT'S ALGORITHM

Hunt's algorithm work based on recursive partition methodology, it has set of training records associated with nodes and trageted variables of various classes.

Here,

D_t - Set of trained records
T - Set of nodes
Y - $\{Y_1, Y_2, Y_3 ..... Y_c\}$ is the target variable of number of classes.

IMPLEMENTATION

Step 1: If all record of training set belongs to same classes, then it will be consider as leaf node of that class.

$D_t \in Y_{t, then}$ node t is a leaf node of class Y_t

Step 2: If all record of training set belongs to more than one classes, then based on attribute test condition partitioned are done. The outcome of training set and test condition are same then the nodes are assembled under same class. This algorithm is a recursive partition based applied to all child node.

Figure 12. Types of decision tree

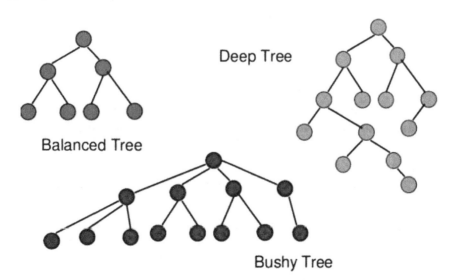

Figure 13. Tree pruning

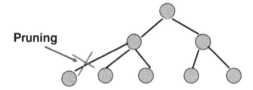

CLASSIFICATION-BACK PROPAGATION

Definition

Back Propagation technique is based on neural network algorithm which has a sequence of input and output with weight. It processes the data in a looping manner by comparing the each tuples predicted value with the target value. The mean squared error between predicted and actual value are reduced in the backward direction of neural network from last layer to first layer hence it is named as back propagation.

Algorithm

Input:
D, a data set consisting of the training tuples and their associated target values;
L, the learning rate;
Network, a multilayer feed-forward network.
Output: A finalized optimized network
Steps shown in Figure 14.

Initializing the Weights

The weight of the edge in the network is assigned with the random numbers ranging from (-1.0 to 1.0 or -0.5 to 0.5) and the bias is also assigned with same criteria.

X is processed with following steps.

Propagation of Inputs

Training tuple is fed as input to the network layers which passes through the input units. Thus, I_j is a input training tuple with input unit j which produces the output O_j will gets computed in a linear combination.

$$I_j = \sum_i w_{ij} O_i + \theta_j$$

Where

W_{ij}-weight of an edge

Figure 14. Back Propagation technique

1) Initialize all weights and biases in network;
2) While terminating condition is not satisfied {
3)   for each training tuple X in D {
4)   //propagate the inputs forward:
5)   for each input layer unit j {
6) $O_j=I_j$;//output of an input unit is its actual input value
7)   for each hidden or output layer unit j {
8) $I_j=\sum_i w_{ij}O_i + \theta_j$; // compute the net input of unit j with respect to the previous layer, i
9) $O_j=\frac{1}{1+e^{-I_j}}$; } // compute the output of each unit j
10)   // BackPropagate the errors;
11)   for each unit j in the output layer
12) $Err_j=O_j(1- O_j)(T_j- O_j)$; // compute the error
13)   for each unit j in the hidden layers, from the last to the first hidden layer
14) $Err_j=O_j(1- O_j)\sum_k Err_k w_{jk}$; // compute the error with respect to the next higher layer, k
15)   for each weight w_{ij} in network {
16) $\Delta w_{ij} = (l)Err_j I_i$; //weight increment
17) $w_{ij} = w_{ij} + \Delta w_{ij}$; } //weight update
18)   for each bias in networkθ_j {
19) $\Delta\theta_j = (l) Err_j$;//bias increment
20) $\theta_j = \theta_j + \Delta\theta_j$; } //bias update
21)   }}

O_j-Output unit

θ_j -Bias(threshold) of the unit

Propagation of Outputs

$$O_j=\frac{1}{1+e^{-I_j}}$$

This formula is also defined as squashing function, because it solves a huge size of input in the ranges of 0 to 1.

Back propagating the error:

On updating the value of weight and bias the error the error is back propagated in the neural network based on the predicted and actual values difference.

The Error Err_j in the Output layer O_j with unit j is computed as follows,

$$Err_j = O_j(1-O_j)(T_j - O_j);$$

The Error Err_j in the middle layers or hidden layers with unit j is computed as follows,

$$Err_j = O_j(1-O_j)\sum_k Err_k w_{jk};$$

Since the errors get propagated the weight of the edge and bias must have to gets updated based on the following,

Weight Updation

$$\Delta w_{ij} = (1) Err_j I_i;$$

$$w_{ij} = w_{ij} + \Delta w_{ij};$$

Bias Updation

$$\Delta \theta j = (1) Err_j;$$

$$\theta j = \theta j + \Delta \theta j;$$

Case Updating: Updating the values of weight and bias based on error propagation.

Epoch Updating: Incrementing the values of weight and bias based on the training samples. Nearly thousands of epoch is necessary to coverage the values of weight.

Terminating Conditions

Training stops when any one of the condition holds

- Values of Δw_{ij} in the previous epoch id too small than the specified threshold.
- Misclassification of epoch value leads the value below the certain threshold.
- Expiration of count of epochs.
- **Note:** Simulated annealing method can be used to converge the solution to the maximum specified threshold, thus it improves the classification based on back propagation.

Example

Back Propagation Algorithm

Figure 15 has given a multilayer forward neural network. Let the learning rate be 0.9. Starting with bias and weight which are shown in Table 9, along with the initial training attribute values, X=(1,0,1), with a class label of 1.

This example shows the calculations for backpropagation, given the first training tuple, **X**. The tuple is fed into the network, and the net input and output of each unit are computed. These values are shown in Table 10. The error of each unit is computed and propagated backward. The error values are shown in Table 11. The weight and bias updates are shown in Table 12.

Figure 15. Multilayer forward neural network

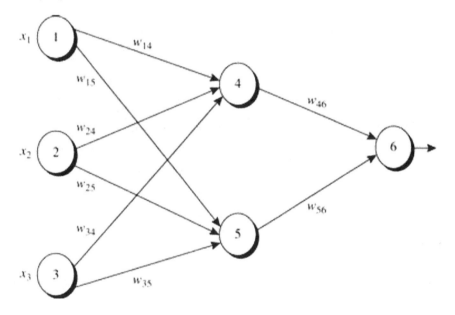

Table 9. Initial input, weight, and bias values

x_1	x_2	x_3	w_{14}	w_{15}	w_{24}	w_{25}	w_{34}	w_{35}	w_{46}	w_{56}	θ_4	θ_5	θ_6
1	0	1	0.2	−0.3	0.4	0.1	−0.5	0.2	−0.3	−0.2	−0.4	0.2	0.1

Table 10. Net input and output calculations

Unit, j	Net Input, I_j	Output, O_j
4	$0.2 + 0 − 0.5 − 0.4 = −0.7$	$1/(1 + e^{0.7}) = 0.332$
5	$−0.3 + 0 + 0.2 + 0.2 = 0.1$	$1/(1 + e^{−0.1}) = 0.525$
6	$(−0.3)(0.332) − (0.2)(0.525) + 0.1 = −0.105$	$1/(1 + e^{0.105}) = 0.474$

Table 11. Calculation of the error at each node

Unit, j	Err$_j$
6	$(0.474)(1 - 0.474)(1 - 0.474) = 0.1311$
5	$(0.525)(1 - 0.525)(0.1311)(-0.2) = -0.0065$
4	$(0.332)(1 - 0.332)(0.1311)(-0.3) = -0.0087$

Table 12. Calculations for weight and bias updating

Weight or Bias	New Value
w_{46}	$-0.3 + (0.9)(0.1311)(0.332) = -0.261$
w_{56}	$-0.2 + (0.9)(0.1311)(0.525) = -0.138$
w_{14}	$0.2 + (0.9)(-0.0087)(1) = 0.192$
w_{15}	$-0.3 + (0.9)(-0.0065)(1) = -0.306$
w_{24}	$0.4 + (0.9)(-0.0087)(0) = 0.4$
w_{25}	$0.1 + (0.9)(-0.0065)(0) = 0.1$
w_{34}	$-0.5 + (0.9)(-0.0087)(1) = -0.508$
w_{35}	$0.2 + (0.9)(-0.0065)(1) = 0.194$
θ_6	$0.1 + (0.9)(0.1311) = 0.218$
θ_5	$0.2 + (0.9)(-0.0065) = 0.194$
θ_4	$-0.4 + (0.9)(-0.0087) = -0.408$

PREDICTION

What Is Prediction?

Predicting the identity of one thing with another, related thing is called Prediction. Not necessarily future events, just unknowns. Based on the relativity between a thing that you can know and a thing you need to predict

Predictor => Predicted

When building a predictive model, you have data covering both. When using one, you have data describing the predictor and you want it to tell you the predicted value.

Classification models predict categorical class labels; and prediction models predict continuous valued functions. For example, we can build a classification model to categorize bank loan applications as either safe or risky, or a prediction model to predict the expenditures in dollars of potential customers on computer equipment given their income and occupation.

COMPARING CLASSIFICATION AND PREDICTION METHODS

Classification and prediction methods can be compared and evaluated according to the following criteria.

Accuracy

The accuracy of a classifier refers to the ability of a given classifier to correctly predict the class label of new or previously unseen data (i.e., tuples without class label information). Similarly, the accuracy of a predictor refers to how well a given predictor can guess the value of the predicted attribute for new or previously unseen data.

Speed

This refers to the computational costs involved in generating and using the given classifier or predictor.

Robustness

This is the ability of the classifier or predictor to make correct predictions given noisy data or data with missing values.

Scalability

This refers to the ability to construct the classifier or predictor efficiently given large amounts of data.

Interpretability

This refers to the level of understanding and insight that is provided by the classifier or predictor. Interpretability is subjective and therefore more difficult to assess. We discuss some work in this area, such as the extraction of classification rules from a "black box" neural network classifier called backpropagation

REGRESSION

Introduction

In general it is a technique for determining the statistical relationship between two or more variables where a change in a dependent variable is associated with, and depends on, a change in one or more independent variables. Khan, Kamran et al.,(2014)

Regression is one of the technique used in data mining to calculate a range of continuous values (also called numeric values),given a particular dataset, eg:regression might be used to predict the cost of a product or service, given other variables.

Regression vs. Classification

- Both techniques are used to solve the same evils but they are frequently confused and used in prediction analysis.
- Regression is used to predict numeric values or continuous values but classification assigns data into discrete categories.
- Example regression would be used to predict a land value based on its location, square feet, price when last sold, price of the similar ;ands and other factors, but classification will order houses into categories, such as walkability, lot size or crime rates.

Regression Analysis

- Regression analysis is a predictive modeling technique which is used to investigate the relationship between a dependent (target) and independent (predictor) variables.
- It is also used for forecasting time series modeling and finding the casual effect relationship between variables. Example relationship between rash driving and number of road accidents by a driver. It is an important tool for modeling and analyzing data

Benefits of Using Regression Analysis

- It specifies the significant relationships between dependent variable and independent variable.
- It specifies the strength of impact of multiple independent variables on a dependent variable.

Types of Regression Techniques

Many types of regression techniques are available to compose predictions. Based on the below metrics the regression techniques are driven.
Metrics are,

- Number of independent variable
- Type of dependent variables
- Shape of regression line

There are seven types of regressions available for predictions.
They are,

- Linear Regression
- Logistic Regression
- Polynomial Regression
- Stepwise Regression
- Ridge Regression
- Lasso Regression
- Elastic Net Regression

ASSOCIATION RULE

Association rule (Figure 16) is a method of rule based machine learning for finding the interesting patterns between the variables in database. The main intend of this machine learning method is to find the strong rules among the items using interestingness measures of support and confident.

Algorithms

Association Rule based machine learning algorithms are

1.   Apriori based Association Rule mining
2.   Association Rule mining based on without candidate set generation

Apriori Based Association Rule Mining

- It is a bottom up approach.
- It is used to mine the frequent item set for Boolean Association Rule.
- Frequent Item sets are calculated for an item one at a is known as candidate generation.
- It is operate on database containing a transaction.

Steps

1.   Scan the database (D) for finding the frequent item set count.
2.   Candidate set Ci using join And Prune
3.   Join:
     if support count of Frequent item set satisfies the min support value (Min Sup)
     Else
     Prune: Remove the frequent item set from the database transaction.
4.   Step 1, 2, and 3 is repeated for getting the proper candidate set.

Example

An example of Apriori based Association Rule mining is shown in Figure 17.

Figure 16. Association rule

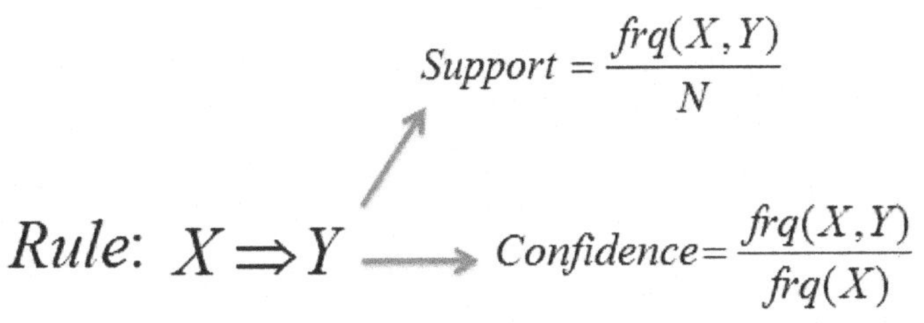

$$Rule: \; X \Rightarrow Y$$

$$Support = \frac{frq(X,Y)}{N}$$

$$Confidence = \frac{frq(X,Y)}{frq(X)}$$

Figure 17. Apriori based Association Rule mining

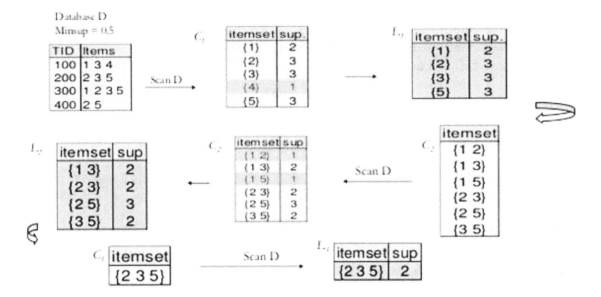

Figure 18. FP tree Construction

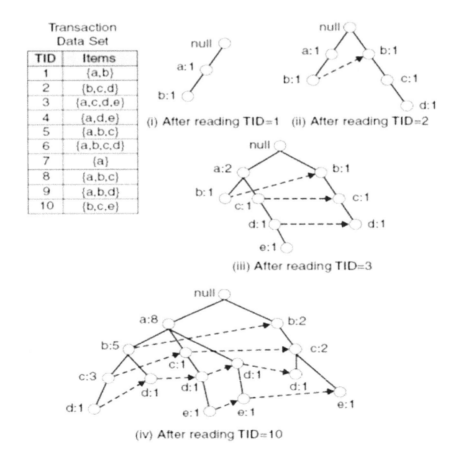

Figure 19. Completion of FP tree

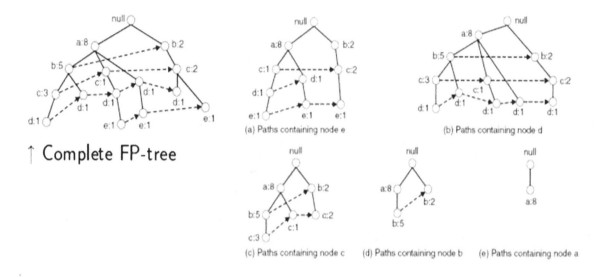

Association Rule Mining Based on Without Candidate Set Generation

It is used to find the frequent item set without candidate generation is called frequent pattern growth.

Two Step Approach

1. Build the FP (Frequent Pattern Tree).
2. Extract the frequent item set from the FP tree.

Example

Step 1: FP tree Construction (Figure 18).
Step 2: Completion of FP tree (Figure 19).

REFERENCES

Ankerst, M., Breunig, M. M., Kriegel, H.-P., & Sander, J. (2011). OPTICS: Ordering Points To Identify the Clustering Structure. *Proc. 4th Int. Conf. on Knowledge Discovery & Data Mining*.

Campello, Moulav, Zimek, & Sander. (2015). Hierarchical Density Estimates for Data Clustering, Visualization, and Outlier Detection. *ACM Transactions on Knowledge Discovery from Data, 10*(1).

Fahad. (2014). *A Survey of Clustering Algorithms for Big Data: Taxonomy and Empirical Analysis*. IEEE.

Finkel, E. J., Eastwick, P. W., Karney, B. R., Reis, H. T., & Spreche, S. (2012). Online Dating: A Critical Analysis From the Perspective of Psychological Science. *Psychological Science in the Public Interest, 13*(1), 3–66. doi:10.1177/1529100612436522 PMID:26173279

Jawak, S. D., Devliyal, P., & Luis, A. J. (2015). A Comprehensive Review on Pixel Oriented and Object Oriented Methods for Information Extraction from Remotely Sensed Satellite Images with a Special Emphasis on Cryospheric Applications. *Advances in Remote Sensing, 4*(03), 177–195. doi:10.4236/ars.2015.43015

Patel & Singh. (2013). New Approach for K-mean and K-medoids Algorithm. *International Journal of Computer Applications Technology and Research, 2*(1), 1-5.

Raut. (2017). A Hybrid Framework using Fuzzy if-then rules for DBSCAN Algorithm. *Advances in Wireless and Mobile Communications, 10*(5), 933-942.

Song & Lu. (2004). Decision tree methods: Applications for classification and prediction. *Medical Decision Making, 24*(4), 386–398. doi:10.1177/0272989X04267009 PMID:15271277

Soni Madhulatha, T. (2012, April). An overview on clustering methods. *IOSR Journal of Engineering, 2*(4), 719–725. doi:10.9790/3021-0204719725

Chapter 13
Remote Elderly Health Monitoring System Using Cloud–Based WBANs

D. Najumnissa Jamal
B. S. Abdur Rahman Crescent Institute of Science and Technology, India

S. Rajkumar
Bhairava Centre for Technology and Research, India

Nabeena Ameen
B. S. Abdur Rahman Crescent Institute of Science and Technology, India

ABSTRACT

Monitoring the physical condition of patients is a major errand for specialists. The development of wireless remote elderly patient monitoring system has been intensive in the past. RPM (remote patient monitoring) is reliant on the person's inspiration to deal with their wellbeing. The flow of patient data requires a group of medicinal services suppliers to deal with the information. RPM sending is reliant on a wireless telecommunication infrastructure, which may not be accessible/practical in provincial territories. Patients' data are shared as service on cloud in hospitals. Therefore, in the current research, a new approach of cloud-based wireless remote patient monitoring system during emergency is proposed as a model to monitor the critical health data. The vital parameters are measured and transmitted. In this chapter, the authors present an extensive review of the significant technologies associated with wireless patient monitoring using wireless sensor networks and cloud.

INTRODUCTION

Remote and rural areas with significant elderly population have challenges getting appropriate and timely care during emergency and critical care as health services in rural and remote areas are very different from the city. Significant progress has been made in RPM which helps the situation with the required data. However, the main challenge is the access and connectivity to the relevant patient data at the point

DOI: 10.4018/978-1-5225-5972-6.ch013

of care in timely manner appropriate to the care parameters. While the patient's clinical history would be available in a particular location, the point of care would be having data which would be required to be presented for drawing relevant expertise from a different location.

During an emergency care requirement, the patient may not be near a location with appropriate connectivity to facilitate reliable RPM, effectively, denying expert care to the patient. In the event that the emergency physician, utilizing sensible judgment, communicates concern about a patient's fast approaching risk of harm to him/herself, the patient ought to be taken for appraisal and treatment. Considering necessary paramedical skill available locally, the remote point of care should be capable of initiating vital RPM with limited energy and bandwidth resources to allow for early-on monitoring until the patient is taken to a care point that allows for a more intensive care. The mode of care could be either in-situ or by tele-medicine or by a combination of both.

John Knight & Yamni Nigam, (2008) states that with increasing age, elderly people experience various anatomical and physiological changes. These changes bring many emotional, behavioral and attitudinal changes in them. As a result, they suffer different physiological problems such as loss of strength and resistance, which turn into more perceptive as they grow older. These conditions further complicate the care requirement multiple fold and will require vast knowledge base to be taken into account before administering care.

Various studies are being conducted in the areas of RPM, Wireless Body Area Networks, QoS in WBAN, Care Scenarios in emergency care, Machine to Machine(M2M) and Cloud Computing as an attempt to improve the quality of care in the above situation.

SCOPE

While the study involves various aspects of the care scenario, this chapter presents the WBAN options available currently, Cloud Computing platforms that enable M2M interaction and also interaction with different health-care and medical information systems in the health-care ecosystem to enable effective RPM and relevant care delivery and aspects in possible emergency care scenarios that necessitate data availability.

Cloud Computing for Patient Monitoring

Cloud computing is characterized as the arrival of computing administrations—servers, stockpiling, databases, organizing, software, examination and the web ("the cloud"). Corporate contributing these computing administrations are called cloud suppliers and normally charge for cloud computing administrations in light of use, like charging for water or power at home.

Cloud Computing provides the following solution choices that can be mashed-up based on relevancy with care scenario that is being addressed. This also empowers the care community to take learned decision relevant to the situation ensuring timely delivery of the care, enabling them in the process to identify and provide quality personalized care. They are monitored via Software-as-a-Service Applications and Platform and Cloud Based M2M and IoT Platform.

Software-as-a-Service Applications and Platforms

Multiple information systems are now being made available as Software as a service (SaaS) applications in the cloud. SaaS is a software distribution model in which a negotiator has applications and makes them accessible to clients over the Internet. These are accessible either privately for a patient or to multiple networked care providers or both. This enables global availability of critical data via internet.

Examples of such information systems, that are now increasingly made available as SaaS applications are Hospital Information Systems, Laboratory Information Systems, Clinical Management, Dispensary Management, Health Care Messaging Systems etc. Such systems are sustained by security, privacy and patient safety regulatory standards which the solution provider must adhere to.

Cloud based systems that provide platforms for exchanging research data, drug information, forms a vital source for diagnostics and treatment planning. Each of these solutions is important for appropriate and relevant care delivery during emergency.

Cloud Based M2M and IoT Platforms

RPM involves a sensor network that is capable of collecting vital patient information adhering to privacy, safety and security standards, machine-to-machine interaction for information interchange and connectivity to the internet to enable data availability across geographically distributed locations. There are multiple technology choices available for sensors and sensor networks, internet connectivity and information system integration. The vital backbone of this comes from a common cloud platform that allows interaction of these equipment and information systems. Such a platform allows for the following:

- Machine-to-Machine interaction
- Internet-of-Things to provide a common format internet connectivity for the variety of devices with the cloud
- Common data format for possible interaction with multiple information systems
- Industry agreed standards and systems for interaction
- Integrated Data Aggregation and Clinical Informatics
- Security and Privacy
- Standardized Physical and Logical Safety Systems
- Authentication of Natural and Machine based Information sources

In general terms, IoT platforms have 3 main layers of technology separation. Edge Systems, Cloud and Fog Providers and Applications

Edge Systems

Edge Systems involves the physical devices that gather vital parameters, deliver drugs, alerts and alarms, automatic and patient-triggered emergency call devices, data network connectivity and devices

Cloud and Fog Providers

Cloud and Fog Providers involves various technology platform vendors who provide the vital link between the monitoring locations and the places where the care planning and delivery can be done. The platforms provide the backbone infrastructure in-terms wireless networks suitable for transmitting the vital parameters in real-time reliably. The providers also include the different technology platforms that allow a service and solution provider to collect and process vast amount real-time data from the edge systems and other information systems across the health-care ecosystem. The data processing involves technology platforms for machine learning, real-time data exchange and security.

Applications

Owing to the complications involved in the patient diagnostics and care, various applications and information systems needs to be integrated and should be analyzed for intelligent, informed and relevant decision making. Table 1 enumerates the different devices and systems involved in the three layers.

Before diving into the technology arena, let us first look at some example care scenarios and parameters associated with RPM.

CARE SCENARIOS IN REMOTE PATIENT MONITORING

Standard Vital Parameters in Patient Monitoring

The vital parameters like heart rate, blood glucose, respiratory rate, blood pressure and body temperature specifies the changes in the health condition (Riazul Islam, Daehan Kwak, MD.Humaun Kabir, Mahmud Hossain, & Kyung-Sup Kwak, 2015). To accomplish the information about the severe health condition of a human being during emergency its measurement is very important. The existence of acute medical problem is identified by the measured parameters. The parameters also quantify the magnitude of illness and are the chronic illness markers (Charlie Goldberg,2009). The measured parameters are compared with the normal values for any variation that indicates illness. These vital parameters will be helpful in making decision for treating the elderly during emergency. They have to be considered because the changes affect the physiological, cognitive and psychosocial health. The normal ranges of the vital parameters are shown in Table 2.

Table 1. The different devices and systems involved in the three layers

Layers	Platforms
Applications	Patient Monitoring, Care Management, Electronic Medical Records, Diagnostics, Therapy and Treatment Plans, Drug Delivery, Drug Database, Research Information Systems, Medicine and Assisted Care
Cloud and Fog Providers	Data Aggregation Platforms, Software Defined Networks, Analytics Platforms, Application Integration Platforms, Deep Learning Platforms, Device and Application Security Platforms
Edge Systems	Health Parameter Sensors (ECG, EKG, EEG, BP, Glucose, Temperature etc.), Sensor Data Acquisition

Table 2. Normal ranges of the vital parameters

Approximate Age Range	Heart Rate	Respiratory rate	Systolic Range	Diastolic Range	Temperature
Newborn	100-160	30-50	75-100	50-70	98-100
0-5 months	90-150	25-40	75-100	50-70	98-100
6-12 months	80-140	20-30	75-100	50-70	98-100
1-3 years	80-130	20-30	80-110	50-80	96.8-99.6
3-5 years	80-120	20-30	80-110	50-80	98.6
6-10 years	70-110	15-30	85-120	55-80	98.6
11-14 years	60-105	12-20	85-120	55-80	98.6
15-20 years	60-100	12-30	95-140	60-90	98.6
Adults	50-80	16-20	95-140	60-90	98.6

In accord to the VI Brazilian Guidelines on Hypertension (2010), a person's blood pressure is satisfactory when the pressure of systolic and diastolic is lower than 130 mmHg and 85 mmHg. Heart rate is appraised on a normal beginning based on the pulse better than a period of 60 seconds and the normal parameter is between 60-100 beats per minute. The respiratory rate as expressed by (Seman, Faria, Paula, Nedel, 2011) is 24 breaths for every moment and typical body temperature is in the vicinity of 36 and 37°C. A typical glucose go for a grown-up is under 100 milligrams for each deciliter when fasting for at least 8 hours, or 140 milligrams for each deciliter after sustenance.

The number of beats per minute denotes the pulse rate. It is measured by placing the index and middle finger tips on to the wrist of the patient. The number of breaths taken for one minute is the respiration rate. It is usually taken when a person is resting and involves counting the number of breaths for one minute.

Conditions like fever, illness, and other medical conditions may increase the Respiration rate (Chapman, 2013). It is used to find the difficulty in breathing of an affected person. The Respiration rate can be observed by the rise and fall of the hospital outfit of the patient while taking their heartbeat. For measuring the temperature an oral thermometer is used to provide a digital reading when the temperature sensor is placed under the patient's tongue. During fever, the temperature of the skin on the forehead is measured quickly using a special thermometer. The estimation of pulse among elderly people is measured with the help of sphygmomanometers and stethoscopes (Cristiane Chagas Teixeira, Rafaela Peres Boaventura, Adrielle Cristina Silva Souza, Thatianny Tanferri de Brito Paranaguá, Ana Lúcia Queiroz Bezerra, Maria Márcia Bachion, & Virginia Visconde Brasil, 2015).

Observing these parameters is imperative on account of the high danger of altered thresholds as a result of growing and is considered the period of most prominent inability because of age and co morbidities (Churpek, Yuen, Winslow, Hall, & Edelson, 2015; Culo, 2011). Because of the loss of homeostasis protection instruments identified with senescence, elderly individuals are more helpless to the eventual outcomes of infections, which add to longer hospitalizations and more noteworthy expenses for the healthcare administrations (Morosini, Marques, Leal, Marino, & Melo 2011;Rantz, Skubic, Popescu, Galambos, Koopman, & Alexander 2015; Dupouy, Moulis, Tubery, Ecoiffier, Sommet, & Poutrain 2013) . The motivation behind serially evaluating a patient's fundamental signs is to maintain a strategic distance from damage and the early affirmation of events with a possibility to impact the nature of medicinal activities. Similarly, the recognition of these parameters encourages to decrease the risk of preventable trouble related with human services to an adequate level, by accomplishing quality care and patient safety which are the main concern for the experts engaged in the concern of the elderly (Dupouy, Moulis, Tubery, Ecoiffier, Sommet, and Poutrain 2013).

Tele-Medicine and Remote Augmented Care Delivery

Cloud and M2M technologies allows patients to be monitored live from M2M enabled hospitals and other plausible care providence centers. The remote monitoring enables to bring in patients to hospitals only when needed critical care and the assisted care scenarios shall be possible with remote augmented care delivery. M2M and wireless network technologies in association with specialized equipment to monitor vital parameters and deliver necessary care are becoming available with multiple vendors bringing in commercial equipment. Further studies are being carried out to bring them to practical use (Abo-Zahhad, Sabah M. Ahmed, & Osama Elnahas,2014; Heba Seddik, & Ayman M. Eldeib., 2016; Medtronic MiniMed).

Beyond Video-Conferencing and Telephony based remote care assistance, Tele-medicine now includes monitoring and care administration. Private companies and institutions come together to bring home grade smart fitness trackers and clinical grade equipment that provide basic clinical data (Nokia Patient Care platform). Specific equipment manufactures additionally bring clinically approved smart devices with embedded bio-sensors for providing the different vital parameters mentioned above. Standard clinical equipment manufacturers provide equipment for diagnostics and drug delivery (Medtronic MiniMed). Some of this equipment also comes with integrated HIPAA compliant information systems that help to log, analyze and consume the data and augmented information for further diagnostics and care planning and delivery (Nokia Patient Care platform).

Structured tele-medicine practices allow for RPM to come together with assisted care for patients requiring monitoring and care at home. Studies are also being conducted for asserting the associated benefits in terms of patient motivation and care efficiency in such scenarios (Deborah A Greenwood, 2014). Considering the technology options available for RPM and Remote Care, one must also have a look at what are the possible types of patients who would be presented before the care personnel during a care episode and would find a RPM and remote augmented care beneficial. We must also bear in mind that age will necessarily impact all the presented care scenarios.

Clinical Care scenarios that benefit RPM and structured remote augmented care includes, but not limited to:

- Treatment and care for Degenerative Disorders like Alzheimer's, Parkinson's, Dementia, Multiple Sclerosis, Progressive Supranuclear Palsy, Cancer, Type II Diabetes
- Rehabilitation and Therapeutic Care for recovery from orthopedic injuries, brain and spinal injuries, post-operative care, rheumatoid arthritis, general aging difficulties
- Chronic Treatment and Therapeutic Care for Respiratory and Digestive Disorders, Endocrine disorders, Cardiac Disorders

Automated Emergency Response

Apart from Structured and ad-hoc planned home care, all the scenarios cited as examples above, also warrant for an emergency response requirement depending upon the individual patient's clinical conditions. In addition, the demography and geo-social structure of the location, connectivity, the availability of facilities and means for treatment and relevant logistics play a pivotal role in planning and execution of an emergency response. This shall include both automated and human initiated emergency response.

An automated emergency response, especially when treating the elderly, requires careful logistics to be arranged. Based on the various factors mentioned, not limited to though, the emergency response shall be planned based on what is exactly needed and what is feasible in the time-line implied by a given emergency situation of interest.

Integration of Systems to Provide New Age Health Care

Industry 4.0 brings together these technologies and the care scenarios together into a planned integration of the three main layers into comprehensive and specific health-care solutions. The integration of these technologies merges these layers and offer no clear distinct line that mark a boundary. The devices often merge with the application layer with integrated data and solution interfaces for collection, aggregation, collaboration, assistance, administration and management. Hospitals, Medical Faculty and Care institutions and agencies, Pharmaceutical Manufacturers, Instrumentation and Technology Providers and Manufacturers, Engineering Institutions, Administration and Financial institutions and Government Policy Administration work together and bring-in a seamless integration of systems that provide new age health care.

A schematic architecture shown in Figure 1 illustrates a typical set of systems and salient technologies. Though not exhaustive, this diagram will help to understand the Cloud based RPM and Remote Health Care ecosystem.

Edge Systems: Sensors and Monitoring Devices

Sensors and Monitoring Devices that are smart form an active part of the remote monitoring scene is the vital component in the cloud based remote monitoring and management for healthcare. Moving further

Figure 1. Schematic Architecture of a typical Cloud based RPM and Remote Health Care

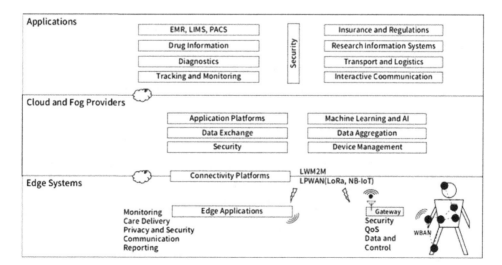

from being simple electro-wetted device, smart sensors and monitoring devices are now powered, contain embedded intelligence and potentially can form part of the drug delivery system as well in addition to their core sensory and monitoring functions.

A typical smart sensor will need to have the following building blocks either in the form of individual components are as an integrated SoC (System-on-Chip). They are typically low powered and optionally have inbuilt communication layer as well.

The devices come in multiple form factors and are of three main types: Contact (Invasive and Non-Invasive), Non-Contact and Implants.

A simple schematic overview given in Figure 2 will give the necessary understanding.

Sensing Element or Delivery Element

The primary sensing or delivery element is essentially the basic device itself that will help sensing the parameter to monitor and/or control.

The term "Delivery Element" is used to define any form of delivery device that can perform an activity like (but not limited to) listed below.

1. Drugs as would be the case of Insulin pumps, where a small low power delivery system administers the drug in a site of interest.
2. Impulse Signals as would be the case of nerve stimulators and pace makers that would directly send an electrical impulse into the site.
3. Control Signals as would be the case of control signals for implants, other associated delivery elements, larger equipment like patient safety and movement alarms for patients and care providers etc.

The term "Sensor Element" is used to define any form of a sensing element that will sense the parameter rof interest. It will be devices that can sense not only vital parameters but also bio markers, movement, statistical and analytical information from peripheral devices and other remote healthcare equipment, ambient information about the patient's environment etc.

Figure 2. Schematic Architecture of a typical Smart Sensor or other Care Delivery Devices

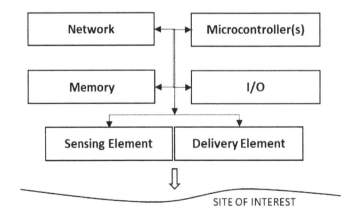

Controller, Memory and I/O

In the case of smart devices, the information from the sensor elements will usually be augmented with information analyzed in-situ by the embedded microcontroller or processing cores and will be proactively sent to the RPM backend. These embedded controllers control the memory, I/O and networking sub systems. Additionally they read and write signals to and from these elements and use it for further processing and communication. The on-board memory is used for computation, storage and buffering.

Network Layer

The network layer component in the smart devices provides the vital link from the device to the BAN and there-on to the cloud or fog gateway. The hardware in this layer supports a predefined set of BAN and/or WBAN protocols based on the manufacturer and the platform in use. At the time of this writing, the security and technical limitations will largely limit the fog capabilities from coming to this layer and have pre-defined layer standards.

Let us have a quick look at the following examples of some of the equipment manufacturers that have different types of such devices. Kindly note that these are only examples and the list is not an exhaustive one. Preparing an exhaustive list would require a specifically designed survey of such equipment and research studies in itself.

Medtronic

Medtronic provides MiniMed series insulin pumps that can feed data for diagnosis and can be used for treatment planning and drug administration via the CareLinkplatform (Medtronic MiniMed).

Nokia Withings

Nokia Withings has a set of home care products that is also clinically approved. Temperature sensors, sleep sensors, weighing scales, and activity trackers (Nokia Withings) form the vital link that are consumer-centric in design but nevertheless provide clinical grade data.

Hospira

Hospira's IV infusion pumps are capable of feeding back data to the EMR to allow for care management, analysis and reporting.

Biotricity

Bioflux from Biotricity provides high precision, clinical grade remote cardiac monitoring device.

Nonin

Nonin has a set of simplistic, clinical grade, Finger Pulse Oximeter capable of RPM.

Edge Systems: WBAN and Gateway

The fundamental part of the ecosystem, next only to the patient himself, is the devices that constitute the WBAN.

There are two main standards, IEEE 802.15.4 and the 802.15.6, that currently define the WBAN area formally. Though limited in application, they are already playing a significant part of the ecosystem. More on the network itself is given further in the chapter.

Wireless BAN

Akin to LAN, a Body Area Network is a very personal system of network that allows inter relationship of sensors and wearable devices for monitoring clinical data and administering drugs.

The miniaturized and lightweight sensors that carry long-term, ambulatory health monitoring data with immediate feedback to the consumer about the present health status and real-time update of the user's medical records are the Wireless body Area Network (WBAN) (Jamil. Y. Khan & Mehmet R. Yuce, 2010). Intelligent heart monitors and accelerometer-based system monitoring physical activity are a few to mention. To build up patient monitoring systems which offer adaptability to medicinal staff and versatility to patients a WBAN can be employed. These frameworks must be sufficiently little to encourage outdoor use and sufficiently precise to give dependable measures. One of the most essential component for any application like web, remote systems, specially appointed systems, remote sensor systems (WSNs), and wireless body area networks (WBANs) is the Quality of service (QoS). However with time, QoS did not get more consideration in WSNs and WBANs like different elements, for example, design, architecture, energy efficient protocol design, nodes' positioning and location (Munir, Yu Wen Bin, Ren Biao & Ma Man, 2007).

In case of Normal data, the physician inspects the data which is provided by the Medical Server and he gives the necessary advice and prescription to the patient through internet thus saving time for the patients as well as doctor. Emergency traffic is unpredictable, not generated on regular basis. Nodes set the threshold level, when the data exceeds that threshold emergency. In this case doctor observes the data and generates an alert signal so that necessary actions can be taken in order to save the patient's life. On-demand data is initiated by the doctor to know some important information for diagnosis (Raju Sharma, Hardeep Singh Ryait, & Anuj Kumar Gupta, 2016). The execution of WSNs is measured by applying three criteria, to be specific the end-to-end reliability, the end-to-end delay and the energy consumption. The two imperatives, energy and delay, are considered as two contending target works that ought to be simultaneously minimized.

The key challenges for a sensor network is the power that a patient is exposed to due to the energy requirements for the network, the patient comfort and the specialized wiring knowledge that would be required for reliable patient monitoring. These restrict monitoring capabilities to specific locations that can guarantee availability of technicians and equipment. WBANs break away from this tradition and brings low-power, clinically compliant wireless network for the devices connected using a BAN. This marks a significant change and provides opportunities to bring devices that can be made as wearable for ubiquitous monitoring of vital parameters. This also makes way for free movement for the patients without compromising on comfort and enables them carry on their daily life without the hassles of sensors and wires.

QoS routing differs from conventional best effort routing mainly because the path selected for forwarding traffic needs to satisfy multiple constraints simultaneously. There has been an increasing demand for network-based tight constrained applications such as digitized multimedia via internet that have stringent QoS requirements. In response to this demand several researchers have been extensively investigating many QoS routing algorithms. One of the important issues is to identify the path between source and destination that can satisfy the QoS constraints imposed which is commonly known as the QoS routing problem (Kuipers, &Van Mieghem, 2003). A mobile ad hoc network offers unique benefits and versatility for certain environments and applications. Since this network has no fixed infrastructure, it can be created and used at anytime and anywhere. This network does not operate under the limitation of fixed topology; hence such a network could be intrinsically fault resilient.

Latré, Braem, & Moerman, (2011)have presented a survey covering the WBAN networks, places it appropriately in reference to the communication network landscape, and comments on the QoS parameters. Remarkably, the survey compares the WBAN against other sensor and actuator networks and mentions the following as main characteristics of WBANs which makes it important: Simple, Heterogeneous, Non-Invasive, Cost and Energy Efficient.

WBAN controllers, at the time of this writing, use predefined set of network topologies with or without adaptive configuration in addition to the adaptive routing control. Reasons like power saving, bandwidth optimization, and manual intervention either by the care providers and care takers or by the patient itself, will cause the devices connected in the network to disconnect and reconnect itself. This will necessitate the controllers to be aware of and allow reconfigurability and adaptability for the network topology. The remote nature also further necessitates the power conservation, reliable connectivity, consistent routing and QoS as part of this adaptability.

Backing the WBANs with cloud using the LPWAN brings the necessary integration feasible. The IEEE WPAN Working Group presents the IEEE standard 802.15.4 and the standard 802.15.6 for the WBAN networks. There are various technology options that are being developed for potential use for and in-conjunction with WBAN.

Hend Fourati, Sabri Khssibi, Thierry Val, Hanen Idoudi, & Adrien Van den Bossche, (2015) are working on project "CANet" - a WBAN platform specifically designed for elderly RPM use case. The work is significant in two salient points from the point of view of this chapter. First is that the study compares the 802.15.4, more widely popular standard in-terms of devices and practical usage penetration, and the more specific 802.15.6 standard which addresses some of the key WBAN requirements highlighted in Latré, B., Braem, &Moerman, (2011). The second salient point from the purview of this chapter is the emphasis given for the native context awareness support in the 802.15.6 which allows us to set priorities for the payload. This is important because a patient's clinical condition contemporary to the RPM and Remote Care need situation that play an important role that needs to be given to the data being transferred and thereby significantly impacting QoS. A context aware standard allows us to transmit and consume data reliably in either direction making the care more relevant and effective in real-time. Any care application that can be developed and deployed on top of such a network shall be capable of giving the freedom for the doctor and the patient to add and remove care specific constraints in-situ while the care procedure is in progress. Thus, the relevancy and timeliness necessary during care is improved.

Gateway: Connecting to the Cloud

The gateway device is the important element that provides the connectivity to the northbound network from the data in the southbound WBAN. The next step from here is backing the WBAN with the fog and the cloud.

Significant technology options are available in this arena mainly due to the availability of the cellular radio network. The cellular network has attained significant maturity and is a widely invested infrastructure by both the private and the government agencies across the world. The fundamental advantage of the cellular network is that they are connected to the world population significantly and, as such, can be improvised and repurposed for LPWAN.

NB-IoT

Narrow Band-IoT is an LPWAN (Low Power Wide Area Network) technology that extends the capabilities of existing LTE networks either by using in-band spectrum allocated for an LTE carrier or in a dedicated spectrum. Re-purposing the existing LTE infrastructure for LPWAN with some alterations makes it a good LPWAN candidate. Standardized in June 2016 by 3GPP (NarrowBand-IoT), the LTE network carriers have made the NB-IoT available for consumption by solution developers and providers.

NB-IoT operates at low bandwidth of 180 kHz and uplink speeds up to 250kbps (Eric Wang,Xingqin Lin, AnsumanAdhikary, Asbjorn Grovlen, Yutao Sui, Yufei Blankenship, Johan Bergman, & Hazhir S. Razaghi, 2017). The protocol supports power saving mode that enables a device to enter power saving mode when idle but still stay registered with the network (LTE evolution for IoT connectivity). Further cost reductions have been achieved by reducing the complexity that calls for simpler cost-effective NB-IoT compliant communication modules that can be embedded into the devices. Security in NB-IoT is provided using LTE security standard.

LoRa

LoRa is a proprietary Long Range radio technology that supports bandwidth up to 500kHz. LoRa provides low-cost, low-power, long range making it suitable for both rural and dense urban settings for collecting device data. LoRa provides end-to-end security with AES128 encryption. Being a spread spectrum technology, LoRa allows any end device can connect to the network in an available frequency and suitable data rate. This significantly increases the possible number of devices that can be connected to the network.

Low-Cost allows LoRa modules to be available for many device manufactures and gateway integrators to support LoRa. The LoRa Alliance member list has a good mix of personnel from the communication and technology space which means will potentially come up with support for various use cases.

LWM2M

Lightweight M2M by Open Mobile Alliance is a LPWAN device management layer that provides the same set of advantages: Simple and Heterogeneous. This allows for developing integrated solutions that enables application users to remotely administer and manage the edge devices based on their quality, reliability, and age of their equipment (Guenter Klas, Friedhelm Rodermund, Zach Shelby, Sandeep-Akhouri, & JanHöller, 2014).

EDGE SYSTEMS: EDGE APPLICATION BACKED SMART SENSOR CASE STUDY

The following case study presents an example ECG Smart Sensor that, along with the ECG data, includes a classification data with possible clinical conditions that the signal exhibits. This sort of augmented information becomes in the case of remote monitoring where the remote monitoring professional or a care giver might not be experienced enough to identify an emergency. The quality of electrodes and signal transport will pose challenges in properly detecting and diagnosing QRS complex and thus an embedded QRS detection algorithm backed estimated diagnostic data would accompany the monitored and transported original signal augmenting it. This augmented information gives the opportunity to forward the signal data to a more qualified professional to seek further guidance and prompt care planning. The edge HMI application in this case shall provide this necessary information to remote care giver.

The sensor uses a pre-built template matching model to identify the possible abnormalities that can be added to the transmitted data in addition to the original signal. The ECG signal changes its physiological and statistical properties and therefore it is said to be a non-stationary signal. The important feature in detecting the abnormalities in the ECG signal is the QRS complex. Morphology and parameters in ECG signals and its segments imitate the working condition of the heart. Detection of QRS complex of the ECG signal and its accurate positioning have a significant practical value in clinical diagnosis. Due to the changeable nature of the QRS complex its detection is difficult and different methods are available like differentiation techniques, classification methods, power spectrum methods and time frequency methods like wavelet transforms. The significant gain of wavelet method above other methods for finding QRS is that wavelet transform provides concurrent time and frequency information. The method is not time consuming and has less processing complexity. This helps us with a relatively simple embeddable implementation. By decomposing the signal the wavelet transform can characterize and localize both in time and frequency domains. Thus the features extracted can be used discriminate ECG waves from noise and movement artifacts.

Significance of QRS Complex Detection

For the past three decades research studies are carried out on the detection of QRS complex of ECG signal. According to the medical depiction the most vital information about ECG signal is concentrated on the QRS complex. The period and amplitude of the QRS morphology is used for diagnosing cardiac arrhythmias, conduction abnormalities, ventricular hypertrophy, myocardial infarction, electrolyte derangements, etc. In processing the ECG signal, like preprocessing, calculation of the RR interval, detection of P and T waves, the detection of the QRS complex is of critical significance. In terms of classification of the abnormality, the QRS complex is of pathological importance from clinician's opinion and its detection provide as an access to almost all of the automated ECG analysis algorithms. On the other hand, the interference, noise and artifacts present in the ECG signal makes the detection of QRS complex more complicated. Also due to the presence of cardiac abnormalities related to the ventricles the duration of the QRS complex can change.

QRS Detection Techniques

Useful information regarding the QRS complex can be obtained from the power spectrum of the ECG signal. The power spectrum provides the information of the frequency and the power spectral density of the signal that exists in the signal. But it does not provide information at what time the particular frequency component exists. The Power spectral density study gives information of different signal components in the ECG signal and with that information a filter can be designed which can select the QRS complex from the ECG signal effectively. A maximum signal to noise ratio (SNR) for a band pass filter can be the observed when we analyze the power spectrum of the ECG signal, QRS complex, and other artifacts. However the QRS wave is indistinguishable by the filter characteristics. Due to intrinsic variability among ECG's from various subjects, as well as variability in the noise, the filter design could be suboptimal in a particular circumstance. Hence, more complex designs may be necessary for filters that must be highly specific to a given recording situation. In addition to detecting the QRS complex, the differentiation technique has the advantage that it produces a pulse which is proportional in width of the complex. A major disadvantage is that the differentiation technique is particularly sensitive to higher-frequency noise.

In another method called the template matching technique one signal is matched with another signal by correlation method and the two signals are aligned with one another. The template of the signal that is necessary to match stores a digitized form of the signal shape. Because the template has to be correlated with the incoming signal, the signal is aligned with the template. The technique of aligning the incoming signal and template of the signal is carried out by using the fiducial points on all signals. An external process assigns these fiducial points to the test ECG signal. If the fiducial points on the template and the signal are aligned, then the correlation can be performed. As this algorithm uses many operations of subtraction the template matching is very sensitive to high frequency noise and baseline wander.

As the Wavelet transform (WT) method provides the time-frequency representation, and it is capable of providing the time and frequency information at the same time, and gives a time-frequency representation of the signal. WT gives a variable resolution. In the time domain the higher frequencies are enhanced and in the frequency domain the lower frequencies are enhanced. The WT uses a short time interval for estimating higher frequencies and a long time interval for lower frequencies. By using this property, high frequency components of short duration can be successfully observed by Wavelet Transform. One of the advantages of the Wavelet Transform is that it can decompose signals at a range of resolutions, which allows accurate feature extraction from non-stationary signals like ECG. From the discussed techniques like template matching, FFT, wavelet, and power spectral density analysis, it is observed that ECG feature extraction using proposed wavelet method behaves significant than other conventional system to find out the proper detection of small abnormalities of the ECG signal.

From Figure 3, we can see that the db2 mother wavelet is applied to the ECG signal for both normal and abnormal conditions. It can be noticed that the high frequency components and unwanted artifacts are removed using wavelet transform technique. Now after removing the unwanted components from the signal, the signal is reconstructed and is further used for feature extraction which are the parameters of the abnormal ECG and normal ECG to be transmitted.

Figure 3. The wavelet transform (db2) is carried out on a normal ECG (left) and an abnormal ECG(right) signal showing three level decomposition

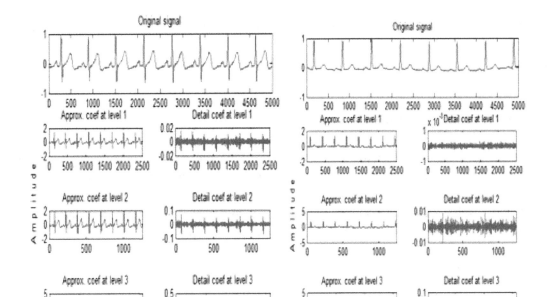

Feature Extraction

The achievement of ECG analysis basically portrays on the quality and the importance of the extracted information. Usually feature extraction computes quantitative information from the decomposed signal. The wavelet coefficients extracted present a solid representation that shows the energy distribution of the ECG signal in both time and frequency. Further in order to decrease the dimensionality of the extracted feature vectors, statistics over the set of the wavelet coefficients is used (Kandaswamy A, Kumar C.S, Ramanathan R. P, Jayaraman S & Malmurugan N, 2004). The statistical features like standard deviation, mean, variance, etc., and frequency domain features like frequency, power spectral density, energy of the signal (Roessgen M, Zoubir M & Boashash, B, 1998) and non-linear features like Hurst exponent, chaos, entropy (Kannathal Natarajan, Rajendra Acharya, Fadhilah Alias, Thelma Tiboleng & Puthusserypady S K, 2004, Osorio I & Frei M G, 2007) are used to signify the time frequency distribution of the ECG signals. The calculated features are directly obtained from the wavelet coefficients. They are Maximum value of the absolute values of the coefficients in each sub-band, Minimum value of the absolute values of the coefficients in each sub-band, Mean value of the absolute values of the coefficients in each sub-band, Variance of the coefficients in each sub band, Standard deviation of the coefficients in each sub band, Energy of the coefficients in each sub-band, Maximum power of PSD of the wavelet coefficients in each sub-band, Frequency at which maximum power occurs in each sub-band and the Entropy of the coefficients in each sub-band.

Multiple features extracted for normal and abnormal variations, modelled and are stored as digital templates in an embeddable light weight database. An edge application shall receive the signal from the sensor via a WBAN and processes the signal and performs template matching using on on-board data decision system using pre-trained models. The data is sent to cloud backend for monitoring and management.

Further work would involve cloud based comprehensive learning for further enhancing diagnostics and clinical study.

Fog: Connectivity Platforms

Platforms like the Nokia IMPACT IoT platform provides the required scalable connectivity vital for the kind of integration that is required in Cloud based RPM. The platform supports multiple connection options, multiple protocols, and multiple LPWAN standards. The platform also allows for easy integration on both the sides of the platform making it simple to integrate. Additionally, the platform provides policy based device management, security and Malware protection.

Cloud Platforms

The most important aspect of any data collection and connectivity is the ability to integrate and put into good use. Multiple Cloud PaaS systems enable solution providers to develop solutions for the ecosystem.

Security

End-to-end security and Malware & Virus protection is a vital baseline feature that is required of any system to reliably be used. The security subsystem needs to be capable of propagating the edge layer security across the PaaS and also should allow for management and control of the security from the various applications in the application layer.

Data Aggregation and Storage

The data aggregation and storage forms a vital bottom layer for the ecosystem. Apart from supporting millions of devices for securely receiving and aggregating the data, a key requirement for the systems is to respond in a timely manner to the data that is being constant pushed into the system without missing the embedded context information.

Data Exchange

Vast data aggregation provides the opportunity to exchange the data with relevant third-party systems in the ecosystem. This kind of data exchange allows for integrated care management and planning, automated supporting intelligence for diagnostics, and information availability. Information availability is a key distinguishing factor when providing and administering remote augmented care.

In elderly care, the clinical symptoms are often complicated with associated psychological and aging related issues, which will prove care planning and providence difficult. Providing care remotely either directly to the patient or via a care assistance personnel, thus involves a lot of information that needs to be consumed for diagnostics and decision making. Timely data exchange capability with multiple systems is thus a key ingredient for integration and solution effectiveness.

Data exchange components in the PaaS shall essentially support industry standard data exchange messaging protocols like HL7, DICOM, etc to allow easy integration with existing systems and also allow for extending purpose of mature protocols to cater to the remote care scenarios.

Regulation Standards compliance (e.g. HIPAA, CFR 21 Part 11) is a must to provide robust and responsible care management.

Analytics, Deep Machine Learning and AI

With the kind of multi-faceted integration the PaaS platforms provide, we now have integration opportunities with systems that would not be integrated before.

Integration with Patient Clinical Statistics, Treatment and Medication Data shall provide the vital clinical history of the patient requiring care. This will be made available at the time of care planning during remote augmented care action. This empowers the doctors and associated care personnel to provide relevant and quality care almost as good as being in person physically to attend the patient requiring care.

Vast volumes of this monitoring data and standard care data gets multiplied when we integrate with Clinical Research Data, Pharmaceutical Data, Drug Databases that provide Side-effects, Indications and Contraindications, Database of Allergies and Symptoms, Demographic Data, Insurance and Policy Data.

The sheer size of this centralized data now poses important and pronounced challenges for any care personnel:

- The means and time to decipher all the information and arrive at a practically suitable plan for the patient of interest in a given scenario.
- Co-relation of all these data.
- Rejection of outlying information in reference to the context of the concurrent need.
- Feasibility, Applicability and Suitability assessment of possible care plans.
- Security and Privacy.
- Challenges Specific to the care episode.

The above requirements and challenges calls for advanced structured and unstructured data analytics. This will require efficient continuous Machine Learning. The number of parameters involved, volume of data from a number of devices and their eccentricity in context makes it a clear candidate for deep machine learning. Such systems require vast computing and storage capacities for analyzing historical data accumulated over a period of time. With the right approach to security and data management, these learned models can selectively be used to enhance the remote monitored data itself by augmenting them with vital insights. Such learning systems allow for use cases such as AI assisted Diagnostics, Analysis of Symptoms, Possible and Suggested Care Plan based on similar experiences elsewhere in the world, Healthcare Management Planning, Planning and Structuring Governmental Policies, Short-term and Long-Term Care Needs Prediction, Identification and Prediction of Social Health care threats like Epidemics and Pandemics etc. Consistent and responsible use shall make these systems more reliable, improving the knowledge base contributing to a dependable AI back-end.

ADVANCED APPLICATIONS AND APPLICATION PLATFORMS

Altogether, we now have a robust and advanced application development platform that would allow us to develop some significant health-care applications on top of it.

Let us look at some of the advanced health-care application platforms that are available for use and are constantly getting better at the time of this writing.

IBM Watson Health and Watson IoT

IBM Watson Health in conjunction with the Watson IoT platform provides an advanced application platform which facilitates development of cognitive health-care solutions. The IBM Watson Health is a comprehensive platform that provides solutions for different verticals within the health care ecosystem. The platform presents capabilities to develop applications for Drug Discovery, Diagnostics, Care Management, Policy Planning and Advanced Image Processing to enhance diagnostics.

Nokia Patient Care

The Nokia Patient Care platform provides clinical and care management solutions backed by data from smart devices and analytics. At the time of this writing, the platform allows collecting data from Nokia Withings Smart Devices worldwide and enables analytics based diagnostics and care management based on the data.

Specialized Care Applications

Apart from the standard vertical user applications like EMR, LIMS, PACS etc, the ecosystem is now capable of providing specialized care applications that involves cross breeding of information and involved stakeholders in the ecosystem hitherto was not possible.

The advanced application platforms available in the cloud and fog, is now capable of catering to specialized care applications.

Some examples are: HCC Profiler, HP Medication Alert & Adherence System (MAAS) and IBM Watson Health for Oncology

HCC Profiler

The Apixio HCC Profiler is a cognitive computing platform that provides HCC (Hierarchical Condition Categories) profiling for commercial risk mitigation helping clinicians mitigate risks and replaces manual coding.

HP Medication Alert and Adherence System (MAAS)

The HP Enterprise Systems deployed a medication alert system in rural Tamilnadu, India in 2013. The system monitors medication adherence using mobile phones and alerts patients using SMS. The backend data collected is used for analyzing clinical observations, outcome analysis and drug efficacy.

IBM Watson Health for Oncology

Backed by analytics and machine learning trained by Memorial Sloan Kettering physicians, the IBM Watson Health for Oncology solution provides clinicians with evidence based treatment options for treating cancer.

FUTURE RESEARCH DIRECTIONS

The current WBAN technology platform does give a variety of advantages over a set use cases. However, further research is needed in terms of bringing a Context Aware, QoS based comprehensive wireless network technology standard. Additionally, the standard must be open to make sure more manufacturers across the globe shall be able to provide equipment and integrate with multiple systems in real-time.

Research is needed especially in-terms of the context awareness and how that can be embedded into a embedded WBAN protocol that still maintain the low-cost, low-bandwidth, low-energy requirements. Although the 802.15.4 (Rim Negra, Imen Jemili, & Abdelfettah Belghith, 2016) based networks are currently trendy, the emphasis on energy requirements in-terms of patient safety, reliability, and device battery life in 802.15.6 is significantly lower (Alam M.M, & Ben Hamida E, 2014). A clear lack of many clinical grade devices in the market clearly highlights the importance in spending quality research and development in this area for hardware implementation.

QoS requirements often tend to impact fidelity and bandwidth. This makes QoS an area to look out and study for making further improvements. Energy requirements, energy provisioning and consumption for wearable sensors and sensor networks is a vital area of study that will have to improve to promise reliable and robust parametric data acquisition and transport. The clinical conditions of elderly make them more sensitive to the energy consumed and dissipated by the sensors and the networks and thus react with enhanced sensitivity. This makes the research in this area to receive a special focus. Improving RPM for elderly care will also help improve the energy requirements, reliability and robustness of the remote care ecosystem as a whole.

Practical Implementation of WBAN enabled clinical grade devices that comply with power requirements to support elderly patient care needs a good deal of research. A structured industry-wide rollout model is required which will involve policy research that would enable a complimentary and healthy ecosystem across multiple players in the field. Beyond health-care and directly associated management and technology, Academic Research, Governmental Policy Research, Investment and Fund Management are also managed and executed mindfully for the convergence of cloud, fog, IoT and health-care will involve a pronounced socio-economic impact.

Short-term and Long-Term technology trends are promising. In the short-term, research works combining Software Defined Radio and FPGA in the field of WBAN implementation is an interesting area opening up opportunities for deeper integration of Fog into the WBAN arena (Priya Mathew, Lismi Augustine, Deepak Kushwaha, Vivian D, & David Selvakumar, 2015). In the long-term, research in the role of grapheme sensors and networks gives interesting possibilities in terms of how deep the WBAN can penetrate and also the efficiency and capabilities of such devices in satisfying the parameters like heartbeat, body temperature or recording a prolonged electrocardiogram (ECG). (Sergi Abadal, Eduard Alarcón, Albert Cabellos-Aparicio, Max C. Lemme, & Mario Nemirovsky, 2013; Latré, Braem, & Moerman,, 2011).

Beyond health care, nanotechnology would significantly impact Cloud and Fog computing in general as the devices would be more miniscule and parallel advances in deep learning shall enable cognitive computing in the nano scale.

CONCLUSION

We are now able to see that treating elderly patient involves a significant set of technologies, equipment, service providers and historical knowledge coming together cohesively to provide the right care. While the younger population, depending on their clinical condition, are usually able to wait for care to arrive owing to age, the elderly patients presents a specific set of challenges that encompasses those that of the younger population and adds a significant set to it.

In spite of being still and evolution, the integration of WBAN with the Cloud and Fog at this early stage means standards and practical adoption can be frame and achieved by systematic research and development. This will enable convergence of the technologies to a practically ubiquitous care situation faster.

The cloud and fog based RPM stack thus opens up an opportunity to integrate various personnel involved in the entire care delivery ecosystem such as patients, doctors/clinicians, scientists, policy makers and fund managers together onto a single delivery platform.

Blurring the differences, the health care community is sincerely working towards a mature and seamless integration, significantly enhancing the capabilities of remote and artificial intelligence aided healthcare. The ecosystem has come a long way and is evolving towards a promising future capable of delivering timely and relevant care to the patient in need.

REFERENCES

80215.4-2015 - IEEE Standard for Low-Rate Wireless Networks, WG802.15 - Wireless Personal Area Network (WPAN) Working Group, C/LM - LAN/MAN Standards Committee, IEEE Computer Society. (n.d.). Retrieved from https://standards.ieee.org/findstds/standard/802.15.4-2015.html

802.15.6-2012 - IEEE Standard for Local and metropolitan area networks - Part 15.6: Wireless Body Area Networks, WG802.15 - Wireless Personal Area Network (WPAN) Working Group, C/LM - LAN/MAN Standards Committee, IEEE Computer Society.

Abadal, S., Alarcón, E., Cabellos-Aparicio, A., Lemme, M. C., & Nemirovsky, M. (2013). Graphene-Enabled Wireless Communication for Massive Multicore Architectures. *IEEE Communications Magazine*, *51*(11), 137–143. doi:10.1109/MCOM.2013.6658665

Abo-Zahhad, Ahmed, & Elnahas. (2014). A Wireless Emergency Telemedicine System for Patients Monitoring and Diagnosis. *International Journal of Telemedicine and Applications, 14*. 10.1155/2014/380787

Alam, M. M., & Ben Hamida, E. (2014). Surveying Wearable Human Assistive Technology for Life and Safety Critical Applications: Standards, Challenges and Opportunities. *Sensors (Basel)*, *14*(5), 9153–9209. doi:10.3390140509153 PMID:24859024

Apixio - HCC Profiler. (n.d.). Retrieved from https://www.apixio.com/solutions/

Biotricity. (n.d.). Retrieved from https://www.biotricity.com/biotricity-bioflux-mwc-2017/

Brazilian Society of Cardiology, Brazilian Society of Hypertension, & Brazilian Society of Nephrology. (2010). VI Brazilian Guidelines on Hypertension. *Arquivos Brasileiros de Cardiologia, 95*(1), 1–51. PMID:21085756

Chagas Teixeira, C., Peres Boaventura, R., Cristina Silva Souza, A., Tanferri de Brito Paranaguá, T., Lúcia Queiroz Bezerra, A., Márcia Bachion, M., & Visconde Brasil, V. (2015). Vital Signs Measurement: An Indicator of Safe Care Delivered To Elderly. *The Scientific Electronic Library Online, 24*(4), 1071–1078.

Chapman, R. A. (2013). Smart textiles for protection. Monitoring vital signs. *Woodhead Publishing Series in Textiles, 133*, 246.

Churpek, M.M., Yuen, T.C., Winslow, C., Hall, J., & Edelson, D.P. (2015). Differences in vital signs between elderly and nonelderly patients prior to ward cardiac arrest. *Crit Care Med., 43*(4), 816-22.

Culo, S. (2011). Risk assessment and intervention for vulnerable older adults. *BCMJ, 53*(8), 421–425.

Dupouy, J., Moulis, G., Tubery, M., Ecoiffier, M., Sommet, A., Poutrain, J. C., ... Lapeyre-Mestre, M. (2013). Which adverse events are related to health care during hospitalization in elderly inpatients. *International Journal of Medical Sciences, 10*(9), 1224–1230. doi:10.7150/ijms.6640 PMID:23935400

Eric, W. Y. P., Lin, X., Adhikary, A., Grovlen, A., Sui, Y., Blankenship, Y., ... Razaghi, H. S. (2017). A Primer on 3GPP Narrowband Internet of Things. *IEEE Communications Magazine, 55*(3), 117–123. doi:10.1109/MCOM.2017.1600510CM

Fourati, H., Khssibi, S., Val, T., Idoudi, H., & Van den Bossche, A. (2015). Comparative study of IEEE 802.15.4 and IEEE 802.15.6 for WBAN-based CANet: 4th Performance Evaluation and Modeling in Wireless Networks (PEMWN 2015), Hammamet, Tunisia. *Proceedings of PEMWN, 2015*, 1–7.

Goldberg, C. (2009). A comprehensive physical examination and clinical education site for medical students and other health care professionals. *A Practical Guide to Clinical Medicine.* Retrieved from https://meded.ucsd.edu/clinicalmed/vital.htm

Greenwood. (2014). Telehealth Remote Patient Monitoring Intervention For People With Type 2 Diabetes. *Conference: 2014 Western Institute of Nursing Annual Communicating Nursing Research Conference.*

Hospira. (n.d.). Retrieved from https://www.hospira.com/en/products_and_services/iv_emr_integration

IBM Watson Health. (n.d.). Retrieved from https://www.ibm.com/watson/health/

IBM Watson Health for Oncology. (n.d.). Retrieved from https://www.ibm.com/watson/health/oncology-and-genomics/oncology/

Kandaswamy, A., Kumar, C. S., Ramanathan, R. P., Jayaraman, S., & Malmurugan, N. (2004). Neural classification of lung sounds using wavelet coefficients. *Computers in Biology and Medicine, 34*(6), 523–537. doi:10.1016/S0010-4825(03)00092-1 PMID:15265722

Khan & Yuce. (2010). Wireless Body Area Network (WBAN) for Medical Applications. In *New Developments in Biomedical Engineering*. InTech. Available from: http://www.intechopen.com/books/new-developments-in-biomedical-engineering/wireless-bodyarea-network-wban-for-medical-applications

Klas, Rodermund, Shelby, Akhouri, & Höller. (2014). *Whitepaper -Lightweight M2M: Enabling Device Management and Applications for the Internet of Things*. Academic Press.

Knight, J., & Nigam, Y. (2008). The anatomy and physiology of ageing. Part 1 - The cardiovascular system. *Nursing Times*, *104*(31), 26–28. PMID:18727348

Kuipers, F. A., & Van Mieghem, P. (2003). The impact of correlated link weights on QoS Routing. *Proceedings - IEEE INFOCOM*, *12*, 1425–1434.

Latré, B., Braem, B., Moerman, I., Blondia, C., & Demeester, P. (2011). A Survey on Wireless Body Area Networks. *Wireless Networks*, *17*(1), 1–18. doi:10.100711276-010-0252-4

LoRa. (n.d.). Retrieved from https://www.lora-alliance.org/What-Is-LoRa/Technology

LoRa Members. (n.d.). Retrieved from https://www.lora-alliance.org/The-Alliance/Member-List

LTE evolution for IoT connectivity A Nokia Whitepaper. (2017). Retrieved from http://resources.alcatel-lucent.com/asset/200178

Mathew, P., Augustine, L., Kushwaha, D., Selvakumar, D. (2015). Hardware Implementation of NB PHY Baseband Transceiver for IEEE 802.15.6 WBAN. *International Conference on Medical Imaging, m-Health and Emerging Communication Systems (MedCom 2014)*. DOI: 10.1109/MedCom.2014.7005977

Mathew, P., Augustine, L., Kushwaha, D., Selvakumar, D. (2015). *Implementation of NB PHY transceiver of IEEE 802.15.6 WBAN on FPGA*. International Conference on VLSI Systems, Architecture, Technology and Applications (VLSI-SATA 2015), Bangalore, India.

Medication Alert & Adherence System (MAAS). (n.d.). Retrieved from http://www8.hp.com/in/en/hp-news/press-release.html?id=1426409#.WR9mU3WGO00

Morosini, S., Marques, A.P.O., Leal, M.C.C., Marino, J.G., & Melo, H.M.A. (2011). Cost and length of hospital stay of elderly residents in Recife-PE. *Geriatrics and Gerontology, 5*(2), 91-98.

Munir, S. A., Yu, W. B., Biao, R., & Man, M. (2007). Fuzzy Logic Based Congestion Estimation for QoS in Wireless Sensor Network. *IEEE Wireless Communications and Networking Conference, WCNC 2007*, 4336-4341. 10.1109/WCNC.2007.791

NarrowBand-IoT. (n.d.). Retrieved from http://www.3gpp.org/news-events/3gpp-news/1785-nb_iot_complete

Natarajan, K., Acharya, R., Alias, F., Tiboleng, T., & Puthusserypady, S. K. (2004). Nonlinear analysis of EEG signals at different mental states. *Biomedical Engineering Online*, *3*(1), 7. doi:10.1186/1475-925X-3-7 PMID:15023233

Negra, R., Jemili, I., & Belghith, A. (2016). Wireless Body Area Networks: Applications and Technologies. *The Second International Workshop on Recent Advances on Machine-to-Machine Communications*, Madrid, Spain. 10.1016/j.procs.2016.04.266

Nokia IMPACT IoT Platform. (n.d.). Retrieved from https://networks.nokia.com/solutions/iot-platform

Nokia Patient Care platform. (n.d.). Retrieved from https://patientcare.withings.com/eu/en/

Nonin Finger Pulse Oximeter. (n.d.). Retrieved from http://www.nonin.com/Finger-Pulse-Oximeter

Osorio, I., & Frei, M. G. (2007). Hurst parameter estimation for epleptic seizure detection. *Communications in Information & Systems*, *7*(2), 167–176. doi:10.4310/CIS.2007.v7.n2.a4

Rantz, M. J., Skubic, M., Popescu, M., Galambos, C., Koopman, R. J., Alexander, G. L., ... Miller, S. J. (2015). A New Paradigm of technology-enabled 'vital signs' for early detection of health change for older adults. *Gerontology*, *61*(3), 281–290. doi:10.1159/000366518 PMID:25428525

Riazul Islam, Kwak, Kabir, Hossain, & Kwak. (2015). The Internet of Things for Health Care: A Comprehensive Survey. IEEE, 3, 678 – 708.

Roessgen, M., Zoubir, A. M., & Boashash, B. (1998). Seizure detection of newborn EEG using a model-based approach. *IEEE Transactions on Biomedical Engineering*, *45*(6), 673–685. doi:10.1109/10.678601 PMID:9609933

Seddik, H., & Eldeib, A. M. (2016). A Wireless Real-Time Remote Control and Tele Monitoring System for Mechanical Ventilators. *IEEE Proceedings of the Conference: 8th Cairo International Biomedical Engineering Conference (CIBEC 2016)*, 64 – 68. 10.1109/CIBEC.2016.7836121

Seman, A. P., Faria, L. F. C., Paula, L. H. B., & Nedel, S. (2011). Hipertermia e hipotermia. In Tratado de Geriatria e Gerontologia (3rd ed.). Rio de Janeiro: Guanabara Koogan.

Sharma, R., Ryait, H. S., & Gupta, A. K. (2016). Wireless Body Area Nework – A Review. *International Journal of Engineering Science*, *17*, 494–499.

Withings. (n.d.). Retrieved from https://www.withings.com/uk/en/

KEY TERMS AND DEFINITIONS

Hospital Information System (HIS): In many implementations, a HIS is a comprehensive, integrated information system intended to manage all the aspects of a hospital's operation, for example, medical, administrative, financial, and legal issues and the comparing preparing of administrations.

M2M: M2M correspondence is regularly utilized for remote checking. M2M correspondence is an imperative part of distribution center administration, remote control, mechanical technology, activity control, calculated administrations, inventory network administration, armada administration, and telemedicine.

Quality of Service (QoS): Refers to the ability of a network to give better support of the selected network traffic over different advances, including Frame Relay, Asynchronous Transfer Mode (ATM), Ethernet and 802.1 networks, SONET, and IP-routed networks that may utilize any or all of these basic technologies.

Remote Patient Monitoring (RPM): It is a technology to facilitate monitoring of patients outside of traditional clinical settings (e.g., in the home), which may build access to care and decline social insurance and conveyance costs.

Telemedicine: Telemedicine permits medicinal services experts to evaluate, diagnose, and treat patients in remote locations using telecommunications technology. Telemedicine enables patients in remote locations to get to medicinal ability rapidly, effectively, and without travel. Telemedicine gives more effective utilization of restricted master assets who can "see" patients in numerous locations wherever they are required without leaving their office.

Vital Parameters: The normal ranges for a person's vital signs differ with age, weight, sexual orientation, and general wellbeing. There are four essential fundamental signs: body temperature, blood pressure, pulse (heart rate), and breathing rate (respiratory rate).

Wireless Body Area Networks (WBAN): A wireless body area network is a special purpose sensor network designed to operate separately to connect different medical sensors and appliances, situated inside and outside of a human body.

Chapter 14
Internet of Things and Smart City Initiatives in Middle Eastern Countries

Khaled Megdadi
Girne American University, Turkey

Murat Akkaya
Girne American University, Turkey

Arif Sari
Girne American University, Turkey

ABSTRACT

This chapter presents a systematic review of prior research work that is closely aligned to the subject of interest related with internet of things (IoT) and smart city initiatives in Middle Eastern countries. Since internet of things technology (IoT) is the new revolution in the existing services provision environment due to increased contact with high-speed internet access, and the need to provide services more quickly and with minimal effort, costs and keeping pace with the development witnessed by the rest of the advanced countries of the world at a time connection is no longer limited by political borders of the states. This encompasses articles, unpublished papers and theses, conference papers, and memos. The chapter is an evaluation of previous research on the current research topic and serves as a space for research gap identification and hypotheses development in the field of IoT with smart city development initiatives.

INTERNET OF THINGS AND FOG COMPUTING

The concept of IoT refers to the ability of physical objects (things) to be connected to the internet (Al-Fuqaha et al., 2015). While IoT is actually not a new technology, it presents a new way of using existing technology to include capabilities of devices to be available over the internet(Whitmore et al., 2015). As depicted in Figure 1, objects embedded with software designed network addressing specific useful information to the object to make independent useful decisions (Huang & Li, 2010). Khan et al., (2012)

DOI: 10.4018/978-1-5225-5972-6.ch014

Figure 1. IoT in picture

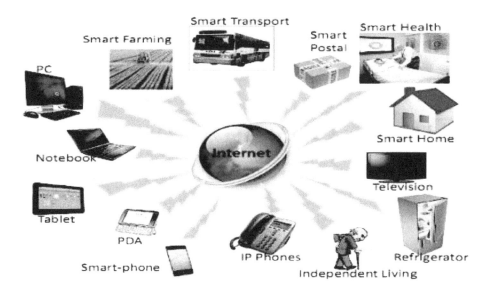

highlighted the basic IoT workflow as sensory, activation and smartness indicating that to an object must be able to sense a data information as required per time autonomously and such input should trigger an action which can be performed automatically and then give status information about output of the system based on the input (Khan et al., 2012).

IoT technology depends on a proper combination of software, hardware, and architectures to function adequately (Whitmore et al., 2015). As we have mentioned, IoT technology uses existing technologies as the foundation upon which its infrastructures are built. Regarding hardware, Near Field Communication (NFC), Radio-Frequency Identification (RFID) and Sensor networks are critical to the deployment of IoT(Whitmore et al., 2015).

RFID uses electromagnetic fields to communicate over a short range between RFID tags and RFID readers. The RFID tag carries varying forms of data which may include electronic product code commonly used in IoT applications.

An electronic product code is a specific identification code implanted in objects to enable it for tracking and communication with RFID technology. RFID has been established for object tracking, and this function is also fundamental to the implementation of IoT technology (Ngai, Moon, Riggins, & Yi, 2008). It can also be used in supply chain management, public utilities, retailing, food safety, aviation and others. Perhaps the most important benefit of RFID is the ability to access the data in RFID tags remotely over the internet (Ngai et al., 2008).

Another important underlining hardware for the deployment of IoT Technology is the NFC, similar to RFID; NFC involves short-range communication mechanism in which devices in proximity can use radio communication. NFC builds on RFID technology in that it also uses the NFC tags that carry the data integrated into smart devices that enable them to communicate when brought in close proximity. A common implementation of NFC tags is in the smart posters where readable data from the poster can be transmitted to smart phones can have NFC tags embedded in it.

The third hardware that IoT technologies rely on is the sensory networks. This refers to devices that have the ability to monitor environmental conditions such as humidity, temperature, quantity, and movement. Wireless sensor network, on the other hand, involves the simultaneous use of multiple sensors. IoT capabilities of machine-to-human communication are achieved through the use of sensory network and actuators. While sensors detect changes, actuators perform required action to affect the change. Both sensors and actuators are often deployed in sensor-actuator networks.

Although IoT depends on existing hardware, the hardware must be used in conjunction with new software to ensure adequate support for all the interoperability between all the different devices and their generated data. In the deployment of IoT, a middleware separates the data generated by various devices and the applications that are designed to use the data. As such, the creation and deployment of new IoT services are harnessed by the use of IoT middleware. Several studies have suggested the use of semantic middleware ensure interoperability of communicating devices across different communication formats. Its main benefit is its ability to create a unified platform for data exchange and sharing on various devices, locations, and application (Gómez-Goiri& López-De-Ipiña, 2010; Ngai et al., 2008). (Aberer et al. 2006; Gómez-GoiriandLópez-de-Ipiña 2010; Huang & Li 2010a; Songetal. 2010)

In light of the world agreement on the necessity to use the cloud computing, especially in the Internet of Things and smart cities environment, which generate a large amount of transferred information, which called the term Big Data, and as millions of devices and humans will interact and connect together in various types of communications (Many to Many, Many to Person and Person to Person) that expected to reach 20 billion things by the year 2025, which showed the need to switch from IP version 4 to IP version 6, all this huge amount of data needs to go through several stages in the Internet of Things environment from the moment the message Launches from the sensor to turn to Data and then Information and passes through several processors and applications of artificial intelligence and others to finally reach appropriate and correct decisions, the challenge here is to make the right decision at the right time without latency responding.

In 2014, CISCO came up with an intermediary interface between the user and the Cloud network that is closer to the edge and faster in data transfer, taking advantage of artificial intelligence applications and non-repetition technologies and able to take decisions faster, which means in the right time.

Fog computing is the computing decentralized infrastructure where data and applications are distributed in the most efficient place intermediary between the data source and the cloud, it primarily expanding cloud computing and services to the edge of the network, driving cloud computing closer to where data is created and worked as shown in Figure 2. In other words, it improves efficiency and reduces the amount of data transferred to the cloud for processing, analyzing and storing, as well as playing a role in solving the problem of security and privacy.

As well as its adoption of faster data transfer technologies based on 4G instead of 3G and we can imagine the time it took to transfer one gigabyte of data via a 3G-based on cloud network

With the existence of many Fog nodes between the edge and the cloud network with different size and location close to the user or cloud network as needed, this idea seems to be efficient, especially in facilitating the process of communication, control and configuration and it will accelerated override the greatest challenge since the creation of cloud computing and stopped controversy the issue of security and privacy or strengthen it, but of course not enough to stop us from thinking about these issues. This challenge will remain a constant subject for discussion, research and development, and as Internet of Things networks and its applications evolve, expand and increase the need for protection and security will become a more urgent need. The two issues are closely linked and the case transformed from talking

Figure 2. Fog Computing in Picture

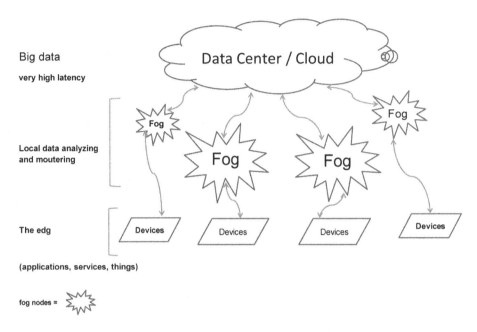

about using a technology to facilitate life to something related to human safety, especially when talking about the umbrella of smart cities and their applications, and we can imagine the speed increasing of a vehicle on a highway that had been hacked and controlled without the will of the driver, or tampering with the transfer of a call whose settings have been set to notify the emergency center of an accident or fire, in this case we will face losses in lives and property. We do not want the Internet of things and its applications and systems to be a killing tool, and this will inevitably happen if there is no concerted effort to solve the problem of security and protection of Internet of things users' data.

As a conclusion the use of Fog networking appears as strong manner because of the rapidly development in this technology and the massive increasing upon it specially in the field of Internet and Things and Smart Cities, by focusing on Fog networking and using it instead of pure and direct cloud networking connectivity we will gain a lot of advantages such as; Law latency, real time interaction, Geo-distribution, local awareness, support for mobility and very low delay jitters in addition to defining security and privacy.

Internet of Things in Numbers

According to a report by Gil Press (2016), about 80% of the organizations have a better positive outlook to IoT in 2016 compare to 2015 based on a survey carried out by CompTIA surveying 512 business and IT executives. The surge in the statistics reflects attention at a greater level from the C-suite and an enhanced perception that the various components that make up the ecosystem of the IoT are beginning to come together.

A yearly compound rate of the number of connected things, from cars to computers to household monitors are projected to grow between 2014 to 2020 from 23.1% in 2014 to 50.1 billion things in the year 2020. As at the time of Gil's report, the IoT adoption level was stated that IoT initiatives had been started by 60% of an organization where 45% of these organizations were funded by new budget apportionment while addition 23% of the organizations were making plans to commence IoT initiatives within a year period. Research exploring how providers of IoT can succeed, 500 executives were surveyed by Bosche, Crawford, Jackson, Schallehn, & Smith (2016)and findings show that about 450 of the executives said they are still in the planning and proof-of-IoT concept stage while just about 90 of the 450 expect implementation by 2020. The utmost five benefits expected were:

1. Cost reduction due to operational effectiveness and efficiency.
2. Improved decision making from better and new streams of data.
3. Staff efficiency benefits.
4. Enhance asset monitoring and visibility throughout the organization.
5. Better and improved customer experience.

Although the projected benefits are unevenly divided between prevailing operations and new revenue or products rivulets, 61% of the businesses which is the majority reported that their initiatives (IoT) as "facilitating and prolonging" technology as opposed to 37% who have their initiatives as a separate and distinct activity. Bosche et al. (2016) also realized high anticipations of the possible IoT benefits which include intensifying the trustworthiness of operations, refining the efficiency of the employees and enhancing products and services quality. Addressing the issue of being pessimistic or optimistic, about 57% of the respondents trust their association is exceptionally very much prepared or for the most part all around prepared to deal with the security segment of IoT. Due to the number of security ambiguities in areas that are beyond the operators' control, confidence might be replaced and Bosche et al. (2016) also found security as the most frequent concerns about IoT because of the citing of about 45% of their respondents that security is one of the topmost three obstacles to IoT application.

Applications

With its ability to allow objects to use hearing, sight, talking and even thinking senses to make a decision within themselves, IoT has empowered those objects with technologies that change the traditional view of objects as inanimate things to smart, living things. As such, IoT applications can be deployed wherever an intelligent decision making is required. Smart objects when specifically deployed for tasks are known as a vertical market. The horizontal market, on the other hand, refers to applications regarding analytical services and universal computing.

Some of the widely known application of IoT are in healthcare, transportation, agriculture, schools, markets, business industry and so on (Al-Fuqaha et al., 2015). IoT is expected to be widely applied business and homes due to its ability to provide good life quality. Deployment in business includes process monitoring where secured communication, remote access controlling and environmental sensing is employed to improve quality of the service delivery (Chen et al., 2014). Similarly, secured communication and location sensing are important areas where IoT deployment will improve logistic management within the business industry (Chen et al., 2014). In healthcare, E-health implies monitoring of patients and delivery of home care services via location monitoring, ad hoc networking, secured communication and environmental sensing while environment monitoring, food traceability, safety and smart agriculture are components of smart city application of IoT. IoT applications capabilities can be summarized as follows:

- **Environment Sensing:** This involves environmental detection and remote medical monitoring. With environment sensing, natural disasters are monitored using automatic alarm systems. Also, data received in the hospital are utilized predict health trend and recommend health advice.
- **Location Sensing and Sharing of Location Info:** The ability of IoT system to gather the specific location details of all smart object nodes allows it to provide location specific informational services accurately. Mobile asset tracking, traffic information system, and fleet management are applications dependent on location sensing and sharing capability of IoT. Drivers can select the most efficient route with the aid of traffic information system because all information regarding road conditions and congestion are provided. Also, fleet management provides room for optimal resources utilization through accurate scheduling process, as well as real-time information on all resources is available. Similarly, all commodity can be tracked and monitor by mobile asset tracking capacity of IoT.
- **Remote Controlling:** Appliance control and disaster recovery are the basic application of this capability of IoT (Chen et al., 2014). It involves execution of commands viz-a-viz termination of such commands from a different location. Such can be employed to minimize disaster losses by monitoring for off-incident location.
- **Secure Communication:** Depending on the required service, IoT systems can provide additional secure transmission between application and service platforms (Chen et al., 2014).
- **Ad Hoc Networking:** The Self-organizing network is used in IoT system. This enable sIoT applications to be able to interoperate between the network or service layer deliver required services (Chen et al., 2014).

Smart City

There are varying concepts of the smart city because it includes different aspects of the urban life such as sustainable development, environment, urban planning, technology, social involvement, economic evolution, energy grid, etc. (Harrison et al., 2010; Hollands, 2008). This concept by researchers includes defining smart cities in different ways such as ubiquitous city, digital city, knowledge city, wired city and intelligent city respectively (Anthopoulos & Fitsilis, 2010; Couclelis, 2004; Ergazakis, Metaxiotis, & Psarras, 2004; Hollands, 2008; Komninos, 2006). According to the researchers, the different concepts can be defined as:

1. **Digital City:** Has Inclusive web-based exemplification but focused on a variety of functions of a definite city and are open to non-experts. The digital city also has different scope: political, social, ideological, theoretical and cultural.
2. **Ubiquitous City:** Is a further extension of the concept of the digital city. It is a city or region that has web-based representation that is present everywhere within the city.
3. **Knowledge City:** Is a city which promotes continuous sharing, creation and evaluation of renewable and updated knowledge with the aim of achieving knowledge-based development.
4. **Wired City:** Literally refers to lying down of connectivity and cables which do not necessarily mean smart.
5. **Intelligent City:** Cities intelligent have a high capacity for innovation and learning. The cities are built-in the inventiveness of their populace, digital infrastructure for knowledge management and communication including their institutions of knowledge creation.

These meanings have shared characteristics of human, institutional and technology dimensions. According to Couclelis (2004), the people are the key driver for smart city and the human dimension is centered on people, learning, knowledge and the education, and this dimension comprises concept about knowledge city while technology dimension basically stands on the usage of infrastructures (principally ICT) to transform work/life inside a city in a significant way and digital city, ubiquitous city, wired city, and intelligent city are concepts included in this dimension.

Lastly, the institutional dimension is founded on policy and governance because the mutual cooperation between the institutional government and stakeholders is crucial to designing and implementing the initiatives. Owing to the fact that there are different concepts of smart cities, there is also different definitions of smart city and will be stated in Table 1, while Caragliu, Del Bo, & Nijkamp (2011) defines operational smart city as a city where there is investment in social and human capital and modern (ICT) as well as traditional (transport) communication infrastructure that promotes high level of living quality in addition to sustainable growth in economy through participatory governance with judicious management of all resources.

According to Giffinger who is one of the most cited researchers identified six dimensions of smart city as shown in Figure 3.

Sharma (2016) identified the key elements in each of the dimensions as shown in Figure 4.

But these dimensions can be further explained as:

1. **Smart Economy:** Providing broadband access for all citizens and businesses, creating business opportunities,, aiding population maintenance in rural areas via leveraging of networks to increase business opportunities beyond the city centre, and using electronic channels in business processes of all sort (e.g., e-shopping, e-banking, e-auction)(Steinert et al., 2011).
2. **Smart People:** This dimension is driven by social capital where social and ethnic diversity, creativity, tolerance and engagement results in smart people. To raise social qualification and capital, cities offer online workshops and courses, programs and services and online assistance with education (Ben Letaifa, 2015).
3. **Smart Governance:** Is information and communication technology-based governance that extensively perform a group of people, technologies, policies, resources, practices, social values and norms and information that interrelate to assist the city's governing activities (Giffinger, 2007).
4. **Smart Mobility:** This is achieved by using urban planning which moves focus from individuals to collective modes of transport via comprehensive extended information usage communication

Table 1. Frequently cited definitions of a smart city

Definition	References
"Smart City is a city of well-performing based on smart combination of the activities and endowments for independent, self definitive and aware citizens."	(Giffinger, 2007)
"Smart City is the product of Digital City combined with the Internet of Things."	(Su, Li, & Fu, 2011)
"Smart City is a well defined geographical area where high technologies such as information, communication technology, energy production, logistics, etc. cooperate in creating benefits for the citizens regarding smart development, well-being concept, participation, environmental quality and inclusion; all Governed by a well specified grouping of topics, and have the ability to provide rules and policies of the city government and development."	(Dameri, 2013)

Figure 3. The smart city dimension (Giffinger, 2007)

Smart environment
smart people
Smart living
Smart governance
Smart economy
Smart mobility

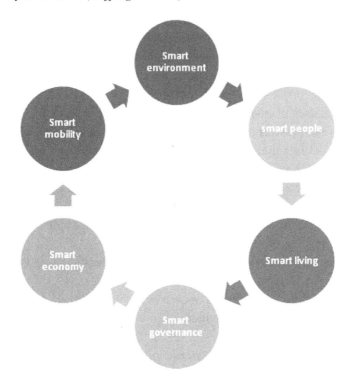

Figure 4. Elements of smart city dimensions (Sharma, 2016)

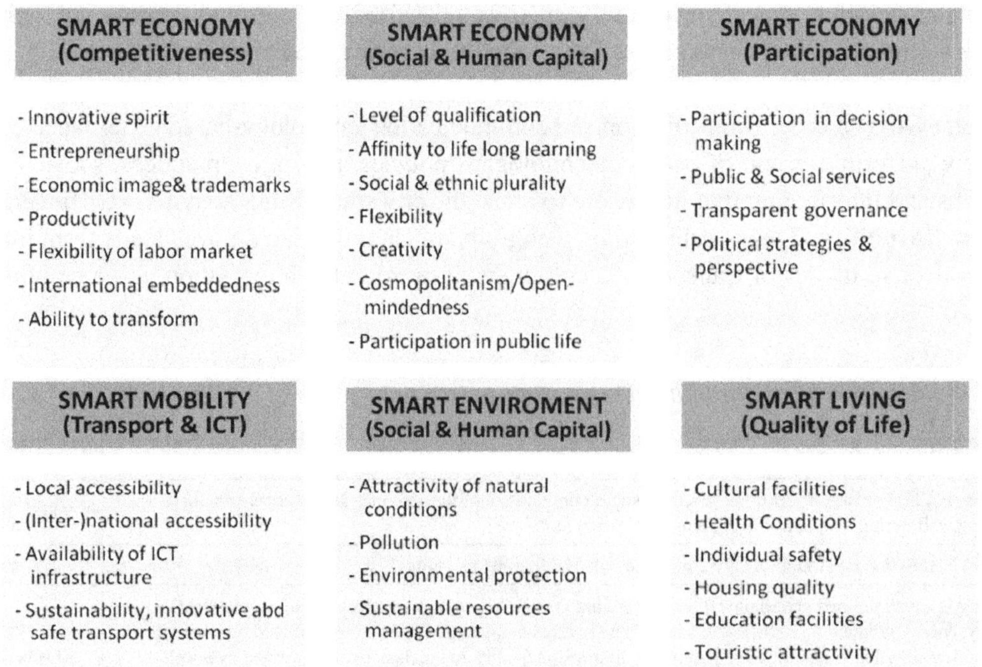

SMART ECONOMY (Competitiveness)
- Innovative spirit
- Entrepreneurship
- Economic image& trademarks
- Productivity
- Flexibility of labor market
- International embeddedness
- Ability to transform
SMART ECONOMY (Social & Human Capital)
- Level of qualification
- Affinity to life long learning
- Social & ethnic plurality
- Flexibility
- Creativity
- Cosmopolitanism/Open-mindedness
- Participation in public life
SMART ECONOMY (Participation)
- Participation in decision making
- Public & Social services
- Transparent governance
- Political strategies & perspective
SMART MOBILITY (Transport & ICT)
- Local accessibility
- (Inter-)national accessibility
- Availability of ICT infrastructure
- Sustainability, innovative abd safe transport systems
SMART ENVIROMENT (Social & Human Capital)
- Attractivity of natural conditions
- Pollution
- Environmental protection
- Sustainable resources management
SMART LIVING (Quality of Life)
- Cultural facilities
- Health Conditions
- Individual safety
- Housing quality
- Education facilities
- Touristic attractivity
- Social cohesion

technologies (Ben Letaifa, 2015). It entails stimulating novel 'social' attitudes such as carpooling, car sharing, and car-bike combinations; and promoting a more intelligent and efficient transportation systems that will effectively leverage networks to guarantee more proficient movement of people, vehicles, and goods, thereby reducing traffic congestion.

5. **Smart Environment:** As Colldahl, Sonya, & Kelemen (2013) clarified, there is an exploration of energy management and building stock by city stakeholders. There is also the use of modern technologies such as renewable sources of electricity to improve the natural environment.
6. **Smart Living:** Comprises of social services, e-health, cultural facilities, and public safety tools, for example, inter-emergency service networks and surveillance systems. Smart living includes enhancing life quality regarding elevating social structure and safety, boosting its attractiveness for tourists, and services (Toppeta, 2010).

In the urban context, people are surrounded by ubiquitous digital system smart buildings, Internet-connected cars and a multitude of other equipment like Smartphone, computer, Global Positioning System (GPS), tablet, sensors, etc. that are ready to interrelate with each other, see Figure 5.

Smart City Challenges

Due to the ever-increasing availability of data with urban environ, research on smart cities has also increased. Reason on the temporal, contextual and spatial; and representation aspects of this data, as well as increasing demand for exploration and search capability are some of the open challenges (Bicer& Lopez, 2013). Cleaning, de-noising, privacy protection and anonymization are ways of managing the

Figure 5. Sample of smart city (Piro, Cianci, Grieco, Boggia & Camarda, 2014)

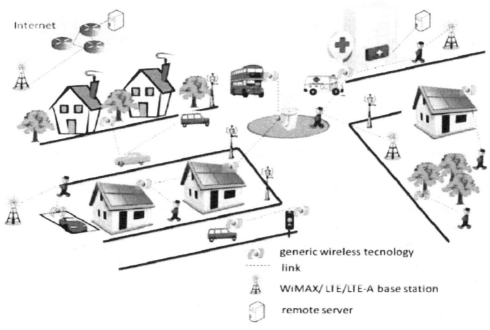

cities' data lifecycle. Assimilating diverse sources of city data – including social media and sensors – justify the need for exploration of interpretation, fusion, aggregation, lifting, correlation and analysis techniques (Kotoulas et al., 2014).

Smart city systems become pervasive and ubiquitous (Kindberg& Chalmers, 2007) which implies the need for optimizations and advances in service-oriented architectures and software engineering with the scalable processing of heterogeneous or dynamic, together with distributed city data. Seeing those cities are fashioned by their residents, it is expedient to investigate the social characteristic of the IoT to their cities which are the essence of this research such as social influence, internet experience, etc. Thriving achievements and outcomes in the topics above are required to convey substantial solutions and services to citizens since research on the smart city is directed more towards producing innovative applications in some pertinent sectors such as commerce, public safety, transportation, government and resource management.

Using a pragmatic, the explorers and developers of smart cities have been looked into. The trends that are outlined in the prior section implied that cities are a spotlight for many sectors extending from environmental and social sciences, economic,, design, urban and architectural planning, to sensor networks, social network analyses and human sensors. Despite the focus, recent encounters with developments of the smart city found that a significant challenge is a use, sharing and exposing of data (Lee, Almirall, & Wareham, 2015). Nonetheless, opening up data is bound to fail if there is not compelling enticement with committed management and clear strategy by data providers (public authorities) for developers, citizens and private companies (Lee et al., 2015).

Masip-Bruin, Ren, Serral-Gracia, &Yannuzzi (2013) itemize three underlying principles that aid open data initiatives: a) open data promotes public participation in data gathering, analysis, and implementation, often reducing the cost of government expenditure or refining efficiency in lieu of that, b) it encourages transparency, collaboration, and participation in government and c) creates an economic growth new source. Janssen, Charalabidis, &Zuiderwijk (2012) identified some possible benefits of smart city open data initiatives and some features covered are: the economic features (such as simulation of innovation), the operational and technical features (such as sustainability of data and external quality checks of data) and the political and social features (such equal access to data and more transparency).

Despite the benefits above of open data to citizens, business, and governments, there are some risk associated with it that needs to be managed (Kucera&Chlapek, 2014). Issues relating to contingency actions, risk and probable opportunities regarding economic issues, governance, legal framework, metadata, data characteristics, skills and access are some of the disadvantages of open data (Martin, Foulonneau, Turki, &Ihadjadene, 2013a). Infringement of trade secret protection, unlawful data disclosure, breaching of infrastructure security and violation of privacy are some of the issues that might have a severe adverse effect.

Therefore, quality control of published data and compliance assessment must be implemented in the publication process especially in places in which the primary essential data has confidential data like individual personal information, application of anonymization is necessary (Kucera&Chlapek, 2014). According to Zuiderwijk and Janssen (2014), a dataset and context-dependent decision-making model should be made to evaluate benefit of open data (e.g., possibility of strengthening economic growth, creating transparency) versus the disadvantages and risks of open data (e.g., misinterpretation of data, invasion of privacy, false impressions possible misuse and mismanagement matters).

Notwithstanding the development of open data platforms, its wider deployment faces major hurdles (Martin, Foulonneau, Turki, &Ihadjadene, 2013b). The gap between the promise of open data and realization day can be explained as the absence of insight into the user's perspective and lack of suitable governance processes (Janssen et al., 2012). Finally, according to (Roberts, 2012), open data can cause intensification social inequality and the digital divide unless approached correctly. Motivating and providing and enabling communities to innovate social enterprise, job creation, and local service provision is the only sustainable means of delivering public benefit from open data.

The challenges of opening up data can be cogitated in two main levels: citizen data and infrastructure data (Lea, 2015). Citizen data is central to cities meaning that it is a 'ground truth' for citizens' desires and activities. Nevertheless, people are not willing to share data due to trust and privacy concerns (Hollands, 2008). Developing trust certifiers and creators will give a feeling of confidence that they have absolute domination over shared data (inclusive of revoking ability of shared data) and usage of data to the citizens. Regrettably, most data infrastructures in cities are still locked due to varying reasons such as shortage of knowledge, resources, vision, technical skills, etc.

Caragliu (2011) expounded on the notion that smart cities are environs of an open and user-driven novelty for investigating and authenticating future Internet-enabled services. It is of necessity that there should be clarification in the way user communities, lab innovation, test-bed facilities and future internet experimentation methods make up a common set of resources (Granell et al., 2016). To achieve elaborate city development goals, it is of importance that these mutual resources should be shared and made accessible in innovation environs; however, it must be safe for security concerns of the citizens (Glasmeier&Christopherson, 2015). This method necessitates sustainable cooperation and partnerships strategies among the key stakeholders. Research carried out by (Naphade, Banavar, Harrison, Paraszczak, & Morris, 2011) also studied perceptions towards targets and goals, limitations, and challenges of smart cities further than technology-intensive and infrastructure visions to an emphasis on citizen empowerment, improvement for life quality and greater equity.

Middle East Countries Initiatives as Smart Cities

The Middle East operates as a proper laboratory of multiplicity in public policies and national experiences. Some common physiognomies are used in "excerpt" fashion to express content, image, and context of the region en-bloc. These usually comprise extensive urbanization, rapid population growth, remarkable young age structure, oil resources, diverse ethnic and religious contentions and configurations, water scarcity, varieties of cross-border immigration and most vital, sustained significance to the global economy. Surpassing such generalities is relevant differential both between and within countries.

There are secular politics and religious ones, poor and wealthy countries, diversified economies and mono-"crop" ones, urban and rural states. Middle East countries are embarking on an intensive drive to move to smart cities buttressed by the support of government and semi-government entities. United Arab Emirates (UAE) and Saudi Arabia are leading the move for developing smart cities in the Middle East by spending heavily on the smart city. Their heavy investment in IoT use cases has resulted in a forecast of 19.3% growth annually until 2019, based on IDC's IoT Spending Guide. The growth of smart cities in the Middle East has drawn the attention of stakeholders. Both public and private sectors are collaborating to organize conferences on smart cities. Even governments services are now available online and on mobile highlighting the level of alignment of the government with the drive for smart cities. The government now operates e-portals to deliver services more efficiently to citizens and also providing a centralized system for information search and government services to the citizens (Romkey, 2015).

Although the impact and effectiveness of adoption of smart cities initiatives in the Middle East vary from country to country, the entire region is unanimous in their drive for the development of smart cities. Most new projects within the region now incorporate the dimensions of smart cities to be able to harness the opportunities of the innovative drive of the projects (Romkey, 2015). In most smart cities initiatives globally, existing cities are upgraded to smart cities by the addition of smart solutions, however, in many Middle East countries, the prevailing opportunity for smart cities development is the opportunity to build from scratch. In trying to implant smart solutions to preexisting cities to make them smart, time is consumed, costs are incurred and sometimes become too complicated, but in the Middle East, such issues have been adequately addressed.

Among the noticeable smart projects on-going in the Middle East is the Dubai design district; a home for creative and design industries. By December 2017, Dubai Silicon Park will be completed. It showcases an integration of residential and business area that reflects smart mobility, sustainability, and lifestyle (Romkey, 2015). The King Abdullah Economic City is the smart cities program in Saudi Arabia. It comprises of a smart city division that builds in the latest ICT infrastructure. There are two main opportunities provided by these Greenfield developments. Firstly, opportunities for innovations to be tested are presented at lower cost, as constructing a brand new ICT infrastructure is much cheaper than retrofitting aged infrastructure.

Secondly and probably most important, provision of opportunities to further developed tested innovations, integration of the innovations into the city's structure and also evaluating the performance on a massive scale. Contrary to the assumption that smart innovation and activeness will be more relevant to developed countries, communities with no history in infrastructural investment and are among the least developed nations of the world are taking the most transformative and innovative initiatives in the adoption of smartness of things. The drive for smart innovations and development in Africa, Middle East and other underdeveloped and developing nations will influence and encourage developed countries to further implement smart city proposals.

Dubai has not only been a big investor in smart technology but has internalized the concept of the smart city into their core vision and value. This is clearly evident in the drive for the Dubai Plan 2021 by Dubai ruler Sheikh Mohammed bin Rashid Al-Maktoum. The plan is envisioned to transform Dubai into the smart, connected and integrated city. To achieve the plan, a strong focus on renewable energy and ensuring sustainable use of the resource is needed. The smart initiative was initiated first in March 2014 in Dubai with the objective of ensuring the place of Dubai as the world's smartest city. Integral to achieving the Dubai plan 2021 is the implantation of mobile and data technologies in the form of smart meter deployment, and the creation of help-2-park apps for real-time monitoring of water and energy consumption. Solar power generation is another crucial component of the plan to provide an additional source of power. Dubai Smart City Establishment was also created to saddle the course of realizing the goal of Dubai smart city by 2018. The last 25 years has seen Dubai transformed from a mere desert to a significant global center for financial services, business, and transport. This transformation has resulted in its designation as an infrastructural city with an enormous capacity to grow and is thus positioned perfectly to grow into a genuine, smart city than other cities of the world.

Qatar, another city in the Middle East, is also embarked on the adoption of smart city initiatives. Their creation of a New Lusail City is a masterpiece of the adoption of the technology. Lusail City is a high-technology center that manages all information technology within the city through both wireless and wired communication networks (Romkey, 2015).

Internet of Things in Services Provision

Due to the recent emergence of varieties of enabling technological devices, Internet of Things (IoT) is close to becoming an essential part of the Future Internet (FI) and a crucial extension to the existing fixed and mobile network infrastructures. Predictions foresaw IoT to become an important part of FI (Toma, Simperl, Filipowska, Hench, & Domingue, 2009)because its connected devices will predominate the mobile devices and computers used by humans by degrees of magnitude. The unfolding of these scenarios makes the design of the FI difficult and the IoT requirements strongly influence its architecture. The major objective of research on IoT is to move from present existing preexisting Intranet to Internet of Things by incorporating these islet technologies into a globally interconnected infrastructure (Zorzi, Gluhak, Lange, & Bassi, 2010). On a different angle, cities are an agglomerate of people, business, organizations, services, organizations and infrastructure; and lately, the use of smart devices such as actuators and sensors.

Just as all complex systems, the cities required adequate management to ensure the incessant interpretation of all crucial activities and consequently incessant living condition for all its stakeholders. The harmonization of these domains and activities is of vital significance to guarantee effective and efficient city service management. Nevertheless, coordination in modern cities is typically done on a more strategic level and not on a daily basis; it is done mostly from the political and administrative perspective with no concurrent feedback. Sections of the public service are governed as a stand-alone activity with walls (administrative) between the different domains which prevents efficient sharing of infrastructures and exchange of information.

In recent times, the European Union (EU) has been devoting steady efforts to create sustainable stratagem for smart urban development in its cities (Caragliu et al., 2011) which is established by the existence of active and just completed projects on smart cities which is shown in Figure 6. On this precept, service provided via the internet of things range from transportation to healthcare, etc. As illustrated in Figure 6, some of the services provided are:

1. **Environmental Monitoring:** The existing proffered solutions to environmental monitoring in cities are centered on few fixed measurement station locations. While there is high accuracy from this measurement equipment, when used at a large scale to obtain measurements at the refined and more accurate level, the cost is obviated. The introduction of IoT infrastructures makes it feasible to deploy low-cost sensors to a great quantity for a little fraction of the expense of the currently used technology. These sensors do not usually give the same level of accuracy as the modern measurement stations but by using the intelligent processing of the measurement, and large quantity of the measurement points will make it probable to achieve sufficiently precise measurements that can be used as a preliminary indicator of the environmental pollution status. Another related case is the scenario of using luminosity sensors around the city to infer a more judgment of the immediate situation of the artificial illumination service on the street. Alternatively, a scenario where there is deployment to aid the use case of environmental monitoring; there has been installation some devices on the municipality vehicles, public transport buses and police cars that give a more efficient coverage of the entire city. Multiple application domains are served with this deployment which enables delivery of supplementary services like traffic condition assessment and smart public transport management.

Figure 6. Most important EU research projects investigated via their uses (Piro et al., 2014).

Category	Use	SMRT SANTANDER	ELLIOT	TEFIS	FIER BALL	IOT	SAFE CITY	OUT SMART	RELY on IT	FINEST	DIGITAL CITIES	MOBINCITY	HOBNET	CITYSDK	LIVE CITY	IES CITIES	PERIPHERIA	ICITY	TV-RING	SMART FREIGHT
TRANSPORTATION	Traffic monitoring situations				x															
	Limited parking management	x						x									x			
	Loading & unloading of areas	x																		
	logistic		x							x										x
	Trip optimization				x						x	x								x
	Transport services (train, bus, plane, etc)		x	x	x		x				x	x				x	x			x
	Parking for people with disabilities	x																		
	Diagnosis and Prediction of Traffic	x							x											
GOVERNMENT & PUBLIC ADMINISTRATION	Automatic & optimized administrative procedure						x					x								
	Document search						x													
	Tax payment						x													
	Election accessibility for people with disabilities																x			
PUBLIC SAFETY	Management of road accidents						x													
	Crime prevention						x													
	Monitoring of public places						x													
	Prediction of climate change effects																x			
SOCIAL	Tourism assistance	x	x										x		x	x				
	Identification of point of interest	x																		
	Location based services	x											x				x			
	Media distribution	x												x					x	
	Retail services & shops discovering		x																	
	Content sharing			x															x	
	Socially sustainable campus																x			
HEALTH-CARE	Dissemination of data about pollution &temperature for patients		x																	
	Remote patients assistance		x	x																
	Remote coordination of surgeries			x																
	Media transmission for hospitals & doctors													x						
	Generic health care services															x				
EDUCATION	Distribution of multimedia contents in a school													x						
SMARTER BUILDING & URBAN PLANNING	Building monitoring & control							x					x							
	Monitoring of electrical devices												x							
	Management of emergency situations												x							
	People & resources tracking												x							
	Park irrigation	x											x							
	Waste management							x												
ENVIRONMENTAL	Environmental monitoring	x	x		x													x		
	Luminosity Measurement	x																		
ENERGY & WATER	Efficient management of artificial lights	x	x				x													
	Efficient management of heating & air conditioning		x		x			x												
	Water distribution						x													
	Optimized energy distribution					x														

2. **Traffic Management:** Classification and counting of vehicles in use on the road in recent times is achieved by placing inductive loops under the asphalt. Nevertheless, there are several disadvantages and problems associated with this method such as high cost, maintenance, deployment, among others. However, the use of Smart Sender project from IoT proffers solution founded on the Wireless Sensor Network. The deployment has the objective of monitoring road occupancy, traffic volume, queue length estimation, vehicle speed as well as traffic distribution (Sánchez et

al., 2013). Furthermore, information received about route times available and vehicle speed from installed nodes on taxis and public buses make the creation of congestion map possible for inner streets in the city.

3. **Augmented Reality:** To optimize the present system in tradition retail shops, especially where customers need to try different clothes and view themselves. This istime-consuming considering the number of clothes they will have to change into to make their choice. The retailers are at risk as different customers put on and take off these clothes either for expensive and not-so-expensive clothes thereby reducing the chances of being purchased by other customers because of possible wear and tear on the clothes. Some customers will also prefer to buy items that are still in their original packing because of the state of hygiene of customers that have tried the clothes on, and this leads to wastage. With intelli-mirror (Lobo, 2016), clothing items are displayed on customers by updating inventory from an external server, then detecting the customer and capturing their image, after this, size and orientation of selected item are selected and inserted, and the image of the customer with the clothing item is displayed. With this customers can know how a particular clothing item will loom on them without actually putting them on which saves both the customer and retailer time and wastage or losses respectively.

4. **Participatory Sensing:** In this case, physical sensing information such as a compass, GPS coordination, environmental data like temperature, noise.etc. is sent by users using their mobile phones. The information received is fed to the Smart Santander rostrum. Services like "pace of the city" are subscribed to by users where they get notifications for specific event types that are happening within the city. User themselves can report the occurrence of the events and subsequently propagate to other users who are subscribed to other events. Via phone calls, smart phone applications, emails and SMS, users receive notifications in the preferred language. For users interested in receiving alerts, they must subscribe to the service by describing their profile; preferred language and choosing information that is of importance to them (Konomi, Wakasa, B, & Sezaki, 2016).

Literature and Hypotheses Development

As aforementioned, Giffinger et al. (2007) noted smart cities as cities that increase life quality for its citizens. This view suggests that the overall goal of the application of information system technology such as IoT in societies as evident in the case of smart cities is to deliver satisfaction to the citizenry of the society. Satisfying human needs is an enormous task. It requires an understanding of the cultural, political, gender, educational and attitudinal peculiarities of individuals that made up the society.

Several researchers have identified key dimensions of a smart city. Giffinger et al. (2007) determined the key dimensions of smart city as environment, economy, people, governance and mobility, where; environmental issues include (energy policies, landscape and waste and water management), the economic stands for (sector strength, GDP, foreign investment and international transactions), when human dimension includes (education, innovation, talent and creativity), social (religions, families, traditions and habits) and institutional which includes (administrative authority, civic engagement and elections). Barrionuevo et al. (2012) identified management and organizations technology governance policy context people and communities economy built infrastructure natural environment. Chourabi et al. (2102) identified quality of life sustainable economic development management of natural resources through participatory policies convergence of economic, social in addition to environmental goals. Thuzar (2011).

All these dimensions as propagated by the scholars helps to understand smart cities as a network of technological infrastructure that permit cultural and social development as well as political efficiency through the inclusion of citizens to achieve the creation of innovative amenities for the use of the citizens.

Demographic Factors and Citizens IoT Satisfaction

Demographic classification of resident or citizens of cities, nations and countries have been in practice for long. Social status and class basically is an end product of demographic classification. More importantly, people's technology affinity and usage is often a function of the generation such person is a member of. For instance, generation Xers are known to be the internet savvies and as such will appreciate smart cities more than their counterpart in generation Y.

Several types of research have had conflicting assertion on the influence of age, gender, status and general demographic factors on people's adoption of technology and their satisfaction of use(Correa, Hinsley, & de Zúñiga, 2010; Jackson, von Eye, Fitzgerald, Zhao, & Witt, 2010; Morris, Venkatesh, & Ackerman, 2005; Palvia & Palvia, 1999; Watson, Rainer, & Koh, 1991; Welch, Hinnant, & Moon, 2005; Zhang, Lee, Cheung, & Chen, 2009). Many opined that older generation is characterized as technophobic because of their high resistance to technology adoption (Correa et al., 2010; Jackson et al., 2010; Morris et al., 2005). Many others suggested no significant relationship between demographic profile and information system use (Palvia & Palvia, 1999; Watson et al., 1991; Welch et al., 2005)

As such, the importance of age in understanding adoption and satisfaction of smart city cannot be overemphasized. Understanding the distinctiveness of age gaps is, therefore, a key to creating and managing citizen's expectation which will, in turn, affect their satisfaction. Because of the fundamental differences in the make-up of men and women, gender disparity often plays an essential and significant role in the adoption in addition to satisfaction derived from the use of technological innovation (Zhang et al., 2009).

According to social role theory, the agentic nature of men enables them to be more instrumentally competent and likely to be more technological savvy than their female counterpart. This is mainly due to the fact that women appreciate relationship and would rather spend time socializing than understanding a technological gadget. This view has been supported by academic researchers in information system fields.

Occupation being a direct result of intense, specified and rigorous training is another demographic factor that we intend to study its impact on the adoption and satisfaction of citizen of the smart city. An engineer is trained to solve problems while an administrator is trained to manage resources. The varying occupation has a specific orientation to life which ultimately influences the actions and behaviors of an individual practitioner of such trade. As we have clearly outlined and explained, with every diversity a perspective difference which overall explains individual actions. Based on the extent theoretical and empirical arguments presented, the following hypothesis is proposed:

- **H1a:** Citizens IoT Satisfaction will differ by age.
- **H1b:** Citizens IoT Satisfaction will differ by gender.
- **H1c:** Citizens IoT Satisfaction will differ by residential area/region.
- **H1d:** Citizens IoT Satisfaction will differ by occupation.

Social/Cultural Factors and Citizens IoT Satisfaction

Theory of planned behavior posit that individual's behavioral inclinations are often predicted by their attitude, individual norms and perceived behavioral control (Morris et al., 2005). Attitudes, norms, and behavior are however shaped by individual's experiences. These experiences are encounter within social circles, family influences, and religious inclination.

All the factors above are an ingredient of the socio-cultural well-being of an individual. Based on the extent theoretical and empirical arguments presented, following the proposed hypotheses, see Figure 6.

- **H2a:** Internet experience will have a positive impact on citizens IoT satisfaction.
- **H2b:** Governmental/Institutional agencies reputation will have a positive impact on citizens IoT satisfaction.
- **H2c:** Social influence will have positive impact on citizens IoT Satisfaction.

Personal Factors and Citizens IoT Satisfaction

Computer self-efficacy stands for the overall assessment of individuals' capacity to use and perform on computer. It is essential the user's perception of their capabilities (Compeau & Higgins, 1995). Self-efficacy refers to own perceived capabilities to execute designated mission. It however not related to one's acquired skills but a perception of the competency of such skills (Imhof, Vollmeyer, & Beierlein, 2007). Choices are decision alternatives evaluated, weighed and integrated based on one's self-efficacy (Bandura, Adams, Hardy, & Howells, 1980; Marakas et al., 1998).

Even though self-efficacy can be positively associated with motivation and performance measurement, domain-specific measures tend to explain self-efficacy more accurately. As such, Compeau & Higgins (1995) studied its application in computer self-efficacy construct. Their empirical findings as well as other studies showed that high computer self-efficacy individuals have a more positive orientation towards IT than others with less computer self-efficacy and are more frequent users than others (Compeau, Higgins, & Huff, 1999; Compeau & Higgins, 1995).

Prior studies of computer self-efficacy also implied a negative orientation toward computer anxiety and positive orientation towards playfulness; both being integral dimensions of IT acceptance (Hackbarth, Grover, & Yi, 2003). Furthermore, intention to use Internet-based applications which are crucial in adoption, use and satisfaction of IoT application in smart cities has also been found to be positively associated with individuals with high computer self-efficacy (Vijayasarathy, 2004).

The decision of acceptance and use of new technology is often made based on users perceive computer self-efficacy threshold and hence impacts their behavioral intention to accept or reject new technology (Shih, 2006). Direct and indirect influence on behavioral intention on acceptance of new technology has been studied and found (Kwon, Choi, & Kim, 2007; Venkatesh, Morris, Davis, & Davis, 2003). Owing to the wealth of studies associating positive relationship between computer self-efficacy and IT acceptance and use, it is safe to propose the hypothesized relation as adopted in this study. Likewise, the level of education is also a determining factor towards adoption and satisfaction of IoT and Smart City technology. Based on the extent theoretical and empirical arguments presented, following the proposed hypotheses, see Figure 7.

Figure 7. Conceptual model for the research

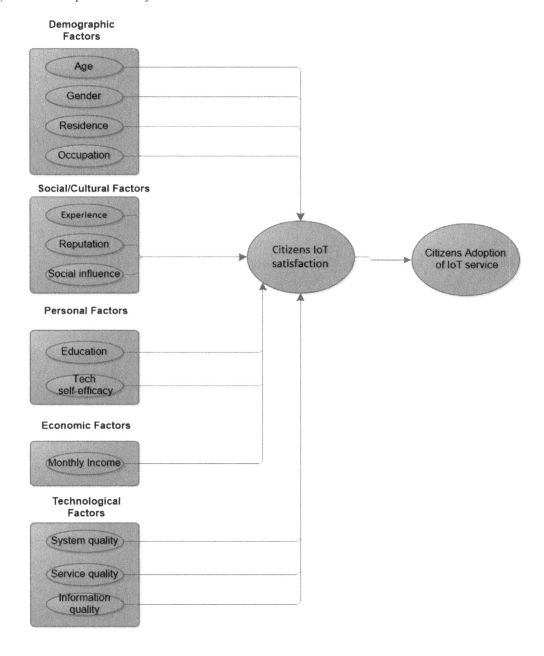

- **H3a:** Computer self-efficacy will have a positive impact on citizens IoT satisfaction.
- **H3b:** Education will have a positive impact on citizens IoT satisfaction.

Economic Factor and Citizens IoT satisfaction

Economic systems, social relations, infrastructures and procedures for the exchange of goods and services form the basic composition of a market. Trading often involves the exchange of value as perceived by both the buyer and seller. The pricing mechanism gives the make the stability and efficiency required for trading. Similarly, in IoT application market, as introduced by Munjin and Morin (2012) imitate the traditional market to ensure transfer of perceived values between different parties.

As money is the legally tenable means of the transaction within a marketplace, it is, therefore, important that financial condition of individual within smart cities as reflected in his/her income should be good enough to consider the purchase of smart technology. As such, the income level of an individual determines the quality of products that can be purchased. If the best quality products are purchased, buyers will have a better satisfaction derived. Hence, we posit that:

- **H4a:** Citizen Income will have a positive impact on citizens IoT satisfaction.

Technological Factors and Citizens IoT Satisfaction

Evaluating information systems such as IoT has widely adopted the usage of DeLone & McLean Model for IS Success (D&M Model for IS Success)(Delone& Mclean, 2004; DeLone& McLean, 2003; Dwivedi, Wade, &Schneberger, 2012). Its initial introduction in 1993 received praises and was adopted in various application of IS. However, based on the criticism the model received, an update was introduced in 2003 to encapsulate all the required input necessary to ensure that quality standards are met. This updated D&M model for IS success has been examined and validated in a different context and with different variables (DeLone & McLean, 2003; Dwivedi et al., 2012; Fang, Chiu, & Wang, 2011; Lin, 2007; Petter& McLean, 2009; Wang & Liao, 2008).

Among the main inputs of D&M model for IS success are system quality, information quality, and service quality. To better understand this concept, we determine system quality as necessary features of the information system. It is concerned with adaptability, usability, system flexibility, data accuracy, system features, uptime, user requirement, data currency, customization, integration, efficiency and response time. In our study context, IoT system quality means the functionality of IoT system that ensures the delivery of sophistication, intuitiveness, flexibility and usability to the users.

Information Quality, on the other hand, encompasses the desired features of the system outputs; graphs, web pages and management reports. For instance: timeliness, importance, completeness, relevance, format, content accuracy, conciseness, usability, consistency, availability, and understandability. Consequently, IoT information quality refers to how IoT systems incorporate the desired features of IS to deliver consistency, availability, usability, and conciseness.

Service Quality on the other hand indicates the level of the upholding and support given to users by IS support personnel. It is concerned with reliability, accuracy, technical competence, empathy in addition to responsiveness. SERVQUAL, adapted from the marketing field is a communal tool for scaling IS service quality (Pitt, Watson, &Kavan, 1995). Findings of several studies on IS success model have shown that an increased information quality will lead to increase net benefit and user satisfaction. Similarly, increase service and system qualities will increase user satisfaction. Consequently, we posit that by prior studies, IoT system quality, IoT service quality, and IoT information quality will result in Smart cities citizens' satisfaction and adoption. Hence, we proposed the following hypotheses:

- **H5a:** IoT System quality will have a positive impact on citizens IoT satisfaction.
- **H5b:** IoT Service quality will have a positive impact on citizens IoT satisfaction.
- **H5c:** IoT Information quality will have positive impact on citizens IoT Satisfaction.

Citizens IoT Satisfaction and Citizens' Adoption of IoT Services

Taking all the argument above and discussion into consideration, we can rightly imply that IoT satisfaction will lead to the adoption of IoT service. Based on the IS success model, increased service, system and information quality will result in net benefit and user satisfaction. Owing to the nature of our study, the net benefit could refer to the overall positive influence of IoT application as reported in wide adoption of IoT services.

- **H6:** Citizens IoT Satisfaction will have positive impact on citizens' adoption of IoT services.

CONCLUSION AND FUTURE RESEARCH DIRECTION

In the digital era, cities are supposing a relevant say as innovation drivers for firms in various segments and industry ranging from construction (i.e., smart building) hostels, city planning, and high tech infrastructures among others. As noted earlier, this dissertation is interested in smart cities. More generally, "smart cities that involve user-driven invention ecosystems and sustainable open to improve firms' innovativeness and improving the quality of living" (Schaffers et al., 2011).People have come to understand that smart cities were design mainly "to reconstruct the rural and urban areas in locations of democratic innovation, in which innovation ecosystems enable intelligence and participated in the creation of communities' capabilities to design creative innovative living and working scenarios.".

The smart cities are setting of open and user-driven innovation for testing and demonstrating the value of future internet enabling service (Schaffers et al., 2011). In a nutshell, "smart cities are composed of smart technologies equipped with the ability to monitor and / or interact with the physical environment and to communicate with other things and objects, are expanding the Internet concept to reach the so-called term (Internet of Things) IoT; which has the potential to influence and change our lives significantly and on our way to interact with the devices like smart phones, sensors, home automation devices and intelligent network devices or smart grid devices

The research has provided evidence of other external factors that have profound effect on citizen's satisfaction with IoT and adoption of IoT services. To wrap up, based on the outcome of this research, the author formulate implications for research and theory, and for society and management.

REFERENCES

Al-Fuqaha, A., Guizani, M., Mohammadi, M., Aledhari, M., & Ayyash, M. (2015). Internet of Things: A Survey on Enabling Technologies, Protocols, and Applications. *IEEE Communications Surveys and Tutorials*, *17*(4), 2347–2376. doi:10.1109/COMST.2015.2444095

Bandura, A., Adams, N. E., Hardy, A. B., & Gary, N. (1980). Test of the Generality of Self-efficacy Theory. *Cognitive Therapy and Research*, *4*(1), 39–66. doi:10.1007/BF01173354

Ben Letaifa, S. (2015). How to strategize smart cities: Revealing the SMART model. *Journal of Business Research*, *68*(7), 1414–1419. doi:10.1016/j.jbusres.2015.01.024

Bicer, V., & Lopez, V. (2013). Searching in the city of knowledge. *Proceedings of the 36th International ACM SIGIR Conference on Research and Development in Information Retrieval - SIGIR '13*, 1123. 10.1145/2484028.2484195

Correa, T., Hinsley, A. W., & de Zúñiga, H. G. (2010). Who interacts on the Web?: The intersection of users' personality and social media use. *Computers in Human Behavior*, *26*(2), 247–253. doi:10.1016/j.chb.2009.09.003

Dameri, R. P. (2013). Searching for Smart City definition: A comprehensive proposal. *International Journal of Computers and Technology*, *11*(5), 2544–2551.

DeLone, W. H., & McLean, E. R. (2003). Journal of Management Information Systems The DeLone and McLean Model of Information Systems Success: A Ten-Year Update. *Journal of Management Information Systems*, *19*(4), 9–30. doi:10.1080/07421222.2003.11045748

Delone, W. H., & Mclean, E. R. (2004). Measuring e-Commerce Success : Applying the DeLone & McLean Information Systems Success Model Measuring e-Commerce Success : Applying the DeLone & McLean Information Systems Success Model. *International Journal of Electronic Commerce*, *9*(1), 31–47.

Dwivedi, Y. K., Wade, M. R., & Schneberger, S. L. (2012). *Information Systems Theory. Springer*.

Ergazakis, K., Metaxiotis, K., & Psarras, J. (2004). Towards knowledge cities: Conceptual analysis and success stories. *Journal of Knowledge Management*, *8*(5), 5–15. doi:10.1108/13673270410558747

Fang, Y.-H., Chiu, C.-M., & Wang, E. T. G. G. (2011). Understanding customers' satisfaction and repurchase intentions: An integration of IS success model, trust, and justice. *Internet Research*, *21*(4), 479–503. doi:10.1108/10662241111158335

Giffinger, R. (2007). Smart cities Ranking of European medium-sized cities. *October, 16*, 13–18.

Gil Press. (2016). *Internet Of Things By The Numbers: What New Surveys Found*. Retrieved December 27, 2016, from http://www.forbes.com/sites/gilpress/2016/09/02/internet-of-things-by-the-numbers-what-new-surveys-found/#5f5270443196

Glasmeier, A., & Christopherson, S. (2015). Thinking about smart cities. *Cambridge Journal of Regions, Economy and Society*, *8*(1), 3–12. doi:10.1093/cjres/rsu034

Gómez-Goiri, A., & López-De-Ipiña, D. (2010). A triple space-based semantic distributed middleware for internet of things. Lecture Notes in Computer Science, 6385, 447–458. doi:10.1007/978-3-642-16985-4_43

Granell, C., Havlik, D., Schade, S., Sabeur, Z., Delaney, C., Pielorz, J., ... Mon, J. L. (2016). Future Internet technologies for environmental applications. *Environmental Modelling & Software*, *78*, 1–15. doi:10.1016/j.envsoft.2015.12.015

Harrison, C., Eckman, B., Hamilton, R., Hartswick, P., Kalagnanam, J., Paraszczak, J., & Williams, P. (2010). Foundations for Smarter Cities. *IBM Journal of Research and Development*, *54*(4), 1–16. doi:10.1147/JRD.2010.2048257

Huang, Y., & Li, G. (2010). Descriptive models for Internet of things. *Proceedings of 2010 International Conference on Intelligent Control and Information Processing, ICICIP 2010, (PART 2)*, 483–486. 10.1109/ICICIP.2010.5564232

Jackson, L. A., von Eye, A., Fitzgerald, H. E., Zhao, Y., & Witt, E. A. (2010). Self-concept, self-esteem, gender, race and information technology use. *Computers in Human Behavior, 26*(3), 323–328. doi:10.1016/j.chb.2009.11.001

Janssen, M., Charalabidis, Y., & Zuiderwijk, A. (2012). Benefits, Adoption Barriers and Myths of Open Data and Open Government. *Information Systems Management, 29*(4), 258–268. doi:10.1080/105805 30.2012.716740

Kindberg, T., Chalmers, M., & Paulos, E. (2007). Urban Computing. *IEEE Pervasive Computing, 6*(3), 18–20. doi:10.1109/MPRV.2007.57

Komninos, N. (2006). The Architecture of Intelligent Cities. *2nd International Conference on Intelligent Environments*, 13–20.

Kucera, J., & Chlapek, D. (2014). Benefits and Risks of Open Government Data. *Journal of Systems Integration, 5*(1), 30–41. doi:10.20470/jsi.v5i1.185

Lee, M., Almirall, E., & Wareham, J. (2015). Open data and civic apps. *Communications of the ACM, 59*(1), 82–89. doi:10.1145/2756542

Lin, H.-F. (2007). Measuring online learning systems success: applying the updated DeLone and McLean model. Cyberpsychology & Behavior: The Impact of the Internet. *Multimedia and Virtual Reality on Behavior and Society, 10*(6), 817–820.

Marakas, G. M., Marakas, G. M., Yi, M. Y., Yi, M. Y., Johnson, R. D., & Johnson, R. D. (1998). The multilevel and multifaceted character of computer self-ef cacy: Toward clari cation of the construct and an integrative framework for research. *Information Systems Research, 9*(2), 126–163. doi:10.1287/ isre.9.2.126

Morris, M. G., Venkatesh, V., & Ackerman, P. L. (2005). Gender and age differences in employee decisions about new technology: An extension to the theory of planned behavior. *IEEE Transactions on Engineering Management, 52*(1), 69–84. doi:10.1109/TEM.2004.839967

Naphade, M., Banavar, G., Harrison, C., Paraszczak, J., & Morris, R. (2011). Smarter cities and their innovation challenges. *Computer, 44*(6), 32–39. doi:10.1109/MC.2011.187

Ngai, E. W. T., Moon, K. K. L., Riggins, F. J., & Yi, C. Y. (2008). RFID research: An academic literature review (1995-2005) and future research directions. *International Journal of Production Economics, 112*(2), 510–520. doi:10.1016/j.ijpe.2007.05.004

Petter, S., & McLean, E. R. (2009). A meta-analytic assessment of the DeLone and McLean IS success model: An examination of IS success at the individual level. *Information & Management, 46*(3), 159–166. doi:10.1016/j.im.2008.12.006

Pitt, L. F., Watson, R. T., & Kavan, C. B. (1995). Service Quality : A Measure of Information Systems Effectiveness. *Management Information Systems Quarterly, 19*(2), 173–187. doi:10.2307/249687

Romkey, M. (2015). Smart cities … Not just the sum of its parts. Beirut: Academic Press.

Schaffers, H., Komninos, N., Pallot, M., Trousse, B., & Nilsson, A. (2011). Oliveira, Smart cities and the future internet: towards cooperation frameworks for open innovation. In Lecture Notes in Computer Science: Vol. 6656. *The Future Internet* (pp. 431–446). Berlin: Springer. doi:10.1007/978-3-642-20898-0_31

Su, K., Li, J., & Fu, H. (2011). Smart city and the applications. *2011 International Conference on Electronics, Communications and Control, ICECC 2011 - Proceedings*, 1028–1031.

Venkatesh, V., Morris, M. G., Davis, G. B., & Davis, F. D. (2003). User Acceptance of Information Technology: Toward a Unified View. *Management Information Systems Quarterly*, *27*(3), 425–478. doi:10.2307/30036540

Wang, Y. S., & Liao, Y. W. (2008). Assessing eGovernment systems success: A validation of the DeLone and McLean model of information systems success. *Government Information Quarterly*, *25*(4), 717–733. doi:10.1016/j.giq.2007.06.002

Welch, E. W., Hinnant, C. C., & Moon, M. J. (2005). Linking citizen satisfaction with e-government and trust in government. *Journal of Public Administration: Research and Theory*, *15*(3), 371–391. doi:10.1093/jopart/mui021

Zhang, K. Z. K., Lee, M. K. O., Cheung, C. M. K., & Chen, H. (2009). Understanding the role of gender in bloggers' switching behavior. *Decision Support Systems*, *47*(4), 540–546. doi:10.1016/j.dss.2009.05.013

Zorzi, M., Gluhak, A., Lange, S., & Bassi, A. (2010). From today's INTRAnet of things to a future INTERnet of things: A wireless- and mobility-related view. *IEEE Wireless Communications*, *17*(6), 44–51. doi:10.1109/MWC.2010.5675777

Zuiderwijk, A., & Janssen, M. (2014). The Negative Effects of Open Government Data - Investigating the Dark Side of Open Data. In *Proceedings of the 15th Annual International Conference on Digital Government Research* (pp. 147–152). Academic Press. 10.1145/2612733.2612761

Chapter 15
Comparison Study of Different NoSQL and Cloud Paradigm for Better Data Storage Technology

Pankaj Lathar
CBP Government Engineering College, India

K. G. Srinivasa
CBP Government Engineering College, India

Abhishek Kumar
M. S. Ramaiah Institute of Technology, India

Nabeel Siddiqui
M. S. Ramaiah Institute of Technology, India

ABSTRACT

Advancements in web-based technology and the proliferation of sensors and mobile devices interacting with the internet have resulted in immense data management requirements. These data management activities include storage, processing, demand of high-performance read-write operations of big data. Large-scale and high-concurrency applications like SNS and search engines have appeared to be facing challenges in using the relational database to store and query dynamic user data. NoSQL and cloud computing has emerged as a paradigm that could meet these requirements. The available diversity of existing NoSQL and cloud computing solutions make it difficult to comprehend the domain and choose an appropriate solution for a specific business task. Therefore, this chapter reviews NoSQL and cloud-system-based solutions with the goal of providing a perspective in the field of data storage technology/ algorithms, leveraging guidance to researchers and practitioners to select the best-fit data store, and identifying challenges and opportunities of the paradigm.

DOI: 10.4018/978-1-5225-5972-6.ch015

INTRODUCTION

In recent years, advancements in Web based technology and the proliferation of sensors and mobile devices interacting with Internet have resulted in immense data sets of user generated content triggered by Web 2.0 companies like Facebook, Google and Amazon.com. Even bigger banking firms like J.P Morgan Chase & Co., Goldman Sachs are facing similar issues of managing intense volume of forex trading and historical financial markets data used in compliance stress testing. These organizations are migrating gradually from traditional relational data base management systems (RDBMS) to more efficient and flexible solutions like NoSQL and Cloud computing. NoSQL solves the basic challenge of storage and retrieval of high-volume dynamic and transactional real time data sets whereas Cloud computing compliments the prior with high on-demand network access to a shared pool of computing resources (e.g., network, storage, applications and services) that can be rapidly used with reduced management effort. Despite the ideal characteristics of NoSQL data stores as cloud data management systems, added with cloud computing competence of shared access, it is difficult to choose an appropriate domain suited model due to the high diversity of these solutions available.

In this chapter, we will deliberate upon the characteristics & classification of NoSQL, as a cloud data management system and Cloud Systems, as the processing unit of the data lake for modern Web. The paper is organized to detail the Data Storage Technologies and Algorithms with focus on the driving factors behind the migration from RDBMS to NoSQL in the industry.

INTRODUCTION OF NOSQL DATABASES

Technology Background of NoSQL Databases

NoSQL as a database facilitates a structure around storage and retrieval of data. This data is organised in logical structures different from tabular relations often found in traditional relational databases. NoSQL database are also referred as Not Only SQL, is an methodology to data management and database design that's useful for fairly large chunks of distributed data. NoSQL can also be called a non SQL or non-relational database. Since the late 1960s, Relational databases have existed but could not gain the title of "NoSQL" till the twenty-first century, emerged by the needs of companies categorised as Web 2.0 such as Amazon, Google and Facebook.

NoSQL databases were triggered due to the exponential growth of the Internet and the rise of traffic generated on web 2.0 applications. Google published the BigTable research in 2006, and Amazon published the Dynamo technical paper in the year 2007. These databases were designed to meet a new generation of enterprise companies.

Conflicting to presumptions caused by its title, NoSQL never prohibited structured query language (SQL). It's a fact that some NoSQL systems are purely non-relational, while others simply avoid use of relational features such as fixed table schemas and operations on join. For example a NoSQL database might structure data into objects, key/value pairs instead of using traditional tabular relation.

The data arrangement used by NoSQL stores (e.g. wide column, key-value, graph or document) are not similar compared to default in relational databases, making some operations faster in NoSQL. The particular use case suitability of a NoSQL database is dependent on the business case it must solve. Occasionally the data arrangement used by NoSQL databases are also considered as "more flexible" when compared to relational database tables.

Various NoSQL databases lack on consistency (Based on CAP Theorem) to provide availability, speed and partition tolerance. Blockers to the increased adoption of NoSQL databases include lack of standardized interfaces, use of low-level query languages and huge prior investments in legacy relational databases. Mostly, NoSQL databases lack true nature of ACID transactions, although a few stores, such as Aerospike, MarkLogic,, Google Spanner, FairCom c-treeACE make up for such transaction based features. Based on the in depth analysis of NoSQL databases, we find they provide a concept of "eventual consistency". Database changes are replicated to all nodes "eventually" (typically within a time frame of milliseconds) so queries on objects might not return latest and updated data points immediately or might result in reading stale data which is inaccurate, a problem called as stale reads. In Addition to this, few NoSQL systems may include lost writes and other types of data loss. To the advantage of NoSQL stores provide features of write-ahead logging to avoid loss of data. For distributed transaction processing across various stores, An even bigger challenge is data consistency. This is difficult for both NoSQL and relational databases. In Comparison to current relational databases there are few systems that maintain both X/Open XA and ACID transactions standards for distributed transaction processing.

Characteristics of NoSQL Databases

Prior to getting into the Characteristics of NoSQL Stores its logical to list a few real world business case scenarios to implement a NoSQL Database as their persistent component for backend Data. One of the most basic and important driver is when a organization has a business scenario which is tough to solve using traditional relational database engineering. For organisations with a stable and mature domain business model supported by a traditional database providing all the required features, use of NoSQL is less probable leading to no change in its data storage mechanism. A few of the business cases are listed below that support the use of a NoSQL database rather than a traditional relational one.

- Cost of relational database is not scalable with increased traffic at an acceptable rate.
- Data is provided in small updates varying over time hence the number of tables required to store a first normal form has become disproportionate to the data being held.
- Dynamic business model providing a huge set of temporary data that should not really belong in the main data schema. Various examples are that of retained searches, shopping carts, incomplete user questionnaires and site personalisation.
- Relational database is denormalised for performance issues or for convenience in data manipulation in web application.
- Dataset has large chunk of images or text and the column definition is a finite large Object (BLOB).
- Business needs to execute queries with your data set that involve complex hierarchical relations; Generic examples are business intelligence queries having an absence or missing piece of data. For the latter consider an example of "All Females in Paris who have a pet dog and whose sister's have not yet purchased a paperback this year".
- If local data transactions where durability is not a required characteristic. For example "liking" items on social websites: creation of transactions for such kind of events are overkill as the action fails the user will mostly repeat it till it works. AJAX-heavy websites tend to showcase these use-cases.

Even though there is no agreement on what exactly constitutes a NoSQL solution, the following set of characteristics is often attributed to them (Hecht R, Jablonski S. (2011), (Cattell R (2010)):

- Flexible and Simple non-relational data models. NoSQL databases provide easy to change schemas or are mostly schema-free and are engineered to manage a wide quality of data structures (Konstantinou I, Angelou E, Boumpouka C, Tsoumakos D, Koziris N (2011)). Existing data structures can be categorized into four broad categories: key-value stores, document stores, column-family stores, and graph databases.
- Horizontal scalability over various commodity servers. A few selective data stores have data scaling, while rest of them focus more with read and/or write scaling.
- Provide Increased availability. Various NoSQL databases are engineered for highly distributed scenarios, and unavoidable partition tolerance. Hence, for providing high availability, these solutions choose to lack consistency in favour of giving more priority to availability. As a result of this NoSQL data stores are AP (Available/ Partition-tolerant) data stores, whereas most RDBMs are CA (Consistent/Available).
- Generally, no support to ACID transactions is provided by NoSQL. They are referred as BASE systems (Basically Available, Soft state, Eventually consistent) (Pritchett D (2008)).Detailing the acronym, *Basically Available* refers to the data store being available all the time when it is accessed, even if its partially unavailable; *Soft-state* emphasizes that consistency is not the highest priority at the times and some inconsistency can be tolerated; and *Eventually consistent* Highlights that after a certain time frame, the data store moves to a consistent state. However, some NoSQL databases are ACID compliant. For e.g. CouchDB.

NoSQL databases are designed to meet the following enterprises software development requirements which mark the reason behind the above characteristics:

1. The need to "develop with agility"!
2. Simplicity for Easier Development.

Develop With Agility

To remain ahead in the current Economy, enterprises must keep innovate – and with a fast pace than ever. Speed is a critical factor, but so is agility, since web 2.0 applications change far more quickly than legacy applications like ERP. Relational databases act as critical roadblock to the required agility, due to their rigid data model.

- **Flexibility for Rapid Development:** A core guiding principle of agile is pacing to evolving application requirements: If requirements change, the domain model tends to changes. Relational databases act as critical roadblock because the data model is rigid and defined by a static schema. Developers have to change the schema, or even worse, "schema change" request is forwarded to the database administrators. This dependency graph leads to slow pace or stops development.

Comparatively a NoSQL document database promotes agile development, Its schema-less nature and absence of static data modelling definition is the key. Data Modelling definition is left to the developer

Figure 1. RDMBS – An Static schema blocks the addition of new attributes on demand

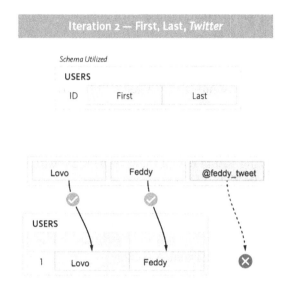

writing the services. With NoSQL, the data model is created by the application model. Applications and services model data as JSON objects.

- **Simplicity for Easier Development:** Applications-Services model data as JSON objects (e.g. employee as an entity), multi-valued data points as collections (e.g., roles), and related data as nested JSON objects or collections (e.g. manager as an entity). The issue with relational databases is that read/write operations are done by "shredding," or disassembling, and reassembling objects. We can term this as object-relational "impedance mismatch." Object-relational mapping frameworks are the workarounds for the same, problematic and inefficient at best.

As an example, consider an resume mapping application. In the given scenario, the Application interacts with resumes and the *user*. Both resume and user are objects. An array for skills with a collection for positions is an internal part of the application. However, the user object needs to be shredded while writing a resume to thid relational database. Application would require to insert six rows into three tables to Store this resume, as illustrated in Figure 3.

Application would require to read six rows from three tables while reading a resume (Figure 4).

A document-oriented NoSQL store performs reads/writes data JSON format. It is the de facto standard for producing and consuming data for mobile, web, and IoT applications. This standard eliminates the object-relational impedance mismatch and removes the overhead of ORM framework, hence simplifying the application development. In contrast to traditional databases, objects are read and written with no "shredding". An Object itself can be read or written as a document with no alterations at service layer. This is illustrated in Figure 5.

All of the above characteristics promote NoSQL databases as a suitable data management system for Cloud. Indeed, various Databases are offered as a Service today, such as Amazon's DynamoDB (Murty J (2008)) and SimpleDB (Apache CouchDB (2013)) are regarded to be NoSQL stores. Though, the ab-

Figure 2. JSON – The data model evolves with easy addition of new attributes

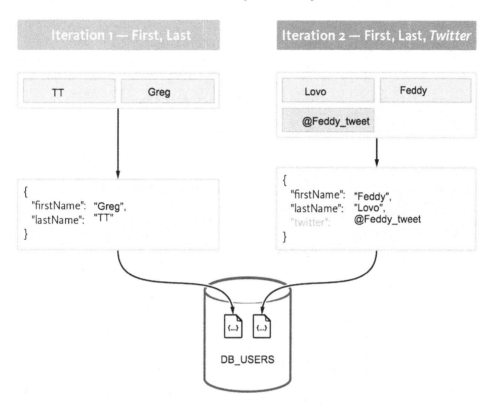

Figure 3. RDMBS – Applications "shred" objects into rows of data stored in multiple tables

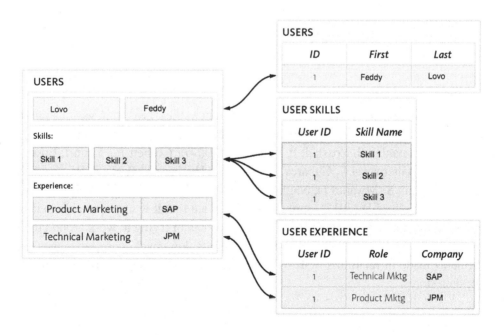

Figure 4. Applications can store objects with nested data as single documents

Lovo	Feddy	Skill 1	Product Marketing	SAP
Lovo	Feddy	Skill 1	Technical Marketing	JPM
Lovo	Feddy	Skill 2	Product Marketing	SAP
Lovo	Feddy	Skill 2	Technical Marketing	JPM
Lovo	Feddy	Skill 3	Product Marketing	SAP
Lovo	Feddy	Skill 3	Technical Marketing	JPM

Figure 5. Transformed objects with nested data as single documents

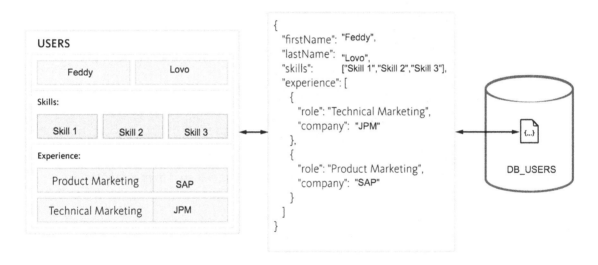

sence of full ACID transactions can be a critical impediment to their growth in various mission-critical systems. For instance, Corbert *et al.* (DeCandia G, Hastorun D, Jampani M, Kakulapati G, Lakshman A, Pilchin A, Sivasubramanian S, Vosshall P, Vogels W (2007))(Corbett JC, Dean J, Epstein M, Fikes A, Frost C, Furman JJ, Ghemawat S, Gubarev A, Heiser C, Hochschild P, Hsieh W, Kanthak S, Kogan E, Li H, Lloyd A, Melnik S, Mwaura D, Nagle D, Quinlan S, Rao R, Rolig L, Saito Y, Szymaniak M, Taylor C, Wang R, Woodford D (2012)) support the argument that it is more suitable to deal with performance problems due to the heavy use of transactions instead of trying to work around the absconded transaction support. However, the lack of interface standards, low-level query languages and the huge legacy investments made in relational SQL by enterprises are other major barriers to the adoption of fresh NoSQL data stores.

Classification of NoSQL Databases

In this brief section of classification we categorize NoSQL databases based on the kind of storage model implemented by them, individually. There are multiple ways to Categorize these Databases which are over 220 in number. The logical reason behind the categorizing methodology is based on "Data Model" or "Domain Driven Design" being the focal point of Data base Technologies in the world of Web 2.0. Each type of NoSQL DB is described with an industrial business case example and its weak points. The description meets the basic objective of providing a perspective in the field of Data Storage Technology/ Algorithms, Leverage guidance to researchers and practitioners to select the best-fit data store.

The categories of NoSQL data stores are as follows:

- Key Value Stores
- Document databases
- Graph databases
- XML databases
- Distributed Peer Stores
- Object Stores

Detailed Analysis of the available data stores:

Key Value Stores

Key-value stores have a uncomplicated data model based on key-value pair logic of data storage, which resembles an associative hash map or a dictionary (Hecht R, Jablonski S (2011)). As per the Key-Value pair methodology, a key is unique identifier of the associated value and is used for storage and retrieval of the value in/out of the data store. The value acts as an opaque object to the data store and can be used for storing any arbitrary data point, including a string, an integer, an array, or an object, hence providing a schema-free domain-data model. Being an static schema-free domain model, key-value stores are efficient in storing data distributed on various clusters, but are unsuitable for business scenarios implementing relations or structures. Any Implementation requiring structures, relations or both must be implemented in the client application interface with the key-value store. However, because the values are opaque objects to them, these data stores cannot handle querying or data-level indexing and can execute queries only with the help of keys. Key-value database stores can be categorized further into 1) *In-memory key-value stores* (Maintains data in memory), like Redis (Redis (2013)) and Memcached (Memcached (2013)) and 2) *Persistent key-value stores* (Stores the data on disk), such as Riak (Klophaus R (2010)), Voldemort (Auradkar A, Botev C, Das S, De Maagd D, Feinberg A, Ganti P, Gao L, Ghosh B, Gopalakrishna K, Harris B, Koshy J, Krawez K, Kreps J, Lu S, Nagaraj S, Narkhede N, Pachev S, Perisic I, Qiao L, Quiggle T, Rao J, Schulman B, Sebastian A, Seeliger O, Silberstein A, Shkolnik B, Soman C, Sumbaly R, Surlaker K, Topiwala S, Tran C, Varadarajan B, Westerman J, White Z, Zhang D, Zhang J (2012)) and BerkeleyDB (Oracle Berkeley DB 12c (2013)).

- **Typical Applications:** Caching of content.
- **Strengths:** Fast Lookups.
- **Examples:** Redis, Voldemort Tokyo Cabinet/Tyrant,, Oracle BDB.

Figure 6. Logical Structure of Key-Value Store

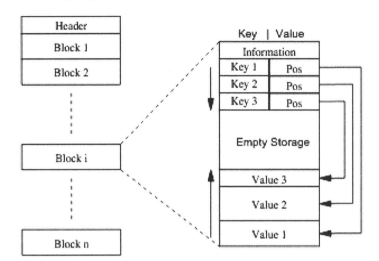

- **Weaknesses:** Maintained Data has no static schema.
- **Practical E.g. Application:** For writing a forum Application with a home profile page that gives the statistics such as user's messages posted, etc. and the top ten messages by them. On hitting the page, it reads on the user's id from a key that is unique and fetches a string of JSON representing all the relevant information. A process running in the background recalculates for every 15 minutes and writes the information to the database independently.

Document Database

The focus point concept of a document database is notion of a "document". Each implementation of document-oriented store differs on the details of its definition, in a common, they are all based around the logic that "documents encapsulate and encode information (or data) in standardized encodings or formats. Most Common Encodings used include YAML, XML, JSON and binary forms of BSON. Similar to a unique primary key, Documents are referred in the store via a *key* that points to that document. An important highlighting characteristics of a document-oriented store is that the store provides an query language or API that fetches documents based on their contents, in addition to the key fast lookups executed by a key-value database.

Various implementations offer multiple ways of grouping and/or organizing documents:

- Collections
- Non-visible metadata
- Directory hierarchies
- Tags

In Comparison with traditional relational databases, for example, tables could be referred analogous to collections and records analogous to documents. Yet they are not the same: Each record in a traditional table has the exactly the same sequence of fields, whereas in a collection documents may have fields which completely different.

Figure 7. Normalized document model

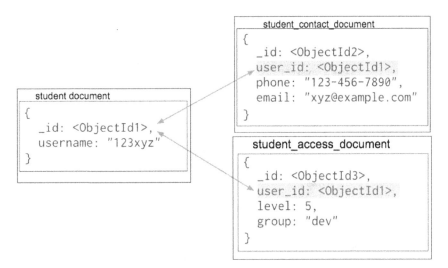

- **Examples:** MongoDb and CouchDB.
- **Typical Applications:** Web applications.
- **Strengths:** Incomplete data tolerance.
- **Weaknesses**: No standard query syntax and Query performance.
- **Practical E.g. Application:** For creating a web application that maintains profiles of refugees. We need to record details of each child with circumstances that vary tremendously, for example a lost child in the camp may know their last name and may not know their parent's last name. Eventually a local may claim to recognise the person and offer you with some extra information which you want to store but unless verified the record, you have to treat it with sceptically.

Graph Database

As the name suggest, Graph stores use graphs as the data model and originated from graph theory. Graph is a mathematical methodology that represents an object set, known as graph nodes or vertices, and the edges (or links) interconnect these vertices. Graph databases can effortlessly maintain the relationships between different graph data nodes which is a wholly different data model than column-family, key-value and document stores. In graph stores, the edge and nodes also have discrete properties entailing of key-value pairs. Graph databases are dedicated in handling highly organized data and hence are very proficient in traversing relationships across various entities. They are relevant in scenarios such as pattern recognition, recommendation systems, social networking applications, dependency analysis and solving path locating problems raised in triangulation systems.

- **Examples:** Infinite Graph, Neo4J, InfoGrid,
- **Typical Applications:** Recommendations and Social networking
- **Strengths:** Graph algorithms e.g. connectedness, n degree relationships, shortest path, etc.
- **Weaknesses:** Has to traverse the complete graph to conclude a definitive answer.

Figure 8. Normalized Weighted Graph

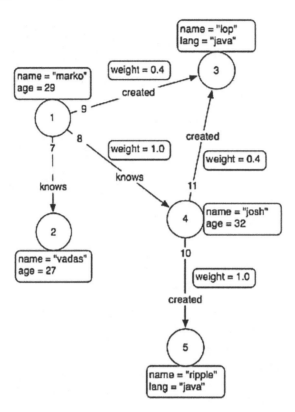

- **Practical E.g. Application:** Web Application that needs social networking is most apt to a graph database. These matching principles can be protracted to any application where we need to comprehend what people are buying, doing or enjoying so that we can suggest further things for them to buy, do or like. Any time you need to reply the query along the lines of "Which malls, do people who are over-50, like skiing and have visited Florida dislike?" a graph database will mostly help.

XML Database

An XML database is a software system that is data persistence and allows data to be quantified, and sometimes stored, in XML format. These data can be fetched, converted, extracted and sent back to a calling system. XML stores are a savour of document-oriented databases.

- **Examples:** Mark Logic, Exist, Oracle,
- **Typical Applications:** Publishing
- **Strengths:** Schema validation and Mature Search technologies
- **Weaknesses**: Re-write is easier than updating the documents, No real binary solution,
- **Practical E.g. Application:** Any publishing entity that uses bespoke XML formats to yield print, web and eBook varieties of their articles. Editors need to rapidly search either semantic or text sections of the mark-up. They persist the XML of completed articles in the XML store and bind it

Figure 9. Example of XML Type Query in IBM DB2 SQL

```
select

    id, vlume, xmlquery('$j/name', parse jnural as "j") as name

from

    dbo.journals

where

    xmlexists('$j[licence="abhishek_crc_publishrs"]', passing jnural as "j")
```

in a readable-URL REST web service for the document production systems. Workflow metadata attributes(e.g. stage of a manuscript) is stored in a isolated RDBMS. When system-wide alterations are required, XQuery re-writes bulk updates all the documents to match the new template.

Distributed Peer Stores

Column Family Stores are also known as distributed peer stores. They are designed to manage large amount of data distributed over several servers. Similar to Key-Value Stores, keys are used as unique binding primary keys. Moreover, the key points to numerous columns of the database. Supreme column-family stores are a derivative of Google Bigtable (Chang F, Dean J, Ghemawat S, Hsieh W, Wallach D, Burrows M, Chandra T, Fikes A, Gruber R (2006)), in which the data are stored in a column-placed way. In Bigtable, the dataset entails of multiple rows, each of which is addressed by a distinctive row key, also known as a *primary key*. Each row is constituted of a set of column families, and diverse rows can have diverse column families. Correspondingly to a key-value store, the row key is similar to the key, and the set of column families similar to the value denoted by the row key. Each column family further provides a key for the one or more columns that it represents, where every column consists of a name-value pair. Google Bigtable concepts are directly implemented by the Hadoop HBase, (Apache HBase (2013)) whereas DynamoDB (DeCandia G, Hastorun D, Jampani M, Kakulapati G, Lakshman A, Pilchin A, Sivasubramanian S, Vosshall P, Vogels W (2007)) and Amazon SimpleDB (Murty J (2008)) have a diverse data model than Bigtable. SimpleDB and DymanoDB have only a set of column name-value pairs in every row, with no column families. On the other hand, Cassandra (Lakshman A, Malik P (2010)) offers an additional functionality of super-columns, which are produced by grouping multiple columns together.

- **Examples:** Riak, Cassandra, HBase.
- **Typical Applications:** Distributed file systems.
- **Strengths:** Good distributed storage of data and Fast lookups.
- **Weaknesses:** Extremely low-level API.
- **Practical E.g. Application:** A news application site where any section of content: comments, author, articles, profiles, can be voted on and a not obligatory comment provided on the vote. We insert one store per user and one store per section of content, using a UUID as the key (produc-

Figure 10. Logical Structure of Distributed Peer data store

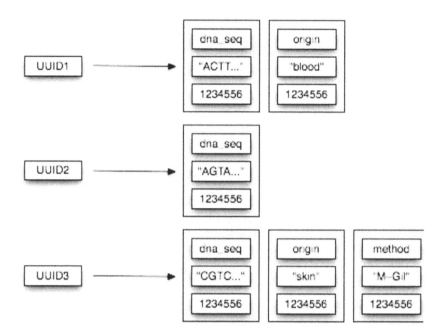

ing one for each section of content and user). The user's store maintains each vote they have ever casted while the content "vessel" holds a copy of each vote that has been casted on the section of content. An overnight batch job is used to detect content that users have voted on, we identify a list of content for each user that has excessive votes but which they haven't voted on. We then push this list of suggested articles into the user's "vessel".

Object Stores

An object store (also known as object-oriented database management system - OODBMS) is a database management system that represents information as objects, as used in object-oriented programming. Object databases are poles apart from relational databases. They are a hybrid version of both approaches.

Object-oriented database management systems (OODBMSs) merge database competencies with object-oriented programming language abilities. OODBMSs allow object-oriented programmers to produce a product, persist them as objects, and modify or replicate prevailing objects to generate new objects within the OODBMS. Because the database is assimilated with the programming language, the developer can persist consistency within single environment, in such a case, both the OODBMS and the programming language maintain the same data model of representation. By way of contrast, Relational DBMS projects maintain a clearer division between the database model and the application.

- **Examples:** ObjectStore, GemStone, Polar, Oracle Coherence, db4o.
- **Typical Applications:** Finance systems.
- **Strengths:** Low-latency ACID, mature technology, Matches OO development paradigm.
- **Weaknesses:** Limited batch-update options and querying.

Figure 11. Logical Structure of Object Store

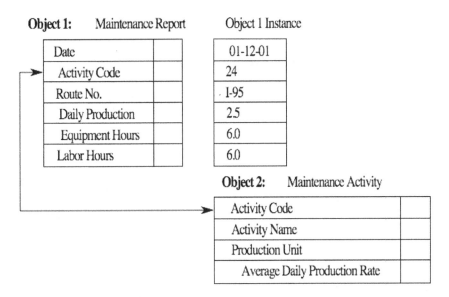

- **Practical E.g. Application:** Global company has a monoculture of trading development and wants to have trades done on desks in New York and Japan go through a risk inspection process in London. An object signifying the trade is pushed into the object store and the risk check listener is listening for modification or appearance of trade objects. As the object is duplicated into the local European space the risk check listener reads the Trade and evaluates the risk. Post this operation it rewrites the object to alert of a trade approval and sends an actual request of trade fulfilment. The trader's client listener waits for changes to be published on objects that contain the trader's id and appends the local information of the trade packet in the client. Hence indicating to the trader of an approved trade.

Query Language Maturity

Analogous to the collection of a data model, the querying abilities of data stores play an vital role when selecting among them for a particular scenario. Various data stores offer different APIs and interfaces to interact with them. This is directly reliant upon the data model that a certain data store owns. For example, a key-value database cannot provide querying built on the contents of the pair's values, as these values are not transparent to the data store. In Contrast, a document database is capable of content based querying as its data model facilitates indexing and querying the document contents. Another vital query-related trait of NoSQL and NewSQL database is their level of assistance for MapReduce. First developed by Google, MapReduce can be defined as a programming model with an associated execution for processing large datasets (Gilbert S, Lynch N (2002)). It is now a widely promoted method for performing distributed data processing on a cluster of servers. Because one of the primary goals of NoSQL data stores is to scale over a large number of computers. Similarly, SQL-like querying is a preferred option due to its rife use over the past decades, and it is now adopted in the world of NoSQL. Therefore, some of the popular NoSQL data stores like MongoDB (MongoDB (2013)) offer a SQL-like query language

Table 1. A Detailed view of the different APIs support provided by the most prominent NoSQL and NewSQL solutions along with other querying capabilities offered.

NoSQL Data Stores		Querying Capabilities of each NoSQL Data Store			
		MapReduce	REST API	Query	Other API
Key-Value Stores	Redis	No	Third Party APIs	Does not provide SQL-like querying	CLI and API in several languages
	Berkely DB	No	Third Party APIs	SQLite	CLI and API in several languages
	Riak	Yes	Yes	Riak search, secondary indices	CLI and API in several languages
Column family stores	Cassandra	Yes	Third Party APIs	Cassandra query language	CLI and API in several languages. Supports Thrift interface
	HBase	Yes	Yes	No, could be used with Hive	Java/Any Writer
	Amazon SimpleDB (Amazon service)	No	Yes	Amazon proprietary	Amazon proprietary
ocument stores	MongoDB	Yes	Yes	Proprietary	CLI and API in several languages.
	CouchDB	Yes	Yes	SQL like UnQL, under development	Memcached API + protocol (binary and ASCII) in several languages
	Couchbase Server	Yes	Yes	No	Memcached API + protocol (binary and ASCII) in several languages
Graph database	Neo4J	No	Yes	Cypher, Gremlin and SparQL	CLI and API in several languages.
	HyperGraphDB	No	Yes	SQL like Querying	Currently has Java API. Could be used with Scala
	Allegro Graph	No	Yes	SparQL and Prolog	API in several languagess

or alike versions such as CQL (Cassandra Query Language (CQL) v3.1.1 (2013)) provided by Cassandra and SparQL (Harris S, Seaborne A (2013)) by Allegro Graph (AllegroGraph 4.11 (2013)) and Neo4j.

INTRODUCTION TO CLOUD SYSTEMS

Understanding Cloud Computing Landscape

Cloud computing is a archetypal for enabling ubiquitous, on-demand, convenient network access to a distributed pool of configurable computing resources (e.g., network, servers, storage, applications, and services) that can be quickly provisioned and released with minimal administrative effort or service provider interaction (Mell P, Grance T (2013)).It represents a archetypal in which a computing infrastructure is regarded as a "cloud", from which individuals and businesses can access applications from anywhere in the world, on demand (Buyya R, Yeo CS, Venugopal S, Broberg J, Brandic I (2009)). Essential features of the cloud-computing archetypal, based on the U.S. National Institute of Standards and Technology (NIST), include (Mell P, Grance T (2013)):

- On-demand self-service, Providing a user to access cloud source services with no human interaction;
- Pooling of service source computing resources to serve various consumers;
- Rapid, Automatic, elastic provisioning of resources;
- Broad network access, Providing both, heterogeneous thin and thick client applications to access the services.
- Measured service in which resource usage is controlled and monitored.

On a High-level a cloud computing archetypal aims to provide aids in terms of ease of access through the Web, lesser up-front venture in infrastructure during deployment, higher scalability, lower operating costs, and reduced maintenance and business risks expenses (Buyya R, Yeo CS, Venugopal S, Broberg J, Brandic I (2009)).

Figure 12. A Typical Cloud Computing Scenario

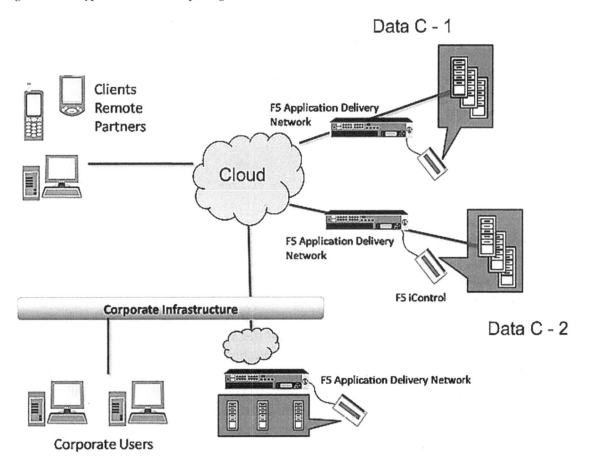

Characteristics of Cloud Systems

Cloud computing has also developed as a computational paradigm for on-call network access to a common pool of computing sources (e.g., storage, network, servers, applications, and services) that can be quickly provisioned with minimal administrative effort(Mell P, Grance T (2013)).

Cloud environments force new requirements to management of data; specifically, a cloud data management system needs to have:

- High performance and Scalability, as today's applications are suffering continuous growth in terms of the data storage, the throughput they should offer and the users they must serve.
- Elasticity, as cloud applications can be exposed to giant fluctuations in their access traffic patterns;
- Need to run on commodity servers that are heterogeneous in nature, Most Cloud environments are based on them;
- Fault tolerance, given that commodity infrastructure is much more prone to fail than high-end servers;
- Security and privacy, As the data storage on a third-party premises is on resources distributed among different consumers;
- Availability, as important applications have also been migrating to the cloud environment and cannot afford extended downtime.

Classification of Cloud Systems (SPI)

As the branch of cloud computing was developing, the systems emerged for the cloud were rapidly stratified into three main subsets of systems. Early on, these three sets of the cloud were developed by several cloud computing experts. The SPI model was formed based on this generic classification of cloud systems, and denotes:

- [S]oftware of the cloud
- [P]latform of the cloud
- [I]nfrastructure systems of the cloud

1. **Cloud Software Systems:** The first subset identifies applications developed and deployed on the Internet for the cloud, which are generally referred to as Software as a Service (SaaS). The focus user of this subset of systems is the end user. These cloud applications are majorly browser based with pre- defined features and scope, and they are accessed for a fee per usage metric predefined in the contract by the cloud SaaS resource provider. Some examples of SaaS are Google Apps like Google Docs and salesforce customer relationships management (CRM) system, SaaS is referred by end users as an smart alternative to desktop applications for various reasons
2. **Cloud Platform Systems:** The second subset of Cloud classification represents the cloud platform systems. In this category of systems, signified as Platform as a Service (PaaS), the supplier provides a platform of Application environments and application programming interfaces (APIs) that can be used for developing cloud applications. Generally, the users of this class of systems are application developers who use certain APIs to build, deploy, test and fine tune their applications on the cloud platform. Google's App Engine is one of the example of systems in this category.The final result

is a browser-based application for the end users. PaaS services provides an APIs for measuring and billing information. This permits software developers to more readily develop a consumption of resource based business model around their application. This support helps enforce and integrate the relationships between end users, developers.

3. **Cloud Infrastructure Systems:** The third subset of systems, based on the SPI classification model, offers infrastructure resources, such as storage, compute and communication services, in a non-rigid manner. These systems are signified as Infrastructure as a Service (IaaS). All software and associated source usage of a particular hardware user to be treated as a schedulable entity, is enabled by OS Virtualization, that is agnostic to the underlying physical sources for being used for scheduling. Therefore, OS Virtualization allows IaaS providers to manage control efficiently the utilization of physical resources by facilitating the exploitation of both statistical multiplexing and time division, while maintaining the flexible and familiar interface of each standard hardware computers and networks for the development of services using existing practices and software. This contract is particularly lucrative to IaaS providers given the underutilization of the high-speed and energy-hungry processors that constitute the infrastructure of data centers.

Hoff's Cloud Model

The SPI model and the UCSB-IBM cloud ontology inspired Christofer Hoff to organize an online discussion and collaboration between various cloud computing experts to develop an ontology upon the earlier archetypes. Figure 13 depicts the Hoff's cloud model. It presents a new cloud ontology in more detail. This model emphasizes on analyzing cloud services: IaaS, PaaS, and SaaS. The model further divides the *IaaS* layer to various other components. Data center provides, which include space power, is the very first component. The second component is the Hardware in the IaaS layer, consisting of data storage compute node, and network subcomponents. The next component is Abstraction that abridges the hardware through systems like grid, VM monitors and cluster utilities. Core connectivity and delivery is the next component, offering the various services like, authentication services and DNS services enabling the systems utilizing the IaaS layer. Hoff's cloud model's abstraction component connectivity and delivery components are interleaving; hence they are closely interdependent on services offered by each other. The API component offers the management services also a simple interface to the successive layer in the cloud. GoGrid CloudCenter API is one of the example systems, that implements this API sub-layer. PaaS is the next layer in Hoff's model. It is constituted of one sub-layer that offers the integration services in the cloud. Several services are provided by this sub-layer like database, authentication and querying services.

The SaaS layer in Hoff's model is auxiliary broken down into various components and sub- layers. The cloud application data sub-layer is shown to consist of the metadata describing the real data, the actual data, and its constituents, which can be in an unstructured or structured form. The SaaS layer's application component is categorized into three sub-categories: web applications, native applications and embedded applications. A native application can be a referred as a desktop application that uses a cloud service. A web application is a cloud application that is read via the web browser. At last, an implanted application is a cloud application that is embedded into another application. The two last sub-layers in Hoff's model's SaaS layer are the presentation sub-layers and the applications' API. Hoff's model can be further divided into the presentation sub-layers into video presentation, data presentation and voice presentation, recognizing the various forms of cloud data presentations. As portrayed in Figure 13, Hoff's

Figure 13. The Hoff's Cloud Ontology

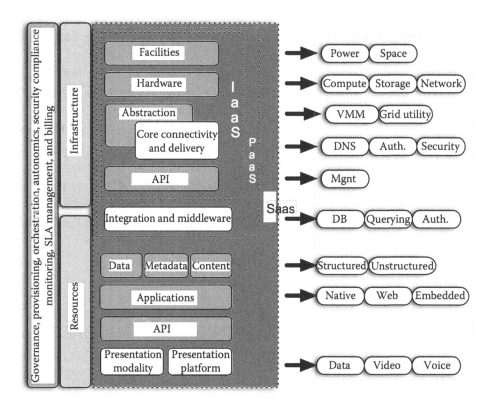

model addresses more details of the composition of the cloud. The amplified detail shows additional challenges and aspects to cloud computing; Moreover, it comes at the cost of simplicity. Nevertheless, the two cloud archetypes detailed in this paper are regarded complementary and depict various viewpoints of the new emerging cloud computing field

UCSB-IBM Cloud Ontology

The UCSB-IBM cloud ontology was developed through a collaboration effort between industry (IBM T.J. Watson Research Center) and academia (University of California, Santa Barbara) in an endeavor to understand the cloud computing topography. The main goal of this effort was to provide the evaluation of the cloud computing area as well as to progress in adopting the cloud computing area and the educational efforts in teaching. In this classification of cloud ontology, the inventors used the basic principle of composability from a Service-Oriented Architecture (SOA) to categorize the various layers of the cloud. Composability in SOA is the ability to assemble and coordinate a collection of services to form services composite in nature. In this viewpoint, cloud services can also be composed of multiple other cloud services.

As per the principle of composability, the cloud model of UCSB-IBM is classified into five layers. Each layer incorporates one or more cloud services. Cloud services are part of the same layer if they have a corresponding level of abstraction, as apparent by their targeted clients. For example, all cloud platforms (also known as cloud software environments) target programmers, while cloud applications target end clients. Therefore, cloud platforms would be categorized in a different layer than cloud applications. In the UCSB-IBM model, the five layers are composed of a cloud stack. In this model, one cloud layer is considered higher in the cloud stack depending on the services it offers can be composed from the services that belong to the underlying child layer.

There is a similarity in the first three layers of the UCSB-IBM cloud and SPI classification, except that the infrastructure layer is broken into three components. The three components that compose the UCSB-IBM infrastructure layer are computational resources, storage, and communications. Brief Explanation of the five layers are as follows:

1. **Applications (SaaS):** The first layer is similar to the SPI model and is referred as the cloud application layer. It is the supreme visible layer to the end consumers of the cloud. Generally, consumers access the services offered by this component using the browser via web based portals and are charged minimum amount to use them.
2. **Cloud Software Environment(PaaS):** The second layer after SaaS is the cloud software environment layer (also referred as software platform layer). The consumers of the second layer are cloud applications' developers, deploying and implementing their applications on the cloud. The service offered by cloud systems in this layer is normally dubbed to as "Platform as a Service (PaaS)".
3. **Cloud Software Infrastructure:** The third layer after PaaS is the cloud software infrastructure layer. This layer's ontology is more unique from the SPI ontology. This layer is composed of three sub-components described below.
    a. **Computational Resources:** Most frequently used form for providing computational resources to cloud users at this layer are VMs. The enabler technology for this cloud layer is OS Virtualization, allowing the consumers extraordinary flexibility in configuration while

Figure 14. UCSB-IBM Cloud Computing Classification Model depicted as five layers with three constituents to the cloud infrastructure layer

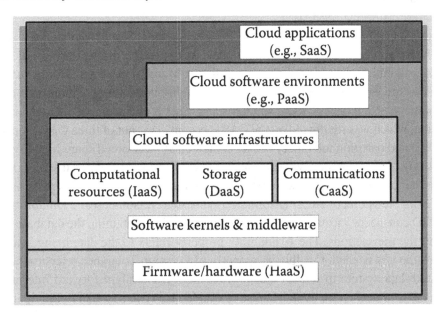

shielding the physical infrastructure data centre of the provider. These services are referred as *IaaS*.

b. **Storage:** Data storage is the second Infrastructure resource that allows consumers to store their data at remotely located disks and access them from any place at any given point of time. Data-Storage as a Service (*DaaS*) is the term used for such a service and it provides cloud applications scalability beyond their limited servers.

c. **Communication:** Quality of service (*QoS*) for network communication should be guaranteed for cloud systems, communication is an important sub-component of the cloud infrastructure. Communication as a Service (*CaaS*) surfaced to support such consumer needs with dynamic provisioning of virtual overlays for traffic isolation, network security, dedicated bandwidth, communication encryption, guaranteed message delay limits and network monitoring.

4. **Software Kernel Layer:** Basic software management for the physical servers is provided by the software kernel layer. Contrasting from the SPI ontology, the UCSB-IBM ontology overtly identifies the software used to manage the hardware resources and its prevailing, choices instead of converging solely on VM instances and how they are used. At this layer, a software kernel is deployed as an OS kernel, VM monitor, hypervisor, and/ or clustering middleware. Typically, grid computing applications were installed and run on the layer with multiple interconnected clusters of machines.

5. **Cloud Hardware/Firmware:** The last but not the least, bottom layer of the cloud mound in the UCSB-IBM ontology is the real switches and physical hardware that define the backbone of the cloud. Consumers of this cloud layer are typically big enterprises with humungous IT requirements in need of sub-renting Hardware as a Service (*HaaS*). Morgan Stanley's sublease agreement with IBM in 2004 is one of the early example of HaaS.

NOSQL AND CLOUD ASSIMILATION

The CAP Theorem

To facilitate storage and processing of enormous datasets, a widely employed strategy is to divide the data and store the partitions across various server nodes. Also these partitions can be replicated in several servers for data availability, even in case of server failures. Many modern data stores, such as BigTable and Cassandra use strategies to implement scalable and high-availability solutions that can be utilized in cloud environments. Nonetheless, these solutions and other replicated networked data stores have an critical restriction, which was reinforced by the CAP theorem: Two out of three CAP properties (consistency, availability, and partition tolerance) can be contented by networked shared-data systems at once.

As interpreted in CAP, Consistency is equivalent to having a single updated instance of the data unit. Therefore, consistency (from CAP viewpoint) has a different meaning to and depicts only a subset of consistency as from viewpoint of ACID (Atomicity, Consistency, Isolation and Durability) transactions of RDBMS. ACID consistency usually refers to the capability of maintaining the database in a consistent state throughout the transactions. The Availability property refers to the data being available to serve a request at the time it is needed. Finally, the property of Partition Tolerance refers to the ability of the networked shared-data system to tolerate network sectors. The straight forward interpretation of the CAP theorem is to ruminate a distributed data store divided into two sectors of participant nodes; if the

Figure 15. The CAP Theorem Representation

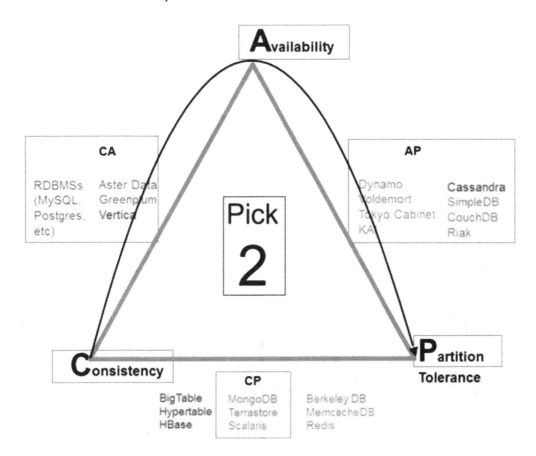

data store rejects all write requests in both partitions, it can be stated as consistent, but it is not available. In contrast, if both (or one) of the partitions admits write requests, the data store is available, but hypothetically inconsistent.

Instead of the relative simplicity of its conclusion, the CAP theorem has had critical implications and has originated a great diversity of distributed data stores focusing to explore the trade-offs amongst the three properties. More granularly, the challenges of RDBMS in managing Big Data and the use of distributed systems techniques in reference of the CAP theorem led to the emergence of new classes of database called NoSQL and NewSQL.

DATA MANAGEMENT IN CLOUD ENVIRONMENTS

Data Consistency

One of the main drivers of the NoSQL movement is scalability. As such, it encompasses distributed system failover, coordination, resource management and several other capabilities. It sounds like a big branch, and it is. Although it can scarcely be said that NoSQL movement got fundamentally different techniques into distributed data processing, it instantiated an avalanche of real-life trials of different combinations of protocols, practical studies and algorithms. These developments slowly highlighted a system of relevant database building slabs with proven practical efficiency. Historically, NoSQL paid a lot of focus to tradeoffs amongst fault-tolerance, consistency and performance to serve low-latency or highly available applications and geographically distributed systems. Fundamentally, these tradeoffs spin around data consistency, so this section is focused on data replication and data repair. It is well known and fairly obvious that in environments with probable network partitions, geographically distributed systems or delays it is not commonly possible to maintain high availability with no sacrificing consistency, as isolated sections of the database have to operate autonomously in case of network partition. This is often defined as the CAP theorem.

Figure 16. Data Consistency in Distributed Computing

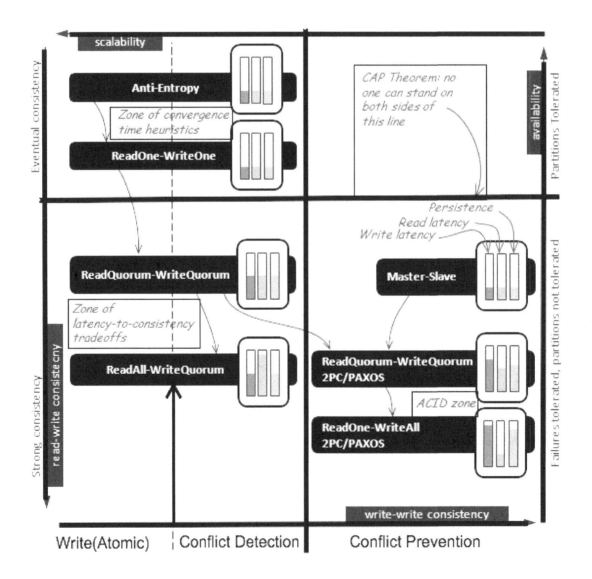

A much more complicated property than the previous ones is Consistency, so we have to discuss different scenarios in detail. It is beyond the scope of the paper to go deeply into concurrency models and theoretical consistency, hence we use a lean framework of simple properties.

- **Read-Write Consistency:** From the perspective of read-write, the main goal of a database is to minimize a replica conjunction time (in simple words how long does it take to propagate to all replicas with a update) and promise eventual consistency. Besides these weak promises, one can be involved in stronger consistency properties:
  - **Read-After-Write Consistency:** The effect of a operation write on data item X, will always be seen by a successive operation read on X.
  - **Read-After-Read Consistency:** If some user reads the value of a data item X, any successive operation- read on X will always result in same or a more recent value.
- **Write-Write Consistency**: Write-write conflicts occur in a case of database partition, so a database should either handle these conflicts somehow or promise that parallel writes will not be handled by different partitions. From this viewpoint, a database can provide several consistency models:
  - **Atomic Writes:** An API where a write request can only be an individual and independent atomic assignment of a value, one possible method to avoid write-write conflicts is to select the "most recent" version of every entity. This promises that all nodes will end up with the exact same version of data unrelatedly to the order of updates which can be altered by network delays and failures. Data version can be mentioned by a application-specific metric timestamps. For example, this approach is used in Cassandra.
  - **Atomic Read-Modify-Write:** Database often receive a do a read-modify-write sequence request instead of unrelated atomic writes. If two users read the same version of data, transform it and write back in-parallel, the most recent update will silently override the first one as per the model of atomic writes. This characteristic can be semantically inappropriate A database can offer at least two approach:
    - **Conflict Prevention:** Read-modify-write can be thought as a one of transaction case, so consensus protocols like PAXOS or distributed locking are both a solution. This is a common technique that can offer both arbitrary isolated transactions and atomic read-modify-write semantics. An alternative approach is to avoid distributed concurrent writes entirely and re-direct all writes of a particular data item to a one global node (global master or shard master). To prevent conflicts, a database must ransom availability in scenario of network partitioning and stop all but one partition. This solutions is used in many systems with strong consistency guarantees (e.g. most MongoDB, RDBMSs, HBase).
    - **Conflict Detection:** A database keeps a track of concurrent conflicting updates. It either rollback one of the inconsistent updates or saves both versions for resolving on the user side. Concurrent updates are usually tracked by using vector clocks (which can be though as a common practice of the optimistic locking) or by saving an entire re-version history. This solution is used in systems like CouchDB, Riak, Voldemort.

Eventually Consistent Data Types

In the above section we worked with the assumption of two nodes always merging their versions of data. However, reconciliation of inconsistent updates is not a trivial task and it is surprisingly tough to make all replicas to join to a semantically true value. Deleted items can resurface in the Amazon Dynamo database, which is a well-known example, is that

Let us take a simple example that demonstrate the problem: a logically global counter and each database node can serve increment/decrement operations is maintained by a database. Although each node can preserve its own local counter as a single value which is scalar in nature, but these local counters cannot be used to merge by straight-forward addition/subtraction. Let's take an example: there are three nodes A, B, and C and operation of type increment was applied thrice, once per node. If A fetches value from B and updates it to the local copy, C fetches from B, C fetches from A, then C ends up with value 4 which is incorrect. One solution to overcome these issues is use of a vector clock like data structure and preserve a pair of counters for each node:

```
class Counter {
    int[] plus
    int[] minus
    int NODE_ID

    increment() {
        plus[NODE_ID]++
    }

    decrement() {
        minus[NODE_ID]++
    }

    get() {
        return sum(plus) - sum(minus)
    }

    merge(Counter other) {
        for i in 1..MAX_ID {
            plus[i] = max(plus[i], other.plus[i])
            minus[i] = max(minus[i], other.minus[i])
        }
    }
}
```

A very similar approach is used by Cassandra to provide counters as a part of its functionality. It is easy to design eventually consistent data structures with increased complexity that can leverage either operation-based or state-based replication principles. For example, A data structure contains a list of such structures that includes:

1. Counters (decrement-increment-operations)
2. Sets (add-remove operations)
3. Graphs (removeEdge/removeVertex- addEdge/addVertex operations)
4. Lists (insertAt(position)-removeAt(position) operations)

However, eventually consistent data types are generally impose performance overheads and are limited in functionality.

Distributed Algorithms in Cloud Data Management

This section focuses on algorithms that manage data placement inside a distributed data store. These algorithms are answerable for mapping between migration of data from one node to another, data items and physical nodes, and allocation of global resources like RAM in the database.

Data Placement: Rebalancing

Let us start with a meek protocol that is focused to provide outage-free data migration amongst cluster nodes. This task arises in scenarios like cluster extension (new nodes are added), failover (few node goes done), or act of rebalancing (data is unevenly distributed across the nodes). Consider a scenario that is depicted in section (A) of the figure below – there are 3 nodes and all nodes contain a section of data (Assumption: A key-value data model with no loss of generality) that is distributed amongst the nodes according to a random data placement policy (Figure 17).

If we do not have a database that offers data rebalancing internally, we will probably deploy multiple instances of the data store to every node as shown in section (B) of the figure above. This enables us to execute a manual cluster extension by turning a discrete instance off, copying it to another new node, and turning it on, as shown in section (C). Though an automatic database has the ability to track every record separately, many systems inclusive of Oracle, MongoDB, Coherence, and Redis Cluster utilize the described method internally, i.e. group records into shards (minimal units of migration for sake of efficiency). Obviously, number of shards should be quite enormous relative to the number of nodes to offer an even load distribution. An outage-free shard migration can be achieved based on the simple protocol that routes client from the exporting to the importing node throughout the migration of shard.

Sharing and Replication in Dynamic Environments

The next query we have to focus is to the mapping of records to the physical nodes. A simple solution is to have a table of key ranges with each range being assigned to a node or to use functions like NodeID = hash(key) % TotalNodes. Though, modulus-based hashing does not explicitly handle cluster reconfiguration as the removal or addition of nodes leads to complete reshuffling of data throughout the cluster. It is difficult to handle replication and failover, as a result of this.

There are different approaches to increase the basic solution from the failover and replication perspectives. Consistent hashing is the most famous technique of all. There are many definitions of the consistent hashing technique on the web, so we provide a basic description just for the sake of completeness.

Consistent hashing is nothing but a mapping schema of key-value stores – Mapping of keys (hashed keys) to physical nodes. Hashed keys is an structured space of binary strings of a definite length, hence

Figure 17. Data Rebalancing through application of Data Migration Technique

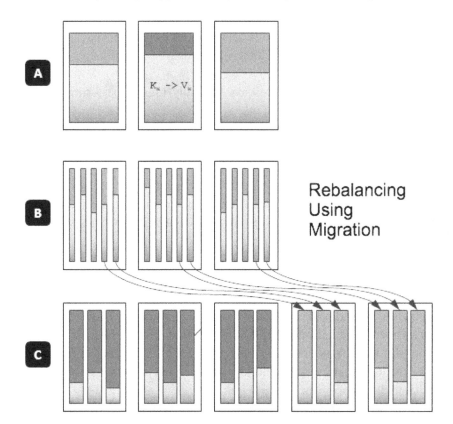

each range of keys is initialized to some node as depicted in the figure (A) for three nodes, namely, A, B, and C. To deal with replication, it is expedient to close a key space into a ring and traversing it clockwise till all replica mapping is completed, as shown in the figure (B). Item Y will be placed on node B as its key points to B's range, Initial and first replica will be placed on C, second replica will be placed on A and so on.

The advantage of this schema is inexpensive addition and removal of a node as it causes data to be rebalanced only in neighboring sectors. As depicted in the figures (C), addition of the node D alters only item X but not Y. Similar to this, failure (or removal) of the node B alters Y and the replica of X, but not X itself. However, the dark side of this advantage is vulnerability to overloads – where all the labor of rebalancing is managed by neighbors only which makes them to replicate high volumes of data. This problem can be assuaged by mapping each node not to a 1 range, but to a collection of ranges, as it shown in the figure (D). This is a collateral damage – it removes skew in loads during rebalancing, but keeps the overall rebalancing effort low in relation with module-based mapping.

Maintaining a coherent complete view of a hash ring may be difficult in huge deployments. Although it is not an issue for data stores due to relatively small clusters, it is noteworthy to study how data placement was merged with the routing of network in peer-to-peer networks. Chord algorithm is a decent example of trades completeness, of the ring view by a single node to efficiency of the query routing. The Chord algorithm's approach is similar to consistent hashing in the sense that it uses a ring based approach for key to node mapping.

Figure 18. Consistent hashing

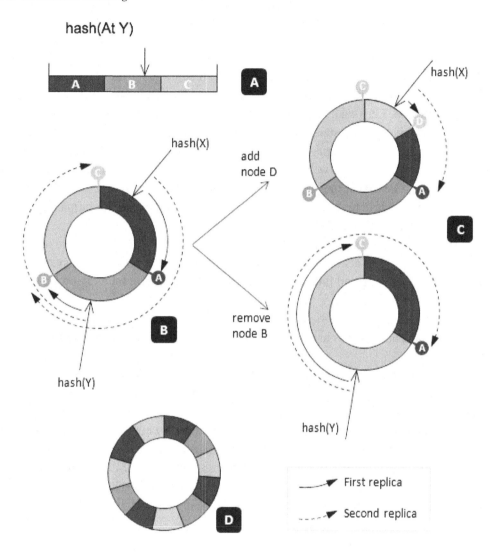

Failure Detection

Failure detection is a building block of any distributed system with fault tolerance. Initially all failure detection protocols are derived from a "heartbeat message" which is a straight forward concept – monitored components sporadically send a heartbeat message to the monitoring process and this process censuses monitored components. An absence of heartbeat messages for a prolonged period is deduced as a failure. However, real distributed systems enforce a number of additional rules that should be addressed during failure detection:

- **Automatic Adaptation:** The process of failure exposure should be robust to the temporary network delays and failures, workload or bandwidth and dynamic changes in the cluster topology.

This is a fundamentally tough problem because there is no solution to distinguish crashed process from a temporary loaded slow one. As a result of this failure detection is always a quid pro quo between a failure detection time and the deceptive-alarm probability. Parameters of this balance should be tuned automatically and dynamically.

- **Flexibility:** At Initial glance, failure detector should result a Boolean output, a registered watch process considered to be either live or dead. Nonetheless, it can be noted that Boolean output is not sufficient in practice. Let's take an example that is similar to Hadoop MapReduce. A distributed application consisting of a master and additional slave workers. The master has a set of jobs and submits them to the slaves. The master can differentiate various "degrees of failure". If the master starts to report that some slave went down, it stops to submit new jobs to this slave. In the next step, if there are no heartbeat messages after a certain time period, the master resubmits jobs that were running on this slave to the other slaves. To conclude, the master is completely assertive that the slave is down and releases all conforming resources.

- **Scalability and Robustness:** Failure detection as a routine process should scale up as well as the system should scale up. It also should be stout and stable, i.e. all nodes in the system should have a update vision of running and failed processes even in case of communication issues.

A possible solution to address the first two requirements is known as Phi Accrual Failure Detector which is used with some adaptations in Cassandra. The elementary workflow is as follows and demonstrated in figure 19.

For each registered watch resource, Detector collects onset times T_i of heartbeat messages. Mean and variance are computed constantly for the recent onset times (on a sliding window of size W) in the block Statistics Estimation.

Assuming that circulation of onset times is known (the figure 19 contains a formula for normal distribution), one can calculate the probability of the recent heartbeat delay (difference between the current time t_now and the last onset time Tc). This probability is a measure of confidence in a failure. The value can be extrapolated using the logarithmic function for usability's sake. In the first case output 1 describes the likeness of the error is about 10%, output 2 means 1% and so on.

CONCLUSION

In recent years, cloud computing has developed as a computational exemplar that can be used to meet the continuously increasing processing and storage requirements of today's applications. This paper has determined on the storage aspect of cloud computing systems, precisely, NoSQL and NewSQL data stores. These elucidations have offered themselves as alternatives to traditional relational databases, capable of managing huge volumes of data by exploring the cloud environment. Specifically, this paper has reviewed NoSQL and NewSQL data stores with the aim of providing a viewpoint on the field, providing direction to practitioners and researchers to choose apt storage solutions, and recognizing challenges and opportunities in the field. An assessment among the most prominent solutions was conducted on a number of dimensions, including querying capabilities data models, security and scaling attributes. Scenarios and use cases in which NoSQL and NewSQL databases have been used were discussed and the suitability of several solutions for different sets of applications was judged. The discussion of the scenarios, as well as

Figure 19. Failure Detection Computation

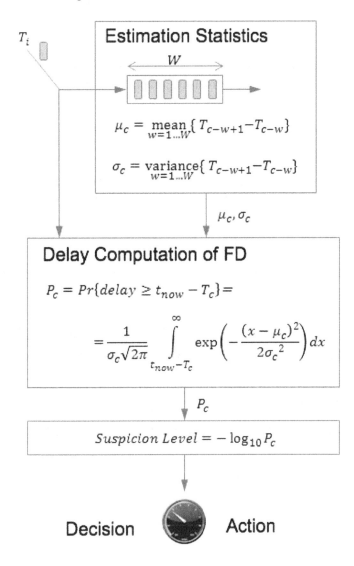

the comparative study of data stores, will assist practitioners in selecting the best storage alternatives for their needs. Additionally, this work has verified challenges in the domain, including inconsistency, sparse comparison, terminology diversity, limited documentation, sparse comparison, occasional immaturity of solutions, benchmarking criteria, lack of support and non-existence of a standardized query language.

REFERENCES

AllegroGraph 4.11. (2013). Retrieved from http://www.franz.com/agraph/allegrograph/

Apache CouchD. B. (2013). Retrieved from http://couchdb.apache.org/

Apache HBase. (2013). Retrieved from http://hbase.apache.org/

Auradkar, A., Botev, C., Das, S., De Maagd, D., Feinberg, A., Ganti, P., ... Zhang, J. (2012). Data Infrastructure at LinkedIn. *Proceedings of 2012 IEEE 28th International Conference on Data Engineering*, 1370–1381. 10.1109/ICDE.2012.147

Buyya, R., Yeo, C. S., Venugopal, S., Broberg, J., & Brandic, I. (2009). Cloud computing and emerging IT platforms: Vision, hype, and reality for delivering computing as the 5th utility. *Future Gen Computer System, 25*(6), 599–616. 10.1016/j.future.2008.12.001

Cattell R (2010). Scalable SQL and NoSQL Data Stores. *ACM SIGMOD Record, 39*(4), 12–27. 10.1145/1978915.1978919

Chang, F., Dean, J., Ghemawat, S., Hsieh, W., Wallach, D., Burrows, M., ... Gruber, R. (2006). Bigtable: A distributed structured data storage system. *7th OSDI, 26*, 305–314.

Corbett, J. C., Dean, J., Epstein, M., Fikes, A., Frost, C., Furman, J. J., ... Woodford, D. (2012). Spanner - Google's globally-distributed database. *Osdi, 2012*, 1–14.

DeCandia, G., Hastorun, D., Jampani, M., Kakulapati, G., Lakshman, A., Pilchin, A., ... Vogels, W. (2007). Dynamo: Amazon's highly available Key-value store. *ACM SIGOPS Operating Syst Rev, 41*, 205. 10.1145/1323293.1294281

Gilbert S, Lynch N (2002). Brewer's conjecture and the feasibility of consistent, available, partition-tolerant web services. *ACM SIGACT News, 33*(2), 51–59. 10.1145/564585.564601

Harris, S., & Seaborne, A. (2013). *SPARQL 1.1 Query Language*. Retrieved from http://www.w3.org/TR/2013/REC-sparql11-query-20130321/

Hecht, R., & Jablonski, S. (2011). NoSQL evaluation: A use case oriented survey. *Proc 2011 Int Conf Cloud Serv Computing*, 336–341. 10.1109/CSC.2011.6138544

Hecht, R., & Jablonski, S. (2011). NoSQL evaluation: A use case oriented survey. *Proc 2011 Int Conf Cloud Serv Computing*, 336–341. 10.1109/CSC.2011.6138544

Klophaus, R. (2010). Core: Building distributed applications without shared state. In *Proceedings of CUFP'10 - ACM SIGPLAN Commercial Users of Functional Programming*. New York, NY: ACM Press. 10.1145/1900160.1900176

Konstantinou, I., Angelou, E., Boumpouka, C., Tsoumakos, D., & Koziris, N. (2011). *On the elasticity of NoSQL databases over cloud management platforms*. ACM Press. doi:10.1145/2063576.2063973

Lakshman, A., & Malik, P. (2010). Cassandra: a decentralized structured storage system. *ACM SIGOPS Operating Syst Rev, 44*(2), 35–40. 10.1145/1773912.1773922

Language, C. Q. (CQL) v3.1.1. (2013). Retrieved from http://cassandra.apache.org/doc/cql3/CQL.html

Mell, P., & Grance, T. (2013). *The NIST definition of cloud computing*. NIST special publication 800–145. Retrieved from http://csrc.nist.gov/publications/nistpubs/800-145/SP800-145.pdf

Memcached. (2013). Retrieved from http://memcached.org/

MongoD. B. (2013). Retrieved from http://www.mongodb.org/

Murty, J. (2008). *SQS, FPS, and SimpleDB*. O'Reilly Media Inc.

Oracle BerkeleyD. B. 12c. (2013). Retrieved from http://www.oracle.com/technetwork/products/berkeleydb/overview/index.html

Pritchett D (2008). BASE: An ACID Alternative. *Queue, 6*, 48–55. doi:10.1145/1394127.1394128

Redis. (2013). Retrieved from http://redis.io/

Venters, W., & Whitley, E.A. (2012). A critical review of cloud computing: researching desires and realities. *J Info Technol, 27*, 179–197. 10.1057/jit.2012.17

Chapter 16
Fast Data vs. Big Data With IoT Streaming Analytics and the Future Applications

A. Jayanthiladevi
Jain University, India

Surendararavindhan
Vignan's University, India

Sakthivel
KSR College of Technology, India

ABSTRACT

Big data depicts information volume – petabytes to exabytes in organized, semi-organized, and un-structured information that can possibly be broken down for data. Fast data are facts streaming into applications and computing environments from hundreds of thousands to millions of endpoints. Fast data is totally different from big data. There is no question that we will continue generating large volumes of data, especially with the wide variety of handheld units and internet-connected devices expected to grow exponentially. Data streaming analytics is vital for disruptive applications. Streaming analytics permits the processing of terabytes of data in memory. This chapter explores fast data and big data with IoT streaming analytics.

INTRODUCTION

Data Is Fast Before It Is Big

Enterprises require an innovation stack that not exclusively is equipped for ingesting and examining fast streams of incoming data,, additionally can enhance live surges of fast data with systematic experiences gathered from big information stores – all as fast data enters the channel. Databases used to deal with fast data and big data are for the most part assembled into two camps: online investigative preparing

DOI: 10.4018/978-1-5225-5972-6.ch016

frameworks (OLAP), and online value-based handling frameworks (OLTP). How about we take a gander at the contrasts between these two ways to deal with data management.

IoT (Internet of Things) is an advanced automation and analytics system which exploits networking, sensing, big data, and artificial intelligence technology to deliver complete systems for a product or service. These systems allow greater transparency, control, and performance when applied to any industry or system.IoT systems have applications across industries through their unique flexibility and ability to be suitable in any environment. They enhance data collection, automation, operations, and much more through smart devices and powerful enabling technology (BhagyaRaju et al.,(2017).

IoT has become so vital in our daily life and it is going to create a big impact in the near future. For example, solutions can be provided instantly for the traffic flows, reminding about the vehicle maintenance, reduce energy consumption. Monitoring sensors will diagnose pending maintenance issues, and even prioritize maintenance crew schedules for repair equipment. Data analysis systems will help metropolitan and cosmopolitan cities to function easily in terms of traffic management, waste management, pollution control, law enforcement and other major functions efficiently. Considering it to the next level, linked devices can help the people personally like you get an alert from the refrigerator reminding you to shop some vegetables when the vegetable tray is empty, your home security systems enables you to open the door for some guest with help of connected devices(IoT) explained by Kundhavai et al.,(2016).

Since there is a massive growth in number of devices day by day, the amount of data generated would also be enormous. Here is where Big Data and IoT go hand in hand. Big Data manages the enormous amount of data generated using its technologies. The Internet of Things (IoT) and big data are two vital subjects in commercial, industrial, and many other applications.

The name IoT was framed in approximately a decade ago and refers to the world of machines or devices connected to the Internet, by which a large amount of big data is collected, stored and managed. Big data additionally refers to the analysis of this generated data to produce useful results. The main motivating power behind the IoT and big data has been the collection and analysis of data related to consumer activities in order to find out why and what customers buy

NECESSITY OF IOT AND BIG DATA IMPLEMENTATION

IoT will enable big data, big data needs analytics, and analytics will improve processes for more IoT devices. IoT and big data can be used to improve various functions and operations in diverse sectors. Both have extended their capabilities to wide range of areas. Figure 1 shows the areas of big data produced. Some or the other way, data is produced through connected devices.

The important basis behind why to implement IoT and big data are: Analytical monitoring, More Uptime, Lower reject rates, Higher throughput, Enhanced safety, Efficient use of labor, Enable mass customization, Analyze the activities for real-time marketing, Improved situational alertness, Improved quality, Sensor-driven decision analytics, Process optimization, Optimized resource utilization, Instant control and response in complex independent systems.

The above are some possible reasons to implement IoT and Big data. As the requirements of both the technologies go hand in hand, a proper improved system is needed to overcome the challenges they pose. Many companies strive to meet the challenges and take possible steps to overcome them.

Figure 1.

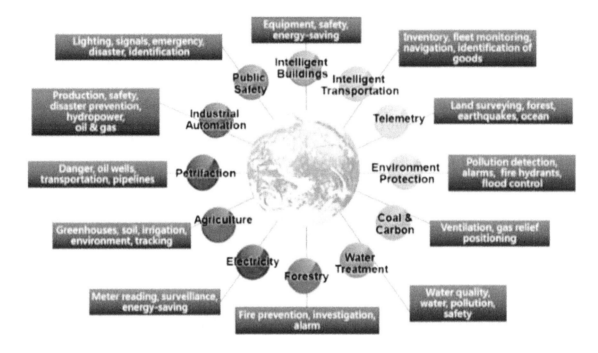

IMPACTS OF IOT ON BIG DATA

IoT is a network consisting of physical devices, which are also implanted with sensors, electronics, and software, thereby allowing these devices to exchange data. This ultimately allows better incorporation between real world physical entities and computer-operated systems. IoT is the next big thing impacting our lives in major ways and number of factors. Technologies like Column-oriented databases, SQL in Hadoop, Hive, Wibidata, PLATFORA, SkyTree, Storage Technologies, Schema-less databases, or NoSQL databases, Streaming Big Data analytics, Big Data Lambda Architecture, Map-reduce, PIG, etc., helps in dealing with the enormous amount of data generated by IoT and other sources.

The main factors that big data is impacted by IoT are:

Big Data Storage

At basis, the key necessities of big data storage are that it can handle very huge amounts of data and continuous balancing to keep up with expansion and that it can provide the input/output operations per second (IOPS) necessary to deliver data to analytics tools. The data is of different form and format and thus, a datacenter for storing such data must be able to handle the load in changeable forms. Obviously IoT has a direct impact on the storage infrastructure of big data. Collection of IoT Big Data is a challenging task because filtering redundant data is mandatorily required. After Collection, the data has to transfer over a network to a data center and maintained. Many companies started to use Platform as a Service (PaaS) to handle their infrastructure based on IT. It helps in developing and running web applications. By this way, Big data can be managed efficiently without the need of expanding their infrastructural facilities to some extent. IoT Big Data Storage is certainly a challenging task as the data grows in a faster rate than expected. Niranjana et al., (2015)

Data Security Issues

The IoT has given new security challenges that cannot be controlled by traditional security methods. Facing IoT security issues require a shift. For instance, how do you deal with a situation when the television and security camera at your home are fitted with unknown Wi-Fi access. Few security problems are:

1. Secure computations in distributed environment
2. Secure data centers
3. Secure transactions
4. Secure filtering of redundant data
5. Scalable and secure data mining and analytics
6. Access control
7. Imposing real time security, etc., (Marc Jonathan Blitz et al., (2013).

A multi-layered security system and proper network system will help avoid attacks and keep them from scattering to other parts of the network. An IoT system should follow rigorous network access control policies and then allowed to connect. Software-defined networking (SDN) technologies should be used for point-to-point and point-tomultipoint encryption in combination with network identity and access policies.

Big Data Analytics

Data analytics is the science of examining raw data with the idea of coming to conclusions about that information. Data analytics is used in many industries to allow them to make better business decisions and in the sciences to verify or disprove existing models or theories. IoT Big data analytics is very much needed to end up in a optimized decision. Big data analytics will help you understand the business value it brings and how different industries are applying it to deal with their sole business necessities. According to the Gartner IT dictionary, Big Data is variety of information assets, high-volume, and high-velocity and, innovative forms of information processing for enhanced approach and decision making. Volume refers to the size of data. Data sources can be social media, sensor and machine-generated data, structured and unstructured networks, and much more (Radha, et al., 2017). Enterprises are flooded with terabytes of big data. Variety refers to the number of forms of data. Big data deals with numbers, 3D data and log files, dates, strings, text, video, audio, click streams. Velocity refers to the speed of data processing. The rate at which data streams in from sources such as mobile devices, click streams, machine-to-machine processes is massive and continuously fast moving. Big data mining and analytics helps to reveal hidden patterns, unidentified correlations, and other business information.

Impact on Day to Day Living

IoT Big Data is slowly redefining our lives. Let us consider a few examples of our lives. At work, the cctv camera in the canteen estimating the time you spend there. The class room sensors can find out how much time you spend in writing on the board. This can be just to measure the productivity of an employee. At home, the home theatre playing the favorite movie of ours as soon as you switch on the television, smart devices could save a lot of power and money by automatically switching off electrical devices when you leave home. A smart wrist band tied to the elder people at home intimates the nearby hospital if they fall sick. The above said is going to happen in a very short time because of the rapid development in IoT and Big Data technologies.

CHALLENGES OF IOT BIG DATA

Major challenges that can fetch momentous rewards when they are solved.

1. Huge data volumes
2. Difficulty in data collection
3. Incompatible standards
4. New security threats
5. No reliability in the data
6. Fundamental shifts in business models
7. Huge amount of data to analyze
8. A rapidly evolving privacy landscape

The above points are some of the challenges that IoT big data faces. The rate in data growth in expanding every second, storage in a big challenge, processing and maintaining is even more tedious. The tools that are developed to manage the both technologies are day by day changing as per the requirements. No doubt, both technologies are going to play a major role in the information technology field.

FAST DATA IN IOT

Fast Data is not a new concept. It has been around before Big Data and IoT came into the picture. Data partitioning, data warehousing and scaling servers were the steps taken to speed up data retrieval prior to IoT and Big Data. The writing on the wall: Big Data volume in no longer the main criteria for gathering quality data. Companies are now vying to build better new platforms to solve data warehousing tasks and in processing analytics.

1. In the modern tech context, Fast Data is about information in real-time or the ability to obtain data insights while it is generated. That is why streaming data is so happening now. Data streams now occur at thousands of times per second, what is now called Fast Data. Brundu, et al.,(2016)
2. The truth is, many companies with big data still don't know what is to be done with it. Most companies use Hadoop for their data storage. Fast Data origins can be linked to Big Data variety, velocity and volume concepts. Fast Data is not just about high frequency data intake. It is about data processing in real-time, arriving at quick action-based results and taking decisions based on these results. All this while dealing with complex analytics. Conclusively, Big Data can only be effective if organizations interpret Big Data findings in real-time.

The Fast/Big Data Channel

Big data systems are centered on a data lake or warehouse, a storage location in which an enterprise stores and analyzes its data. This component is a critical element of a data channel that must capture all information. The big data platform's core requirements are to store historical data that will be sent or shared with other data management products, and also to support frameworks for executing jobs directly against the data in the data lake.Fast data systems include a fast in-memory database component. These Fast data databases have a number of critical requirements, which include the ability to ingest and interact with live data feeds, make decisions on each event in the feeds, and apply real-time analytics to provide visibility into fast streams of incoming data explained by DeFries et al(2010).

The Fast data/big data channel supports fast incoming streams of live data created in a multitude of new end points. It operationalizes the use of that data in applications, and exports data to a data lake or data warehouse for deep, long-term storage and analytics. The Fast/Big data channel unifies applications, analytics, and application interaction across multiple functions, products, and disciplines.

The Future of Applications

Applications are the most purpose of entry for data streaming into the enterprise. They are the initial assortment purpose for data, and are accountable for interactions – personalized offers, decisions, updates to balances or accounts, changes to the distribution of power in electrical grid. Application interaction has identical characteristics as those delineated for fast data—it ingests events, interacts with data for choices, uses period analytics to reinforce the expertise, and exports the information for storage and additional analysis. The application is both the organization's and the consumer's "interface" to the data. Applications are responsible for interaction. The greatest value from applications and the data they process comes with interactions that are accurately performed in real time. Fast data systems make better, faster real-time applications. The application is each the organization's and therefore the consumer's "interface" to the data. Applications are responsible for interaction. The best worth from applications and therefore the data they method comes with interactions that are accurately performed in real time. Fast data systems build higher, quicker time period applications. Here are the five steps I propose as part of your fast data strategy: Ashton et al.,(2009)

Figure 2. Fast Data vs. Big Data

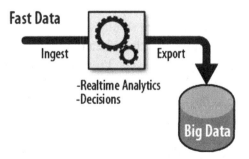

Fast Data: The Velocity Side of Big Data

- Identify your fast data opportunity
- Assess and leverage your existing infrastructure
- Understand the (business implications of) alternatives
- Get agreement on success criteria for project
- Prototype, pilot, refine
- Provide Visibility into Fast-Moving Data with Real-Time Analytics
- Real-time analytics analyze streams of incoming data, per-event, at ingestion. Analytic results are used in real-time to guide application interactions.
- Export Processed Data to Long-Term Analytics Systems
- Once Fast Data analytics are completed, the data moves through the channel for storage long-term analytical processing; data ingestion and export flow at the same rate.

DATA PROCESSING TIMELINESS

Picture an online shopping company that wants to recommend its products to a customer. Recommendations are based on the customer's latest purchases. Only, the shopping website can't make these recommendations fast enough. How soon in real-time can the website collect data, summarize and then provide the shopping options – preferably in real-time? Unless they want to lose the customer. This is where Fast Data comes in, adding immediacy to the proceedings. Timeliness and accuracy are two prime Fast Data attributes. Fast Data includes sampled recommendations, sensors that pass on instant trend changes and choices. When it comes to pinpointing loopholes or instances of inefficiency, go for Fast Data. Giusto, et al.,(2010)

DATA ANALYTICS

More focused analytics is now possible, thanks to Fast Data. Analytics enables customization of services or products. It enables better decision-making, leading to better customer service and faster fraud detection, among other things. The question you need to ask is, at what particular time do you go for analytics? The more you are able to analyze in real-time, the more easier it becomes to take action on the basis of analytic results. Eastman et al.,(2010)

STREAMING DATA ANALYTICS

Fast Data makes a critical difference in obtaining results within a limited time span. For example, why would you want information on a customer who has already left the store or website? Fast Data helps organizations make similar make-or-break decisions. Processing streaming data is a vital part of Fast Data. Making automated decisions based on streaming machine data is important for the process. You may call this streaming analytics. At the same time, human intervention in the automated decisions are necessary. That is why the automated dashboards and streaming data sources need to be interactive for that ever important human tweaking and final authorization.

Figure 3.

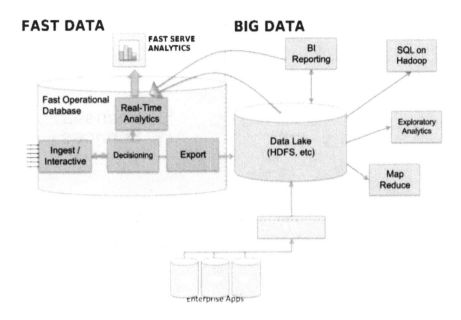

FAST DATA ARCHITECTURE

When we look at Fast Data architecture, it will feature real-time analytics, taking in information, and giving immediate results and resultant decisions. Instant, real-time solutions are possible if you integrate your Big Data system (consisting of a Hadoop database, SQL on Hadoop, MapReduce and related big data components) to the company's applications. This whole set up can then be connected to the Fast Data architecture as displayed in the illustration above.

FAST DATA USAGE

Elements like dashboards can be served quickly, with Fast Data usage. The operations systems can be constantly powered by instant analytics, the entire system thus working at a rapid pace. Building this big data dependent application combined with fast data capability applications can entirely change its efficiency. Architecture plays a key role here.

THE EMERGING BIG DATA (FAST DATA) STACK

Finally, Fast Data is Big Data that is constantly moving. Imagine a pipeline through which data is flowing in great speed. Here are the Emerging Big Data (Fast Data) Stack details:

Figure 4.

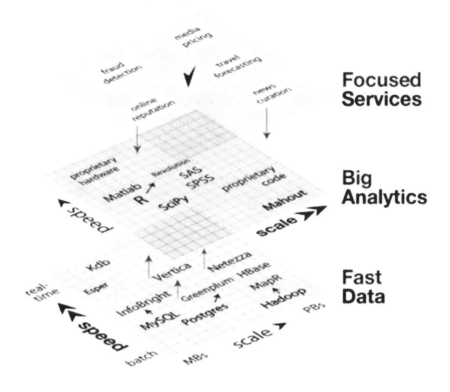

1.   The first level concerns focused services. It concerns applying key processes and functions to obtain significant value from streaming data. Fraud detection, travel forecasting and similar services can thus be availed faster.
2.   The second layer consists of real-time analytics based on the streaming data. The company's business logic is then put to use to make real-time decisions.
3.   In the Fast Data layer, the data is then exported for analytics and long term storage to Hadoop and other data storage options.Speed, real-time and accuracy are key elements of the entire stack.

Streaming is however just a part of the Fast Data solutions. OLTP databases are the in thing for processing streaming data. You can thus have speed and scale using an in-memory database, designed to handle data streaming at great speed. One popular Fast Data database is VoltDB.

The Challenge of Fast Streaming Data

When we talk about fast data, we're not measuring volume in the typical gigabytes, terabytes, and petabytes common to data warehouses. We're measuring volume in terms of time: the number of megabytes per second, gigabytes per hour, or terabytes per day. Fast data means velocity as well as volume -- thousands of events per second, millions of transactions per hour -- which gets to the core of the difference between big data and fast data. The challenge for today's businesses is to capture intelligence from streaming data while it's still live, before it ages and flows into the big data "lake" (Tomlinson et al., 2001).

Streaming Data?

Streaming Data is data that is generated continuously by thousands of data sources, which typically send in the data records simultaneously, and in small sizes (order of Kilobytes). Streaming data includes a wide variety of data such as log files generated by customers using your mobile or web applications, ecommerce purchases, in-game player activity, information from social networks, financial trading floors, or geospatial services, and telemetry from connected devices or instrumentation in data centers. This data needs to be processed sequentially and incrementally on a record-by-record basis or over sliding time windows, and used for a wide variety of analytics including correlations, aggregations, filtering, and sampling. Information derived from such analysis gives companies visibility into many aspects of their business and customer activity such as –service usage (for metering/billing), server activity, website clicks, and geo-location of devices, people, and physical goods –and enables them to respond promptly to emerging situations. For example, businesses can track changes in public sentiment on their brands and products by continuously analyzing social media streams, and respond in a timely fashion as the necessity arises.

Benefits of Streaming Data

Streaming data processing is beneficial in most scenarios where new, dynamic data is generated on a continual basis. It applies to most of the industry segments and big data use cases. Companies generally begin with simple applications such as collecting system logs and rudimentary processing like rolling min-max computations. Then, these applications evolve to more sophisticated near-real-time processing. Initially, applications may process data streams to produce simple reports, and perform simple actions in response, such as emitting alarms when key measures exceed certain thresholds. Eventually, those applications perform more sophisticated forms of data analysis, like applying machine learning algorithms, and extract deeper insights from the data. Over time, complex, stream and event processing algorithms, like decaying time windows to find the most recent popular movies, are applied, further enriching the insights. Kamilaris et al.,(2011).

Challenges in Working With Streaming Data

Streaming data processing requires two layers: a storage layer and a processing layer. The storage layer needs to support record ordering and strong consistency to enable fast, inexpensive and replay able reads and writes of large streams of data. The processing layer is responsible for consuming data from the storage layer, running computations on that data, and then notifying the storage layer to delete data that is no longer needed. You also have to plan for scalability, data durability, and fault tolerance in both the storage and processing layers. As a result, many platforms have emerged that provide the infrastructure needed to build streaming data applications.

Trends in the World of Big and Fast Data Analytics

Big data analytics is moving beyond the realm of intellectual curiosity and is beginning to tangibly affect business operations, offerings, and outlooks. No longer merely hype or a buzzword, big data analytics will soon become a central tenet for every sort of business enterprise. Meanwhile, real-time analytics has become a hot requirement. For example, factories require the use of real-time data such as sensor data to detect abnormalities in plant and machinery.

OPEN ISSUES OF BIG DATA

The analysis of big data is confronted with many challenges but the current research is still in the beginning phase. Considerable research efforts are needed to improve the efficiency of data display, data storage, and data analysis. Although big data is a hot research area in both academia and industry, there are many important problems remain to be solved, which are discussed below

- **Fundamental Problems:** There is compelling need for a rigorous definition of big data, a structural model of big data, formal description of big data, and a theoretical system of data science, etc. At present, many discussions of big data look more like commercial speculation than scientific research. This is because big data is not formally and structurally defined and not strictly verified.
- **Standardization:** An evaluation system of data quality and an evaluation standard of data computing efficiency should be developed. Many solutions of big data applications claim they can improve data processing and analysis capacities in all aspects, but there is still not a unified evaluation standard and benchmark to balance the computing efficiency of big data with rigorous mathematical methods. The performance can only be evaluated by the system is implemented and deployed, which could not horizontally compare advantages and disadvantages of various solutions and compare efficiencies before and after the use of big data. In addition, since data quality is an important basis of data preprocessing, simplification, and screening, it is also an urgent problem to effectively evaluate data quality.
- **Evolution of Big Data Computing Modes:** This includes external storage mode, data flow mode, PRAM mode, and MR mode, etc. The emergence of big data triggers the development of algorithm design, which has transformed from a computing-intensive approach into a data-intensive approach. Data transfer has been a main bottleneck of big data computing. Therefore, many new computing models tailored for big data have emerged and more such models are on the horizon.

TECHNOLOGY DEVELOPMENT

The big data technology is still in its infancy. Many key technical problems, such as cloud computing, grid computing, stream computing, parallel computing, big data architecture, big data model, and software systems supporting big data, etc. should be fully investigated.

- **Format Conversion:** Due to wide and various data sources, heterogeneity is always a characteristic of big data, as well as a key factor which restricts the efficiency of data format conversion. If such format conversion can be made more efficient, the application of big data may create more values.

- **Big Data Transfer:** Big data transfer involves big data generation, acquisition, transmission, storage, and other data transformations in the spatial domain. As discussed, big data transfer usually incurs high costs, which is also the bottleneck for big data computing. However, data transfer is inevitable in big data applications. Improving the transfer efficiency of big data is a key factor to improve big data computing.

- **Real-Time Performance:** The real-time performance of big data is also a core problem in many different application scenarios. Ways to define the life cycle of data, compute the rate of depreciation of data, and build computing models of real-time applications and online applications, will influence the values and analytical and feedback results of big data. As big data research is advanced, new problems on big data processing arise from the traditional simple data analysis, including:
  - Data re-utilization, since big data features big value but low density, with the increase of data scale, more values may be mined from re-utilization of existing data;
  - Data re-organization, datasets in different businesses can be re-organized, with the total re-organized data values larger than the total datasets' value;
  - Data exhaust, unstructured information or data that is a by-product of the online activities of Internet users.

In big data, not only correct data should be utilized, but also the wrong data should be utilized to generate more value. Collecting and analyzing data exhaust can provide valuable insight into the purchasing habits of consumers.

PRACTICAL IMPLICATIONS

- **Big Data Management:** The emergence of big data brings about new challenges to traditional data management. At present, many research efforts are being made on consider big data oriented database and Internet technologies, management of storage models and databases of new hardware, heterogeneous and multistructured data integration, data management of mobile and pervasive computing, data management of SNS, and distributed data management.

- **Searching, Mining, and Analysis of Big Data:** Data processing is always a research hotspot in the big data field, e.g., searching and mining of SNS models, big data searching algorithms, distributed searching, P2P searching, visualized analysis of big data, massive recommendation systems, social media systems, real-time big data mining, image mining, text mining, semantic mining, multistructured data mining, and machine learning, etc.

- **Integration and Provenance of Big Data:** As discussed, the value acquired from a comprehensive utilization of multiple datasets is higher than the total value of individual datasets. Therefore, the integration of different data sources is a timely problem to be solved. Data integration is to integrate different datasets from different sources, which are confronted with many challenges, such as different data patterns and large amount of redundant data. Data provenance is to describe the process of data generation and evolution over time. In the big data era, data provenance is mainly used to investigate multiple datasets other than a single dataset. Therefore, it is worth of study on how to integrate data provenance information featuring different standards and from different datasets.

- **Big Data Application:** At present, the application of big data is just beginning and we shall explore and more efficiently ways to fully utilize big data. Therefore, big data applications in science, engineering, medicine, medical care, finance, business, law enforcement, education, transportation, retail, and telecommunication, big data applications in small and medium-sized businesses, big data applications in government departments, big data services, and human-computer interaction of big data, etc. are all important research problems.

CHALLENGES AND FUTURE DIRECTIONS OF IOT

The IoT offers several new prospects to the industry and end user in many application fields. The IoT needs theory, technology, architecture, and standards that join the virtual world and the real physical world in a merged outline. Some key challenges are listed in the following subsections.

1. **Architecture Challenge:** IoT covers an extensive variety of technologies. IoT includes a cumulative number of smart interconnected devices and sensors such as cameras, biometric, physical, and chemical sensors. They are often nonintrusive, visible, and hidden. The devices are connected in a wireless or ad hoc manner as the communication may occur at any time and the facilities turn into mobile dependent and more complex. In IoT, data collected from different resources so it will be difficult to integrate these heterogeneous data. The solution is collecting data from various sources and determining the common characteristics between them to explain data and find the associations for support decision-making. The existence of heterogeneous reference architectures in IoT is important. IoT architecture must be reliable and elastic to suit all cases as RFID, Tags, intelligent devices, and smart hardware and software solutions .

2. **Environment Innovation Challenge:** IoT is a complicated network that might be achieved by some sponsors, where services should be openly produced. Therefore, new services or applications should be supported without resulting loads for the market accesses or other operation blocks. So, the cross-domain systems supporting innovation is still deficient.

3. **Technical Challenge:** There are several technical challenges as Heterogeneous architecture in the network technologies and applications. IoT contains different types of networks that are not easy to integrate them. The cost of communication technology should be small and connections must be reliable. Defining the form of suitable security and privacy solution is a complicated process. Activation of automated services stills a challenge.

4. **Hardware Challenge:** Smart devices with enhanced inter-device communication will lead to smart systems with high degrees of intelligence. There are five challenges that face hardware in IoT, cost, electricity and energy, environment related problems, connectivity, and maintenance. IoT connections depend on wireless that somewhat low cost and low size. Hardware devices must be designed to use the smallest amount of power and longtime battery. The outer environment may

affect the hardware efficiency as pollution, humidity, and heating. The connection must be reliable and flexible and not depend only on wireless, the Internet or data should be allowed. It is expensive to maintain damages in sensing devices, so maintenance and support should be local.

5. **Privacy and Security Challenge:** Problems of security and privacy in IoT become more obvious than a traditional network. Despite there exist a great number of researchers in security and privacy, there is a continuous demand for security protection and confidential privacy of data. Todays, user's information has an extensive privacy, so privacy protection is a significant issue. There are many issues should be considered in IoT and need new technologies to be solved as the definition of privacy and security, trust mechanism, the privacy of common and user data, and security of services and applications. Security architectures that are designed now may not be suited for IoT systems. Approval of new technologies and services depend on trustfulness of information and protection of data and its privacy.

6. A standard is important to permit easy and equal access and use to all actors. Standard and proposal developments will encourage the development of IoT infrastructures and applications, services and devices. Standardization permits product and services to do the best. The standardization will be difficult because of vast speed in IoT. Protocols and multi-parities can develop standardization. It should be open. In addition, the standard development process should be open to all actors and the resulting standard should be public and free.

7. **Business Challenge:** For advanced application, it is easy to convert business model and application scenario into technical requirements. So the developers do not want to waste time on business aspects. In IoT, there exist many uncertainties in business models and application scenarios. The problem is that there is no solution of business technology algorithm to suit all. The IoT is a prevention to traditional business model. In the first step in business model development in IoT, business requirements must begin with reducing system failure.

8. **Development Strategies:** IoT has been developed in different areas and states in three main plans and chances financing approach. In the states such as the US, the short-term yield to finance drive of the progress of smart energy, smart cities, and RFIDs. Through the social media network, some services, and applications, such as location-based services, augmented reality, and smartphones, are leading to the development of IoT. Although it is not yet obvious which strategy is more effective, all of them can encourage IoT and its applications. However, how to determine the efforts of available resources at a planned level acquires another challenge.

9. **Data Processing Challenges:** Data processing is an essential property in the IoT. By observing the interconnecting devices and objects that exchange different forms of data, the resulting gathered data has an intensive volume. The storage data centers that store this resulting data will need extra spaces, energy and power sources. This data require organization and processing. Semantic data fusion models may be used for extracting meaning from data. Also, artificial intelligence algorithms should be implied to obtain meaning from this redundant data. Data storage and analysis will be a problem during all world will be connected through IoT

Handling out all of the data from the IoT is a practice in Big data that applied three main steps: data ingestion, data storage, and analytics. Thus, enterprises must assimilate new technologies like Hadoop, and MapReduce. It should be able to provide sufficient disk, network, and compute capacity to continue with the inflow of new data, many data processing challenges are listed in the following subsections: a) Heterogeneous Data Processing In IoT applications, the enormous data are gathered from heterogeneous sensors such as cameras, vehicles, drivers, passengers, and medical sensors. It results in heterogeneous sensing data like text, video, and voice. Heterogeneous data processing as fusion, classification gets exclusive challenges and also provides many advantages and new opportunities for system enhancement. An IoT system may include many types of sensors whose data have heterogeneous data structures. For example, IoT system may contain many forms of sensors, such as traffic sensors, hydrological sensors, geological sensors, meteorological sensors, and biomedical sensors. Each category can be separated into different forms of sensors. For example, traffic sensors can include GPS sensors, RFID readers, video-based traffic-flow analysis sensors, traffic loop sensors, road condition sensors, and so on. The sampling data from different sensors may have dissimilar semantics and data structures that critically rises the troubles in data processing .Noisy Data Noisy data is irrelevant data. The term was often used as a replacement for abnormal data, but its meaning has extended to contain data from the unstructured text that cannot be understood by machines. Its meaning has extended to contain any data that cannot be recognized and translated correctly by machines, such as unstructured text. Slightly data that has been collected, stored, or altered in such a manner that it cannot be recognized or used by the program that originally made it can be identified as noisy. Statistical analysis can use the information collected from old data to clear noisy data and simplify data mining .

Anomaly detection is the detection of irregular events or patterns that is not considered as expected events or patterns. Detecting anomalies are significant in a broad range of different fields, such as diagnosing medical problems, bank, insurance fraud, network intrusion, and object imperfections. Algorithms for anomaly detection are employed based on one type of learning formation: supervised, semi-supervised and unsupervised. These techniques vary from training the detection algorithm using completely unstructured data to having a preformed dataset with entries structured normal or abnormal.

In an IoT system, there could be a considerable amount of connected sensors, and these sensors incessantly send sampling data to the data center. The data center needs to save the latest forms of the sampling data. It also needs to save past forms of the data for some period say one week to offer query processing, state monitoring, and data analyzing. The size of data can be visualized to be massive and processing them effectively is a significant challenge.

SUMMARY

Since there is a major impact of IoT on big data we need to quickly improvise the complete structure to manage the daily changing circumstances. There are a few areas of concern and security and privacy and data collection efficiency are probably the most difficult problems we are facing. Security compromise and inefficiencies in data collection mechanisms result in a loss of status, money, time and effort. But there is hope because both the IoT and the big data are at an emerging stage and there will be upgrade.

Fast Data is powering innovation, while using Big Data to obtain key insights and conclusions. Anything real-time, be it security, fraud surveillance, risk analytics, customer choices, etc – Fast Data helps deliver instant, accurate solutions. The Big Data and Fast Data challenge is finally about concurrency.

REFERENCES

Ashton, K. (2009). That Internet of Things Thing. *RFID Journal*. Retrieved from http://www. rfidjournal. com/articles/view

Blitz. (2013). *The Fourth Amendment Future of Public Surveillance: Remote Recording and Other Searches in Public Space.* Academic Press.

Brundu, F. G., Patti, E., Osello, A., Del Giudice, M., Rapetti, N., Krylovskiy, A., ... Acquaviva, A. (2016). IoT Software Infrastructure for Energy Management and Simulation in Smart Cities. *IEEE Transactions on Industrial Informatics*.

DeFries, R. S., Rudel, T., Uriarte, M., & Hansen, M. (2010). Deforestation driven by urban population growth and agricultural trade in the twenty-first century. *Nature Geoscience, 3*(3), 178–181. doi:10.1038/ngeo756

Eastman, C. M., Eastman, C., Teicholz, P., Sacks, R., & Liston, K. (2011). *BIM handbook: A guide to building information modeling for owners, managers, designers, engineers and contractors.* John Wiley & Sons.

Giusto, D., Iera, A., Morabito, G., & Atzori, L. (Eds.). (2010). *The internet of things: 20th Tyrrhenian workshop on digital communications.* Springer Science & Business Media.

Kamilaris, A., Pitsillides, A., & Trifa, V. (2011). The smart home meets the web of things. *International Journal of Ad Hoc and Ubiquitous Computing, 7*(3), 145–154. doi:10.1504/IJAHUC.2011.040115

Kundhavai & Sridevi. (2016). IoT and Big Data- The Current and Future Technologies: A Review. *International Journal of Computer Science and Mobile Computing, 5*(1), 10-14.

Niranjana. (2015). Big data analytics – Tools, techniques and challenges. *International Journal of Advance Research in Science and Engineering, 4*(3).

Radha, B. S., & Bharathi, T. (2017). A Study On Corporate Valuation On Selected Indian Firms. *Indian Journal of Commerce and Management, 3*(6).

Raju. (2017, November). A Mutational Approach to Internet of Things. *International Journal for Research in Applied Science and Engineering Technology, 5*(11).

Tomlinson, R. F. (2001). A geographic information system for regional planning. *The Journal of Geography, 78*(1), 45–48. doi:10.5026/jgeography.78.45

Chapter 17
Voice Biometrics:
The Promising Future of Authentication in the Internet of Things

Saleema A.
Indian Institute of Information Technology and Management Kerala, India

Sabu M. Thampi
Indian Institute of Information Technology and Management Kerala, India

ABSTRACT

Biometric technology is spearheading the existing authentication methods in the IoT. Considering the balance between security and convenience, voice biometrics seems to be the most logical biometric technologies to be used. The authors present an extensive survey to identify, analyze, and compare various methods and algorithms for the different phases in the process of speaker identification/recognition, which is the part and parcel in voice biometrics. The chapter is intended to provide essential background information to those interested in learning or planning to design voice authentication systems. The chapter highlights the need for a biometric authentication system, the reason why we prefer voice, its present state of affairs, and its scope with fog computing to be used in IoT.

INTRODUCTION

The drastic increase of online profiles and websites necessitates remembering a number of passwords for authentication. Users are now being displeased by the minimum recommended password setting criteria enforced by the authorities for preserving security. Many companies use security questions to confirm identities. These questions are usually personal in nature, asking about the user's background. Considering privacy, users tend to lie to such questions. The problem is that you will forget your lie, because you are not a pathological liar! In recent times, hundreds of millions of passwords have been leaked online, including more than a hundred million LinkedIn logins and tens of millions of Twitter logins put on the Darknet. It's high time we should think about the large scale adoption of an authentication system that is able to resist the future network breaches.

DOI: 10.4018/978-1-5225-5972-6.ch017

Studies found out that card fraud is on the rise in Asian countries, mirroring a global trend. External threats such as spoofing, pharming, phishing, randsomeware etc. are premeditated and they instigate risky actions to a larger degree rather than leveraging on consumers' own carelessness(Weekly & Asia, 2016).

Analysis reveals that biometric technology has now become a viable alternative to traditional identification systems in many government and commercial application domains. Biometrics use physiological or behavioral characteristics to recognize who you are, and provide highly secure identification and personal verification solutions. The focus is not on 'what you know' - which can be stolen and misused, rather verifies you based on features that are unique to you i.e. 'what you are'. It is found out that a best voice authentication system will outperform all other biometric systems. The easiness in installation, data collection and usage makes voice biometrics more preferable in the scenario of Internet of Things (IoT).

A glance through the current applications of voice biometrics reveals the fact that it can provide a seamless and frictionless customer experience. The merits of voice biometric systems include increased security and decreased fraud, improved customer experience, reduced costs, accuracy etc. While thinking about the integration of this authentication method in Internet of Things, the major challenges we could spot out include degradation by background noise, voice imitation, codec degradation, short term and long term variations in voice, attacks on devices, link, hosts and workstations, replay attacks, Trojan etc. Recent advancements in this scenario could solve some of the listed problems to a certain extent. But the use of voice biometrics based authentication system in IoT is still in its infancy. Although the modern voice recognition technologies are evolving rapidly, the companies developing such technologies still face information security challenges.

The chapter starts with a brief overview of voice biometrics, the reason why we prefer voice, its present state of affairs and the scope of voice biometrics with fog computing to be used in IoT. Then it gives an outlook to the merits, demerits, existing applications and the traditional as well as emerging features, the existing ways of feature extraction and speaker modeling. Finally, the necessity of multimodal systems and some future directions are discussed.

BACKGROUND

Evolution

Recognition of voice started when introducing the first automatic voice recognition device in 1952.This non computerized machine was capable to recognize human voice pronouncing single digits. Later in 1992 the first prototype of a modern voice recognition system, Sphinx-II, was created which could perform real-time voice recognition and became suitable for using in modern software application.

In 1867, for instance, Alexander Melville Bell laid the groundwork for future voice biometrics research by inventing a language called Universal Alphabetic. Using this system, which replicates the position a mouth makes when speaking a certain speech pattern, it's possible to transcribe not only what a person is saying, but how they are saying it ("A Brief History of Voice Biometrics - VoiceVault Voice Authentication," n.d.)

The first use cases of voice biometric identity verification emerged by the introduction of machines called spectrographs during World War II. It was used by the American soldiers to intercept voice transmissions and track enemy movements. It didn't provide accurate results as it was primitive at the time.

Later the first modern voice biometrics engine capable of accurately registering and determining an end user's voiceprint was created by Texas Instruments in 1976.

Why We Opt Voice???

The ability to work with standard equipment makes it possible to support broad-based deployments of voice biometrics applications in a variety of settings. In contrast, most other biometrics require proprietary hardware, such as the vendor's fingerprint sensor or iris-scanning equipment (Markowitz, 2000). The Characteristics of various biometric authentication schemes are compared in the Table 1("Top Five Biometrics: Face, Fingerprint, Iris, Palm and Voice," n.d.)

Present State of Affairs

The identification and verification strategies (ID&V) currently available are more or less creating a frustrating customer experience and at the same time costly for the enterprises. In the United States alone, contact centers spend $12.4 billion annually verifying the caller is who they say they are. Callers meanwhile have to endure an average of 23 seconds of interrogation, beginning each call with a negative experience(Nuance, 2011). A quick look into Nuance's Voice Biometrics solutions profile make us realize that voice biometric systems offer organizations a secure and convenient way of authenticating users providing the caller with a faster and more pleasant experience. Figure 1 illustrates the significance of automated identity verification using voice biometrics by Nuance.

WHEN VOICE BIOMETRICS WITH FOG MEET IoT

IoT evolves as an attractive next generation network paradigm where physical objects are seamlessly integrated in order to provide advanced and intelligent services for human beings. The need for security and privacy is increasing day by day with the emerging applications of IoT in the fields of surveillance, healthcare, distant object monitoring, traffic management, transport etc. Since a large number of applications are accessed through smart devices which necessitate keeping a lot of personal and confidential

Table 1. Characteristics of various biometric authentication schemes

Characteristic	Fingerprints	Hand Geometry	Retina	Iris	Face	Signature	Voice
Ease of Use	High	High	Low	Medium	Medium	High	High
Error incidence	Dryness, dirt, age	Hand injury, age	Glasses	Poor Lighting	Lighting, age, glasses, hair	Changing signatures	Noise, colds, weather
Accuracy	High	High	Very High	Very High	High	High	High
Cost	Medium	Medium	Medium	Medium	Medium	Medium	Low
User acceptance	Medium	Medium	Medium	Medium	Medium	Medium	High
Required security level	High	Medium	High	Very high	Medium	Medium	Medium

Figure 1. Automated vs. manual Identity Verification

Automated Identity Verification using Voice Biometrics

5 Seconds[1]

Manual Identity Verification Performed by Agent

23 Seconds[2]

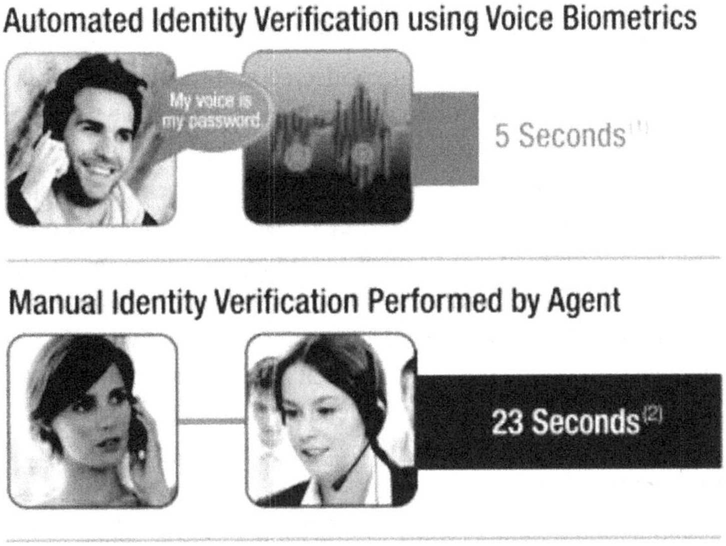

information, attackers extend their scope of invasion to extract the stored user information. In such a scenario where everything is accessed through smart devices, it's highly advantageous to incorporate biometric applications in the IoT environment.

With the advent of biometrics, strong easy and scalable authentication systems began to provide viable solutions for ensuring privacy and security in IoT networks. Voice biometrics is found to be best suited in IoT since it is a "dynamic biometric" in the sense that we have an infinite number of spoken words which we can set as our passwords unlike face,iris and fingers("Viewpoint: Why we need voice biometrics | IDG Connect," n.d.). Voice is integrated to already existing digital assistants like Alexa, Cortana ansd Siri and it is expecting to authorize critical applications like accessing a bank account to transfer funds (Gaubitch, 2017). The possibilities of voice biometrics are endless as it can be used in new voice services such as smart home inspired environments, giving virtual customer assistance, launching application subscriptions to our device controlled by voice etc... Current research and market trends indicate that future applications of voice-biometrics will be text independent and incorporate other speech-processing and biometric technologies. Such applications are already in demand in several markets. For example, health-care, financial services, and other industries that handle large numbers of sensitive documents have begun to incorporate multiple biometrics into their security strategies (Markowitz, 2000).

The major obstacles in deploying biometric authentication in IoT are the scalability and computational complexity. Such issues can be resolved by moving the computational part of the biometric authentication to a cloud platform where ubiquitous computing can be carried out in a more flexible way. In the case of voice biometrics, the processes of feature extraction and modeling where majority of the computation is concentrated, can be offloaded to a cloud. The Figure 2 illustrates the incorporation of a recognition module on cloud with authentication carried on cloud providing high performance and scalability of the biometric system. Various cloud centric biometric architectures have been proposed in the literature which shows the effective integration of cloud computing, biometrics and IoT.

In new age terminology, an architecture which manages access control to IoT objects via biometric authentication is termed as "Internet of Biometric Things (IoBT)." The concept of IoBT was first introduced in (Kantarci, Erol-Kantarci, & Schuckers, 2015). They have mentioned a cloud centric IoT architecture in which data from smart devices are collected and transmitted to a cloud where liveness detection and protection against spoofing attacks are performed. They have well illustrated some context aware authentication techniques with behaviourometrics as well as biometrics.

Later on, owing to the recent advancements in IoT, new requirements such as mobility support, geo distribution, location awareness etc.. became critical and the use of cloud computing seemed to be insufficient. The search for a new platform to meet the emerging requirements led to fog computing. Fog, being a cloud closer to the ground, will be enabling a new breed of applications and services in the future. In addition to mobility support, geo distribution and location awareness, fog computing brings properties like efficient real time interaction, heterogeneity, low latency, interoperability, predominance of wireless access etc.. (Bonomi, Milito, Zhu, & Addepalli, 2012). An alternative solution is edge computing where the intelligence lies in the edge devices. Nowadays, fog and edge computing is being used interchangeably by many researchers.

Matt Newton had explained the difference between Fog and Edge Computing in its real essence ("Fog Computing vs. Edge Computing: What's the Difference? | Automation World," n.d.).

Fog computing pushes intelligence down to the local area network level of network architecture, processing data in a fog node or IoT gateway.

Edge computing pushes the intelligence, processing power and communication capabilities of an edge gateway or appliance directly into devices like programmable automation controllers (PACs). - Matt Newton

Figure 2. Voice based Authentication in Cloud Centric IoT

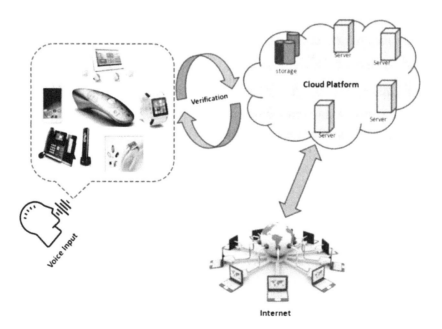

Nowadays, fog is used as the best platform to offload the computational processes of biometric authentication rather than doing it alone in the cloud. Offloading from a cloud to the network edge devices not only improves processing efficiency, but also reduces network transmission. A fog based face identification and resolution based on Local Binary Patterns and Euclidian Matching is described in (Hu, Ning, Qiu, Zhang, & Luo, 2017). Since fog provides location awareness, mobile users can make use of its applications through biometric authentication in a convenient way. Figure 3 illustrates a fog based architecture for authentication in IoT smart environments.

The major challenges identified in deploying fog computing are application, scaling and placement(Luan et al., 2015).The network operator should customize the applications embedded in each fog servers based on the demand at a specific location. Also he must ensure sufficient resources anticipating the demands in each fog. For nearby mobile users, we can employ a group of fog servers, but their collaboration should be efficiently managed according to the demands and location. A three dimensional service oriented recourse allocation should be done as the fog server posses hardware in three dimensions namely storage, computation and communication.

Another fog based biometric authentication is presented in (Abdul et al., 2017), which shows a biometric security solution for face images using visual cryptography. Here the basic security functions are employed in the fog and sharing is achieved by cloud. A Fog Computing Architecture(FIT) is introduced in (Monteiro, Dubey, Mahler, Yang, & Mankodiya, 2016) which analyses speech data from a remote site. The clinical features were extracted in the fog and are sent to the cloud. Functionalities like configurability, computational intelligence and interoperability make FIT a suitable interface for remote monitoring of speech treatments.

Figure 3. Fog based Architecture to be used in Smart Environments

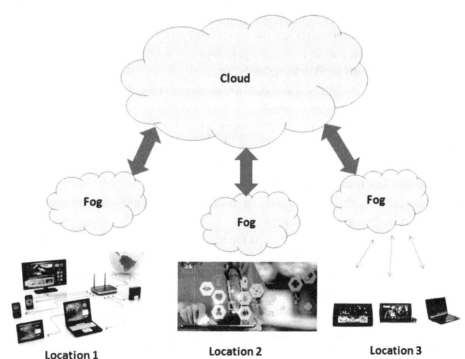

MERITS, APPLICATIONS AND CHALLENGES IN VOICE BIOMETRICS

The major advantages of voice biometrics are

- **Increased Security and Decreased Fraud:** Here involves no disclosure of personal information such as name, age, race, gender, health or immigration status. Hence it seems to be highly secure, privacy preserving and fraud resistant.
- **Improved Customer Experience:** By the use of voice based authentication system the time taken to verify a caller's identity became 10 seconds to several minutes. Also the callers no longer need to provide passcodes or PINs or provide answers to challenge questions.
- **Reduced Costs:** Its found out that the verification time is reduced by 70-80%. The decrease in time needed to authenticate customers have led to savings of millions of dollars.
- **Accuracy:** Voice based authentication systems are achieving near perfect performance in terms of accuracy.
- **No Lengthy Enrollments or High Implementation Costs:** In most cases, voice prints are collected as part of normal conservations and securely encrypted and stored. So there are no long procedures for its enrollment and authentication. Also there is no need of additional devices for the enrollment and verification purposes

The applications of biometrics based authentication system is widespread, among which some of them are listed below(Babich, 2012; Reynolds, 2002).

- **Transaction Authentication:** For telephone banking, in addition to account access control, higher levels of verification can be used for more sensitive transactions. More recent applications are in user verification for remote electronic and mobile purchases (e- and m-commerce).
- **Marketing:** (Methods of biometrics are used to identify owners of loyal cards)
- **Law Enforcement:** Home parole monitoring, prison call monitoring etc.
- **Time Accounting Systems at Work, Schools, etc.**
- **Security Systems:** Used to control the access to the rooms and control access to internet resources and for automated password reset services.
- **Speech Data Management:** In voice mail browsing or intelligent answering machines, use speaker recognition to label incoming voice mail with speaker name for browsing and/or action (personal reply). For speech skimming or audio mining applications, annotate recorded meetings or video with speaker labels for quick indexing and filing.
- **Voting System:** (During the functionality of voting system identification/authentication of people, that take part in voting is demanded)
- **Registration:** Biometric identifiers are used for registration of immigrants and foreign workers. It allows identifying people even without documents.
- **Personalization:** In voice-web or device customization, store and retrieve personal setting/preferences based on user verification for multi-user site or device (car climate and radio settings). There is also interest in using recognition techniques for directed advertisement or services, where, for example, repeat users could be recognized or advertisements focused based on recognition of broad speaker characteristics (e.g. gender or age).

Voice plays a crucial role in the field of forensics as it can act as an efficient tool in commission of criminal offences such as kidnapping, extortion, blackmail threats, obscene calls, anonymous calls, harrassent calls, random calls, terrorist calls, match fixing etc (Tiwari, Hasan, & Islam, 2013).

The major challenges that we could spot out in a voice based authentication system are as follows.

- **Highly Affected by Background Noises:** Since the background and channel noises affects the quality of the signal, the software and algorithms should be highly efficient to compensate for them.
- **Recordings and Voice Imitation:** Someone could obtain a high quality recording of your pronunciation of the password phrase in case of a text dependent voice authentication system and use it to hack your accounts. So new methods providing security measures like liveness detection, playback detection and fraudster detection is being obligatory.
- **Short Term and Long Term Variations in Voice:** Due to aging, weight changes and other physiological changes, the voice of a person may change in long term. So technologies to compensate for such short term and long term variations are in the bottom-line.
- **Codec Degradation:** The voice recordings usually undergo many processing and compression stages (Eg: the transmission over GSM followed by some form of perceptual encoding). Signals of poor quality and high SNRs are produced as a result.

Recent researches show that biometric technology acquires a huge potential in IoT environment. The use of voice biometrics in IoT opens a number of research issues which include:

- **Sensor Interoperability:** Since the sensors connected to IoT that collect data vary greatly, their interoperability is being a major concern.
- **Attacks:** Attacks on the device, links between devices, hosts and workstations are evolving crucially. Although the resolution of replay attacks can be done by using some digital encryption and time stamping, some other attacks like Trojan seems dreadful. It may give false data to the system so that the calculated biometric print corresponds an authorized person and it may not be able to actually recognize the honest owner.

VOICE FEATURES

The two major processes in a speaker recognition system are feature extraction and decision. Generally, Tone, pitch, cadence, prosody, speaking rate etc. are considered to be the things characterizing voice. Voice features for recognition means parameters of the speech signal that carries speaker specific information. The information contained in a speech signal can be high level like dialect, accent, talking style, the subject manner of context, phonetics, prosodic and lexical information or low level like fundamental frequency, formant frequency, pitch, intensity, rhythm, tone, spectral magnitude and bandwidth for an individual's voice. Among these, features are selected by assigning priority to those having lower intra speaker variability and higher inter speaker variability. The other concerns while selecting a feature include robustness against noise and distortion, frequency of occurrence in natural speech, difficulty in mimicry, unaffected by health and easiness in measurability. There are different ways to categorize the features (Kinnunen & Li, 2010).

1. **Short Term Spectral Features:** As the name suggests, they are computed from the short frames of about 20 to 30 milliseconds in duration. These actually describe the resonance properties of the supralaryngeal vocal tract. MFCC is a conventional short term spectral feature.
2. **Voice Source Features:** characterize the glottal excitation signal of voiced sounds such as glottal pulse shape and fundamental frequency. Hence it is reasonable to assume that they carry speaker-specific information.
3. **Spectro-Temporal Features:** These constitute signal details such as formant transitions and energy modulations that contain useful speaker-specific information.
4. **Prosodic Features:** It includes syllable stress, intonation patterns, speaking rate and rhythm. These features depends upon the long segments like syllables, words, and utterances and reflects differences in speaking style, language background, sentence type and emotion of the speaker
5. **High Level Features:** These features attempt to capture conversation-level characteristics of speakers, such as characteristic use of words ("uh-huh", "you know", "oh yeah", etc.). Other features are the dialect of any language used in the conversation by the speaker, accent of the speaker and the style of speaking.

FEATURE EXTRACTION TECHNIQUES

Traditional Feature Extraction Processes: MFCC, LPC, LPCC, PLP

Mel Frequency Cepstral Co-Efficient: MFCC is one of the most successful methods of feature extraction due to its high success rate of recognition and strong robustness against noise in the lower frequency regions. It captures speaker characteristics information from the high frequency regions less effectively. MFCC is based on the human peripheral auditory system. It is derived from the interesting fact that human hearing behaves in a nonlinear way. The Process of feature extraction sing MFCC can be summarized as in Figure 4.

Since majority of the energy of a speech signal is in the low frequencies, using a filter bank the energy of high frequencies are raised. Then frame blocking is done to divide the signal into small blocks. Each frame will be multiplied by a hamming window in order to make the signal continuous. Then FFT is used to convert the time domain to frequency domain. Then the Mel Filter bank is applied.DCT is used to get the Mel-scale cepstral coefficients. Thus the information in the low frequency part is highlighted than the noise contents in the high frequency part.

Present day researchers concentrate on advanced methods for feature extraction by making conjunctions with several other methods. Some make use of the Intrinsic Mode Functions (IMFs) of the speech signals in conjunction with MFCC to get a performance enhanced speaker verification system which works well not only with the normal speech but also for the fast and whispered speech.

(Wang & Lawlor, 2017) discusses a latest work in 2017 using the MFCC and Back Propagation Neural Network. The important inference obtained from this work is that if the number of MFCC coefficients is increased, the number of questionable speakers increases. The paper also suggests investigating the use of the Winger Distribution Function to give increased joint time-frequency resolution on the input to the neural networks, which may increase the rate of recognition.

Figure 4. Process of Extraction of MFCC Coefficients

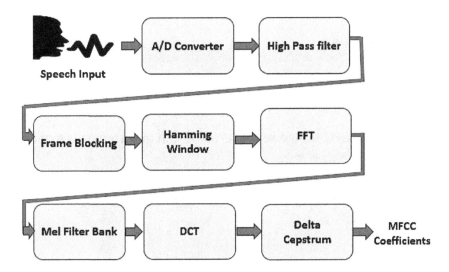

- **Linear Predictive Coding:** Being a method for spectrum feature extraction, LPC provides good interpretation for both time and frequency domain. It mimics the human voice production system and gives accurate estimation of speech spectra, pitchs and formants (Sremath, Reza, Singh, & Wang, 2017). The transfer function of the vocal tract in the z domain using the all pole autoregressive model can be represented as

$$H(z) = \frac{X(z)}{E(z)} = \frac{1}{1 - \sum_{k=1}^{p} a_k z^{-k}} = \frac{1}{A(z)}$$

where $X(z), E(z)$ are the z domain representations of the output and the excitation signals respectively. P is the LPC order and A(z) is the inverse filter. Taking inverse, we will arrive at

$$E[n] = x[n] - \sum_{k=1}^{p} a_k x[n-k]$$

From which we can calculate the LPC coefficients a_k, k=1,...p by minimizing e[n] using the autocorrelation method.

- **Linear Predictive Cepstral Coefficients:** LPCC is a powerful feature extraction process derived from LPC and it reflects the differences of the biological structure of the human vocal tract. LPCC computing method is a recursion from LPC parameter to LPC cepstrum according to All-pole model. Its recursion is as follows.

$$\begin{cases} c_1 = a_1 \\ c_n = a_n + \sum_{k=1}^{n-1} \frac{k}{n} c_k a_{n-k}, 1 < n \le p \\ c_n = \sum_{k=1}^{n-1} \frac{k}{n} c_k a_{n-k}, n > p \end{cases}$$

where $a_1, \ldots \ldots a_p$ is p order LPC feature vector, c_n, n=1,.....p (p corresponds to the first p values of the cepstrum) $c_m(t) = \sum_{i=-k}^{k} i.c_m(t+i) \Big/ \sum_{i=-k}^{k} i^2$

The definition of the differential cepstrum coefficient of *LPCC is as follows.

$$c_m(t) = \sum_{i=-k}^{k} i.c_m(t+i) \Big/ \sum_{i=-k}^{k} i^2$$

Here $c_m(t)$ and $c_m(t+i)$ both expresses a frame of speech parameter, k is a constant usually chosen as 2(Yuan, Zhao, & Zhou, 2010)

Researches show that a combination of LPCC and MFCC methods could achieve higher recognition rates and lesser recognition times. In (Yuan et al., 2010), when MFCC parameters were used, the system tends to judge speakers as legal speakers even if he embezzles the password. So the use of LPCC which reflects the biological differences of vocal tract enhanced the system's security.

- **Perceptual Linear Predictive:** PLP was proposed by Hynek Hermansky in 1989. Although PLP was initially used to suppress speaker dependent components, later proved to be efficient for speaker recognition tasks. It is similar to LPC except that PLP also uses three concepts from psychophysics of hearing, which are critical-band spectral resolution, equal loudness curve, and intensity loudness power law.LPC and PLP are similar in the sense that both use the autoregressive all-pole model to estimate the short-term power spectrum of speech. Hermansy pointed out that the LPC all-pole model is not consistent with human auditory perception because it does not consider the non-uniform frequency resolution and intensity resolution of hearing (Abdulla, 2007). But unlike LPC, PLP alleviates this problem by applying the all-pole model to the auditory spectrum. The auditory spectrum is designed to be an estimate of the mean rate of firing of auditory nerve fibers. The Figure 5 shows the illustration of PLP.

A modified version of PLP called MPLP is presented in (Abdulla, 2007). In MPLP analysis, two processes equal loudness pre-emphasis and intensity loudness conversion are applied to the power spectrum P(x) of the speech signal in order to account for the characteristics of human perception of sound .

RECENT ADVANCED FEATURE EXTRACTION PROCESSES

- **Gammatone Frequency Cepstral Coefficients:** GFCC has recently shown a promising recognition performance in such speaker recognition applications, especially in noisy acoustical environ-

Figure 5. Process of Extraction of PLP Coefficients

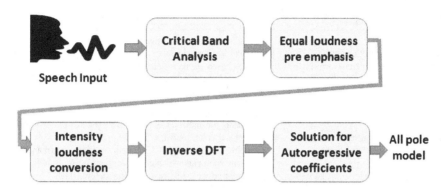

ments. GFCCs were tested for text-independent speaker identification over VoIP Networks and found successful (Ayoub, Jamal, & Arsalane, 2016).

The main idea of the GFCCs is based on an auditory periphery model that imitates the human cochlear filtering mechanism. Improved GFCCs also have been explored to increase the recognition accuracy and robustness (Shi, Yang, & Zhou, 2016). It has been found out that methods like multitaper estimation, normalized Gammatone filter bank, dynamic feature and MVA can improve robustness of GFCC in order to make it suitable for speaker recognition. Table 2 shows some recent significant works on GFCC and their discussion.

- **Log Area Ratio:** LAR is an effective feature for recognizing speakers as it embodies the geometry and dynamics of the vocal tract, which are very much person-dependent. LAR has linear spectral sensitivity and it is more robust to quantization noise (Abdulla, 2007). In LAR modeling technique, the vocal cord of a person is modeled as a non-uniform acoustic tube formed by cascading p uniform equal- length cylindrical tubes with different cross-section areas. The length of each cylindrical tube is closely related to the frames sampling period and the number of coefficients in the LP model. The LAR coefficients are calculated by the log area ratio between the cross-sections of every two consecutive tubes. From Recent studies, LAR is found to be more robust to quantization noise than LPC.

PLAR or Perceptual LAR proved to be another promising and superior feature over MFCC and LPCC. This depends on notions from psychoacoustics where the robustness can be assured. PLAR is calculated By deriving the LAR feature from PLP coefficients. Table 3 shows some recent works on LAR based speaker identification.

- **Wavelet Based Methods:** Wavelets and WP analysis has been used in the field if signal processing for a variety of problems. Combining modified LPC and Wavelet transforms, a novel method was suggested in (Daqrouq & Al Azzawi, 2012)termed as average framing linear prediction Coding(AFLPC). The vocal characteristics of speakers were extracted using AFLPC and the

Table 2. Significant Works on GFCC

Sl No:	Approaches	Results and Discussion
1	Gammatone Frequency Cepstral Coefficients for Speaker Identification over VoIP Networks (Ayoub et al., 2016)	• GFCCs are studied and evaluated text independent speaker identification task over VoIP networks. • GMM based speaker modeling process. • Finding: It appears that each increase in the number of coefficients is accompanied by a decrease in the identification performance of the system.
2	Robust Speaker Recognition Based on Improved GFCC (Shi et al., 2016)	• An improved GFCC is proposed based on methods like multitaper estimation, normalized Gammatone filter bank, dynamic feature and MVA. • I-vector speaker modeling is used. • Findings: improved GFCC obtains the relative permanent improvements under environments which contains music noise, Babble noise, White noise and Pink noise, especially the SNR is below 10dB.
3	Hindi vowel classification using GFCC and formant analysis in sensor mismatch condition (Biswas, Sahu, Bhowmick, & Chandra, 2014)	• Used auditory based feature extraction procedure GFCC for Hindi phoneme classification based on recognition of frequencies of first three formants that are present in vowels along with their cepstral feature. • Finding: Formant based GFCC has shown best classification efficiency across all testing conditions.
4	Analyzing noise robustness of MFCC and GFCC features in speaker Identification(X. Zhao & Wang, 2013)	• Compared MFCC and GFCC to analyze why GFCC appear to be more robust than MFCC. • Findings: The nonlinear rectification mainly accounts for the noise robustness differences. The cubic root rectification provides more robustness to the features than the log.
5	An Auditory-Based Feature For Robust Speech Recognition (Shao, Jin, Wang, & Srinivasan, 2009)	• CASA-based speech segregation and robust speech recognition. • Compared GFCC with PLP and MFCC • Finding: integrating the feature (GFCC) with a computational auditory scene analysis system yields promising recognition performance.
6	CASA-Based Robust Speaker Identification (X. Zhao, Member, Shao, & Wang, 2012)	• Applied CASA separation and then either reconstruct or marginalize corrupted components indicated by a CASA mask. • Further combined the two methods into a single system • Finding: GFCC captures speaker characteristics and performs substantially better than conventional speaker feature under noisy conditions. The combined system achieves significant performance improvements over related systems under a wide range of signal-to-noise ratios.

Table 3. Significant Works on LAR based identification.

Sl No:	Approach	Results and Description
1	Robust speaker modeling using perceptually motivated feature (Abdulla, 2007)	• Deduced Perceptual LAR feature from LAR. • Used GMM and OGMM classifiers. • Finding: PLAR proved its superiority over the commonly-used features such as MFCC and LPCC.
2	Speaker Identification Based on Log Area Ratio and Gaussian Mixture Models in Narrow-Band Speech (D. Chow & Abdulla, 2004)	• Used LAR feature for speaker identification. • LAR and MFCC feature vectors are compared using F-ratio feature analysis. • Finding: Speaker identification rate using LAR: 98.8%, Speaker identification rate using MFCC: 96.73%
3	Robust Speaker Identification Based on Perceptual Log Area Ratio and Gaussian Mixture Models (David Chow & Abdulla, 2004)	• PLAR feature is investigated using F-ratio analysis. • Modelled using GMM • Finding: To derive speaker related information, lower order PLAR coefficients are more efficient than lower order MFCC.

feature vector size was optimized using Genetic Algorithm. Further classification was done using Probabilistic Neural Network and deduced at the fact that PNN in conjunction with AFLPC could achieve a better recognition rate up to 97.36%.

Fuzzy Wavelet transforms also have been experimented in speaker recognition tasks for feature extraction. An adaptive fuzzy wavelet algorithm is used for text independent speaker recognition is carried out in (Lung, 2004). Here Adaptive fuzzy c means algorithm (AFCM) is combined with wavelet to attain a recognition rate of 95%. Also an attempt to combine DWT with MFCC has been discussed in (Al-Ali, Dean, Senadji, Chandran, & Naik, 2017) for enhanced forensic speaker verification. The common problems of forensic speaker recognition reverberation conditions and environmental noise could greatly be eliminated by this method. In (Lung, 2010), an improved wavelet algorithm for feature extraction with a kernel canonical correlation analysis with underlying GMM is performed. A unique method with wavelet decomposition and Volterra adaptive model is introduced in (Jun Juo,Shuying Yang, 2016). The method gained accuracy and lowered distortion among features.

- **Spectral Subband Centroids:** The centroid frequencies of the subband spectra are computed which represents the locations of the local maxima of the power spectrum. The advantage of high recognition accuracy with this approach in noisy conditions is proven to outperform MFCC. The problem of optimizing the parameters of the filterbank is noted and attempts to simplify the parameter settings has been initialized (Kinnunen, Zhang, Zhu, & Wang, 2007). A self adaptivity method is mentioned which considers subbands as partitions of a scalar quantizer.

Empirical experiments were conducted in (Thian, Sanderson, & Bengio, 2004) and found out that SSC on concatenation with MFCC and LFCC gives high robustness. They stated that speaker discriminative information are contained in SSCs which are represented by dominant frequencies unlike MFCC and LFCC. Studies about the time trajectory of SSCs are forecasting. An audio fingerprinting method based on normalized SSC is proposed in (Seo et al., 2006) and tested several audio processing methods like compression, equalization, random start etc showing its reliability as well as robustness. They also claims the outperformance of SSC over other widely used features such as tonality, MFCC etc. (Gajic & Paliwal, 2006) is a similar work proving SSCs robustness over MFCC.

SPEAKER MODELING TECHNIQUES

Automatic speaker recognition technology had its beginning from human aural and spectrogram comparisons and then turned to simple template matching and dynamic time warping approaches and further spanned to modern statistical pattern recognition methods such as Neural Networks and Hidden Markov Models. (Kinnunen & Li, 2010).

- **Spectrogram Based:** The concept of using spectrograms for speaker identification has been around for decades. The attempts for speaker recognition using spectrograms have begun from 1960s. Spectrograms are meant for describing how the spectral density of a signal varies with time. The most commonly used form of a speech spectrogram is the frequency versus time plot with a third dimension indicating the amplitude of a particular frequency at a particular time represented by the intensity or color of each point in the image (Kekre, 2012). The generated spectrogram of a particular speaker is transformed into another domain where comparison with the test sample is performed. Various transformations used include DCT, Haar, Walsh, Kekre, Radon etc. Feature vectors are extracted and matching is performed using Manhattan distance, Euclidian distance etc. in traditional approaches. Sometimes the spectrogram features are reduced in dimension using operators like Local Binary pattern operator (LBP) (Li, Li, Luo, & Luo, 2015). Studies to explore methods for feature extraction from spectrograms are still ongoing.

The concept of modulation spectrogram (MSG) was first introduced by Kingsburey et al (Kingsbury, Morgan, & Greenberg, 1998) and provides an alternative and complementary representation of the speech signal with a focus on temporal structure. Literatures have filed MSG based methods in combination with commonly used MFCCs could achieve significant results in processes like speaker diarization (Vinyals & Friedland, n.d.). Table 4 summarizes some recent approaches based on spectrograms with a brief description.

- **Gaussian Mixture Models:** GMM is the commonly used statistical modeling technique in speaker recognition applications with speaker adaptation. It possesses the advantage of using every speech frames without any segmentation or transcription for the estimation of speaker information and build GMMs. The problem identified with GMM is that it won't consider the acoustic vari-

Table 4. Significant Works on Spectrogram based identification

Sl No:	Approach	Results and Description
1	Speaker Identification using Spectrograms of Varying Frame Sizes (Kekre, 2012)	• Spectrogram generation using DFT for varying frame sizes with 25% and 50% overlap between speech frames. • Feature extraction: row mean vector • Feature matching: Euclidean and Manhattan distance • The maximum accuracy is 92.52% for an overlap of 50% between speech frames with Manhattan distance as similarity measure.
2	Modulation Spectrogram Features for Improved Speaker Diarization(Vinyals & Friedland, n.d.)	• Uses modulation spectrogram features in speaker diarization. • The long term characteristics extracted from it along with MFCCs provides potential improvement in speaker diarization. • An improvement of 20.77% relative DER is obtained with respect to MFCC only systems.
3	Spectrogram patch based acoustic event detection and classification in speech overlapping conditions (Workshop, Communication, & Arrays, 2014)	• Focuses on the task of detecting and classifying acoustic events in a conversation scene • Learns hidden features directly from spectrogram patches. • Integration within the deep neural network framework to detect and classify acoustic events. • Conclusion: narrow and deep architectures achieve better performance in terms of both computational efficiency and detection performance.
4	Speaker Identification Using FrFT-based Spectrogram and RBF Neural Network (Li et al., 2015)	• Uses optimized spectrogram and RBF neural network. • Applies fractional Fourier transform (FrFT) to obtain spectrograms. • Converts spectrogram features to lower dimension using local binary patterns operator, optimized using PSO and fed to RBF network. • Achieved Acceptable recognition rate with high accuracy
5	Feature Extraction Using Image Processing Techniques for Speaker Identification System (Sekar, 2012)	• Radon transform and DCT applied to extract spectrogram features. • After applying RT, the two dimensional DCT has been applied on Radon projections yields low dimensional feature vectors.

ability of phonetic events while comparisons with different speakers(Huang, Wang, & Ma, 2016). Studies to solve this problem have been carried out to improve the performance by focusing on the use of specific constrained data. Table 5 depicts some recent works on GMM based speaker recognition.

- **Dynamic Time Warping:** This approach is mostly used in text dependent applications. A sequence of feature vectors from a fixed phrase is extracted which is called template. During verification a match score is produced by using dynamic time warping (DTW) to align and measure the similarity between the test phrase and the speaker template. DTW is based on the idea of dynamic programming, which is perfect for solving the matching problem of difference of length of speech. It is preferred when it comes to comparison of speech from the same speaker, which is limited in application. Besides heavy computation, lack of dynamic training and excessive reliance on speech from original speaker also accounts to its disadvantages

In the current context where mobile and wearable computing devices being prevalent, natural interaction with such devices using speech is needful.(Lopez-Meyer, Cordourier-Maruri, Quinto-Martinez, & Tickoo, 2016) presents the analysis of ANN and DTW for spoken keyword recognition for wearable devices under transient noise conditions. In addition to selecting the first 12 MFCC features from the extracted, they derived additional features such as energy, deltas (velocity), and double deltas (acceleration), to have a 36 dimensional vector per frame. Some works from the literature based on DTW are shown in Table 6.

- **Vector Quantization:** Being an important method of signal processing, Vector Quantization gives significant results in speaker recognition. Training and recognizing are the two steps in VQ. The speaker models are formed by clustering the speaker's feature vectors in K non-overlapping clusters. Each cluster C_i is represented by a code vector c_i, which is the centroid. The resulting set of code vectors $\{c_1, c_2, \ldots\ldots\ldots c_k\}$ is called a codebook, and it serves as the model of the speak-

Table 5. Significant Works on GMM based speaker recognition

Sl. No:	Approach	Results and Description
1	Ensemble based speaker recognition using unsupervised data selection(Huang et al., 2016)	• Applied LTF analysis on MFCC • Used ensemble method in GMM-UBM architecture with unsupervised data collection. • Finding: Improved speaker recognition performance.
2	Speaker recognition based on GMM and SVM (Huo & Zhang, 2012)	• A model combining GMM and SVM is used for speaker recognition • Finding: Achieved better performance than both using separately.
3	Structural MAP Adaptation in GMM-Supervector based Speaker Recognition (Ferràs, Shinoda, & Furui, 2011)	• Approach to tackle data scarceness issues using Structural MAP (SMAP), Maximum a Posteriori adaptation. • Used GMM-SVM for modeling. • Finding: Using GMM-SVM with a linear kernel outperforms the existing state of the art systems.
4	Speaker Recognition System Using the Improved GMM-based Clustering Algorithm (Xin-Xing Jing, Ling Zhan, Hong Zhao, Ping Zhou, 2010)	• Applied improved GMM based clustering algorithm • Used subtractive clustering for centroid initialization. • Finding: Higher clustering accuracy and speaker recognition rate than traditional GMM.

Table 6. Significant Works on DTW based speaker recognition

Sl No:	Approach	Results and Discussion
1	Personal Threshold in a Small Scale Text-dependent Speaker Recognition (Chen, Heimark, & Gligoroski, 2013)	• Text dependent speaker recognition system which uses Modular Audio Recognition framework (MARF) • DTW is used in the training and comparison processes to create reliable feature references and generate countable distance information • Personal thresholds used for individual users. • Achieved optimal tradeoffs of FAR and FRR(13% and 12% respectively)
2	Analyzing Artificial Neural Networks and Dynamic Time Warping for Spoken Keyword Recognition Under Transient Noise Conditions(Lopez-Meyer et al., 2016)	• Analyses the tradeoffs in performance between ANN and DTW under three different transient noise conditions. • Analyzed how the different types of transient noise affect the recognition methodologies of interest. • Finding ; In the case of storage both methodologies used comparable memory for Speaker Dependent systems, but Speaker Independent model needed more memory with DTW methodology
3	Speaker Recognition Based on Combination of LPCC and MFCC (Yuan et al., 2010)	• LPCC and MFCC used for text independent speaker recognition. • Compared the recognition rates for LPCC, MFCC and their combination by using VQ and DTW • Finding: Combination of LPCC and MFCC gave higher recognition rates.

er. The model size (number of code vectors) is significantly smaller than the training set. The distribution of the code vectors follows the same underlying distribution as the training vectors. Thus, the codebook effectively reduces the amount of data by preserving the essential information of the original distribution. The matching function in VQ-based speaker recognition is typically defined as the quantization distortion between two vector sets $X = \{x_1, x_2, \ldots\ldots x_T\}$ and $C = \{c_1, c_2, \ldots\ldots\ldots c_k\}$. Table 7 summarizes some works based on Vector Quantization.

- **Neural Networks:** The model can take many forms such as multi-layer perceptions or radial basis functions. models are explicitly trained to discriminate between the speaker being modeled and some alternative speakers. Training can be computationally expensive and models are sometimes not generalizable. The ability to process uncertain information, system flexibility, self-learning and organizing makes neural networks suitable for automatic recognition.

The inference from (Lopez-Meyer et al., 2016) is that simplicity and robustness of the ANN methodology make it more suitable for "always-listening" speaker independent acoustic front-end applications from a hardware implementation perspective, particularly when compared to computationally heavier methods like Gaussian Mixes models and ANN-Hidden Markov Models hybrids, usually used for larger vocabulary tasks like continuous speech to text.

The use of Deep Neural Networks (DNN) is gaining impression in the field of biometrics for past few decades. Due to its wide range of impacts in machine learning and pattern recognition, it could achieve successful applications in image and automatic speech recognition. There are two general methods of applying DNN to the speech recognition tasks. The first or "direct" method uses a DNN trained as a classifier for the intended recognition task directly to discriminate between speakers for SR. The second or "indirect" method uses a DNN possibly trained for a different purpose to extract data that is then used to train a secondary classifier for the intended recognition task (Richardson, Member, Reynolds, & Dehak, 2015). With recent developments of DNN, the feature extraction and pattern classification can be unified in one learning framework, i.e., learning efficient discriminative feature as well as clas-

Table 7. Significant Works on VQ based speaker recognition

Sl No.	Approach	Findings and Description
1	Vector Quantization Approach for Speaker Recognitionusing MFCC and Inverted MFCC (Singh, 2011)	• shown that the inverted Mel-Frequency Cepstral Coefficients is one of the performance enhancement parameters for speaker recognition, which contains high frequency region complementary information in it. • Uses Gaussian shaped filter while calculating MFCC and inverted MFCC instead of traditional triangular shaped bins. • VQ feature matching technique is used which resulted in high accuracy and simplicity. • achieved 98.57% of efficiency with a very short test voice sample of 2 seconds.
2	Vector Quantization Approach for Speaker Recognition (Kamale & Kawitkar, 2013)	• Feature extracted by MFCC • Vector Quantization (VQ) approach is used for mapping vectors from a large vector space to a finite number of regions in that space • LBG algorithm due to Linde, Buzo and Gray is used for clustering a set of L training vectors into a set of M codebook vectors. • 75% accuracy using VQLBG algorithm.
3	Speaker Recognition using Vector Quantization by MFCC and KMCG Clustering Algorithm (Kekre H.B,Bharadi V A, Sawant A R et al.(2012)	• A combination of MFCC and Kekere's Median Codebook Generation Algorithm (KMCG). • Achieved an EER of 84% for True Acceptance Rate (TAR) Vs True Rejection Rate (TRR) analysis. • Finding:KMCG is simpler to generate and faster calculations can be achieved; it gives results better than the existing LBG algorithm for Vector Quantization
4	Comparison of Indonesian Speaker Recognition Using Vector Quantization and Hidden Markov Model for Unclear Pronunciation Problem (Handaya, Fakhruroja, Muhammad, Hidayat, & Machbub, 2016)	• a comparison of two classifier methods based on accuracy level in Indonesian speaker recognition for unclear pronunciation problem in a word, simple sentences, and complete sentences. • VQ based on distortion distance and the second method is Hidden Markov Model (HMM) based on the probability value of the data is observed. • Finding: HMM method has better accuracy than VQ method especially for pronunciation of simple sentences.

sification simultaneously(Lu, Shen, Tsao, & Kawai, 2016). It is inferred that multi-task learning can be used for improving generalization ability of the model for each task.

Besides DNN, other Deep Learning techniques like Deep belief Networks and Restricted Boltzmann Machines (RBM) are also being explored in the field of speech processing especially in speech recognition (Ghahabi & Hernando, 2017). DBNs and RBMs are generative models where DBMs have multiple hidden layers of stochastic units above a visible layer which represents a data vector and RBMs are constructed from two undirected layers of stochastic hidden and visible units. The success use of i-vectors in speaker recognition and DL techniques in speech processing applications has encouraged the research community to combine those techniques for speaker recognition. Two kinds of combination can be considered. DL techniques can be used in the i-vector extraction process, or applied as a backend. Some significant works using Neural networks are summarized in Table 8.

- **Hidden Markov Models:** Based on the literature, HMM based models produces the best performances. HMM is used to encode the temporal evolution of the features and efficiently model statistical variations of features to provide a statistical representation of how a speaker produces sounds. HMM parameters are estimated from the speech using automated algorithms. During verification, the likelihood of the test feature sequence is computed against the speaker's HMMs. For text dependent applications, whole phrases or phonemes may be modeled using multi-state left-

Table 8. Significant Works on Neural Network based speaker recognition

Sl No.	Approach	Findings and Description
1	A Pseudo-task Design in Multi-task Learning Deep Neural Network for Speaker Recognition (Lu et al., 2016)	• Applied multi-task learning strategy in DNN learning for speaker recognition • Feature extraction by MFCC • Voice Activity Detection Algorithm is applied on each utterance to remove long duration silence in speech. • a pseudo-task was designed as an auxiliary task to the main task in a multi-task learning framework. • Finding: the auxiliary task can have effect as parameter space constraint for improving the generalization ability of the DNN model.
2	Deep Learning Backend for Single and Multi-Session i-Vector Speaker Recognition (Ghahabi & Hernando, 2017)	• make use of deep architectures for backend i-vector classification • took the advantage of unsupervised learning of DBNs to train a global model referred to as Universal DBN (UDBN) and DNN supervised learning to model each target speaker discriminatively • DL technology is used as a backend in which a two-class hybrid DBN-DNN is trained for each target speaker to increase the discrimination between target i-vector/s and the i-vectors of other speakers (non-targets/impostors) • Finding: the proposed hybrid system fills approximately 46% of the performance gap between the cosine and the oracle PLDA scoring systems in terms of min DCF.
3	Deep Neural Network Approaches to Speaker and Language Recognition (Richardson et al., 2015)	• Developed a DNN BNF i-vector system and demonstrated substantial performance gain when applying the system to both the DAC13 SR and LRE11 LR benchmarks. • 55% reduction in EER for the DAC13 out-of-domain condition and a 48% reduction in on the LRE11 30 s test condition. • Inference: further gains are possible using score or feature fusion leading to the possibility of a single i-vector extractor producing state-of-the-art SR and LR performance

to right HMMs. For text-independent applications, single state HMMs, also known as Gaussian Mixture Models (GMMs), are used. Some relevant works on HMM based recognition are depicted in Table 9.

Recent Research Trends in Speaker Recognition

In addition to the above discussed, ensemble based learning methods also have been experimented in the area of speaker recognition to attain improved performance. A recent work which uses ensemble based learning by dividing the speech utterance into several subsets based on the acoustic characteristics is provided in (Huang et al., 2016).Applying long term feature (LTF) analysis on traditional MFCC, discriminative acoustic features are extracted and similarity metric are calculated using vector-based and likelihood-based distance metrics. After applying the clustering algorithm, they used ensemble classifiers. The speaker recognition performance is found to be improved while using the ensemble classifiers with unsupervised data selection.

Alternative methods to improve i-vector space and solve the case of low discrimination by class imbalance are continued to be investigated in the field of automatic speaker recognition. A recently developed system (Sheng, K., Dong, W et al .2017). used centroid aware balanced boosting to solve class imbalance and thereby increase efficiency of learning. Techniques like Adaptive Neighborhood component analysis (AdaNCA) and Linear Magnet Loss (LMNL) are used with ASV to strengthen local discriminative modeling. The work insights into its future modification using deep learning and some efforts to exploit intrinsic data structure.

Table 9. Significant Works on HMM based speaker recognition

Sl No:	Approach	Results and Discussion
1	HMM-Based Phrase-Independent i-vector Extractor for Text-Dependent Speaker Verification(Zeinali, Sameti, & Burget, 2017)	• HMM based extension of the I vector approach • HMM-UBM is used to collect statistics for I vector extraction • Normalized I vectors using phrase-dependent Within-Class Covariance Normalization (WCCN) • Findings: I vector/HMM works much better than I vector/GMM.
2	Comparison of Indonesian Speaker Recognition Using Vector Quantization and Hidden Markov Model for Unclear Pronunciation Problem (Handaya et al., 2016)	• Compares VQ method and HMM method • Feature extraction based on MFCC. • Finding: HMM outperforms VQ
3	Speech and Speaker Recognition System using Artificial Neural Networks and Hidden Markov Model (Dey, Mohanty, & Chugh, 2012)	• Spectrogram analysis of speech signal is performed. • Signal is noise reduced and normalized • Mapping using ANN and HMM • Finding: For more than 80% cases, recognition was success, the remaining 15% needed additional features for training.
4	Support Vector Machines Based Text Dependent Speaker Verification Using HMM Supervectors (Dong, Dong, Li, & Wang, 2008)	• HMM supervectors are used as feature vectors in SVM • Used two SVM kernels: Linear Kernel and Dynamic time alignment kernel. • Normalized SVM output scores using speaker independent HMM supervectors. • Finding: HMM supervectors in SVM had lower performance than conventional GMM and realized that their fusion can give a slight improvement.

Adaptive Neuro Fuzzy Inference Systems (ANFIS) has been tried in the field of speaker as well as speech recognition. In (Pandey, 2010) Features extracted using LPC,LPCC,RC,LAR,LSF and ARSCIN are fed to ANFIS. The structure of ANFIS was designed by setting the premise parameters using subclustering method and hybrid learning algorithm was used. Their model obtained a minimum and maximum of 73.91% and 95.65% accuracies respectively. A Genetic Wavelet Adaptive Network based on Fuzzy inference systems (GWANFIS) which consists of three layers such as genetic algorithm, wavelet and adaptive net- work based on fuzzy inference system (ANFIS) is introduced in (Avci & Avci, 2009). The system was shown to be very effective in detecting real speech signals. A low overhead voice authentication system based on equalization and scaling of voice harmonics is studied in (Adibi, 2014).

The authors propose a context and language independent speaker recognition method with its computations and verification processes integrated in a cloud platform. Since feature selection is the highest impacting factor in Speaker recognition, Optimization methods such as Particle Swarm Optimization, Genetic Algorithm, Ant Colony etc are to be used for selecting optimal features. Realizing the fact that recognition rates depends on the precision of the feature vector values, application of fuzzy logic before inputting to the traditional speaker models seems to improve the results considerably. This is because the voice feature values we obtain from different devices differ for the same speaker itself. Also the same speaker's voice through the same device differs in different pathological conditions. By fuzzifying the input features the recognition rates are expected to surpass the existing ones.

MULTIMODAL AUTHENTICATION SYSTEMS

The analysis of parallel evolution of the biometric identification technologies has revealed the fact that the use of a single hardware modality for identification purposes may no longer be the most intelligent choice for many industries. Single modality biometric systems have to contend with a variety of problems such as noisy data, intra class variations, non-universality, spoof attacks, and distinctiveness. In IoT scenario single modal systems degrade in the presence of sensory noise and mismatch between training and testing environments. Some of these limitations can be addressed by deploying multimodal biometric systems that integrate multiple biometric modalities in a single scan to alleviate the challenges of a unimodal system (W. Zhao & Chellappa, 2006a).

Multi-modal biometric are capable of using more than one physiological or behavioral characteristic for enrollment, verification, and identification. The integration of voice biometrics with any other authentication system improves the overall recognition performance. Listed below are the advantages of multimodal systems over single modal systems identified from the recent researches(W. Zhao & Chellappa, 2006b)(Morgera, 2009).

- **Accuracy:** As biometric traits remain independent of each other; it results in higher accuracy while identifying a person.
- **Security:** By eliminating attacks like spoofing, the level of security for a multimodal system is higher. It is unable to spoof multiple biometric traits at once by a person.
- **Liveness Detection:** Multi-modal biometric systems ask end users to submit multiple biometric traits randomly which ensures strong liveness detection to protect from spoofing or hackers.
- **Universality:** A multimodal biometric system is universal in nature, even if a person is unable to provide a form of biometric due to disability or illness, the system can take other form of biometric for authentication.
- **Cost Effectiveness:** Multimodal biometric systems are cost effective by providing higher levels of security to lessen the risk of breaches or criminal attacks.

In sensor level fusion, the raw data from multiple biometric sensors are combined to generate new data from which features are extracted. For example, combining 2D face images from more than one cameras, we can generate a 3D face input for a 3D face recognition system. Sensor-level fusion is extremely rare in multimodal biometric systems because the raw data obtained from the various sensors are not usually compatible (W. Zhao & Chellappa, 2006b).

For biometric fusion at the feature level, the features extracted from multiple sensors are concatenated to form a high dimensionality feature vector in a hyperspace. The problem of efficient fusion when the multiple sensors are incompatible is still open. However, the integration of multiple features is expected to perform better than fusion at score and decision levels, because the features extracted from different signals contain much richer information than those in higher level (Kung, Mak, & Lin, 2005). An effective method of feature level fusion by integrating features of static face images and text-independent speech segments using Genetic Algorithm for optimization is discussed in (Morgera, 2009). In this work, the weights of individual feature vectors are obtained with a GA algorithm and subsequently used in a classification procedure for person recognition. Different algorithms like Tabu Search (TS), Least Square (LS), Weighted Least Square (WLS), Probabilistic Neural Network Methods(PNN) can be used for the procedures of feature fusion.

In matching score level fusion, each modal unit provides a matching score and the fusion mechanism combines these matching scores to determine the identity. A great amount of work has been done in score level fusion. A recent work on score level biometric fusion considered 4 different biometric traits(Elmir, Elberrichi, & Adjoudj, 2012). They considered iris, palm print, left and right fingerprints as input which are converted into different color spaces. The features were extracted using Thepade's sorted ternary block truncation coding. It shows a clear evidence of improvement in the true acceptance rate of recognition. A score level fusion based on triangular norms is proposed in (Peng, El-Latif, Li, & Niu, 2014) with four finger biometric traits. T-norms are considered as most suitable general candidates for generalized intersection operations of fuzzy sets in the mathematical fuzzy community. T-norms are preferred as no learning or training is needed and the reduction in computational complexity. It is inferred that score level fusion is easy to be utilized to obtain effective performance by the discriminated availability between genuine and imposter scores uses the face biometric Feature Extraction by using PCA (Principle Component Analysis) approach as well as the fingerprint recognition by using Minutiae Extraction approach and the fingerprint recognition by using Gabor Filtering. A sum score level fusion is carried out in (Telgad, Deshmukh, & Siddiqui, 2014) where face and fingerprint multimodalities are used.

There are three categories of score level fusion such as

1. **Transformation Based Fusion:** To obtain effective performance by the discriminated availability between genuine and imposter scores.
2. **Classifier-Based Fusion:** Scores from multiple matchers are treated as a feature vector and a classifier is constructed to discriminate genuine and impostor scores.
3. **Density-Based Fusion:** This is based on the likelihood ratio test and it requires explicit estimation of genuine and impostor match score densities.

Present day researches deviate to combining feature level fusion and score level fusion in multimodal biometrics. (Daniel, Mihaela, & Romulus, 2015) presents such a system which takes the advantages of both the techniques to achieve a biometric system which is more accurate and efficient. A comparison of feature and score level fusion in multimodal biometric identification using iris and palmprint traits with fractional transformed energy content is discussed in (Thepade, Bhondave, & Mishra, 2016).

At decision level, each modal provides its classification result which will be fed to a decision block. Later strategies like majority voting, conduct information space and OR rules are employed for final ruling. Because of the lack of information content, fusion at decision level is considered to be rigid. A decision level fusion is performed using KNN and Neural classifiers using logical conjunction and disjunction methods (Garg, 2016). The work shows that logical conjunction based decision fusion achieve higher performance as compare to logical disjunction based methods. A novel feature extraction technique for finger vein and iris traits is discussed in (Venkatesha, 2014)combines the decisions from the individual modalities using the conventional AND rule. Significant improvements in FAR and FRR is shown in this work. Multimodal systems can be classified as in Figure 6 based on the level at which the fusion is carried out (Morgera, 2009).

Figure 6. Classification of Multimodal Systems

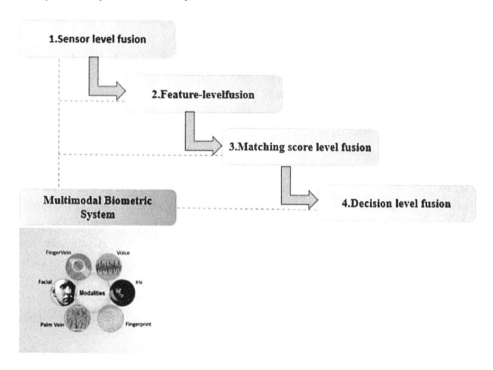

FUTURE TRENDS

- **Exploitation of Features:** Apart from the low level spectral features, some high level features carrying speaker specific information has to be explored. It is obvious that exploring robust and less noise susceptible features will improve the accuracy.
- **Real World Robustness:** Obtaining real world data from IoT environment, their examination and development of new improved methods.
- **Language Independency:** It should be feasible to recognize speakers even if the speech samples are of different languages.
- **Context Independency:** Recognition systems independent of the physical conditions of the speaker like speaker's health, ageing, extreme emotional conditions, the attitude of the speaker and situations like channel mismatch or mismatch in recording conditions are future expectations.
- **Enhanced Features and Modeling:** Discovering advanced voice features that possess enhanced discriminative ability will unearth new research paradigms. Also new signal processing alternatives that well suit the speaker verification systems should be explored to provide excellent recognition rates.
- **Fog-Centric Authentication:** Developing Biometric authentication and verification on a Fog-centric IoT architecture which provides high storage capacity and computing capability and inter operability of sensing objects.
- **Context Aware Authentication:** To be used with IoT which is dynamic and heterogeneous in nature, authentication methods adapting to changing contexts are appropriate.

- **Challenging Ageing:** The human voice's ever changing nature is challenging customer service departments. An effort to well overcome the problem will be of great acceptance in the coming days.
- **Challenging Voice Morphing:** Recent Research showed the use of an off the shelf tool attempting to penetrate automated human verification system using voice (Gaubitch, 2017). It has been found that voice morphing can transform the attacker's voice to the victim's voice to utter any word. So, challenging voice morphing will be of future interests.
- **Countering Replay/Spoofing:** The often neglecting less sophisticated attacks like spoofing and replay causes huge loses. Also the majority of literature concentrates on specific spoofing attacks while variants of spoofing attacks like combined spoofing can be expected in practice. So generalized countermeasures should be taken to eliminate such more frequent and less detecting attacks.

CONCLUSION

The chapter presents a pervasive review on the development of Voice Biometrics as an authentication system with focus on its deployment in the field of Internet of Things. With a brief introduction specifying the need of Voice Biometrics and its evolution, the authors tried to give an insight into the current state of affairs and made discussions about merits, demerits and applications in the scenario of IoT. The authors have analyzed and evaluated various traditional as well as emerging methods for feature extraction, speaker modeling, current research trends etc, giving a short proposal for developing a context and language independent speaker recognition system. In addition the necessity of a multimodal biometric authentication and a brief review of their types are mentioned. Further, the authors tried to identify the gaps in the field and specified some future research directions.

ACKNOWLEDGMENT

This research was supported by the Kerala State Council for Science, Technology and Environment [KSCSTE/5623/2017-FSHP-ES].

REFERENCES

A Brief History of Voice Biometrics - VoiceVault Voice Authentication. (n.d.). Retrieved October 20, 2017, from http://voicevault.com/a-brief-history-of-voice-biometrics/

Abdul, W., Ali, Z., Ghouzali, S., Alfawaz, B., Muhammad, G., & Hossain, M. S. (2017). Biometric Security Through Visual Encryption for Fog Edge Computing. *IEEE Access: Practical Innovations, Open Solutions*, 5, 5531–5538. doi:10.1109/ACCESS.2017.2693438

Abdulla, W. H. (2007). Robust speaker modeling using perceptually motivated feature. *Pattern Recognition Letters*, 28(11), 1333–1342. doi:10.1016/j.patrec.2006.11.018

Adibi, S. (2014). A low overhead scaled equalized harmonic-based voice authentication system. *Telematics and Informatics*, *31*(1), 137–152. doi:10.1016/j.tele.2013.02.004

Al-Ali, A. K. H., Dean, D., Senadji, B., Chandran, V., & Naik, G. R. (2017). Enhanced Forensic Speaker Verification Using a Combination of DWT and MFCC Feature Warping in the Presence of Noise and Reverberation Conditions. *IEEE Access: Practical Innovations, Open Solutions*, *5*, 15400–15413. doi:10.1109/ACCESS.2017.2728801

Avci, E., & Avci, D. (2009). Expert Systems with Applications The speaker identification by using genetic wavelet adaptive network based fuzzy inference system. *Expert Systems with Applications*, *36*(6), 9928–9940. doi:10.1016/j.eswa.2009.01.081

Ayoub, B., Jamal, K., & Arsalane, Z. (2016). Gammatone frequency cepstral coefficients for speaker identification over VoIP networks. *2016 International Conference on Information Technology for Organizations Development, IT4OD 2016*. 10.1109/IT4OD.2016.7479293

Babich, A. (2012). *Biometric Authentication. Types of biometric identifiers* (Thesis). University of Applied Science.

Biometrics, T. F. Face, Fingerprint, Iris, Palm and Voice. (n.d.). Retrieved November 30, 2017, from https://www.bayometric.com/biometrics-face-finger-iris-palm-voice/

Biswas, A., Sahu, P. K., Bhowmick, A., & Chandra, M. (2014). Hindi vowel classification using GFCC and formant analysis in sensor mismatch condition. *WSEAS Transactions on Systems*, *13*(1), 130–143.

Bonomi, F., Milito, R., Zhu, J., & Addepalli, S. (2012). Fog Computing and Its Role in the Internet of Things. *Proceedings of the First Edition of the MCC Workshop on Mobile Cloud Computing*, 13–16. 10.1145/2342509.2342513

Chen, Y., Heimark, E., & Gligoroski, D. (2013). Personal threshold in a small scale text-dependent speaker recognition. *Proceedings - 2013 International Symposium on Biometrics and Security Technologies*, 162–170. 10.1109/ISBAST.2013.29

Chow, D., & Abdulla, W. (2004). Robust speaker identification based on perceptual log area ratio and gaussian mixture models. *Eighth International Conference on Spoken Language Processing*, 2–5. Retrieved from http://www.isca-speech.org/archive/interspeech_2004/i04_1761.html

Chow, D., & Abdulla, W. H. (2004). Speaker identification based on log area ratio and Gaussian mixture models in narrow-band speech speech understanding / interaction. Lecture Notes in Artificial Intelligence, 3157, 901–902.

Daniel, D. M., Mihaela, C., & Romulus, T. (2015). Combining feature extraction level and score level fusion in a multimodal biometric system. *2014 11th International Symposium on Electronics and Telecommunications, ISETC 2014 - Conference Proceedings*. 10.1109/ISETC.2014.7010807

Daqrouq, K., & Al Azzawi, K. Y. (2012). Average framing linear prediction coding with wavelet transform for text-independent speaker identification system. *Computers & Electrical Engineering*, *38*(6), 1467–1479. doi:10.1016/j.compeleceng.2012.04.014

Dey, N. S., Mohanty, R., & Chugh, K. L. (2012). Speech and Speaker Recognition System Using Artificial Neural Networks and Hidden Markov Model. *2012 International Conference on Communication Systems and Network Technologies*, 311–315. 10.1109/CSNT.2012.221

Dong, C., Dong, Y., Li, J., & Wang, H. (2008, January). *Support vector machines based text dependent speaker verification using HMM supervectors*. Odyssey.

Elmir, Y., Elberrichi, Z., & Adjoudj, R. (2012). Score level fusion based multimodal biometric identification (Fingerprint & voice). *2012 6th International Conference on Sciences of Electronics, Technologies of Information and Telecommunications (SETIT)*, 146–150. 10.1109/SETIT.2012.6481903

Ferràs, M., Shinoda, K., & Furui, S. (2011). Structural MAP adaptation in GMM-supervector based speaker recognition. *ICASSP, IEEE International Conference on Acoustics, Speech and Signal Processing - Proceedings*, 5432–5435. 10.1109/ICASSP.2011.5947587

Fog Computing vs. Edge Computing: What's the Difference? | Automation World. (n.d.). Retrieved November 30, 2017, from https://www.automationworld.com/fog-computing-vs-edge-computing-whats-difference

Gajic, B., & Paliwal, K. K. (2006). Robust speech recognition in noisy environments based on subband spectral centroid histograms. *IEEE Transactions on Audio, Speech, and Language Processing*, *14*(2), 600–608. doi:10.1109/TSA.2005.855834

Garg, S. N. (2016). *Multimodal Biometric System Based On Decision Level Fusion*. Academic Press.

Gaubitch, N. (2017). How voice ageing impacts biometric effectiveness. *Biometric Technology Today*, *2017*(6), 8–9. 10.1016/S0969-4765(17)30115-7

Ghahabi, O., & Hernando, J. (2017). Deep Larning Backend for Single and Multisession i-Vector Speaker Recognition. *IEEE/ACM Transactions on Audio Speech and Language Processing*, *25*(4), 807–817. 10.1109/TASLP.2017.2661705

Handaya, D., Fakhruroja, H., Hidayat, E. M. I., & Machbub, C. (2016, December). Comparison of Indonesian speaker recognition using vector quantization and Hidden Markov Model for unclear pronunciation problem. In *Frontiers of Information Technology (FIT), 2016 International Conference on* (pp. 39-45). IEEE. 10.1109/ICSEngT.2016.7849620

Hu, P., Ning, H., Qiu, T., Zhang, Y., & Luo, X. (2017). Fog computing based face identification and resolution scheme in internet of things. *IEEE Transactions on Industrial Informatics*, *13*(4), 1910–1920. doi:10.1109/TII.2016.2607178

Huang, C.-L., Wang, J.-C., & Ma, B. (2016). Ensemble based speaker recognition using unsupervised data selection. *APSIPA Transactions on Signal and Information Processing*, *5*, e10. doi:10.1017/ATSIP.2016.10

Huo, C. B., & Zhang, C. J. (2012). The research of speaker recognition based on GMM and SVM. *Proceedings 2012 International Conference on System Science and Engineering, ICSSE 2012*, 373–375. 10.1109/ICSSE.2012.6257210

Jing, X.-X., Zhan, L., Zhao, H., & Zhou, P. (2010). Speaker recognition system using the improved GMM-based clustering algorithm. *IEEE International Conference on Intelligent computing and Integrated systems,ICISS 2010*. doi: 10.1109/ICISS.2010.5655122

Juo, J., & Yang, S. (2016). Speaker recognition based on wavelet packet decomposition and Volterra adaptive model. *IEEE International Conference on Computer and Communications(ICCC)*. doi: 10.1109/ CompComm.2016.7925042

Kamale, H. E., & Kawitkar, R. S. (2008). Vector quantization approach for speaker recognition. *International Journal of Computer Technology and Electronics Engineering*, 110-114..

Kantarci, B., Erol-Kantarci, M., & Schuckers, S. (2015). Towards secure cloud-centric Internet of Biometric Things. *2015 IEEE 4th International Conference on Cloud Networking, CloudNet 2015*, 81–83. 10.1109/CloudNet.2015.7335286

Kekre, H. B. (2012). Speaker Identification using Spectrograms of Varying Frame Sizes. *International Journal of Computer Applications, 50*(20), 27-33.

Kekre, H. B., Bharadi, V. A., & Sawant, A. R. (2012) Speaker Recognition using Vector Quantization by MFCC and KMCG Clustering Algorithm. *IEEE International Conference on Communication, Information, Information and Computing Technology, ICCICT 2012*. 10.1109/ICCICT.2012.6398146

Kingsbury, B. E., Morgan, N., & Greenberg, S. (1998). Robust speech recognition using the modulation spectrogram. *Speech Communication, 25*(1), 117–132. doi:10.1016/S0167-6393(98)00032-6

Kinnunen, T., & Li, H. (2010). An overview of text-independent speaker recognition: From features to supervectors. *Speech Communication, 52*(1), 12–40. doi:10.1016/j.specom.2009.08.009

Kinnunen, T., Zhang, B., Zhu, J., & Wang, Y. (2007). Speaker verification with adaptive spectral sub-band centroids. *Advances in Biometrics*, 58-66.

Kung, S. Y. (Sun Y., Mak, M. W., & Lin, S.-H. (2005). *Biometric authentication: A machine learning approach*. Prentice Hall Professional Technical Reference.

Li, P., Li, Y., Luo, D., & Luo, H. (2015). Speaker Identification Using FrFT-based Spectrogram and RBF Neural Network. *Proceedings of the 34th Chinese Control Conference*, 3674–3679. 10.1109/ ChiCC.2015.7260207

Lopez-Meyer, P., Cordourier-Maruri, H., Quinto-Martinez, A., & Tickoo, O. (2016). Analyzing Artificial Neural Networks and Dynamic Time Warping for spoken keyword recognition under transient noise conditions. *Proceedings of the International Conference on Sensing Technology*, 274–277. 10.1109/ ICSensT.2015.7438406

Lu, X., Shen, P., Tsao, Y., & Kawai, H. (2016). A Pseudo-task Design in Multi-task Learning Deep Neural Network for Speaker Recognition. *10th International Symposium on Chinese Spoken Language Processing(ISCSLP)*. 10.1109/ISCSLP.2016.7918433

Luan, T. H., Gao, L., Li, Z., Xiang, Y., Wei, G., & Sun, L. (2015). *Fog Computing: Focusing on Mobile Users at the Edge*. Academic Press. 10.1016/j.jnca.2015.02.002

Lung, S. Y. (2004). Adaptive fuzzy wavelet algorithm for text-independent speaker recognition. *Pattern Recognition, 37*(10), 2095–2096. doi:10.1016/j.patcog.2004.03.015

Lung, S. Y. (2010). Improved wavelet feature extraction using kernel analysis for text independent speaker recognition. *Digital Signal Processing: A Review Journal, 20*(5), 1400–1407. 10.1016/j.dsp.2009.12.004

Markowitz, J. A. (2000). Voice biometrics. *Communications of the ACM, 43*(9), 66–73. doi:10.1145/348941.348995

Monteiro, A., Dubey, H., Mahler, L., Yang, Q., & Mankodiya, K. (2016). Fit: A Fog Computing Device for Speech Tele-Treatments. *2016 IEEE International Conference on Smart Computing, SMARTCOMP 2016*, 10–12. 10.1109/SMARTCOMP.2016.7501692

Morgera, S. D. (2009). A method towards biometric feature fusion. *International Journal of Biometrics, 1*(4), 2009.

Nuance. (2011). *Nuance Voice Biometrics: Improving the Caller Experience*. Academic Press.

Pandey, B. (2010). Multilingual Speaker Recognition Using ANFIS. *2010 2nd International Conference on Signal Processing Systems (ICSPS)*, 714–718.

Peng, J., El-Latif, A. A. A., Li, Q., & Niu, X. (2014). Multimodal biometric authentication based on score level fusion of finger biometrics. *Optik (Stuttgart), 125*(23), 6891–6897. doi:10.1016/j.ijleo.2014.07.027

Reynolds, D. a. (2002). An overview of automatic speaker recognition technology. *IEEE International Conference on Acoustics Speech and Signal Processing, 4*, IV-4072-IV-4075. 10.1109/ICASSP.2002.5745552

Richardson, F., Member, S., Reynolds, D., & Dehak, N. (2015). Deep Neural Network Approaches to Speaker and Language Recognition. *IEEE Signal Processing Letters, 22*(10), 1671–1675. doi:10.1109/LSP.2015.2420092

Sekar, K. (2012). Techniques for Speaker Identification System. *XI Biennial Conference of the International Biometric Society (Indian Region) on Computational Statistics and Bio-Sciences*, 88–94.

Seo, J. S., Member, A., Jin, M., Lee, S., Member, S., Jang, D., … Yoo, C. D. (2006). Audio Fingerprinting Based on Normalized Spectral Subband Moments. *Proceedings of IEEE International Conference on Acoustics, Speech, and Signal Processing*, 209–212. doi: 10.1109/ICASSP.2005.1415684

Shao, Y., Jin, Z., Wang, D., & Srinivasan, S. (2009). An auditory-based feature for robust speech recognition. *ICASSP, IEEE International Conference on Acoustics, Speech and Signal Processing - Proceedings*, (1), 4625–4628. 10.1109/ICASSP.2009.4960661

Sheng, K., Dong, W., Li, W., Razik, J., Huang, F., & Hu, B. (2017). Centroid-aware local discriminative metric learning in speaker verification. *Pattern Recognition, 72*, 176–185. doi:10.1016/j.patcog.2017.07.007

Shi, X., Yang, H., & Zhou, P. (2016). Robust Speaker Recognition Based on Improved GFCC 27r J. *IEEE International Conference on Computer and Communications (ICCC)*, 1927–1931. doi: 10.1109/CompComm.2016.7925037

Singh, S. (2011). Vector Quantization Approach for Speaker Recognition using MFCC and Inverted MFCC. *International Journal of Computer Applications, 17*(1).

Sremath, S., Reza, S., Singh, A., & Wang, R. (2017). Speaker identification features extraction methods : A systematic review. *Expert Systems with Applications*, *90*, 250–271. doi:10.1016/j.eswa.2017.08.015

Telgad, R. L., Deshmukh, P. D., & Siddiqui, A. M. N. (2014). Combination approach to score level fusion for Multimodal Biometric system by using face and fingerprint. *International Conference on Recent Advances and Innovations in Engineering, ICRAIE 2014*. 10.1109/ICRAIE.2014.6909320

Thepade, S. D., Bhondave, R. K., & Mishra, A. (2016). Comparing Score Level and Feature Level Fusion in Multimodal Biometric Identification Using Iris and Palmprint Traits with Fractional Transformed Energy Content. *Proceedings - 2015 International Conference on Computational Intelligence and Communication Networks, CICN 2015*, 306–311. 10.1109/CICN.2015.68

Thian, N. P. H., Sanderson, C., & Bengio, S. (2004). Spectral subband centroids as complementary features for speaker authentication. *Biometric Authentication Proceedings*, *3072*, 631–639. doi:10.1007/978-3-540-25948-0_86

Tiwari, A. K., Hasan, M. M., & Islam, M. (2013). Effect of ambient temperature on the performance of a combined cycle power plant. *Transactions of the Canadian Society for Mechanical Engineering*, *37*(4), 1177–1188. doi:10.4172cientificreports

Venkatesha, M. K., Radhika, K. R., & Sudhamani, M. J. (2014, December). Fusion at decision level in multimodal biometric authentication system using Iris and Finger Vein with novel feature extraction. In *India Conference (INDICON), 2014 Annual IEEE* (pp. 1-6). Academic Press.

Viewpoint: Why we need voice biometrics | IDG Connect. (n.d.). Retrieved December 4, 2017, from http://www.idgconnect.com/abstract/10564/viewpoint-why-voice-biometrics

Vinyals, O., & Friedland, G. (2008). *Modulation spectrogram features for improved speaker diarization* (pp. 630–633). INTERSPEECH.

Wang, Y., & Lawlor, B. (2017). Speaker recognition based on MFCC and BP neural networks. *2017 28th Irish Signals and Systems Conference (ISSC)*, 1–4. doi:10.1109/ISSC.2017.7983644

Workshop, J., Communication, H. S., & Arrays, M. (2014). Spectrogram patch based acoustic event detection and NTT. Communication Science Laboratories, NTT Corporation.

Yuan, Y., Zhao, P., & Zhou, Q. (2010). Research of speaker recognition based on combination of LPCC and MFCC. *Proceedings - 2010 IEEE International Conference on Intelligent Computing and Intelligent Systems, ICIS 2010, 3*, 765–767. 10.1109/ICICISYS.2010.5658337

Zeinali, H., Sameti, H., & Burget, L. (2017). HMM-based phrase-independent i-vector extractor for text-dependent speaker verification. *IEEE/ACM Transactions on Audio Speech and Language Processing*, *25*(7), 1421–1435. doi:10.1109/TASLP.2017.2694708

Zhao, W., & Chellappa, R. (2006a). *Face processing: Advanced modeling and methods*. Elsevier / Academic Press. Retrieved from https://books.google.co.in/books?hl=en&lr=&id=ZRw9dP7nj2kC&oi=fnd&pg=PP1&dq=)+Face+Processing:+Advanced+Modeling+and+Methods,+Academic+Press.&ots=6KhJxnC-O3&sig=v0NWu0HCdS7BuE5an6CQjFr1rk8#v=onepage&q=) Face Processing%3A Advanced Modeling and Methods%2C Academic Press.&f=false

Zhao, W., & Chellappa, R. (2006b). *Face processing : advanced modeling and methods.* Elsevier / Academic Press.

Zhao, X., Shao, Y., & Wang, D. (2012). CASA-based robust speaker identification. *IEEE Transactions on Audio, Speech, and Language Processing, 20*(5), 1608–1616. doi:10.1109/TASL.2012.2186803

Zhao, X., & Wang, D. (2013). Analyzing noise robustness of MFCC and GFCC features in speaker identification. *ICASSP, IEEE International Conference on Acoustics, Speech and Signal Processing - Proceedings,* 7204–7208. doi:10.1109/ICASSP.2013.6639061

KEY TERMS AND DEFINITIONS

Behaviometrics: Derived from the two words *behavior* and *biometrics*, behaviometrics means the analysis of a person's behavior rather than physical characteristics in order to identify him uniquely.

Internet of Biometric Things: An architecture that supports the accessibility of applications in IoT through biometric authentication schemes.

Liveness Detection: The detection of whether an acquired biometric sample data is coming from a currently active live user.

Multimodal Biometric Authentication: Refers to the use of more than one physiological or behavioral biometric characteristic for authentication purposes.

Speaker Diarization: The process of identifying and labeling different speakers from a speech segment by segmentation and clustering methods.

Speaker Recognition: The process of recognizing a speaker from his own voice characteristics.

Voice Morphing: The process of generating a person's voice using software in order to impersonate or obscure his identity.

Chapter 18
Text, Images, and Video Analytics for Fog Computing

A. Jayanthiladevi
Jain University, India

S. Murugan
Mewer University, India

K. Manivel
United Health Corporation, India

ABSTRACT

Today, images and image sequences (videos) make up about 80% of all corporate and public unstructured big data. As growth of unstructured data increases, analytical systems must assimilate and interpret images and videos as well as they interpret structured data such as text and numbers. An image is a set of signals sensed by the human eye and processed by the visual cortex in the brain creating a vivid experience of a scene that is instantly associated with concepts and objects previously perceived and recorded in one's memory. To a computer, images are either a raster image or a vector image. Simply put, raster images are a sequence of pixels with discreet numerical values for color; vector images are a set of color-annotated polygons. To perform analytics on images or videos, the geometric encoding must be transformed into constructs depicting physical features, objects and movement represented by the image or video. This chapter explores text, images, and video analytics in fog computing.

INTRODUCTION

Image analysis (also known as "computer vision") is the ability of computers to recognize attributes within an image.Image analysis methods extract information from an image by using automatic or semiautomatic techniques termed: scene analysis, image description, image understanding, pattern recognition, computer/machine vision etc. Image analysis differs from other types of image processing methods, such as enhancement or restoration in that the final result of image analysis procedures is a numerical output rather than a picture. The steps for image analysis are Preprocessing, Segmentation,

DOI: 10.4018/978-1-5225-5972-6.ch018

Feature extraction, Classification and interpretation. Image analytics can also identify faces within photos to determine sentiment, gender, age, and more. It can recognize multiple elements within a photo at the same time, including logos, faces, activities, objects, and scenes. It is the automatic algorithmic extraction and logical analysis of information found in image data using digital image processing techniques. The use of bar codes and QR codes are simple examples, but interesting examples are as complex as facial recognition and position and movement analysis. These constructs can then be logically analyzed by a computer (Er. Anjna, Er.Rajandeep Kaur, et al.,(2007).

Text analytics or text mining is the process of determining and collecting high-quality information from unstructured text such as a mass of Twitter posts, a collection of scientific papers, or restaurant reviews, depending on the focus of the organization conducting the analysis.Text analytics can be performed manually, but it is an inefficient process as expressed in Dr.V.Sankaranarayanan,(2010) et al., Therefore, text analytics software has been created that uses text mining and natural language processing algorithms to find meaning in huge amounts of text.Text analytics is the way to unlock the meaning from all of this unstructured text. Video is a major issue when considering big data. Videos and images contribute to 80% of unstructured data. Now days, CCTV cameras are the one form of digital information and surveillance. All these information is stored and processed for further use, but video contains lots of information and is generally large in size. Apart from videos, surveillance cameras generate a lot of information in seconds. Even a small Digital camera capturing an image stores millions of pixel information in mille seconds.

TEXT ANALYTICS

In the middle of 1980's the text mining was evolved but it was not well developed due to lack of sophisticated technology. Later the technology developed and along with it, the text mining was also developed. In text analytics Most of all information or data is available in textual form in databases. From these contexts, manual Analytics or effective extraction of important information are not possible. For that it is relevant to provide some automatic tools for analyzing large textual data. Text analytics or text mining refers process of deriving important information from text data. It will use to extract meaningful data from the text in Dilpreet Kaur, (May- 2014) et al., Text analytics widely use in government, research, and business needs. Data simply tells that what people did but text analytics tell you why. The text analytics is also called as "text mining" and is a way that has the unstructured data.From unstructured or semi structured text data all information will retrieve. From all textual data it will extract important information. After extracting information it will be categorized.

Working in Text Mining

The text mining has many processes or working methods and all these are combined to obtain the results that are nothing but the working of text mining. The stages involved in it are shown in Figure 1.

Information Retrieval System

The initial step in text mining is to search the body of documents and this happens in the information retrieval systems.Information retrieval is regarded as an extension to document retrieval where the docu-

Figure 1. Text mining areas

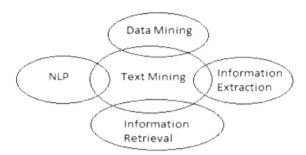

ments that are returned are processed to condense or extract the particular information sought by the user. Thus document retrieval could be followed by a text summarization stage that focuses on the query posed by the user, or an information extraction stage using techniques. IR systems help in to narrow down the set of documents that are relevant to a particular problem. As text mining involves applying very complex algorithms to large document collections, IR can speed up the analysis significantly by reducing the number of documents for analysis.

Natural Language Processing

It is the study of human language so that computers can understand natural languages as humans do. The natural language processing permits the computer to perform grammatical testing of a sentence towards the text of a document or file. While words of nouns, verbs, adverbs and adjectives are the building blocks of meaning, it is their correlation to each other within the structure of a sentence in a document, and within the context of what we already know about the world, that provides the true meaning of a text in M.Radha,(Dec 2011) et al., The role of NLP in text mining is to deliver the system in the information extraction phase as an input.

Information Extraction

The information extracting involves in the operation of data structuring. Thus, data structuring is considered as its vital performance. It is automatically extracting structured information from unstructured and/or semistructured machine-readable documents.

Data Mining

The data mining finds the patterns in huge data to find the new knowledge.It can be more fully characterized as the extraction of hidden, previously unknown, and useful information from data. The overall goal of the data mining process is to extract information from a data set and transform it into an understandable structure for further use by Kompal Ahuja, (June 2014).

Text Analytics System

Figure 2 shows steps for Text Analytics system.

Figure 2. Steps for Text Analytics system

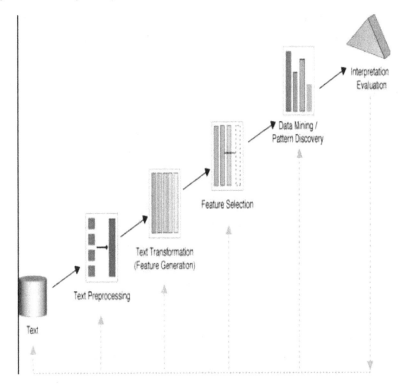

Text

In the first step, the text documents are collected which are present in different formats. The document might be in form of pdf, word, html doc, css etc.

Text Processing

The input to natural language processing will be a simple stream of Unicode characters is described by V. Verma, (August 2014)et al.,. Basic processing will be required to convert this character stream into a sequence of lexical items (words, phrases, and syntactic markers) which can then be used to better understand the content.Preprocessing is one of the key components in many text mining algorithms. For example a traditional text categorization framework comprises preprocessing, feature extraction, feature selection and classification steps. Although it is confirmed that feature extraction, feature selection and classification algorithm have significant impact on the classification process. The preprocessing step usually consists of the tasks such as tokenization, filtering, lemmatization and stemming.

Kirti Joshi,(Jul-Aug 2015)et al., suggested that *Tokenization* is the task of breaking a character sequence up into pieces (words/phrases) called tokens; it can be words, numbers, identifiers or punctuation (depending on the use case) and perhaps at the same time throws away certain characters such as punctuation marks. The list of tokens then is used to further processing.*Filtering* is usually done on documents to remove some of the words. A common filtering is stop-words removal. Stop words are the words frequently appear in the text without having much content information (e.g. prepositions, conjunctions, etc.). *Lemmatization* is the task that considers the morphological analysis of the words. In other words lemmatization methods try to map verb forms to infinite tense and nouns to a single form. *Stemming* methods aim at obtaining stem (root) of derived words. Stemming algorithms are indeed language dependent.

Text Transformation

A text document is collection of words (feature) and their occurrences. There are two important ways for representations of such documents are Vector Space Model and Bag of words.

Bag-of-Words

For image analysis, a visual analogue of a word is used in the BoW model, which is based on the vector quantization process by clustering low-level visual features of local regions or points, such as color, texture, and so forth.

To extract the BoW feature from images involves the following steps by Ho KANG, (April, 2007) et al.,:

- Automatically detect regions/points of interest,
- Compute local descriptors over those regions/points,
- Quantize the descriptors into words to form the visual vocabulary, and
- Find the occurrences in the image of each specific word in the vocabulary for constructing the BoW feature (or a histogram of word frequencies).

Figure 3 describes these four steps to extract the BoW feature from images.

Figure 3. Bag-of-words document representation

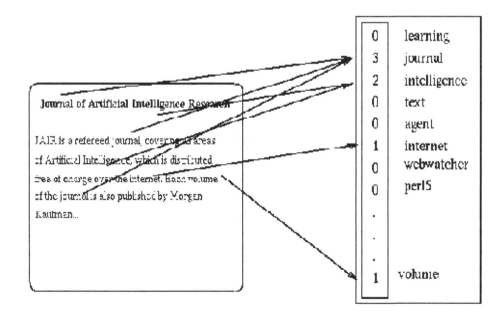

The Bag of Words (BoW) model learns a vocabulary from all of the documents, and then models each document by counting the number of times each word appears by Geethu P. C.,(February 2017). The BoW model is a simplifying representation used in NLP and IR. In this model, a text (such as a sentence or a document) is represented as the bag (multiset) of its words, disregarding grammar and even word order but keeping multiplicity. The BoW model is commonly used in methods of document classification, where the (frequency of) occurrence of each word is used as a feature for training a classifier.For example, consider the following two sentences:

- **Sentence 1:** "The cat sat on the hat".
- **Sentence 2:** "The dog ate the cat and the hat"

From these our vocabulary is:{the, cat, sat, on, hat, dog, ate, and}

To get our bags of words, we count the number of times each word occurs in each sentence. In Sentence 1, "the" appears twice, and "cat, "sat", "on", and "hat" each appears once, so the feature vector for Sentence 1 is:{The, cat, sat, on, hat, dog, ate, and} Sentence 1: {2, 1, 1, 1, 1, 0, 0, 0} Similarly, the features for Sentence 2 are: {3, 1, 0, 0, 1, 1, 1, 1}

Vector Space Model

It is a generalization of the Bag of Words model. Each document is represented as a multidimensional vector. Each unique term represents one dimension of the vector space. Term can be a single word or a sequence of words (phrase). The number of unique terms determines the dimension of the vector space. Vector elements are weights associated with individual terms; these weights reflect the relevancy of the corresponding terms.

If a document consists of n terms (ti), document d would be represented with the vector: d = {w1, w2,..., wn}, where wi are weights associated with terms ti. Distance among vectors in this multidimensional space represents the relationships among the corresponding documents.

In VSM, it is represented in the form of Term Document Matrix, i.e., an m x n matrix with following features are Rows (i=1,m) represent terms, Columns (j=1,n) represent documents and Cell i,j stores the weight of the term i in the context of the document j.

Naveen Aggarwal, (February 2016) et al., explained that before creating the TDM matrix, documents need to be preprocessed. The Preprocessing includes the Normalizing the text, removing terms with

Figure 4. Vector Space Models

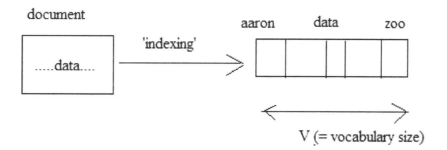

Figure 5. Term Document Matrix

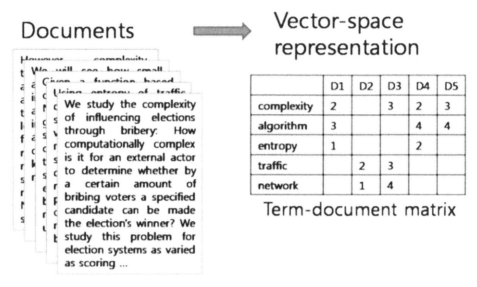

very small / high frequency, removing the stop-words and reducing words to their root form through stemming or lemmatization

Feature Selection

Atul Patel(2001) et al., explained Feature selection helps in the problem of text classification to improve efficiency and accuracy. In feature selection technique, a subset of original features is selected, and only the selected features are used for training and testing the classifiers. The removed features are not used in the computations anymore. There are two methods in feature selection i.e. filtering and wrapping methods

Filter Method

Filter methods is defined as using some actual property of the data in order to select feature using the classification algorithm. Features selected using the filter approach is the input variables to the different classifiers. The various Filter methods are Correlation Coefficient method, Chi- Squared, Information Gain, Gain Ratio. In the filter techniques the feature relevance score is calculated, and the low features are removed.

Correlation Coefficient Method

Correlation coefficient is simplest criteria and it is defined by the equation:

$$R(i) = \frac{\text{cov}(x_i, Y)}{\sqrt{\text{var}(x_i) * \text{var}(Y)}}$$

Where, xi is ith variable, Y is the output class, var() is the variance and cov() denotes covariance. The disadvantage is that correlation ranking can only detect linear dependencies between variable and target.

The Chi-Square (χ2)

The Chi-Square (χ2) is evaluates features individually by computing chi square statistics with respect to the classes. It means that the chi-squared score, analysis the dependency between the term and the class. If the term is independent from the class, then its score is equal to 0, other wise 1. A term with a higher chi-squared score is more informative as suggested by Dr. R. Manicka chezian, et al.,(August 2015)

Information Gain (IG)

Information Gain is a feature selection technique that can decrease the size of features by computing the value of each attribute and rank the attributes. Then it simply decides a threshold in the metric and keeps the attributes with a value over it. It just keeps those top ranking ones. Generally, it selects the features through this scores.

Document Frequency (DF)

Document frequency is the number of documents in which a term occurs in a dataset. It is the simplest criterion for term selection and it can easily scales to a large dataset with linear computational complexity. It is simple but effective feature selection method for text categorization.

Term Strength (TS)

Term strength is originally evaluated for vocabulary reduction in text retrieval. It is computed based on the conditional probability that a term occurs in the second half of a pair of related documents. Since need to calculate the similarity for each document pair, the time complexity of TS is quadratic to the number of documents. Because the class label information is not required, this method is also suitable for term reduction in text clustering.

Term Contribution (TC)

Term Contribution takes the term weight into account. Because the simple method like DF assumes that each term is of same importance in different documents, it is easily biased by those common terms which have high document frequency but uniform distribution over different classes. TC is used to deal with this problem; the result of text clustering is highly dependent on the documents similarity. The similarity between documents di and dj is computed by dot product.

$$TC\left(t\right) = \sum_{i,j \cap i \neq j} f\left(t,d_i\right) * f\left(t,d_j\right)$$

Entropy Based Ranking

Entropy Based Ranking (EN) term is measured by the entropy reduction when it is removed. The entropy is defined as the equation

$$E\left(t\right) = -\sum_{i=1}^{N}\sum_{j=1}^{N}\left(S_{i,j} * \log\left(S_{i,j}\right) + \left(1 - S_{i,j}\right) * \log\left(1 - S_{i,j}\right)\right)$$

where $S_{i,j}$ is the similarity value between the document d_i and d_j. $S_{i,j}$ is defined as

$$S_{i,j} = e^{-a*dist_{i,j}}, \ a = -\frac{\ln\left(0.5\right)}{dist}$$

where $dist_{i,j}$, is the distance between the document d_i and d_j after the term t is removed. The most serious problem of this method is its high computation complexity. It is impractical when there is a large number of documents and terms, and therefore, sampling technique is used in real experiments.

WRAPPER METHOD

Wrapper method is a simple and effective way for variable selection. A wide range of search strategies can be used, including branch-and-bound, best-first and genetic algorithm simulated annealing to find a subset of variables which maximizes the classification performance.Some common examples of wrapper methods are forward feature selection, backward feature elimination, recursive feature elimination, etc.

Forward Selection is an iterative method in which itstarts with having no feature in the model. In each iteration, it keep adding the feature which best improves the model till an addition of a new variable does not improve the performance of the model. *Backward elimination* starts with all the features and removes the least significant feature at alliteration which improves the performance of the model. *Feature elimination* is a greedy optimization algorithm which aims to find the best performing feature subset. It repeatedly creates models and keeps aside the best or the worst performing feature at each iteration. It constructs the next model with the left features until all the features are exhausted. It then ranks the features based on the order of their elimination Dr. Deepa Raj et al., (July- August 2017).

Though wrapper methods are computationally expensive and take more time compared to the filter method, it gives more accurate results than filter model. And also maintain dependencies between features and feature subsets. Wrapper methods are broadly classified as sequential selection algorithms and heuristic search algorithms as follows:

Sequential Selection Algorithms

The Sequential Feature Selection algorithm starts with an empty set and adds one feature for the first step which gives the highest value for the objective function. After the first step, the remaining features are added individually to the current subset and the new subset is evaluated. The individual features that give maximum classification accuracy are permanently included in the subset. The process is repeated until itgets required number of features. This algorithm is called a naive SFS algorithm since the dependency between the features is not taken into consideration.A Sequential Backward Selection algorithm is exactly reverse of SFS algorithm. Initially, the algorithm starts from the entire set of variables and removes one irrelevant feature at a time whose removal gives the lowest decrease in predictor performance by Manisa Mal, et al.,(May 2016).

Heuristic Search Algorithms

Heuristic search algorithms include Genetic algorithms, Ant Colony Optimization, Particle Swarm Optimizationetc.A genetic algorithm is a search technique used in computing to find true or approximate solution to optimization and search problems. It is based on the Darwinian principle of survival of the fittest theory. ACO is based on the shortest paths found by real ants in their search for food sources. ACO approaches suffer from inadequate rules of pheromone update and heuristic information. They do not consider random phenomenon of ants during subset formations. PSO approach does not employ crossover and mutation operators, hence is efficient over GA but requires several mathematical operators. Such mathematical operations require various userspecified parameters and dealing with these parameters, deciding their optimal values might be difficult for users. Although these ACO and PSO algorithms execute almost identically to GA, GA has received much attention due to its simplicity and powerful search capability upon the exponential search spaces.

Data Mining/Pattern Selection

In this stage the conventional data mining process combines with text mining process. Structured database uses classic data mining technique that resulted from previous stage. Data Mining is defined as the procedure of extracting information from huge sets of data. In other words, data mining is mining knowledge from data.

The Applications of Text Analytics

1. **Security Application:** It willbe monitoring and analyzing internet blogs, news, social sites etc. for national security purpose. It will beuseful to detect unethical thing on internet.
2. **Marketing Application:** By analyzing text data it can identify which type of product customers most like.
3. **Analyzing Open – Ended Survey Responses:** In survey research one company ask to customer some question like, pros and cons about some products or asking for suggestion. For analyzing these types of data, text analytics is requiring.
4. **Automatic Process on Emails and Messages:** By using big data analytics it can filter huge amount of emails based on some terms or words. It is also useful to automatically divert messages or mails to appropriate department or section.

Text analytics has its applications in spam filtering, monitoring the public opinion, customer services and also in the e-mail support.

IMAGE ANALYTICS

An introductory definition of image analytics is a transformation from images to analytically prepared data. It defines an image as the rendering of a non-moving scene. More specifically, the objective of image analytics is to bring an unstructured rendition of reality in the form of images.

In computer science or engineering, the detection of objects, faces, movement and so on in images has many labels including image processing or computer vision. Figure 6 frames the steps followed by an image analytics system in transforming images to analytically prepare a dataset (a set of time series, one per variable).

At this level, image analytics continues to be a set of transformations on image-input that add value and creates a rich set of time series as analytically prepared data output. The first transformation step segments images into structured elements and prepares them for feature extraction. The second transformation step is the detection of relationships between these features, variables and time. The third transformation step is the extraction of variables with time-stamped values.

Image Segmentation

Images are segmented using algorithms and digital processing techniques known as image segmentation. Segments are spatially relevant regions of image that have a common set of features. These can be color distributions, intensity levels, texture, moving and stationary parts of an image. There are numerous image segmentation algorithms, each with a specific purpose and deep technical application. These techniques process a gray scale or color version of an image to identify edges, boundaries, regions, movement and many other important criteria. Some of the most important and widely used image segmentation techniques are shown in Figure 7.

Threshold Based Image Segmentation

Histogram thresholding is used to segment the given image; there is certain preprocessing and post-processing techniques required for threshold segmentation. The thresholding method is broadly classified into three categories.

Figure 6. Steps for Image Analytics system

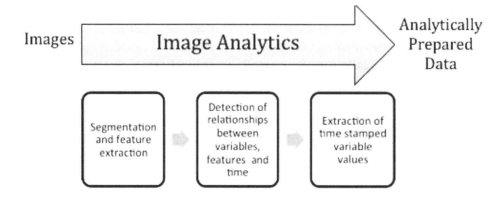

Figure 7. Various image segmentation techniques

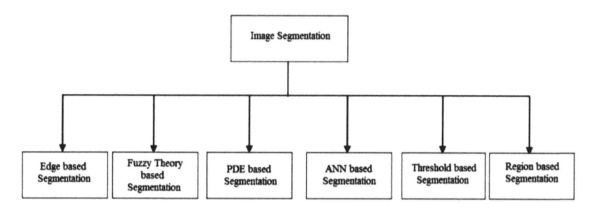

1. **Global Thresholding:** Global Thresholding is based on selecting an appropriate threshold value i. e. T. This T is a constant and output image depends upon this T value.
2. **Variable Thresholding:** In this method, the value of T varies over an image. It is further divided into two categories namely local threshold and adaptive threshold. In local Threshold the value of T depends upon the neighborhood of x and y. In adaptive Threshold the value of T is a function of x and y.
3. **Multiple Thresholding:** In this type of thresholding, there are multiple threshold values like T0 and T1. Threshold values can be calculated with the help of peaks of histogram.

Region Based Image Segmentation

Region based segmentation is simple compared to other methods and also noise resilient. It divides an image into different regions based on pre-defined criteria, i.e., color, intensity, or object. Region based segmentation methods are categorized into three main categories, i.e., region growing, region splitting, and region merging.

Region Growing

The region growing based segmentation methods are the methods that segments the image into various regions based on the growing of initial pixels. These pixels can be selected manually (based on prior knowledge) or automatically (based on particular application). Then the growing of pixels is controlled by connectivity between pixels and with the help of the prior knowledge of problem, this can be stopped.

Region Splitting and Merging

Splitting stands for iteratively dividing an image into regions having similar characteristics and merging contributes to combining the adjacent similar regions. Figure 8 shows the division based on quad tree.

Figure 8. Division of regions based on quad tree

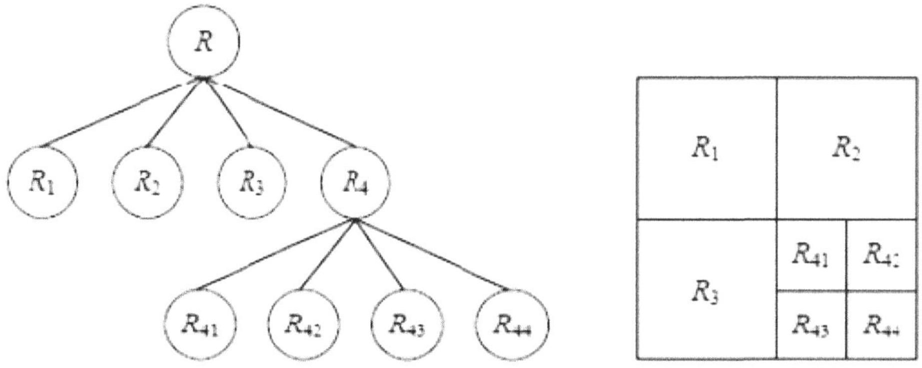

Edge Based Image Segmentation

Edge detection is a basic step for image segmentation process. It divides an image into object and its background. Edge detection divides the image by observing the change in intensity or pixels of an image. Gray histogram and gradient are two main methods for edge detection for image segmentation. Several operators are used by edge detection method, i.e., Roberts's edge detection, Sobel Edge Detection, Prewitt edge detection, Kirsh edge detection, Robinson edge detection, Marr-Hildreth edge detection, LoG edge detection and Canny Edge Detection.

Roberts Edge Detection

The Roberts edge detection performs a simple, quick to compute, 2-D spatial gradient measurement on an image. This method emphasizes regions of high spatial frequency which often correspond to edges. The input to the operator is a grayscale image the same as to the output is the most common usage for this technique. Pixel values in every point in the output represent the estimated complete magnitude of the spatial gradient of the input image at that point.

Sobel Edge Detection

The Sobel method of edge detection for image segmentation finds edges using the Sobel approximation to the derivative. It precedes the edges at those points where the gradient is highest. The Sobel technique performs a 2-D spatial gradient quantity on an image and so highlights regions of high spatial frequency that correspond to edges. In general it is used to find the estimated absolute gradient magnitude at each point in n input grayscale image. Dr. S. Pushpa et al.,(Nov 2015)

The Prewitt Edge Detection

The Prewitt is used to estimate the magnitude and orientation. Even though different gradient edge detection wants a time consuming calculation to estimate the direction from the magnitudes in the x and y-directions, the compass edge detection obtains the direction directly from the kernel with the highest response. It is limited to 8 possible directions; however knowledge shows that most direct direction estimates are not much more perfect. This gradient based edge detector is estimated in the 3x3 neighborhood for eight directions. Prewitt detection is slightly simpler to implement computationally than the Sobel detection, but it tends to produce somewhat noisier results.

Kirsch Edge Detection

The masks of Kirsch technique are defined by considering a single mask and rotating it to eight main compass directions of North, Northwest, West, Southwest, South, Southeast, East and Northeast. The edge magnitude is defined as the maximum value found by convolution of each mask with the image. The direction is defined by mask that produces the maximum magnitude.

Robinson Edge Detection

The Robinson method is similar to Kirsch masks but is easier to implement because they rely only on coefficients of 0, 1 and 2. The masks are symmetrical about their directional axis, the axis with the zeros. One need only to compute the result on four masks and the result from other four can be obtained by negating the result from the first four. The magnitude of the gradient is the maximum value gained from applying all eight masks to the pixel neighborhood, and the angle of the gradient can be approximated as the angle of the line of zeroes in the mask yielding the maximum response.

Marr-Hildreth Edge Detection

The Marr-Hildreth technique is a method of detecting edges in digital images that is continuous curves wherever there are well-built and fast variations in image brightness. It is an easy and it operates by convolving the image with the LoG function.Subsequently the zero-crossings are discovered in the filtered result to find the edges. The LoG method is sometimes as well referred to as the Mexican hat wavelet due to its image shape while turned up-side-down.

LoG Edge Detection

he LoG of an image f(x,y) is a second order derivative defined as,

$$\nabla^2 f = \frac{\partial^2 f}{\partial x^2} + \frac{\partial^2 f}{\partial y^2}$$

It has two effects; it smooths the image and it computes the Laplacian, which yields a doubleedge images. Locating edges then consists of finding the zero crossings between the double edges. The Laplacian is generally used to found whether a pixel is on the dark or light side of an edge.

Canny Edge Detection

The Canny edge detection technique is one of the standard edge detection techniques. To find edges by separating noise from the image before find edges of image the Canny is a very important method. Canny method is a better method without disturbing the features of the edges in the image afterwards it applying the tendency to find the edges and the serious value for threshold.

Fuzzy Theory Based Image Segmentation

Fuzzy set theory is used in order to analyze images, and provide accurate information from any image. Clustering function can be used to remove noise from image as well. A gray-scale image can be easily transformed into a fuzzy image by using a Clustering function. Different morphological operations can be combined with fuzzy method to get better results. Fuzzy k-Means and Fuzzy C-means (FCM) are widely used methods in image processing.

ANN Based Image Segmentation

In Artificial Neural Network, every neuron is corresponding to the pixel of an image. Image is mapped to the neural network. Image in the form of neural network is trained using training samples, and then connection between neurons, i.e., pixels is found. Then the new images are segmented from the trained image. Some of the mostly used neural networks for image segmentation are Hopfield, BPNN, FFNN, MLFF, MLP, SOM, and PCNN. Segmentation of image using neural network is perform in two steps, i.e., pixel classification and edge detection.

PDE Based Image Segmentation

PDE equations or PDE models are used widely in image processing, and specifically in image segmentation. They uses active contour model for segmentation purpose. Active Contour model or Snakes transform the segmentation problem into PDE. Some famous methods of PDE used for image segmentation are Snakes, Level-Set, and Mumford shah method.

Feature Extraction

To assist in the detection of higher-level characteristics, low-level features are extracted and stored with each instance. Some of the commonly used methods are Spatial features, Transform features, Edge and boundary features, Color features, Shape features, Texture features.

Spatial Features

Spatial features of an object are characterized by its gray level, amplitude and spatial distribution. Amplitude is one of the simplest and most important features of the object. In X-ray images, the amplitude represents the absorption characteristics of the body masses and enables discrimination of bones from tissues.

Transform Features

Generally the transformation of an image provides the frequency domain information of the data. The transform features of an image are extracted using zonal filtering. This is also called as feature mask, feature mask being a slit or an aperture. The high frequency components are commonly used for boundary and edge detection. The angular slits can be used for orientation detection. Transform feature extraction is also important when the input data originates in the transform coordinate.

Edge and Boundary Features

Edges in images are areas with strog intensity contrast and a jump in intensity from one pixel to the next can create major variation in the picture quality. Edge detection of an image significantly reduces the amount of data and filters out unimportant information, while preserving the important properties of an image. Edges are scale dependent and an edge may contain other edges, but at a certain scale, an edge still has no width. If the edges in an image are identified accurately, all the objects are located and their basic properties such as area, perimeter and shape can be measured easily. Therefore edges are used for boundary estimation and segmentation in the scene.

Color Features

Color is a visual attribute of object things that results from the light emitted or transmitted or reflected. From a mathematical viewpoint, the color signal is an extension from scalar-signals to vector-signals. Color features can be derived from a histogram of the image. The weakness of color histogram is that the color histogram of two different things with the same color can be equal. The color features are still useful for many biomedical image processing applications such as cell classification, cancer cell detection and CBIR systems.

Shape Features

The shape of an object refers to its physical structure and profile. Shape features are mostly used for finding and matching shapes, recognizing objects or making measurement of shapes. Moment, perimeter, area and orientation are some of the characteristics used for shape feature extraction technique. The shape of an object is determined by its external boundary abstracting from other properties such as color, content and material composition, as well as from the object's other spatial properties.

Texture Features

In a general sense, texture refers to surface characteristics and appearance of an object given by the size, shape, density, arrangement, proportion of its elementary parts. A basic stage to collect such features through texture analysis process is called as texture feature extraction. Due to the signification of texture information, texture feature extraction is a key function in various image processing applications like remote sensing, medical imaging and CBIR.

Relationships Among Variables, Features and Time

The relationships among variables, features and time in image analytics are represented as a predictive model. Before a predictive model can be created, a set of instances are extracted from all the given images. An instance isan image (one of all the given images),a part (one or more segments) of an image, and a sub-set of all the given images. From this predictive modeling, three sub-sets of all extracted instances are of interest:training instances,test instances andPredicted instances.

Modeling algorithms are based on known techniques including neural networks, scalable vector machines, function learning, Bayesian networks, regression and many more. Test instances are used to calculate the accuracy of a predictive model created by a modeling algorithm. The training process is often repeated with different sets of training and test instances and/or algorithm parameters until the accuracy of the predictive model is at an acceptable level. After the predictive model has been trained, it is used to classify predicted instances.

The final step of the image analytics process is to create the analytically prepared data. This final output is created by using these predictive models to predict a time series of variable values for every variable from the remaining set of instances called predicted instances.

VIDEO ANALYTICS

It is the science of using technology to analyses and manages video, often in large volumes and in multiple formats, from CCTV to mobile phone footage. This transforms video information into intelligence and potential evidence upon which to make decisions.Video analytics can be real-time: using technology configured to track and provide alerts to specific incidents as they happen; or post event: retrospectively searching for incidents that have already occurred.

Types of Video Analytics

Video analytic algorithms could be best described in 3 main categories – Rule Based analytics, Machine Learning Based Analytics and Multi Modal analytics. These could be effectively applied in different scenarios to achieve desired outcomes or to drive the creation of useful metadata.

Rule Based Analytics

Rule based analytics are best used in deployments where you want to detect a specific behavior of a subject or vehicle. It is commonly deployed by drawing Areas of Interest (AOI) within a camera's Field of View (FOV) and applying specific rule sets to detect specific activities.

Machine Learning Based Analytics

With the advancement of computation power and a decline in the cost of computational resources gave rise to a new breed of Video analytics engines based on computer vision or machine based learning technologies. Though relatively new, we have seen strong market demand in this area and have commissioned several projects with government agencies using machine learning based video analytics.

Multi Modal Analytics

The next generation system is that effectively combines vision, sound and passive sensor analytics to provide a multi-modal sensor based application for behavioral monitoring and detection in an enclosed space. The solution employs an integrated approach using the Microsoft Kinect for both video and sound.

Video Analysis Approach

There are three video analysis approaches namely,

1. Whole-to-part inductive(grounded analysis).
2. Part-to-whole inductive(content analysis).
3. Manifest content(critical incident approach).

Grounded Theory Work Using Rich Video Data

The video was recorded with four cameras from different angles. The analysis involved four analysts and three steps. (1) One analyst identified video segments with interesting verbal or non-verbal team interactions. (2) Two analysts created conceptual descriptions of the segments by consensus. (3)Taxonomies for leadership actions from the conceptual descriptions were developed.

Video Content Analysis

Video content analysis (VCA) is the capability of automatically analyzing video to detect and determine events not based on just a single image. As such, it can be seen as the automated process unlike human's ability to see objects and activities and then ascribe meaning to them. This technical capability is widely used in the security industry for better situation awareness. The video data generated by IP CCTV cameras are used for data analysis to process, categorize and analyses the objects and activities captured. The algorithms can be implemented as software on general purpose machines, or can be embedded in the IP CCTV camera's video processing units. Many different capabilities can be implemented in VCA, some of them are as follows:

Motion Detection

Video Motion Detection is one of the simpler forms of video analysis where motion is detected with regard to a fixed background scene.

People / Object Counter

This is an ability to count the number of people / object pass through a defined region in the camera's field of view.

Trip Wire

The crossing of a boundary by any moving object within the camera's view can be detected.

Heat Maps

It is an ability of the video analysis software algorithm to overlay heat maps on the video in a defined area of the camera's view. The data analyzed by the software will provide information on varying density of the object / people within the camera's field of view in a given time interval.

The Dimensions of Video Analytics

The dimensions of video analytics are volume, variety and velocity. Volume defines the size of video it being more. Variety defines the format of videos such as HD videos, Blu-ray copies etc. and velocity gives the speed of data. Now days, Digital cameras process and capture videos at a very high quality and high speed. Video editing makes it to grow in size as it contains other extra information about the videos. Videos grow in size faster as they are simply nothing but collection of images.

Applications of Video Analytics

1. **Useful in Accident Cases:** With the use of CCTV cameras we can identify what happened at the time of accident it is also used for security reason and parking vehicles etc. and also useful in schools, traffic police, business, security etc.
2. **Video Analytics for Investigation:** Video analytics algorithms is implemented to analyze video, a task that is challenging and its very time consuming for human operator especially when there is large amount of data are available using video analytics.
3. **Video Analytics for Business Intelligence:** It uses to extracts statistical and operational data. Rather than having operator that review all the video and tally all the people or cars moving in certain area, or checking which traffic routes are most commonly taken, video analytics can do it automatically.
4. **Target and Scene Analytics:** Video Analytics for business Intelligence involves target and scene Analytics. Target Analytics provides details information about the target movement, patterns, appearance and other characteristics which can be used for identification of target.
5. **Direction Analytics:** Direction Analytics is the ability to distinguish behavior by assigning specific values (low to high) to areas within a camera's field of view.
6. **Remove the Human Equation Through the Automation:** It removes the tedium involved in giving one or more set of eyes on a monitor for an extended period of time. The automation of video analytics allows the insertion of human judgment at the most critical time in the surveillance process.

REFERENCES

Allahyari, M., Pouriyeh, S., Assefi, M., Safaei, S., Trippe, E. D., Gutierrez, J. B., & Kochut, K. (2017). A Brief Survey of Text Mining: Classification, Clustering and Extraction Techniques. Bigdas at KDD 2017, Halifax, Canada.

Anjna & Kaur. (2007). Review of Image Segmentation Technique. *International Journal of Advanced Research in Computer Science, 8*(4).

Balamurugan & Pushpa. (2015). A Review On Various Text Mining Techniques And Algorithms. *2nd International Conference on Recent Innovations in Science, Engineering and Management,* 22.

Borgo, Chen, Daubney, Grundy, Heidemann, Höferlin, … Xie. (n.d.). A Survey on Video-based Graphics and Video Visualization. *EUROGRAPHICS.*

Divya & Nanda Kumar. (2015). Study on Feature Selection Methods for Text Mining. *International Journal of Advanced Research Trends in Engineering and Technology, 2*(1).

Jadhav Swapnil & Verma. (2014). Revived Fuzzy K-Means Clustering Technique for Image Segmentation. *International Journal of Engineering Research & Technology, 3*(8).

Kanakalakshmi & Chezian. (2015). Feature Selection Approaches With Text Mining For Categorical Variable Selection. *IJRSET, 2*(6).

Kang. (2007). A Review on Image and video processing. *International Journal of Multimedia and Ubiquitous Engineering, 2*(2).

Kaur, & Kaur. (2014). Various Image Segmentation Techniques: A Review. *International Journal of Computer Science and Mobile Computing, 3*(5), 809–814.

Kaur & Joshi. (2015). Review On Image Segmentation Techniques. *International Journal of Computer Science Trends and Technology, 3*(4).

Kumar & Raj. (2017). Video Processing and its Applications: A survey. *International Journal of Emerging Trends & Technology in Computer Science, 6*(4).

Kumar & Bhatia. (2013). Text mining: Concepts, process and applications. *Journal of Global Research in Computer Science, 4*(3).

Kumbhar & Mal. (2016). A Survey on Feature Selection Techniques and Classification Algorithms for Efficient Text Classification. *International Journal of Science and Research, 5*(5).

Lakshmi & Sankaranarayanan. (2010). A study of Edge Detection Techniques for Segmentation Computing Approaches. *IJCA.*

Macnamara. (n.d.). Media content analysis: Its uses; benefits and best practice methodology. *Asia Pacific Public Relations Journal, 6*(1), 1–34.

Muthukrishnan & Radha. (2011). Edge Detection Techniques For Image Segmentation. *International Journal of Computer Science & Information Technology, 3*(6).

Preeti, K. A. (2014). Colour Image Segmentation Using K-Means, Fuzzy C-Means and Density Based Clustering. *International Journal For Research In Applied Science And Engineering Technology, 2*(6).

Raj & Rajaraajeswari. (n.d.). A Framework for Text Analytics using the Bag of Words (BoW) Model for Prediction. *International Journal of Advanced Networking & Applications.*

Singh, R. D., & Aggarwal, N. (2016, February). Video content authentication techniques: A comprehensive survey. *Multimedia Systems.* doi:10.100700530-017-0538-9

Sonawane, Shirole, Patil, Patil, & Patil. (2017). Effective Pattern Discovery for Text Mining. *International Research Journal of Engineering and Technology, 4*(4).

Swathy, M., Nirmala, P. S., & Geethu, P. C. (2017). Survey on Vehicle Detection and Tracking Techniques in Video Surveillance. *International Journal of Computer Applications, 160*(7).

Verma, Agrawal, Patel, & Patel. (n.d.). Big Data Analytics: Challenges And Applications For Text, Audio, Video, And Social Media Data. *International Journal on Soft Computing, Artificial Intelligence and Applications, 5*(1).

Compilation of References

802.15.6-2012 - IEEE Standard for Local and metropolitan area networks - Part 15.6: Wireless Body Area Networks, WG802.15 - Wireless Personal Area Network (WPAN) Working Group, C/LM - LAN/MAN Standards Committee, IEEE Computer Society.

80215.4-2015 - IEEE Standard for Low-Rate Wireless Networks, WG802.15 - Wireless Personal Area Network (WPAN) Working Group, C/LM - LAN/MAN Standards Committee, IEEE Computer Society. (n.d.). Retrieved from https://standards.ieee.org/findstds/standard/802.15.4-2015.html

A Brief History of Voice Biometrics - VoiceVault Voice Authentication. (n.d.). Retrieved October 20, 2017, from http://voicevault.com/a-brief-history-of-voice-biometrics/

Aazam, M., & Huh, E. N. (2014, August). Fog computing and smart gateway based communication for cloud of things. In *Future Internet of Things and Cloud (FiCloud), 2014 International Conference on* (pp. 464-470). IEEE. doi:10.1145/2757384.2757397

Abadal, S., Alarcón, E., Cabellos-Aparicio, A., Lemme, M. C., & Nemirovsky, M. (2013). Graphene-Enabled Wireless Communication for Massive Multicore Architectures. *IEEE Communications Magazine, 51*(11), 137–143. doi:10.1109/MCOM.2013.6658665

Abdulla, W. H. (2007). Robust speaker modeling using perceptually motivated feature. *Pattern Recognition Letters, 28*(11), 1333–1342. doi:10.1016/j.patrec.2006.11.018

Abdul, W., Ali, Z., Ghouzali, S., Alfawaz, B., Muhammad, G., & Hossain, M. S. (2017). Biometric Security Through Visual Encryption for Fog Edge Computing. *IEEE Access: Practical Innovations, Open Solutions, 5*, 5531–5538. doi:10.1109/ACCESS.2017.2693438

ABI. (2013). *Billion Devices Will Wirelessly Connect to the Internet of Everything in 2020.* ABI Research. Available: https://www.abiresearch.com/press/more-than-30-billion-devices-willwirelessly- conne/

Abo-Zahhad, Ahmed, & Elnahas. (2014). A Wireless Emergency Telemedicine System for Patients Monitoring and Diagnosis. *International Journal of Telemedicine and Applications, 14.* 10.1155/2014/380787

Adibi, S. (2014). A low overhead scaled equalized harmonic-based voice authentication system. *Telematics and Informatics, 31*(1), 137–152. doi:10.1016/j.tele.2013.02.004

Advanced Message Queuing Protocol. (2008). AMQP-Protocol specification Version 0-9-1, 13.

Agrawal, D., Das, S., & El Abbadi, A. (2011, March). Big data and cloud computing: current state and future opportunities. In *Proceedings of the 14th International Conference on Extending Database Technology* (pp. 530-533). ACM. 10.1145/1951365.1951432

Agrawal, R., Imienski, D., & Swamy, A. (1991). *Database Mining: A Performance Perspective. IEEE Tran. on Knowledge and Data Engg.*

Ahuja, S. P., Mani, S., & Zambrano, J. (2012). A survey of the state of cloud computing in healthcare. *Network and Communication Technologies*, *1*(2), 12.

Ajit, A., Chavana, Mininath, K., & Nighotb. (2015). *Secure and Cost-effective Application Layer Protocol with Authentication Interoperability for IOT.* ICISP 2015, Nagpur, India.

Ala, A. F., Guizani, M., & Mohammadi, M. (2015). Internet of Things: A Survey on Enabling Technologies, Protocols, and Applications. *IEEE Communications Surveys and Tutorials.* doi:10.1109/COMST.2015.2444095

Al-Ali, A. K. H., Dean, D., Senadji, B., Chandran, V., & Naik, G. R. (2017). Enhanced Forensic Speaker Verification Using a Combination of DWT and MFCC Feature Warping in the Presence of Noise and Reverberation Conditions. *IEEE Access: Practical Innovations, Open Solutions*, *5*, 15400–15413. doi:10.1109/ACCESS.2017.2728801

Alam, M. M., & Ben Hamida, E. (2014). Surveying Wearable Human Assistive Technology for Life and Safety Critical Applications: Standards, Challenges and Opportunities. *Sensors (Basel)*, *14*(5), 9153–9209. doi:10.3390140509153 PMID:24859024

Al-Fuqaha, Guizani, Mohammadi, Aledhari, & Ayyash. (2015). *Internet of Things: A Survey on Enabling Technologies, Protocols, and Applications.* Academic Press.

Al-Jarrah, O.Y., Yoo, P. D., Muhaidat, S., Karagiannidis, G. K., & Taha. (2015 Efficient machine learning for big data: A review. *Big Data Res., 2*(3), 87-93.

Allahyari, M., Pouriyeh, S., Assefi, M., Safaei, S., Trippe, E. D., Gutierrez, J. B., & Kochut, K. (2017). A Brief Survey of Text Mining: Classification, Clustering and Extraction Techniques. Bigdas at KDD 2017, Halifax, Canada.

AllegroGraph 4.11. (2013). Retrieved from http://www.franz.com/agraph/allegrograph/

Almobaideen, W., Allan, M., & Saadeh, M. (2016). Smart archaeological tourism: Contention, convenience and accessibility in the context of cloud-centric IoT. *Mediterranean Archaeology & Archaeometry, 16*(1).

Alrawais, A., Alhothaily, A., Hu, C., & Cheng, X. (2017). Fog Computing for the Internet of Things: Security and Privacy Issue. *IEEE Internet Computing*, *21*(2), 34–42. doi:10.1109/MIC.2017.37

Alur, R., & Berger, E. (2015). Systems Computing Challenges in the Internet of Things. Academic Press.

Anjna & Kaur. (2007). Review of Image Segmentation Technique. *International Journal of Advanced Research in Computer Science, 8*(4).

Ankerst, M., Breunig, M. M., Kriegel, H.-P., & Sander, J. (2011). OPTICS: Ordering Points To Identify the Clustering Structure. *Proc. 4th Int. Conf. on Knowledge Discovery & Data Mining.*

Apache CouchD. B. (2013). Retrieved from http://couchdb.apache.org/

Apache HBase. (2013). Retrieved from http://hbase.apache.org/

Apixio - HCC Profiler. (n.d.). Retrieved from https://www.apixio.com/solutions/

Armbrust, M., Fox, A., Griffith, R., Joseph, A. D., Katz, R., Konwinski, A., ... Zaharia, M. (2010). A view of cloud computing. *Communications of the ACM*, *53*(4), 50–58. doi:10.1145/1721654.1721672

Ashton, K. (2009). That Internet of Things Thing. *RFID Journal.* Retrieved from http://www.rfidjournal.com/articles/view

Atzori, L., Iera, A., & Morabito, G. (2010). The internet of things: A survey. *Computer Networks*, *54*(15), 2787–2805. doi:10.1016/j.comnet.2010.05.010

Auradkar, A., Botev, C., Das, S., De Maagd, D., Feinberg, A., Ganti, P., ... Zhang, J. (2012). Data Infrastructure at LinkedIn. *Proceedings of 2012 IEEE 28th International Conference on Data Engineering*, 1370–1381. 10.1109/ICDE.2012.147

Avci, E., & Avci, D. (2009). Expert Systems with Applications The speaker identification by using genetic wavelet adaptive network based fuzzy inference system. *Expert Systems with Applications*, *36*(6), 9928–9940. doi:10.1016/j.eswa.2009.01.081

Ayodele, T. O. (2010). Introduction to machine learning. In *New Advances in Machine Learning*. InTech.

Ayoub, B., Jamal, K., & Arsalane, Z. (2016). Gammatone frequency cepstral coefficients for speaker identification over VoIP networks. *2016 International Conference on Information Technology for Organizations Development, IT4OD 2016.* 10.1109/IT4OD.2016.7479293

Aziz, B. (2016). A formal model and analysis of an IoT protocol. *Ad Hoc Networks*, *36*, 49–57. doi:10.1016/j.adhoc.2015.05.013

Aziz, H. A., & Guled, A. (2016). *Cloud Computing and Healthcare Services. Academic Press.*

Babich, A. (2012). *Biometric Authentication. Types of biometric identifiers* (Thesis). University of Applied Science.

Baccarelli, E., Vinueza Naranjo, P. G., Scarpiniti, M., Shojafar, M., & Abawajy, J. H. (2017). Fog of Everything: Energy-Efficient Networked Computing Architectures, Research Challenges, and a Case Study. *IEEE Access: Practical Innovations, Open Solutions*, *5*, 9882–9910. doi:10.1109/ACCESS.2017.2702013

Balamurugan & Pushpa. (2015). A Review On Various Text Mining Techniques And Algorithms. *2nd International Conference on Recent Innovations in Science, Engineering and Management, 22.*

Bandura, A., Adams, N. E., Hardy, A. B., & Gary, N. (1980). Test of the Generality of Self-efficacy Theory. *Cognitive Therapy and Research*, *4*(1), 39–66. doi:10.1007/BF01173354

Baranwal, T., & Pateriya, P. K. (2016, January). Development of IoT based smart security and monitoring devices for agriculture. In *Cloud System and Big Data Engineering (Confluence), 2016 6th International Conference* (pp. 597-602). IEEE. 10.1109/CONFLUENCE.2016.7508189

Barbera, M. V., Kosta, S., Mei, A., & Stefa, J. (2013). To offload or not to offload? The bandwidth and energy costs of mobile cloud computing. *2013. Proceedings - IEEE INFOCOM*, 1285–1293.

Barroso, L. A., Clidaras, J., & Hölzle, U. (2013). The datacenter as a computer: An introduction to the design of warehouse-scale machines. *Synthesis Lectures on Computer Architecture, 8*(3), 1-154.

Bee, X. (n.d.). *Digi XBee Ecosystem - Everything you need to explore and create wireless connectivity - Digi International.* Retrieved from https://www.digi.com/xbee

Ben Letaifa, S. (2015). How to strategize smart cities: Revealing the SMART model. *Journal of Business Research*, *68*(7), 1414–1419. doi:10.1016/j.jbusres.2015.01.024

Berryand, M. J., & Linoff, G. S. (1997). *Data mining techniques: For marketing, sales, and customer support.* John Wiley & Sons, Inc.

Bhardwaj, A., Bhattacherjee, S., Chavan, A., Deshpande, A., Elmore, A. J., Madden, S., & Parameswaran, A. G. (2014). *Datahub: Collaborative data science & dataset version management at scale.* arXiv preprint arXiv:1409.0798

Bhardwaj, S., Jain, L., & Jain, S. (2010). Cloud computing: A study of infrastructure as a service (IAAS). *International Journal of Engineering and Information Technology*, *2*(1), 60–63.

Bhide, V. H., & Wagh, S. (2015, April). i-learning IoT: An intelligent self learning system for home automation using IoT. In *Communications and Signal Processing (ICCSP), 2015 International Conference on* (pp. 1763-1767). IEEE.

Bicer, V., & Lopez, V. (2013). Searching in the city of knowledge. *Proceedings of the 36th International ACM SIGIR Conference on Research and Development in Information Retrieval - SIGIR '13*, 1123. 10.1145/2484028.2484195

Biometrics, T. F. Face, Fingerprint, Iris, Palm and Voice. (n.d.). Retrieved November 30, 2017, from https://www.bayometric.com/biometrics-face-finger-iris-palm-voice/

Biotricity. (n.d.). Retrieved from https://www.biotricity.com/biotricity-bioflux-mwc-2017/

Bishop, C. M. (2006). *Pattern recognition and machine learning*. New York: Springer.

Biswas, A., Sahu, P. K., Bhowmick, A., & Chandra, M. (2014). Hindi vowel classification using GFCC and formant analysis in sensor mismatch condition. *WSEAS Transactions on Systems*, *13*(1), 130–143.

Blitz. (2013). *The Fourth Amendment Future of Public Surveillance: Remote Recording and Other Searches in Public Space*. Academic Press.

Bluetooth Low Energy Protocol Stack. (2016). Bluetooth Low Energy Software Developer's Guide. *Texas Instruments*. Retrieved November 14, 2017, from http://dev.ti.com/tirex/content/simplelink_cc2640r2_sdk_1_00_00_22/docs/blestack/html/ble-stack/index.html

Bonomi, F., Milito, R., Natarajan, P., & Zhu, J. (2014). Fog Computing: A Platform for Internet of Things and Analytics. Big Data and Internet of Things: A Roadmap for Smart Environments. *Studies in Computational Intelligence*, *546*, 169–186.

Bonomi, F., Milito, R., Zhu, J., & Addepalli, S. (2012, August). Fog computing and its role in the internet of things. In *Proceedings of the first edition of the MCC workshop on Mobile cloud computing* (pp. 13-16). ACM. 10.1145/2342509.2342513

Borgo, Chen, Daubney, Grundy, Heidemann, Höferlin, … Xie. (n.d.). A Survey on Video-based Graphics and Video Visualization. *EUROGRAPHICS*.

Bormann, C., Castellani, A. P., & Shelby, Z. (2012). CoAP: An application protocol for billions of tiny Internet nodes. *IEEE Internet Computing*, *16*(2), 62–67. doi:10.1109/MIC.2012.29

Brazilian Society of Cardiology, Brazilian Society of Hypertension, & Brazilian Society of Nephrology. (2010). VI Brazilian Guidelines on Hypertension. *Arquivos Brasileiros de Cardiologia*, *95*(1), 1–51. PMID:21085756

Breiman, L., Friedman, J., Olshen, R., & Stone, C. (1984). *Classification and Regression Trees*. Wadsworth Int. Group.

Brundu, F. G., Patti, E., Osello, A., Del Giudice, M., Rapetti, N., Krylovskiy, A., ... Acquaviva, A. (2016). IoT Software Infrastructure for Energy Management and Simulation in Smart Cities. *IEEE Transactions on Industrial Informatics*.

Burgess, L. (2015). How Does Sensor Data Go From Device To Cloud? *readwrite*. Retrieved November 22, 2017, from https://readwrite.com/2015/10/13/sensor-data-device-to-cloud/

Business Insider. (2016). *The US government is pouring money into the Internet of Things*. Retrieved from http://www.businessinsider.com/the-us-government-is-pouring-money-into-the-internet-of-things-2016-5?IR=T

Butler, B. (2017). *Internet of Things. What is edge computing, how it's changing the network?* Retrieved November 1, 2017, from https://www.networkworld.com/article/3224893/internet-of-things/what-is-edge-computing-and-how-it-s-changing-the-network.html

Butler, B. (2017). *Internet of Things. What is edge computing, how it's changing the network?* Retrieved November 3, 2017, from https://www.networkworld.com/article/3224893/internet-of-things/what-is-edge-computing-and-how-it-s-changing-the-network.html

Buyya, R., Calheiros, R. N., Son, J., Dastjerdi, A. V., & Yoon, Y. (2014, September). Software-defined cloud computing: Architectural elements and open challenges. In *Advances in Computing, Communications and Informatics (ICACCI, 2014 International Conference on* (pp. 1-12). IEEE.

Buyya, R., Yeo, C. S., Venugopal, S., Broberg, J., & Brandic, I. (2009). Cloud computing and emerging IT platforms: Vision, hype, and reality for delivering computing as the 5th utility. *Future Gen Computer Syst*em, *25*(6), 599–616. 10.1016/j.future.2008.12.001

Buyya, R., Yeo, C. S., Venugopal, S., Broberg, J., & Brandic, I. (2009). Cloud computing and emerging IT platforms: Vision, hype, and reality for delivering computing as the 5th utility. *Future Generation Computer Systems*, *25*(6), 599–616. doi:10.1016/j.future.2008.12.001

Campello, Moulav, Zimek, & Sander. (2015). Hierarchical Density Estimates for Data Clustering, Visualization, and Outlier Detection. *ACM Transactions on Knowledge Discovery from Data, 10*(1).

Cao, Y. (2015). FAST: A Fog Computing Assisted Distributed Analytics System to Monitor Fall for Stroke Mitigation. *Proc. 10th IEEE Int'l Conf. Networking, Architecture and Storage (NAS 15)*, 2–11. 10.1109/NAS.2015.7255196

Catarinucci, L., De Donno, D., Mainetti, L., Palano, L., Patrono, L., Stefanizzi, M. L., & Tarricone, L. (2015). An IoT-aware architecture for smart healthcare systems. *IEEE Internet of Things Journal*, *2*(6), 515–526. doi:10.1109/JIOT.2015.2417684

Cattell R (2010). Scalable SQL and NoSQL Data Stores. *ACM SIGMOD Record*, *39*(4), 12–27. 10.1145/1978915.1978919

Chagas Teixeira, C., Peres Boaventura, R., Cristina Silva Souza, A., Tanferri de Brito Paranaguá, T., Lúcia Queiroz Bezerra, A., Márcia Bachion, M., & Visconde Brasil, V. (2015). Vital Signs Measurement: An Indicator of Safe Care Delivered To Elderly. *The Scientific Electronic Library Online*, *24*(4), 1071–1078.

Chang, F., Dean, J., Ghemawat, S., Hsieh, W., Wallach, D., Burrows, M., … Gruber, R. (2006). Bigtable: A distributed structured data storage system. *7th OSDI*, *26*, 305–314.

Chapman, R. A. (2013). Smart textiles for protection. Monitoring vital signs. *Woodhead Publishing Series in Textiles*, *133*, 246.

Chatrapathi, C., Rajkumar, M. N., & Venkatesakumar, V. (2015, February). VANET based integrated framework for smart accident management system. In *Soft-Computing and Networks Security (ICSNS), 2015 International Conference on* (pp. 1-7). IEEE. 10.1109/ICSNS.2015.7292411

Chen, F., Xiang, T., Lei, X., & Chen, J. (2010). Highly Efficient Linear Regression outsourcing to a cloud. *IEEE Transactions on Cloud Computing, 2*(4), 499-508.

Chen, Y., Heimark, E., & Gligoroski, D. (2013). Personal threshold in a small scale text-dependent speaker recognition. *Proceedings - 2013 International Symposium on Biometrics and Security Technologies*, 162–170. 10.1109/ISBAST.2013.29

Chen, Y., & Kunz, T. (2016). Performance Evaluation of IoT Protocols under a Constrained Wireless Access Network. In *International Conference on Selected Topics in Mobile and Wireless Networking*. Cairo, Egypt. IEEE. 10.1109/MoWNct.2016.7496622

Cherkassky, V., & Mulier, F. M. (2007). *Learning from data: concepts, theory, and methods. John Wiley & Sons.* doi:10.1002/9780470140529

Cheshire, S., & Krochmal, M. (2013). *Rfc 6762: Multicast dns.* Internet Engineering Task Force (IETF) standard.

Chhabra, J., & Gupta, P. (2016). IoT based Smart Home Design using Power and Security Management. 2016 *1st International Conference on Innovation and Challenges in Cyber Security (ICICCS 2016).*

Chiang, M., & Zhang, T. (2016). Fog and IoT: An Overview of Research Opportunities. *IEEE Internet of Things Journal*, *3*(6), 854–864. doi:10.1109/JIOT.2016.2584538

Cho, K., Park, G., Cho, W., Seo, J., & Han, K. (2016). Performance analysis of device discovery of Bluetooth Low Energy (BLE) networks. *Computer Communications*, *81*, 72–85. doi:10.1016/j.comcom.2015.10.008

Chow, D., & Abdulla, W. (2004). Robust speaker identification based on perceptual log area ratio and gaussian mixture models. *Eighth International Conference on Spoken Language Processing*, 2–5. Retrieved from http://www.isca-speech.org/archive/interspeech_2004/i04_1761.html

Chow, D., & Abdulla, W. H. (2004). Speaker identification based on log area ratio and Gaussian mixture models in narrow-band speech speech understanding / interaction. Lecture Notes in Artificial Intelligence, 3157, 901–902.

Chowdhary, S. K., Yadav, A., & Garg, N. (2011, April). Cloud computing: Future prospect for e-health. In *Electronics Computer Technology (ICECT), 2011 3rd International Conference on* (Vol. 3, pp. 297-299). IEEE.

Chun, B., Ihm, S., Maniatis, P., Naik, M., & Patti, A. (2011). CloneCloud. *Proceedings of the sixth conference on Computer systems - EuroSys '11*, 301–314. 10.1145/1966445.1966473

Churpek, M.M., Yuen, T.C., Winslow, C., Hall, J., & Edelson, D.P. (2015). Differences in vital signs between elderly and nonelderly patients prior to ward cardiac arrest. *Crit Care Med., 43*(4), 816-22.

Collotta, M., & Pau, G. (2015). Bluetooth for Internet of Things: A fuzzy approach to improve power management in smart homes. *Computers & Electrical Engineering*, *44*, 137–152. doi:10.1016/j.compeleceng.2015.01.005

Corbett, J. C., Dean, J., Epstein, M., Fikes, A., Frost, C., Furman, J. J., ... Woodford, D. (2012). Spanner - Google's globally-distributed database. *Osdi, 2012*, 1–14.

Correa, T., Hinsley, A. W., & de Zúñiga, H. G. (2010). Who interacts on the Web?: The intersection of users' personality and social media use. *Computers in Human Behavior*, *26*(2), 247–253. doi:10.1016/j.chb.2009.09.003

Couldry, N., & Turow, J. (2014). Advertising, big data, and the clearance of the public realm: Marketers' new approaches to thecontent subsidy. *International Journal of Communication*, *8*, 1710–1726.

Cuervo, E., Balasubramanian, A., Cho, D., Wolman, A., Saroiu, S., Chandra, R., & Bahl, P. (2010). Maui. *Proceedings of the 8th international conference on Mobile systems, applications, and services - MobiSys '10*, 49-62.

Culo, S. (2011). Risk assessment and intervention for vulnerable older adults. *BCMJ, 53*(8), 421–425.

Dameri, R. P. (2013). Searching for Smart City definition: A comprehensive proposal. *International Journal of Computers and Technology*, *11*(5), 2544–2551.

Daniel, D. M., Mihaela, C., & Romulus, T. (2015). Combining feature extraction level and score level fusion in a multimodal biometric system. *2014 11th International Symposium on Electronics and Telecommunications, ISETC 2014 - Conference Proceedings.* 10.1109/ISETC.2014.7010807

Daqrouq, K., & Al Azzawi, K. Y. (2012). Average framing linear prediction coding with wavelet transform for text-independent speaker identification system. *Computers & Electrical Engineering*, *38*(6), 1467–1479. doi:10.1016/j.compeleceng.2012.04.014

DeCandia, G., Hastorun, D., Jampani, M., Kakulapati, G., Lakshman, A., Pilchin, A., ... Vogels, W. (2007). Dynamo: Amazon's highly available Key-value store. *ACM SIGOPS Operating Syst Rev, 41,* 205. 10.1145/1323293.1294281

DeFries, R. S., Rudel, T., Uriarte, M., & Hansen, M. (2010). Deforestation driven by urban population growth and agricultural trade in the twenty-first century. *Nature Geoscience, 3*(3), 178–181. doi:10.1038/ngeo756

DeLone, W. H., & McLean, E. R. (2003). Journal of Management Information Systems The DeLone and McLean Model of Information Systems Success: A Ten-Year Update. *Journal of Management Information Systems, 19*(4), 9–30. doi:10.1080/07421222.2003.11045748

Delone, W. H., & Mclean, E. R. (2004). Measuring e-Commerce Success : Applying the DeLone & McLean Information Systems Success Model Measuring e-Commerce Success : Applying the DeLone & McLean Information Systems Success Model. *International Journal of Electronic Commerce, 9*(1), 31–47.

Dey, N. S., Mohanty, R., & Chugh, K. L. (2012). Speech and Speaker Recognition System Using Artificial Neural Networks and Hidden Markov Model. *2012 International Conference on Communication Systems and Network Technologies,* 311–315. 10.1109/CSNT.2012.221

Dhanya, N.M., & Kousalya, G. (2016) Context Aware Offloading Decision and Partitioning in Mobile Cloud Computing. *Asian Journal of Information Technology, 15*(13), 2177-2185.

Dhanya, N. M., Kousalya, G., & Balakrishnan, P. (2017). Dynamic mobile cloud offloading prediction based on statistical regression. *Journal of Intelligent & Fuzzy Systems, 32*(4), 3081–3089. doi:10.3233/JIFS-169251

Dhar, P., Gupta, P., (2016). Intelligent Parking Cloud Services based on IoT using MQTT Protocol. *Int. J. of Engineering Research, 5*(6/12), 457-461.

Divya & Nanda Kumar. (2015). Study on Feature Selection Methods for Text Mining. *International Journal of Advanced Research Trends in Engineering and Technology, 2*(1).

Dong, C., Dong, Y., Li, J., & Wang, H. (2008, January). *Support vector machines based text dependent speaker verification using HMM supervectors.* Odyssey.

Duffy, A. H. (1997). The "what" and "how" of learning in design. *IEEE Expert, 12*(3), 71–76. doi:10.1109/64.590079

Dunkels, A., Eriksson, J., & Tsiftes, N. (2011). Low-power interoperabilityfor the IPv6-based Internet of Things. *Proc. 10thScandinavian Workshop Wireless ADHOC,* 10-11.

Dupouy, J., Moulis, G., Tubery, M., Ecoiffier, M., Sommet, A., Poutrain, J. C., ... Lapeyre-Mestre, M. (2013). Which adverse events are related to health care during hospitalization in elderly inpatients. *International Journal of Medical Sciences, 10*(9), 1224–1230. doi:10.7150/ijms.6640 PMID:23935400

Dwivedi, Y. K., Wade, M. R., & Schneberger, S. L. (2012). *Information Systems Theory.* Springer.

E. (n.d.). Retrieved December 22, 2017, from http://www.eclipse.org/kura//

Eastman, C. M., Eastman, C., Teicholz, P., Sacks, R., & Liston, K. (2011). *BIM handbook: A guide to building information modeling for owners, managers, designers, engineers and contractors.* John Wiley & Sons.

Edwards-Murphy, F., Magno, M., Whelan, P. M., O'Halloran, J., & Popovici, E. M. (2016). b+ WSN: Smart beehive with preliminary decision tree analysis for agriculture and honey bee health monitoring. *Computers and Electronics in Agriculture, 124,* 211–219. doi:10.1016/j.compag.2016.04.008

Elarabi, T., Deep, V., & Rai, C. K. (2015, December). Design and simulation of state-of-art ZigBee transmitter for IoT wireless devices. In *Signal Processing and Information Technology (ISSPIT), 2015 IEEE International Symposium on* (pp. 297-300). IEEE. 10.1109/ISSPIT.2015.7394347

Ellouze, A., Gagnaire, M., & Haddad, A. (2015). A Mobile Application Offloading Algorithm for Mobile Cloud Computing. *2015 3rd IEEE International Conference on Mobile Cloud Computing, Services, and Engineering*, 34-40.

Elmir, Y., Elberrichi, Z., & Adjoudj, R. (2012). Score level fusion based multimodal biometric identification (Fingerprint & voice). *2012 6th International Conference on Sciences of Electronics, Technologies of Information and Telecommunications (SETIT)*, 146–150. 10.1109/SETIT.2012.6481903

Eman, E. E., Koutlo, M., Kelash, H., & Allah, O. F. (2009). A Network Authentication Protocol Based on Kerberos. Int. *J. of Computer Science and Network Security.*, *9*(8/12), 18–26.

Ergazakis, K., Metaxiotis, K., & Psarras, J. (2004). Towards knowledge cities: Conceptual analysis and success stories. *Journal of Knowledge Management*, *8*(5), 5–15. doi:10.1108/13673270410558747

Eric, W. Y. P., Lin, X., Adhikary, A., Grovlen, A., Sui, Y., Blankenship, Y., ... Razaghi, H. S. (2017). A Primer on 3GPP Narrowband Internet of Things. *IEEE Communications Magazine*, *55*(3), 117–123. doi:10.1109/MCOM.2017.1600510CM

Esposito, C., Russo, S., & Di Crescenzo, D. (2008). Performance assessment of OMG compliant data distribution middleware. *Proc. IEEE IPDPS*, 1–8. 10.1109/IPDPS.2008.4536566

European Research Commission. (2015). *European Research Cluster on Internet of Things*. Retrieved from http://www.internet-of-things-research.eu/

Extensible Messaging Presence Protocol. (n.d.). Retrieved from http//tools.ietf.org.rfc6120

Fahad. (2014). *A Survey of Clustering Algorithms for Big Data: Taxonomy and Empirical Analysis*. IEEE.

Fang, Y.-H., Chiu, C.-M., & Wang, E. T. G. G. (2011). Understanding customers' satisfaction and repurchase intentions: An integration of IS success model, trust, and justice. *Internet Research*, *21*(4), 479–503. doi:10.1108/10662241111158335

Fernandes, J. L., Lopes, I. C., Rodrigues, J. J. P. C., & Ullah, S. (2013). Performance evaluation of RESTful web services and AMQP protocol. *Proc. 5th ICUFN*, 810–815.

Ferràs, M., Shinoda, K., & Furui, S. (2011). Structural MAP adaptation in GMM-supervector based speaker recognition. *ICASSP, IEEE International Conference on Acoustics, Speech and Signal Processing - Proceedings*, 5432–5435. 10.1109/ICASSP.2011.5947587

Fielding, A. H., & Bell, J. F. (1997). A review of methods for the assessment of prediction errors in conservation presence/absence models. *Environmental Conservation*, *24*(1), 38–49. doi:10.1017/S0376892997000088

Finkel, E. J., Eastwick, P. W., Karney, B. R., Reis, H. T., & Spreche, S. (2012). Online Dating: A Critical Analysis From the Perspective of Psychological Science. *Psychological Science in the Public Interest*, *13*(1), 3–66. doi:10.1177/1529100612436522 PMID:26173279

Fog Computing and the Internet of Things. (n.d.). Retrieved from www.cisco.com/go/iot-Whitepaper

Fog Computing vs. Edge Computing: What's the Difference? I Automation World. (n.d.). Retrieved November 30, 2017, from https://www.automationworld.com/fog-computing-vs-edge-computing-whats-difference

Fourati, H., Khssibi, S., Val, T., Idoudi, H., & Van den Bossche, A. (2015). Comparative study of IEEE 802.15.4 and IEEE 802.15.6 for WBAN-based CANet: 4th Performance Evaluation and Modeling in Wireless Networks (PEMWN 2015), Hammamet, Tunisia. *Proceedings of PEMWN, 2015*, 1–7.

Gade, Gade, & Ugander Reddy. (2016). *Internet of Things (LOT) for Smart Cities- The Future Technology Revolution.* Academic Press.

Gajic, B., & Paliwal, K. K. (2006). Robust speech recognition in noisy environments based on subband spectral centroid histograms. *IEEE Transactions on Audio, Speech, and Language Processing, 14*(2), 600–608. doi:10.1109/TSA.2005.855834

Garg, S. N. (2016). *Multimodal Biometric System Based On Decision Level Fusion.* Academic Press.

Garimella, D., Kumar, R., (2015). Secure Shell-Its significance in Networking (SSH). *Int. J. of Application or Innovation in Engineering & Management, 4*(3/12), 187-196.

Gaubitch, N. (2017). How voice ageing impacts biometric effectiveness. *Biometric Technology Today, 2017*(6), 8–9. 10.1016/S0969-4765(17)30115-7

Gerardo, P. C., Farabaugh, B., & Warren, R. (2005). *An Introduction to DDS and Data-Centric Communications.* Real Time Innovations.

Ghahabi, O., & Hernando, J. (2017). Deep Larning Backend for Single and Multisession i-Vector Speaker Recognition. *IEEE/ACM Transactions on Audio Speech and Language Processing, 25*(4), 807–817. 10.1109/TASLP.2017.2661705

Giffinger, R. (2007). Smart cities Ranking of European medium-sized cities. *October, 16*, 13–18.

Gil Press. (2016). *Internet Of Things By The Numbers: What New Surveys Found.* Retrieved December 27, 2016, from http://www.forbes.com/sites/gilpress/2016/09/02/internet-of-things-by-the-numbers-what-new-surveys-found/#5f5270443196

Gilbert S, Lynch N (2002). Brewer's conjecture and the feasibility of consistent, available, partition-tolerant web services. *ACM SIGACT News, 33*(2), 51–59. 10.1145/564585.564601

Giusto, D., Iera, A., Morabito, G., & Atzori, L. (Eds.). (2010). *The internet of things: 20th Tyrrhenian workshop on digital communications.* Springer Science & Business Media.

Glasmeier, A., & Christopherson, S. (2015). Thinking about smart cities. *Cambridge Journal of Regions, Economy and Society, 8*(1), 3–12. doi:10.1093/cjres/rsu034

Goldberg, C. (2009). A comprehensive physical examination and clinical education site for medical students and other health care professionals. *A Practical Guide to Clinical Medicine.* Retrieved from https://meded.ucsd.edu/clinicalmed/vital.htm

Gomez, C., & Paradells, J. (2010). Wireless home automation networks: A survey of architectures and technologies. *IEEE Communications Magazine, 48*(6), 92–101. doi:10.1109/MCOM.2010.5473869

Gómez-Goiri, A., & López-De-Ipiña, D. (2010). A triple space-based semantic distributed middleware for internet of things. Lecture Notes in Computer Science, 6385, 447–458. doi:10.1007/978-3-642-16985-4_43

Granell, C., Havlik, D., Schade, S., Sabeur, Z., Delaney, C., Pielorz, J., ... Mon, J. L. (2016). Future Internet technologies for environmental applications. *Environmental Modelling & Software, 78*, 1–15. doi:10.1016/j.envsoft.2015.12.015

Granjal, J., Monteiro, E., & Silva, J. (2015). Security for the Internet of Things: A Survey of Existing Protocols and Open Research Issues. *IEEE Communications Surveys and Tutorials, 17*(3), 1294–1312. doi:10.1109/COMST.2015.2388550

Greenwood. (2014). Telehealth Remote Patient Monitoring Intervention For People With Type 2 Diabetes. *Conference: 2014 Western Institute of Nursing Annual Communicating Nursing Research Conference.*

Guo, Y., Kuo, M. H., & Sahama, T. (2012, December). Cloud computing for healthcare research information sharing. In *Cloud Computing Technology and Science (CloudCom), 2012 IEEE 4th International Conference on* (pp. 889-894). IEEE. 10.1109/CloudCom.2012.6427561

Gupta, G. K. (2015). *Introduction to data mining with case studies.* Delhi: PHI Learning Private Limited.

Gurun, S., Wolski, R., Krintz, C., & Nurmi, D. (2008). On the Efficacy of Computation Offloading Decision-Making Strategies. *International Journal of High Performance Computing Applications, 22*(4), 460–479. doi:10.1177/1094342007095289

GV, R. L., & Annappa, B. (2015, November). An Efficient Framework and Access control scheme for cloud health care. In *Cloud Computing Technology and Science (CloudCom), 2015 IEEE 7th International Conference on* (pp. 552-557). IEEE.

H. (2017, June 17). *Harshitgupta1337/fogsim.* Retrieved December 22, 2017, from https://github.com/harshitgupta1337/fogsim

Ha, K., Chen, Z., Hu, W., Richter, W., Pillai, P., & Satyanarayanan, M. (2014, June). Towards wearable cognitive assistance. In *Proceedings of the 12th annual international conference on Mobile systems, applications, and services* (pp. 68-81). ACM.

Han, J., & Yu, P. S. (1996). Data Mining: An Overview from a Database Perspective. *IEEE Tran. on Knowledge and Data Engg.*

Handaya, D., Fakhruroja, H., Hidayat, E. M. I., & Machbub, C. (2016, December). Comparison of Indonesian speaker recognition using vector quantization and Hidden Markov Model for unclear pronunciation problem. In *Frontiers of Information Technology (FIT), 2016 International Conference on* (pp. 39-45). IEEE. 10.1109/ICSEngT.2016.7849620

Han, J., Kamber, M., & Pei, J. (1996). *Data Mining Concept and Technique* (3rd ed.). Morgan Kaufmann.

Hao, Q., Zhang, F., Liu, Z., & Qin, L. (2015). Design of chemical industrial park integrated information management platform based on cloud computing and IOT (the internet of things) technologies. *International Journal of Smart Home, 9*(4), 35–46. doi:10.14257/ijsh.2015.9.4.04

Harris, S., & Seaborne, A. (2013). *SPARQL 1.1 Query Language.* Retrieved from http://www.w3.org/TR/2013/REC-sparql11-query-20130321/

Harrison, C., Eckman, B., Hamilton, R., Hartswick, P., Kalagnanam, J., Paraszczak, J., & Williams, P. (2010). Foundations for Smarter Cities. *IBM Journal of Research and Development, 54*(4), 1–16. doi:10.1147/JRD.2010.2048257

Haughn, M. (2015). Wireless Sensor and Actuator Network. IoT Agenda. *TechTarget Network.* Retrieved November 20, 2017, from http://internetofthingsagenda.techtarget.com/definition/WSAN-wireless-sensor-and-actuator-network

Haut, Paoletti, Plaza, & Plaza. (2017). Cloud implementation of the K-means algorithm for hyperspectral image analysis. *Journal of Supercomputing, 73,* 514–529. DOI: 10.1007/s11227-016-1896-3

Hecht, R., & Jablonski, S. (2011). NoSQL evaluation: A use case oriented survey. *Proc 2011 Int Conf Cloud Serv Computing,* 336–341. 10.1109/CSC.2011.6138544

He, W., Yan, G., & Da Xu, L. (2014). Developing vehicular data cloud services in the IoT environment. *IEEE Transactions on Industrial Informatics, 10*(2), 1587–1595. doi:10.1109/TII.2014.2299233

Hitachi Data System. (2016). *How to improve health care with cloud computing.* Author.

Hospira. (n.d.). Retrieved from https://www.hospira.com/en/products_and_services/iv_emr_integration

Hou, X., Li, Y., Chen, M., Wu, D., Jin, D., & Chen, S. (2016). Vehicular fog computing: A viewpoint of vehicles as the infrastructures. *IEEE Transactions on Vehicular Technology*, *65*(6), 3860–3873. doi:10.1109/TVT.2016.2532863

Hu, X., & Qian, S. (2011, November). IOT application system with crop growth models in facility agriculture. In *Computer Sciences and Convergence Information Technology (ICCIT), 2011 6th International Conference on* (pp. 129-133). IEEE.

Hu, Y. C., Patel, M., Sabella, D., Sprecher, N., & Young, V. (2015). *Mobile edge computing—A key technology towards 5G*. ETSI White Paper, 11.

Huang, Y., & Li, G. (2010). Descriptive models for Internet of things. *Proceedings of 2010 International Conference on Intelligent Control and Information Processing, ICICIP 2010, (PART 2)*, 483–486. 10.1109/ICICIP.2010.5564232

Huang, C.-L., Wang, J.-C., & Ma, B. (2016). Ensemble based speaker recognition using unsupervised data selection. *APSIPA Transactions on Signal and Information Processing*, *5*, e10. doi:10.1017/ATSIP.2016.10

Huo, C. B., & Zhang, C. J. (2012). The research of speaker recognition based on GMM and SVM. *Proceedings 2012 International Conference on System Science and Engineering, ICSSE 2012*, 373–375. 10.1109/ICSSE.2012.6257210

Hu, P., Ning, H., Qiu, T., Zhang, Y., & Luo, X. (2017). Fog computing based face identification and resolution scheme in internet of things. *IEEE Transactions on Industrial Informatics*, *13*(4), 1910–1920. doi:10.1109/TII.2016.2607178

IBM Watson Health for Oncology. (n.d.). Retrieved from https://www.ibm.com/watson/health/oncology-and-genomics/oncology/

IBM Watson Health. (n.d.). Retrieved from https://www.ibm.com/watson/health/

IEEE 802.15.4 (2015). *IEEE Standard for Low-Rate Wireless Networks*. Retrieved from https://standards.ieee.org/find-stds/standard/802.15.4-2015.html

IEEE Standards Association. (2016). *Standard for an Architectural Framework for the Internet of Things (IoT)*. New York: Institute of Electrical and Electronics Engineers.

Ikram, M. A., Alshehri, M. D., & Hussain, F. K. (2015, December). Architecture of an IoT-based system for football supervision (IoT Football). In *Internet of Things (WF-IoT), 2015 IEEE 2nd World Forum on* (pp. 69-74). IEEE.

IoT Analytics Across Edge and Cloud Platforms. (n.d.). Retrieved December 22, 2017, from https://iot.ieee.org/newsletter/may-2017/iot-analytics-across-edge-and-cloud-platforms.html

Islam, S., Keung, J., Lee, K., & Liu, A. (2012). Empirical prediction models for adaptive resource provisioning in the cloud. *Future Generation Computer Systems*, *28*(1), 155–162. doi:10.1016/j.future.2011.05.027

Jackson, L. A., von Eye, A., Fitzgerald, H. E., Zhao, Y., & Witt, E. A. (2010). Self-concept, self-esteem, gender, race and information technology use. *Computers in Human Behavior*, *26*(3), 323–328. doi:10.1016/j.chb.2009.11.001

Jadhav Swapnil & Verma. (2014). Revived Fuzzy K-Means Clustering Technique for Image Segmentation. *International Journal of Engineering Research & Technology, 3*(8).

Jain, R., & Paul, S. (2013). Network virtualization and software defined networking for cloud computing: A survey. *IEEE Communications Magazine*, *51*(11), 24–31. doi:10.1109/MCOM.2013.6658648

Janssen, M., Charalabidis, Y., & Zuiderwijk, A. (2012). Benefits, Adoption Barriers and Myths of Open Data and Open Government. *Information Systems Management*, *29*(4), 258–268. doi:10.1080/10580530.2012.716740

Japkowicz, N., & Shah, M. (2009). *Evaluating Learning Algorithms: a classification perspective*. Cambridge, UK: Cambridge University Press.

Jara, A. J., Martinez-Julia, P., & Skarmeta, A. (2012, July). Light-weight multicast DNS and DNS-SD (lmDNS-SD): IPv6-based resource and service discovery for the Web of Things. In *Innovative mobile and internet services in ubiquitous computing (IMIS), 2012 sixth international conference on* (pp. 731-738). IEEE.

Jara, A. J., Ladid, L., & Gómez-Skarmeta, A. F. (2013). The Internet of Everything through IPv6: An Analysis of Challenges, Solutions and Opportunities. *JoWua, 4*(3), 97–118.

Jarmakiewicz, J., Parobczak, K., & Maślanka, K. (2016, May). On the Internet of Nano Things in healthcare network. In *Military Communications and Information Systems (ICMCIS), 2016 International Conference on* (pp. 1-6). IEEE. 10.1109/ICMCIS.2016.7496572

Jawak, S. D., Devliyal, P., & Luis, A. J. (2015). A Comprehensive Review on Pixel Oriented and Object Oriented Methods for Information Extraction from Remotely Sensed Satellite Images with a Special Emphasis on Cryospheric Applications. *Advances in Remote Sensing, 4*(03), 177–195. doi:10.4236/ars.2015.43015

Jing, X.-X., Zhan, L., Zhao, H., & Zhou, P. (2010). Speaker recognition system using the improved GMM-based clustering algorithm. *IEEE International Conference on Intelligent computing and Integrated systems,ICISS 2010*. doi: 10.1109/ICISS.2010.5655122

Ji, Y.-K., Kim, Y.-I., & Park, S. (2014). Big Data Summarization Using Semantic Feature for IoT on Cloud. *Contemporary Engineering Sciences, 7*(22), 1095–1103. doi:10.12988/ces.2014.49137

Joshi, M., & Kaur, B. P. (2015). CoAP Protocol for Constrained Networks. Int. *J. of Wireless and Microwave Technologies, 6*, 1–10.

Juo, J., & Yang, S. (2016). Speaker recognition based on wavelet packet decomposition and Volterra adaptive model. *IEEE International Conference on Computer and Communications(ICCC)*. doi: 10.1109/CompComm.2016.7925042

Kalaivanan, S., & Manoharan, S. (2016). Monitoring and Controlling of Smart Homes using IoT and Low Power Wireless Technology. *Indian Journal of Science and Technology, 9*(31). doi:10.17485/ijst/2016/v9i31/92701

Kamale, H. E., & Kawitkar, R. S. (2008). Vector quantization approach for speaker recognition. *International Journal of Computer Technology and Electronics Engineering*, 110-114..

Kamilaris, A., Pitsillides, A., & Trifa, V. (2011). The smart home meets the web of things. *International Journal of Ad Hoc and Ubiquitous Computing, 7*(3), 145–154. doi:10.1504/IJAHUC.2011.040115

Kanakalakshmi & Chezian. (2015). Feature Selection Approaches With Text Mining For Categorical Variable Selection. *IJRSET, 2*(6).

Kandaswamy, A., Kumar, C. S., Ramanathan, R. P., Jayaraman, S., & Malmurugan, N. (2004). Neural classification of lung sounds using wavelet coefficients. *Computers in Biology and Medicine, 34*(6), 523–537. doi:10.1016/S0010-4825(03)00092-1 PMID:15265722

Kang. (2007). A Review on Image and video processing. *International Journal of Multimedia and Ubiquitous Engineering, 2*(2).

Kantarci, B., Erol-Kantarci, M., & Schuckers, S. (2015). Towards secure cloud-centric Internet of Biometric Things. *2015 IEEE 4th International Conference on Cloud Networking, CloudNet 2015*, 81–83. 10.1109/CloudNet.2015.7335286

Karnwal, T., Sivakumar, T., & Aghila, G. (2011). Cloud Services in Different Cloud Deployment Models. An Overview. *International Journal of Computer Applications*.

Kaur & Joshi. (2015). Review On Image Segmentation Techniques. *International Journal of Computer Science Trends and Technology, 3*(4).

Kaur, & Kaur. (2014). Various Image Segmentation Techniques: A Review. *International Journal of Computer Science and Mobile Computing, 3*(5), 809–814.

Kaur, N., & Sood, S. K. (2015). Cognitive decision making in smart industry. *Computers in Industry, 74*, 151–161. doi:10.1016/j.compind.2015.06.006

Kekre, H. B. (2012). Speaker Identification using Spectrograms of Varying Frame Sizes. *International Journal of Computer Applications, 50*(20), 27-33.

Kekre, H. B., Bharadi, V. A., & Sawant, A. R. (2012) Speaker Recognition using Vector Quantization by MFCC and KMCG Clustering Algorithm. *IEEE International Conference on Communication, Information, Information and Computing Technology, ICCICT 2012.* 10.1109/ICCICT.2012.6398146

Kemp, R., Palmer, N., Kielmann, T., & Bal, H. (2012). Cuckoo: A Computation Offloading Framework for Smartphones. *Lecture Notes of the Institute for Computer Sciences, Social Informatics and Telecommunications Engineering Mobile Computing, Applications, and Services,* 59-79.

Khan & Yuce. (2010). Wireless Body Area Network (WBAN) for Medical Applications. In *New Developments in Biomedical Engineering.* InTech. Available from: http://www.intechopen.com/books/new-developments-in-biomedical-engineering/wireless-bodyarea-network-wban-for-medical-applications

Khan, Parkinson, & Qin. (2017). Fog computing security: a review of current applications and security solutions. *Journal of Cloud Computing Advances, Systems and Applications, 6*(1), 6-19.

Khan, M., Din, S., Jabbar, S., Gohar, M., Ghayvat, H., & Mukhopadhyay, S. C. (2016). Context-aware low power intelligent SmartHome based on the Internet of things. *Computers & Electrical Engineering, 52*, 208–222. doi:10.1016/j.compeleceng.2016.04.014

Kiefer, C., & Behrendt, F. (2016). Smart e-bike monitoring system: Real-time open source and open hardware GPS assistance and sensor data for electrically-assisted bicycles. *IET Intelligent Transport Systems, 10*(2), 79–88. doi:10.1049/iet-its.2014.0251

Kim, D. Y., & Jung, M. (2017). Data transmission and network architecture in long range low power sensor networks for IoT. *Wireless Personal Communications, 93*(1), 119–129. doi:10.100711277-016-3482-7

Kindberg, T., Chalmers, M., & Paulos, E. (2007). Urban Computing. *IEEE Pervasive Computing, 6*(3), 18–20. doi:10.1109/MPRV.2007.57

Kinetic, C. (2017, December 15). Retrieved December 22, 2017, from http://www.cisco.com/c/en/us/solutions/internet-of-things/iot-kinetic.html

Kingsbury, B. E., Morgan, N., & Greenberg, S. (1998). Robust speech recognition using the modulation spectrogram. *Speech Communication, 25*(1), 117–132. doi:10.1016/S0167-6393(98)00032-6

Kinnunen, T., Zhang, B., Zhu, J., & Wang, Y. (2007). Speaker verification with adaptive spectral subband centroids. *Advances in Biometrics,* 58-66.

Kinnunen, T., & Li, H. (2010). An overview of text-independent speaker recognition: From features to supervectors. *Speech Communication, 52*(1), 12–40. doi:10.1016/j.specom.2009.08.009

Klas, Rodermund, Shelby, Akhouri, & Höller. (2014). *Whitepaper -Lightweight M2M: Enabling Device Management and Applications for the Internet of Things.* Academic Press.

Klophaus, R. (2010). Core: Building distributed applications without shared state. In *Proceedings of CUFP'10 - ACM SIGPLAN Commercial Users of Functional Programming.* New York, NY: ACM Press. 10.1145/1900160.1900176

Knight, J., & Nigam, Y. (2008). The anatomy and physiology of ageing. Part 1 - The cardiovascular system. *Nursing Times, 104*(31), 26–28. PMID:18727348

Komninos, N. (2006). The Architecture of Intelligent Cities. *2nd International Conference on Intelligent Environments,* 13–20.

Konstantinou, I., Angelou, E., Boumpouka, C., Tsoumakos, D., & Koziris, N. (2011). *On the elasticity of NoSQL data-bases over cloud management platforms.* ACM Press. doi:10.1145/2063576.2063973

Kucera, J., & Chlapek, D. (2014). Benefits and Risks of Open Government Data. *Journal of Systems Integration, 5*(1), 30–41. doi:10.20470/jsi.v5i1.185

Kuipers, F. A., & Van Mieghem, P. (2003). The impact of correlated link weights on QoS Routing. *Proceedings - IEEE INFOCOM, 12,* 1425–1434.

Kumar & Bhatia. (2013). Text mining: Concepts, process and applications. *Journal of Global Research in Computer Science, 4*(3).

Kumar & Raj. (2017). Video Processing and its Applications: A survey. *International Journal of Emerging Trends & Technology in Computer Science, 6*(4).

Kumar, N., Kaur, K., Jindal, A., & Rodrigues, J. J. (2015). Providing healthcare services on-the-fly using multi-player cooperation game theory in Internet of Vehicles (IoV) environment. *Digital Communications and Networks, 1*(3), 191–203. doi:10.1016/j.dcan.2015.05.001

Kumar, S., & Goudar, R. H. (2012). Cloud Computing-Research Issues, Challenges, Architecture, Platforms and Ap-plications: A Survey. *International Journal of Future Computer and Communication, 1*(4), 356–360. doi:10.7763/IJFCC.2012.V1.95

Kumbhar & Mal. (2016). A Survey on Feature Selection Techniques and Classification Algorithms for Efficient Text Classification. *International Journal of Science and Research, 5*(5).

Kundhavai & Sridevi. (2016). IoT and Big Data- The Current and Future Technologies: A Review. *International Journal of Computer Science and Mobile Computing, 5*(1), 10-14.

Kung, S. Y. (Sun Y., Mak, M. W., & Lin, S.-H. (2005). *Biometric authentication: A machine learning approach.* Prentice Hall Professional Technical Reference.

Kushalnagar, N., Montenegro, G., & Schumacher, C. (2007). *IPv6 over low-power wireless personal area networks (6LoWPANs): overview, assumptions, problem statement, and goals* (No. RFC 4919).

Kuswantoa, H., Asfihanib, A., Sarumahab, Y., & Ohwada, H. (2015). Logistic Regression Ensemble for Predicting Customer Defection with Very Large Sample Size. *Proceedings of Third Information Systems International Conference, 72,* 86 – 93. 10.1016/j.procs.2015.12.108

La, H. J. (2016). A conceptual framework for trajectory-based medical analytics with IoT contexts. *Journal of Computer and System Sciences, 82*(4), 610–626. doi:10.1016/j.jcss.2015.10.007

Lakshman, A., & Malik, P. (2010). Cassandra: a decentralized structured storage system. *ACM SIGOPS Operating Syst Rev, 44*(2), 35–40. 10.1145/1773912.1773922

Lakshmi & Sankaranarayanan. (2010). A study of Edge Detection Techniques for Segmentation Computing Approaches. *IJCA.*

Langley, P., & Simon, H. A. (1995). Applications of machine learning and rule induction. *Communications of the ACM, 38*(11), 54–64. doi:10.1145/219717.219768

Language, C. Q. (CQL) v3.1.1. (2013). Retrieved from http://cassandra.apache.org/doc/cql3/CQL.html

Lashkari, A. H., & Danesh, M. M. S. (2009). A Survey on Wireless Security Protocols (WEP, WPA and WPA/802.11i). *2nd Int. Conf. on Computer Science and Information Technology (ICCSIT)*, 49-52.

Latré, B., Braem, B., Moerman, I., Blondia, C., & Demeester, P. (2011). A Survey on Wireless Body Area Networks. *Wireless Networks, 17*(1), 1–18. doi:10.100711276-010-0252-4

Lee, H., Yoo, S., & Kim, Y. W. (2016, January). An energy management framework for smart factory based on context-awareness. In *Advanced Communication Technology (ICACT), 2016 18th International Conference on* (pp. 685-688). IEEE.

Lee, W., Nam, K., Roh, H. G., & Kim, S. H. (2016). A gateway based fog computing architecture for wireless sensors and actuator networks. In *Advanced Communication Technology (ICACT). 18th Int. Conf. on Advanced Communication Technology (ICACT)*. Pyeongchang, South Korea: IEEE. doi: 10.1109/ICACT.2016.7423331

Lee, B. M., & Ouyang, J. (2014). Intelligent healthcare service by using collaborations between IoT personal health devices. *International Journal of Bio-Science and Bio-Technology, 6*(1), 155–164. doi:10.14257/ijbsbt.2014.6.1.17

Lee, M., Almirall, E., & Wareham, J. (2015). Open data and civic apps. *Communications of the ACM, 59*(1), 82–89. doi:10.1145/2756542

Lemey, S., Agneessens, S., Van Torre, P., Baes, K., Vanfleteren, J., & Rogier, H. (2016). Wearable flexible lightweight modular RFID tag with integrated energy harvester. *IEEE Transactions on Microwave Theory and Techniques, 64*(7), 2304–2314. doi:10.1109/TMTT.2016.2573274

Lengyel, L., & Ekler, P. (2015). SensorHUB: An IoT Driver Framework for Supporting Sensor Networks and Data. Hindawi Publishing Corporation.

Lerche, C., Hartke, K., & Kovatsch, M. (2012). Industry adoption of the Inter-net of Things: A constrained application protocol survey. *Proc. IEEE17th Conf. ETFA*, 1–6.

Li, H., Chen, Q., & Zhou, X. (2017, June). An analysis of the health care platform in the cloud environment. In *Software Engineering Research, Management and Applications (SERA), 2017 IEEE 15th International Conference on* (pp. 99-102). IEEE. 10.1109/SERA.2017.7965713

Li, H., & Hu, X. M. (2008). Analysis and comparison between ID3 Algorithm and C4.5 Algorithm in Decision Tree. *Water Resources and Power, 26*(2), 129–132.

Lin, H.-F. (2007). Measuring online learning systems success: applying the updated DeLone and McLean model. Cyberpsychology & Behavior: The Impact of the Internet. *Multimedia and Virtual Reality on Behavior and Society, 10*(6), 817–820.

Li, P., Li, Y., Luo, D., & Luo, H. (2015). Speaker Identification Using FrFT-based Spectrogram and RBF Neural Network. *Proceedings of the 34th Chinese Control Conference*, 3674–3679. 10.1109/ChiCC.2015.7260207

Li, S., Wang, H., Xu, T., & Zhou, G. (2011). Application study on internet of things in environment protection field. *LectureNotes in Electrical Engineering*, *133*(2), 99–106.

Liu, Q., Ma, Y., Alhussein, M., Zhang, Y., & Peng, L. (2016). Green data center with IoT sensing and cloud-assisted smart temperature control system. *Computer Networks*, *101*, 104–112. doi:10.1016/j.comnet.2015.11.024

Locke, D. (2010). *MQ telemetry transport (MQTT) v3. 1 protocol specification.* Available Http://Www.Ibm.Com/Developerworks/ Webservices/Library/Ws-Mqtt/Index.Html

Lopez-Meyer, P., Cordourier-Maruri, H., Quinto-Martinez, A., & Tickoo, O. (2016). Analyzing Artificial Neural Networks and Dynamic Time Warping for spoken keyword recognition under transient noise conditions. *Proceedings of the International Conference on Sensing Technology*, 274–277. 10.1109/ICSensT.2015.7438406

LoRa Members. (n.d.). Retrieved from https://www.lora-alliance.org/The-Alliance/Member-List

LoRa. (n.d.). Retrieved from https://www.lora-alliance.org/What-Is-LoRa/Technology

LoRaWAN. (2017). *The Things Network*. Retrieved November 11, 2017, from https://www.thethingsnetwork.org/wiki/LoRaWAN/Home

LTE evolution for IoT connectivity A Nokia Whitepaper. (2017). Retrieved from http://resources.alcatel-lucent.com/asset/200178

Luan, T. H., Gao, L., Li, Z., Xiang, Y., Wei, G., & Sun, L. (2015). *Fog Computing: Focusing on Mobile Users at the Edge*. Academic Press. 10.1016/j.jnca.2015.02.002

Lung, S. Y. (2010). Improved wavelet feature extraction using kernel analysis for text independent speaker recognition. *Digital Signal Processing: A Review Journal*, *20*(5), 1400–1407. 10.1016/j.dsp.2009.12.004

Lung, S. Y. (2004). Adaptive fuzzy wavelet algorithm for text-independent speaker recognition. *Pattern Recognition*, *37*(10), 2095–2096. doi:10.1016/j.patcog.2004.03.015

Lupşe, O. S., Vida, M. M., & Tivadar, L. S. (2012). Cloud computing and interoperability in healthcare information systems. In *The First International Conference on Intelligent Systems and Applications* (pp. 81-85). Academic Press.

Lu, X., Shen, P., Tsao, Y., & Kawai, H. (2016). A Pseudo-task Design in Multi-task Learning Deep Neural Network for Speaker Recognition. *10th International Symposium on Chinese Spoken Language Processing(ISCSLP)*. 10.1109/ISCSLP.2016.7918433

Luzuriaga, J. E., Perez, M., Boronat, P., Cano, J. C., Calafate, C., & Manzoni, P. (2015, January). A comparative evaluation of AMQP and MQTT protocols over unstable and mobile networks. In *Consumer Communications and Networking Conference (CCNC), 2015 12th Annual IEEE* (pp. 931-936). IEEE. 10.1109/CCNC.2015.7158101

Macario, H. R., & Srirama, S. (2013). Adaptive code offloading for mobile cloud applications. *Proceeding of the fourth ACM workshop on Mobile cloud computing and services - MCS '13*, 9-16. 10.1145/2497306.2482984

Macnamara. (n.d.). Media content analysis: Its uses; benefits and best practice methodology. *Asia Pacific Public Relations Journal*, *6*(1), 1–34.

Mano, L. Y., Faiçal, B. S., Nakamura, L. H., Gomes, P. H., Libralon, G. L., Meneguete, R. I., ... Ueyama, J. (2016). Exploiting IoT technologies for enhancing Health Smart Homes through patient identification and emotion recognition. *Computer Communications*, *89*, 178–190. doi:10.1016/j.comcom.2016.03.010

MapR. (n.d.). *The only converged data platform*. Retrieved from https://mapr.com/

Marakas, G. M., Marakas, G. M., Yi, M. Y., Yi, M. Y., Johnson, R. D., & Johnson, R. D. (1998). The multilevel and multifaceted character of computer self-ef cacy: Toward clari cation of the construct and an integrative framework for research. *Information Systems Research, 9*(2), 126–163. doi:10.1287/isre.9.2.126

Markowitz, J. A. (2000). Voice biometrics. *Communications of the ACM, 43*(9), 66–73. doi:10.1145/348941.348995

Martins, J., Ahmed, M., Raiciu, C., Olteanu, V., Honda, M., Bifulco, R., & Huici, F. (2014, April). ClickOS and the art of network function virtualization. In *Proceedings of the 11th USENIX Conference on Networked Systems Design and Implementation* (pp. 459-473). USENIX Association.

Mathew, P., Augustine, L., Kushwaha, D., Selvakumar, D. (2015). Hardware Implementation of NB PHY Baseband Transceiver for IEEE 802.15.6 WBAN. *International Conference on Medical Imaging, m-Health and Emerging Communication Systems (MedCom 2014)*. DOI: 10.1109/MedCom.2014.7005977

Mathew, P., Augustine, L., Kushwaha, D., Selvakumar, D. (2015). *Implementation of NB PHY transceiver of IEEE 802.15.6 WBAN on FPGA*. International Conference on VLSI Systems, Architecture, Technology and Applications (VLSI-SATA 2015), Bangalore, India.

Medication Alert & Adherence System (MAAS). (n.d.). Retrieved from http://www8.hp.com/in/en/hp-news/press-release.html?id=1426409#.WR9mU3WGO00

Mell, P., & Grance, T. (2013). *The NIST definition of cloud computing*. NIST special publication 800–145. Retrieved from http://csrc.nist.gov/publications/nistpubs/800-145/SP800-145.pdf

Memcached. (2013). Retrieved from http://memcached.org/

Ministry of Industry and Information Technology of China. (2012). *The National 12th Five-Year Plan Including IoT Development (2011–2015)*. Retrieved from http://www.gov.cn/zwgk/2012-02/14/content2065999.html

Mireku, K., FengLi, Z., NiiAyeh, M. D., Khan, A., & Khan, I. (2016, March). Secured cloud database health care mining analysis. In *Computing for Sustainable Global Development (INDIACom), 2016 3rd International Conference on* (pp. 3937-3740). IEEE.

Mitchell, T. M. (1997). *Machine learning*. New York: McGraw-Hill.

Mitchell, T. M. (2006). *The discipline of machine learning*. Carnegie Mellon University, School of Computer Science, Machine Learning Department.

Modadugu, N., & Rescorla, E. (2004). The Design and Implementation of Datagram TLS. *Proceedings of the Network and Distributed System Security Symposium.*

MongoD. B. (2013). Retrieved from http://www.mongodb.org/

Monteiro, A., Dubey, H., Mahler, L., Yang, Q., & Mankodiya, K. (2016). Fit: A Fog Computing Device for Speech Tele-Treatments. *2016 IEEE International Conference on Smart Computing, SMARTCOMP 2016*, 10–12. 10.1109/SMARTCOMP.2016.7501692

Morabito, V. (2015). Managing Change for Big Data Driven Innovation. In *Big Data and Analytics* (pp. 125–153). Springer International Publishing. doi:10.1007/978-3-319-10665-6_7

Morgera, S. D. (2009). A method towards biometric feature fusion. *International Journal of Biometrics, 1*(4), 2009.

Morosini, S., Marques, A.P.O., Leal, M.C.C., Marino, J.G., & Melo, H.M.A. (2011). Cost and length of hospital stay of elderly residents in Recife-PE. *Geriatrics and Gerontology, 5*(2), 91-98.

Morris, M. G., Venkatesh, V., & Ackerman, P. L. (2005). Gender and age differences in employee decisions about new technology: An extension to the theory of planned behavior. *IEEE Transactions on Engineering Management, 52*(1), 69–84. doi:10.1109/TEM.2004.839967

Mozaffarian, D., Benjamin, E. J., Go, A. S., Arnett, D. K., Blaha, M. J., Cushman, M., ... Howard, V. J. (2016). Heart disease and stroke statistics—2016 update. *Circulation, 133*(4), e38–e360. doi:10.1161/CIR.0000000000000350 PMID:26673558

Mukherjee, A., Gupta, P., & De, D. (2014). Mobile cloud computing based energy efficient offloading strategies for femtocell network. *2014 Applications and Innovations in Mobile Computing (AIMoC)*, 22-33.

Munir, S. A., Yu, W. B., Biao, R., & Man, M. (2007). Fuzzy Logic Based Congestion Estimation for QoS in Wireless Sensor Network. *IEEE Wireless Communications and Networking Conference, WCNC 2007*, 4336-4341. 10.1109/WCNC.2007.791

Muralidharan, S., Roy, A., & Saxena, N. (2016). An Exhaustive Review on Internet of Things from Korea's Perspective. *Wireless Personal Communications, 90*(3), 1463–1486. doi:10.100711277-016-3404-8

Murty, J. (2008). *SQS, FPS, and SimpleDB*. O'Reilly Media Inc.

Muthukrishnan & Radha. (2011). Edge Detection Techniques For Image Segmentation. *International Journal of Computer Science & Information Technology, 3*(6).

Naik, A. (2016). *k-Means Clustering Algorithm*. Retrieved June 14,2016, from https://sites.google.com/site/dataclusteringalgorithms/k-means-clustering-algorithm

Nandimath, J., Banerjee, E., Patil, A., Kakade, P., Vaidya, S., & Chaturvedi, D. (2013, August). Big data analysis using Apache Hadoop. In *Information Reuse and Integration (IRI), 2013 IEEE 14th International Conference on* (pp. 700-703). IEEE. 10.1109/IRI.2013.6642536

Naphade, M., Banavar, G., Harrison, C., Paraszczak, J., & Morris, R. (2011). Smarter cities and their innovation challenges. *Computer, 44*(6), 32–39. doi:10.1109/MC.2011.187

NarrowBand-IoT. (n.d.). Retrieved from http://www.3gpp.org/news-events/3gpp-news/1785-nb_iot_complete

Natarajan, K., Acharya, R., Alias, F., Tiboleng, T., & Puthusserypady, S. K. (2004). Nonlinear analysis of EEG signals at different mental states. *Biomedical Engineering Online, 3*(1), 7. doi:10.1186/1475-925X-3-7 PMID:15023233

Negra, R., Jemili, I., & Belghith, A. (2016). Wireless Body Area Networks: Applications and Technologies. *The Second International Workshop on Recent Advances on Machine-to-Machine Communications*, Madrid, Spain. 10.1016/j.procs.2016.04.266

Ngai, E. W. T., Moon, K. K. L., Riggins, F. J., & Yi, C. Y. (2008). RFID research: An academic literature review (1995-2005) and future research directions. *International Journal of Production Economics, 112*(2), 510–520. doi:10.1016/j.ijpe.2007.05.004

Nie, P., (2006). *A Open Standard for Instant Messaging: eXtensible Messaging and Presence Protocol*. TKK T-110.5190 Seminar on Internetworking.

Niedermayer, M. (n.d.). *Cloud Computing Based Systems for Healthcare*. Academic Press.

Nikam, V. R., Katkar, G. S., & Umathe, M. K. (2016). Statistical Pattern Classification and Data Mining Approach through Cloud Computing. *IOSR Journal of Computer Engineering*, 24-29.

Niranjana. (2015). Big data analytics – Tools, techniques and challenges. *International Journal of Advance Research in Science and Engineering, 4*(3).

Nokia IMPACT IoT Platform. (n.d.). Retrieved from https://networks.nokia.com/solutions/iot-platform

Nokia Patient Care platform. (n.d.). Retrieved from https://patientcare.withings.com/eu/en/

Nonin Finger Pulse Oximeter. (n.d.). Retrieved from http://www.nonin.com/Finger-Pulse-Oximeter

Nuance. (2011). *Nuance Voice Biometrics: Improving the Caller Experience.* Academic Press.

Nunes, B. A. A., Mendonca, M., Nguyen, X. N., Obraczka, K., & Turletti, T. (2014). A survey of software-defined networking: Past, present, and future of programmable networks. *IEEE Communications Surveys and Tutorials, 16*(3), 1617–1634. doi:10.1109/SURV.2014.012214.00180

Okay, F. Y., & Ozdemir, S. (2016). A Fog Computing Based Smart Grid Model. *International Symposium on Networks, Computers and Communications (ISNCC).* 10.1109/ISNCC.2016.7746062

Olariu, S., Khalil, I., & Abuelela, M. (2011). Taking VANET to the clouds. *International Journal of Pervasive Computing and Communications, 7*(1), 7–21. doi:10.1108/17427371111123577

Oracle BerkeleyD. B. 12c. (2013). Retrieved from http://www.oracle.com/technetwork/products/berkeleydb/overview/index.html

Osanaiye, Chen, Yan, Lu, Choo & Dlodlo (2017). From Cloud to Fog Computing: A Review and a Conceptual Live VM Migration Framework. *Recent Advances in Computational Intelligence paradigms for Security and Privacy for Fog and Mobile Edge Computing, 5,* 8284 – 8300.

Osorio, I., & Frei, M. G. (2007). Hurst parameter estimation for epleptic seizure detection. *Communications in Information & Systems, 7*(2), 167–176. doi:10.4310/CIS.2007.v7.n2.a4

Oueis, J., Strinati, E. C., & Barbarossa, S. (2014). Multi-parameter decision algorithm for mobile computation offloading. *2014 IEEE Wireless Communications and Networking Conference (WCNC),* 3005-3010. 10.1109/WCNC.2014.6952959

Ovidiuvermison & Friess. (2014). Internet of things-From research, innovation to market deployment. River Publishers.

Pan, Y., Beyah, R. A., Goscinski, A., & Ren, J. (2017). Edge Computing for the Internet-of-Things. *IEEE Network.* Retrieved November 3, 2017, from https://www.comsoc.org/netmag/cfp/edge-computing-internet-things

Pandey, B. (2010). Multilingual Speaker Recognition Using ANFIS. *2010 2nd International Conference on Signal Processing Systems (ICSPS),* 714–718.

Park, Chen, & Yu, S. (1995). An effective hashbased algorithm for mining association rules. *Proceedings of ACM-SiGMOID international Conference on Management of Data.*

Patel & Singh. (2013). New Approach for K-mean and K-medoids Algorithm. *International Journal of Computer Applications Technology and Research, 2*(1), 1-5.

Patel, K., & Srivastava, R. (2013). Classification of Cloud Data using Bayesian Classification. *International Journal of Science and Research, 2*(6), 80–85.

Patil, P. V. (2015). Fog Computing. *National Conference on Advancements in Alternate Energy Resources for Rural Applications,* 1-6.

Peng, J., El-Latif, A. A. A., Li, Q., & Niu, X. (2014). Multimodal biometric authentication based on score level fusion of finger biometrics. *Optik (Stuttgart), 125*(23), 6891–6897. doi:10.1016/j.ijleo.2014.07.027

Peter, N. (2015). FOG Computing and Its Real Time Applications. *International Journal of Emerging Technology and Advanced Engineering, 5*(6), 266–269.

Petter, S., & McLean, E. R. (2009). A meta-analytic assessment of the DeLone and McLean IS success model: An examination of IS success at the individual level. *Information & Management, 46*(3), 159–166. doi:10.1016/j.im.2008.12.006

Pham, H. N., & Triantaphyllou, E. (2008). The Impact of Overfitting and Overgeneralization on the Classification Accuracy in Data Mining. *Soft Computing for Knowledge Discovery and Data Mining,* 391-431.

Pitt, L. F., Watson, R. T., & Kavan, C. B. (1995). Service Quality : A Measure of Information Systems Effectiveness. *Management Information Systems Quarterly, 19*(2), 173–187. doi:10.2307/249687

Poole, I. (2015). *RFID Standards. Radio-Electronics.* Retrieved November 11, 2017, from http://www.radio-electronics.com/info/wireless/radio-frequency-identification-rfid/iso-epcglobal-iec-standards.php

Predix | Cloud-Based Platform for the Industrial Internet. (2017, December 11). Retrieved December 22, 2017, from http://www.ge.com/digital/predix

Preeti, K. A. (2014). Colour Image Segmentation Using K-Means, Fuzzy C-Means and Density Based Clustering. *International Journal For Research In Applied Science And Engineering Technology, 2*(6).

Pritchett D (2008). BASE: An ACID Alternative. *Queue, 6,* 48–55. doi:10.1145/1394127.1394128

Qiu, X., Luo, H., Xu, G., Zhong, R., & Huang, G. Q. (2015). Physical assets and service sharing for IoT-enabled Supply Hub in Industrial Park (SHIP). *International Journal of Production Economics, 159,* 4–15. doi:10.1016/j.ijpe.2014.09.001

Quinlan, J. R. (1983). *C4.5: Programs for Machine Learning.* Los Altos, CA: Morgan Kaufmann.

Quinlan, J. R. (1986). Induction of decision trees. *Machine Learning, 1*(1), 81–106. doi:10.1007/BF00116251

Quinlan, J. R. (1990). Decision trees and decision-making. *IEEE Transactions on Systems, Man, and Cybernetics, 20*(2), 339–346. doi:10.1109/21.52545

Quinlan, J. R. (1993). *C4.5 programs for machine learning.* Morgan Kaufmann Publishers.

Quinlan, J. R. (1996). Improved use of continuous attributes in C4.5. *Journal of Artificial Intelligence Research, 4*(1), 77–90.

Rad, C. R., Hancu, O., Takacs, I. A., & Olteanu, G. (2015). Smart monitoring of potato crop: A cyber-physical system architecture model in the field of precision agriculture. *Agriculture and Agricultural Science Procedia, 6,* 73–79. doi:10.1016/j.aaspro.2015.08.041

Radha, B. S., & Bharathi, T. (2017). A Study On Corporate Valuation On Selected Indian Firms. *Indian Journal of Commerce and Management, 3*(6).

Raghupathi. (2014). Big data analytics in healthcare: Promise and potential. *Health Inf. Sci. Syst., 2*(1).

Raj & Deka. (2014). *Cloud Infrastructures for Big Data Analytics.* IGI Global. Retrieved from http://www.igi-global.com/book/cloud-infrastructures-big-data-analytics/95028

Raj & Rajaraajeswari. (n.d.). A Framework for Text Analytics using the Bag of Words (BoW) Model for Prediction. *International Journal of Advanced Networking & Applications.*

Raj & Raman. (2016). *The Internet of Things (IoT): the Technologies and Tools.* CRC Press. Retrieved from https://www.crcpress.com/The-Internet-of-Things-Enabling-Technologies-Platforms-and-Use-Cases/Raj-Raman/p/book/9781498761284

Raj. (2015). *High-Performance Big Data Analytics: the Solution Approaches and Systems.* Springer-Verlag, UK. Retrieved from http://www.springer.com/in/book/9783319207438

Raju. (2017, November). A Mutational Approach to Internet of Things. *International Journal for Research in Applied Science and Engineering Technology, 5*(11).

Rantz, M. J., Skubic, M., Popescu, M., Galambos, C., Koopman, R. J., Alexander, G. L., ... Miller, S. J. (2015). A New Paradigm of technology-enabled 'vital signs' for early detection of health change for older adults. *Gerontology, 61*(3), 281–290. doi:10.1159/000366518 PMID:25428525

Rao, C. C., Leelarani, M., & Kumar, Y. R. (2013). Cloud: Computing Services and Deployment Models. *International Journal Of Engineering And Computer Science, 2*(12), 3389–3390.

Ratasuk, R., Vejlgaard, B., Mangalvedhe, N., & Ghosh, A. (2016). NB-IoT System for M2M Communication. *Workshop on Device to Device Communications for 5G NETWORKS.*

Rauscher, R., & Acharya, R. (2013, December). Performance of private clouds in health care organizations. In *Cloud Computing Technology and Science (CloudCom), 2013 IEEE 5th International Conference on* (Vol. 1, pp. 693-698). IEEE. 10.1109/CloudCom.2013.113

Raut. (2017). A Hybrid Framework using Fuzzy if-then rules for DBSCAN Algorithm. *Advances in Wireless and Mobile Communications, 10*(5), 933-942.

Razzaque, M. A., & Clarke, S. (2015, December). A security-aware safety management framework for IoT-integrated bikes. In *Internet of Things (WF-IoT), 2015 IEEE 2nd World Forum on* (pp. 92-97). IEEE. 10.1109/WF-IoT.2015.7389033

Reddy, B. E., Kumar, T. S., & Ramu, G. (2012, December). An efficient cloud framework for health care monitoring system. In *Cloud and Services Computing (ISCOS), 2012 International Symposium on* (pp. 113-117). IEEE. 10.1109/ISCOS.2012.11

Reddy, G. N., & Reddy, G. J. (2014). *Study of Cloud Computing in HealthCare Industry.* arXiv preprint arXiv:1402.1841

Redis. (2013). Retrieved from http://redis.io/

Reynolds, D. a. (2002). An overview of automatic speaker recognition technology. *IEEE International Conference on Acoustics Speech and Signal Processing, 4*, IV-4072-IV-4075. 10.1109/ICASSP.2002.5745552

Riahi, Challal, Natalizio, Chtourou, & Bouabdallah. (2013). A systemic approach for IoT security. IEEE.

Riazul Islam, Kwak, Kabir, Hossain, & Kwak. (2015). The Internet of Things for Health Care: A Comprehensive Survey. IEEE, 3, 678 – 708.

Richardson, M., & Robles, I. (n.d.). *RPL- Routing over Low Power and Lossy Networks.* Retrieved November 21, 2017, from https://www.ietf.org/proceedings/94/slides/slides-94-rtgarea-2.pdf

Richardson, F., Member, S., Reynolds, D., & Dehak, N. (2015). Deep Neural Network Approaches to Speaker and Language Recognition. *IEEE Signal Processing Letters, 22*(10), 1671–1675. doi:10.1109/LSP.2015.2420092

Roessgen, M., Zoubir, A. M., & Boashash, B. (1998). Seizure detection of newborn EEG using a model-based approach. *IEEE Transactions on Biomedical Engineering, 45*(6), 673–685. doi:10.1109/10.678601 PMID:9609933

Romkey, M. (2015). Smart cities ... Not just the sum of its parts. Beirut: Academic Press.

Ruan, J., & Shi, Y. (2016). Monitoring and assessing fruit freshness in IOT-based e-commerce delivery using scenario analysis and interval number approaches. *Information Sciences, 373*, 557–570. doi:10.1016/j.ins.2016.07.014

Rudin, C., & Wagstaff, K. L. (2014). Machine learning for science and society. *Machine Learning, 95*(1), 1–9. doi:10.100710994-013-5425-9

Russell, S., & Norvig, P. (1995). *Artificial intelligence: a modern approach.* Englewood Cliffs, NJ: Prentice-Hall.

Ryu, M., Yun, J., Miao, T., Ahn, I. Y., Choi, S. C., & Kim, J. (2015, November). Design and implementation of a connected farm for smart farming system. In SENSORS, 2015 IEEE (pp. 1-4). IEEE.

Saint-Andre, P. (2009). XMPP: Lessons learned from ten years of XML messaging. *IEEE Communications Magazine, 47*(4), 92–96. doi:10.1109/MCOM.2009.4907413

Salman, O., Elhajj, I., & Kayssi, A. (2015). Edge computing enabling the Internet of Things. In *IEEE 2nd World Forum on the Internet of Things (WF-IoT)*. Milan, Italy. IEEE. 10.1109/WF-IoT.2015.7389122

Samsung Corporation. (2017). *Samsung Shows Dedication to IoT with $1.2 Billion Investment and R&D*, Retrieved from https://news.samsung.com/global/samsung-electronics-announces-vision-for-a-human-centered-internet-of-things-planning-1-2-billion-for-u-s-research-and-development-of-iot

Schaffers, H., Komninos, N., Pallot, M., Trousse, B., & Nilsson, A. (2011). Oliveira, Smart cities and the future internet: towards cooperation frameworks for open innovation. In Lecture Notes in Computer Science: Vol. 6656. *The Future Internet* (pp. 431–446). Berlin: Springer. doi:10.1007/978-3-642-20898-0_31

Schmidt, S. (2016). *6LoWPAN: An Open IoT Networking Protocol.* Open IoT Summit. Retrieved November 14, 2017, from http://events.linuxfoundation.org/sites/events/files/slides/6lowpan-openiot-2016.pdf

Scholkopf, B., & Smola, A. J. (2002). *Learning with kernels.* MIT Press.

Seddik, H., & Eldeib, A. M. (2016). A Wireless Real-Time Remote Control and Tele Monitoring System for Mechanical Ventilators. *IEEE Proceedings of the Conference: 8th Cairo International Biomedical Engineering Conference (CIBEC 2016)*, 64 – 68. 10.1109/CIBEC.2016.7836121

Sekar, K. (2012). Techniques for Speaker Identification System. *XI Biennial Conference of the International Biometric Society (Indian Region) on Computational Statistics and Bio-Sciences*, 88–94.

Seman, A. P., Faria, L. F. C., Paula, L. H. B., & Nedel, S. (2011). Hipertermia e hipotermia. In Tratado de Geriatria e Gerontologia (3rd ed.). Rio de Janeiro: Guanabara Koogan.

Seo, J. S., Member, A., Jin, M., Lee, S., Member, S., Jang, D., … Yoo, C. D. (2006). Audio Fingerprinting Based on Normalized Spectral Subband Moments. *Proceedings of IEEE International Conference on Acoustics, Speech, and Signal Processing*, 209–212. doi: 10.1109/ICASSP.2005.1415684

Seo, S. M., Kim, S. W., Jeon, J. W., Kim, J. H., Kim, H. S., Cho, J. H., ... Paek, S. H. (2016). Food contamination monitoring via internet of things, exemplified by using pocket-sized immunosensor as terminal unit. *Sensors and Actuators. B, Chemical, 233*, 148–156. doi:10.1016/j.snb.2016.04.061

Sethi, P., & Sarangi, S.R. (2017). Internet of Things: Architectures, Protocols, and Applications. *Journal of Electrical and Computer Engineering, 17*.

Shao, Y., Jin, Z., Wang, D., & Srinivasan, S. (2009). An auditory-based feature for robust speech recognition. *ICASSP, IEEE International Conference on Acoustics, Speech and Signal Processing - Proceedings*, (1), 4625–4628. 10.1109/ICASSP.2009.4960661

Sharma, R., Ryait, H. S., & Gupta, A. K. (2016). Wireless Body Area Nework – A Review. *International Journal of Engineering Science, 17*, 494–499.

Shearer, C. (2000). The CRISP-DM model: The new blueprint for data mining. *Journal of Data Warehousing, 5*, 13–22.

Shelby, Z., Hartke, K., & Bormann, C. (2014). *The constrained application protocol (CoAP).* Academic Press.

Sheng, K., Dong, W., Li, W., Razik, J., Huang, F., & Hu, B. (2017). Centroid-aware local discriminative metric learning in speaker verification. *Pattern Recognition, 72*, 176–185. doi:10.1016/j.patcog.2017.07.007

Shih, C. W., & Wang, C. H. (2016). Integrating wireless sensor networks with statistical quality control to develop a cold chain system in food industries. *Computer Standards & Interfaces, 45*, 62–78. doi:10.1016/j.csi.2015.12.004

Shi, X., Yang, H., & Zhou, P. (2016). Robust Speaker Recognition Based on Improved GFCC 27r J. *IEEE International Conference on Computer and Communications (ICCC)*, 1927–1931. doi: 10.1109/CompComm.2016.7925037

Singh, S. (2011). Vector Quantization Approach for Speaker Recognition using MFCC and Inverted MFCC. *International Journal of Computer Applications, 17*(1).

Singh, A., & Gahlawat, M. (2012). Internet Protocol Security (IPSec). *International Journal of Computer Networks and Wireless Communications., 2*(6), 717–720.

Singh, R. D., & Aggarwal, N. (2016, February). Video content authentication techniques: A comprehensive survey. *Multimedia Systems.* doi:10.100700530-017-0538-9

SmartThings | Home automation, home security, and peace of mind. (2014). Available: http://www.smartthings.com

Sobhy, D., El-Sonbaty, Y., & Elnasr, M. A. (2012, December). MedCloud: healthcare cloud computing system. In *Internet Technology And Secured Transactions, 2012 International Conference for* (pp. 161-166). IEEE.

Sonawane, Shirole, Patil, Patil, & Patil. (2017). Effective Pattern Discovery for Text Mining. *International Research Journal of Engineering and Technology, 4*(4).

Song & Lu. (2004). Decision tree methods: Applications for classification and prediction. *Medical Decision Making, 24*(4), 386–398. doi:10.1177/0272989X04267009 PMID:15271277

Soni Madhulatha, T. (2012, April). An overview on clustering methods. *IOSR Journal of Engineering, 2*(4), 719–725. doi:10.9790/3021-0204719725

Spanò, E., Di Pascoli, S., & Iannaccone, G. (2016). Low-power wearable ECG monitoring system for multiple-patient remote monitoring. *IEEE Sensors Journal, 16*(13), 5452–5462. doi:10.1109/JSEN.2016.2564995

Sremath, S., Reza, S., Singh, A., & Wang, R. (2017). Speaker identification features extraction methods : A systematic review. *Expert Systems with Applications, 90*, 250–271. doi:10.1016/j.eswa.2017.08.015

Stantchev, V. (2015). Smart Items, Fog and Cloud Computing as Enablers of Servitization in Healthcare. *J. Sensors & Transducers, 185*(2), 121–128.

Stantchev, V., Barnawi, A., Ghulam, S., Schubert, J., & Tamm, G. (2015). Smart items, fog and cloud computing as enablers of servitization in healthcare. *Sensors & Transducers, 185*(2), 121.

Stantchev, V., Colomo-Palacios, R., & Niedermayer, M. (2014). Cloud computing based systems for healthcare. *The Scientific World Journal.* PMID:24892070

Stojmenovic, I., & Wen, S. (2014, September). The fog computing paradigm: Scenarios and security issues. In *Computer Science and Information Systems (FedCSIS), 2014 Federated Conference on* (pp. 1-8). IEEE.

Su, K., Li, J., & Fu, H. (2011). Smart city and the applications. *2011 International Conference on Electronics, Communications and Control, ICECC 2011 - Proceedings*, 1028–1031.

Sun, Y., Song, H., Jara, A. J., & Bie, R. (2016). Internet of things and big data analytics for smart and connected communities. *IEEE Access: Practical Innovations, Open Solutions, 4*, 766–773. doi:10.1109/ACCESS.2016.2529723

Swathy, M., Nirmala, P. S., & Geethu, P. C. (2017). Survey on Vehicle Detection and Tracking Techniques in Video Surveillance. *International Journal of Computer Applications, 160*(7).

Telgad, R. L., Deshmukh, P. D., & Siddiqui, A. M. N. (2014). Combination approach to score level fusion for Multimodal Biometric system by using face and fingerprint. *International Conference on Recent Advances and Innovations in Engineering, ICRAIE 2014.* 10.1109/ICRAIE.2014.6909320

The Internet of Things becomes the Internet that thinks with Watson IoT. (n.d.). Retrieved December 22, 2017, from http://www.ibm.com/internet-of-things

Thepade, S. D., Bhondave, R. K., & Mishra, A. (2016). Comparing Score Level and Feature Level Fusion in Multimodal Biometric Identification Using Iris and Palmprint Traits with Fractional Transformed Energy Content. *Proceedings - 2015 International Conference on Computational Intelligence and Communication Networks, CICN 2015*, 306–311. 10.1109/CICN.2015.68

Thian, N. P. H., Sanderson, C., & Bengio, S. (2004). Spectral subband centroids as complementary features for speaker authentication. *Biometric Authentication Proceedings, 3072*, 631–639. doi:10.1007/978-3-540-25948-0_86

Tiwari, A. K., Hasan, M. M., & Islam, M. (2013). Effect of ambient temperature on the performance of a combined cycle power plant. *Transactions of the Canadian Society for Mechanical Engineering, 37*(4), 1177–1188. doi:10.4172cientificreports

Tomlinson, R. F. (2001). A geographic information system for regional planning. *The Journal of Geography, 78*(1), 45–48. doi:10.5026/jgeography.78.45

Townsend, K., Cufi, C. A., & Davidson, R. (2016). Bluetooth Low Energy - Part 1: Introduction to BLE. *MikroElektronika*. Retrieved November 14, 2017 from https://learn.mikroe.com/bluetooth-low-energy-part-1-introduction-ble/

Treadway, J. (2016). Using an IoT gateway to connect the "Things" to the cloud. IoT Agenda. *TechTarget Network*. Retrieved November 21, 2017, from http://internetofthingsagenda.techtarget.com/feature/Using-an-IoT-gateway-to-connect-the-Things-to-the-cloud

Ullah, S., & Xuefeng, Z. (2013). *Cloud Computing Research Challenges*. arXiv preprint arXiv:1304.3203

Valluri, S. P. (2014). Secure Internet of Things Environment using XMPP Protocol. *International Journal of Computers and Applications, 106*(4). doi:10.5120/18511-9589

Vaquero, L. M., Rodero-Merio, L., Caceres, J., & Lindner, M. (2009). A break in the clouds: Towards a cloud definition. *Computer Communication Review, 39*(1), 50–55. doi:10.1145/1496091.1496100

Velte, A. T., Velte, T. J., Elsenpeter, R. C., & Elsenpeter, R. C. (2010). *Cloud computing: a practical approach*. New York: McGraw-Hill.

Venkatesha, M. K., Radhika, K. R., & Sudhamani, M. J. (2014, December). Fusion at decision level in multimodal biometric authentication system using Iris and Finger Vein with novel feature extraction. In *India Conference (INDICON), 2014 Annual IEEE* (pp. 1-6). Academic Press.

Venkatesh, V., Morris, M. G., Davis, G. B., & Davis, F. D. (2003). User Acceptance of Information Technology: Toward a Unified View. *Management Information Systems Quarterly, 27*(3), 425–478. doi:10.2307/30036540

Venters, W., & Whitley, E.A. (2012). A critical review of cloud computing: researching desires and realities. *J Info Technol, 27*, 179–197. 10.1057/jit.2012.17

Ventura, D., & Martinez, T. R. (1995). An empirical comparison of discretization methods. *Proceedings of the tenth international symposium on Computer and information sciences*, 443-450.

Verma, Agrawal, Patel, & Patel. (n.d.). Big Data Analytics: Challenges And Applications For Text, Audio, Video, And Social Media Data. *International Journal on Soft Computing, Artificial Intelligence and Applications, 5*(1).

Verma, P. K., Verma, R., Prakash, A., Agrawal, A., Naik, K., Tripathi, R., ... Abogharaf, A. (2016). Machine-to-Machine (M2M) communications: A survey. *Journal of Network and Computer Applications, 66*, 83–105. doi:10.1016/j.jnca.2016.02.016

Viewpoint: Why we need voice biometrics | IDG Connect. (n.d.). Retrieved December 4, 2017, from http://www.idgconnect.com/abstract/10564/viewpoint-why-voice-biometrics

Vinoski, S., (2006). Advanced Message Queuing Protocol. *IEEE Internet Computing, 10*(6).

Vinyals, O., & Friedland, G. (2008). *Modulation spectrogram features for improved speaker diarization* (pp. 630–633). INTERSPEECH.

Wang, Y., & Lawlor, B. (2017). Speaker recognition based on MFCC and BP neural networks. *2017 28th Irish Signals and Systems Conference (ISSC)*, 1–4. doi:10.1109/ISSC.2017.7983644

Wang, D., Lo, D., Bhimani, J., & Sugiura, K. (2015, July). Anycontrol--iot based home appliances monitoring and controlling. In *Computer Software and Applications Conference (COMPSAC), 2015 IEEE 39th Annual* (Vol. 3, pp. 487-492). IEEE. 10.1109/COMPSAC.2015.259

Wang, W., He, G., & Wan, J. (2011). Research on Zigbee Wireless Communication Technology. In *Int. Conf. on Electrical and Control Engineering (ICECE)*. Yichang, China: IEEE. doi: 10.1109/ICECENG.2011.6057961

Wang, Y. S., & Liao, Y. W. (2008). Assessing eGovernment systems success: A validation of the DeLone and McLean model of information systems success. *Government Information Quarterly, 25*(4), 717–733. doi:10.1016/j.giq.2007.06.002

Wei, Y., & Blake, M. B. (2010). Service-oriented computing and cloud computing: Challenges and opportunities. *IEEE Internet Computing, 14*(6), 72–75. doi:10.1109/MIC.2010.147

Welch, E. W., Hinnant, C. C., & Moon, M. J. (2005). Linking citizen satisfaction with e-government and trust in government. *Journal of Public Administration: Research and Theory, 15*(3), 371–391. doi:10.1093/jopart/mui021

What the Internet of Things (IoT) needs to become a reality. (2015). Retrieved from www.freescale.com-White paper-2015

Withings. (n.d.). Retrieved from https://www.withings.com/uk/en/

Witten, H. I., & Frank, E. (2005). *Data Mining: Practical machine learning tools and techniques*. Morgan Kaufmann.

Wolski, R. (2003). Experiences with predicting resource performance on-line in computational grid settings. *Performance Evaluation Review, 30*(4), 41. doi:10.1145/773056.773064

Wolski, R., Gurun, S., Krintz, C., & Nurmi, D. (2008). Using bandwidth data to make computation offloading decisions. *2008 IEEE International Symposium on Parallel and Distributed Processing*, 1–8. 10.1109/IPDPS.2008.4536215

Wolski, R., Spring, N. T., & Hayes, J. (1999). The network weather service: A distributed resource performance forecasting service for metacomputing. *Future Generation Computer Systems, 15*(5-6), 757–768. doi:10.1016/S0167-739X(99)00025-4

Woo, J. (2012). Apriori-Map/Reduce Algorithm. *WORLDCOMP'12 - The 2012 World Congress in Computer Science, Computer Engineering, and Applied Computing*.

Workshop, J., Communication, H. S., & Arrays, M. (2014). Spectrogram patch based acoustic event detection and NTT. Communication Science Laboratories, NTT Corporation.

Wu, F., & Sun, G. (2013). *Software-defined storage. Report*. Minneapolis, MN: University of Minnesota.

Wu, H., Huang, D., & Bouzefrane, S. (2013). Making Offloading Decisions Resistant to Network Unavailability for Mobile Cloud Collaboration. *Proceedings of the 9th IEEE International Conference on Collaborative Computing: Networking, Applications and Worksharing*, 168 - 177. 10.4108/icst.collaboratecom.2013.254106

Xia, F., Tian, Y. C., Li, Y., & Sun, Y. (2007). Wireless Sensor/Actuator Network Design for Mobile Control Applications. *Journal of Sensors*, 7(10), 2157–2173. doi:10.33907102157 PMID:28903220

Yi, S., Li, C., & Li, Q. (2015, June). A survey of fog computing: concepts, applications and issues. In *Proceedings of the 2015 Workshop on Mobile Big Data* (pp. 37-42). ACM.

Yuan, Y., Zhao, P., & Zhou, Q. (2010). Research of speaker recognition based on combination of LPCC and MFCC. *Proceedings - 2010 IEEE International Conference on Intelligent Computing and Intelligent Systems, ICIS 2010, 3*, 765–767. 10.1109/ICICISYS.2010.5658337

Zao, J. (2014). Augmented Brain Computer Interaction Based on Fog Computing and Linked Data. *Proc. 10th IEEE Int'l Conf. Intelligent Environments (IE 14)*, 374–377. 10.1109/IE.2014.54

Zao, J. K., Gan, T. T., You, C. K., Chung, C. E., Wang, Y. T., Méndez, S. J. R., ... Chu, S. L. (2014). Pervasive brain monitoring and data sharing based on multi-tier distributed computing and linked data technology. *Frontiers in Human Neuroscience*, 8. PMID:24917804

Zeinali, H., Sameti, H., & Burget, L. (2017). HMM-based phrase-independent i-vector extractor for text-dependent speaker verification. *IEEE/ACM Transactions on Audio Speech and Language Processing, 25*(7), 1421–1435. doi:10.1109/TASLP.2017.2694708

Zhang, D., Yu, H., & Zheng, L. (2014). Apriori Algorithm Research Based on Map-Reduce in Cloud Computing Environments. *The Open Automation and Control Systems Journal, 6*(1), 368–373. doi:10.2174/1874444301406010368

Zhang, K. Z. K., Lee, M. K. O., Cheung, C. M. K., & Chen, H. (2009). Understanding the role of gender in bloggers' switching behavior. *Decision Support Systems, 47*(4), 540–546. doi:10.1016/j.dss.2009.05.013

Zhang, Q., Cheng, L., & Boutaba, R. (2010). Cloud computing: State-of-the-art and research challenges. *Journal of Internet Services and Applications, 1*(1), 7–18. doi:10.100713174-010-0007-6

Zhao, W., & Chellappa, R. (2006a). *Face processing: Advanced modeling and methods.* Elsevier / Academic Press. Retrieved from https://books.google.co.in/books?hl=en&lr=&id=ZRw9dP7nj2kC&oi=fnd&pg=PP1&dq=)+Face +Processing:+Advanced+Modeling+and+Methods,+Academic+Press.&ots=6KhJxnC-O3&sig=v0NWu0HCdS7-BuE5an6CQjFr1rk8#v=onepage&q=) Face Processing%3A Advanced Modeling and Methods%2C Academic Press.&f=false

Zhao, W., Ma, H., & He, Q. (2009). Parallel K-Means Clustering Based on MapReduce. *IEEE International Conference on Cloud Computing.*

Zhao, X., & Wang, D. (2013). Analyzing noise robustness of MFCC and GFCC features in speaker identification. *ICASSP, IEEE International Conference on Acoustics, Speech and Signal Processing - Proceedings*, 7204–7208. doi:10.1109/ICASSP.2013.6639061

Zhao, W., & Chellappa, R. (2006b). *Face processing : advanced modeling and methods.* Elsevier / Academic Press.

Zhao, X., Shao, Y., & Wang, D. (2012). CASA-based robust speaker identification. *IEEE Transactions on Audio, Speech, and Language Processing, 20*(5), 1608–1616. doi:10.1109/TASL.2012.2186803

Zhu, J., Chan, D. S., Prabhu, M. S., Natarajan, P., Hu, H., & Bonomi, F. (2013, March). Improving web sites performance using edge servers in fog computing architecture. In *Service Oriented System Engineering (SOSE), 2013 IEEE 7th International Symposium on* (pp. 320-323). IEEE.

Zhuang, Y., Wang, Y., Shao, J., Chen, L., Lu, W., Sun, J., ... Wu, J. (2016). D-Ocean: An unstructured data management system for data ocean environment. *Frontiers of Computer Science*, *10*(2), 353–369. doi:10.100711704-015-5045-6

Zomya, A. Y., Ghazawi, T. E., & Frieder, O. (1999). Parallel and Distributed Computing for Data Mining. *IEEE Concurrency*, *7*(4), 11–13. doi:10.1109/MCC.1999.806974

Zorzi, M., Gluhak, A., Lange, S., & Bassi, A. (2010). From today's INTRAnet of things to a future INTERnet of things: A wireless- and mobility-related view. *IEEE Wireless Communications*, *17*(6), 44–51. doi:10.1109/MWC.2010.5675777

Zuiderwijk, A., & Janssen, M. (2014). The Negative Effects of Open Government Data - Investigating the Dark Side of Open Data. In *Proceedings of the 15th Annual International Conference on Digital Government Research* (pp. 147–152). Academic Press. 10.1145/2612733.2612761

Index

A

administration 109, 117, 119-120, 132, 139, 162

Algorithms 7, 10, 15, 17, 28, 73, 121, 145-146, 158, 166, 178, 188, 190-191, 195, 199, 205-206, 391-394, 398-400, 406-407

architecture 4, 18, 20, 38, 40, 44, 46-47, 51, 53, 56, 60-63, 68, 71, 78-80, 89, 92, 95, 97, 103, 119, 125, 128-130, 132-135, 143, 146, 149-153, 158-160, 163, 165-166, 169, 175, 177-180, 185-186, 188

B

Bandwidth 2-4, 7, 18, 27, 34, 40, 50, 54, 57, 59, 75, 119, 121, 124, 128-129, 142, 145-146, 165, 177-180, 182-183, 185-186, 190, 192, 196, 206

Big Data 7, 13, 17, 39, 51, 59, 143-144, 149, 151, 166-167, 175, 195, 390-391

Biometrics 13, 139

C

Cameras 7, 13, 15-16, 31, 55, 75, 78, 139, 159-160, 163, 391, 407-408

Cloud Computing 4, 18, 32-34, 36, 38, 40, 46-47, 49-50, 53, 55-56, 58-59, 73, 77-78, 108-109, 113-117, 119-121, 142, 162, 175-176, 178, 196, 200, 206

Connectivity 2-3, 7, 13, 18, 27, 34, 45, 53, 55, 70, 73-74, 78, 82, 86, 88-89, 93, 125, 134, 139, 141-142, 146, 150, 159-160, 179, 401

consumer 2, 18, 20, 31, 88, 100, 134, 165

context-awareness 3, 12, 15, 73

D

Data Distribution Service 95, 127, 134

decentralized 12, 18, 34, 47, 77, 95

Deployment 20-21, 27-28, 31, 33, 41, 61, 66, 74, 81-82, 86, 88, 96, 114-116, 142, 146, 198

Development 17, 25, 27, 33, 45, 68, 74, 81, 83, 91, 99-100, 104, 108, 136, 139, 141, 150, 153, 158, 164, 177, 195

E

Edge Computing 3-4, 7, 10, 12, 18, 28, 30, 32-33, 35, 55-56, 73, 76-78, 81, 83, 85-87, 105, 145, 168, 205

E-Healthcare 108

Embedded 2, 13, 17, 20, 34, 53, 55, 69, 71, 73-74, 78, 85, 91, 93, 97, 125, 138-139, 160, 407

Energy Efficiency 86, 88, 178, 194

F

Filter 4, 7, 45, 89, 396, 398

Fog Computing 1-4, 7-8, 10, 12, 18-20, 28, 32-40, 42-43, 45-51, 53, 55-59, 63-65, 68-69, 73, 75-79, 82-83, 85-86, 124, 141-146, 151, 167-169, 175-176, 179, 194, 195-196, 199, 205-206, 390

Fuzzy Logic 160, 175-176, 179, 181, 183-187, 191, 194

G

gateway 2-3, 20, 24-27, 35, 72, 74-75, 82, 86-87, 89-90, 126, 131, 150, 152-153, 159, 161-162, 164-166

H

Hardware 27-28, 48, 60, 71, 74, 81, 96, 109, 112, 142, 176, 196

health care 37, 39, 58-59, 77, 121, 142, 145, 154, 159-160, 165, 169

Heterogeneous 7, 12, 18-19, 34, 40, 55, 72-74, 88, 142, 144

Historical 5, 10, 25, 39, 42, 46, 51, 56, 83, 143, 166, 195

I

Iaas 108-112
Identifying 10, 138, 159, 166, 196, 202
Infrastructure 1, 12, 16, 18, 34, 47, 53-56, 58, 60-61, 70-71, 74, 76, 78, 95-96, 108-114, 116-120, 126, 128, 136-138, 142, 156, 159, 162, 164, 177, 181, 196, 206
infrastructures 1, 3, 5, 7, 15, 18, 28, 33, 50, 53, 56, 58, 163-164
innovation 7, 139-141
Internet of Electricity 137
IOT Application 34, 39, 42, 51, 73, 136, 141, 143, 146, 150, 152-153, 157-159, 161, 163-164, 166-167, 169, 175-176, 185-189, 194
IoT protocols 127

L

Latency 3, 9, 18-19, 33-34, 40, 43, 45-46, 50, 54-56, 58-59, 64, 74, 77, 81, 87, 96, 128, 134, 142, 144-145, 176, 196, 206
Local 2-4, 12, 17-19, 31, 35, 40, 53, 56, 59, 68, 71, 73-74, 83, 86, 97-98, 135, 159-161, 176-178, 181-188, 190-191, 200, 206, 394

M

M2M 69-70, 97, 100, 130, 134, 138, 150, 158
maintenance 10, 12, 16-17, 25, 110, 114, 119, 158, 160, 163
Management 13-14, 17-18, 20-22, 27, 40, 47-48, 51, 63, 66, 73, 77, 81-83, 86, 103, 110, 116, 119-120, 134-138, 143-144, 149, 159-160, 162-164, 169, 196, 206
Mining 145, 160, 163, 195-199, 202-203, 205-206, 391-393, 399
Mobile Cloud Offloading 175, 194
Monitoring 7, 18, 28, 58-59, 64, 71, 81, 91, 136-139, 142, 145, 150, 154, 158-166, 399, 407
multi-structured 1-2, 12

N

Networking 3, 12, 27, 34, 38, 51, 55, 60-62, 71-72, 86, 88, 93, 95, 101, 114, 116-119, 121, 132, 139, 152, 196
Nodes 18, 33-34, 39-41, 45-48, 55, 57, 59, 63, 66, 72, 74-75, 78, 82, 88, 93, 95-97, 100, 103, 142-143, 145-146, 150, 153, 158, 163, 168, 196, 199, 203

O

Offloading Decision Making 177-179, 181, 191, 194

P

Paas 108-112
Protocols 22, 25, 27, 34, 41, 47, 60, 63, 65-66, 85, 89, 91-93, 95-96, 101, 105, 116, 124-125, 127, 130, 146, 149, 151, 153, 155-156, 168-169

Q

Quality of Service (QoS) 34, 36, 40, 60, 74, 114, 118, 154

R

Real-Time 1, 3, 7, 9-10, 12, 15-16, 18-19, 25, 28, 30, 33-34, 39, 45, 48, 50, 53, 55, 59, 64, 74-75, 77, 83, 131, 135, 145, 406
records 10, 104, 124, 135-140
Remote Patient Monitoring (RPM) 164
resource-constrained 2, 18, 20, 85
resource-intensive 4-5, 18-19, 35, 175
retrieval 391-392, 397

S

Saas 108-110, 112
semi-structured 196, 206
Smart Agriculture 149, 153, 157-158
Smart City 8, 74, 90, 138, 145-146, 150, 153
Smart Industry 149-150, 153, 161
Smart Vehicle 150, 153, 157, 163
Software Defined Networks 121
standards-compliant 2, 13

T

Time Efficiency 176, 191, 194
Traditional 3, 5, 18-19, 26, 28, 32-33, 38, 42, 55, 59, 86, 89, 118, 142, 150, 153, 393
Traffic 3, 7-8, 15, 18, 26, 38, 40, 45-46, 51, 55, 61, 63, 86-87, 96, 138-139, 142, 144-146, 163, 177, 205

U

Unstructured 196, 206, 390-392, 400

V

VANETS 45-47, 57, 63, 163
virtual 4, 53, 55, 61, 66, 69-70, 81, 86, 112, 116, 118-119, 139, 141, 163, 179, 181
Virtualization 13, 48, 53, 60-61, 112, 114, 117-118

W

Wireless 3, 7, 37, 45, 50, 68-71, 82, 88, 91-93, 99-101, 125, 138, 142, 150, 152, 158, 161-162, 165-166, 187, 206

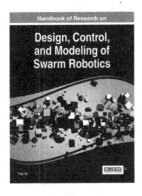

 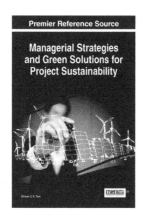  

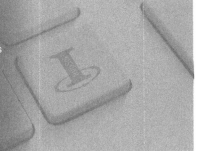

Printed in the United States
By Bookmasters